SILENT COUP

Len Colodny and Robert Gettlin

SILENT COUP

THE REMOVAL OF A PRESIDENT

ST. MARTIN'S PRESS
NEW YORK

Design by Glen Edelstein

Library of Congress Cataloging-in-Publication Data

Colodny, Len.
    Silent coup : the removal of a president / Len Colodny and
Robert Gettlin.
       p.   cm.
    Includes index.
    ISBN 0-312-05156-5
    1. Watergate Affair, 1972–1974.   2. Nixon, Richard M. (Richard
Milhous), 1913–   .   I. Gettlin, Robert.   II. Title.
E860.C635   1991
364.1′32′0973—dc20   90-49208
                                                                    CIP

First Edition: June 1991

10 9 8 7 6 5 4 3 2 1

DEDICATION—LEN COLODNY

For Sandy Colodny
Sherry and Jerry Hollis
John and Robin Colodny
Ethel Colodny
and in memory of Sam Colodny and
Fanny and Seymour Price
for their loving support, faith, and values
[Bandit]

DEDICATION—ROBERT GETTLIN

For Arlene, Adam, Alex,
Sunny, Leo, and Esther
and in everlasting memory of
Shirley Gettlin, Alex and Sylvia Gettlin,
Rae Frantz, Joe Goodstein, and Doris Perlstein

CONTENTS

Acknowledgments   viii

Foreword by Roger Morris   xiii

Book One: Spy Ring   1

1. Spying on the White House   3
2. Carrying the Contraband   21
3. The Admiral's Confession   32
4. Nixon Orders a Burial   47
5. The Woodward-Haig Connection   69

Book Two: Golden Boy   91

6. The President's Private Eye   93
7. Sandwedge Becomes GEMSTONE   111
8. The Bailley Connection   123
9. The Last Break-In   142
10. Los Angeles and Manila: The Cover-up Begins   161
11. A Walk in the Park   173
12. "The Smoking Gun"   195
13. Hush Money—for Hunt   205
14. Damage Control Action Officer   215
15. The Pressure Mounts   233
16. Confession Time   248
17. The Cancer Within the Presidency   260

Book Three: Exit the President 277

18. The Return of Alexander Haig 279
19. Stewart Shakes Up the White House 304
20. Five Days in July 316
21. The Saturday Night Massacre 337
22. The Eighteen-and-a-Half-Minute Gap 360
23. Moorer-Radford Disinterred 373
24. Senator Stennis Holds a Hearing 390
25. The Real Final Days 404

Epilogue: . . . And Throw Away the Key 426

Appendix A: List of Interviewees 441

Appendix B: Welander Confessions 445

Notes 475

Bibliography 487

Index 491

ACKNOWLEDGMENTS

The investigation from which *Silent Coup* was born began a decade ago. At that time we had no interest in Watergate. We were immersed in a story about journalistic ethics involving one of America's most influential reporters, Bob Woodward of the *Washington Post*, and it was about that topic that we hoped to write a book. But when one looks closely at Woodward, we eventually discovered, the trail inevitably leads back to Watergate and the events that brought down Richard Nixon.

What turned our attention was the publication in November 1984 of Jim Hougan's ground-breaking book, *Secret Agenda: Watergate, Deep Throat, and the CIA*. Hougan accomplished what no other investigator had attempted to do—he investigated the events and circumstances of the June 17, 1972, break-in at Democratic headquarters, reporting in scrupulous detail that the accepted version of the crime was riddled with contradictions, flaws, and inaccuracies. Hougan's work was revelatory, showing that the Watergate story rested upon myths that had obscured the public's understanding of a great national calamity. Hougan also raised the first questions about Woodward's background, and it was this clue that launched us on the path that led to the writing of *Silent Coup*.

A first-rate journalist, Hougan generously shared with us the product of his own investigative efforts and provided sound advice and unflagging support. He is among those to whom we have accumulated a serious debt during our half-dozen years of work on this book.

Roger Morris is a scholar and journalist of great intellectual depth whose contribution to our work was immeasurable. As he does in his own critically acclaimed writings, Morris constantly inspired us to see the larger picture. Not only had we uncovered startling new facts about an old political story, but also a compelling tale about the way in which power is wielded inside the U.S. government. Morris' firsthand knowledge of the National Security Council under Richard Nixon and Henry Kissinger was invaluable, giving us—and thus our readers—a deeper understanding of the key players in this book. A man of sensitivity and wit, Morris' insights and boundless enthusiasm for our work helped sustain us through years of arduous research and writing.

Len Colodny's childhood friend Benton Becker was initially asked to advise and assist us, even though he had worked with individuals in the Department of Justice and in the Nixon and Ford administrations whose actions we examined. Becker's knowledge of the pathways of government, his tenacity for tracking down a story, and his desire to expose the truth were always at our disposal. He helped direct the search for information, interpreted evidence, and, opened doors to other sources before, in the final months of the project, putting aside his private law practice to become a full-fledged collaborator. We also thank Becker's colleague, attorney Peter Collins, and administrative aide Melissa Hodes for their assistance, and acknowledge the help of Becker's longtime friend Eric Jimenez.

At a critical time in the preparation of the manuscript, we consulted Tom Shachtman, a writer of exceptional talent. The author of a wide-ranging examination of the entire era, *Decade of Shocks, 1963–1974*, published in 1983, as well as several other books on twentieth-century American history, Shachtman was called upon to help Colodny write eight chapters in the Golden Boy section of this book, and, later, to work with Gettlin on revision and completion of the entire manuscript. Shachtman is a masterful storyteller, and without his enormous contribution we might still be typing away.

Phil Stanford, who followed up on Hougan's findings, provided crucial assistance that helped us discover the reason for the Watergate break-ins. It was Stanford who first found the critical link between "Mo Biner" and attorney Phillip Bailley. And it was his basic research that led to our writing of what the reader will come to know as the "Bailley connection" to Watergate. Now a columnist for *The Oregonian* in Portland, Oregon, Stanford graciously provided advice and help over the past two years.

Nat Sobel served as much more than our literary agent. He assisted in the careful preparation of our proposal, guided us through the tricky waters of the publishing world, and contributed greatly to the strengthening of our manuscript. He has been an adviser and friend, providing at the appropriate times both sound criticism and nourishing praise. We also thank others at Sobel Weber Associates, especially Craig Holden and Wanda Cuevas.

We can not imagine a publisher demonstrating a more unswerving commitment to a book than St. Martin's Press has shown with *Silent Coup*. We are deeply indebted to our skillful and diligent editor, George

Witte, and to the always-encouraging St. Martin's President, Roy Gainsburg, for their dedication to quality, their remarkable patience, and for allowing us to build the book even as we were writing. General Counsel David Kaye and Associate General Counsel Lotte Meister made tremendous contributions, spending many painstaking hours meticulously reviewing our research and helping to sharpen the story that appears in the following pages. We thank Pat Modigliani for her careful transcription of a particularly important section of the book. We owe special thanks to St. Martin's Chairman Tom McCormack, who believed in this project from day one, who shepherded it through trying periods, and who pushed for the highest quality in our work.

Before his death at the end of 1988, John Mitchell was an especially valuable source. Until we contacted him, Mitchell had said little about his association with Richard Nixon or his involvement in Watergate. But in more than three years of dealings with Mitchell we found him to be forthright, sometimes brutally frank, about that often painful period of his life. Mitchell provided access to other sources, and after his death many of them continued to assist us. We acknowledge the help of Jack Brennan, Steve Bull, Dwight Chapin, Harry Flemming, Steve King, Dick Kleindienst, Jerris Leonard, Bob Mardian, Powell Moore, Sandy Perk, and Lee (Jablonski) Uhre. Special thanks goes to John Mitchell's daughter, Marty Mitchell, and to his longtime companion, Mary Gore Deane.

Bob Sherrill, one of the country's great investigative writers, gave us early encouragement and criticism that helped launch our research and then kept us going long before we knew we would produce *Silent Coup*. We also thank his wife, Mary, for her continuing kindness.

Philip Simon, a close and longtime friend of Bob Gettlin, tracked down crucial documents for us from the government of the Philippines. We thank Simon, who lives in Manila, for his extraordinary ingenuity and persistence, as well as his friend, Evelyn Villa, for her own diligent efforts in the securing of this information.

During years of investigation and research, we found the Nixon Presidential Materials Staff, an arm of the National Archives, located in Alexandria, Virginia, to be an invaluable resource. We gratefully acknowledge those staff members who assisted us. Supervisory Archivist Dr. Byron A. Parham deserves special recognition for his professionalism, thoroughness, and ever-present good humor. Audiovisual archivist Dick McNeill and photo specialist Mary Young provided materials from which we selected a number of photographs for the book.

At the Center for Legislative Archives, also part of the National

Archives, Robert Coren, chief of the reference branch, his predecessor, David Kepley, and archivist Rodney Ross were extremely helpful over the years in providing and interpreting the files of the Senate Watergate committee. Similarly, David Paynter of the archives' textual reference division, and his predecessor Steve Tilley, provided documents from the files of the Watergate Special Prosecution Force and tracked down those that had been difficult to find. In sum, all of the professionals with whom we dealt at the various archives branches contributed greatly to our research efforts.

Finally, we are grateful to each person on the interview list located in the appendix of this book (as well as those few whose names are not listed) for their cooperation over the years. Our debt to them is substantial, for their separate stories enabled us to uncover many of the hidden truths of Watergate. Only by stripping away historical falsehoods and misconceptions can the United States, or any nation, hope to avoid repeating its mistakes and secure a brighter future.

A Personal Acknowledgment by Len Colodny

In a book with few heroes, there is one person who truly is a hero— my wife, Sandy Colodny. Without her there would have been no *Silent Coup*. Through the early 1980s, in turmoil and strife, Sandy stood by me, her faith and love sustaining me. When necessary, her financial support kept us going. No individual deserves more credit, and there is no one I love and respect more than her. I owe Sandy a lot and so, too, does any American who might regard this book as contributing to an understanding of our history.

My children, Sherry and John, went through some very difficult and trying periods of my life and were rocks of love and support, and have been a source of great pride to me. They, too, played an important role in the making of this book. Their spouses, Jerry and Robin, have given me love and friendship.

My late father, Sam Colodny, instilled in me by word and by deed a strong set of values, stressing the importance of honesty and integrity over the all-too-common pursuits of money and power. He loved the give and take of politics, but he understood its dark side—that the bottom line for most politicians is personal gain and getting reelected. My father had great insights into human nature, and a sense of humor second to none. It was his legacy that enabled me to uncover the truths found in *Silent Coup*.

Although we left Washington, D.C., in 1984, we have very special friends there who stuck with us through the tough times. My love and thanks go out to Sue and Dick, Phyllis and Teddy, Audrey and Joe, David and Rosemary, Ed and Sue, John and Maryann, Marion and Hugh, Leila and Dan, and Jo and, in memorium, Don.

In Tampa, there are wonderful friends who welcomed us and made our new home a joy. Many thanks to Kay and Pete, Alma and Ernie, George and Joan, Carol and Richard, Charlotte and Al, Kathy and Bill, and Richard and Betty.

Last but not least, we acknowledge our old antiwar friends now residing in Maine, Irene and Ben.

A Personal Acknowledgment by Bob Gettlin

Writing a book is an intensely personal and satisfying experience, but one that is far more arduous than the uninitiated could ever know. This being my first book, I went through many trials, learned many lessons. That I survived the process is due in great measure to the unbending love and support of my wife, Arlene Gettlin. Her faith and positive outlook were a reassuring beacon during difficult periods, and she constantly shared in the excitement of the project even though I spent many hours away from home doing battle with the word processor.

My sons, Adam and Alex, did not see me as much as they would have liked, but when I was around their enthusiasm and love was more sustenance.

Amid the satisfaction of producing this book, I regret that my mother, Shirley, who died in my early childhood, is not able to see its publication. Her memory has been a lifelong source of inspiration. My mother Sunny, who raised me and taught me how to believe in myself, and my father, Leo, who passed on to me a thirst for the study of history, deserve all the thanks a son can give.

I am deeply grateful to my siblings and relatives in California, Pennsylvania, New Jersey, Illinois, Massachusetts, and Maryland who have been incredibly supportive over the years, as have my colleagues and friends in California, Washington, D.C., and Virginia.

Finally, I owe a special debt to my co-author, Len, a man of remarkable strength whose keen intellect and burning desire to pursue the truth kept us on course. He has shown me the meaning of friendship.

FOREWORD

Daniel Boorstin, the eminent historian and Librarian of Congress, said it well in a work called *Hidden History*. "Our past is only a little less uncertain than our future," he wrote, "and, like the future, it is always changing, always revealing and concealing."

Silent Coup is the excavation of some vital hidden history, of a national scandal within a scandal, and of a literary-journalistic atrocity of revealing while concealing.

There are several virtues that make this book quite remarkable among political writing of our era. What follows is a finely styled, fast-paced narrative, gripping as it is disturbing. Distinguished from so much written about Watergate and Richard Nixon, it also happens to be true.

You are about to read the story of a coup d'état, of all political events the most dramatic, suspenseful, sinister. To make the subject even more ominous, this is an American coup, albeit carried out (for a change) in the United States itself.

The means and methods are appropriate to the setting. No conspirators steal away to some secret command post. No tanks crouch among the tree-shaded streets behind the Capitol. We are witnessing the classically American genus of the coup d'état, achieved by folly as well as cunning, by commercial calculus and public relations, by both the manipulation of institutions and their own craven abdication, by cold intention and no little inadvertence, and—perhaps most essential—at no sacrifice of the popular mythology. (A distinguishing mark of the American coup is that it should remain concealed from its victims and history even *after* its successful execution.)

Among several dimensions, this book is a portrait of Richard Milhous Nixon. Of many remarkable United States presidents in this century, he remains in many respects the most intriguing, seemingly the most elusive. He emerges in these pages as a tortured, torturing man of historic paradox. A kind of political prodigy, Mr. Nixon is in many ways a misfit in public life. Widely respected and widely abhorred, he appears here as a statesman coasting to reelection, yet a politician lethally anxious about his place and future. Most important for purposes of the coup, he has been strikingly adept at concentrating power and sometimes almost magisterial in its use, yet strangely inept in understanding the inner realities of government, feebly unable to cope with the supreme crisis of his own removal.

Even those who know well the provenance of Richard Nixon will find in this book an unexpected figure. His rise, it is true, gave premonition of his fall. But no other portrayal has provided us such a gritty, authentic montage of the tottering ruler, the old predator at bay. It is this president—the would-be visionary, the punitive and the pathetic—very much as he was. That he was never seen so clearly at the time, viewed through the lens of other ambitions, other reckonings of power, is part of the considerable revelation of *Silent Coup*.

Yet the following pages are far more than a major contribution to the history of the American presidency—though that would be enough. Above all, this is a book about a larger reality of government and politics in the United States.

Mr. Nixon himself has been fond of saying that history if not historians would somehow vindicate him, that most of the first scathing verdicts on his regime have come from those whom he dismisses with that old sneer as "on the left." Like his fitful grasp of governance, his sense of what really happened to him turns out to be sadly superficial, and ironic. As *Silent Coup* shows so compellingly, Watergate was acted out—and its early ersatz history dictated, as it were—by those of far more reactionary views, and by some far closer to the Oval Office.

Nothing, in fact, was quite what it seemed, from spies in gold braid to the manipulation of a presidential pardon, from the chaotic White House cover-up to the matching confusion and concealment of Congress and the prosecutors. Even the famous break-in itself was born of an urge still seedier than party espionage. In a sense, an American president was toppled by the world's oldest profession.

Not least—and this much Mr. Nixon may yet come to appreciate—the regime was replaced because of its policies as well as its squalid politics. However petty the maneuvers, there was grim substance to this coup d'état. One of its purposes was not only to rid us of an awkward leader and his extra-Constitutional excursions, but in the first instance to check some unwanted statesmanship, and thus to maintain a prescribed course for America and the world.

As the hidden history of Watergate unfolds in *Silent Coup*, there seems little doubt about the base motives of the participants. One is tempted to blame much on power and greed. The Joint Chiefs of Staff and their agents-in-place had authority and appropriations at stake. Reporters with laggard or uncertain careers, publishers hungry for industry sensation and profits, bureaucrats behaving bureaucratically—all, in a way, are recognizable. There is something fetid in the released odor, personal aggrandizement, dishonesty, and corruption as old as the Republic.

Yet what became decisive in the end was relatively modern, the stunning superficiality of Washington's political culture in this last half of the American Century. Events depended upon the absence or subversion of what the Founders trusted rather hopefully to be the guardians—the press, the Congress, and Judiciary. Washington's journalists of the 1970s were no more co-opted than their predecessors, and in some ways less so than the snap-brimmed barkers of an earlier era who took their leaks whole from J. Edgar Hoover or flush, back-slapping senators. But their chemistry in Watergate was typically banal: a conspiracy of accepted convention, a conjunction of careers, the arrogance, presumption, and opportunism of an insular capital.

Messrs. Colodny and Gettlin perform no black magic in righting the record. What they do is a meticulous and thoughtful weighing of the evidence, almost all of it available at the time to enterprising reporters, or to subsequent scholars and investigators, most of whom glided languidly past. It was—and has been—a cruel hoax to pretend that the most powerful institutions of the media did not have the wherewithal to uncover this story, not to mention the train of putative historians and writers who have rehearsed the fiction since. The result has been an American version of *treason of the clerks*, nothing less than a Constitutional betrayal of trust.

The implications have been far-reaching. Reputations and fortunes were made. Books and movies were confected. A generation of students stood inspired by discreet fraud. Reaction and machination passed blithely as the legitimate Constitutional process. A government was overthrown not in the clear light of democratic day—where its abuses might have compelled its recall anyway—but in the shadows of myth and factional intrigue. Public ignorance, democracy's lethal draft, was served and drunk.

There was indispensable common ground on which the players met, hunters and prey alike. Each was still in the grip of the great national security myth of postwar America, the whole elaborate construct of power and patriotism, fear and ignorance, that has so manacled governance—until, in end-of-the-century America, a sentient public scarcely exists. *Silent Coup* lists no "military party" of plotting colonels and generals, at least in the crude caricatures in which we usually prefer to view them. But it does reveal a formidable *national security party*, civilian and uniformed, Republican and Democrat, that governs when it chooses, whenever it believes it must. (It is in the process once again in the wake of the Persian Gulf war—incredibly with some of the same techniques and mouthpieces—of foisting off a fresh mythology of power and personality.)

This book will not rescue Richard Nixon from posterity, not salvage the reputations of his men. Nor will it confirm with its real-life complexity Mr. Nixon's own demonology of partisan or ideological animus. But in its sheer authenticity it retrieves something invaluable for the rest of us. The ultimate price of the coup was to defraud a nation of its past, its one true and common patrimony. Colodny and Gettlin are giving back what was stolen.

The revelations here are a coming to terms with what we have been, and thus are becoming—an anguishing self-examination of the kind our old rivals are now conducting from Berlin to Moscow, from the Katyn Forest to the graveyards of the Gulag. Hiding history was the common scourge of the Cold War, plaguing winners no less than losers. And from the cost of such national distortion in hypocrisy and political, moral decay, there has been no real escape on either side. The reclaiming of America's democracy, like the birth of other's, begins with telling the truth.

That is why *Silent Coup* is not only history, but a fateful current event—a precious omen, Boorstin would say, of "how much still remains to be discovered about our past, and how uncertain is our grip on the future."

—ROGER MORRIS

It's just the way you put it. It was his [Nixon's] personality and his mode of operation that did him in.

—John N. Mitchell, to the authors
July 1988

BOOK ONE

SPY RING

1

SPYING ON THE WHITE HOUSE

ON Thursday afternoon, December 16, 1971, Navy Yeoman Charles Edward Radford left his house at Bolling Air Force Base on the edge of Washington, D.C., and steered his blue Datsun toward the Pentagon. It seemed like springtime; the temperature had climbed to a record 74 degrees, and as he passed the Tidal Basin and then crossed the Potomac River Radford could see a few cherry blossoms sprouting on the trees, and joggers running along the Mall near the Lincoln Memorial. The lanky, mustachioed twenty-seven-year-old with the friendly open manner had made the routine commute many times since arriving in Washington fifteen months earlier, but this was a special trip, one that made Radford too tense to enjoy the balmy weather. A day earlier, the Navy had placed him under virtual house arrest, and he dreaded what was now about to happen. He was on his way to an interrogation by Defense Department investigators who suspected that Radford had leaked classified documents to columnist Jack Anderson.

Radford had never liked Washington. He had enlisted in the Navy in 1963, and four years later the Navy had sent him to Defense

3

Intelligence School near the capital. He'd developed a strong dislike of the city, and was glad when his administrative training ended. In May 1967, he was posted to the defense attaché's office in the United States Embassy in New Delhi, India. He liked New Delhi, where he met and married the daughter of a U.S. Navy officer. The first two of their eight children were born in India. After three years, when the assignment to India ended, Radford sought the job of "admiral's writer," a post that involved clerical work, dictation, and memo writing, and that would make him personal aide to a flag officer; that was the route, Chuck Radford thought, to earning an officer's commission. The Navy agreed to give him such training at a school in Bainbridge, Maryland, and Radford hoped that after it he would land a post in the Pacific Northwest, close to his own family and that of his in-laws.

The Navy had other plans for him. In the summer of 1970 a prestigious and highly sensitive assignment linking the Pentagon and the White House opened up, and Radford, third in his class at the "admiral's writer" school, became a leading candidate. Offered the job, he was urged to take it. In the Navy you don't say no very often if you want to get ahead, so he accepted the post.

Upon arriving in Washington in September 1970, with his wife Toni and two children, he went to work in an office that directly served the nation's senior military man, the chairman of the Joint Chiefs of Staff (JCS). Radford became the personal aide to Rear Admiral Rembrandt C. Robinson, an ambitious and politically savvy officer, who served as a top assistant to the chairman, Admiral Thomas H. Moorer. Moorer was the boss, an ardent anticommunist who concealed tenacity and a thirst for bureaucratic combat beneath a thick Alabama drawl.

Admiral Robinson and Yeoman Radford were a two-man team that ran the Joint Chiefs' liaison office to the National Security Council (NSC). Their assignment didn't amount to much on the organizational chart, but it connected them on one side to the highest reaches of the military, and on the other to the White House and its powerful national security adviser, Henry A. Kissinger. Robinson and Radford handled the flow of classified documents and messages between the Joint Chiefs and the NSC. Though small in size, under Kissinger the NSC wielded far more power than the mammoth bureaucracies of the departments of Defense and State, principally because President Richard M. Nixon wanted it that way.

The two-man team was Moorer's eyes and ears at the NSC, and Robinson stressed to his yeoman that his loyalty to Moorer stood above all else. "It was his responsibility to keep the chairman informed, and I was to help him to do this," Radford later testified of his instruction from Robinson. Though Radford performed all the usual menial tasks of an assistant, from taking dictation to typing, filing, pouring coffee, serving lunch, and arranging Robinson's transportation, the yeoman understood that his main job was to assist Robinson by ensuring that everything they saw and heard inside the White House was promptly passed on to Chairman Moorer.

The Robinson-Radford team would begin each morning at the Joint Chiefs' suite on the second floor of the E-Ring of the Pentagon, then drive to their NSC office, 376A of the old Executive Office Building (EOB) just west of the White House; later in the day they would return to the Pentagon. They often worked past dark, and usually had long, grueling schedules that allowed Radford little time for his family. That loss was offset by his continguity to power and the intimate secrets of the nation's foreign policy. His dedicated service to Robinson, Moorer, and the Joint Chiefs earned him Robinson's praise and the promise of an officer's commission.

Chuck Radford was a sensitive young man, the product of an unusual childhood and a broken home. His father was a Native American, his mother descended from Slavic, Irish, and Jewish ancestors, and Radford had had difficulty gaining acceptance at the places to which his family moved, and at the foster homes to which he had occasionally been sent. Perhaps that was why, from the very outset, Yeoman Radford was enthralled by his new job. "It's a long way from an Indian reservation to a position like that," he remembers. "I thought, my gosh, I've finally broken those ties with my past, and I can really be better than a lot of my cousins and a lot of my family had been. I can finally accomplish something. I even stopped reading newspapers—that's how exciting it was—because the stuff in the newspapers was boring; they didn't know what they were talking about."

The fall of 1970, when Yeoman Radford took up his post, was a pivotal time for the Joint Chiefs of Staff. From their point of view, the president of the United States was out of control.

On January 20, 1969, Richard M. Nixon had become the thirty-seventh president of the United States. Earlier, as a private citizen, Nixon had contemplated several historical foreign policy shifts, including new relationships with the United States' cold war adversaries, China and the Soviet Union, an end to the war in Vietnam, and an attempt to stop bloodshed in the Middle East. Though long regarded as a conservative anticommunist, Nixon actually had a world view that favored diplomacy and arms control over confrontation and a continued arms race. He cultivated a public image of anticommunism because he found it useful, but privately was more flexible in his thinking.

His slim electoral victory in 1968, with a margin of only a half-million votes, represented a tremendous comeback from defeats in the presidential election of 1960 and in the California gubernatorial race in 1962. As he entered the White House, Nixon was full of bitterness and anger about these past defeats, and about years of perceived slights from others in the political establishment. He believed he had never been treated with the respect that a former vice-president should have received. He viewed the nation's capital as a hostile territory populated by his enemies. "Washington is a city run primarily by Democrats and liberals, dominated by like-minded newspapers and other media," Nixon wrote in his autobiography, *RN*. He urged his cabinet to replace holdover bureaucrats with "people who believed in what we were trying to do," and insisted they do so quickly, or the old establishment would "sabotage" their intended reforms. What he wanted from these new people was "undivided loyalty."

Nixon's need to control his political destiny and to prevent the blunting of his agenda by bureaucrats pushed him toward the establishment of what was, in effect, a secret government. An intensely private and withdrawn man, almost the opposite of the usual gregarious politician, Nixon often recoiled from social situations and preferred to be closeted with familiar aides or to sit alone with a pad and pen and jot down his own thoughts. "Meeting new people filled him with vague dread, especially if they were in a position to rebuff or contradict him," Henry Kissinger observed of his former chieftain in the first volume of his own memoirs, *White House Years*. Nixon usually directed his chief of staff H. R. "Bob" Haldeman, his counsel and later domestic adviser John D. Ehrlichman, or his attorney general and close friend John N. Mitchell to carry out the dirty work of imparting bad news or even somewhat unpalatable directives to subordinates.

Both Nixon and Kissinger saw the government bureaucrats as roadblocks to be circumvented. To Nixon, Congress was under the thumb of the Democrats; the Department of State and the Central Intelligence Agency were havens for Eastern Establishment liberals who hated him; and the military was full of doctrinaire, inflexible anticommunists. To circumvent them all, Nixon determined to use an agency first established in 1947 that had lain dormant in the Kennedy and Johnson years but was under the complete control of the White House—the National Security Council. For a man who loved secrecy, it was perfect. While the statutory members of the NSC were officers of the cabinet, the national security adviser and his staff were presidential appointees who did not have to be confirmed by Congress. The NSC was chartered as a clearinghouse for information from State, the Pentagon, and the intelligence community flowing to the White House, and it could take action quickly. Nixon had seen the NSC work under President Dwight D. Eisenhower, but then it had been balanced by the power and influence of Secretary of State John Foster Dulles.

Nixon constructed a cabinet that could be ignored or easily manipulated, depending on the whim of the White House. Generally, the most important cabinet post for an incoming administration is the secretary of state. Nixon appointed to that post William P. Rogers, attorney general under Eisenhower, and a man who had befriended Nixon at a time when he had needed friends, after the gubernatorial defeat in 1962. In the opening hours of Rogers' tenure as secretary of state, Nixon had Kissinger send letters to many leaders of foreign nations, without advising Rogers or his department that he was doing so. Rogers' refusal to show outrage at this deliberate slight assisted in his department's emasculation. Rogers' complete eclipse occurred less than a month later, when Nixon met with Soviet Ambassador to the United States Anatoly Dobrynin without Rogers present, and told the ambassador that Kissinger would meet regularly with him from then on. As Kissinger reports in his memoirs, after that, Rogers was routinely left out of all important initiatives having to do with foreign policy, or informed only after they had been irretrievably set in motion. Items on which Rogers was kept in the dark included the strategic arms limitation talks (SALT) with the Russians that aimed to put a ceiling on nuclear arsenals, the secret negotiations with China and the trip to Peking, and the secret peace talks with the North Vietnamese in Paris.

Whereas Bill Rogers had no real foreign policy experience, the man selected by Nixon as secretary of defense had considerable experience in military affairs. Melvin R. Laird had spent eight terms as a congressman sitting on the powerful House Appropriations Committee, which handled the funding of the Pentagon and the intelligence agencies. He understood the military bureaucracy far better than Nixon or Kissinger. He also appears to have understood the way Nixon planned to work, and though he protested being cut out of many decisions, he decided to continue on in his post in an attempt to make his own imprint on winding down the war in Vietnam.

Nixon's agreement to let Johnson holdover Richard M. Helms remain as the director of the CIA was among his most astounding appointments. "The two were polar opposites in background," Haldeman wrote in his memoir, *The Ends of Power*, "Helms the aloof, aristocratic, Eastern elitist; Nixon the poor boy (he never let you forget

it) from a small California town." The appointment was especially
puzzling in light of Nixon's deep-seated belief that the CIA had
contributed to his loss in the 1960 election. Back then, Nixon told
friends, the CIA had played politics with the Bay of Pigs operation,
briefing candidate John Kennedy on it to the point where he was able
to take a strong anti-Castro stand that Nixon did not want to take
because it might jeopardize the impending Bay of Pigs invasion; the
CIA had also given Kennedy ammunition for his accusations about a
"missile gap" that he exploited in similar fashion. On both of these
issues, sabotaged by the CIA, Nixon believed he had appeared weak or
uninformed during the televised debates, which were widely credited
with having won Kennedy the election. That the election had turned
on a number of factors, not the least among them Nixon's physical
appearance on television rather than the content of his remarks, did
not prevent Nixon from continuing to believe that the CIA had done
him in. Nixon planned to ignore the CIA as much as he could, and
leaving Helms in place—where he and his agency could be embarrassed—became part of the plan. Nixon and Helms thought little of
each other; there was at least one near-confrontation between them.
According to Nixon's memoirs, when Nixon requested the complete
Bay of Pigs files, Helms, after initially balking, turned over what the
president believed to be a sanitized file.

Nixon's relationships with the senior military officers of the nation
were the most complex of those within the upper echelon. It was
impossible to carry out the war in Southeast Asia without cooperation
from the Pentagon, and such matters as the secret bombings in
Cambodia and the air war against North Vietnamese cities required
the support of the Joint Chiefs of Staff. But Kissinger courted individual service chiefs and encouraged them to report directly to him rather
than to Secretary Laird. He also, on behalf of the president, requested
that the JCS set up a "backchannel" through which he and Nixon could
transmit private messages within the government and abroad. Such
backchannels were normally operated for the government by the CIA
and the National Security Agency (NSA), but Nixon wanted to circumvent those intelligence agencies. Using special codes, teletypes, and
secure terminals located at the Pentagon and in the White House
Situation Room, the president and his national security adviser could
send and receive messages to selected American officials and members
of foreign governments around the world without alerting the rest of
the United States government.

This backchannel for transmitting and receiving messages was
under the control of the JCS and physically located in the Digital

Information Relay Center in the Pentagon basement. Operated under a twenty-four-hour guard and open only to those with the highest security clearances, the center was linked to military commanders and installations worldwide. It allowed senior officers to communicate in single-copy messages that were not filed or retained and could not be read by others in the government. At banks of code machines, terminals, and teletypes, technicians would decipher incoming messages using a card system and then route the information via pneumatic tube to the proper location within the Pentagon. Or it would be sent to compatible equipment located in the West Wing basement of the White House, adjacent to Kissinger's office. One of the most secret links at the center was the Navy's SR-1 channel, which Kissinger would use on his first secret trip to the People's Republic of China because it could not be monitored by the State Department or the CIA. The secretary of defense normally had access to the Relay Center, but, according to a technician who worked there at the time, in late 1970, the guards at the main doors were given orders—apparently from the White House—to prevent Laird or any of his aides from entering the facility.

Kissinger wrote that "extraordinary procedures" were necessary for a president who didn't trust his cabinet and wouldn't give cabinet officers direct orders:

> Nixon feared leaks and shrank from imposing discipline. But he was determined to achieve his purposes; he thus encouraged procedures unlikely to be recommended in textbooks on public administration, that, crablike, worked privily around existing structures. It was demoralizing for the bureaucracy, which, cut out of the process, reacted by accentuating the independence and self-will that had caused Nixon to bypass it in the first place.

To the Joint Chiefs, the backchannel and the Kissinger overtures to the service chiefs provided the military with special access to the commander in chief, a wondrous thing at a time when they were engaged in a war that was not being won. Yet these backchannel operations also provided the chiefs with indelible evidence that the president was circumventing other officials in the government, and was probably doing the same to them.

The Pentagon brass faced a dilemma. On the one hand, they approved of the president's and Kissinger's readiness to use military force in an effort to rejuvenate the United States' efforts to win the grinding, frustrating war in Southeast Asia. They secretly applauded when in March 1969 the president charged them, through backchannels, with conducting secret bombing missions over neutral Cambodia. These missions would continue for the next fourteen months, and had as their target suspected North Vietnamese and Vietcong "sanctuaries" in that country. But even when the brass was included as a partner in White House machinations—used to create a second set of reports to conceal the actual targets of the air strikes, or asked to provide military communications links for secret diplomatic forays—the brass was an uneasy partner in the alliance. Military officers sensed that they were merely being used as instruments to further Nixon's own ends; their belief that this was the case was furthered by the events of ensuing months, during which they saw themselves being ignored, cut out, and circumvented on all the important issues—the conduct of the war, troop withdrawals, the peace negotiations, and SALT, just to name the most important ones. The members of the Joint Chiefs of Staff watched with rising frustration as the president and the former Harvard professor—whom they especially disliked—exerted dictatorial control over the military bureaucracy by telling the brass how to run the war.

One of the men who served on the Joint Chiefs, former Chief of Naval Operations Admiral Elmo R. Zumwalt, Jr., wrote of the problem in his 1976 memoir, *On Watch*. He described

> the deliberate, systematic and, unfortunately, extremely successful efforts, of the President, Henry Kissinger, and a few subordinate members of the inner circle to conceal, sometimes by simple silence, more often by articulate deceit, their real policies about the most critical matters of national security: the strategic arms limitation talks (SALT) and various other of the aspects of "detente," the relations between the United States and its allies in Europe, the resolution of the war in southeast Asia, the facts about America's military strength and readiness. Their concealment and deceit was practiced against the public, the press, the Congress, the allies, and even most of the officials within the executive branch who had a statutory responsibility to provide advice about matters of national security.

The Joint Chiefs, the military advisers to the president, consisted of the chairman, the chiefs of staff of the Army and the Air Force, the chief of naval operations, and the Marine Corps commandant. The men in what was known as the Tank, the windowless room in the Pentagon where the Joint Chiefs of Staff met, grew increasingly desperate through the first years of the Nixon administration, believing that the political side of the United States governing elite was undermining the military's legitimate efforts to conduct a war and to keep the country safe from external threats of harm.

Admiral Thomas H. Moorer was appointed by Nixon to be chairman of the Joint Chiefs of Staff in July of 1970, after a period of months in which he had done the job on a day-to-day basis because of the illness of his predecessor, Army General Earle G. Wheeler. A swaggering former aviator who had survived Pearl Harbor and wore that as a badge of honor, Moorer constantly made reference to that Japanese attack as the reason why the United States must build its war machine and be prepared for a global battle with the communists. Moorer "made no pretense of academic subtlety," Kissinger wrote; rather, "he exaggerated the attitude of an innocent country boy caught in a jungle of sharpies." The admiral was known for his tough talk, especially his insistence that the U.S. could still prevail in Vietnam through effective use of its military might. Because of this Moorer stance, Nixon and Kissinger believed they could convince him to carry out certain secret military operations that would be kept from the Pentagon bureaucracy. Upon his elevation, Moorer decided to cooperate with the White House. However, Moorer must have recognized that Nixon's and Kissinger's penchant for secrecy was resulting in the military being denied the information it thought it needed to win the war and to keep the country safe from the communist threat worldwide.

Moorer must have felt desperate, but desperation is often born when men are in the dark, as the JCS was in those days. While Kissinger and Nixon reassured military and congressional conservatives about their dealings with the Russians, they told liberals and arms control advocates that assuaging these same conservatives was making progress difficult on SALT, which involved complex formulas to limit warheads, bombers, submarines, and the defensive weapons system called ABM, the antiballistic missile. This strategy of telling each end of the spectrum that the other was at fault left hawks and doves screaming at each other, and Kissinger and Nixon free to do whatever they wanted in the SALT negotiations. The JCS's sense of betrayal intensified during 1970. They felt beleaguered by an unpopular war that seemed only to expend lives and weapons; while the military services took the casualties and the brunt of the public's antipathy, behind the chiefs' backs, Nixon and Kissinger were negotiating away everything for which American and South Vietnamese blood had been spent. To the JCS, the fact that the Nixon-Kissinger secret diplomacy was being conducted to end the war while at the same time White

House instructions were in place to escalate the war on the battlefield was tantamount to treason.

The backchannel existed, and so did the liaison office that consisted of Admiral Robinson and Yeoman Radford. The office provided a home for the JCS inside the White House and, as Radford later explained, shortly after he arrived at his post in September 1970, JCS Chairman Moorer became the beneficiary of an espionage operation run by Robinson and Radford and directed against President Nixon and National Security Adviser Kissinger.

The very chaos attendant on Kissinger's effort to control foreign policy and expand his NSC empire gave the spy ring breathing room at its birth. During the Kissinger-led expansion, Robinson managed to establish himself and Radford in an office in the EOB from which Robinson was able to remove all the civilians. Now, Robinson could handle the flood of paperwork between the Pentagon and the NSC as a lean, all-military operation. Unseen by civilians, the office faded into the background, and Robinson liked it that way, for he enjoyed the intrigue and secrecy attendant upon acting behind the scenes. Robinson's attitude became evident shortly after Radford started work at the liaison office. The yeoman had innocently told a caller that the admiral was unavailable because Robinson was then out of the office at a meeting with Kissinger's deputy, Brigadier General Alexander Meigs Haig. When Radford later informed Robinson of the call he was reprimanded and reminded not to reveal Robinson's whereabouts to anyone. If Robinson received a visitor at the office, Radford was not to tell anyone that the person had been there. "He [Robinson] said that if the wrong person found out" about the visitor, "they might think that something was going on."

That was before Radford himself found out what was "going on." The first sign was the removal of the last civilian secretary from the liaison office, who was bitter about losing the job. Admiral Robinson had done his best to make her feel unwanted, for instance by refusing to let her type his most sensitive memos. Chuck Radford liked the secretary, for despite her anger, she even helped Radford learn his duties so he could properly replace her.

Radford was able to make friends with the woman he replaced because he had a gift for disarming people and collecting information, traits that served him well as Robinson's aide—and that also served Robinson's purposes. The senior officer told the yeoman he must be wary of everyone else, and he must not let himself be pumped for information, especially by Kissinger's NSC civilians who would inevitably try to query him about the JCS. At the same time, Robinson instructed, Radford should collect information and gossip from the NSC and make sure that Robinson "saw or knew about what I saw by bringing him a copy or asking him if he had seen what I had seen. . . . He made it clear . . . that he expected my loyalty, and that I wasn't to speak outside of the office about what I did in the office."

Radford attacked the task with gusto, getting to know many people on the EOB staff, "people in the reproduction center and the burn center and in the bookkeeping center. You know, I was everywhere. Always constantly moving and talking." Radford fed back to Robinson the substance of these conversations and was praised, and came to feel he was "pretty well liked."

Yeoman Chuck Radford, the straight arrow, was an espionage controller's dream, a barely noticed secretary who traveled easily through NSC staff offices. It wasn't long before he was converted from a passive to an active spy. It happened around the time Radford was taking dictation, a memo to Moorer about a conversation Robinson had had with a defense contractor; as Radford scribbled in shorthand, he mentioned that he had picked up some information on the same subject in conversation with an NSC staffer. Robinson stopped dictating and told Radford never to hold back anything he'd heard, no matter how minor it seemed. Radford understood that he was now to do more than look or listen. That was when he began to steal information actively, taking documents from burn bags, making extra copies in the reproduction center, peering over the shoulders of bookkeepers. As the yeoman grew more adroit at gathering information, he earned ever greater praise from his admiral.

"You have to understand," says retired Rear Admiral Gene R. LaRocque, "that with the military it's 'us versus them.' The Navy in particular. Civilians are all to be feared and distrusted and guarded against. . . . So that reading their traffic and taking it out of their burn bags was all considered legitimate. They [the military] saw themselves as beleaguered." LaRocque, who first learned about Radford's activities when pieces of the story broke publicly, deplores the spying, but understands it as an extension of Robinson's personality. Robinson was, LaRocque says, "totally blind-doggedly loyal to Moorer."

When Rear Admiral Robert O. Welander replaced Robinson, who was being given a cherished sea command, the praise for Radford became fainter—but the job was still there to be done. From late 1970 to late 1971, Yeoman Radford collected literally thousands of documents from the White House and, while on foreign trips, documents that ranged from private messages between Kissinger and Nixon that involved their secret China gambit, to negotiating stances over sensitive

European military bases, to closely guarded policy papers put together by Kissinger's staff, to Nixon's strategy and timetables for withdrawing troops from Southeast Asia.

On the morning of December 14, 1971, Yeoman Chuck Radford read Jack Anderson's column and realized it was trouble. Anderson had obtained explosive White House and Defense Department documents on the Nixon strategy of secret support and a "tilt" to Pakistan in its South Asian border war with India. One of these was a memo on naval ship movements written days earlier by Admiral Welander. Cited in the column were also four more top-secret government memos, and their accumulated weight blew away Nixon's public stance of neutrality in the conflict.

The Anderson column embarrassed Nixon and Kissinger at a time when Nixon was already enraged because the "tilt" as a strategy was failing. After two weeks of fighting, Pakistani forces had been routed by the Indian army and a final surrender was imminent. The Washington Special Action Group (WSAG), a crisis management team of senior bureaucrats established by Kissinger, had met on December 3 and 4, and Anderson had obtained minutes of these meetings. They contained Kissinger's complaint that he was "getting hell every half hour from the president that we are not being tough enough on India. He doesn't believe we're carrying out his wishes. He wants to tilt in favor of Pakistan. He feels everything we do comes out otherwise." The Anderson column also revealed that Nixon had sent a naval task force to the Bay of Bengal, risking a "dangerous confrontation" with Soviet vessels stationed there in support of India.

Part of the reason Nixon and Kissinger were so embarrassed was that West Pakistan's president Yahya Khan was involved on the losing side of the conflict. In fact, the "tilt" had been ordered to support Khan, whose army had been inflicting atrocities on tens of thousands of East Pakistani separatists and ordinary citizens in West Pakistan, and whose outrages had induced India to enter and prevail in the conflict. Why support such a butcher? Nixon and Kissinger backed Khan because he had provided the link to the Peking leadership through which the president and Kissinger had negotiated his stunning diplomatic opening to China.

To get away from the now-public disparity between his stance of neutrality and his open tilt to Pakistan, Nixon flew to Key Biscayne and sailed aboard his friend Bebe Rebozo's cabin cruiser, the *Coco Lobo III*. And Kissinger and the Department of Defense issued orders to find and punish whoever had leaked the memos to Anderson.

Radford knew he had not been Anderson's source, and planned to say so as he completed his drive to the Pentagon for interrogation on December 16. Chuck had never discussed the details of his job with any outsider, not even with his wife, Toni. Moreover, this incident had blown up just when he thought he was on the verge of getting away from clandestine work. He'd been trying to get a new assignment since Admiral Robinson had gone to sea and been replaced by Welander. His new boss was a tall, studious, career destroyer officer who came reluctantly to the liaison job; to Radford, Welander appeared indecisive and nervous about the work they were called on to do for Chairman Moorer. "He wasn't careful like Robinson," Radford remembers; "He just didn't seem very astute." By the fall of 1971 Radford had begun to seek a transfer and the commission he'd been promised. His fitness reports glowed with praise from both Robinson before he'd left and Welander, as recently as December 1, when the admiral had judged Radford "hardworking and reliable . . . displays initiative and imagination in performance of assigned duties . . . has performed exceptionally well in a unique and demanding assignment." The transfer didn't come, but Radford continued to seek it. Welander didn't assist him in that search, saying a transfer would have to wait because Radford was too important in his present post.

When Welander read the Anderson column on December 14, and before he'd actually talked to Radford, Welander rushed to accuse Radford of the leak, and did so to an officer to whom he had close ties, General Haig, deputy to Kissinger. Haig called presidential assistant John Ehrlichman, who immediately assigned White House aide David R. Young to investigate the leak. Young was a Kissinger protégé who had worked at the NSC and had transferred to Ehrlichman's staff. In July 1971, with Nixon's approval, Ehrlichman had appointed Young and another aide, Egil "Bud" Krogh, Jr., to be codirectors of a new Special Investigations Unit and to investigate the leak of what became known as the Pentagon Papers; Daniel J. Ellsberg, the former government analyst accused of leaking the documents, was also targeted for study. With their office in the basement of the EOB, Young and Krogh were later dubbed the Plumbers, because they were assigned to stop news leaks, and because Young had a self-deprecating sense of humor and had placed a sign on the door that read PLUMBER. Krogh and Young had worked closely with Haig on the Pentagon Papers–Ellsberg investigation and on a leak to *The New York Times* concerning the SALT talks. Thus, when Welander came to him about the Anderson column on December 14, Haig immediately turned to Ehrlichman, the boss of the leak investigators Krogh and Young.

The top civilian investigator at the Defense Department was W. Donald Stewart, an irrepressible, tenacious, and earthy former FBI man whose honesty and blunt language often rankled the high-ranking military officers and senior bureaucrats who became the targets of his probes. Stewart also had been involved in the Pentagon Papers–Ellsberg investigation, as well as that on the SALT leak, and had been trying to track down the source of eleven other Jack Anderson columns published between March and May 1971 that contained classified information from the Defense Department. In his job, Stewart often dealt with the department's general counsel, J. Fred Buzhardt, who reported directly to Secretary Melvin Laird.

To investigate this new Anderson column Stewart quickly assembled a four-man support team that included Raymond J. Weir, Jr., a polygraph expert from the National Security Agency, the Defense Department's code-breaking and communications arm. Stewart and his support team joined Young from the White House and decided to question all officers and enlisted men assigned to the suite of offices in which Chairman Moorer's staff at the Pentagon worked. Based on Welander's assertion, Chuck Radford was the prime suspect.

Welander was outraged; as he told Haig on the morning of the fourteenth, the column "could only have come from my files." He thought so because the Anderson column cited or quoted five documents: 1) a Welander memo to Haig, dated December 10, that detailed the movements of the USS *Enterprise* carrier task force as it steamed toward the Indian Ocean; 2) the minutes of the December 3 meeting of the Washington Special Action Group; 3) a separate JCS memo on the December 4 WSAG meeting; and 4 and 5) two State Department cables from the U.S. Embassy in New Delhi. The presence in the column of his memo gave Welander the idea that Radford had been the leaker, for that memo (and no other one cited) contained a phrase that Anderson had repeated but misconstrued. Welander had talked of the ships being armed "with Tartar Sam," by which he meant that they carried surface-to-air missiles (SAMs) that went by the name of Tartars. Anderson had mistaken Tartar Sam for the name of one of the ships.

Welander was certain the leaker was Radford, but there was room for doubt. At least five people had seen the "Tartar Sam" memo— Welander, Radford, Haig, Kissinger, and an aide to Haig. Moreover, the prevalence of photocopying machines in all of their offices argued that far more people might have had copies of the memo. And the other documents cited by Anderson spread the net of suspicion even wider; for instance, the minutes of the December 3 WSAG meeting had been written by a civilian assistant secretary of defense, and the memo on the December 4 meeting had been produced by one of Moorer's aides. Questioned later, Welander admitted that about fifty Pentagon officials had access to each of these documents, and ten to both; that many people on the Haig or Kissinger staffs could have copied Welander's memo; and that several persons in the Pentagon could have had access to his files, safes, and the burn bags in which he ordered Radford to place rough drafts of documents.

The people who had a clear motivation to make the leak were the Joint Chiefs. On December 10, and without any consultation with Laird or any senior Navy commanders—or even a meeting of the NSC or of the WSAG—Nixon had sent the *Enterprise* and nine accompanying warships filled with two thousand combat-ready Marines to the Bay of Bengal. The group was known as Task Group 74. The action outraged the Joint Chiefs, as Admiral Zumwalt reported in his memoir, *On Watch*. They were especially concerned because in response a Russian task group also moved into the area, making it possible that a confrontation could happen, one about which the Joint Chiefs had little information. "Perhaps the President and Kissinger, both of whom were quite clearly frustrated by their inability to influence events on the subcontinent, impulsively organized TG 74 and sent it on its way in a final effort to show the world that America was not to be taken lightly," Zumwalt wrote.

The investigators were convinced that Radford had been responsible for the leak to Anderson in December and for those in the spring of 1971. As it turned out, the source for the eleven earlier columns was an Army enlisted man at the time, a communications specialist named Stephen W. Linger, who had worked at the Digital Information Relay Center, the room through which Moorer provided the backchannel to Kissinger and Nixon. Linger insists that he never gave Anderson anything that threatened the lives of U.S. servicemen and never turned over top-secret documents, but that he had given important material to Anderson because he had become disillusioned with the Pentagon and the conduct of the Vietnam War. Linger had nothing to do with the India-Pakistan leak, since he had left the military in March 1971. But he has admitted to making the eleven others to Anderson, which revealed the Air Force cloud-seeding program over Laos, U.S. monitoring of South Vietnamese President Thieu's private conversations, and Admiral Moorer's receipt of FBI surveillance reports on antiwar and black dissident groups in the U.S. These FBI reports involved domestic political activity and were outside the purview of the chairman of the JCS. Linger handled the reports when they came over the teletypes at the Pentagon Relay Center. "I grew up real fast at the Pentagon,"

Linger told us. "I saw the government was doing things that were wrong."

But Radford was the prime suspect in the December leak at the time, and not only because of his contiguity to Welander. He had two strikes against him: He had been stationed in India, and he had some social contact with Jack Anderson.

The social contact had come about by accident. While attending a Mormon service in New Delhi, Radford and his wife had met Jack Anderson's parents, who were traveling through India en route to Ethiopia. The Andersons needed help with their visas, and Radford, who worked at the embassy, was able to lend a hand. Correspondence and exchanges of Christmas cards followed, and, soon after the Radfords were posted to Washington in the fall of 1970, the elder Andersons, while visiting their son, invited the young couple and their children to the columnist's Bethesda home. It was not until he arrived at the suburban home that Radford realized that the man he was visiting, and to whom the elder Andersons had referred, was the famed investigative reporter. Jack thanked Radford for the help he had given the elder Andersons in India, and his parents spent most of the evening talking to Radford about the Mormon Church and India. Anderson confirms that he hardly talked to the yeoman at all that night, and not at all about journalism or the military.

Next day the yeoman told Admiral Robinson where he'd been the previous evening. "Robinson was surprised," Radford told us, and Robinson then called Moorer to report. Word came back from Moorer that Chuck was to keep his job separate from his social activities. Radford recalls, "I felt better for having told him. I wanted to make sure that he could count on my loyalty."

After several more months of no contact with the Andersons, Chuck Radford was doing some research on his great-great-grandfather and called Libby Anderson, the columnist's wife and a Mormon, for help with the family genealogy; later, Toni Radford talked on the phone with Libby about how to conduct the research, which is required of Mormons. Then, on December 5, 1971, Jack called to extend an invitation to his parents' fiftieth wedding anniversary in Utah; the Radfords declined, unable to make the trip. A week later, on December 12, Anderson called again and asked the Radfords to come to dinner that very night. Radford thought it odd to get such an invitation on short notice, but he and Toni met the Andersons at a Chinese restaurant of which Anderson was a part-owner.

That dinner two nights before the column appeared would provide investigators with their strongest evidence linking Anderson and Radford. But Radford said he had no idea of the forthcoming column, and didn't discuss India or Pakistan or any other aspect of his job at dinner. Moreover, if he had been the source, he surely would not have accepted a dinner invitation from Anderson and then been seen with the famous columnist in such a public way at a time close to the column's release. Anderson denies ever receiving material from Radford. "I got those documents from at least five or six sources," he says. Although even many years after the event he would not name the real sources, he did say that "You don't get these kind of secrets from an enlisted man. You get them from generals and admirals. You don't get them from the little guys."

On December 14, when he read the column, Radford knew it was trouble, and focused, as Welander had, on the reference to "Tartar Sam." When he and Welander made their daily ride from the Pentagon to the EOB, the atmosphere in the car was tense and the conversation brief.

"Radford, did you give my memo to Jack Anderson?" Welander asked.

"No, sir, I didn't," Radford said.

Despite his denial, Radford was ordered to stay home the next day and wait for a call from the Navy. "I was under virtual house arrest. I felt humiliated. . . . I felt things were going on around me that I couldn't control. I felt helpless."

So it was that around three in the afternoon of that balmy December 16 he arrived at the Pentagon for interrogation. The event was held in a two-room suite on the second floor of the E-Ring, in a green-walled office furnished with standard furniture and military pictures. Stewart, chief of Defense's investigative division, and Weir from the NSA were accompanied by Young from the Plumbers and Stewart's assistant Joseph D. Donohue. Immediately on arriving, Radford admitted that he was in a vulnerable position because he had known Anderson for about a year. This information startled the investigators, because no one in the Navy had told them of the relationship, even though Radford just as quickly told them that he had relayed news of his meeting Anderson to his former superior, Admiral Robinson. The investigators called Welander, who said that he had not been apprised of the relationship when he took over the liaison office. Radford insisted that he'd told Welander of the December 12 meeting with Anderson, just as he'd reported his first dinner at Anderson's home to Robinson.

Investigator Stewart was upset by Radford's claim of having told Robinson of the first dinner, because earlier in the year, when he'd been looking into the sources for those earlier Anderson columns, he had questioned Robinson, and Robinson had never mentioned that his yeoman was a social acquaintance of the columnist. Once the initial interrogation concluded on December 16, Stewart asked his immediate superior, D. O. Cooke, to call Robinson in San Diego and ask him about this lapse. Cooke made the call, and Robinson verified Radford's story, even remembering that the columnist had met the yeoman through Anderson's parents. But, as Stewart's investigative report concludes, "It was never made quite clear . . . why [Robinson] had not furnished this information during the [earlier] investigation." A year later, Robinson would tell an investigator that he hadn't told Stewart in early 1971 about the Radford-Anderson acquaintance because he had not been specifically asked if he knew anyone acquainted with the columnist.

That afternoon of December 16, Stewart, Young, and the rest of the team asked Radford to take a polygraph examination about his contacts with Anderson. He was willing to do so, believing he would pass with flying colors. Weir and Radford moved to an adjacent office and the yeoman was strapped to the lie detector. What Radford did not consider, and what the investigators did not know, was that an ancillary question about to be asked while Radford was "on the box" would uncover the deeper and more explosive secrets that Radford knew all too well—the extent to which he was spying for the Joint Chiefs of Staff on the president of the United States.

2

CARRYING THE CONTRABAND

A polygraph test is a quiet affair—no bright lights, no shouted accusations, the fewest number of people possible in the room. Stewart and Young waited outside while expert polygrapher Ray Weir calmly asked Yeoman Radford nine questions. Strapped to the lie detector, the yeoman easily answered those that had to do with Anderson; no, he had not passed classified information to Anderson or to any other member of the press, Radford responded, and the needle didn't jump. It also stayed in the truth zone when he was asked if he'd had unauthorized contact with foreign nationals, or had been involved in espionage against the United States, or had ever taken classified documents home.

Then, according to the test report, Weir asked another standard question: "Have you ever furnished classified documents to uncleared persons?"

Radford had felt comfortable talking about Anderson because he'd had nothing to hide, but this question struck to the heart of his job. He believed the question was not a standard one, but, rather, reflected possible knowledge by Stewart's team of his clandestine activities. "I remember feeling, Uh-oh, the data I'm taking from Kissinger and giving to Admiral Welander has somehow been exposed. They caught me." Months earlier, Radford had broken through the rationalization that his job had not been particularly sinister, that it was only a matter of "taking from this branch of the government and giving it to that branch." In that earlier moment of revelation, he had told himself, "Well, no. You're being stupid because this branch [the White House] doesn't want that branch [the Joint Chiefs] to have it." That realization put him "in a vise," but back then he'd still considered himself under Robinson's original junction, "never to speak to anybody," so he'd remained silent. Now, during the lie detector test, in the split second between the time the question was asked and he had to answer it, he reviewed all these emotions. "I couldn't talk about this, but yet how could I deny it, because [if I did] I'd be lying. I was stuck."

So he answered "Yes" to whether he'd ever furnished classified documents to uncleared persons. But he wouldn't give details.

Following this admission by Radford, the report reads,

> he [Radford] became emotionally disturbed and it was deemed advisable to continue no further testing on this statement. He was interrogated concerning these reactions, and he stated that he was concerned about his activity in this area but that he did not feel free to discuss this matter. He further advised that the cause of his concern was a very sensitive operation which he could not discuss without direct approval of Admiral Welander.

As Weir went into the next room to report the surprising nature of the polygraph results to Stewart and Young, Radford became increasingly distraught. "I wanted to talk to Admiral Welander before I said anything more. I wanted to make sure it was all right with him if I went through this."

Thus the stage was set for one of those small misinterpretations of information on which great events sometimes hinge.

"David Young called me," Welander recalls, "and said, 'Radford has admitted to everything but he won't go beyond a certain point without talking to you.'" What Young did *not* tell Welander was the subject of Radford's admissions—and Welander assumed they had to do with Jack Anderson, not with the secret spying Radford had done for the JCS. Welander remembers that Radford was put on the telephone and posed the following question: "'Admiral, they are asking me all about our job at the Pentagon. What should I do?'" Welander, of course, thought

Radford was guilty of the leak, so he responded, "Chuck, all you can do is tell the truth."

Radford took in that instruction and became even more upset. "I started to doubt myself," he later told us. "Was that his [Welander's] voice? Because I was receiving conflicting information and it did not compute. Because I had been told, 'Don't say anything about what you're doing,' and then the same guy is saying, 'Tell them whatever they need to know.' " Radford resolved that conflict on the side of truth and began talking. In the first blush of confession he revealed that he had stolen confidential documents and private correspondence from White House desks, "out" baskets, burn bags, and—in his boldest thefts—from Henry Kissinger's briefcase. He'd also typed cover memos from Admirals Robinson and Welander that went on top of the stolen papers they conveyed to Chairman Moorer and to Admiral Zumwalt, the chief of naval operations.

Though the questioning had started calmly, it soon escalated when Stewart got into the act. The beefy former FBI man was an aggressive interrogator. He urged the yeoman on, and remembers that the interrogation had to be stopped several times when Radford broke down in tears. The source of the tears was religious. As the polygraph report notes, the "subject advised that he felt very guilty about this, since he only enjoyed the freedom which permitted this activity because people trusted him. He stated that these thefts were certainly contrary to his religious faith and he hoped to obtain absolution through prayer."

It was a wrenching experience akin to penance, Radford remembers of that first interview. Once he began to talk, "There was nowhere to draw the line. I just couldn't say 'I did this' and not talk about that. And I didn't want to quit. I wanted to get it off my chest." When he finished, he was drained, hardly able to walk.

Stewart, a hardened investigator, was shocked by Radford's story. That evening he talked in guarded terms about it to his wife, who happened to be the personal nurse to FBI Director J. Edgar Hoover. Stewart told her, "This is a goddamned *Seven Days in May*. We've got the military spying on the president." He was, he recalled to us, "literally shook," and decided that from that moment on, his investigation would concentrate "on the military conspiracy." Though he was a part of the Pentagon bureaucracy, he was "going after the military."

Welander quickly realized that he had made a mistake in advising Radford to talk, and the next day tried to stop Stewart from further questioning the yeoman. He reached Radford early the next morning and told him to get an attorney and to stop talking to the investigators. And he directly challenged Stewart's authority to conduct the interrogation, telling Stewart that he didn't have the proper clearances, and implying that Radford's operation had sanction from the highest levels.

"The day after we first interviewed Radford," Stewart recalls, "I get in bright and early and then Welander is all over me. He was like a madman." Stewart had already learned from Radford that the admiral had advised him to get a lawyer. "I flew off at Welander and told him to shut up and stay out of our business. I told him that in two minutes I'd get whatever damn security clearances I needed."

The secret report on the matter made by Stewart at the time is consistent with what Stewart told us, and shows for the first time what has not been known before now, that under questioning by Stewart and Donohue, Welander admitted receiving the bootlegged documents. Initially, the "quite defensive" Welander would only discuss the Jack Anderson column, but, braced with the substance of Radford's confession, "he did, however, admit receiving classified documents to which Radford referred," but refused to say more because "he had certain confidential relationships with Dr. Kissinger and General Haig." Despite this partial demurrer, the second link in the clandestine chain had definitely been verified.

Over the course of four interviews and lie detector tests from December 16 to 23, 1971, Yeoman Chuck Radford told his story to Stewart, Young, and the investigators. "We're talking about a library," Radford said to us as he summarized his pilfering, "uncounted documents—just thousands, thousands of documents. The safes [at the Pentagon] were full of the stuff." John Ehrlichman, who was responsible for the White House's investigation of the matter, concurred with Radford's assessment: "Radford would go to the staff secretary's office of the NSC and just wander around and take stuff out of baskets. He would take them out and xerox them and put them back. And that [NSC office] was the clearinghouse. That's where all the paperwork went to be redistributed. [Radford] used that like a cafeteria." Don Stewart adds that Radford had a source in the NSC mail room who was "at the focal point," because this person handled the distribution of classified correspondence, including that to and from Kissinger, and was able to "hand [originals or copies] to Radford."

When Radford first started the job at the liaison office, he began immediately to follow Robinson's instruction to report on everything. Soon, he was stealing documents. Then, in December of 1970, Radford was selected for an unusual assignment, as military aide-de-camp to Kissinger's deputy, General Haig, on a trip to Saigon and Phnom Penh. Haig and Robinson were friends. Both were high-ranking military hawks who had offices in the White House complex; Radford remembers that sometimes after work the general and the admiral would share drinks and freewheeling conversations. They had worked together under Kissinger's direction in 1969 to draw up the "Duck Hook" plan, a top-secret study on escalation of the war against North Vietnam. Though Robinson participated with the blessing of Admiral Moorer, then chief of naval operations, the effort was carried out secretly in order to keep knowledge of it hidden from Secretary of Defense Laird. By 1970, Kissinger viewed Robinson as a trustworthy staff member as loyal to the NSC as he was to the Pentagon. That fall, Robinson helped draft Nixon's secret warning to the Soviets to keep their missiles out of a disputed Cuban submarine base—and, without Kissinger's knowledge, Robinson showed the memo to Zumwalt, who had recently been appointed CNO, even though Kissinger did not want the JCS to see it. Zumwalt asked Robinson why such a delicate matter had been kept away from the JCS, and Robinson replied that Kissinger "did not want any policy discussion on the matter."

Haig brought Robinson into a number of highly sensitive NSC operations and therefore at least implicitly, if not explicitly, vouched to Kissinger for Robinson's discretion and allegiance. Haig and Robinson collaborated on the establishment of the military backchannel that allowed Kissinger to circumvent Laird and Secretary of State Rogers in his communications with foreign governments. Kissinger noted in his memoirs that when they were looking for a way to do this during the February 1971 negotiations over the status of West Berlin, Haig "found a solution" by having Robinson set up the link through a Navy channel.

As Radford prepared to accompany Haig on his trip to Southeast Asia, Robinson told him to keep his "eyes and ears" open for information on two subjects of particular interest to the Joint Chiefs, the administration's orchestration of the plan for an all-volunteer army and the schedule for troop withdrawals from Vietnam.

"So I did," Radford recalls, "but I went a little further [and] kept notes as I went along. . . . The information was so overwhelming that I couldn't absorb it all and keep it factual. And what Robinson wanted to know was who said it, when they said it, and where they said it, who they talked to. So what I [gave] Robinson was grass roots data, feedback."

Amazing though it might sound, the Joint Chiefs had little knowledge about the planned withdrawals of their own troops. "We wondered who the hell is the son of a bitch who is coming up with the information" to justify the withdrawals, Welander told us. "The chiefs' viewpoint was being disregarded. If they [Nixon and Kissinger] weren't listening to the chiefs, where were they getting the information to base their decisions?" Welander told us that the Joint Chiefs sought to learn who was developing the data that refuted the military's own numbers on required troop strength. The admiral's comments underscore the desperate position of the Joint Chiefs, and the reason they went to the extraordinary measure of spying on the White House. In their eyes, it was self-defense.

On this first trip with Haig, Radford handled the chores of stenographer, courier, and "baggage boy." Everything from top-secret papers to the general's dirty socks went through his hands. Beyond his primary assignment from Robinson, there were other instructions for the yeoman: to report on agreements in the making with South Vietnamese President Nguyen Van Thieu, and progress in Haig's talks with Cambodian Premier Lon Nol. Robinson had asked Radford for information. Radford, "as cunning as I could be," rationalized, "Well, what's information? Is it written, is it verbal, what is it? So whatever I typed for General Haig I made a carbon copy of. In one case, I couldn't save the carbon copy so I saved the carbons. It worked just as well. . . . If I was asked to put [copies] in the burn bag, well, I would put it in the burn bag, but I made a xerox copy of it first." This was a bold, even reckless course for Radford to pursue, one that led to having to carry back from Southeast Asia a huge government envelope overflowing with hundreds of pages of documents dealing with troop withdrawals, movements, and the eventual winding down of the war. The booty also included information on a more legitimate problem that was vexing the Joint Chiefs, how the Vietcong seemed to learn in advance of the bombing raids what arms caches and base camps the Americans had targeted; often, by the time the bombers made their runs, previously identified targets had been abandoned. Radford brought back information on how American security had been breached on this matter. The bulging envelope also contained private communications and cables that would allow insight into the thinking at high levels.

When Robinson saw what the yeoman had brought, he was stunned and overjoyed. Together, he and Radford spent hours preparing the documents for transmission to Admiral Moorer. Radford felt exalted at Robinson's excitement, expressed in the way Robinson would light up his pipe, puff it "like a steam engine," and pace around the room firing questions as to how and where Radford had obtained the material, so they could put the document into context for Moorer.

"I gave him much more than he could ever get on his own," Radford recalls. The reception by Robinson helped him shake the doubts of his childhood. "I thought, I scored! I'm in now. He likes me. You know, it feels good to be accepted by the guy you work for. . . . Ever since I was a child it's been important to me to be accepted, and I always worked extra hard to be accepted. Especially by the white community. . . . To be accepted by an Anglo with very high standing in the government and who was dynamic and going places—I felt really good about that. I really felt like I was assimilating."

After that, Radford had an open license to purloin documents, and the secure feeling that his superiors wanted him to do so and prized him for his busy hands as well as for his "eyes and ears." Robinson's appetite for the stolen material increased, and as Radford grew more confident of his ability to obtain material, he widened the compass of his search. He established a network of secretaries and clerks throughout the NSC complex, people from whom he could steal documents. If they had a piece of mail to deliver, he'd offer to carry it for them; if they had documents to be photocopied, he'd handle that chore for them. It was as easy as taking candy from a baby—he'd go to the copying machine, make his duplicates, keep the duplicates for Robinson and Moorer, and then deliver the originals and expected copies to the intended party.

To guard against discovery of the pilfering operation, Robinson told Radford to "sanitize" the papers by cutting off the letterhead and other identification symbols, and then to photocopy the excised document with a white piece of paper behind it. The idea may have come from a practice of Admiral Moorer's. According to Admiral Zumwalt's memoir, Moorer told him of an NSC meeting at which a senior civilian Defense official had glanced at Moorer's briefing book and had seen a document with a White House letterhead that had not been sent to Secretary Laird's office. "From then on," Zumwalt wrote, "the Robinson-Welander liaison office made sure to cut off the letterhead before photocopying NSC documents for Moorer."

On the first trip with Haig, Radford recalls, he was selective because Robinson had been specific about what to look for; later, he just took everything:

> If it became available, I took it. [The activity of stealing] became intense . . . all out. I made a career out of it. Everyday. Constantly. Every minute. . . . It was coming in so fast that they couldn't digest it. They were so delighted to have the data . . . and each time I came back they were even more delighted. It was like they were a bunch of buzzards waiting around an empty carcass, waiting to jump in and start biting on it.

The report of the polygraph test supplies a list of the types of documents Radford sent through to Moorer: contingency plans, political agreements, troop movements, behind-the-scenes politics, and security conferences going on between the U.S. government and foreign governments. Radford later told investigators he also had taken memoranda of conversations of private, top-level meetings, cables, secret channel papers involving negotiations with foreign governments, memos regarding internal White House political dealings, and defense budget papers. The yeoman was privy to some of the most sensitive secrets in the White House. He recalls seeing documents discussing the possibility of assassinating Chilean President Salvador Allende; documents on the government's spy satellite network; on the CIA–Howard Hughes project to retrieve a sunken Soviet submarine from the floor of the Pacific Ocean. "There was so much [that] I would see . . . and say to myself, My gosh, you're kidding me! I would grab it. They're doing *what* to the people in Britain? I grabbed it. They're doing *what* with the people in Israel? I grabbed it."

Radford knew that his actions gave his superiors "an excellent overview of what was going on in the White House. . . . Knowledge is power and the more they knew about all this peripheral data [regarding the White House's operations] the more they were able to circumvent and to maneuver and to accomplish their own ends."

And what, we asked him, did he think those ends were? He told us, "Well, bringing Nixon down. Really, getting rid of Kissinger—Kissinger was a real monkey wrench in things."

Radford himself never passed documents directly to Moorer; that task was reserved for Robinson and Welander, and occasionally for Moorer's senior aides at the Pentagon, such as Captain Arthur K. Knoizen, who once told Radford to "keep up the good work." Radford would later testify that that sentiment was echoed by another Moorer aide who he believes saw the documents, Captain Harry D. Train II; "You do good work," he told the yeoman. Admiral Welander acknowledges that Knoizen "knew that Radford was seeing things. I sometimes transmitted material to the chairman through him [Knoizen]." In Chairman Moorer's absence, material was generally held for his return, but on occasion it was sent directly to Admiral Zumwalt, the CNO.

One particularly sensitive subject for the Navy in this period was a bitter dispute with the State Department over the Navy's ability to use a harbor in Greece as the home port for the Sixth Fleet. The Navy wanted pressure put on Athens to comply; the State Department refused, citing the right-wing military dictatorship then in power in Greece. Radford says he was told to obtain information on discussions on this matter being held among senior NSC officials. He did, and documents were immediately sent to Zumwalt. The Navy ultimately prevailed in this dispute.

Radford cannot remember ever sending specific items to the Army or Air Force chiefs; if those services ever received information, he says, they would have done so only through Moorer's office.

In March of 1971 Radford took a second trip with Haig. While in his instructions he was "cautioned several times and told not to take any chances," on this trip, he later admitted, Haig's briefcase was "always open to" him, and he didn't hesitate to dip into it. He also worked tirelessly for Haig, buying his liquor, doing his laundry, and carrying sensitive messages from Haig to the communications center at the U.S. Embassy in Saigon or to American military headquarters and seeing that these messages were transmitted, logged, and safeguarded.

Radford's exertions on this trip yielded material about Haig's discussions with South Vietnamese leaders, military officials, and U.S. Embassy personnel, all of which Robinson routed through to Moorer.

Haig was so pleased with the yeoman's assistance on the trip that he sent a letter to Robinson on March 21, 1971, saying that Radford "was given many requirements at all hours of the day and accomplished them all with enthusiasm and cheerfulness," and that Radford had handled the sensitive messages "in a diligent and expeditious manner. . . . Please extend my personal thanks to Yeoman Radford for a job well done."

That "job well done" got Radford assigned to accompany Haig's boss on another similar trip. It is not clear whether or not Haig recommended this arrangement to Kissinger, but it is likely. By June of 1971 Admiral Robinson had left for his sea duty and been replaced by Admiral Welander, who made the arrangements with Haig for Radford to accompany Kissinger and an entourage of fifteen people on a swing through Southeast Asia from July 1 to July 17. "Be careful and don't get caught," Radford later testified that Welander had instructed him. "Don't take any chances."

The official itinerary for the Kissinger trip listed South Vietnam, Thailand, India, West Pakistan, Paris, and then on to San Clemente to report to the president. However, once in Pakistan, Kissinger made a secret flight to Peking to wrap up the details of the soon-to-be-announced "opening to China." This was one of the most closely held secrets of Nixon's first term—and Radford found out about it.

As he had on the Haig trips, Radford was given unlimited access to Kissinger's personal papers, including his briefcase and luggage. Before the trip was half over, Radford had collected so much material that he had to send it back to Washington via diplomatic pouch. He did so with the assistance of a friend still stationed in the U.S. Embassy in New Delhi. Radford crammed the stolen papers into envelopes and addressed them to himself at the Pentagon, and his friend arranged for the pouch to be sent through the secure courier system.

Then came the prize. Once the plane left Pakistan, Radford rifled Kissinger's briefcase and discovered a document addressed to the president and marked EYES ONLY—Kissinger's report on his talk with Chinese Premier Chou En-lai. Radford scanned it and made notes for Welander, but did not copy it. During the stop in Paris, Radford also obtained details of Kissinger's private talks with North Vietnamese negotiator Le Duc Tho about a possible settlement to the war.

Radford and Kissinger arrived at San Clemente together. Welander and Moorer flew in separately. A National Security Council meeting had been scheduled by the president for Kissinger's return. Radford was summoned to Moorer's suite; there, he saw the chairman in another room, waiting to talk to Welander. It was then that Radford turned over the bulky package of documents he had stolen on the trip. From these documents, the Joint Chiefs learned of the content of the secret talks between Kissinger and Chou, something they could not have otherwise known. Depending on whose version you believe, this either was or was not the first time the Joint Chiefs heard anything at all about the opening to Peking. The documents also gave the Joint Chiefs new information about Kissinger's Paris talks with Le Duc Tho.

A third document obtained by Radford was also welcomed by Moorer—the agenda for the forthcoming NSC meeting. "Kissinger wanted to control those meetings," Radford says, "Just like he wanted to control everything else. . . . My obtaining the agenda put Admiral Moorer in a very powerful position [to] anticipate what Kissinger was going to say and do." During his deft-handed period, Radford obtained several such agendas for his patrons.

On a third trip to Vietnam with Haig, in September of 1971, Radford was able to steal information regarding another matter of prime importance to Moorer, the "Vietnamization" of the war, a strategy in which control of the ground war was progressively turned over to the South Vietnamese; Radford obtained this information from a memo of Haig's conversation (addressed to Kissinger) on his discussion of this issue with President Nguyen Van Thieu. Additional booty from Haig's briefcase included papers pertaining to troop strengths and intended withdrawal rates of American forces.

* * *

Three months later, with the publication of Anderson's column on the Pakistan "tilt," Radford's tenure at the liaison office ended. Though after his confession his progress toward a commissioned officership was obviously halted, Radford chose to remain in the Navy, and did so for five more years, returning to civilian life in 1976. He worked at a nuclear power plant and at a lumber mill and held other jobs. All the while he remained in the naval reserves, and when the Navy instituted a search for submarine yeomen, a local recruiter asked him to reenlist. He did so in July 1982 and today serves as a senior chief yeoman at a naval base on the West Coast. His application for a commission as a chief warrant officer is under consideration. At the time of his reenlistment, he told us, no mention was made of his troubles in the 1970s, and no mention has been made of it to him since by the Navy. He has received all the requisite security clearances to serve on nuclear subs, for instance, and his clearance has been regularly renewed. Though he hasn't been dogged in recent years by what happened in the early 1970s, Radford nonetheless remains bitter about the treatment he received from the Navy at the time of his confession. He had obeyed his superiors but was pilloried for it, and never allowed to rise above an enlisted man's rank.

Radford believes the stealing from the White House was made necessary by decisions on the part of Nixon and Kissinger to withhold vital information from the Joint Chiefs. Radford argues that the president and his national security adviser showed so much contempt for the chiefs, and had so "fragmented the government," that the military was forced to react. "The military had to intervene because if they hadn't, I'm afraid what would have happened. When I first went there [the liaison office] it was all blue sky and apple pie and 'I'm supporting the United States Constitution; I'm up here working with this team.' It didn't take long for me to learn they weren't a team at all. It was factions and splinter groups, and egos, and professional jealousies . . . a sewer. How does a government operate like that?"

When Richard Nixon found out about the military espionage ring that was feeding information to Admiral Moorer, he was faced with a similar question: how to operate a government infected with such profound distrust of the president and his top adviser.

3

THE ADMIRAL'S CONFESSION

AFTER his vacation on Key Biscayne, President Nixon flew briefly to New York for an evening of dinner, sightseeing, and theater with his wife Pat and his daughters Julie and Tricia and their husbands. He flew back to Washington on Sunday, December 19, five days after the damaging Anderson column. He had not been told of the Radford interrogation or confession, and was not told then, because he had to go with Kissinger to Bermuda for two days of meetings with British leaders. Only when Nixon returned to the White House late on Tuesday, December 21, 1971, did he learn of the Radford espionage, in a 6:00 P.M. meeting with his three top advisers: John Ehrlichman, who had been closely following the investigation through David Young; Chief of Staff Bob Haldeman; and Attorney General John Mitchell, who was also the president's closest personal friend in the administration.

Ehrlichman laid out the story from Radford, who by this time had undergone three examinations by Stewart and his team.

Nixon's response to the story was characteristically cautious. He did not become enraged. What Radford was presenting to his investigators were bombshells that in Nixon's view had to be carefully handled. According to Ehrlichman's recollections, the president wondered if Radford was truthfully recounting a clandestine operation by Moorer, or were these merely the exaggerations of a frightened yeoman trying to save himself. Nixon's deeper concern was whether further investigation of the military espionage would expose the supersensitive backchannel that he and Kissinger had set up with the aid of Moorer. To resolve both of these problems, Nixon decreed that Admiral Welander should be questioned to see if he could corroborate Radford's story.

The following day, Ehrlichman summoned the admiral from the Pentagon to Ehrlichman's own large, paneled office on the third floor of the West Wing of the White House, the traditional office for the domestic adviser to the president, located directly above the Oval Office. In nearly three years as Nixon's counsel and domestic chief, Ehrlichman had conducted many sensitive discussions in this comfortable room with its dark mahogany walls, low ceiling, and Queen Anne furniture; few had been as traumatic or would leave as many scars on the administration as the one he conducted with Admiral Welander starting at one in the afternoon of December 22, 1971.

Welander arrived to find Young seated in one wing-backed chair and Ehrlichman on a sofa. The admiral took the other wing chair, and could not help but notice the bulky recorder with a large spool of tape that lay on the coffee table in front of them; a microphone protruded from a nearby stand. Ehrlichman began the interview in a deliberately stern manner. After pleasantries, he handed the admiral a document drafted by Young and based on Radford's confessions. It was to be a "statement of Rear Admiral Robert O. Welander" of the office of the chairman of the Joint Chiefs, and it read, in full:

> Yeoman Charles Radford, while my aide in my capacity as Liaison Officer between the National Security Council and the Office of the Chairman of the Joint Chiefs of Staff, did obtain unauthorized copies of various documents and memoranda relating to, among other matters, memcons [memos of conversations] of private top-level meetings, internal White House political dealings, secret negotiations with foreign governments, contingency plans, political agreements, troop movements, telcons [memos of telephone conversations], secret channel papers and defense budget papers. These papers were obtained surreptitiously from a variety of senior members of the NSC staff and without their knowledge or consent.
>
> Radford furnished me with copies of the foregoing described papers. As I considered it part of my job to inform the Chairman of the Joint

Chiefs, I either directly or indirectly passed those papers of particular interest on to him, or to whomever happened to be Acting Chairman at the time.

Ehrlichman asked Welander to read the statement, correct any inaccuracies, and sign it. Welander read the statement but refused to sign it, and said later that Ehrlichman had been trying to force him to "admit to the wildest possible, totally false charges of 'political spying' on the White House." And so, he later testified, he found himself "trying to put gross distortions of fact and circumstances into some reasonable and rational perspective." Ehrlichman would have preferred that Welander sign the document, but he mainly wanted to impress the admiral that this meeting was held "at the president's request," and that the situation was viewed "very, very seriously." Today, Ehrlichman muses, he would have read him his rights, "but that wasn't the vogue in those days."

Instead, Ehrlichman proceeded to disarm Welander so completely that the admiral's initial refusal to sign the statement proved only prelude to a confession that lasted more than an hour and was much more detailed than the admissions on the statement. As Ehrlichman began the questioning, he carefully asked the admiral if the recorder could be turned on. Welander agreed that it could.

This tape of Admiral Welander's confession was to become one of the greatest secrets of the Nixon years, one so closely held that its very existence forced many important people to actions they might otherwise never have taken, and which eventually contributed substantially and directly to Nixon's resignation. The tape and its transcript have never before been made public, and although the existence of Welander's confession has been known for some time, the story of the tape and its precise contents has never been fully told prior to the publication of this book. Appendix B of this book contains this Welander confession, as well as a later one.

Ehrlichman began by asking Welander to give him "a feel for this man Radford," and "a little bit about the Joint Chiefs of Staff liaison operation and how that works."

Welander described his "two hats and two offices," one title as assistant for national security affairs to the chairman of the Joint Chiefs, and the other as a senior member of the National Security Council staff, with offices in both the Pentagon and the EOB. A JCS liaison office had been established inside the White House ten years earlier, and its occupant had performed the role of military adviser to the head of the NSC. That function changed "rather significantly" when Nixon became president in 1969 and Alexander Haig became Kissinger's military assistant, Welander explained. The office had remained but now reported through Haig as a conduit for information between the NSC and the JCS. It was seemingly because both Robinson and Welander had reported to the NSC through Haig that Welander appeared insistent in the interview/confession that Ehrlichman talk to Haig, "really about some of the other things I do specifically for Henry [Kissinger]. . . . many times there are things which he wants to come to the attention of the chairman." Well, yes, that avenue was there for Kissinger, Welander added later in the interview, but messages to and from Kissinger went through Haig. "Nine-tenths of the things that I do I give to Al, and then it's a matter of his judgment whether or not it goes to Henry." Most of this work was "outside the correspondence system," meaning that it was confidential information rarely made available to anyone else on the NSC staff other than Haig.

After setting out his legitimate function, the admiral spoke of Radford as "one of the finest young fellows" he had ever worked with, praising him as "extremely conscientious" and "completely selfless." He related how Radford had wanted to get out of his assignment because the hours were so demanding, but that a transfer had been denied. He pointed out that he had tried to loosen the reins on Radford so the yeoman could spend more time with his family, and had then been chagrined to learn that Radford had been moonlighting to earn money. "That disappointed me a little bit," Welander said.

We asked Radford about this recently, and he says Welander "never said anything to me about my working at those other jobs. I never heard any criticism about it." He undertook those jobs in a drugstore, as a newspaper delivery man, and as a security guard, because "it was expensive living in Washington. I had two kids and my wife wasn't working."

In Ehrlichman's comfortable office, after dispensing with Radford, they were ready for the larger issues. Welander said his relationship with Moorer was so exclusive that it sometimes sparked battles within the JCS, especially when Moorer was away. At such times, Welander was technically subject to the orders of the acting chief, a title that rotated alternately from one service chief to another; Welander would usually withhold from the acting chief the information he got from Radford, even when Welander was subjected to "knock-down and drag-out fights" in the halls of the Pentagon from an acting chief who demanded the "sensitive" information. Welander's ability to hold back the material stemmed from his powerful personal relationship with Moorer. Ehrlichman asked him specifically if he reported to the Joint

Chiefs or to Moorer. "There's nobody between me and Admiral Moorer," Welander explained. "I mean it's a direct personal liaison." He only gave materials to the acting chairman when it was absolutely unavoidable, and even then, "I very carefully paraphrase it or just give him exactly what he needs to have to act as chairman."

Welander told Ehrlichman and Young that he had "agonized a hell of a lot over this thing," that it was "personally embarrassing to me, and I think it could be potentially embarrassing to Admiral Moorer, whom I think the world of." Welander was good at knowing where to put his loyalty. It was one of the qualities that recommended him to Moorer and Zumwalt for the highly sensitive liaison and espionage operation at the NSC. Immediately prior to that appointment, Welander had worked for Zumwalt in the CNO's office, and for Moorer when he had been CNO. Earlier in his career Welander had followed the standard route to advancement, a degree from the Naval Academy, a career in the destroyer fleet; he had come to Washington to have his ticket punched, that is, to hold down a Pentagon desk assignment, a prerequisite in the modern Navy for being awarded the rank of admiral.

Welander gave no sign to Ehrlichman and Young that he had not wanted the liaison office assignment. It was a job that was "very much in demand," supposedly "the finest job for a flag officer." But years later Welander insists he was essentially pressured into taking the position. "I wanted to go to sea," he told us, but Moorer's assistant Captain Harry Train had reminded him, " 'You're the only guy that Bud Zumwalt and Moorer agree on. They both trust you.' I knew that [the job] would help me get what I wanted, which was to command a task force."

Welander arrived at the post in early May 1971, and his month-long apprenticeship in the liaison office under Robinson was difficult. Welander was tall, bookish, and inclined to overly study a matter before making a move, while Robinson was short, brash, decisive— "very abrasive," Welander called him, and disparaged Robinson's proclivity for convincing other admirals to do "something to advance his career."

Radford later provided his own insights on the contrasts between the two men. The yeoman liked Robinson and admired the care with which Robinson would meticulously review, analyze, and catalog what had been purloined, and then deliver it personally to Moorer. Welander, says Radford, was less disciplined and less careful about the material, and would see that the material was often passed to Moorer through aides such as Knoizen and Train.

Despite what Radford referred to as Welander's "cold feet," the admiral carefully followed Robinson's instructions during the month-long training period, which included sessions on the "gossip" among the NSC staff. Welander says Robinson instructed him on "who was doing what to who" at the NSC and "who had what kinds of information." Robinson hadn't relied solely on Radford in the gathering of information, but also had developed his own sources, and, Welander says, Robinson would trade a piece of information about the Pentagon to a civilian NSC aide in exchange for a piece from within that organization. Welander took over that operation as well, which allowed him—as Robinson had done—to come into the possession of "talking papers," or summaries of topics and likely debate on them that would ensue during forthcoming policy meetings. Such "talking papers" had been prepared for Kissinger, and by rushing them to Moorer the chairman was enabled to prepare his own strategic responses to the initiatives Kissinger would launch at NSC meetings.

There was a conscious decision on the part of Moorer to sacrifice certain privileged Pentagon information in order to obtain the more valuable talking papers. "It was a *quid pro quo* arrangement," Welander told us; when he first began at the liaison office, he was told by Robinson and by Moorer's aide Harry Train that it would be his decision as to what they would put out as bait. He had to be sure they didn't go too far and offer up really sensitive JCS material—but, he reported, he did give up everything from backchannel messages between General Creighton W. Abrams in Vietnam and Chairman Moorer to position papers on troop movements. NSC staffers "came to me with all kinds of requests, all the time. I often felt I was giving up more to them than I was getting," Welander recalls.

Amid the confusion of the NSC staff, Welander thought that it was only Haig who understood his role completely. He reported to Haig virtually every day, and "oftentimes in the evening, when things had quieted down." As Robinson had, Welander forged a close relationship with Haig. It was Haig who had "pressed" him to provide Radford for the Kissinger trip, and because of Welander's own close relationship with Haig, he could hardly refuse such a request.

After having plunged into confession in Ehrlichman's West Wing office, Welander pulled back later in the interview and became coy, claiming he had only agreed to send Radford on the Haig and Kissinger trips to "keep his ears open, his eyes open."

Radford scoffs when shown these partial demurrals. Of course Welander knew what he was up to, Radford told us: "Robinson explained to him what was happening and when they were relieving each other he [Robinson] said, and I remember this very clearly, that I

[Radford] would be glad to fill Welander in on the mechanics of how it was done. And I did. I told Welander how I did it."

Ehrlichman, familiar through Young with Radford's own confession, carefully prodded Welander as to Moorer's knowledge of Radford's activities. He focused on what had happened after they'd all met in San Clemente following the July 1971 Kissinger trip. Welander avowed that it was only at that time, when he saw Radford's bulging envelopes, that he first realized the extensive nature of Radford's eyes and ears. Welander kept insisting that it was all Radford's doing and initiative:

> The Chairman and I flew out to the NSC meeting out in San Clemente and that was the day that the announcement was made about Henry's first trip to Peking. So I only had a chance to talk with Radford very briefly. . . . when he came back he had an envelope full of things, and he said perhaps you might care to go through some of these things. They may be of interest to you; and I started to go through them and I was very much startled. . . . I said, "Chuck, where did you get these things?" He said, "Well, I used to take the burn bags out for disposal and things of that sort, and I'd kind of go through them and as far as typing I'd keep a flimsy or whatever." . . . I spent a night culling through this and 90 percent of it I just had burned. There were a few things that gave some fairly significant insights on some things that were going on, which I assembled and made some comments on a cover sheet and I showed to Admiral Moorer. And when he had read them we discussed them. Then he gave them all back to me and I have them all locked in my personal safe over at the Pentagon.

Welander opened up a little more, admitting to Ehrlichman and Young that he'd given instructions to Radford before the yeoman traveled with Haig to Vietnam that fall. He told Radford that the Joint Chiefs were "concerned about the troop withdrawal rate," and to bring back any information he could get on the matter. Radford returned with more purloined papers, one of which was a "significant" memo on Haig's discussions with President Thieu. "That I made available to the Chairman," Welander said, ". . . and he [Moorer] back to me." The material was in Welander's safe at the Pentagon.

Ehrlichman wanted to know about more than Radford's success on the trips, and asked if the yeoman had ever picked up materials around the White House. Yes, Welander conceded, "every now and then" when Radford delivered documents for White House secretaries he would bring the papers to Welander and ask, " 'Admiral, is this of any interest to you?' "

Welander maintained that he would only "scan" the papers and then give them back to Radford. But Ehrlichman wasn't satisfied, and while he didn't rant and rave, he kept up the pressure. Ehrlichman pressed for an admission that Welander had actually transmitted materials that Radford had stolen to Moorer, as is evident in the following exchanges:

> **E:** If it [what Radford showed you] were something of interest, did you take it out?
>
> **W:** I would look at it and occasionally I'd say, "Okay, Chuck, would you make a xerox of this one portion of it?" Or something of that sort.
>
> **E:** And send it over to the chairman?
>
> **W:** (Nodded yes.)
>
> **E:** So he [Radford] has had some access that is outside of your ordinary channels. . . . So he would be bird-dogging occasionally and bring you things?
>
> **W:** I'm obviously not happy about having to relate that.
>
> **E:** I understand. But he, of course, has gone into this in his testimony and he testified that he had actually delved into people's briefcases and come up with material which he had duplicated and turned over to Captain Robinson in some cases.

Welander hemmed and hawed and attempted to distance himself from Radford. "I never delved into it, you know, to find out specifics of anything," he insisted, but then confessed that Radford had brought him "annotated first drafts" of documents from the Kissinger trip that Radford "assured me that he got" from rifling the burn bags. Radford had also brought him "complete copies of memcons" from the fall trip, Welander added, but nothing that "would have come directly from busting into somebody's luggage."

> **E:** But there isn't any question in your mind, though, that he has brought you stuff from time to time that has been obtained from . . .
>
> **W:** Surreptitiously and everything else.
>
> **E:** Now, does Admiral Moorer know that this kind of source has been available to the JCS?

W: I have shown him, as I say, some of the most significant things that I felt that he had to know.

E: Sure, but again he is aware that the source is irregular.

W: He knows that Radford picked this up on a trip.

The Kissinger trip fascinated Ehrlichman and Young as they questioned Welander in the West Wing office, and squeezed an admission from the admiral that "one piece of paper" on Kissinger's secret negotiations from that trip, in Ehrlichman's words, "advised you of something that you were not privy to."

"That's right," Welander responded. "Nor to the best of my knowledge had the Chairman been privy to it."

During a more recent interview with us, Welander was far less hesitant than he was that day in the room with Ehrlichman, going so far as to admit that "When Admiral Moorer asked me I told him where Radford got this stuff and that Radford had taken it from the burn bags." Yet he still maintains the posture that what he and Radford did wasn't espionage. "Getting stuff out of the burn bags was snooping, but if I had known about Radford going into Kissinger's briefcase I would have fired him. . . . There was nothing wrong with Radford mooching around to find out what was going on." As for his own role, he is adamant: "I didn't do anything illegal. I was keeping my boss informed and I never intended to do anything otherwise."

However, Radford says, "I was completely aboveboard with [Robinson and Welander]. . . . If they wanted to know the exact second I picked [a document] up, I annotated it right on the piece of paper in the upper right-hand corner, the name of the guy who wrote it, where I got it, whether it was on the plane, out of his briefcase or whether I got it in his hotel room. Which city we were in. I gave them specific data so they could judge the chronology as well as the actual value of the document."

As Welander opened up during his White House interview, Ehrlichman continued to press the admiral, eliciting an admission that Welander had instructed Radford to gather information on a matter "the Navy was highly interested in." Welander asked the yeoman to find out if Kissinger was likely to side with the Pentagon in a dispute with the State Department over naval bases in the Mediterranean. "In about five minutes," Welander told Ehrlichman and Young, Radford returned with a copy of an NSC staff paper on the matter.

Perhaps understanding that he had already incriminated himself, Welander softened as his interview with Ehrlichman and Young continued. When Ehrlichman handed the statement Welander had originally refused to sign to him a second time, the admiral began to elaborate on the various types of documents Radford had stolen. " 'Memcons of private top-level meetings,' " he read, as if it were a question, and then told Ehrlichman and Young the answer, "Yes, from his trips."

" 'Political agreements,' " Welander read, and answered immediately after, "In the international sense. You mean Al's most recent trip and his discussions with Thieu?"

"Exactly," said Ehrlichman.

" 'Telcons.' I can't think of any unless there were from the trip or something of that sort. I think on one occasion there was some reference made in a message to a telephone conversation with the White House and Ambassador Smith with regard to the SALT negotiations."

They went on ticking off the types of purloined secrets—backchannel papers on talks with foreign governments, troop movements and withdrawals, and so on. Welander confirmed that Moorer had learned of Kissinger's secret peace talks with Le Duc Tho, one of the most closely guarded White House initiatives. Learning that Kissinger was talking secretly with the enemy could only have increased the Joint Chiefs' anxiety that the civilians were making deals with the enemy while American soldiers died in the jungle. After Ehrlichman and he had been through the list, Welander finally admitted directly, "I have in fact either shown or discussed these papers with Admiral Moorer, as I say, not with the Acting Chairman at the time. . . . The literal papers and everything else I only show to Admiral Moorer."

After this ultimate admission, Welander returned to his opening theme, Radford's culpability, which he still thought hinged on Radford's supposedly having given things to Jack Anderson. "I do feel that some punitive action ought to be taken if in fact there is a substantial case against him," Welander concluded.

The tape reveals that Ehrlichman and Young weren't as certain that this was a wise course. Ehrlichman put it to Welander this way:

E: Supposing he [Radford] says I didn't feel too badly about turning this stuff over to Anderson because I was a spy for the Joint Chiefs. I used to turn stuff over to them all the time. And the morals involved in one is about the same as the other as far as I'm concerned.

"Do you have qualms about that?" Ehrlichman asked Welander rhetorically, and then answered, "We have qualms about that."

*   *   *

There followed in the conversation a remark of Welander's that evoked no real comment from Ehrlichman or Young at the time, a reference to Welander's warning that the whole affair "exposes some very, very sticky relationships and the function here that has been going on." It was an alarm bell, to Young particularly—repeated elsewhere in the taped conversation—about the central and mysterious role played in the private channel communications of the White House and the Pentagon by Alexander Haig, who had more "sticky relationships" than anyone else in the White House. The "two-way street" to which Welander referred, the one that allowed the brass to receive as well as send information, depended on Haig. The general conveyed information from the JCS to the NSC, and from the White House to the Pentagon.

Haig was ambitious, and the assignment to the NSC and the frequent private meetings with Kissinger and Nixon that he held placed him at the center of power. By 1971, with Kissinger frequently abroad, Haig often supplanted Kissinger as the president's sounding board. Nixon liked Haig, because Haig had just the sort of tough, military mind that Kissinger lacked. Nixon consulted Haig readily, and by his closeness with Haig kept Kissinger off guard; it was a tactic to prevent Kissinger from having too much power. The three men engaged in an intricate dance—though neither Kissinger in those early years nor Nixon during his entire presidency seems to have entertained the notion that General Haig's loyalty might lie somewhere other than with his White House patrons.

Haig's loyalty was principally to the military establishment that had brought him to his present position, and he allayed some of the fears of his Pentagon brethren about his privileged access to Nixon by passing on to them intimate details about the man they preferred to hate, Professor Henry Kissinger.

"The Pentagon was terrified of Kissinger," wrote William Gulley in his book *Breaking Cover*; Gulley served in the White House as director of the Military Office in the Nixon-Kissinger years, and explains why Haig was so important as a counterweight to Kissinger. The military brass, Gulley contended, didn't want Kissinger

telling them what to do with their missiles and their submarines or who should be promoted. That was their department, and they wanted to keep it that way. Kissinger was just National Security Advisor to the President, and his role didn't include disposing of bombs, or armies and navies. But he sure as hell had the ear of the Commander in Chief. But now they had their own boy [Haig] in a substantial position over there at the White House. He could jump in his car and brief the Secretary of Defense or a few carefully selected generals on what Kissinger was up to, what was coming down the road to meet them.

Egil Krogh, who as one of the Plumbers had worked with Haig on the SALT leak and similar investigations, recalls that "Haig was really the JCS guy inside Kissinger's staff right from the beginning. He rose fast but he was the guy that certainly would take care of his military superiors."

Buried in Welander's confession to Ehrlichman and Young were some subtle, but in retrospect very telling, references to Alexander Haig. Welander raised the subject of Haig several times, volunteering how Welander obtained certain NSC information other than through Radford's surreptitious activities.

One subject always of interest to the JCS was "the interplay between Secretary Laird and Henry and the president and the chairman." Ehrlichman asked him about the form that information took, and Welander replied that it was "my conversations with Al." Ehrlichman asked if Radford ever brought him bootlegged copies of "contingency plans," and Welander responded forthrightly: "Al Haig has cut me in on what we've been thinking about on the most recent thing and given me a copy of game plans and so on."

Commenting on Radford's take from Haig's most recent trip, Welander sought to minimize the significance of the information Radford had brought back, saying, "We knew pretty much what the game plan was going to be. Al related to me orally his discussions and some observations that the staff people had made."

In response to Welander's reference to the "very, very sticky relationships" concerning the liaison office, Ehrlichman wondered: If the JCS office at the White House was eliminated, could the function of the conduit still exist? "Really I think you ought to talk to Al Haig on this," Welander responded.

Ehrlichman didn't attach significance to Welander's references to Haig, but Young, who worked more closely with Kissinger and had viewed with suspicion Haig's meteoric rise in the White House, asked an important question. Could Haig have truly not been cognizant of Radford's surrepitious activities? "Do you think Al is in any way aware that when [Radford] was on a trip with him, that he might come back and bootleg a copy and give it to you?" asked Young.

Welander, who already had said that Haig was the person who had requested Radford for the trips, gave a reply that was both to the point and oblique. "You can only ask Al; I've never discussed it with him," the admiral began, but then launched into a discussion of what a male assistant would have had to do on that trip, and made a most important observation: "Were I in the same case and having borrowed a yeoman, I think I would have concluded that most of the things the yeoman might have been exposed to would in turn be exposed to the guy he normally works for."

Welander was saying that had he been in Haig's place, knowing all he knew about how the military operated, and how senior officers could command complete and unquestioning obedience from their subordinates, he would have been forced to assume the yeoman must be reporting to his superior.

The access given to Radford on Haig's trips was remarkable; even Radford believed at the time that it was unusual. "I thought [that Haig] was placing quite a bit of trust in somebody that he really didn't know that well," Radford says.

We asked Welander about his interview with Ehrlichman and Young, and whether Haig knew that Radford was collecting documents and that whatever Radford saw would get back to the JCS. In hindsight, he was more direct than he'd been in 1971. "I think Haig knew that Radford was observing things," Welander told us. "I think it was stuff that Haig expected me to see and that I would make available to the chairman." Welander recalls, too, that Haig would oftentimes tell him things for the chairman's ears, though "sometimes he would say, 'Don't tell the chairman,' which probably meant I was supposed to tell the chairman; that's the way things worked sometimes in the White House at that time."

Accepting Welander's belief that Haig must have known at least some of what Radford was doing has a number of important consequences. For example, Haig had known of the secret diplomatic initiative to China when he had arranged for Radford to accompany Kissinger. But Nixon had ordered that the Pentagon be cut out of the attempt to play the China card. If Haig still wanted information about what happened on the China trip to go to Moorer, but in a way that he himself was not suspected of leaking and that would allow him to retain the confidence of Nixon and Kissinger, what better way than to send along the military's eyes and ears?

Today, Admiral Moorer insists he knew of the opening to China even before Radford departed on the July 1971 trip, during which Kissinger secretly flew to Peking. This idea, however, flabbergasted one of the few people who knew of the opening, Attorney General John Mitchell; before his death, Mitchell insisted to us that Moorer could not have known in advance of Nixon's plan to open the door to

Peking. Moorer disagrees. "I can tell you right now that Mitchell wouldn't have known what I knew. I did know about it. Let me just tell you that. I'm not going to tell you how I knew about it—I knew about it."

There is evidence—some of which we will take up now and some of which we will get to later—to support Welander's belief that Haig knew of Radford's activities. Recently, Moorer confirmed that when Radford returned from his trip with Kissinger, Welander delivered to him a sheaf of materials Radford had collected while traveling with Kissinger. Normally, when Moorer received these sensitive papers he instructed Welander to place them in a Pentagon safe, but in this instance Moorer turned over the purloined documents to Haig. Welander "did carry [the documents] to me," Moorer told us; "I had been told every damn thing that was in there." He then blurted out, "I gave the things back to Haig."

By handing the hot documents back to Haig, Moorer in effect shouted that he was not worried that Haig would ask how Moorer had obtained them. If Moorer had had a moment's concern that Haig would ask embarrassing questions that would uncover the yeoman's activities, Moorer would have kept the sensitive papers in the safe. But he says he "gave the things" to Haig.

If, as Moorer says, Haig had received the purloined documents from him, Haig would have been obligated to report the leak to Nixon or Kissinger. But Nixon's and Kissinger's memoirs of the period suggest that neither the president nor the national security adviser knew anything of the spying until Radford's confession in December 1971. Interviews of others in the White House inner circle confirm there was no report of the military's surreptitious activities before Radford confessed.

Moreover, a former staff colleague of both Haig and Kissinger at the NSC in those years who was familiar with the operations of the military liaison office revealed to us that Rembrandt Robinson and Alexander Haig had a special relationship. He recalls that many people would come to see Haig at his office in the White House, but whenever Robinson came over to talk, "Haig would shut the door. No one else was allowed in. It was fundamentally different from the way Haig dealt with other people at the NSC. In other cases, he might close the door, but there might be traffic in and out of the office. Not with Robinson."

While the JCS was quite specifically excluded from the Nixon-Kissinger plans to make an opening to China, Alexander Haig was not. Kissinger's memoirs recount that Haig sent backchannel messages to Kissinger on the trip, "held the fort heroically and efficiently in my absence," and received from Kissinger via cable the one-word message, "Eureka," that told Haig and Nixon that Kissinger's mission had succeeded and that the Chinese had approved a forthcoming trip to Peking by the president.

Nixon's near-obsession with secrecy for Kissinger's China negotiations have been well documented, and both men have written at great length in their memoirs on their rationale for developing this historic opening to China without including in the plans any other key foreign policy figures in the government. In his memoirs, Kissinger explained that by going it alone, Nixon had taken a huge political gamble; should the gambit fail, "Having made the decisions without executive or Congressional consultation, Nixon left himself quite naked should anything go wrong; in such lonely decisions he was extremely courageous." And as Nixon well knew, the new relationship with Peking was sure to anger critics on the right who felt that the U.S. had an obligation to continue close ties to Taiwan; senior military officers, including the hard-line anticommunist Chairman Moorer, were among the most ardent supporters of Taiwan and of its strategic value to America.

But according to John Ehrlichman, the Joint Chiefs "knew the secret details of the new China opening before most of the senior people in the White House did." Such knowledge by the JCS was one of the things Nixon sought to prevent by the extreme secrecy that surrounded the Kissinger mission. "If somebody had said to the president, 'Do you want the Joint Chiefs to know what Henry is doing,' " Ehrlichman says, "he would have said, 'Absolutely not.' "

Thus when Ehrlichman and Young concluded their interview with Admiral Welander, they were aghast on their president's behalf at the breach of faith that the spying represented. They sent the admiral packing—Welander returned to the Pentagon to tell Chairman Moorer what had just happened to him. In the White House, Young took the tape to have it transcribed, and even before the transcript was in hand Ehrlichman made preparations to see the president about the matter, that very afternoon. "I had the sense that we got a lot more from Welander than we had any right to expect," Ehrlichman recalls for us. He remembers thinking at the time, "It was bigger because it involved Moorer. I had to warn the president."

4

NIXON ORDERS A BURIAL

LESS than two hours after they had obtained Admiral Welander's taped confession on the afternoon of December 22, 1971, John Ehrlichman and David Young sat in Nixon's hideaway office in the Executive Office Building. The transcription of the tape would not be ready until the following day, but Ehrlichman thought he had a political disaster on his hands, and insisted on bringing the bad news immediately to the president. Bob Haldeman and John Mitchell, the two senior members of the administration on whom Nixon most usually relied, were also in attendance as Ehrlichman laid out the story for the president as he and Young had heard it from Welander. Ehrlichman was clearly disposed toward pursuing a thorough investigation. Now, what would the president do?

Looking to precedent, Nixon knew all too well the actions of one of his predecessors, President Harry S. Truman, in regard to the insubordination of General Douglas MacArthur during the war in Korea. When the Supreme Commander of U.S. and Allied forces in Korea publicly challenged Truman's conduct of that war, Truman summarily fired him, even though the action brought down on the president a firestorm of negative publicity. Historians have said in retrospect that the firing of the popular MacArthur was among Truman's most important acts, one that strengthened the presidency and the president's authority under the Constitution. Arguing from precedent and citing massive insubordination, Nixon could well have fired Moorer and gained from the episode.

However, in this meeting with his top advisers, the first signals that the president put out were not in that direction. Ehrlichman recalls that Nixon did not ask to hear the tape recording, and evidenced no interest in reading the transcript when it became available. The reason for this would soon become evident: His mind was already made up as to the course of action he would have to take.

Nixon's reactions to this crisis, John Mitchell told us after reviewing our evidence, went to the core of his being—they were political. He was concerned with how this affair might hurt him, or help him. Could the situation be turned to his advantage? Where could blame be placed, and for what purpose?

The president's chain of logic in the crisis would soon become apparent. John Ehrlichman, who met with the president several times during the first days of what became known as the Moorer-Radford affair, offered us in a recent interview the following analysis. As a political man, Nixon was convinced that the matter of utmost importance was his reelection in 1972, and he was also convinced that what would most recommend him to the electorate for reelection were foreign policy triumphs. He was scheduled to visit Peking in February 1972, to hold a summit in Moscow in the late spring at which he would sign the SALT and ABM treaties, and he was also hoping that the secret talks with Le Duc Tho would bear fruit before the following November. He envisioned a steady series of these foreign policy thunderclaps, and riding them easily to reelection. In his mind those triumphs, in turn, depended on backchannel communications of the sort enabled by the JCS. Nixon also feared, Ehrlichman says, that "if he disciplined Moorer for conducting espionage activity against the president and Henry" it would expose the backchannel, reveal publicly how Secretary Laird had been repeatedly circumvented, and ultimately "give Laird a whip hand over the Joint Chiefs." Therefore, Ehrlichman concludes that Nixon reasoned, the backchannel must be protected. Guaranteeing the continued existence of the backchannel then became the engine that drove Nixon's actions. In his autobiography, RN, Nixon wrote he was "disturbed" to learn "the JCS was spying on the White House" but offered two additional reasons for keeping the scandal quiet. First, he worried that exposure of it would further demoralize the military at a time when the armed services were already under attack by the antiwar movement. Second, he believed that top-secret information would leak out if the case was pursued. Ehrlichman and Mitchell offered a third reason: Nixon did not want the world to know that he had been spied upon; it would be embarrassing to him, and undermine the image of a strong leader that he was trying to protect.

We have been told that at the December 22 meeting the president, seated at his EOB office desk, turned in his chair, stared out the window, and rhetorically asked, "Why did Tom do this?" referring to Moorer.

Later, he told everyone at the meeting to keep quiet about the espionage; news of it was not to go beyond the room. Yet Nixon also instructed Young to write a full report, a directive with which Young enthusiastically began to comply, and eventually produced quite a thick day-to-day account of the investigation that contained all the evidence of the spying. Nixon also decided that Moorer had to be spoken to, but the president didn't want to do it himself. A key Nixon personality trait was the avoidance of personal confrontation at almost any cost. Among Nixon's first decisions was to give the job of bracing Moorer to John Mitchell. But even before the attorney general summoned the chairman of the Joint Chiefs, Nixon had made up his mind not to fire or discipline Moorer.

The reason was not then apparent to those in the room, but did emerge in later discussions. If Nixon kept Moorer in office after bloodying the chairman's nose a bit, Ehrlichman remembers that the president argued, the chairman would be even more pliant than he had been in the past, and that would be good for Nixon. "He had two ways of going. He could either tear up the Joint Chiefs or he could continue to do business with them. And he says to himself, 'I've got to keep that [backchannel] in place and keep doing business with them. And maybe it turns out to be an advantage for me because they know that I know [about the spying].' "

A Nixon diary entry from December of 1971, reprinted in *RN*, gives further inkling of Nixon's analysis of the crisis. He declared that Radford's "spying on the White House for the Joint Chiefs is something that I would not be surprised at, although I don't think it's a healthy practice."

Having decided to bury the spy ring but to keep alive the recipient of the stolen documents, Nixon nevertheless had to deal with the other people touched by the affair. In his autobiography, Nixon suggested the train of thought that led to his next actions. "Whether or not [Radford] had disclosed classified information to Anderson, the fact remained that he had jeopardized the relationship of the JCS to the White House," Nixon wrote. Having twisted the facts to fit his preconceptions about the origins, dimensions, and dangers of the scandal, Nixon now proceeded to vent his ire on the press and the yeoman rather than to discipline Moorer, Welander, or Robinson.

Nixon ordered Ehrlichman to have the investigators uncover what the president was sure existed, a homosexual liaison between Radford and Jack Anderson; Ehrlichman bucked that task down to David Young, who relayed the request to Pentagon investigator Don Stewart. There was no prior evidence of such a relationship between Radford and Anderson, and Stewart refused to try and "find" one. Ehrlichman was put in the unfortunate position of having to follow up on this presidential imperative, and found that Mel Laird thought it was a terrible idea and resisted asking Radford to take a lie detector test about it. Laird pointed out that the subject matter of a polygraph test must first be disclosed to the person who is going to take it, and that person may refuse to take it if he doesn't want to risk self-incrimination—or for any other reason. Suppose, Laird suggested to Ehrlichman in a telephone call on the morning of December 23, just suppose that "if [Radford] decides not to take the test and then he goes out and tells the press that that's what we're running here, I think we just get in a hell of a lot of— We blow the lid." Ehrlichman had to instruct Laird to try anyway, because it was the president's wish, and because Nixon felt "there is no apparent motive for this fellow turning these papers over to Anderson."

So they were searching for a motive that didn't exist, and they were looking in the wrong direction, away from the spy ring. The homosexuality premise had been pursued with Welander, who told Ehrlichman and Young he had seen no evidence to support the idea that Radford and Anderson were so linked. Radford only learned about the thesis of homosexuality much later, and now laughs about such an idea. "It's comical," he told us, pointing out that he and Toni have been married twenty years and have together raised eight children. When advised that the possible homosexual link had been Nixon's idea, Radford responded, "It's embarrassing."

Nixon seemed obsessed with Jack Anderson. He asked Ehrlichman, who had begun in the administration as counsel to the president, if the columnist had committed a crime in publishing the White House documents on the India-Pakistan situation, and what the statute of limitations was on such a crime. Ehrlichman understood the reference: Nixon had spoken to him several times about Anderson and other "enemies" to be targeted for punishment after reelection in 1972, when

Nixon would be in a position to disregard any negative public reaction to such treatment. Currently, though, Nixon wanted Ehrlichman to come down hard on the one known connection between Radford and Anderson: the Mormon Church. In a move that Ehrlichman characterized to us as "Nixon's typical generic revenge," the president ordered all Mormon clergymen barred from performing services at the White House. "Don't use Mormon Bishop," states one of Ehrlichman's notes of his meeting with Nixon.

There remained several other major players who had to be handled. John Mitchell was dispatched to question Moorer. Interestingly, when Mitchell summoned Moorer, he did so, he told us just before his death in 1988, without having learned any details of what Welander had said in his interview with Ehrlichman and Young.

The chairman of the Joint Chiefs hurried to see Mitchell, flatly denied any knowledge of the stealing, and said that if he had ever been shown contraband material the blame lay with Welander, who should be disciplined. Because he never heard the tape or saw the transcript of Welander's interview, Mitchell believed the chairman and reported Moorer's denial back to Nixon. This report by the attorney general may have been the flimsy evidence on which Nixon relied when six months later, and to the astonishment of many of his aides, he reappointed Moorer for a second term as chairman of the Joint Chiefs. But, as Ehrlichman succinctly told us in an interview, this was to Nixon's advantage because he had a "pre-shrunk admiral" as head of the JCS.

Then there was Secretary of Defense Mel Laird. Nixon worried that exposure of the backchannel would strengthen the hand of Laird, whom the president deeply distrusted. Laird had known about the liaison office through coming into contact with it in prior administrations, during his eight terms as a congressman who sat on a defense-related subcommittee. Laird had argued with Nixon at the outset of this administration that the liaison office should be closed because it always had been a nuisance and a source of leaks. But Nixon needed the backchannel that the liaison office helped to enable, and his disagreement with Laird over the necessity of such a channel was part of the reason for his distrust. Nixon wanted to keep the secretary on board but not cognizant of the matters being discussed through the backchannel. It was obvious to Ehrlichman from his December 23 phone call to Laird that the secretary knew what was going on. Laird said he was "sure that Robinson bootlegged things" to the Pentagon brass, but "not to me. I never saw any of it." He knew that "somebody was giving them [the Joint Chiefs] information" and was certain "that the president wasn't calling them directly and giving them this sort of information." In a later White House meeting, Nixon would dispatch Mitchell to neutralize Laird and to tell him to keep the lid on the espionage story.

Nixon's major personnel problem stemming from this crisis, everyone agreed, was Henry Kissinger. The national security adviser hated leaks other than his own and would be apoplectic when he learned that he had been spied upon, that his briefcase had been rifled, and that his diplomatic initiatives had been known to the JCS. Typically, Nixon refused to deal with Kissinger personally until Ehrlichman had given the national security adviser precise instructions on how to behave in Nixon's presence. In an early afternoon meeting on December 23, Nixon issued his instruction to Ehrlichman. First, Kissinger must be told that he should never mention the espionage mess to the president. That tactic would work, because Kissinger was always circumspect when addressing the president, who was the source of whatever power Kissinger possessed. Next, Ehrlichman reports, the president "wanted me to tell Henry that I was handling the situation [together] with Mitchell and that the president is aware of the situation because of his backchannel relationship with the Joint Chiefs." Third, Nixon told Ehrlichman not "to let Henry get involved in the question of, Do we keep Moorer or not." However, Kissinger was to be thrown a bone— allowed to shut down the JCS liaison office at the NSC—but was to see to it that the backchannel to the JCS was not dismantled.

Nixon's final order, as reflected in Ehrlichman's notes of the meeting, was odd: "Don't let K blame Haig." The president had obviously concluded that Kissinger would indeed try to fault Haig, the assistant who had the closest ties to the JCS, for having permitted a situation to exist in which Radford could steal from Kissinger.

In retrospect, Ehrlichman told us recently, it was clear to him that the president's instruction was "a very explicit injunction from Nixon, intended to protect Haig." This was the first time, Ehrlichman recalls, that he ever saw Nixon protect Haig, and at the time Ehrlichman dismissed the action as a simply logical one: Nixon didn't want Kissinger blaming his chief military aide because the espionage had been conducted by the military.

Haig, Kissinger, and Nixon had a complex three-way relationship. When Nixon had hired Kissinger as national security adviser, the Harvard professor had sought a military aide not only to liaise with the JCS, but also because he and Nixon would need a backchannel communications capability, and that military aide would have to be privy to it and might help facilitate it. The military at first thought they'd better suggest a man with advanced degrees who would be comfortable with Kissinger, but Kissinger wanted what he described in his memoirs as "a more rough-cut type," preferably with combat experience, someone who didn't have the same academic viewpoint as he did and could provide a new perspective. Colonel Al Haig, then on the staff at West Point, was recommended by a mutual friend, and that nomination was seconded by Robert S. McNamara, secretary of defense under Kennedy and Johnson, and Joseph A. Califano, Jr., who had been Haig's boss at the Pentagon in the early 1960s when they served McNamara and Army Secretary Cyrus R. Vance. Kissinger liked that Haig had been endorsed by both conservatives and liberals, and hired him after one interview, and, as Kissinger himself wrote, "Haig soon became indispensable. He disciplined my anarchic tendencies and established coherence and procedure in an NSC staff of talented prima donnas." Within months, the army colonel, who had not been initially seen as a threat by Kissinger's civilian staff, had elbowed all of them out of the way and become Kissinger's principal deputy.

Then came a moment, former Nixon speechwriter William Safire reports in his book *Before the Fall*, when the balance changed. Nixon, Kissinger, and Safire were working on a speech and needed a figure on troop strength. Haig was called into the room. He delivered the figure and was about to withdraw, but Nixon asked him to stay, then turned to Safire and murmured "thought and action." It was a phrase from another speech Nixon and Safire had discussed, one that contrasted the man of thought with the man of action; Haig, Nixon implied, was a man of action who counterbalanced Kissinger. But Nixon, Safire wrote, also wanted to include Haig "not as a messenger but as an adviser." Shortly thereafter, John Ehrlichman remembers, whenever Nixon was displeased with Kissinger on any account, he would have Haig brief him for five or six days, until Kissinger was softened up enough to be allowed to come back into the president's good graces. An NSC aide close to Kissinger recalls that "Henry would be an absolute wreck, he'd be close to a nervous breakdown because the president was meeting with Haig." Talk of urging Kissinger to see a psychiatrist was also rampant in the Oval Office—simply another instance of Nixon's sadistic treatment of his chief foreign policy adviser. Ehrlichman wrote that Nixon told him to bring the subject up with Kissinger but "I could think of no way to talk to Henry about psychiatric care."

Being in the White House was good for Haig. He "earned his star," that is, jumped from colonel to brigadier general, in less than a year, and earned a second star, making him a major general, in 1972. As Haig continued to rise in the White House hierarchy, Kissinger worried about his aide. "Can I trust Haig?" he would wonder, according to one NSC staff member who talked privately with Kissinger. No one could give the professor complete assurance on that score. In public, say in front of the staff or Haldeman or Ehrlichman, Kissinger would often berate Haig for minor mistakes and seem to humiliate him, describing military officers as "animals" who were too "dumb" to understand the intricacies of foreign policy. (This is the view of the Haig-Kissinger relationship portrayed in the Bob Woodward and Carl Bernstein book *The Final Days*.)

We have learned that in private, however, Haig was the more dominant character, acting as what one source who knew both men called "a schoolyard bully." This source recalls angry, nasty screaming matches between the two men in which Haig threatened to punch Kissinger out, and Kissinger cowered. "Haig took the crap in public; Henry took it in private," this source told us.

Why would Kissinger take insubordination in any form from Haig? Because, this source insists, "Haig could leak so many things about Henry's personal behavior or the secret way he was carrying out [foreign] policies. On an emotional level, Henry would ask himself, 'Do I really want to cross him?' " But on the other side of the coin, "Haig himself knew that if he wanted another star he had to get along with Kissinger, too."

Kissinger and Haig shared many secrets, and this sharing had begun in the early days of the administration. Nixon had authorized (and Kissinger and Haig encouraged) an enormous bombing campaign against suspected North Vietnamese and Vietcong havens and supply lines in neutral Cambodia. The air strikes continued for seven weeks, unknown to the American public until May 9, 1969, when William Beecher, the Pentagon correspondent for *The New York Times*, broke the story with a front-page article on the secret raids.

Kissinger was on vacation with Nixon in Florida, and when they read the story both were enraged. During that day, Kissinger had four conversations with FBI Director J. Edgar Hoover. Hoover wrote memos of his Kissinger calls to his senior officials. In the first call, Kissinger asked Hoover to use "whatever resources" were necessary to find Beecher's source, although Kissinger expected this to be done "discreetly." By the fourth call, Kissinger was vowing to Hoover that the White House would "destroy whoever did this if we can find him, no matter where he is." Hoover, in turn, suggested a possible leaker, a former Harvard associate of Kissinger's who was then on the NSC staff, Morton H. Halperin.

Unfortunately, Kissinger had to agree with the assessment. Halperin had been in the Pentagon during the Johnson administration, and had advocated a halt to the bombing of North Vietnam, a strategy that angered many military and civilian defense officials in Washington. When Kissinger announced his intention of bringing Halperin to the NSC, the proposed appointment drew criticism from General Wheeler, then chairman of the Joint Chiefs, from Senator Barry Goldwater, and from Director Hoover. To defend Halperin now, Kissinger believed, would undercut his position with Haldeman and Nixon. By six that evening, the FBI managed to activate a tap on Halperin's home telephone.

The very next morning, Alexander Haig went to Assistant FBI Director William C. Sullivan with the names of three more individuals to be tapped, NSC aides Daniel I. Davidson and Helmut Sonnenfeldt, and Air Force Colonel Robert E. Pursley, military assistant to Secretary of Defense Laird; Pursley was distrusted by Haig and other military hardliners who scorned him as a dove on Vietnam and for being too close to civilian officials. Kissinger's deputy told Hoover's deputy that the taps on all four men were ordered "on the highest authority," and that the matter should be handled "on a need-to-know basis, with no record maintained." The desire for secrecy, Haig later testified in a civil suit, arose from his own experience in the Pentagon in the early 1960s when Hoover circulated through upper levels of the government a damaging report on Martin Luther King, Jr., which "just about blew the Pentagon apart." The Hoover report was "flushed all through the bureaucracy," Haig testified, adding, "I think that is the kind of concerns we had" about the new wiretapping effort in May 1969.

Ten days after his first meeting with Sullivan, Haig, accompanied by Kissinger, showed up at Sullivan's office to give him the names of two more NSC staffers to be tapped, and to read the first logs of the in-place taps. Sullivan's memo of the meeting quotes Kissinger as saying, "It is clear that I don't have anybody in my office that I can trust except Colonel Haig here."

During the next two years, Haig transmitted more names of the seventeen government officials and newsmen whose phones were tapped at various times over a period of twenty-two months from May 1969 to February 1971. Some of those tapped had ties to high Democratic party powers such as Senator Edmund S. Muskie and former ambassador W. Averell Harriman, some were Republicans such as speechwriter William Safire, and some were reporters whom the White House disliked.

Haig effectively became the operations officer of the wiretapping program. Periodically he would visit Sullivan, read dozens of wiretap summaries, and take some to Kissinger. In his biography of Haig, *The General's Progress*, Roger Morris described what happened after Kissinger had read the reports. Morris was at that time a fellow NSC staff member; he remembers the reports being kept in "a small, wired safe in the West Basement situation room," and wrote that while by mid-1969 the wiretap reports were "an open secret among the NSC staff," no one but Haig and Kissinger knew who had been targeted.

Nixon later wrote that he authorized the wiretapping to stop news leaks and to protect "national security." But no leakers were ever discovered, and the surveillance seemed openly political, especially since in several cases, such as that of Halperin and NSC staff member W. Anthony Lake, the taps were continued after the subject had left the government and had gone to work for Muskie, or had ceased to have any access to classified material.

In any event, on February 8, 1971, Haig finally called Sullivan to order that the program be discontinued, and the taps were shut off two days later. The logs were not destroyed, however, and six months later Sullivan's copies as well as those from Haig's safe were placed at the instruction of Nixon into Ehrlichman's safe, where they lay for two years, a secret bomb waiting to explode. In later testimony, Haig would say that the wiretap reports were "an awful lot of garbage," and that whatever he had done had been on behalf of Dr. Kissinger—but, as the FBI records show, over a two-year period Haig encouraged the collection of the garbage and pored over the results.

Considering their close linkage, it was no wonder that, in thinking about Kissinger's reaction to the spy ring in December 1971, Nixon would consider Haig in almost the same breath.

Moments after seeing the president on the afternoon of December 23, Ehrlichman and Haldeman briefed Kissinger. In his 1982 memoir, *Witness to Power*, Ehrlichman described Kissinger at this meeting as "calm, almost sleepy, as I recounted what we'd learned. His only reaction was to remark, almost indifferently, that the Joint Chiefs' liaison office must be closed at once." Ehrlichman was surprised at the mildness of Kissinger's reaction, for "I had expected a huge eruption of emotion. Haldeman had told me that Henry was being a tremendous problem for the President that week. He had been mounting elaborate, daily tirades about [Secretary of State] Bill Rogers; Nixon, Haldeman reported, was nearly to the point of firing Henry, just to end the wear and tear." Although it seems clear that such sentiments were just a way of venting presidential spleen, and that Nixon never seriously considered sacking Kissinger, it was obvious that in late 1971 Kissinger was under considerable stress and that the public exposure of the ill-fated tilt to Pakistan had severely strained his relationship with Richard Nixon.

In the meeting with Haldeman and Ehrlichman, Kissinger displayed his diplomatic face, but when he returned to his own quarters he exploded into angry action. That very afternoon, he closed the JCS liaison office and ordered Welander's files and safes seized. Unfortunately, this order was not completely carried out. Though Kissinger got many materials, more remained in Welander's hands. In mid-January, Welander was given a sea command and transferred away from Washington. Before he left, though, he was ordered by the secretary of defense to turn over materials from his safes. Instead, Welander asked Al Haig what to do, and an edict came down from Ehrlichman to hand over the remaining materials to the White House. Welander gave the documents to Haig, and Haig gave a packet of materials to an Ehrlichman aide who placed them directly in Ehrlichman's safe. Today, Ehrlichman says he never reviewed that material, and doesn't know whether he got all of what Welander had turned over to Haig, or if the batch was sanitized by either man. At the time, Ehrlichman points out, his main concern was the president's fiat to keep those files out of the hands of Secretary of Defense Melvin Laird.

The next casualty of the Kissinger explosion was Yeoman Radford. Within days of Kissinger's learning of Radford's involvement, the yeoman was hustled out of the capital, together with his wife and children, and sent to a new assignment at a Naval Reserve Training Center in Oregon.

By the time he arrived at the base, Radford had figured out that he held a few good cards, and when an effort was made to yank his security clearance—a move that would have effectively gutted his ability to work as a yeoman—he played them. He threatened to cause trouble for the upper echelon if the Navy didn't continue his clearance, and the Navy quickly backed down. Nonetheless, a White House–approved tap was placed on his home telephone and remained in operation for the next six months. It caught two calls between Radford and Anderson. In the first, Radford declined an invitation to visit the elder Andersons. In the second, in May of 1972, Radford congratulated the columnist on winning the Pulitzer Prize for the "tilt to Pakistan" column. Some investigators tried to make hay of that call, saying it was evidence of complicity in the affair, but there was overwhelming evidence to the contrary—dramatized by the fact that the tap was discontinued a month later, in June 1972, as completely useless.

Ehrlichman had urged Nixon to hold off any questioning of Moorer until after Rembrandt Robinson had been interrogated, "but Nixon couldn't be patient." When Admiral Robinson, who was then stationed in San Diego, finally arrived for his interview on December 27, Ehrlichman wrote in his memoirs, the "self-assured" admiral was in full uniform "complete with gold braid and battle stars." In an unpublished diary entry, Ehrlichman recorded that Robinson admitted receiving "one set of trip papers" from Radford, "but denies animus." Robinson was "voluble, articulate, pushed all the right buttons"; those "buttons," Ehrlichman reported in his diary, included Robinson's assurance that he was "the president's man for four more years, etc.," and that Robinson expressed "concern for Moorer and the system." Ehrlichman ended the entry with the observation that Robinson "can't explain disparity" between his testimony and that of Radford and Welander. Ehrlichman later learned that Robinson had been to the Pentagon and had seen Defense Department general counsel Fred Buzhardt before arriving to see Ehrlichman; therefore, Ehrlichman now concludes, Robinson was primed for his questions. Confirmation that Robinson had been in the Pentagon on the day in question was provided to us by investigator Don Stewart, who had come across him in the halls and had been surprised to see Robinson running off to Buzhardt's office. Robinson managed to avoid the questions of both Ehrlichman and Stewart, and to salvage his sea duty. Later in 1972, however, he was posted to Vietnam, where he was subsequently killed in a helicopter crash in the Gulf of Tonkin.

The firing of Welander and the closing of the liaison office by Kissinger did not please Brigadier General Haig. Though it had been Haig who had initiated the investigation into the leak to Anderson, it was Haig who, in the hours following the moment when Kissinger learned of the espionage, conversely began a desperate, emotional attempt to protect Welander. That evening, December 23, Haig called David Young in a rage and accused him of impugning Welander on naught but circumstantial evidence. Young did not inform Haig that he and Ehrlichman had interviewed Welander or that a tape of that interview existed. From what Haig said and did not say, Young concluded that Haig had probably talked to Laird, and had thought that the only evidence of espionage was the Radford confession. The call shook the White House aide, but also fed Young's growing conviction that Haig was doing more than coming to the defense of an embattled fellow officer—that he was pressing his own agenda, one that to Young clearly showed that Haig's loyalties lay more with the JCS than with Kissinger or Nixon.

Ehrlichman knew of Young's suspicions. "David Young suggested to me that Al Haig had probably planted Radford to help the military spy on Henry," Ehrlichman wrote in his memoir, "but that did not seem logical to me because I assumed Haig had full access to Henry's papers and files. Young insisted that Haig constantly sold Henry out to the military." Ehrlichman wrote that at the time he "discounted" Young's allegation because he thought Young was a rival of the rapidly rising Haig, and he knew that there was "obviously bad blood between them."

That evening of December 23, while Haig berated Young, Kissinger was also heating up the telephone wires. Ehrlichman was at home in the midst of a Christmas party, he wrote, when Kissinger called to say that he had fired Welander and closed the liaison office. Haig had obviously been talking to Kissinger, because Kissinger now asked if there was "hard evidence" of Welander's culpability. Ehrlichman told Kissinger that there was a tape of Welander's confession, and that he'd be glad to play it for Kissinger the next day in his office. Kissinger said he'd be there, and, "Would it be all right if I bring Al Haig along?" The tape-play was arranged to take place just after the early morning senior-staff meeting.

Ehrlichman's next call at the party was from "a badly shaken" David Young, who related his own conversation with the agitated Haig in some detail. "I suggested to Young that he not attend in the morning when I played the tape for Henry and Haig," Ehrlichman wrote in his memoirs.

Young agreed, but he remained troubled about the entire affair and early the next morning, December 24, he wrote a remarkable short memorandum for Ehrlichman that he hoped Ehrlichman would read before playing the tape:

JDE

EYES ONLY

8 AM
Fri 12/24

John,

1.) After reflecting on yesterday's events and particularly last night's call to me by Haig, I am all the more convinced that it is now up to only you and Bob [Haldeman] to protect Henry; i.e., it is very difficult for him to say no to Haig.

2.) Haig's change <u>from</u> enthusiastic retribution against Welander <u>to</u> outrage over the dismissal of Welander is odd.

3.) The imminent return of Adm. Robinson and the possibility that we might talk more with Welander especially about his "confidential relationships with Haig" may be the cause of Haig's concern.

David

When Ehrlichman played the tape for Kissinger and Haig at 9:00 A.M. the general said almost nothing, but "this time Henry wasn't so calm," Ehrlichman wrote in his memoir. "When the tape ended he began striding up and down loudly venting his complaints," among them that Nixon now wouldn't fire Chairman Moorer. Ehrlichman quotes Kissinger as saying, "They can spy on him and spy on me and betray us and he won't fire them! If he won't fire Rogers—impose some discipline in this Administration—there is no reason to believe he'll fire Moorer. I assure you all this tolerance will lead to very serious consequences for this Administration!"

Ehrlichman dutifully conveyed Kissinger's desire that Moorer be fired to Nixon when the president returned that morning from his annual physical at Bethesda Naval Hospital. "Ch JCS must go," read Ehrlichman's note of Kissinger's demand. Nixon had no intention of firing Moorer, for all the reasons noted earlier in this chapter, but neither did he have any intention of telling that to Kissinger right away, because he seems to have enjoyed watching Kissinger rant and rave and display his insecurity. Such Kissinger tantrums reinforced Nixon's confidence that he held the upper hand over his volatile national security adviser.

Later in the meeting, Kissinger crashed the gathering, though not happily. "Mood indigo," Ehrlichman cryptically noted of Kissinger's demeanor. Speaking in what Ehrlichman later wrote was "a very low, somber voice," Kissinger spread "gloom and doom" for the president and urged him to take some action. Nixon tried to joke with Kissinger and offer him some encouragement, but when Kissinger left the meeting, he showed no signs of having been relieved of his distress.

As was his wont, Nixon now spent some time weighing the pros and cons of sacking Moorer, and by this process reaffirmed to himself the wisdom of the decision he had already made: He'd keep Moorer, albeit on a tighter leash. It was at this meeting that Nixon decided to send Mitchell to direct Laird to "keep quiet" about the spying. Mitchell, Nixon instructed Ehrlichman, was to tell Laird that public exposure would hurt Laird himself, the administration, and "the uniform," by which he meant the entire military apparatus of the United States.

Laird was prepared to agree, even though he was in the process of learning rather completely what had happened in the liaison office—something Nixon did not want him to do. He was receiving briefings from Defense Department general counsel Buzhardt, who oversaw the Don Stewart investigatory team. Buzhardt had the polygraph examinations of Radford, and through the White House had somehow obtained the most damning evidence, Welander's confession, and had listened to it—something Nixon did not know, and would have preferred not to have happened. This last piece of evidence was so secret that it was not even known to investigator Stewart, nor did Ehrlichman and Young, who had interrogated Welander, know that Buzhardt had obtained it. Later, the transcript of the Ehrlichman-Young-Welander interview was included in Buzhardt's report to Laird of January 10, 1972. It is not clear where Buzhardt got the transcript. However, Ehrlichman says that if Nixon had known about it, he would have been angry. As we shall shortly see, the Buzhardt report also contained some further material.

Laird says today that he still has that report, to which was attached the transcript of Welander's confession, but won't release it. He told us that when Buzhardt brought him a copy of the tape, he listened to it. We asked whether Buzhardt had told him that Moorer was involved in the espionage, and Laird responded, "Fred Buzhardt told me yes, that he [Moorer] was."

Buzhardt knew that fact in his bones, because he was from the military, too, even if he no longer wore a uniform, and he understood as well as Admiral Welander the degree of compulsion inherent in the chain of command. Originally from South Carolina, Buzhardt graduated from West Point just a year before Alexander Haig, and had known Haig at the academy and kept in touch with him afterward. Buzhardt wore spectacles, had slightly stooped shoulders, and spoke in a drawl that reflected his home county. From the academy he went into the Air Force and became a pilot, then left the military entirely to go to law school. A protégé of the ultraconservative senator from his home state, Strom Thurmond, he then served as Thurmond's aide and developed close contacts with Thurmond's colleagues on the Hill, such as Representative Melvin Laird and Senator John Stennis, who also sat on defense committees, and with civilian and uniformed Pentagon officials. He went to the Pentagon in 1969 as a special assistant to the secretary, and Laird chose him as Defense Department general counsel in August 1970.

Since starting at the Pentagon, Buzhardt had been a fireman, helping Laird and the military to stave off or limit the fallout from a variety of scandalous episodes including the Army's domestic spying program against the political left, the My Lai massacre, and the publication of the Pentagon Papers. Buzhardt collaborated directly with the White House Plumbers to find the source of news leaks including the Pentagon Papers leak. Buzhardt's brief in the Moorer-Radford affair was the same as it had been in these other disasters: to determine the extent of the damage and then work to contain it. His secret report to Laird told the secretary more than what he was being told by the White House, and it verified Laird's good sense in having earlier prophesied to Nixon that the liaison office would cause more harm than good.

In January of 1972, Buzhardt suddenly decided that he needed to interview Welander, much as Ehrlichman and Young had done two weeks earlier, and even though he had their interview in hand. The ostensible reason for the reinterview was to verify independently the Radford information—but as we shall see, there may well have been a hidden reason.

While Stewart was on vacation in January of 1972, he received a call telling him to rush back to Washington, and when he got there, Stewart was told that he and Buzhardt would together question Welander. Stewart remembers being told by Buzhardt that this was being done "at the request of the president." That was untrue, but Stewart didn't know it, and was specifically *not* told that Welander had already confessed on tape to Ehrlichman and Young. Buzhardt and Stewart proceeded to interview Welander on January 7, 1972, and a report was written of the interview.

We have obtained the report. Welander again admitted that Radford brought him documents to which the admiral himself did not have access. He boasted to Buzhardt and Stewart that Radford "had great contacts amongst the White House people," that the yeoman had routinely picked up documents from NSC secretaries, and that Welander would photocopy the most interesting ones. Welander discussed Radford's activities on trips and confessed to tabbing and indexing the papers that Radford stole before passing them to Moorer and then locking some of the documents in his safe.

The material he provided to Moorer from the Kissinger and Haig trips, the report said, "was so sensitive that the chairman did not keep it overnight." In conclusion, the report added, "Admiral Welander stated that no one knew Radford was conducting his clandestine operation" and that while he had "not praised Radford directly," he had told the yeoman that the material "was important and significant and made many things understandable."

Stewart recalls that Buzhardt pressed Welander on one document the admiral may have received from Radford—the memo on General Haig's private conversation with South Vietnamese President Thieu. Buzhardt insisted to Welander that "the president has to know" if Radford stole the document. "He [Buzhardt] hammered away at that," says Stewart, who didn't know at the time that Buzhardt was only using Nixon's name to pull the information out of Welander. The admiral then admitted he had gotten the memo from Radford, had shown it to Moorer, and then locked it in his safe.

The two most striking things about the reinterview of Welander are the matter of who ordered it, and the matter of what was *not* said in it. Both matters are interlinked.

Ehrlichman says that neither he nor the president ordered such a reinterview, and in fact they were unaware of it at the time, and so was David Young. The president, Ehrlichman points out, was trying to bury the whole affair, and would have vetoed the idea of a further interview of Welander if he'd known about it. Nor would Kissinger have wanted it, and Laird says he didn't order it.

Examining the two interviews of Welander side by side, we found that in the Buzhardt-Stewart reinterview Haig was mentioned several times in passing—but all references to Welander's confidential dealings with Haig were omitted. There could possibly have been an innocent reason for this—maybe Buzhardt did not bring up his friend Haig's name, and Stewart, unaware of what Welander had actually said to Ehrlichman, didn't see fit to introduce Haig's name. But that is unlikely. The most likely candidate to have ordered the reinterview was Haig himself.

To see why, we must jump ahead in time to a congressional hearing in March 1974. The military spy ring was being investigated, and Fred Buzhardt was testifying. He had become the counsel to the president, and Alexander Haig was White House chief of staff. Buzhardt baldly told the Senate Armed Services Committee on March 7 that there was "no material substantive difference" between his reinterview of Welander and Ehrlichman's. Buzhardt waved a copy of his reinterview about in the faces of the senators, and if they had insisted on having a document, would have given that to them (rather than the Ehrlichman-Young-Welander interview). And the only person who would have benefited from that would have been his old comrade and current superior, Alexander Haig. Thus, the reinterview seems to have been conducted for the purpose of shielding the Welander tape of December 22 on the chance that some document of Welander's admissions would one day have to be disclosed.

Queried by us about the military spy ring, Laird now says that Buzhardt's contemporary report to him was "full" of references to Haig, but not because Laird specifically asked Buzhardt to look into matters concerning the general; rather, because in the Ehrlichman-Young interview of Welander, as Laird put it, "Haig was drawn in through the back door on the thing. . . . If you've listened to the tape you certainly know what the problem is." Laird told us he was "disappointed" by what Welander had to say about Haig, but added, "I think that's enough to say." But we pressed on. Why was he disappointed? "I didn't think it was fair to the president." Despite his reluctance to elaborate, Laird then made it plain that he believed that Haig knew what was going on and Laird emphasized that his disappointment was specifically with Haig not telling the president, and not just with the activities of Robinson, Welander, and Radford.

"Are you saying you didn't think it was fair to the president that they were collecting the material?" we asked.

"Without Haig telling the president," Laird responded.

"That he knew about the Radford situation?" we asked.

"Yeah," Laird said.

Welander had confessed twice, to two different sets of interrogators, that Chairman Thomas Moorer was aware of the espionage—but Moorer has always refused to acknowledge that what Radford, Robinson, and Welander stole amounted to more than a small whitecap on a vast ocean. Yes, he agrees he did see material collected by Radford on Kissinger's China trip, but he insists that he learned nothing new from those documents or from any of the others Welander confessed to conveying to him. "I met with Kissinger frequently, every week, and went into his office, the two of us, and talked about these things, and I'm not aware of anything that I ever learned from Radford that I didn't know already, and let's leave it at that," Moorer told us in an interview.

But why would Welander assert that Moorer had learned new things from these documents and had reacted as if the information was fresh? "[Welander] didn't know what I was doing either." Moorer challenged the assumption, made by Radford and Welander, that he benefited from the pilferings. "It wasn't a spy case or anything like that. . . . You can go around, I imagine, in our bureaucratic system and if you were trying to prove, whatever in the hell you're trying to prove, you can find people who'll say everything. I can build up just as many people to say the opposite." When we tried to proceed with our telephone interview, Moorer said, "Look . . . you can write any damn thing you want about me," and hung up the phone.

Before John Mitchell's death in 1988 we laid out the evidence for Moorer's complicity, and asked Mitchell about his 1971 interview with Moorer. He reiterated that it had been done before he learned the details of Welander's confession, and that when he had determined that Moorer's denial was plausible, he had done so in the absence of crucial evidence to the contrary. "If I had heard that tape or heard it discussed, I would have had to follow an entirely different course than I did," he told us. After reading a copy of the transcript of the Ehrlichman-Young-Welander conversation, Mitchell concluded, "the president played a game with me" by not disclosing all the facts at the time Mitchell was sent to brace Moorer. "It sounds like I was set up," Mitchell said.

Why would that happen? The answer, Mitchell thought, had to do with Nixon's personality and style of governance. In 1971, had Nixon laid out all the evidence for Mitchell and asked his advice, the ex-attorney general said in 1988, he would have strongly pushed for the dismissal of Moorer. But that's not what happened, and so Mitchell reached the conclusion that Nixon never intended to seek his guidance on how to handle the military spying crisis, because he already knew what he wanted to do. Mitchell based this conclusion on the fact that at the time of the crisis, Nixon sent Mitchell—unencumbered by evidence—to ask Moorer a few questions and obtain a cursory denial, because Nixon did not want to hear what he expected Mitchell would have to say had the attorney general become convinced of Moorer's culpability. The president used him as a prop, Mitchell asserted in retrospect—as a vehicle through which Moorer could assert that he was clean. In the Moorer-Radford affair, then, Mitchell, one of Nixon's closest friends, said he was used by the president to justify the clearing of the admiral who held one of the dirtiest secrets of the Nixon years.

Why didn't Nixon listen to the Welander tape? Mitchell thought it was a deliberate refusal to face the facts. Mitchell agreed that had Nixon listened to the tape, or allowed an aggressive pursuit of all the leads on Welander's tape by his own investigators operating under Ehrlichman, or by Mitchell himself, the consequences would have been severe. Severe for whom? For Alexander Haig. "It would have taken and put Haig in a different light and probably gotten him the hell out of there," Mitchell told us.

The transcript of the Welander interview, said Mitchell after reading it, bolstered his preexisting belief that "Haig was no great supporter of Richard Nixon's; he was in business for himself."

However, Nixon was intent on burial of the episode, not exposure, and the actions he took to cover the traces of the matter ensured that Welander's admissions and his references to Haig were not explored.

On only one point in his assessment of the affair can Mitchell be faulted—what Nixon would have done if he had learned what Welander had to say about Haig, and on this, the former attorney general may have been blinded by his loyalty to Nixon. All the evidence suggests that the president would have dealt with Haig precisely as he dealt with Moorer: kept him around, and shortened his leash. This was the conclusion reached by John Ehrlichman. He imagined for us the scenario that would have unfolded if Nixon had listened to the tape, and he invented what Nixon would most likely have said to Haig: "I know what you're doing and I'm going to keep you in place anyway, but you better realize that I'm looking down your throat." Had Haig's relationships with Robinson and Welander been exposed, Ehrlichman contends, even if Nixon kept Haig on after 1972, he would never have been allowed to become chief of staff, as he did in May 1973.

"I missed the boat on Al Haig at the time," Ehrlichman told us recently, after reviewing the transcript of his old interview with Welander, and David Young's worried early morning memo, and all the other warning signs. At the time, he muses, "I heard what Welander was saying, but I didn't fully realize its implications in terms of Haig's role as an agent for the Joint Chiefs." Rather, he was focused on Welander's confirmation of the spying, on Moorer's complicity, and on dealing with the Anderson leak. He now concludes that Welander, while at pains not to appear disloyal to a fellow officer, was trying to show Ehrlichman and Young the path to the truth about Al Haig. "The implications are that Haig was a prime source for the Joint Chiefs," Ehrlichman now understands. "I think it's pretty clear on the four corners of the interview with Welander that Haig had an enormous conflict of interest between his loyalty to the president, who had really sponsored him and fostered his career on the one hand, and the Joint Chiefs on the other. . . . Haig had an impossible situation—which I guess he resolved in favor of the Joint Chiefs."

Ehrlichman is adamant that Nixon did not have any sense of what Welander had said about Haig, because the president had not reviewed either the tape or the transcript, and because the subject of Welander's veiled accusations didn't really come up in Ehrlichman's conversation with the president. "Nixon didn't want to know anything," Ehrlichman recalls. And so Nixon didn't know that the man he would later appoint as his chief of staff previously had had "confidential relationships" with those implicated in the military spy ring that had operated against Nixon in 1970-71.

Alexander Haig has repeatedly refused to comment or to answer any of our questions about the Moorer-Radford affair, or on any other subject, either orally or in writing. His assistant Woody Goldberg advised us that Haig is writing his memoirs and that everything he has to say about the Nixon years will be contained in that work.

By Christmas Day of 1971, Richard Nixon had made his decision and had begun his burial of Moorer-Radford. He would protect the back-channel that was so vital to his secret foreign policy, and in order to do so he would not disrupt the Joint Chiefs of Staff by publicly exposing or punishing their espionage. The following day Nixon left for a vacation in Key Biscayne, but not before issuing one last instruction to Ehrlichman about the crisis: He asked the domestic adviser to oversee a detailed security review of the NSC.

This was a deliberate needle in the heart of Henry Kissinger, but Ehrlichman recalls that Nixon both wanted to insert it and to slip it in gently, for Nixon needed Kissinger as much as he needed Moorer. "The president wanted it done delicately. He did not want Henry to feel that his shop was being totally torn up by this process," Ehrlichman told us.

A retired Air Force colonel conducted the review, questioning scores of Kissinger staffers and reporting back to the president in February of 1972 that the NSC staff suffered from low morale. Kissinger later testified that he never saw the report because Haig got hold of it first "and told me there was nothing in it of significance." A few procedural changes were implemented, Haig was left in place, and the report was shelved. The crisis was past, and no one wanted to hear anything more about it.

By early 1972 Nixon's attention had turned to his upcoming Chinese summit and his reelection. The White House machinery was geared toward those goals and the military spying episode, seemingly contained, quickly receded. Reflecting on those events, however, John Ehrlichman says he now realizes how vulnerable the White House was to military surveillance. "All the cars that we rode in at the White House were driven by military drivers," Ehrlichman recalls. "All of the telephone calls that we made in and out of our homes, in and out of Camp David, were through a military switchboard. It was a little bit like the purloined letter. It was there so plain nobody noticed it most of the time. We talked in the cars, we talked on our phones, we talked from Camp David, and thought nothing about it. This was part of the warp of the place, that you had military listening or in a position to listen to everything."

5

THE WOODWARD-HAIG CONNECTION

WHEN twenty-six-year-old Naval Lieutenant Robert U. Woodward arrived to take up a new and prestigious post at the Pentagon in August of 1969, he appeared to be just one more eager young lieutenant among the thousands already stationed in the capital. There was a war on, and junior officers were everywhere. Woodward was boyish-looking and just off the boat, having come from four years of sea duty as a communications officer, which followed four years at Yale and a childhood in the Chicago suburb of Wheaton, Illinois. He blended in with the rest of the fresh-faced young officers who hurried through the Pentagon's labyrinthine corridors and the mazes of offices in the White House complex. John Ehrlichman remembers that soldiers and sailors seemed so ubiquitous at the White House in those days, and blended so easily into the everyday hustle and bustle of government, that they were barely noticed.

Woodward's arrival in Washington coincided with a turning point for the military and for Admiral Thomas Moorer, the chief of naval operations who was exerting ever more control over the operations of the executive body of which he was a member, the Joint Chiefs of

Staff, and which he would soon head. This was when the JCS was in the first blush of its astonishment at the way Nixon and Kissinger were seizing power and freezing out of the decision-making process in foreign policy the usual bureaucracies of State and Defense—and the JCS. Woodward came on good recommendations, and found at the Pentagon his first skipper, Rear Admiral Francis J. Fitzpatrick, who had become assistant chief of naval operations for communications and cryptology, and his second, Rear Admiral Robert Welander, who had similarly become one of Moorer's other top aides.

The Navy brought Woodward to the Pentagon ostensibly as a communications watch officer responsible for overseeing approximately thirty sailors who manned the terminals, teletypes, and classified coding machines at the naval communications center through which all Navy traffic flowed, from routine orders to top-secret messages. It was a sensitive position that afforded Woodward access to more than a hundred communications channels, among them, according to Admiral Fitzpatrick, the top-secret SR-1 channel through which the Navy sent and received its most important messages, for instance, those which served to operate its covert global spy unit known as Task Force 157. SR-1 was the channel that Moorer provided to the White House when Kissinger and Nixon pushed him for backchannel communications capability. When Kissinger conducted his delicate and highly secret negotiations with China during 1971, SR-1 carried Kissinger's message back to his deputy Al Haig that the Peking mission had succeeded.

In addition to being one of the officers charged with managing the communications center, Woodward had another job. The young lieutenant was one of Moorer's specially selected briefing officers. A briefer is an officer who sees, hears, reads, and assimilates information from one or a variety of sources, and who conveys it succinctly and intelligibly to more senior officers. This was not only a highly prized assignment, since it often entailed close contact with very senior men who could advance a junior officer's career, but was also an enormously sensitive one, because the information conveyed was frequently top secret.

On his briefing assignment from Admiral Moorer, Woodward was often sent across the river from the Pentagon to the basement of the White House, where he would enter the offices of the National Security Council. There, Woodward would act as briefer to Alexander Haig.

The Woodward-Haig connection, that of the briefer and the officer he briefed, is one that Woodward has labored to keep secret, for reasons that will become ever clearer as this book unfolds. Over the intervening years, Woodward has vehemently denied the existence of the relationship. When we informed Woodward that we had information linking him to Haig, he issued his denial, saying, "Now what the hell are my ties to Haig?" He has even gone so far as to deny to us that he was a briefer at all and issued to us the following challenge: "I defy you to produce somebody who says I did a briefing."

However, that Woodward was a briefer and that some of those briefings were to Alexander Haig can no longer be in doubt. Admiral Moorer has confirmed to us what other sources had told us, that Woodward had been a briefer and that his duties included briefing Haig.

"He was one of the briefers," Moorer told us. Did he brief Haig? "Sure, of course," Moorer said. Woodward was instructed to brief Haig "because I was on the telephone with Haig eight or nine times a day" and there was even more to convey to Haig, so Haig could in turn relay information to Kissinger and ultimately to the president. "You don't have four-star generals lugging papers back and forth between the Pentagon and the White House," Moorer told us, you "pick up a junior-grade lieutenant and tell him to do that." But Woodward was a full-grade lieutenant, not a junior one, and especially selected for the job. What sort of briefing would Woodward normally give to Haig? "Probably the same briefing he'd just given me at nine o'clock," Moorer said, referring to the daily 9:00 A.M. briefing attended by the CNO and other flag officers at the Pentagon.

Bob Woodward was a senior at Wheaton Community High School just outside Chicago when he decided to join the Navy. It was 1961. To attend one of the country's most prestigious schools, Yale University, he needed a scholarship, and Navy ROTC would provide one, so he signed up and passed the rigorous entrance exam. His father, Al Woodward, had seen such continuous duty in the Navy during World War II that Bob had had no glimpse of him from the time he was born in 1943 until 1946. When the senior Woodward returned home and pursued a career as a lawyer, he kept photos around the house that showed himself in uniform as a fighter in the Pacific, photos Bob later remembered as urging him toward the Navy.

Bob Woodward was the oldest of Al and Jane Woodward's three children. When Bob was twelve, his parents divorced, and, in a move unusual at that time, Al Woodward retained custody of the three children. Then Al married a second time, to a woman who brought her own three children into the household; later, the couple had a child of their own, so Bob Woodward became the oldest of seven children in his home.

Alfred E. Woodward was a leading citizen of Wheaton, a chief judge of the county circuit court, and he expected his son to be an achiever. Bob tried hard to meet these expectations, but was uncomfortable in his new family situation. One Christmas, Bob Woodward told a *Playboy* interviewer in 1988, he was dismayed to discover that the presents that he and his natural brother and sister had received didn't measure up to those given to his new stepbrothers and stepsisters. "I looked up the prices of all the presents in the gift catalog," Woodward said. "It was a moment of great emotional distress for me and my father when I confronted him and showed him that the money he'd spent on them and on us was so dramatically out of balance. . . . It was kind of sad, but the fact is that it's a very competitive world when two families are brought together that way. You end up feeling like an outsider in your own family."

Nevertheless, Bob emulated Al in his Republican conservative politics, and tried to do so in his attempt to play on the football team— Al had been captain of the team at Oberlin College. Bob wasn't as athletically talented, and though he made it onto the team, he almost never played. In this matter, he told *Playboy*, he believed he had disappointed his father. "So I spent a lot of time up in my room as a radio ham, talking in Morse code around the world." He characterized the members of the ham radio club as classic "outsiders" with "slide-rules on their belts."

Woodward's portrait of himself as a tortured yet intellectual outsider is fine psychologically, but, as with so much that he has told interviewers of his own past, is incomplete and misleading. In fact, the adolescent Woodward was a definite insider, elected to the student council each year at Wheaton, the general chairman of the prom, one of four commencement speakers from his class—"one of the greatest honors to be bestowed on a senior," the school yearbook describes this privilege—and a member of several clubs (none of them for ham radio operators) as well as a member of several athletic teams and of the National Honor Society.

For that commencement speech, Bob Woodward adapted his remarks from Senator Barry Goldwater's book *The Conscience of a Conservative*, decrying the intrusion of the federal government into the lives of everyday citizens. Beside his name in the senior yearbook he printed the motto, "Though I cannot out-vote them, I will out-argue them."

His girlfriend in high school, later his first wife, Kathleen Middle-kauff, says he was popular, though "it wasn't the kind of popularity that made him liked by everyone. But he was known as an intellectual. You don't get elected to student government if you're an outsider."

Middlekauff was a year behind Bob at Wheaton, and they kept up a correspondence when she moved with her family to New Jersey after her sophomore year. Bob matriculated at Yale in 1961, and Kathleen at Smith College, in 1962. They continued to see one another.

Bob Woodward attended Yale on a scholarship from the Naval Reserve Officers Training Corps program. The NROTC program was the most highly competitive "officer candidate procurement program" in that service; only about 10 percent of the applicants were accepted, according to a 1965 guide. Approximately one thousand new officers were graduated from it each year, and these were meant to supplement those graduated from the U.S. Naval Academy. The corps at Yale provided about seventy-five of these officers per year, and, says a 1958 Yale NROTC graduate, John McAllister, "the competition was very fierce and intense. You didn't go into the program as a lark." Yale NROTC students took one course per semester in some naval science such as engineering and propulsion, gunnery skills, military history, navigation, or naval operations and tactics. They also learned to march and drill in their uniforms, and had to attend six-to-eight-week training cruises each of three summers. Woodward's first summer was spent aboard an aircraft carrier, the second in a Marine and flight-training program, the third on a destroyer in the Mediterranean.

Midshipman Woodward was also a thoroughgoing Yalie who seemed at home in the Ivy League atmosphere of the early 1960s. His major concentrations were in history and English literature, and he was a member of Yale Banner Publications, the group that produced all campus publications except for the daily newspaper. As a senior, he was the chairman of Banner.

During this period, Woodward wrote a novel, which Kathleen remembers as a deeply emotional work. He sent the manuscript to publishers in New York, but it was rejected. In his *Playboy* interview, Woodward sloughed off the novel as "silly" and "garbage," but said that it contained "all the painful material of Wheaton and childhood and divorce and families in which all the innocent are wounded, because children are innocent, and it inflicts great pain." He said he later turned to journalism and its concern with the "external" world rather than have to continue his examination of the internal world represented by that novel. In that interview, Woodward admitted that after its rejection he shed his literary ambitions somewhat and the notion of himself as an intellectual. He was actively political only as a freshman, as a member of the Yale Political Union. His conservative stance may have set him apart; after hearing Woodward speak in class one day, a political science professor called him a "crypto-fascist."

In the carefully constructed version of his own life that he gave to interviewers, Woodward recalled a sea change while at Yale. His tale was recorded by Leonard Downie, Jr., a colleague at the *Washington Post*, in the 1976 book *The New Muckrakers*. "I had a crisis at Yale when it became clear what the Vietnam war was really all about, but I never considered going to Canada or anything like that," Woodward recalled. The version he told David Halberstam three years later, condensed in *The Powers That Be*, was slightly different. In his last two years at Yale, Halberstam wrote, Woodward "had watched what was happening in Vietnam and he did not like anything about it. He thought for a time about going to Canada, but that was not the sort of thing a Wheaton boy did."

John McAllister, the 1958 Yale NROTC graduate, notes that at Yale in 1963-64 the campus was still relatively docile about the Vietnam War; McAllister knows, because as a Yale man and a Vietnam War veteran he took part in the first teach-in at the campus, in 1965. Captain Andrew Coombe, a 1965 Yale NROTC graduate who knew Woodward at Yale, said there was no antimilitary activity on campus at the time Woodward claims to have undergone the sea change; in fact, he points out, the ROTC units marched at one of the football games "and there was no big deal about it."

Kathleen visited Bob at Yale, and didn't note a change in his attitude toward the war either. "He still remained very conservative," she recalled, and was quite definite in her memories of this because *she* had changed. Kathleen said she had become a little involved with one of the most radical of campus organizations, the Students for a Democratic Society (SDS). "We used to have arguments about it. He didn't think that was something that was wise for me to be doing." Had Bob ever considered going to Canada to avoid the war? "Heavens, no," Kathleen Woodward told us.

Rather than experiencing a crisis of the soul at Yale and veering to the left, at Yale Bob Woodward became ever more closely tied to the establishment environment in which he had been raised. For decades, Yale had been a prime recruiting ground for the Central Intelligence Agency; professors and athletic team coaches would openly seek candidates for the Agency. The Navy, too, considered Yale good hunting grounds on which to find future officers. Many graduates who did not go into the Navy or the CIA often filled important posts in the government or in business, and all of these constituted an "old boy network" to rival those of the graduates of Oxford and Cambridge among the ruling elite of Great Britain. In many ruling elites, a large proportion of the members are initiated into the networks through secret societies. Legendary secret societies have long been a fixture of Yale life, mysterious, closed fraternities that enjoyed connections to powerful government figures who had been members in their own college days. Bob Woodward was "tapped" to join Book and Snake in his junior year.

Though Book and Snake was not as well known as Skull and Bones, which counts George Bush among its members, "It is certainly among the top four," says Yale professor Robin Winks, author of *Cloak and Gown*, which documented Yale's ties to the intelligence community in the years 1939–1961. No evidence has emerged that Woodward was recruited from Book and Snake for the intelligence community, but from his year in Book and Snake he got a good grounding in an environment founded on secrecy, exclusivity, and the burnishing of old boy network ties. Founded in the 1880s and based on the Italian secret societies, those at Yale each have their own building, usually a windowless structure designed to keep its activities secret. The Book and Snake building is adjacent to the law school library, and across from a cemetery, and has a marble facade that makes it resemble a mausoleum.

Of approximately twelve hundred men in a class, the secret societies would tap about 10 percent, or twelve men for each society. Meetings were held twice a week, and on those occasions the chosen dozen would dine and drink together, or hold group discussions in which they would criticize one another or share secrets about themselves. In these societies, bonds were formed that lasted well after a member's departure from the campus.

In 1965, Bob Woodward graduated from Yale. He owed the Navy four years of active duty, and although he never planned to make the Navy his career—he thought he might write fiction, or study law as his father had done—he determined to make the most of his assignments. His first post was aboard the USS *Wright*, one of two ships designated as a National Emergency Command Post Afloat. Woodward was circuit control officer on this rather odd-looking vessel, a refitted aircraft carrier with five enormous antennae that rose above an otherwise empty deck. The venerable publication *Jane's Fighting Ships* declared that the *Wright* had "the most powerful transmitting antennae ever installed on a ship," the tallest of which was 83 feet high and designed to withstand 100-mph winds. The *Wright*'s mission was to handle "world-wide communications and rapid, automatic exchange, processing, storage and display of command data," and to serve in times of emergency as a floating command post for top military officials and the president, according to a dictionary of naval fighting ships. One admiral described it as "a mini-headquarters facility in case of nuclear war." Stationed at the Norfolk, Virginia, naval base, it mostly cruised the Virginia capes, but occasionally ranged the entire seaboard from Maine to Florida, and sometimes as far south as Guantanamo Bay in Cuba and Rio de Janiero. In April 1967, with Woodward aboard, the *Wright* was at anchor off Punta del Este, Uruguay, serving as a command center for President Lyndon Johnson, who was attending a Latin American summit conference.

Woodward held a "top-secret crypto" security clearance and commanded the enlisted men who operated the ship's radio circuits. According to its skipper at that time, because the *Wright* had to be ready for the president at any time, it was privy to the same information that flowed daily into the Situation Room at the White House. That skipper, Captain Francis Fitzpatrick, who shortly rose to admiral and served as assistant CNO for communications and cryptology, remembers Woodward "pushing traffic" on the ship, that is, supervising the processing of sensitive messages and coded cables that flowed into the ship from all points around the globe.

According to Woodward, it was no big deal, and neither was the security clearance, then or afterward at the Pentagon. He insists that it was "not an intelligence . . . clearance at all. It's for the cryptographic machines and code cards that are used in communications."

For nearly twenty years, ever since achieving fame for his reporting about Watergate, Woodward has said his naval career was an era of his life during which he was "miserable." Over the course of several interviews, he insisted to us that he was never anything more in the Navy than an officer in charge of men who handled communications traffic.

In evaluating Woodward's naval career and his own estimate of it, we must be as careful as in evaluating his career as a student, for Woodward's version has all the hallmarks of a disinformation campaign designed to hide, rather than to illuminate, the essential points.

Admiral Welander, who later commanded Woodward on another ship, says the *Wright* was a plum assignment for an officer fresh out of Yale, because though there were periods of relative inactivity, the *Wright* was nevertheless plugged into the same communications network that fed the White House. And former Green Beret Shelby Stanton, author of several books on military matters, says that "To go to a command ship right off the bat is a top job. It's like going to work for a corporation and being assigned right away to headquarters and getting the inside track. It sounds like he [Woodward] was being groomed. They would not have assigned just anybody to that ship."

Woodward says he has "no idea" how he was selected for the job. "I was a radio ham when I was a kid. . . . Maybe that was the connection." It was while stationed in Norfolk in 1966 that he married Kathleen Middlekauff, his childhood sweetheart, after her graduation from Smith. Kathleen said she hated their tiny apartment and the regimentation of Navy life. Things were better for her on Bob's next assignment, which allowed the Woodwards a home in San Diego at the end of 1967.

How Woodward obtained this second assignment, and what he made of it, is the subject of some confusion. He told Leonard Downie that he had received orders to go to Vietnam to serve as a tactical watch officer at a "jungle command center" in the Can Tho province located in the Mekong Delta. "I knew it would be a death trap," Woodward told Downie. "To get out of that I asked to be transferred instead to a destroyer, which apparently pleased the Navy." Woodward's second version, given to Halberstam, was more detailed: The post would have entailed "going out in the canals of the Mekong Delta at night on Navy riverboats," and, Woodward believed, it almost certainly would have resulted in his death. So he looked for a way out. According to the Halberstam account, that way was "to imply that he wanted to go career Navy," and thereby earn assignment to a destroyer. To do so, Halberstam's account says, Woodward "got hold of the Pentagon phone book and he made a list of everyone who might have some control over his destiny, and he sat down and wrote each of them a letter."

To us, Woodward reported a different set of events and motives. The proposed duty in the Mekong Delta had never been one that was directly in the line of fire, but was merely at an operations center; moreover, he wrote only one letter to get the orders changed, and that was to his Navy detailer, the personnel specialist who helps set assignments for each officer. "I didn't want to go to Vietnam," Woodward told us in 1989; "I wrote a letter and sat down and talked to the guy." Just a request to his detailer for a different assignment? "Correct," Woodward says. He also denied any attempt on his part to imply to the Navy that he wanted to be a career officer and thus needed a destroyer assignment, and he says no higher officers played a role in the decision to get him such an assignment.

Retired Rear Admiral Gene LaRocque, a flag officer in that era, says that writing letters and promising to go career Navy could have made an impression, but that it was difficult to get out of such an assignment without help from a sympathetic senior officer, such as the captain of your ship. Retired Rear Admiral Eugene J. Carroll, Jr., former assistant director of naval personnel—that is, the director of all detailers—says it was almost inconceivable in that era for a junior officer to get out of duty in Vietnam by relying simply on his detailer. "I was a detailer," Carroll insists, "and in almost every case you had to be adamant about the original orders unless a very senior officer requested a man for his ship or staff. I can't think of a situation in which a detailer changed those kinds of orders on his own."

Admiral Welander says Woodward's story doesn't make much sense to him, either—even though it was to Welander's ship, the USS *Fox*, that Woodward was sent when he didn't want to go to Vietnam. Furthermore, though Woodward served under Welander at sea, later socialized with him in Washington, and worked near him at the Pentagon during the period from late 1967 to mid-1969, Woodward never mentioned to him any story of having his orders changed from Vietnam to destroyer duty.

The *Fox* was a guided-missile frigate based in San Diego that made cruises to the South China Sea to provide targeting information in support of air strikes in Vietnam. Woodward, now a lieutenant junior grade, became the ship's communications officer, responsible for maintaining the ship's state-of-the-art electronics gear. The *Fox* accompanied aircraft carriers in the Tonkin Gulf and also provided communications for highly classified intelligence operations. According to Welander, Woodward "had a lot of potential as a good officer," an opinion shared by the man who took over command of the *Fox* from Welander in May of 1968, M. D. Ward, and by the Navy itself, which gave Woodward his second promotion in three years in July 1968, a promotion to lieutenant that put him about a year ahead of the normal rate of elevation, according to a Navy personnel document. Woodward earned a Navy Commendation Medal during this period, and its citation reflects "exceptional zeal and ingenuity in developing methods which enabled his ship to . . . retransmit important operational messages to other units . . . in a more timely manner than normally available through regular communications channels." The citation celebrated a special talent that Woodward would display frequently in later years and in other than military situations.

About six months before his four-year obligation was to conclude, on January 29, 1969, Woodward submitted a letter of resignation to the Navy, but when it came time to leave, in the summer of 1969, he didn't go. Though he has consistently said to interviewers that he found the service oppressive, he nonetheless stayed on a year after he could have left. Why?

According to Woodward, it was red tape that kept him in place—a 1967 order signed by the secretary of the Navy that extended all regular officers to an additional twelve months of service because of the war in Vietnam. However, that 1967 NAVOP, as it is known in the Navy, was not a blanket extension of all service. Officers were to be extended "on a selective basis," and "subject to the needs of the Navy." In fact, Admiral Carroll says that the policy was administered only on a case-by-case basis. Once an officer had requested to resign, Carroll maintains, the Navy would have determined whether or not he held a crucial job or was about to be assigned to one, and if that were so, it would invoke the secretary's policy and extend him for another year; if not, he would normally be allowed to go.

Al Woodward proudly says his son volunteered for that fifth year after the Navy offered Bob the prestigious assignment linking the Pentagon and the White House. "I don't think he was ordered. He had an option to do it or not, and he decided to do it," the senior Woodward told us. "I guess it was considered somewhat of an honor, and he accepted it." Did he accept because it was a White House assignment? "Right," says Al Woodward, who emphasized that "the assignment [Bob] had was in the basement of the White House."

On the other hand, Kathleen Woodward had always believed that the Navy "made him stay for another year." She would have preferred for him to have left the Navy, for, as it turned out, Bob's assignment to Washington broke their marriage apart. However, informed of Al Woodward's view that Bob volunteered for the fifth year, Kathleen said it was possible that Bob didn't tell her the whole story about the assignment.

It was 1969, and they had talked of moving to Berkeley after Bob was discharged; there, she could continue her studies in economics, and he could write. "I was going to make money so that my husband could write," she remembers. But that dream evaporated when Bob announced quite suddenly that he was taking a "good assignment [that] involved this work at the White House." Rather than spending that fifth year in California or in any of the several other locations among which, Kathleen says, he was allowed to choose, he said he was going to Washington. After Bob left, Kathleen remembers, "I tried to visualize what he was doing in the basement of the White House."

"I can't conceive of a case in which a man was given an option of choosing his assignment in a situation like that," Admiral Carroll comments; "It could only happen if his commanding officer or someone from the Pentagon requested him for a particular assignment."

In any event, the transfer to the capital was the effective end of Woodward's first marriage. Kathleen visited him once in Washington during the latter part of 1969, and left for France shortly thereafter for a year of study abroad. During that year, they divorced. Today, as Kathleen Woodward, she is a professor at the University of Wisconsin, in Milwaukee, where she is also head of The Center for Twentieth Century Studies. Kathleen remains fond of Woodward, has maintained contact with him over the years, and considers herself still "loyal to Bob." Nonetheless, she assesses him as "ruthless . . . extremely ambitious . . . immensely controlled. All of his passion has been channeled into his ambition."

When Woodward arrived in Washington he went on the staff of Admiral Moorer, together with his two former skippers, Fitzpatrick and Welander; he reported to Fitzpatrick through Commander John J. Kingston, chief of all the watch officers, and supervised the people manning terminals in the CNO's communications center. It was Woodward's job as communications watch officer to route incoming messages to the proper person on the staff of the chief of naval operations or the secretary of the Navy, and to be aware of particular sensitive areas or "hot spots" about which the CNO or his flag officers must be alerted. Most of the messages were classified, and some were top secret. They also included, according to Kingston, "personal, exclusive-type messages. A lot of negotiations at the time. What the Navy thought about this, that, or the other thing. It was all in personal messages between flag officers."

According to Charles Hunnicut, who held a similar position to Woodward's at that time, because of the many terminals and the messages coming and going, even from the special adjoining room for secure voice communications to the White House, "There was something different happening all the time. You had stuff coming in from all over the world. You knew what was going on in the world for real." These particular watch officers were at the nexus of a constant stream of communications. They presided over its acquisition and transmittal, they reviewed the raw traffic that flowed into and out of the CNO's office to and from the fleet, the CIA and the NSA, the State Department, and the NSC. Most watch officers, however, had very little direct contact with the White House; occasionally they would be in touch with the White House Communications Agency—Kingston says that someone would be assigned to drop off a package at the WHCA perhaps once a week, and that this *never* involved going into the basement offices of the White House or the NSC.

Woodward insists that he loathed the assignment. To Leonard Downie he said the job was "awful and boring . . . I was miserable." In an interview he told us that the courier duty to the White House amounted to "scut work" in which he sometimes carried "some documents or a folder. . . . Strictly nuts and bolts. It's not substantive."

Asked if he had any responsibilities in his fifth year in the Navy beyond that of the ordinary communications watch officer, Woodward said, "No. Nothing at all." Did he perform as a briefing officer? "Never," he shot back. It was at this point that he issued his challenge defying us to produce anyone who confirmed he did a briefing. "Have you got somebody who says I did a briefing?" Assured that we had, Woodward pushed harder. "Who says that? What sort of people?" We reminded him that throughout his career as a reporter he had steadfastly refused to disclose his sources, and refused to tell him ours, but assured him that his full denial of the briefing assignment would be published. "I wasn't [a briefer]," he insisted. "It never happened. I'm looking you in the eye. You have got bad sources. . . . Call up and find out who does the communications watch officer work now and find out if they're briefers, if they give briefings. It just isn't so."

Woodward is partially correct, for communications watch officers do not normally give briefings, but the job title can be misleading. L. Fletcher Prouty, retired Air Force colonel and one of the top briefing officers for the JCS from 1955 to 1963, says he never formally held the title of briefing officer, because "Briefer is not a job description, it's something that somebody does. I had the title of chief of special operations for the Joint Chiefs of Staff, and you wouldn't know from that that I was a briefer. . . . It's easy to hide behind words and say somebody didn't do something because they didn't have a title, but it's meaningless."

But of course, Admiral Moorer, as noted above, has confirmed that Woodward was indeed a briefer. Moorer described for us the qualities required of briefers such as Woodward. First, the briefer "had to be articulate"; then, "you have to be able to stand on your two feet without beating around the bush and taking up people's time. Give the information out, that's all. Some people are good at communications and decoding messages . . . and some people are good at standing on their two feet in front of the admiral and giving the summary of the latest messages that came in during the night. And Woodward could do that."

To be a briefer was "a marvelously challenging job," recalls Dr. William Bader of the Stanford Research Institute, who served as a Navy briefer in the 1950s and 1960s. He notes that the old boy network of former Navy briefers includes Senator Richard Lugar of Indiana and Admiral Bobby Ray Inman, former deputy director of the CIA and head of the NSA. It was an incredibly important job for a young man in his twenties, Bader says, "very heady business." He has always been amazed by the Navy's capacity to find good men and bring them "into the system" through "a very interesting and intricate job." Bader describes the task as part presentation of data, part entertainment. "They considered that you had the intelligence and analytical ability to take vast amounts of information and process it, collate it, and present it. Perhaps 'entertaining' is a bit flip—but they really wanted you to have a certain amount of the Dan Rather in you." Most briefers, Bader says, continued to stay in touch with one another through the old boy network; it was through this network, Bader says, that he learned that Woodward "was one of us."

Fletcher Prouty, himself a former briefer, described in his book *The Secret Team* that, within the government's power centers, "one of the most interesting and effective roles is that played by the behind-the-scenes, faceless, ubiquitous briefing officer" who sees the important people "almost daily." Moreover, the briefer "comes away day after day knowing more and more about the man he has been briefing and about what it is that the truly influential pressure groups at the center of authority are trying to tell these key decision makers." Prouty recalls that he was the focal point for contact between the CIA and the Department of Defense in cases where the military was involved in covert operations; at the time he held the job, he considered himself "perhaps the best informed liaison officer among the few who operated in this very special area."

Prouty the briefer described his formal job as that of liaison officer. Downie, reflecting on his interview with Woodward, described Woodward's job in Washington as a "communications liaison officer between the Pentagon and the White House." In 1983, Woodward spoke to reporter Jim Hougan, then researching his book entitled *Secret Agenda*. Hougan had learned of Woodward's briefing assignment, and asked him about it. "He admitted to me that his assignment included a responsibility to brief," Hougan told us recently. "He would not, however, identify the people he did brief." In his later conversation with us, Woodward would not even admit to having acted as a liaison officer. But some senior officials at the Pentagon knew of Woodward's assignment, including former secretary of defense Melvin Laird, who told us, "Yes, I was aware that Haig was being briefed by Woodward," and Laird's aide at the time, Jerry Friedheim, who agreed that Woodward "was one of several briefers. Briefers were identifiable. That's how they came to the notice of senior officials."

However, Woodward's briefing assignment was kept secret from his fellow officers and from some of his superiors. "If he did it," fellow watch officer Hunnicut avows, "he did it other than when he was relieving me. Because he relieved me personally on almost every watch. I knew Bob Woodward and he had the same job that I did, and I had none of those duties, and none of the other [communications watch officers] had it either." Woodward's superior, Kingston, is more circumspect: "Anything is possible," he told us in regard to Woodward's briefing assignment, "but if he did those briefings I didn't know about it." Admiral Fitzpatrick says if Woodward did White House briefings, "he did it behind my back," but admits that he saw very little of Woodward directly while at the Pentagon, principally only when Bob came into Fitzpatrick's office to say hello to another junior officer with whom he'd served on the *Wright*. Even Admiral Welander says there was "never any indication" that Woodward briefed anyone in the White House, and reminds us that his office was a mere forty to fifty feet from Woodward's in the Pentagon.

That Woodward had a secret assignment and that it was kept from his fellow officers and from some of his superiors argues that his true assignment was extremely sensitive. That he would go to such lengths to deny having briefed Haig further argues that the sensitivity about his secret assignment might well have to do with precisely this point: that Woodward briefed Haig. We can't prove it, but the evidence suggests that Woodward might well have served as a human backchannel between Haig and the JCS, carrying information so sensitive that it could only be conveyed by a specially selected briefing officer.

Woodward was an insider in high school and college, but insists to recent interviewers that he was an outsider; he tells one story about dissent during the Vietnam War to one interviewer, another to a second; he says at one time that he wrote letters to everyone he could find in a Pentagon phone book to get out of duty in Vietnam, and at a second time that he only spoke to his detailer; he was a well-placed junior officer who briefed Admiral Moorer and other senior military officials at the Pentagon and at the White House, yet insists that his military career was boring and that he couldn't wait to get out.

Why does Woodward dissemble? Why hide your light under a bushel basket—especially if it is a fine, smart, highly trained, well-connected light? Why downplay an insider's school career? Why discount or refuse to acknowledge the sort of military assignments about which others would like to be able to boast? Woodward's description of his life prior to the time he sprang into fame as the investigative reporter of Watergate resembles the cover identities and complete past histories chosen by moles in tales of espionage: It is drab to the point of the subject vanishing into the wallpaper. Woodward seems to cover his past associations with shadows in order to conceal strong, ongoing connections to the military hierarchy, and to protect people in that hierarchy who are or have been his journalistic sources.

The confusion about Woodward's life extends even into the early stages of his journalistic career. He received his discharge from the Navy in August 1970. His NROTC contract obligated him to six years of service—four years' active, two years' inactive reserve—but Woodward only served five years. The sixth year remains a mystery; it may be that the reserve obligation was waived because Woodward served five years on active status, but that is unclear. We asked Woodward if that sixth year was waived, and he said, "I don't know what happened. But I know I had an option about going into the reserve or not and I chose not to." That summer Woodward was accepted at Harvard Law School and thought briefly of attending, but did not do so. He told Downie that he turned to journalism because "newspaper work was something I thought I could do right away." With no reporting experience, he nonetheless managed to get an interview with *Washington Post* metropolitan editor Harry Rosenfeld, who gave him a two-week tryout without pay—it was Woodward's idea. None of what he wrote during that period was printed, and the tryout was terminated.

Woodward was then hired at the *Montgomery County Sentinel*, a suburban Maryland weekly. Woodward told Downie that *Post* editors "helped me get a job" at the *Sentinel*, and in 1987 upped the ante by telling *Miami Herald* reporter Ryan Murphy that Rosenfeld had written a glowing recommendation that helped him land the suburban job. "I distinctly remember when he was telling me about the Rosenfeld letter," Murphy recalls. "He [Woodward] described it as if it were a really superlative, high-praise letter." Rosenfeld, who is no longer with the *Post*, says he cannot remember writing such a letter for Woodward and denies playing any role in helping Woodward get a job at the *Sentinel*.

Roger B. Farquhar, who hired Woodward for the *Sentinel*, says, "I got no word from the *Post* at all" about Woodward. He picked Woodward from forty applicants because Woodward was a Yale man, because he seemed an eager beaver—Woodward stood in the doorway and declared, "I want to work here so much that I can taste it," Farquhar recalls—and because Woodward produced a Navy document that praised his abilities. In an interview with us in 1984, Farquhar described this document as a letter from a senior officer who "just raved" about Woodward, "particularly how hard he worked, how he had the work ethic."

Asked about his hiring at the *Sentinel*, Woodward said that a "number of people," perhaps one being Rosenfeld, suggested it was a good place to start his career. Rosenfeld, Woodward recalled, "may have called" Farquhar, "or written him a letter. I don't remember. . . . It's possible I may have had a recommendation from somebody in the Navy." Told that Farquhar said he saw a letter from a Navy officer, Woodward responded, "I don't think that's true. I may have shown him my fitness report, or something like that. . . . I don't think there was a letter."

After our interview with Woodward, and after seeing some of our written materials, Farquhar denied that he had been shown a letter and said the document Woodward had shown him was a personnel form from Woodward's service record that contained the statement about his "incredible" work habits. He also told us that he'd had no recent contact with Woodward on the matter.

After one year at the *Sentinel*, Woodward joined the *Washington Post* on September 14, 1971.

After briefing Moorer at nine in the morning in 1969 and 1970, Woodward would often travel to the West Basement offices of the White House, carrying documents from Moorer, and would then deliver these and brief Alexander Haig about the same matters he had earlier conveyed to Moorer.

Among those who saw Woodward enter Haig's room was Roger Morris, then a member of Kissinger's NSC staff. (Morris later resigned from his position in protest at the bombing of Cambodia.) When pictures of Woodward began to appear in the newspapers in the 1970s, Morris recognized him as a young Navy officer he had seen going into Haig's office. "I learned through friends that this was the same guy who had been one of Moorer's aides, and had worked at the Pentagon and so forth, and knew Al Haig well, and had been back and forth in the West Basement in those early days," Morris told us recently.

Morris told us that Haig's briefers "came from all the services, from the Air Force, the Army, as well as the Navy, and of course there were guys from CIA and NSA, who gave these kinds of briefings." In the early days, Morris recalled, "Haig took all of the military briefings . . . and intelligence briefings" personally, "on a very frequent basis" because of the ongoing war in Vietnam. For the NSC, Kissinger had his own office, and Haig shared one with Lawrence Eagleburger; other personnel were in the large bullpen area of the Situation Room, where they could monitor incoming cable traffic and the hot line to Moscow, guard safes containing highly classified material, and send or receive the Nixon-Kissinger backchannel messages. The briefing area was a small conference room adjacent to this bull pen. Here, Morris says, "Haig took his briefings from people like Woodward always behind closed doors," most often alone, but sometimes with a military aide; after these briefings, Haig would then "delegate various things and act on whatever he got from [the briefer]." In addition to being briefed by the military, Haig was also briefed by the FBI and the CIA. "He was the conduit, which gave him a great deal of information . . . probably 90 percent of the intelligence material. . . . It was very, very heavy traffic." As a result of these frequent briefings, Morris says, Haig "became not just a conduit but he became an active liaison and a kind of representative of and to the Joint Chiefs and to the [armed] services themselves."

The NSC's staff secretary at the time, William Watts, told us that Colonel Haig made it "very clear, very early" in his tenure at the White House that no one should tread on "his turf," which was the Pentagon and all military information. Watts had a direct line from his office to Air Force Colonel Robert Pursley, military aide to Laird. Haig openly disdained Pursley by name, but was annoyed that Watts had such direct access to Pursley. Haig, Watts says, "was just very effective at establishing the fact that he was the guy who was going to be dealing with the Pentagon. . . . He was keeping his line over there very much open, and he was very effective at doing that."

Alexander Meigs Haig, Jr., was then forty-four and a career army officer. His early childhood had been spent in a Catholic, upper middle-class suburb of Philadelphia, where his father was a lawyer. The father died when his namesake was ten, and this caused financial hardships for the family. An uncle became Haig's early benefactor, and from then on, throughout Haig's career, he found and nurtured mentor-protégé relationships with powerful men.

Haig entered West Point at the age of twenty in 1944, after having previously been rejected by the academy. The course had been condensed into three years because of the war, and in 1947 Haig graduated 214th in the class of 310. First Lieutenant Haig was sent to Tokyo in 1948, and became aide-de-camp to General Alonzo Fox, deputy chief of staff to Douglas MacArthur, the supreme Allied commander. Haig later married Fox's daughter.

In Japan, Roger Morris noted in his biography of Haig, the young officer learned how to cater to the "personal and professional whims of his superiors," especially MacArthur, who viewed himself as a sovereign and the ultimate ruler of Japan, and to maneuver from within among the jealous ranks of MacArthur's courtiers. "In that sense, Haig was given a taste of both the pomp and the politics of a veritable presidency two decades before he joined the White House staff," Morris concludes.

When war broke out in Korea, Haig went to it as an aide to another of MacArthur's favorites, General Edward Almond. Other assignments in the 1950s included three years in Europe, a stint as a company commander at West Point and one as an executive officer at Annapolis. In 1959, after attending the Naval War College, he enrolled in what Morris described as an "undemanding" master's degree program in international relations at Georgetown University. Advanced degrees were thought desirable to enable an officer to enter the upper ranks.

Haig's 1962 master's thesis was a virtual blueprint of the officer and politician he would become. The topic was the role of the military man in the shaping of national security policy, and he called for "a new breed" of soldier who could "continually appraise military policy in terms of its political implications." In his *tour d'horizon* of the relationships between the civilian and military authorities in the United States since the turn of the century, Haig criticized past "civilian interference" in military decision-making, and declared that the civilians "must consistently include vital military considerations" in dealing with political matters. General George Marshall erred in the other direction, Haig wrote, bowing too far to too many political considerations of the civilian leadership in World War II. Haig deplored Truman's recall of MacArthur as further tipping the scales to the side of the civilians. Yet he was particularly laudatory to the man who would shortly become his boss, civilian Robert McNamara, while another future boss, Henry Kissinger, appears in a gracious footnote as a keen academic strategist.

To Haig, in his thesis, the State Department's dominance in foreign affairs must be ended; moreover, the military's many voices should be distilled into one—a single presidential adviser, more influential than the chairman of the Joint Chiefs, who would give his counsel directly and continuously. This would give the Pentagon a "seat at the pinnacle" of government. Haig fretted that there were currently several levels of people keeping the military from the president's ear; that had to be eliminated. "There is a growing danger that future policy may lack the military contribution called for by the challenge that confronts our nation," Haig wrote in summation, and this was a challenge that would have to be met by civilians assisted at the highest level by military men "skilled in the management of violence."

General Fox, although by then retired from the military, still had ties to McNamara, and he backed Haig's first posting to the Pentagon after his son-in-law had earned his master's degree. It was in the

International and Policy Planning Division, and although Haig's title sounded impressive, he was just one of a multitude of middle-rank officers who shuffled between such desk jobs, making the Army's contingency plans for Berlin and for an invasion of Cuba. Working in the Pentagon, Haig came in contact with several men he had known since West Point days, such as Fred Buzhardt, who was then on the staff of Senator Strom Thurmond.

In the halcyon summer of 1963, Haig was, in Morris' words, "rescued . . . from the army's oblivion" by "the most decisive patronage of his career," that of Cyrus Vance, then secretary of the Army, through Vance's counsel, Joe Califano. Califano put him to work on assimilating into the army some of the Cuban exile veterans of the Bay of Pigs, discovered that Haig "was more of a workaholic than I was," and touted him to Vance as one of the "Maxwell Taylors of tomorrow."

Vance, Califano, and company were up to their neck in brushfire problems in Central and South America in the year Haig worked for them, and took Haig along in 1964 when Vance was promoted by McNamara to be deputy secretary of defense. In the next year, as the United States was drawn increasingly into the maelstrom of Vietnam, Haig was a small cog in the decision-making hierarchy of the Pentagon. To his bosses, Vance and McNamara, he declared that the military men must not be excluded from "key decision-making" on the war, urging in a memorandum that the chairman of the Joint Chiefs should attend the weekly meetings "of high-level advisers at the White House." In June 1965, Haig went off to the Army War College, and was replaced in his post by an Air Force officer named Alexander P. Butterfield, with whom he became friends. Eleven months later, Haig headed to Vietnam for his first true battle command. It proved in retrospect to be a great time to get out of the Pentagon, for those who remained were later tarred by their association with disastrous war policies.

Battalion Commander Lieutenant Colonel Haig and his troops saw heavy action in the spring of 1967, and Haig was cited for bravery. In 1968 he returned to the United States, was promoted to full colonel, and went to West Point as deputy commander of cadets, the number-two position at West Point. In late 1968, he received the call from Henry Kissinger summoning him to a position in the Nixon White House.

We asked Woodward when he first met or first talked to Haig; he said it was "some time in the spring of 1973." Did he remember the circumstances? "I don't. I don't." Had Haig become White House chief of staff by that time? "Don't know. Don't know," Woodward responded, and reasserted that "the idea that I had a tie to him [earlier] is false." And he wouldn't answer any other inquiries about his dealings with Haig after that spring 1973 time "because it's complicated."

We'll skip over for the moment what has long been suspected—that Haig was "Deep Throat," the source that gave to Woodward nearly every investigative break on the Watergate affair and was immortalized in *All the President's Men*—and jump ahead to the controversy surrounding a later book by Woodward and his *Post* colleague, Carl Bernstein, *The Final Days*, in which the investigative reporters chronicled the last fifteen months of the Nixon presidency. Articles and reviews in 1976 and since that time have wondered whether Haig was a key source for that book, because on page after page the authors reconstructed what they said were White House meetings and conversations of the most intimate and sensitive kind, many of which involved Haig. Since there is rarely any attribution of sources in the book, it is impossible to state conclusively who those sources were—but some passages include private scenes between Nixon and his chief of staff, Haig, in which the thoughts and feelings of both men are described.

Nixon was not interviewed, and Haig has denied being a source for that book or for any later material that Woodward has written about him. Upon publication of *The Final Days*, Haig was supreme commander of Allied Forces in Europe, and he sent Nixon a cable that read: "I . . . want to assure you that I have not contributed in any way to the book." Conservative journalist and author Victor Lasky got a letter from Haig in April 1976 that contained a similar denial; Haig told Lasky he had rebuffed Woodward's strenuous effort to get him to talk. In the letter, Haig told the story, repeated elsewhere, that Woodward flew to NATO headquarters in Europe hoping for an interview, but that the general, with a witness present, refused to have anything to do with the reporter.

This story of a public rebuff to Woodward has been repeated to us by associates of both men as the quintessential proof that Haig refused to have any dealings with Woodward. David Korn, a longtime personal friend and former special assistant to Haig, says "Woodward came to see him [Haig] in Brussels and he threw him [Woodward] out. He refused to talk to him . . . I heard it directly from Haig. You know, sometimes people exaggerate, but he [Haig] claims he never wanted to talk to him [Woodward]." Korn says Woodward was "persona nonwelcome, non grata, as they say, in Haig's entourage," but acknowledges that he may not know the whole story. "Now if there were three faces of Haig, that's a different story," he adds. "You know, [Haig] telling me one thing and dealing with Woodward on the other hand."

The scene of Woodward jetting to Brussels but being forced by a stonewalling Haig to cool his heels and then getting tossed out of the general's office was simply theater, acted for public consumption. Haig might not have said a single word to Woodward at that moment, but he had talked to him copiously at other times. Asked if Haig talked to Woodward for *The Final Days*, attorney Leonard Garment, Haig's colleague in the White House during the final days, who acknowledges speaking to Woodward for the book, told us recently, "Of course Haig talked to Woodward." Garment was aware that the Haig-Woodward connection dated back to the days when Woodward had been a naval officer.

Lawrence Higby had been a principal aide to H. R. Haldeman, and stayed on after Haldeman resigned and became a colleague of Haig's during the last months of the Nixon presidency. In a recent interview with us, Higby recalled getting a call from Woodward requesting an interview for *The Final Days*, and, before consenting, "I asked Haig, and he said, 'Oh, yeah. You ought to talk to them. It's all over now, anyway.' "

Bob Woodward was right: His relationship to Alexander Haig certainly was "complicated."

BOOK TWO

GOLDEN BOY

6

THE PRESIDENT'S PRIVATE EYE

AS Richard Nixon's predilection for secrecy and intrigue were the hallmarks of his operation of foreign policy, so they also became the distinguishing characteristics of certain actions he pursued in the domestic arena. He entered the White House with deep suspicion of his "enemies" on the left, the opponents he had fought throughout his political career, from the supporters of Jerry Voorhis in 1946 to the partisans of Hubert Humphrey in the 1968 presidential campaign, and who he believed made up the bulk of the bureaucrats in the government. Henry Kissinger, the former Harvard professor who moved easily within the Eastern Establishment, recognized that Nixon felt "shunned" by that same group, and, he wrote, "this rankled and compounded his already strong tendency to see himself beset by enemies." Chief of Staff H. R. "Bob" Haldeman similarly wrote that Nixon "would despair at his lack of natural charisma, and realize that if he was to win he would have to attack and destroy the enemy." Whoever seemed to be on the opposite side, Nixon pursued, often with what Haldeman observed were "petty, vindictive orders." If Nixon had endured a time of negative press coverage, he would seek to bar all

93

reporters from *Air Force One*. If a senator made a speech against the president's policies in regard to Vietnam, Nixon would issue an order to Haldeman: "Put a twenty-four-hour surveillance on that bastard."

Why a surveillance? To obtain deleterious information that could be used against the senator. Nixon liked that sort of secret, intrigue-related intelligence, and fostered an environment within the White House that put a premium on it. The president believed that the domestic information-gathering arms of the government—the FBI and other federal policing agencies—could not be counted on to undertake confidential assignments of the sort he had in mind. J. Edgar Hoover, Nixon believed, had files on everybody, but even though Hoover often cooperated with Nixon, the FBI director was reluctant to release any of those files to Nixon even after he became president, just as reluctant as Director Richard Helms would be in 1971 to release the CIA's Bay of Pigs files when Nixon instructed him to do so.

And so, just weeks after Nixon's inauguration, the president directed White House counsel John Ehrlichman to hire a private eye. "He wanted somebody who could do chores for him that a federal employee could not do," Ehrlichman says. "Nixon was demanding information on certain things that I couldn't get through government channels because it would have been questionable." What sort of investigations? "Of the Kennedys, for example," Ehrlichman wrote in *Witness to Power*.

Ehrlichman quickly found a candidate, a well-decorated, forty-year-old Irish New York City cop, John J. Caulfield. Caulfield had been a member of the NYPD and its undercover unit, the Bureau of Special Services and Investigations (BOSSI). He had made cases against dissident and terrorist organizations, and BOSSI as a whole was known for its ability to penetrate and keep track of left-wing and black groups. One of the unit's jobs was to work closely with the Secret Service and guard political dignitaries and world leaders who frequently moved through the city. During the 1960 election, Caulfield had been assigned to the security detail of candidate Richard Nixon. He had befriended Nixon's personal secretary, Rose Mary Woods, and her brother Joe, the sheriff of Cook County, Illinois. In 1968, after leaving the New York City Police Department, Caulfield had served as a security man for the Nixon campaign.

But when Ehrlichman approached him in early 1969 and asked Caulfield to set up a private security firm to provide services for the Nixon White House, Caulfield declined, and instead suggested that he join Ehrlichman's staff and then, as a White House employee, supervise another man who would be hired solely as a private eye. Ehrlichman agreed, and when Caulfield arrived at the White House to start work in April 1969, he said he had the ideal candidate for presidential gumshoe, a BOSSI colleague, Anthony T. Ulasewicz.

In May 1969, Ehrlichman and Caulfield flew to New York and met Ulasewicz in the American Airlines VIP lounge at LaGuardia Airport. Ulasewicz was ten years older than Caulfield, just as streetwise, and even saltier, with a thick accent picked up from his youth on the Lower East Side and twenty-six years of pounding the pavement on his beats. He was told in the VIP lounge that he would operate under a veil of tight secrecy. He would receive orders only from Caulfield though he could assume that those came from Ehrlichman, who would, in turn, be acting on instructions from the president. Ulasewicz would keep no files and submit no written reports; he later wrote in his memoirs that Ehrlichman said to him, "You'll be allowed no mistakes. There will be no support for you whatsoever from the White House if you're exposed." Ulasewicz refused an offer of six months' work, and insisted on a full year, with the understanding that there would be no written contract, just a verbal guarantee. It was also agreed that to keep everything away from the White House, Ulasewicz would work through an outside attorney. In late June 1969, Caulfield directed Ulasewicz to come to Washington and meet a man named Herbert W. Kalmbach at the Madison Hotel. Kalmbach was Nixon's personal attorney in California, and he told Tony that he would be paid $22,000 a year, plus expenses, and that the checks would come from Kalmbach to Tony's home in New York. To avoid putting the private eye on the government payroll, Kalmbach was to pay him out of a war chest of unspent Nixon campaign funds. Ulasewicz requested and was promised credit cards in his own name and in that of a *nom de guerre*, Edward T. Stanley. Shortly, he started on his first job for the Nixon White House. One day after Senator Edward M. Kennedy's car plunged off a bridge, killing a young woman, Tony Ulasewicz was at Chappaquiddick, Massachusetts, posing as a reporter, asking a lot of questions and taking photographs. He stayed a week, and phoned reports to Caulfield thrice daily.

Thereafter, he crisscrossed the country, investigating whatever the president or his subordinates thought proper targets for information—such Democrats as George Wallace, Hubert Humphrey, Edmund Muskie, Vance Hartke, William Proxmire, and Carl Albert, Republican representatives John Ashbrook and Paul McCloskey, antiwar groups, entertainers, think tanks, reporters, even members of Nixon's own family. For instance, when it was feared that the president's nephew, Donald Nixon, Jr., might fall prey to an embarrassing business deal,

Ulasewicz went to California to look into the matter. When a Florida teachers' union complained of the ease with which Julie Nixon Eisenhower landed a job, Ulasewicz was there to investigate the accusation and the resulting news coverage. When the satirical film *Millhouse: A White Comedy* was released, Tony had to go and see it. When the comic and presidential imitator known as Richard M. Dixon became popular, Tony was charged with looking into his background.

He was asked to dig up information on one of Nixon's favorite targets, columnist Jack Anderson, and then to search the backgrounds of Anderson's brothers. Ulasewicz also pried into a group that sold presidential emblems on walnut plaques, tried to discover how the My Lai massacre story had leaked out, and hung around with demonstrators from the Vietnam Veterans Against the War and the National Peace Action Coalition. Ulasewicz was dispatched to investigate a former lobbyist who had written a book in which he alleged that he had conveyed gifts to many Capitol Hill politicians. Even a band of Quakers—members of Nixon's own religion—were targeted when they held a prayer vigil in front of the White House. In most of these instances, Ulasewicz was told to find out what he could about these groups or individuals, to dig for information that could be used against them, and report his findings to Caulfield.

After a year and a half as presidential counsel and then assistant to the president for domestic affairs, John Ehrlichman was appointed head of the new White House Domestic Council, in effect, the number-three man in the White House managerial hierarchy, just behind Bob Haldeman. It was July 1970, and the White House looked to replace Ehrlichman with a man who—in the mold of all the newer Nixon appointees—would be competent but not a threat to the president. Ehrlichman, who had known Nixon since the 1960 campaign, had had the president's ear, but the new counsel would not. He would be among the loyal staff, a detail man who would report to Ehrlichman and Haldeman. A prime candidate was one among the dozens of bright-eyed young Republicans of good background who had been attracted to the political arena, John Wesley Dean III.

Dean came from a family of some means and had attended a military prep school in Virginia, where he had roomed with Barry M. Goldwater, Jr., son of the Arizona senator. He remained close to the Goldwater family for many years. He graduated from Georgetown Law School and married the daughter of a Democratic senator from Missouri. There was one child, and a divorce. He landed a position at a Washington, D.C., law firm specializing in communications law, but lasted only six months before he was fired when it was discovered that Dean was secretly working on a television station license application for a competitor of one of his firm's clients.

But Dean landed on his feet and through his connections soon became minority counsel to the House Judiciary Committee, and, after Nixon's election, moved rather easily into the Department of Justice, then under the direction of Attorney General John Mitchell. Obviously bright and ambitious, Dean picked up the sense of ruthlessness that seemed to be in favor in the Nixon administration. After little more than a year as a deputy assistant attorney general, Dean made a list of candidates for a job at the White House being compiled by Bud Krogh, another White House aide of about Dean's age, who had bumped into him on Justice Department matters. Because he was on this list, Dean became the leading candidate for the job of counsel to the president.

Ehrlichman and Haldeman, to whom Krogh reported, both assumed that Dean was a Mitchell man because he worked at Justice, but this wasn't precisely the case, for Dean was only at Justice thanks to Republican connections. Nor did Mitchell recommend him to the White House. In fact, both Dean and Mitchell later reported that Mitchell had tried to discourage him from taking the job. Dean told that to the Senate Select Committee on Presidential Campaign Activities, known as the Watergate committee, and recalled in an interview with us that Mitchell had advised him to stay where he was, saying, "I hate to see you go to the White House, because that's an awful place. . . . You're going to go on up in the Department of Justice—you'll have a better job here."

But for a young man who wanted power, the White House seemed the place to be, and when Bud Krogh offered to have him flown to San Clemente to meet with Haldeman, Dean jumped. Haldeman, who wore his own hair in a close-cropped military cut, didn't like Dean's long blond hair, and joked that Dean would be the resident "hippie." At San Clemente, Dean had a perfunctory interview with Nixon, and was then officially hired.

Dean's first day at the White House was July 27, 1970, and from the outset, he determined to make the most of his position. A flashy figure in an environment filled with drab ones, he eventually became known around the White House as the "golden boy," and not only for his long, thin blond hair. Youthful and dashing in appearance, Dean developed a reputation as a playboy, a notion he did not try to discourage. "He lived a little fancier than the rest of us," recalls Gordon C. Strachan, who was about Dean's age and worked as an assistant to Bob Haldeman. Ehrlichman wrote that Dean "lived beyond his salary.

He owned an expensive town house in Alexandria [Virginia]. Dean's Porsche, Gucci loafers, and tailored sports clothes should have raised more eyebrows than they did." In those days Dean wore contact lenses and his suits were crisp and a bit flashy; only later, when he was to appear before the Watergate committee, did he don owlish glasses, conservative suits, and cut his hair so that it didn't fall below his collar.

Shortly after assuming his position, Dean began thinking about expanding his domain, and hired former Army officer Fred F. Fielding as an assistant lawyer in the counsel's office. They became close friends. In Dean's 1976 memoir, *Blind Ambition,* he recounted how he explained to his new associate the way in which their careers could quickly rise: "Fred, I think we have to look at our office as a small law firm. . . . We have to build our practice like any other law firm. Our principal client, of course, is the president. But to convince the president we're not just the only law office in town, but the best, we've got to convince a lot of other people first." Especially Haldeman and Ehrlichman.

But how to convince them? As Dean tried to assess the situation at the White House, events soon showed him that intelligence gathering was the key to power in the Nixon White House. One of Dean's first assignments from Haldeman was to look over a startling proposal to revamp the government's domestic intelligence operations in order to neutralize radical groups such as the Black Panthers and the Weathermen.

The scheme had been the work of another of the White House's bright young stalwarts, Nixon aide Tom Charles Huston. The impetus was a meeting chaired by Nixon in the Oval Office on June 5, 1970, attended by J. Edgar Hoover, Richard Helms, and the chiefs of the NSA and the Defense Intelligence Agency (DIA). The various agencies were almost at war with one another; just a few months earlier, for instance, Hoover had cut all FBI communication with the CIA. Nixon wanted the agencies to work together against the threat from the "New Left." In the aftermath of Nixon's decision in May 1970 to invade Cambodia, and the killings of several students at Kent State University, colleges all over the country were again being rocked by riots and demonstrations as they had been in the last year of Lyndon Johnson's presidency, and for the same reason—young people were objecting to the president's war policies. In Nixon's view, the threat was grave and must be attacked; therefore the agencies must find some way to bury their differences and concentrate on the true enemy. Huston was assigned to help Hoover and the intelligence chiefs clear obstacles to their working jointly on these matters.

In early July, Huston sent a long analysis to the president, endorsed by Hoover and the other intelligence agency directors, on how to enhance cooperation. To this memo Huston added his own secret one that became known as the "Huston Plan." It called for six activities, some of which were clearly illegal. They included electronic surveillance of persons and groups "who pose a major threat to internal security"; monitoring of American citizens by international communications facilities; the relaxation of restrictions on the covert opening of mail by federal agents; surreptitious entries and burglaries to gain information on the groups; the recruitment of more campus informants; and, to ensure that the objectives were carried out and that intelligence continued to be gathered, the formation of a new interagency group consisting of the agencies at the June 5 meeting and military counter-intelligence agencies. Nixon endorsed these measures in the Huston Plan on July 14, 1970, because, as he put it in his memoir, "I felt they were necessary and justified by the violence we faced."

The secret plan angered J. Edgar Hoover, not because he objected to coming down hard on dissidents, but, rather, because he felt that any new interagency group would encroach on the turf of the FBI and because he was concerned about the negative public reaction should any of the activities be exposed. On July 27, the day Dean began work at the White House, Hoover took the unusual step of venturing out of his own domain to visit his nominal superior, Attorney General John Mitchell. As Hoover learned, Mitchell did not know anything about the Huston Plan at the time. "I was kept in the dark until I found out about it from Hoover," Mitchell later told us. But as soon as he was apprised of the plan, Mitchell agreed with Hoover that it must be stopped—not for Hoover's reasons, but because it contained clearly unconstitutional elements—and immediately visited Nixon and told him it could not go forward. In testament to Mitchell's arguments and good sense, Nixon canceled the plan shortly thereafter and Huston was relieved of his responsibilities in the area of domestic intelligence.

Coordination of official domestic intelligence from various federal agencies concerning antiwar activists and other "radicals" was then handed to the new White House counsel, John Dean, along with a copy of the rejected Huston Plan. But it seemed that the president was still not satisfied with the quality of domestic intelligence, because in August and September Haldeman pushed Dean to try and find a way around the Hoover roadblock. In pursuit of a solution, on September 17, 1970, Dean went to see his old boss, John Mitchell. Hours earlier, Mitchell had lunched with Director Helms and other senior CIA officials who had all agreed that the FBI wasn't doing a very good job of collecting domestic intelligence.

Dean and Mitchell spoke, and the next day Dean prepared a memo to Mitchell with several suggestions: There should be a new committee set up, an interagency group to evaluate the government's domestic intelligence product, and it should have "operational" responsibilities as well. Both men, Dean's memo said, had agreed that "it would be inappropriate to have any blanket removal of restrictions" such as had been proposed in the Huston Plan; instead, Dean suggested that "The most appropriate procedure would be to decide on the type of intelligence we need, based on an assessment of the recommendations of this unit, and then to proceed to remove the restraints as necessary to obtain such intelligence."

Dean's plan languished and was never put into operation. Years later, in the spring of 1973, when Dean was talking to federal prosecutors and preparing to appear before the Senate committee investigating Watergate, he gave a copy of the Huston Plan to Federal Judge John J. Sirica, who turned it over to the Senate committee. Dean's action helped to establish his bona fides as the accuser of the president and was the cause of much alarm. In his testimony and writings thereafter, Dean suggested that he had always been nervous about the Huston Plan and that he had tried to get around it, and as a last resort had gotten John Mitchell to kill the revised version. In an interview, Dean told us, "I looked at that goddamn Tom Huston report," went to Mitchell and said, "General, I find it pretty spooky." But as the September 18, 1970, memo to Mitchell shows, Dean actually embraced rather than rejected the removal of "restraints as necessary to obtain" intelligence.

A small matter? A minor divergence between two versions of the same incident? As will become clear as this inquiry continues, Dean's attempt to gloss over the actual disposition of the Huston Plan was a first sign of the construction of a grand edifice of deceit.

When John Dean took over the office of counsel to the president, says his predecessor John Ehrlichman, it was an office that "was really vacant . . . it was essentially unsupervised." Ehrlichman had left to set up the new Domestic Council, taking with him his own small staff, and thus "Dean was pretty much on his own." But Jack Caulfield had stayed behind and Dean soon was supervising his intelligence work. Dean looked in all the nooks and crannies and cabinets and found whatever assets the office possessed. Hanging in a forgotten closet was Tony Ulasewicz.

Later, in 1973, appearing before the Senate, Dean testified to little knowledge about Ulasewicz, saying he didn't know or remember his full name until that year. In *Blind Ambition*, he wrote that in July 1971—one year after he had become counsel—he only knew that one of Caulfield's "operatives" was named Tony, "but I didn't find out his last name, Ulasewicz, until years later." Dean's Senate testimony about Ulasewicz befuddled Haldeman aide Gordon Strachan. "That kind of surprised me," Strachan told us. "I thought [Ulasewicz] was [Dean's] guy." Strachan was right: Ulasewicz *was* Dean's guy.

In fact, Dean knew all about Ulasewicz, as can be seen from Dean's comments to the former detective when Caulfield introduced them at the White House. Ulasewicz later described this meeting to a Senate investigator, who recorded in his notes that "He [Ulasewicz] remembers his conversation with Dean as being short and pleasant, indicating that Dean was aware of what Ulasewicz had been doing, and was appreciative of his work." The investigator's notes, located in the National Archives, also record that Ulasewicz quoted Dean as telling him: "You've been doing good work. May get better." Yet another note reads, "Dean knew of his [Ulasewicz's] travels, assignments."

Dean's claims of noninvolvement with Ulasewicz are further controverted by portions of Dean's own book, in which he wrote of some of the assignments he undertook as White House counsel—assignments that match many of the investigations carried out by Ulasewicz, such as those aimed against the Vietnam Veterans Against the War, impersonator Richard M. Dixon, and so on. Dean even boasts of having had to investigate Representative Richard Poff of Virginia, for whom he'd once worked as a legislative aide, when Poff was under consideration by Nixon for a seat on the Supreme Court. A Senate committee staff memorandum of seventy-three Ulasewicz assignments, compiled by the investigators from long conversations with Tony, lists his Number 37 assignment as "Background investigation into Congressman Richard Poff in his hometown in Virginia." As we will see, despite Dean's denials, Dean knew precisely who Ulasewicz was, often ordered him into action through Caulfield, and later issued orders directly to him without an intermediary.

Dean, Caulfield, and Ulasewicz were also involved in a Nixon attempt to settle an old score. Back in 1956, Nixon's brother Donald had received a secret loan from Howard Hughes; when this loan was revealed during the 1960 campaign, it caused some embarrassment. Eleven years later, Nixon determined to make the Democrats pay for having revealed that loan. His friend Bebe Rebozo had convinced Nixon that Democratic Party chairman Lawrence F. O'Brien had been secretly retained by Hughes to represent his interests in Washington. "It would seem that the time is approaching when Larry O'Brien is held accountable for his retainer with Hughes," Nixon wrote in a memo to Haldeman in January 1971; the president suggested that Charles W. Colson, Nixon's special counsel, could obtain the proof of the O'Brien-Hughes deal, expose it, and thereby damage the Democrats. "Let's try Dean," Haldeman scribbled on the bottom of the memo, and the next day gave the assignment to the White House counsel.

It has long been believed that this early investigation of Larry O'Brien was the germ of the seed that became the Watergate affair, and that it led to the break-in of Democratic Party headquarters in June of 1972. As we will see in later chapters, and demonstrate conclusively for the first time, the target of the two Watergate burglaries was specifically *not* O'Brien. This 1971 investigation of O'Brien led precisely nowhere.

To be sure, Ulasewicz, who had been put on O'Brien's trail two years earlier, did more fieldwork, and so did Dean. The most promising lead, provided by Colson, was Robert F. Bennett, son of Utah Senator Wallace F. Bennett and the man who had just taken over Mullen & Company, a Washington public relations firm that had strong connections to the CIA and that had just signed Howard Hughes as a client. Bennett claimed to Dean that he knew all about the O'Brien-Hughes relationship, and promised to obtain documentation for it, but never did so. Much later, Nixon obtained IRS records that showed that O'Brien had indeed received a retainer from Howard Hughes for $160,000. By that time, however, Dean, Caulfield, and Ulasewicz had gone on to other investigations.

Within six months of arriving, Dean had made the counsel's office into a small but growing power center. He had sufficiently impressed Haldeman enough to merit more perks, such as being allowed to have an Army Signal Corps telephone in his home. He knew he had a loyal staff of three lawyers, plus Caulfield, and, as he wrote in *Blind Ambition*, "it did not take [my superiors] long to notice that the counsel's office could perform intelligence work for the White House. . . . [We] built up a reputation for such intelligence investigations— some juicy, many simply laborious—and we handled them while the ordinary legal work hummed along."

In April 1971, Dean was summoned to Haldeman's office and given specific instructions on his role in the Nixon reelection campaign. "He knew what he wanted from me," Dean wrote, describing Haldeman's worry that the Republican convention would be ruined by antiwar protests as the Democratic gathering had been in 1968. " 'One thing that can be improved, for example, is demonstration intelligence,' Haldeman told him. 'We're not going to have a convention like the one the Democrats had in Chicago.' "

Dean soon had a chance to prove himself during the massive antiwar demonstration of May 3, 1971, that followed Nixon's decision to order military "incursions" into Laos. Dean's office became the focal point for intelligence gathered about the demonstrators, who had vowed to shut down Washington for a day by blocking roads and bridges. Special telephone lines in the command centers of the FBI, the District of Columbia police headquarters, and the Department of Justice all were linked to Dean's White House office. During that day of protest, Dean and his staff received data from the field and sent reports directly to the president; later, Dean received word that Nixon was pleased with his performance.

Haldeman patted Dean on the head, too, and tried to spur him to even greater efforts against the demonstrators, but Dean was becoming antsy with chasing protestors and felt such actions would not gain for his "law firm" the senior status he desired. But perhaps he could transfer the success in the antiwar demonstrations to a larger role for himself in the 1972 presidential election campaign, something already under intense consideration in the summer of 1971.

"I reflected on how I might take advantage of Haldeman's preoccupation" with political intelligence, Dean wrote in his memoirs.

I knew the campaign would be a steppingstone for those who distinguished themselves. . . . If the counsel's office could play the same role at the Republican convention we had played on Mayday—special White House tie-lines, half-hourly reports—I knew we would be in the thick of things. We had a jump on other White House offices in demonstration intelligence. Why not expand our role to all intelligence that would be of interest to the President in a campaign?

In July 1971, Dean took the idea to Haldeman, seeking "a grant of authority" to prepare a regular confidential digest for the president on all domestic intelligence, from crime and drugs through "civil rights problems of note" and "political intelligence." Dean's mixed bag of types of intelligence was a cover for what Dean really sought, that is, to be the focal point for political intelligence (that would, for example, reveal the identity of contributors to opposing campaigns, personal dirt on Nixon's opponents, and Democratic and dissident Republican campaign secrets). Haldeman said such information was already being compiled by Gordon Strachan, who worked more closely with the chief of staff, and Haldeman shot down the Dean Plan.

There is a saying in Washington that in the capital, nothing is ever completely dead. John Mitchell thought he had shot down the Huston Plan, but aspects of it came creeping back into administration policy. Haldeman thought he had shot down Dean's plan, having told the counsel to stick to demonstration intelligence. But Haldeman did not understand the degree to which Dean saw his dream of becoming campaign intelligence czar as his own ticket to the top, and what Dean would do to keep that dream alive. And Haldeman had inadvertently shown Dean the way to get what he wanted—to go through Gordon Strachan. As time went on, Dean would facilitate a misunderstanding between Haldeman and Strachan, causing Strachan to believe that Dean had been placed in charge of political intelligence, not just demonstration intelligence.

Undaunted by Haldeman, Dean soon devised a project to help get his foot in the door. On August 16, 1971, he produced a memorandum titled "Dealing with our Political Enemies," that in his own words addressed "how we can use the available federal machinery to screw our political enemies." Dean suggested that key White House staff members collect names of administration opponents whom "we should be giving a hard time" and then use various government departments and agencies to "screw them." This Dean memo was the germ that led to a White House "enemies list."

Testifying in 1973, Dean admitted he had written the document, which was not signed and listed no addressee, but insisted he had been pushed into doing it by others in the White House. As far as he could remember, he told the Senate Watergate committee, he had sent the memo to Haldeman and Ehrlichman for approval, disapproval, or comment. But the only copy that ever surfaced was one in which the approve, disapprove, and comment lines were blank. In his own testimony, Ehrlichman denied ever seeing the memo.

Dean's testimony included the claim that "I was a restraining influence at the White House to many wild and crazy schemes," and as for the enemies list "I also made it very clear . . . I just didn't want to get involved in doing the sort of things they wanted." A skeptical Senator Daniel K. Inouye, the Hawaii Democrat, questioned Dean about that, but Dean's claim stood, even though the committee had White House memos addressed to Dean that indicated he was very much involved.

Two of those were memos by Gordon Strachan, who by the fall of 1971 was working more closely with Dean. In one, Strachan wrote to

Dean that "you have the action on the political enemies project" while in another Strachan forwarded a list of "fat cats" supporting Muskie and scribbled at the top of the page, "The attached should be of interest to you and the political enemies project." This interest in Muskie led to three Tony Ulasewicz assignments that focused on financial backers of the Maine Democrat.

As the reader will recall, in *Blind Ambition* Dean openly admitted to participating in intelligence assignments, including "juicy" ones, and to a desire to expand his intelligence portfolio to encompass "all intelligence that would be of interest to the President in a campaign." Strikingly, before the Senate Watergate committee, Dean did his best to portray his political intelligence role as at best peripheral.

Despite Dean's partial retreat in his book from his earlier testimony, for the past eighteen years Dean has consistently sought to bury his true relationship to Caulfield and, more to the point, Ulasewicz. He trumpeted this position first to the Senate investigating committee, suggesting, for instance, that when he took over the counsel's office the use of Caulfield and Ulasewicz diminished, that "Caulfield seldom informed me of his findings," and that "the persons on the White House staff who were most interested in political intelligence were Ehrlichman, Haldeman, and Colson." In his memoir, published after he had served a short prison term, Dean maintained the same line. He continued to adhere to it in a recent interview. Regarding Caulfield's investigative work, Dean insisted to us, "I was never in the loop on any of that" and "I scratched my head for a long time before it just sort of came out in dribs and drabs as to what he [Caulfield] was doing." As for his interest in gathering intelligence as White House counsel, Dean declared, "It just wasn't my bag. It was something I just didn't know how to do."

But we have pored over the mountains of testimony and documents, and have interviewed Caulfield, Ulasewicz, Haldeman, Ehrlichman, Mitchell, and many others, and can now present a more accurate picture of what Dean did to get around Haldeman's blocking him from the arena of overseeing the collection of politically important intelligence.

"I was working for Dean, just as I had for Ehrlichman," Caulfield told us recently. "He knew somebody was doing it. He's full of shit when he says he knew very little about Ulasewicz." In fact, said Caulfield, Dean "at my behest renegotiated the continuation of Ulasewicz's contract."

One of the more interesting of the Caulfield-Ulasewicz assignments from Dean came in October 1971. Acting on a request and a tip from

Colson, Dean had asked Caulfield to investigate the "Happy Hooker" ring in New York, with an eye toward finding out if any clients of Xaviera Hollander had been high-ranking politicians. Caulfield sent Ulasewicz, but later told Dean that the material Tony had obtained was useless because the names of too many prominent members of both parties were present in Hollander's appointment books: dirt on the Democrats would be canceled out by dirt on the Republicans. Dean didn't use the material as he had planned, in order to raise his stock with Colson, Haldeman, and Ehrlichman, but he did hint at a bit of it to scare press secretary Ronald L. Ziegler. Pulling someone else's chain was part of the macho game at the Nixon White House.

As 1971 waned Caulfield saw that Dean's appetite for political intelligence continued to increase. "I saw a desire to take greater chances as [Dean] saw the potential rewards. And the key to the ball game was intelligence—who was going to get it and who was going to provide it. Dean saw that and played the game heartily. . . . I was getting my instructions from Dean. I did whatever Dean asked . . . I would put Tony to work."

On only one job suggested by Dean did Caulfield have qualms, he told us, and that was an assignment to determine "the feasibility of getting information out of the Watergate," by which Caulfield meant the headquarters of the Democratic National Committee. It was November of 1971, that is, seven months before the actual break-ins at the DNC office. "The more I thought about the thing, the more I saw the hazards. In my view, it was a goddamn good chance if that thing failed you could bring down the president," Caulfield remembered with perfect 20-20 hindsight.

Tony Ulasewicz recalled in his book that Caulfield told him that "Dean wants you to check out the offices of the Democratic National Committee." (Caulfield places Ulasewicz's entry in November of 1971. Ulasewicz told us that it was in April of 1972, but wrote in his book that it was the end of May of 1972. We are convinced that Caulfield and not Ulasewicz is correct because, among other reasons, Caulfield left the White House in March of 1972.) There was no break-in; Ulasewicz simply walked in as a visitor and noted the location of various offices within the floor that was occupied by the DNC. He reported back, Ulasewicz told us, telling Caulfield "there was nothing that would be of particular interest. It was a business office, it was a kind of a place you would send donations, it was a similar business office to what the Republicans would have, a place for records of donors, sending out brochures, making arrangements for dinners and fund-raising programs, hiring people out in the field, contacts with newspapers and all the routine matters."

Ulasewicz says he reported, " 'I don't know what you think is in this office.' My street smarts told me when Dean's asking me this kind of thing, there's something that they are after. Something hot. I told him, 'It's not there.' "

We asked Dean about these Caulfield and Ulasewicz accounts that he assigned Tony to check out the DNC offices at the Watergate. "I can absolutely flat out tell you that isn't true," he first responded. When the subject came up a second time Dean said, "I don't have any knowledge" of sending Ulasewicz in but that perhaps Caulfield "came into my office and said, 'John, I think Tony should go in' [to the DNC]." At that moment, Dean suggested, he may have been "in the middle of something else. [I] don't even reflect on it, and say, 'Whatever you think, Jack.' You know, which I did a lot. 'Just go and do it.' "

The story of Tony Ulasewicz's visit to the Democratic National Committee represents the first time anyone in the Nixon administration had mentioned the Watergate complex as a target of investigation. We will come back to this unusual Ulasewicz walk-through in later chapters, and ascertain its full significance then.

By the spring of 1971, Caulfield had begun to think about leaving the White House in order to set up the private security business that Ehrlichman had suggested to him in 1969. He'd create an outside entity that could provide security to the 1972 Nixon campaign, and much more. He wrote up his suggestions in a memo for John Dean, suggesting $500,000 to fund what he called Operation Sandwedge.

Sandwedge would provide "offensive intelligence and defensive security" to counteract what Caulfield warned could be "a strong, covert intelligence effort mounted against us in 1972 by the Democratic nominee." He had looked into a security firm organized by former Robert Kennedy–era Justice Department employees known as Intertel. Howard Hughes was an Intertel client, and the Sandwedge memo analyzed Intertel and concluded that it was a group controlled by Larry O'Brien and the Kennedys. Sandwedge's offensive side included clandestine operations: "penetration of nominees [sic] entourage and headquarters; 'Black Bag' capability . . . to minimize Democratic voting violations in Illinois, Texas, etc.; surveillance of Democratic primaries, convention, meetings, etc.; and derogatory information investigative capability world-wide." Caulfield suggested that the principals in the Sandwedge organization include Rose Mary Woods's brother Joe the former sheriff, and IRS official Vernon Acree.

Caulfield told us that Sandwedge was "my initiative, but it really involved a lot of discussions with John Dean about what I would do after my departure from the White House." Dean tried to sell Sandwedge to Mitchell and Haldeman, but both rejected it. Having struck out with the senior people, Dean dropped down a level, pushing the Sandwedge proposal to Gordon Strachan, Haldeman's eyes and ears on political matters, and to Jeb Magruder, a former Haldeman aide who now worked for the Nixon reelection committee as deputy campaign director. But, though Strachan queried Haldeman repeatedly about increasing Dean's involvement in intelligence-gathering, Dean once again found no takers for the Sandwedge operation that Caulfield had proposed.

As an alternative, Dean arranged for Caulfield to have an interview with John Mitchell, who was slated to leave Justice in early 1972 to become the head of Nixon's reelection campaign. That interview was held on November 24, 1971.

In later testimony before the Senate, Dean would claim that he was not present during the entire meeting, but that Caulfield had reported to him that Mitchell had wanted Caulfield to do some investigative work on the New Hampshire campaign of Paul N. "Pete" McCloskey, the California congressman who was challenging Nixon for the Republican nomination.

Caulfield says that on November 24 he only discussed with Mitchell the possibility of his working on the forthcoming campaign as a security official. Did Mitchell ever ask him to penetrate the McCloskey campaign? "No," Caulfield told us. "I'm certain that he didn't." Caulfield assumes that it was Dean who ordered the McCloskey probe "because that was the guy I was working for at the time." Mitchell also confirmed that future security work was the substance of their conversation, and that there was no discussion of snooping around McCloskey or of any other investigative task.

It's an important distinction, because Dean later used this meeting between Caulfield and Mitchell effectively to shift responsibility for initiating intelligence-gathering activities to Mitchell and to exculpate himself. To support his position, Dean submitted to the Senate Watergate committee a memo of an "investigative report that Mr. Caulfield prepared for Mitchell on the McCloskey New Hampshire campaign."

The committee didn't look at the memo very carefully, for the document clearly showed it could not have resulted from the November 24 meeting, as Dean claimed. It actually described an investigation conducted (by Tony Ulasewicz) from November 18 to November 21, three days prior to the date that Mitchell saw Caulfield in his office.

Dean submitted to the committee a second memo addressed to the attorney general from Dean dated December 1, 1971, attaching "some additional information which Jack [Caulfield] has collected re McCloskey's operation."

There is also a problem with this second memo. The memo bears no trace of having come from the White House—no letterhead, and no initials, such as characterize other documents that originated in the White House during that period of time. Did Dean prepare this memo after leaving the White House, for the purpose of shoring up his contention that it was Mitchell who ordered the McCloskey investigation?

He may well have done so. Dean submitted to the committee another of his memos addressed to Mitchell, dated January 12, 1972, that—again—was not written on White House letterhead and bears no initials. This was a memo on a purported Dean-Mitchell conversation that said, "As a result of our recent conversation, I asked Jack Caulfield to prepare a summary of his activities so that you could review them. However, because of the sensitivity of this information, I would like to suggest that you briefly meet with Jack and go over this material. Operation Sandwedge will be in need of refunding at the end of this month so the time is quite appropriate for such a review." This does not square with two facts.

First, Dean testified that Sandwedge had been killed by November of 1971, in part because Mitchell rejected it. When asked by the skeptical Democratic Senator Inouye to explain why Mitchell would want to refund Sandwedge in January of 1972 if the plan had died "a natural death" months earlier, Dean again implicated Mitchell by transferring his own actions to the attorney general. Dean first concocted the story that Caulfield "continued to do various investigative assignments" for Mitchell after the November 24 meeting. And he then said that Mitchell assumed that Operation Sandwedge was a handy label for all the Caulfield-Ulasewicz activities, and so Dean's mention of it in the January 12 memo to Mitchell was merely a shorthand device. However, at that time the label "Sandwedge" was a code name used by Dean and Caulfield for Tony Ulasewicz investigations; the label was not something Mitchell would have known.

Second, Sandwedge-Ulasewicz had in fact been refunded months earlier in the fall of 1971 in the amount of $50,000. Caulfield says that Dean himself was involved in getting Ulasewicz's contract extended through 1972, renegotiating the continuation with Herb Kalmbach. It was not the half-million that Caulfield had originally envisioned for Sandwedge, but it was enough to keep Ulasewicz on board. In his book, Ulasewicz described meeting with Kalmbach and Caulfield in September of 1971 for the purpose of arranging his payments through the upcoming election. And Gordon Strachan, reflecting a conversation he'd had with Dean, wrote a memo on October 27 saying that "Sandwedge has received an initial 50," meaning $50,000.

Furthermore, the "summary of [Caulfield-Ulasewicz] activities" Dean claimed to have "asked Jack Caulfield to prepare" so that "you [Mitchell] could review them" was unavailable to the Senate committee. Dean had promised that summary to them, but couldn't produce it. "I thought earlier I did have a list," he testified. "I have searched my records that were available and I have no such list available." No such list was ever given to the committee. But Dean's testimony on the matter stood, and so he had implicated John Mitchell as Caulfield's action officer for campaign espionage and covered up his own role as director of the Caulfield-Ulasewicz operation.

Mitchell denied he had anything to do with Ulasewicz's activities. "No, sir," he answered to Watergate committee chief counsel Sam Dash when asked if he was aware that Tony Ulasewicz was working at the White House for Dean, or for anybody else. "I didn't know who Ulasewicz was until the spring of 1973," Mitchell told us. Caulfield insists that it was Dean who initiated all such operations and received reports on them. The president's private eye, though hired by Ehrlichman and paid by Kalmbach, had become for all intents and purposes the exclusive gumshoe of White House counsel John Dean.

7

SANDWEDGE BECOMES GEMSTONE

JACK Caulfield's desire to leave the White House and the rejection of his Operation Sandwedge plan were a large blow to John Dean, who envisioned the collection and purveying of intelligence as the route to power. Bob Haldeman had rejected his request to handle all intelligence for the forthcoming battle for Nixon's reelection, but Dean had the resources to continue gathering information on his own, the private investigators Caulfield and Ulasewicz. Now Caulfield was going to leave, and Dean had to have a replacement. Opportunity presented itself in the form of G. Gordon Liddy.

Liddy was a weapon waiting to be aimed and fired. Then forty-one, he had been an FBI agent, a firearms expert, a pilot, an upstate New York prosecutor, and the unsuccessful conservative candidate for a Republican congressional nomination. He had a reputation for blunt honesty and unconventional derring-do. After his defeat in the New York primary, by calling in political favors Liddy landed a job in Washington at the Treasury Department, working on firearms and narcotics matters. In his position he came into contact with many mid-level Justice Department officials including Dean, who was then an associate deputy attorney general. Donald Santarelli, also an associate deputy at Justice who worked with Liddy on firearms matters, warned Liddy about Dean. In his autobiography, *Will*, Liddy wrote that Santarelli labeled Dean an "idea thief" and told Liddy that if "one mentioned a good idea in Dean's presence, one remotely in Dean's official area of interest, before one's memorandum was out of the typewriter, Dean's would be on the appropriate desk, crediting himself with the idea." As is clear from that passage, Liddy didn't like Dean much, even then. When Dean was on the Hill, one source who worked with him told us, he would "come in early in the morning before anybody else and go around and look on their desks to see what they were working on," in order to steal their ideas, and then "hog" the credit in the service of "promoting himself."

Another Dean strategy, frequently in evidence before he reached the White House, was a propensity for unauthorized use of his superior's name. "Either [Dean] would just lie about it," said this former Dean colleague, who prefers anonymity, "or he would mention something obliquely to the person whose name he was going to use and would do it in such a way that the guy wouldn't notice that Dean was going to extrapolate authority from it. It's an old trick in Washington." This was done, said the source, in an indirect way "that would not get your attention or not warn you that you were making a commitment to something you didn't want to commit to." Because of this behavior "we all formed a rather arm's length attitude toward John Dean because you couldn't believe him," says Robert T. Hartmann, one of Dean's fellow staffers on Capitol Hill, who later became a top aide to Gerald R. Ford.

At Justice, Liddy didn't think much about Dean, and when the former FBI man transferred into the White House in June 1971, to work for Bud Krogh, Dean was only a figure to pass in the hall or to be seen across the White House mess. Krogh, who had dealt with Liddy on firearms matters, got Liddy assigned to the newly formed Special Investigations Unit, the one that was later dubbed the Plumbers. Liddy started at a critical time. On June 13, 1971, *The New York Times* and other newspapers began publishing excerpts from the secret Defense Department study that became known as the Pentagon Papers. National Security Adviser Henry Kissinger was enraged by this publication, even though it had little to do with his current employer, Richard Nixon, for Kissinger had been a consultant to the Kennedy and Johnson administrations and the Pentagon Papers dealt at length with those administrations' involvement in Vietnam. Evidently fearing that his own role in shaping Vietnam policy would be revealed,

Kissinger convinced Nixon that the publication was a grave threat to national security. When it was discovered that the Pentagon Papers had been given to the press by Kissinger's past colleague, Daniel Ellsberg, a furious campaign to discredit Ellsberg was launched from the Oval Office. Don Stewart and Fred Buzhardt at the Pentagon and others at the Justice Department and at the FBI were all investigating the leak, but Krogh and David Young, the former Kissinger aide who would help break open the Moorer-Radford affair, were asked to look into the leak as well. When Liddy came on board, the onetime FBI investigator was assigned to help in the task.

The Plumbers were well equipped. Room 16 of the old EOB was a suite of three offices that contained a KYX scramble phone, used mostly to speak securely to the CIA at Langley. "It sounded as if we were speaking to each other from opposite ends of a long drainpipe," Liddy recalled in his autobiography. The pressure on the Plumbers to do something intensified in July, when *The New York Times* reported the administration's confidential fallback negotiation position in the on-going SALT talks with the Soviets. This revelation infuriated Nixon more than the Pentagon Papers, as it undermined a current negotiation strategy. Word came down to the Plumbers that the stories and leaks must be stopped at all costs.

The Plumbers now got some additional help. His name was E. Howard Hunt, a former CIA agent, recently retired and working for a fellow alumnus of Brown University, presidential aide Chuck Colson. On July 6, Hunt wandered over to Room 16 looking for information on Ellsberg.

Ex-FBI man Liddy and ex-CIA man Hunt recognized one another as comrades in arms. But whereas Liddy was firmly out of the FBI, Jim Hougan persuasively argues in his 1984 book *Secret Agenda* that Hunt's ties with the CIA had not ended when he officially retired from the agency in April of 1970. While working for Colson, Hunt also worked for the Mullen public relations firm, owned by Robert Bennett, which was being used as a front by the CIA, and had many other continuing connections to the agency.

Plumbers Hunt and Liddy served together on one of the most sensitive investigations then under way, "Project Jennifer," in which the *Glomar Explorer* ship was to retrieve a Soviet submarine from the Pacific floor bed, under the guise of a Howard Hughes–financed mining operation. They also worked to locate evidence that might link President John Kennedy to the assassination of former South Vietnamese President Ngo Dinh Diem in 1963—anything deleterious to any Kennedy was highly prized within the Nixon White House. While pursuing these matters, they also kept Ellsberg in their sights. "We became fast friends and our families visited each other," Liddy recalled. "Even on social occasions, when Howard and I would be alone together, we'd talk about the Ellsberg case." They were unable to resolve the basic question of whether Ellsberg had acted as a "romantic rebel of the left and lone wolf," or as "part of a spy ring that had deliberately betrayed top secret information in unprecedented quantity to the Soviet Union."

Unsure as to Ellsberg's motives, the Plumbers, at the suggestion of Hunt, asked the CIA to draw up a psychological profile of Ellsberg. Two were done, and both were deemed unsatisfactory not only by Hunt and Liddy but also by Young and Krogh. Hunt and Liddy then decided what was needed was a black bag job on the offices of Ellsberg's psychiatrist Dr. Lewis J. Fielding; it was hoped that Fielding's files might contain information on Ellsberg's motivations and contacts. Liddy put a proposition to Bud Krogh.

Much later, a memo from Bud Krogh and David Young to Ehrlichman surfaced, a memo that covered several matters relating to the leak of the Pentagon Papers. Young and Krogh recommended "that a covert operation be undertaken to examine all the medical files still held by Ellsberg's psychoanalyst covering the two-year period in which he [Ellsberg] was undergoing analysis." A space was provided for Ehrlichman to approve or disapprove, and he put his "E" in the approve box, and added the handwritten comment, "If done under your assurance that it is not traceable." Ehrlichman admits checking that box, but says that what he approved was merely an investigation of Ellsberg by Liddy and Hunt, not a burglary. It was his understanding that Liddy and Hunt would go and talk to Dr. Fielding, and he remembers the "not traceable" warning as really being an admonition that the clandestine-minded duo of Hunt and Liddy shouldn't try to pass themselves off as "White House cops." Eventually, Ehrlichman went to jail for his role in this break-in.

Outfitted with CIA-furnished disguises, aliases, and small cameras, Hunt and Liddy flew to Los Angeles, convinced a cleaning woman to let them into Fielding's office, and snapped photos that were turned over to the CIA for processing. Hunt then recruited a handful of Miami-based Cubans known to Hunt from the time of his involvement in the Bay of Pigs. Trained in clandestine work, these Cubans were fiercely loyal to Hunt.

Over the 1971 Labor Day weekend the Cubans broke into Fielding's office as Hunt and Liddy remained outside as guards, Liddy with a knife and ready to kill, if necessary, to protect the operation. On emerging, the Cubans told Liddy they had found nothing, though they had severely damaged some file cabinets; to cover their traces they had ransacked the office, dumping pills and papers about to make it appear as if the entry had been that of a drug addict searching for narcotics.

Liddy thought the Fielding office episode a failure, and was puzzled because back at the hotel room, Hunt and the Cubans celebrated with champagne. Today, Liddy wonders whether Hunt and the Cubans may well have concealed the fruits of the Fielding break-in from him, found just what they had sought, photographed it, and whisked the results back to their true employer, the CIA. Otherwise, what was there to celebrate?

The ex–FBI man consoled himself with a new project handed him by Krogh, an analysis of the current state of the FBI and the future of Director J. Edgar Hoover. Nixon was trying to decide if he should retain Hoover, then well past retirement age. Liddy's critique of the Bureau's internal politics was incisive, and his recommendation that his former boss (and an idol of his boyhood) be replaced stirred admiring comment from Nixon, though for many reasons the president felt himself unable to get rid of Hoover.

Just at this time, John Dean was being pressured by Jeb Magruder, the Nixon deputy campaign director, to give up the junior partner in his "law firm," Fred Fielding—no relation to Ellsberg's psychiatrist—so Fielding could become general counsel to the president's reelection committee. Dean countered with the suggestion that the committee try to take David Young, but Krogh refused to give his partner up and instead suggested to Dean that the proper candidate was G. Gordon Liddy.

Liddy as counsel to the Committee to Re-elect the President (CRP) was the answer to several of Dean's problems. If he recommended Liddy, he would have a man somewhat beholden to him who could be asked to do intelligence gathering on someone else's nickel—while leaving intact Dean's "law firm" in the White House. Since the demise of Caulfield's proposed Operation Sandwedge, Dean had been searching for a way to undertake the gathering of political intelligence. Magruder reported in his book that when he approached Dean about finding a lawyer for the CRP, Dean said, "Maybe we could combine the intelligence job with the general counsel . . . I'll check into it." Though Mitchell and Haldeman had rejected Sandwedge, both men continued to envision some sort of operation capable of gathering information on the Democrats and also able to neutralize expected antiwar demonstrations at the Republican convention. For instance, Haldeman would shortly approve the hiring of Donald H. Segretti and the funding of his dirty tricks against Democratic candidates, as well as the infiltration into Senator Edmund Muskie's campaign by John Buckley, a former private investigator who planted an operative inside the Muskie camp. Liddy and Dean were only casually familiar to one another, so Krogh set up a meeting between the two men in November of 1971 to discuss the CRP general counsel job. Liddy insisted that Krogh himself sit in because, as he later wrote, "with Dean, it's always best to have a witness anyway."

Dean later claimed, in his testimony and in his book, that this meeting in Bud Krogh's office was the first time he had ever met Liddy, but, as we have seen, the two had known one another for more than a year.

Liddy reported in his own book, *Will*, that immediately upon entering the room, Dean told Liddy that both Liddy and Caulfield might be required "to go into the closet for a while" to create for the campaign an "absolutely first-class intelligence operation." Was Dean talking about Sandwedge? Liddy asked. Dean responded that something more sophisticated was required. Liddy recollects that Dean encouraged him to think bigger, and then gave him a copy of Sandwedge and said, "This has been judged inadequate, so you'll have a pretty good idea of what you'll have to come up with to be adequate." When Liddy said that thinking big would cost money, Dean mentioned "half a million for openers," and Liddy topped him by suggesting that an additional half-million would probably be required. "No problem," Liddy quoted Dean as replying.

Dean's recollection of this meeting contains no suggestion of his own pushing of an intelligence operation or of any mention of money. Had he testified to those things, he might have placed himself squarely in the planning of the intelligence operations that got out of hand in the spring of 1972. Did Dean help transform Sandwedge into another intelligence operation, or not? In 1973 and 1974, while Dean was spinning his own tale to the Senate and to the prosecutors, Liddy was in jail and had vowed to maintain silence on all matters pertaining to Watergate. Krogh says he simply can't remember which man's version is true. Liddy's version of this meeting is a late one, published in his 1980 book. But there is corroboration for Liddy's side from E. Howard Hunt. In his own memoir, *Undercover*, published in 1974, Hunt recounted the story of an excited Liddy, fresh from this November 1971 meeting. "I've just come from John Dean's office, and you'll never guess what the Attorney General wants me to do," Hunt quoted Liddy as saying. "The AG wants me to set up an intelligence organization for the campaign that'll be big, Howard, and important." Asked for details,

Liddy replied, "Dean tells me there's plenty of money available—half a million for openers, and there's more where that came from. A lot more."

That meeting between Liddy, Krogh, and Dean occurred in late November, evidently just before Dean and Liddy met with Attorney General John Mitchell, on November 24—moments after Mitchell had talked to Caulfield about the job as a security man for the campaign.

There is some dispute as to what happened when Liddy, Dean, and Mitchell met. The conferees had eighteen items on their agenda; most involved legal matters Liddy would handle as the new CRP attorney, and only one item was labeled "intelligence." Both Liddy and Mitchell told us that they had so much else to discuss that they never got to that one. Dean's own version, given to the Senate committee, differs only slightly: "There was virtually no discussion of intelligence plans, other than that Liddy would draw up some sort of plans." Liddy says there wasn't even that. He was so upset about the lack of mention of the subject that he pressed Dean for word on whether there would be a further meeting "to discuss what I understood to be my principal mission, intelligence," and, according to Liddy, Dean then— on his own—ordered him to start work "as soon as possible" on a plan that could be submitted to Mitchell.

With the help of Hunt, and mindful of the $1 million Dean had promised would be "no problem," Liddy did let his imagination loose. He called his plan GEMSTONE; the plan contained a bracelet of related surreptitious notions (OPAL, EMERALD, GARNET) including infiltration of Democratic campaigns, electronic eavesdropping on Democrats in airplanes and on their telephones, use of prostitutes to compromise the Democrats, counterdemonstrations, sabotage of air-conditioning units at the Democrats' convention hall, and clandestine entries at the headquarters of Senators Muskie and George McGovern, at a hotel near the convention, and at a fourth site later to be determined. Liddy wanted to present this to Mitchell for funding, but kept getting delayed by other jobs.

One of these was a direct request from Dean to accompany Jack Caulfield to New York to audit the operations of Tony Ulasewicz. Liddy decided to present himself to the president's private eye as "Mr. George." In his memoir, Liddy reported that the man called Tony kept first-rate records in which he accounted meticulously for every cent he'd spent above his then-current $36,000 annual salary. These records, Liddy wrote, were "a time bomb, waiting to go off; everywhere he had gone, and virtually everything he had done, could be reconstructed from them. I approved the audit on the spot and urged him to destroy the records and not to generate any more like them."

For his part, Ulasewicz was not about to destroy those records, for they were good insurance against being dropped suddenly by his White House patrons. After the January 10, 1972 audit, when he had evidently gained his auditor's confidence, Tony listened, fascinated but somewhat appalled, as Mr. George described the more fanciful aspects of an offensive intelligence plan for the reelection campaign. Ulasewicz thought Mr. George's "screws were coming loose," and when asked if he would be ready for duty in the "war" against the Democrats, Tony said that as a private eye he was available for assignments, but made a mental promise to himself that his answer to any of the specific requests by Mr. George would be "*nyet*."

On January 27, 1972, two months after Dean had stirred Liddy to begin work on a plan, Liddy presented his $1 million scheme, together with charts professionally drawn by Hunt's CIA cohorts, to a group gathered in the attorney general's office that included Mitchell, Magruder, and Dean. Mitchell, whose interest was in collecting information on potential demonstrations and disruptions at the Republican convention, listened patiently, puffing on his pipe, but even Liddy could see that the AG was more troubled than pleased by the presentation.

When later questioned by the Senate, Mitchell characterized Liddy's imaginative plan as

> a complete horror story that involved a mish-mash of code names and lines of authority, electronic surveillance, the ability to intercept aircraft communications, the call-girl bit and all the rest of it. . . . The matter was of such striking content and concept that it was just beyond the pale. . . . As I recall, I told him [Liddy] to go burn the charts and that this was not what we were interested in. What we were interested in was a matter of information gathering and protection against the demonstrators.

Asked why he did not throw Liddy out of his office, Mitchell told the committee, "In hindsight, I not only should have thrown him out of the office, I should have thrown him out of the window." In their own appearances before the Senate, both Dean and Magruder agreed that Mitchell had been appalled by Liddy's presentation.

At the time, though, when the meeting ended Liddy angrily castigated Dean for not having supported him after he had earlier given Liddy reason—and a proposed dollar figure—to believe the AG wanted such a plan. Dean and Magruder mollified Liddy by suggesting that he cut the budget in half, down to the size of Sandwedge, and try again. A week later, on February 4, in a meeting with the same cast of characters, Liddy did so. As described by Liddy in *Will*, Mitchell looked at the papers Liddy brought and said he'd have to "think about it." Dean then cut in and, in a grandstanding manner, shot Liddy down in midflight, interrupting the presentation with the observation that this was not fit subject matter to be decided by the office of the attorney general of the United States but that the decision should come from "completely unofficial channels." Angry and frustrated, Liddy left the meeting.

According to Dean's Senate committee testimony, after the February 4 meeting Dean supposedly reported to Haldeman what had occurred. Dean later claimed to have told Haldeman that what Liddy had presented to Mitchell was "incredible, unnecessary and unwise," and that "no one at the White House should have anything to do with this." Having obtained Haldeman's agreement on this point, Dean then said he had "no further dealings on the matter."

It was a good story Dean told, but it wasn't true. Haldeman had no memory of this meeting with Dean in early February—a meeting that would have exculpated him. Haldeman wrote in his book that Dean later "reminded" him so many times about the meeting, "I eventually believed it." Only when he reviewed his office logs years after the event was Haldeman "surprised" to learn that "no such meeting with Dean took place. It just didn't happen." It is likely that Dean made up the Haldeman meeting so that he could say that he, Dean, had said no to Liddy in February, and backed up that no by reporting it to his superior, Haldeman.

Back at the Committee to Re-elect the President, Liddy had taken over control of Donald Segretti, and in mid-February Magruder instructed him to grab potentially damaging information "that would blow Muskie out of the water," documents that supposedly lay in the safe of Las Vegas newspaper publisher Hank Greenspun. The tip had come from Robert Bennett, head of Mullen & Company, through Hunt. That should have made it suspect of itself, since the public relations agency was a CIA front and Hunt was still working for the Mullen firm, but it did not. Liddy and Hunt flew first to Los Angeles to confer with a security man for Howard Hughes, who wanted other documents thought to be in Greenspun's safe, and they all agreed to work together, but the caper was aborted before it went any further.

Another plum given to Liddy by Magruder was to be, in effect, operations officer for SEDAN CHAIR, which placed an infiltrator in the Muskie camp, and for the project run by former private investigator

John Buckley, alias "Fat Jack," which passed documents from the Muskie camp to the CRP and which Liddy dubbed RUBY I in his GEMSTONE plan. Shortly, Magruder placed under Liddy another operative, Thomas J. Gregory, a friend of Robert Bennett's nephew, who was also sent into Muskie's organization as a spy and code-named RUBY II.

Another assignment had to do with an investigation of the Democrats' campaign financing, which Liddy wrote up as a memo for Mitchell, routed through Magruder, dated March 15, 1972.

Liddy assumed that this memo was going to be taken to John Mitchell, but it was not. There was another sponsor. In fact, Magruder was keeping Liddy and all Liddy operations away from Mitchell; by his own admission, for instance, Magruder would later keep yet a third revised GEMSTONE plan from being reviewed by Mitchell for nearly two more months after the February 4 meeting. But the very day he got Liddy's memo of March 15, Magruder walked it over to John Dean—as Dean would later testify to the Watergate committee. At the side of one paragraph of the memo, which described an alleged 25 percent kickback to the Democrats from an exposition to be held at the Fontainebleu Hotel and Convention Hall during the time of the Democratic convention in Miami, Dean scribbled, "Need more info." Dean sent Tony Ulasewicz to Florida to get the same information. Dean often utilized two routes to obtain something he wanted.

Why would Magruder bring a memo to Dean that was addressed to Mitchell and accept it back with only Dean's comments, if Jeb thought he was supposed to report such matters to anyone else? And why would Dean have commented on the matter if—as he testified—after February he "had no further dealings" on Liddy's work?

That spring of 1972 was a difficult time for Gordon Liddy; he felt uneasy, because as long as Magruder controlled the purse strings of these piecemeal operations he was conducting, and he himself had no authorized budget, Liddy was not in control. As the day-to-day manager at the CRP, Magruder had near-blanket authority to dispense funds, and indeed he had authorized committee official Herbert L. "Bart" Porter to dole out money to Liddy for his various undercover projects. By March, Liddy had drawn about $25,000, but was angry because "Magruder was in a position to call the shots. I began to suspect he was delaying a decision on GEMSTONE deliberately, to maintain this control over intelligence operations. He was, after all, a Haldeman man."

As the quote shows, for more than a decade after the events of Watergate, Gordon Liddy believed that Magruder had been acting for

Haldeman, and that the refusal to fund GEMSTONE came about because Haldeman was trying not to let Mitchell have complete command of the reelection campaign.

In fact, Magruder did continue to report to Haldeman after he left the White House for CRP, but through Gordon Strachan, whom Haldeman designated as liaison with the CRP. Magruder didn't like this arrangement one bit, for Strachan was junior to him and several years younger. However, Strachan later told the Senate Watergate committee that although he reported to Haldeman on all matters political, that did not include intelligence operations. "As to the subject of political intelligence gathering, however, John Dean was designated as the White House contact for the Committee to Re-elect the President," Strachan testified, adding that,

> As a result, my inquiries about political intelligence were slight. Mr. Haldeman seldom had me attend meetings on the subject. He rarely asked me a question about the subject and so I seldom reported about it to him. Nor did Mr. Dean report to me about all his activities in the area of political intelligence. . . . On those occasions when I made such follow-up inquiries with Mr. Haldeman about political intelligence operations, he responded that I should let Dean handle it. When I followed up with Mr. Dean, he rarely advised me in any detail about the status of intelligence matters. Instead, he dealt directly with Mr. Haldeman.

In this same passage of testimony, Strachan also advised the Senate investigators "where the documentary proof on this point is located," but the Senate committee did not follow a lead that might have badly impugned their major witness against the president. What the committee might have learned was not as Strachan thought—that Haldeman had placed Dean in charge of political intelligence. Rather, the committee might have discovered, as we have, that Haldeman had done no such thing—but that Dean had convinced Strachan otherwise.

Eventually, Liddy's frustration with Magruder grew, and he threatened—Liddy says jokingly—to kill Magruder.

"This isn't working out, Gordon," Magruder remembered responding. "I can't work with people who talk about killing me. We've got to have a change."

"That's fine with me," Liddy said (in the version of the story that Magruder reported in his book), "I'm sick of screwing around with a punk like you."

Both men decided Liddy would be better off elsewhere. Liddy admired Maurice H. Stans, who had recently resigned as secretary of commerce to become the chairman of the CRP finance committee, which because of a new campaign finance law was shortly going to need a general counsel of its own. Liddy says that he decided to ask for that job. Magruder claims he opened it up as a possibility. Even if Magruder did not originate it, he was clearly delighted at any idea that would get rid of Liddy, and knew from being in the previous two GEMSTONE meetings that perhaps Mitchell also would not mind.

Opposition to losing Liddy entirely from the intelligence operation came from the White House, from Dean and Strachan. Upon learning of the possibility of Liddy's departure, Dean called Magruder and told him, "Don't let your personal feelings about Liddy get in the way of an important operation."

Magruder agreed that the operation was indeed important, and as he recounts in his memoir, "That afternoon I went to see Strachan at the White House and we discussed the Liddy problem." Haldeman's deputy Strachan echoed precisely what Dean had said on the phone, and in virtually the same phrases. Strachan, reports Magruder, "urged me to put aside my personal feelings, because we needed the intelligence-gathering program and Liddy was our number-one professional in that area."

Magruder wrote that it was finally agreed that Liddy should transfer to the finance committee "but continue to report to me as our intelligence chief," a decision that Magruder also noted was taken without informing Mitchell.

Shortly, Magruder, under pressure from Dean and Strachan at the White House, told Liddy to try formulating a third intelligence plan, with an even further reduced budget, that they could again present to Mitchell.

8

THE BAILEY CONNECTION

ON March 30, 1972, there was an important meeting in Key Biscayne, Florida, that, through a circuitous route, eventually led to the Watergate break-in. Reports of this meeting differ dramatically, one from another, and the substance of their differences is what has laid a cover of fog over the real Watergate story from 1972 to the present day.

To put the meeting in context, back at the CRP headquarters, Gordon Liddy's transfer to Maurice Stans's finance committee took effect on Monday, March 27. Liddy believed he was through with Jeb Magruder, though he still expected to be in the campaign intelligence business if there was approval of a modified GEMSTONE plan. In the White House, as we shall see, John Dean also was thinking about GEMSTONE and hoping for its approval, but for another reason.

Gathered in shirt-sleeves and casual wear at John Mitchell's quarters at Key Biscayne on March 30 were Mitchell, who had recently left the Justice Department to become head of CRP, and his chief lieutenants, Frederick C. LaRue and Jeb Magruder, as well as another Mitchell aide, Harry S. Flemming. Mitchell appeared tired and haggard, the result of two factors: his grilling by the Senate over allegations of a secret deal between the Nixon administration and the International Telephone and Telegraph Corp. to help finance the Republican convention, and the deterioration into alcoholism of his wife, Martha. There were about thirty items—two full Magruder briefcases of material—to be gone over and decided upon, and the men went through them one by one for many hours, including a break for lunch.

When it came time to discuss the GEMSTONE plan, through prior arrangement of LaRue and Magruder, a way was found to excuse Flemming from the room so that only three men would discuss the plan. LaRue had placed it at the end of the long agenda.

Magruder has in the past claimed that Mitchell authorized a modified GEMSTONE plan of this meeting, and, specifically, a break-in at the Watergate. Magruder remembered ten minutes of discussion on the Liddy proposal and Mitchell scribbling on the paper outlining the proposal. In his book, Magruder commented, "I assumed that Haldeman wanted it, because I had asked Strachan if Haldeman had any comments to make on the proposal, and Strachan replied that the plan was all right with Haldeman if it was all right with Mitchell."

In testimony, under questioning by Watergate committee chief counsel Sam Dash, Magruder said that this was when Mitchell approved the plan. Later, braced by Senator Howard H. Baker, Jr., vice chairman of the committee, he testified that Mitchell had specifically identified the DNC as a break-in target. Magruder adhered to the same story in his book, writing that Mitchell personally approved a quarter-million-dollar budget for the scaled-down GEMSTONE.

Mitchell consistently denied that he ever discussed an illegal break-in with anyone, and insisted that he never granted an approval. He told the Watergate committee that the GEMSTONE paper he saw contained no mention of break-ins or wiretaps and that Magruder must have been under pressure by someone to get some sort of Liddy plan okayed. Mitchell testified he forcefully rejected the plan and told Magruder, "We don't need this, I am tired of hearing it out, let's not discuss it any further."

In fact, Magruder *was* under extreme pressure from the White House. And, as Magruder has now admitted to us, Mitchell did not approve the DNC as a break-in target. "We [CRP] weren't the initiators," Magruder told us, and reminded us that "the first plan we got had been initiated by Dean. Mitchell didn't do anything. All Mitchell did is just what I did, was acquiesce to the pressure from the White House." At a later point in our interview, he confirmed this again, saying, "The target never came from Mitchell." We believe that Magruder has not gone far enough in his partial retreat from his earlier claims. Mitchell did not approve GEMSTONE at all, but pushed off the plan that he had been led to mistakenly believe Haldeman wanted.

LaRue told the Watergate committee that he had read the plan, and that when Mitchell sought his opinion of it, LaRue said he didn't think much of it and that Mitchell then responded, "Well, this is not something that will have to be decided at this meeting." When asked by Dash if Mitchell had rejected the plan out of hand at the meeting, LaRue said no. In an interview with us, LaRue explained that Mitchell could not have identified a target because "he didn't even approve the bugging." He insists that he has a vivid recollection of the meeting and that Mitchell did not approve the plan at that meeting. "I have no doubt in my mind about my recollection of that meeting," he told us.

In fact, Magruder was trapped between the pressure from Dean at the White House and Mitchell's repeated annoyed refusals to approve GEMSTONE on behalf of the CRP. So trapped, we believe, that Magruder gave the CRP's go-ahead to fund the scaled-down GEM-STONE without Mitchell's approval, using the funds that were already under Magruder's own control.

In his book, Magruder claims he tried to call Liddy about the plan's approval, was unable to reach him, and sent word through Robert Reisner, Magruder's assistant. Magruder also wrote that he did call Strachan at the White House to inform him of this and other Mitchell "decisions." As we have seen, Strachan was reporting to Haldeman about intelligence matters through Dean, so Magruder's call was really a report to Dean that the revised GEMSTONE had been approved.

Gordon Liddy now thinks that Magruder didn't try very hard to reach him in person just then, because Magruder "couldn't stand to be in my presence, especially after the time I told him I'd tear his arm off." He also recalls that the week prior to the Magruder-Mitchell meeting in Key Biscayne—when he wasn't talking to Magruder—he was talking to Dean. Furthermore, Liddy says, he had no knowledge that the Key Biscayne meeting of Mitchell and Magruder was going to take place. When Bob Reisner called to give Liddy a "go" on his project, some time around the first of April, the approval came out of the blue.

Moreover, Liddy understood this "go" as enabling action at the forthcoming Democrats' convention in Miami, especially since Reisner made no mention of any other target, such as the headquarters of the Democratic National Committee at the Watergate. As far as Liddy was concerned, the "project" was in Miami. Since he knew that the Democratic convention, always the primary target of GEMSTONE, was not going to convene until July, and it was just the beginning of April, he didn't drop everything and proceed with haste, as he would have if the target had been the DNC headquarters. Swamped with other business, Liddy relayed the "good news" to Hunt, asked him to alert his team of Miami operatives, and dove back into collecting campaign money for Stans.

The new federal election law was to take effect April 7. After that date, all donations would have to bear a donor's name, and might be made public, an exposure that some potential contributors to Nixon's reelection wished to avoid. So, many large donations to the CRP had to be arranged and collected before April 7; Liddy served as a prime collection man for that effort.

Once the deadline passed, Liddy showed Stans's deputy Hugh W. Sloan, Jr., his now approved $250,000 intelligence budget and asked for an immediate $83,000. In short order, Sloan gave him 830 one-hundred-dollar bills, most of which Liddy conveyed to the CRP security chief, former CIA agent James W. McCord, Jr., to buy equipment, especially a $30,000 bug-and-transmitter. When Sloan asked for an accounting, and Liddy started to detail just what was being done with the money, Sloan backed away and told him the accounting wouldn't be necessary after all.

In early April, at about the same time as the Liddy-Hunt-McCord plans for infiltrating the Democratic convention were being readied, other events were taking place that would shortly, and very drastically, alter the target of that infiltration. Those events concerned a young Washington attorney named Phillip Mackin Bailley.

Bailley was in his late twenties, a handsome, liberal, long-haired, wide-tied Catholic University Law School graduate with a modest practice in the district that others described as "small-time, small crime." He represented petty criminals, drug dealers, and prostitutes, though a large portion of his practice was the representation of indigent defendants assigned to him by the courts. His business card was emblazoned with the word *peace*, and the number and variety of his female conquests was the stuff of legends. He had an inordinate ability to persuade young women to sleep with him, then to pose nude as he photographed them. Interested in politics, he was always on the fringe of people who were going somewhere, though he himself was not. In his college and law school days he had attached himself to such young Maryland Democrats as Stenny Hoyer, later to become a congressman, and R. Spencer Oliver, who ran successfully for the national presidency of the Young Democrats. Bailley claimed to have been a lieutenant of these men; others point out that most of his duties seemed those of a hanger-on and chauffeur. His model, Bailley said, was not Bobby Kennedy but Bobby Baker, the friend of Lyndon Johnson's who had parlayed his connections into a lucrative lobbying career before he landed in jail. In law school, Bailley had been voted the classmate "most likely to be disbarred."

Phil Bailley's practice included representing many prostitutes and party girls, and this, plus his free-swinging lifestyle, had spilled over into an alliance with a group of women headed by one who called herself "Erika," or Cathy Dieter.

Bailley did not know it at that time, but Cathy Dieter's true identity and real name was Erika L. "Heidi" Rikan, a woman who between 1964 and 1966 had performed as a stripper at Washington's Blue Mirror club in the notorious 14th Street district.

Cathy/Heidi was forced to leave another sex-for-money operation that had been closed by the police, and was about to manage a new one at an apartment complex known as the Columbia Plaza. Often in the company of Bailley, Cathy/Heidi recruited at such Georgetown bars as Nathan's, where the line between young women out to have a good time and those not adverse to going to bed with a man for pay was often hard to discern. One evening in the summer of 1971, at Nathan's, Cathy/Heidi showed Bailley photographs of herself with another young woman, taken at Lake Tahoe. According to Bailley's later written recollection, they were in a chorus line pose, "both in bikinis with right legs raised off ground to their left and hands on each other's shoulders." Cathy/Heidi said the name of the other woman was "Catherine."

Cathy/Heidi's women friends became known to Bailley by code names and nicknames. "Catherine" soon was given the nickname of "Clout." The nickname was significant and reflective of what Cathy/Heidi believed to be Clout's power in town. Bailley did not ask what the Clout nickname meant, and would not find out until more than a decade had passed.

Bailley kept a small pocket address book that soon became overloaded with names, nicknames, and code names matched with phone numbers. Some denoted acquaintances, some girlfriends, some party girls, some prostitutes, and some law clients; there was no attempt to segregate the names by categories. Because of the overload of names, Bailley's younger sister Jeannine, who functioned as the secretary in his office, from time to time transferred information from his pocket address book to another address book that was kept in his office. It contained more than two hundred names, together with a key for understanding to whom those names referred.

Shortly after Labor Day of 1971, Bailley met Clout and Cathy/ Heidi at Nathan's. Clout was curvaceous, wearing a "white tight blouse" and jeans that were "painted on," and sporting shoulder-length light brown hair tied in a red bandana, long red fingernails, black mascara, and red rouge. She talked slowly and was quite poised.

At subsequent meetings between Bailley and Cathy/Heidi, there was talk of a new source of business for Cathy's ring. Bailley had boasted to Cathy of his former political connections, and she now wanted him to make use of his claimed friendship with Spencer Oliver, who was currently working as the executive director of the Association of State Democratic Chairmen in the DNC headquarters at the Watergate, a short walk away from the Columbia Plaza, the headquarters of Cathy's call-girl ring. The thought was that someone—perhaps Oliver himself, perhaps another employee—would be able to steer "high rolling pols" to Cathy's Columbia Plaza operation. Bailley, with his well-known powers of persuasion, was asked to go in and find such a person, who could be promised a commission on any customers.

It was during this period that Bailley entered the telephone number for Clout into his pocket address book. Jeannine Bailley remembers specifically transferring into the second address book the nickname Clout, to key with the identification of this woman as "Mo Biner." She remembers writing "Clout" with the name "Mo Biner." She also recalls taking messages from "Clout" for her brother on many occasions. She told us that that woman left messages under the nickname "Clout" as well as under "Ms. Biner" and most frequently as "Mo."

In the winter of 1971, Bailley went to the DNC to see Oliver, who was away at the time; unable to get to him, he chatted with the receptionist about the good old days working on Bobby Kennedy's 1968 campaign, and took a brief walk-through of the DNC offices. In late February 1972, he tried again, with more success. Oliver was away, though his secretary, Ida M. ("Maxie") Wells, was in, and she agreed, Bailley says, to see him and to give him a full tour of the premises.

It's important to note (as Bailley did, just then, and later reported back to Cathy) the locations of Wells and Oliver and the adjacent office used by the chairman of the Democratic State Governors organization in the DNC offices. Wells's desk was near the central reception area, between Oliver's and the Governors' private, enclosed offices. The whole area was backed by an outside wall that gave onto a terrace overlooking Virginia Avenue, on which several secretaries were sitting, having snacks on that warm day. The most important offices, of course, were on the outside corners of the space—those of DNC Chairman Larry O'Brien, the campaign treasurer, and two other officials. O'Brien's office was as far away from the Oliver/Wells/Governors' area in the physical setup as mathematically possible; it did not face Virginia Avenue at all, as the reader will see from the diagrams reprinted following this page.

It was clear from the location of offices that Oliver was a middle-rank man at best, though he had the perk of an office that backed on the shared terrace. Bailley told us he learned that Oliver traveled a lot and that the Governors' office was almost always vacant. It was, in short, a perfect setup for what Cathy Dieter had in mind.

Bailley says he then found someone at the DNC with whom he could do business, telling her, "I have friends who can make your out-of-town people happy at night." He stressed that these were college-educated ladies and that they were just across the street, referring to the Columbia Plaza. According to Bailley, at this and in subsequent meetings and phone calls with Cathy and Bailley, the DNC contact agreed to take part in the operation.

Though her major telephonic contact would be Cathy Dieter, messages from Bailley's DNC contact or the party girls themselves could also be relayed through Bailley and his office. Often, Bailley recalls, his contact wanted to talk directly to the nicknamed women to explain dates, times, and sexual preferences. After the dates, Cathy would frequently call to see if the men had had a good time. Bailley believed that such calls were invariably made or received, unobserved, from the private phone in Oliver's office while Oliver was away, although the calls may actually have been made from the nearly always vacant Governors' office.

Crucial to understanding what follows is this: Mo Biner's code name Clout referred to her ongoing romance with White House Counsel to the President John Dean. Dean would later become her husband.

In her own book, *"Mo," A Woman's View of Watergate*, Maureen Elizabeth Kane Owen Biner Dean related that she had met John Dean in California in 1970, fallen in love, and at his behest had come to Washington in January of 1971. She had taken a low-level secretarial job at the Bureau of Narcotics and Dangerous Drugs, one that did not require a background check to be done by the FBI. At twenty-five, according to her own story, Biner had already been married twice. The first marriage was annulled on the grounds that George Owen, her first husband, had not previously and properly divorced another woman; the second was ended by Michael Biner's death in an automo-

DEMOCRATIC NATIONAL COMMITTEE HEADQUARTERS

*Watergate Office Building
2600 Virginia Avenue, N.W.
Washington, D.C.*

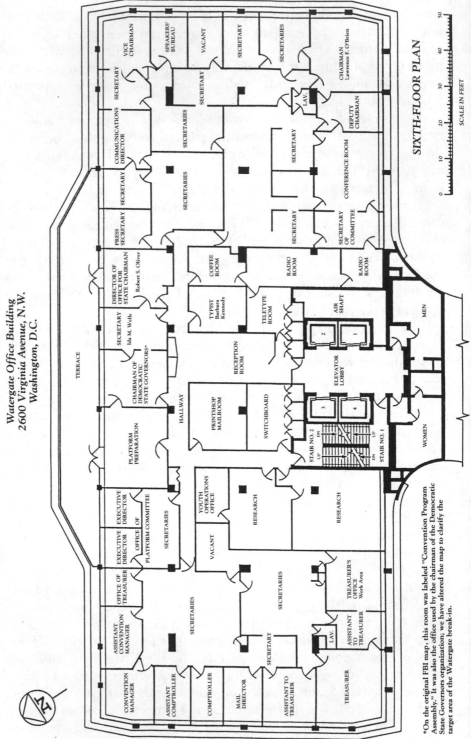

SIXTH-FLOOR PLAN

SCALE IN FEET

0 10 20 30 40 50

*On the original FBI map, this room was labeled "Convention Program Assembly." It was also the office used by the chairman of the Democratic State Governors organization; we have altered the map to clarify the target area of the Watergate break-in.

WATERGATE OFFICE BUILDING
AND
HOWARD JOHNSON'S MOTOR LODGE

2600 block of Virginia Avenue, N.W., Washington, D.C.

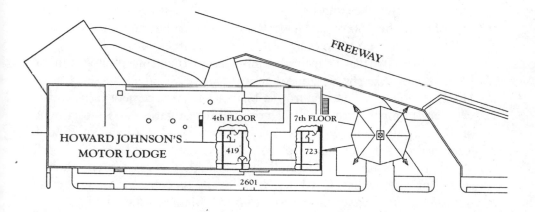

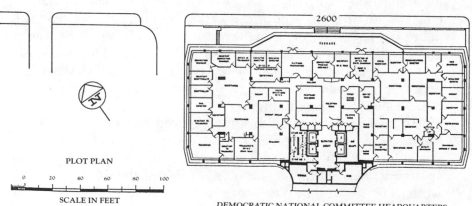

bile accident. A former stewardess and insurance agency employee, she had stayed in her first Washington job only a few weeks before moving up to a $10,000-a-year post as assistant to the director of the new National Commission on Marijuana and Drug Abuse. She traveled a great deal, just as Dean also was required to do a lot of traveling by his own job. She recounts that she lived with John at his two-bedroom town house in Alexandria, but since the straitlaced men of the Nixon administration frowned on premarital alliances, she also stayed frequently in the Washington apartment of a friend. That friend she identifies in her book as Heidi Rikan, whom she had met in Lake Tahoe. There is even a picture of Heidi in Maureen Dean's book.

Recently, we have received confirmation that this photograph of Heidi Rikan is a photograph of the woman who called herself Cathy Dieter. Confirmation came from a former law enforcement officer who was very familiar with the 1972 criminal investigation and indictment of Bailley and who had personally interviewed Cathy Dieter and identified the Rikan photograph as being that of Cathy Dieter.

Maureen Biner met Heidi Rikan through George Owen, then a scout for the Dallas Cowboys who would become Maureen's first husband. After her second marriage ended, Maureen stayed with Rikan in Lake Tahoe for several months. She also spent a month with her in Washington during the first half of 1969, and in her book describes that at that time, "Heidi was single, well-to-do, and had plenty of spare time." The two women drove across the country.

From the late 1960s onward, Erika L. "Heidi" Rikan/Cathy Dieter lived a life in Washington, D.C., on the fringes of the law. In Washington, Heidi/Cathy was a girlfriend of Joe Nesline, who was called by police and reporters "the godfather of illegal gambling" in the capital, and the District's best-known underworld figure. The relationship between Heidi/Cathy and Nesline was confirmed to us by a Washington police detective who had investigated Nesline in the early 1970s and by others who knew Heidi/Cathy.

At the beginning of 1971, after Maureen had met John Dean in California, fallen in love, and agreed to come with him to Washington, she wrote, "I 'moved in' with Heidi . . . My mail came to Heidi's apartment, most of my clothes were deposited there." However, she wrote, most of her time was spent with Dean at his two-bedroom town house in Alexandria—except when Dean was on a trip. Then she stayed with Rikan. She also borrowed some of Heidi's glamorous clothes, such as a black sable coat, for formal occasions at the White House.

Maureen Biner's acquaintanceship with Bailley, and the true identity of her friend Heidi, have never previously been revealed. They are the keys to understanding all the events of the break-ins and cover-ups that we know under the omnibus label of Watergate.

At about the same time that Bailley was helping to set up an arm of Cathy/Heidi's Columbia Plaza operation at the DNC, John Dean also developed an interest in the Watergate headquarters. The roots of his interest had been demonstrated earlier, in October 1971, when, as the reader will recall, based on a Colson tip Dean had asked Jack Caulfield to investigate the "Happy Hooker" ring in New York. This was when Caulfield had come back with nothing that could be used, because the dirt obtained on the Democratic clients of the ring would be canceled out by the dirt on the Republican clients.

Dean continued to be interested in salacious political material, and that interest also pointed him toward the Watergate, at just about the same point in time at which Cathy/Heidi's Columbia Plaza operation was getting started. That was when he had Caulfield send Ulasewicz on the walk-through of the DNC described in an earlier chapter.

With this order, Dean effectively left his fingerprints all over what would become the target of the Watergate break-ins—the DNC. Even Dean himself has not claimed that Haldeman, Ehrlichman, Mitchell, or any other CRP or Nixon administration official was involved prior to the time of the Ulasewicz walk-through in any of the events that would lead directly to the Watergate break-ins, nor that any of those officials had identified the DNC as a potential target. In November 1971, when Ulasewicz took his walk through the DNC, Gordon Liddy had not yet been hired to work at CRP, John Mitchell was still attorney general, and GEMSTONE had not yet even been proposed.

We asked Dean about this, and included in our question the information that Caulfield had told us he had received the order from him. Dean at first "unequivocally" denied giving any such instruction to Caulfield, but toward the end of our interview suggested that there were a number of occasions on which Caulfield (and, separately, Liddy) would come to him when he was very busy, and sort of half-mention an idea:

> I've watched them both, take, ah, you know, just, ah, the tiniest thing, you know, ah, you know, when I'm off doing 400 other things, or anybody else, a Mitchell or a Magruder, busy on other things, and then coming by and, you know, [saying] "Hey, John, what do you think about this, is that a good idea?" And, you know, a grunt [from me, meaning], "Whatever you think, Jack." And [him] going off and doing something, taking [my grunt] like a damn command. . . .

If it was not Dean who asked Caulfield to go into the Watergate, then who was it? Who among his superiors knew or even suspected that valuable intelligence information could be gleaned from the DNC at that point in time? Asked by us if they had been aware of, let alone ordered, a Caulfield pass-through, Haldeman, Ehrlichman, Mitchell, and Magruder all said no. Had Dean learned that lonely out-of-town Democrats were using his girlfriend's roommate's call-girl ring through an in-house operative at the DNC? We do not know, but we have been informed by another source, who agreed to speak only if not identified, that Dean and Heidi Rikan were "great friends."

During the winter of 1971–1972, Cathy/Heidi's business continued apace, with what Bailley says was at least one client a day being referred through the DNC connections. Other clients included men from the State Department, major hotels in town, a private club, and the Library of Congress. According to Bailley, as the operation grew, pictures and other materials about the women—some taken by him— were given to Bailley's DNC contact, so that prospective clients could choose among possible dates. Bailley says these photos were concealed by his contact in a safe place in the DNC offices.

Bailley's own conquests also were continuing, and as the spring of 1972 began, so did a time of reckoning for them: He would shortly stand accused of violations of the Mann Act, the transporting of young women across state lines for immoral purposes. On the morning of April 6, 1972, four special agents of the FBI entered Bailley's law office and executed search warrants for his office and his home. Bailley was at neither place, but his sister was at the office when the agents seized a number of items. Included among them were the two address books— Bailley's pocket address book and the other address book into which Jeannine had copied the names. Both address books contained the names, nicknames, and telephone numbers of hundreds of women. One was black with gold lettering on the cover, and the second was black with gold letters on a red background. Jeannine Bailley signed a receipt for these few items. At Bailley's residence, the haul was considerably larger and of more obvious sexual content: a movie projector, motion picture and still photographic equipment, more than a hundred photos of women, and a "black and white rawhide whip."

Bailley himself was not arrested at that time.

When the prosecuting attorneys got hold of these Bailley address books, they evolved their own, military-type way of referring to the women named in them so as to protect their identities. Recently, we asked John Rudy, who was the assistant U.S. attorney in charge of the Bailley investigation, whether any of the code names in the Bailley address books were familiar to him. He remembered "Greenhouse Nymph" and some others, and then we asked—without elaboration— if he knew the nickname "Clout."

"Yeah, that was another one that sounded familiar. That was, we called her something else, though. That was M.B. No, not M.B.—no, hold on, I'll get it—Mike Bravo. That's who we called Mike Bravo— that's military for M.B."

We asked him to further identify M.B.

"We knew that to be a lady by the name of—oh, hell—that was Biner, Binner, Bomer. No . . ."

"Biner?"

"Biner," Rudy affirmed.

"Maureen Biner?" we asked again.

"Yeah," said Rudy. "I've identified it, that's Maureen Biner."

A few weeks after the search of Bailley's home and office, Liddy reports, he was called in by Jeb Magruder and asked, "Gordon, do you think you could get into the Watergate?" This was a switch, and Liddy didn't like it. Earlier in the month Liddy had been given a "go" on a target he thought to be the Miami Democratic convention, and had asked McCord to order equipment for it. Now, in his view, the target was being changed.

Going into the Watergate was not an entirely new thought. Liddy had considered a surreptitious entry there, but in his mind it was something to do later in the year, when and if it had become the headquarters of the Democratic standard bearer as well as the national committee. At the moment, the center of the political stage was occupied by the Democratic primaries, hotly contested between Hubert Humphrey, Edmund Muskie, and George McGovern. The DNC was engaged in setting up a convention for July, and would have to wait until a nominee was chosen to really get into action. Liddy replied that an entry was certainly feasible, though, and Magruder asked him if he could place a bug in Larry O'Brien's office. Liddy objected that it was too late for placing such a bug, since O'Brien was spending most of his time in Miami, readying the convention. Magruder pursued the matter anyway; though O'Brien might be away, Liddy quotes Jeb as saying, "There's still plenty of activity over there. We want to know whatever's said in his office, just as if it was here; what goes on in this office." Liddy thought the demand strange, but acquiesced to it because at least it was action, and was told, "Get in there as soon as you can, Gordon. It's important."

It was clear to Liddy that Magruder was not acting on his own, but simply passing on orders from someone else. At the time, Liddy assumed the directive had come from Mitchell, and in the years that followed, most people have erroneously accepted that idea. But Magruder's order had not come from Mitchell. As we have shown earlier in this chapter, even Magruder, who continues to incorrectly maintain that Mitchell approved GEMSTONE, recently admitted to us that pressure to go into the Watergate had come from the White House, and specifically from John Dean, noting, "The target never came from Mitchell."

But there was a specific target when Magruder instructed Liddy, and it was "important."

A properly cautious break-in would take a few weeks to set up, Liddy thought. A wire-man and the Cubans from Miami would actually go into the DNC. Responding to the need to shield all higher-ups from a connection to this operation, Liddy did not plan to accompany the burglars inside but (as in the instance of Dr. Fielding's office) would remain outside, in case there was any trouble. The point was to ensure that even if someone inside were to be caught, it would not be possible to connect them to the CRP.

That was how Liddy understood the task. However, unbeknownst to him (and, most likely, to Magruder, too), although the ostensible focus of this first break-in was the office of Larry O'Brien, the actual target was quite different. As Howard Hunt and two of the burglars recently told us, the real target was the frequently used telephone that was in the portion of the DNC that contained the offices of R. Spencer Oliver, his secretary Maxie Wells, and the chairman of the State Democratic Governors organization.

In the interim between the enabling order from Magruder and the first Watergate break-in, Liddy was kept busy on related matters. He was asked by Magruder on behalf of White House special counsel Charles Colson to provide men to muck about in antiwar demonstrations being planned in Washington for the first week in May. A Vietcong flag had been displayed on the Mall at an earlier demonstration, and one was expected this time; Colson wanted to seize it to present to Nixon. Bernard L. Barker, a former CIA employee from Miami whom Howard Hunt had recruited for the Dr. Fielding break-in and now for GEMSTONE operations, took a group of men and mixed roughly with the crowd, enough so for Barker to injure a hand and for Frank A. Sturgis, another Miami recruit, to be detained by police, but that was all. Hunt and Liddy drove the Miamians around McGovern headquarters and around the DNC offices at the Watergate complex, indicating these as the sites of future break-ins.

In other clandestine matters, Liddy was asked by Hugh Sloan to cash some signed traveler's checks made out before the April 7 deadline, and after he had done this successfully through Barker, had a second request from Sloan for help on a similar matter. Stans's assistant showed Liddy five checks. One was a cashier's check for $25,000, bearing the name Kenneth H. Dahlberg and dated April 10; this, said Sloan, represented a contribution made in the Midwest prior to April 7 that had been converted by Dahlberg, the Nixon campaign's Midwest finance chairman, to conceal the name of the donor. The other four checks, totaling $89,000, had the same purpose but had been made out to Mexican attorney Manuel Ogarrio Daguerre and drawn on Ogarrio's bank account in Mexico City. Sloan wanted Liddy to convert these five checks to $114,000 in cash. Several trips to Miami were necessary before Liddy returned to Sloan's office with $111,500 in brand-new $100 bills (after paying $2,500 in expenses) that had consecutive serial numbers. In addition to this money-laundering, Liddy and Hunt also planned and were about to execute a surreptitious entry into McGovern's headquarters. This entry was aborted because they learned that a recent burglary had caused a Burns Agency guard to be stationed inside the front door every hour of the day.

Such shenanigans kept Liddy busy until Monday, May 22, when Barker and the rest of his clandestine team—Sturgis, Eugenio Rolando Martinez, Virgilio R. Gonzalez, Felipe De Diego, and Reinaldo Pico—came to Washington and moved into the Manger-Hamilton Hotel. Acting as tourists, the contingent signed the log in the Watergate complex and went upstairs to get a glimpse of the DNC layout from the hall; Hunt, Liddy says, took an impression of the front-door lock with soft clay. The group also made "familiarization tours" of the Howard Johnson's Motor Inn across the street from the Watergate, which was to serve as a lookout post for the team and the place from which the bugs to be placed inside the DNC offices would be monitored. Finally, the men toured the Watergate itself, in darkness as well as in daylight. On May 26, four days after they arrived, the group checked into the Watergate hotel under their aliases.

During this period of setup and casing the joint, James McCord, who had joined the group, did some things that Liddy found odd. Liddy was able to stop his friend before he did something truly dumb: seek FCC approval for the frequencies on which the transceivers were to be operated. Liddy was not able to prevent McCord from disappearing frequently in between assigned meeting times or from reporting delays in obtaining the correct bugging equipment for the DNC penetration. Liddy expressed his annoyance at McCord for not renting a room at the Howard Johnson's that was properly situated for line-of-sight transmission of stolen conversations from the DNC; McCord's room was on the fourth floor, while the target was on the sixth floor across Virginia Avenue. (Liddy, who believed the target was O'Brien, had not seen the DNC floor plan and did not know that O'Brien's office, which was on the opposite side from the Howard Johnson's, could not be seen at all from the motel.) McCord was able to transfer into a room on the seventh floor, which was better for the clandestine purposes, but Liddy continued to bristle at McCord's sloppiness.

There were other mistakes that smacked more of amateurs than professionals. It was difficult to get into the Watergate office building unobserved, but an underground corridor connected the Watergate hotel with the office building; to utilize it, the visitors boldly rented a banquet room with the notion of keeping the fun going until a late hour when all the waiters would have gone home and left them alone, and then traveling through the corridor. The plan went awry. Hunt and McCord blamed an activated building alarm system for scuttling the plan, but author Jim Hougan has revealed that no such alarm existed, and that some other, reason wrecked the scheme.

In any case, Saturday night, May 27, they tried again and Liddy was elated when he believed that the team had actually gotten in—until they returned to the "command post" at Liddy's Watergate hotel room with the news that the team hadn't entered the Democrats' stronghold because Gonzalez hadn't brought the proper lock-picking tools. Angry, Liddy sent Gonzalez back to Miami to get the right tools. When Gonzalez returned it was Sunday afternoon. At 9:45 that evening, McCord reported to Liddy that all the lights were out in the DNC. Liddy decreed they should wait until eleven, and go in through the garage-level entrance doors, a route previously suggested by Hunt, that would give the men an hour before the midnight shift change and regular round of inspection made by the new shift of security guards.

As Liddy later wrote,

To Hunt's and my delight, that's exactly how it went. McCord reported success [the bugs had been placed], and Barker had two rolls of 36-exposure 35-mm film he'd expended on material from O'Brien's desk, along with Polaroid shots of the desk and office before anything was touched so that it could all be returned to proper order before leaving. I congratulated them all and we had a small victory celebration in the command post before going home. The Watergate entry had been successful. Or so I thought.

Liddy did not then know how wrong his estimate was. Although Barker had given him a Polaroid shot of O'Brien's office to show to Magruder—which Liddy did, on Monday morning, May 29—the two rolls of 35-mm film didn't surface for several weeks. When they did, they showed photographs that Liddy (and perhaps Magruder) thought had been taken in O'Brien's office, but, as we shall see, had been taken somewhere other than that. Frustrated by the slowness the Miamians demonstrated in getting the film developed, Liddy was even more annoyed when by Wednesday McCord had told him nothing about what the bugs were transmitting. With his Walther air pistol in his briefcase, Liddy went to the Howard Johnson's, where he was ushered into the darkened inner sanctum and spoken to in a hushed voice. McCord showed him complex equipment and a man—they all used aliases—trying to tune in on the signals coming from the DNC. Two bugs had been planted, McCord said, but only one was being picked up. To Liddy's surprise, there was no tape recorder visible, and he asked why. McCord replied "that while he had a recorder, it proved to be incapable of adaptation to his receiver because the resistance, stated in ohms, was mismatched."

This explanation was technological sand thrown in Liddy's eyes, and Liddy called McCord on it. McCord then floated a second explanation, saying that a compatible recorder was unnecessary in any event because so much of the information coming over from the DNC was useless, and the man at the headphones would type a log of it and "edit out the junk." Liddy responded that he wanted it all, and would do his own editing, and took some of the logs with him. He later wrote that "the logs revealed that the interception was from a telephone rather than a microphone that relayed all conversation in the room, and that the telephone tapped was being used by a number of different people, none of whom appeared to be Larry O'Brien."

Precisely so. In a recent interview given for the purpose of this book, and breaking silence after many years, Watergate burglar Rolando Martinez told us that the tap was not placed on Larry O'Brien's telephone, but on one in the Oliver/Wells/Governors' area. We showed him an FBI diagram of the DNC replete with the names and titles of those who occupied the offices at the time and he identified without doubt that area as the target of the bugging. This area was the perfect target for a tap, given that it was directly across Virginia Avenue from the receiving equipment in the Howard Johnson's. O'Brien's office was

unsuitable because it was obviously shielded from line-of-sight transmission by a myriad of intervening walls, beams, electrical cables, and
so on. Martinez also confirmed that the photographs had not been
taken in O'Brien's office. A second man in the break-in, Frank Sturgis,
recently told us that he had never "been in or near O'Brien's office"
and said that he had received no instructions to enter or to search it. A
source within the DNC has told us that she was informed by the FBI
in 1972 that the actual bugging target was a phone in the office of the
chairman of the Democratic State Governors organization, noting that
Spencer Oliver, among others, sometimes used a phone in that nearly
always vacant office.

The man who sat in the darkened surveillance room in the late
spring and summer of 1972 was identified as Alfred C. Baldwin III, a
former FBI agent recruited by McCord. Baldwin would later assume
the unique historical position of being the sole Watergate burglary co-
conspirator to be neither indicted nor tried for the crime.

When questioned by the Senate, Baldwin testified that the bug that
had been placed during the first break-in had worked. In a recent
conversation with us, Howard Hunt said that the bugging target was
not Wells or Oliver, "they just happened to be on the same phone,
that's all."

For corroboration that the phone tapped was in this area, and that
the overheard conversations pertained to Cathy/Heidi's call-girl operation, we have to leap ahead in time to the days and weeks after the
burglars had been caught on their second entry into the DNC headquarters in mid-June 1972. We'll return to that entry in detail in the
next chapter. The evidence establishes that in the period just after the
burglars had been caught and identified, and their criminal trial was
imminent, the government's lead prosecutor, Assistant U.S. Attorney
Earl J. Silbert, believed that the fruits of the Watergate break-in were
embarrassing tapes of a sexual nature. Baldwin had turned himself in
to Silbert, who was preparing to use him as the key witness against
Howard Hunt. Silbert believed that Hunt had intended to use the
telephone conversations that Baldwin had overheard for purposes of
blackmail.

The evidence includes the fact that Baldwin characterized the
conversations he overheard as "explicitly intimate." In addition, federal
prosecutors have confirmed that the telephone tap conversations were
"primarily sexual" and "extremely personal, intimate, and potentially
embarrassing." Another piece of evidence comes from a lunch Silbert
had with lawyer Charles Morgan, Jr., who was representing Oliver,
Wells, and some Democratic officials in several pending cases stemming

from the break-in. At this lunch on December 22, 1972—a month before the trial of the burglars was scheduled to begin—Morgan was accompanied by his associate Hope Eastman. Silbert told them, as Morgan later wrote in his book, that "he [Silbert] wanted to use the Democrats' conversations to prove that blackmail was indeed the motive for the Watergate burglary. Exasperated and angry, he looked across the table at me and blurted out, 'Hunt was trying to blackmail Spencer [Oliver] and I'm going to prove it!' " Morgan's book also noted that Morgan had checked with Eastman and she had confirmed to him that his recollection of that important moment was accurate.

Howard Hunt vehemently denies that he had any intention to blackmail anyone at the DNC, and we do not have any evidence that he was actually planning to do so.

Silbert wanted Baldwin to repeat in open court his recollection of the conversations he overheard. When Baldwin took the stand, Morgan made an objection. Since Morgan was not representing any of the defendants in the criminal case before Judge John Sirica, as Morgan himself admitted in his book, his objection was an "unprecedented long shot." Sirica denied the objection but suspended the trial so that his ruling could be immediately appealed to the U.S. Court of Appeals. During the oral argument of that appeal, Chief Judge David L. Bazelon, reviewing the request to allow Baldwin to testify, asked Silbert, "Is the government interested in whether this information [that Baldwin had overheard] would be used to compromise these people [Oliver and the DNC]? That is a euphemism for blackmail." Silbert replied that the conversations were "highly relevant" in his quest to lay "a factual foundation so that we can suggest that is what they were interested in . . . We believe this information goes to the motive and intent." The Court of Appeals overturned Sirica's ruling, thereby prohibiting Baldwin's testimony at the trial of the burglars.

As a result of the Court of Appeals ruling, prosecution attempts to pursue theories based on the contents of what Baldwin heard came to an immediate and permanent end.

Today, Silbert declines to discuss the case at all.

In early June 1972, as far as the insiders were concerned, there was a bug in the DNC headquarters, and it was transmitting to a receiving room in the Howard Johnson's across the avenue. Liddy was dissatisfied with what he thought were its results, and amazed that no one in the CRP seemed to be pestering him for what information it might be revealing. He had his secretary type up Baldwin's logs, which he had further edited, and retained those in a safe spot. On his own, he kept asking McCord for the photographic fruit of the break-in, and received rather lame excuses about the difficulty of having such photographs developed by an expert who knew how to keep his mouth closed. He had no need for making another surreptitious entry into the Watergate, and thought no one else did, either.

But Liddy was really in the dark on this one. Liddy had intentionally been excluded from the knowledge that the target had been switched from O'Brien to a phone in the Oliver/Wells/Governors area. More than that, no one in the CRP knew that CRP employees Liddy and Magruder, and the CRP-funded GEMSTONE operation, were being used as a shield for a criminal act directed from the White House. Recently, Hunt, Martinez, and Sturgis have all confirmed to us that Hunt gave the specific targets for the Watergate break-ins to the burglars. But who above Hunt had given this order?

To discuss that vital question, we must again jump ahead in time to the period after the burglars had been apprehended and identified. At that time, feeling the pressure, E. Howard Hunt looked for a way to justify, excuse, and possibly to negotiate away the responsibility for his actions. He knew he had the evidence to back him up, evidence that would put knowledge of his actions squarely in the lap of higher-ups. First, however, he had to locate it. Accompanied by his attorneys, in November of 1972 Hunt went to the U.S. Courthouse to examine evidence that had been seized from his safe in the White House. As he described the scene in his autobiography (italics in original),

> I searched the seized material for my operational notebook, files and telephone list, but did not find them. Bittman [Hunt's attorney] asked Silbert if he was holding them in another area, but Silbert declared that what I had reviewed was all there was. It was sufficient to convict me, *but any material that could have been used to construct a defense for me was missing:* my operational notebooks, telephone lists and documents in which I had recorded the progress of Gemstone from its inception, mentioning Liddy's three principals by name: Mitchell, Magruder and Dean.

At the Senate hearings, Senator Howard Baker listened to Hunt tell that these materials were gone, and asked Hunt, "Can you give me any idea why those notebooks disappeared? What was in them that would cause them to be so sensitive if they were found or why they would be a candidate for destruction, if they were not destroyed?"

"Certainly, Senator," Hunt replied. "They would provide a ready handbook by which any investigator with any resources at all could quickly determine the parameters of the GEMSTONE operation."

Recently, in an interview with us, Hunt was even more specific. The notebooks, he said, held "the full operational story of Watergate as he knew it." Moreover, these notebooks "would have implicated Dean long before there was a Watergate cover-up."

John Dean did eventually admit that he had destroyed Howard Hunt's notebooks. They were distinctive notebooks, known and referred to as "Hermès notebooks" because they were made by only one company and different from many other types. John Dean shredded them, and told the prosecutors that he had done so—but he *"remembered"* this crucial fact in late 1973, only after he had pleaded guilty to one and only one count of an indictment, and the government had agreed to drop the other counts.

We'll examine in a later chapter, and in more detail, the timing of Dean's disclosure of his destruction of Hunt's notebooks, but for the moment let's note only that they were the main documentary evidence that could link Dean directly with orders to E. Howard Hunt about the Watergate break-in.

9

THE LAST BREAK-IN

IT was early June 1972. A federal grand jury had been investigating Phillip Mackin Bailley since the April seizure of records and photographs from his office and home. Although there had been only one original complainant and the seized materials, Assistant United States Attorney John Rudy had developed charges against Bailley through the testimony of friends and acquaintances, and from several women who were prepared to testify about Bailley's sexual practices. The allegations included luring women somewhere for sex, photographing them in the nude, then threatening to release the photos unless the women engaged in sexual activities with other people. (None of these allegations were ever proven, nor constituted acts for which Bailley was convicted.)

Rudy took his time and proceeded carefully, for he knew he would be indicting a practicing lawyer, not some ordinary pimp. In his view, Bailley was a bad apple in the legal system who practiced before the very court that would soon have to bring him to justice. Rudy readied and the grand jury returned on June 9, 1972, a twenty-two-count indictment of Bailley charging violations of the Mann Act, the federal

142

Travel Act, the federal extortion statute, the District of Columbia blackmail statute, the District pandering statute and the District procuring statute. The actions covered in the indictment spanned the period from Bailley's induction into the Washington, D.C., bar in 1969 right up to February of 1972.

To the public at large this was, at best, news of only modest importance. Mary Ann Kuhn wrote up the indictment and an interview with Bailley for a late edition of the June 9 Washington *Daily News*, headlined D.C. LAWYER CHARGED WITH WHITE SLAVERY, and the newspaper printed it on an interior page. The first three editions of the Washington *Star* went to press before the story broke; then, rather suddenly, it became page-one news for the *Star*. The "night final" edition replaced a top-of-the-paper story about the bombing of Haiphong and Hanoi with the lurid headline CAPITOL HILL CALL-GIRL RING UNCOVERED. The story was written by reporters Winston Groom and Woody West. Its lead paragraph read, "The FBI here has uncovered a high-priced call girl ring allegedly headed by a Washington attorney and staffed by secretaries and office workers from Capitol Hill and involving at least one White House secretary, sources said today." It named Bailley as head of that operation and reported that Bailley had denied the charges entirely. "Sources close to the investigation" were cited as saying that clients of the operation were prominent D.C. attorneys and that

> no high officials either on Capitol Hill or at the White House were involved in running the ring, but they did indicate that a White House lawyer was a client. It was learned that a subpoena several weeks ago of a White House employe prompted a phone call from White House aide Peter Flanigan to the U.S. Attorney's Office.
>
> No one in the [U.S. Attorney's] office would acknowledge that such a phone call was made. But sources outside the office said Flanigan apparently called to find out if there was any chance of embarrassment to the Nixon administration.

How had the *Star* found out about Bailley's involvement in the call-girl operation when the Columbia Plaza ring was not mentioned in the indictment? Rudy appears not to have known about it, and his office had not told the reporters, nor had Bailley. Bailley was actually peripheral to the call-girl ring and was not charged with anything having to do with it; he was faced with jail time, disbarment, and fines for his involvement with women who were not part of Cathy/Heidi's Columbia Plaza ring. He would even make this very point much later, from the federal prison in Danbury, Connecticut, when trying to get his sentence reduced.

Peter M. Flanigan, the White House aide referred to in the *Star* article, has denied to us any call from him at the White House to Rudy's office while the grand jury was sitting in order to learn if anyone in the Nixon administration was implicated. All sorts of bells would have gone off if there had been that danger, Flanigan says: "A story this weird I believe I would have remembered it, if it had happened, but I have absolutely no memory of it whatsoever. I never heard of Mr. Bailley until [this interview]. I never saw this [newspaper] story until today nor did any reporter at any time before or after . . . ever contact me on this matter."

According to the *Star* reporters, the story developed in the following manner. Around nine or nine-thirty in the morning, Groom picked up the indictment from the court, but although it involved a lawyer it was otherwise so ordinary that he filed something similar to what Kuhn had written for the *Daily News*. Back at the city room, Woody West believes he must have received other information that took what was actually a second story given or relayed to him from another direction, commingled it with Bailley's indictment, and made the whole thing page-one news. West thought the call-girl information might have come from a reporter that the *Star* had stationed in the press room at the White House, but can't recall.

The *Star* made plain in the article itself that the information had not come from the U.S. Attorney's office. Moreover, Rudy denies that any such suggestion of a Capitol Hill call-girl ring would have come from his office. Actually, he remembers repeating that denial to John Dean, later on the day that the indictment and article appeared, June 9.

In an extraordinary move, Dean telephoned Rudy directly. He said right off the bat that he was "calling on behalf of the president of the United States," and demanded—citing the *Star* story of the ring as his rationale for the call—that the prosecutors come right over and bring "all documentary evidence identified with people involved in the [Bailley] investigation," so he could determine if anyone in the White House was involved in the ring. The night final edition of the *Star* did not hit the streets until about 1:30 P.M., and this telephonic summons was issued shortly thereafter. Records from the Executive Office Building show that John Rudy and his superior, Don Smith, visited John Dean at 4:00 P.M. on Friday, June 9, 1972, and we have interviewed John Rudy about that meeting.

According to Rudy, after discussing the request with criminal division head Don Smith and possibly with First Assistant U.S. Attorney Harold Titus, he and Smith traveled to the White House in a limousine sent for that purpose. As demanded by Dean, the prosecutors brought with them Bailley's address book and fifty to sixty of the nude photos, which had been seized in early April.

Rudy remembered the entire incident with great clarity, down to the gray pin-striped suit and blue shirt Dean was wearing, and the layout of the office. He had never before been summoned by the White House, and this was a big deal for him. "That's the kind of stuff," he told us, about which "you stand up and salute and say, 'Yes, sir!' That was heady stuff."

Dean's first inquiry after greeting the men was a question: Who did they think leaked the information on the call-girl ring to the press? Rudy didn't know, and Dean replied that he thought it had been the *Democrats*.

Dean then asked to whom at the White House the story referred. From the materials Rudy brought, Dean selected a possibility. The person Dean picked out was neither a male White House lawyer nor a White House secretary, as the *Star* had reported and as the *Washington Post* would report the next day. Rather, the person was a female employee in an agency across the street, whose picture Rudy had brought with him. Dean noted this, and looked at the other photos. Then he saw the Bailley address book, and it was this that became his main focus.

Dean looked closely at the address book and the photos, and informed the men that he wanted to keep the materials over the weekend. This, of course, would have been a gross violation of the maintenance of evidence in a currently pending case, and Smith quite properly said that could not be allowed. As a lawyer, Dean would have known full well that taking possession of the evidence was improper, but he asked for it anyway. When that idea was scotched, Dean returned to staring intently at the address book.

Though he concealed any sense of this from Rudy and Smith, he could not have avoided seeing the name of his live-in girlfriend, Mo Biner—"Clout"—and the alias of her close friend Heidi Rikan—"Cathy Dieter."

When he couldn't get hold of the address book for the weekend, he came down to the next level. He asked if he could copy the address book so he could compare the names in it to "a list of personnel in the White House, to see if the same names appear in both places." Ordinarily, such a request would be summarily denied, but the prosecutors were, after all, dealing with the president's lawyer, and Dean's request was considered reasonable. Dean called in an "older woman" who took the address book to another room and photocopied it.

John Rudy later told us he had not known at the time he sat in Dean's EOB office that "Mo" Biner was personally connected to John Dean. Had he known, he said, "That would have changed the picture a whole lot." Rudy stated that the entire proceedings would have had a different character if he had known that Maureen Biner was Dean's lover; that is to say, if Rudy knew that Dean had a personal interest in Bailley's records. Then he would have more properly understood that Dean's motives were personal and that he was *not* acting "on behalf of the president of the United States." But this was not revealed by Dean.

The secretary soon returned with Bailley's address book and the copies of its pages, which Dean then checked to see if all the pages were there, and then against the White House personnel list, circling certain names with a pen as he did so. "He was very meticulous," Rudy told us. After about forty-five minutes, Rudy and Smith went back to their offices, taking the book and photos but leaving with Dean the photocopied pages.

A few days later, Rudy wrote a five-page summary of the Bailley case for the file, in which he spent a paragraph detailing the meeting with Dean at the EOB. In a recent interview, he remembered this document especially, because others involved with the prosecution of Bailley complimented him and called it the best summary of the case.

As for John Dean, immediately after Rudy and Smith left the EOB, he called a middle-level official in an independent agency across from the White House and told him that one of the female attorneys who served under him had her name in Bailley's book and that he, Dean, had seen her nude picture as taken by Bailley. Called on the carpet, the female attorney, who had no connection to any call-girl ring, said she had briefly been in love with Bailley and denied any wrongdoing. By 5:30 P.M. that afternoon, she had been forced to resign. Now Dean had a scalp to show for the meeting with Rudy, should he ever be asked what action he had taken as a result of it. But he did not create any permanent record of his meeting with Rudy and Smith through memos to the file, to his superiors, or to the Department of Justice—as he normally did with important matters—and has not spoken publicly, written, or testified about it, ever since.

Recently, we asked Haldeman and Lawrence Higby (Haldeman's top aide, and the proper channel for something like the Bailley case) about this matter. They knew nothing of a Dean meeting with local prosecutors to request evidence earmarked for a pending criminal case. We pressed further: Was that the proper way for Dean to go about the task of protecting the White House in such a sensitive matter? Both men responded that it was not, that a standard procedure had been established and promulgated. Under it, Dean would be in touch with them, to ask for and receive from them permission to call Assistant Attorney General Henry E. Petersen, head of the criminal division at Justice, and make the request to the prosecutors through that correct channel. Petersen could have been urged to make haste, to answer Dean's question and possibly to provide a copy of the address book, and all the answers and materials would have come back through the same channel from Justice. But if it had been done that way, other people would have known of John Dean's extraordinary interest in the affairs of Phillip Mackin Bailley.

Liddy had been having problems with McCord and the material coming from the bug in the DNC. The logs from McCord, which he said came from Baldwin and which Liddy reedited and had his secretary type up, showed nothing of interest. Liddy was almost embarrassed to pass them on. Yet he felt he had to show something, and on June 8 put the transcribed logs in an envelope for Magruder, with expectations that Jeb would give it to Mitchell.

According to Magruder, he did pass it on, in two directions. He first showed it to Strachan, who reported back that "It was junk." The next day, in Magruder's account, he had a private meeting at the CRP offices with John Mitchell in which they reviewed the logs. Mitchell then supposedly called Liddy in and said, "This stuff is not worth the paper it's printed on." Magruder told us that he has a vivid recollection of this meeting and added that it happened so quickly that Liddy didn't even get a chance to sit down.

This account, of course, at least implicitly tied John Mitchell to the second break-in.

Once again, however, we do not believe Magruder's account. In his Senate testimony and later interviews with us, Mitchell denied this meeting with Liddy, or reviewing the logs of the bugging. Liddy also contradicts Magruder and says that this meeting never occurred.

In Liddy's account, he was called in to Magruder's office on June 12 and asked by Magruder if the bug could be replaced. Liddy said that it could, but there was no money in the budget for another Watergate entry, and besides, they wanted to go into McGovern's headquarters. Magruder ignored this and asked him how many file cabinets were in the DNC. Then he got to the heart of the matter. Banging the lower left drawer of his own desk, Jeb told Liddy, "Here's what I want to know. I want to know what O'Brien's got right here."

Liddy understood the reference completely, for in that drawer, he knew, Magruder kept his own derogatory information on the Democrats.

Liddy bought the idea hook, line, and sinker—so completely that he was convinced when he wrote in 1980 that this was the previously unknown key to the break-in. He shouted it in his book by italicizing his conclusion: *"The purpose of the second Watergate break-in was to find out what O'Brien had of a derogatory nature about us, not for us to get something on him or the Democrats."* Liddy says that it was not until June 15 that he briefly got to see Mitchell and to slip on the corner of Mitchell's desk a blank envelope containing the bugging logs; even at that moment, Liddy says, he was not able to discuss the bugging, and certainly did not receive any direct authorization to go in a second time from Mitchell. He didn't even ask for it, since he already had such authorization from Magruder.

Confronted by us with these contradictions, Magruder refused to give up the idea that he had met with Mitchell and Liddy about the logs, but he admitted to us that Liddy's version of the events was correct—and that he, Magruder, had been told by John Dean to obtain derogatory information about Republicans that the Democrats kept at their Watergate headquarters, and that Dean, not Mitchell, had directed him to have Liddy and his men go back into the DNC to obtain this information.

Magruder was not eager to give us that acknowledgment. At first he said only that the order to go back into the Watergate "came from Strachan or Dean," but when pressed, he amended his attribution of the order and said, "I'm sure it was Dean."

Maxie Wells went on vacation in early June, and she gave a key to her desk to another woman at the DNC, Barbara Kennedy, for use in case the desk had to be opened while she was away. Maxie was back at work by June 12, and on that day received at the DNC a visitor who announced himself as "Bill Bailey."

He was actually McCord's man Alfred Baldwin, and he bore a strong physical resemblance to Phil Bailley. He had been sent into the DNC, he later told the Senate investigating committee, by McCord, in order to get the layout of the place. He knew before he entered that both Larry O'Brien and Spencer Oliver were out of town. To receptionist Clota Yesbeck he expressed disappointment, and was passed on to Maxie Wells. Later, in her own debriefing by the Senate committee, Yesbeck said that she believed Baldwin had been in the DNC to see Maxie many times before—but she may well have been confused by the name he gave her on entering and his physical resemblance to Phil Bailey, who had been in and out of the DNC more than a few times. Then too, the Bailey name was one to conjure with inside the Democratic stronghold, for it was borne by an important Democrat from Connecticut; Baldwin has at times said that he claimed to have been that Bailey's nephew, though at other times has not pressed this notion.

But why would McCord have sent Baldwin in to get the lay of the land, if there had already been a break-in and the burglars already knew the setup? There must have been another reason.

Baldwin made sure that he saw Maxie Wells by telling Yesbeck that he was a friend of Spencer Oliver's. Yesbeck passed him on, and returned to her duties in the reception area. Then something happened either between Baldwin and Wells, or while Baldwin was in proximity to Wells's desk. We can't say precisely what, but we do know that after the burglars were caught, the key to Maxie's desk was found in the possession of burglar Rolando Martinez.

The presence of the key was one startling thing. Another was the absence of any in-place bug or transmitting device. Just a day or two before the second break-in on June 17—but after Baldwin's visit—the telephone company swept the DNC phones for bugs and found none. And just after the break-in, the police and the FBI made their own sweeps and found no in-place bugs. In other words, the bug that had been installed during the first break-in, on the frequently used phone in the office of the chairman of the State Governors, the bug from which Baldwin overheard conversations and passed on logs about them to McCord and Liddy—that bug was *not* found at all. It seems likely, though we cannot prove it, that Baldwin either somehow obtained a key from Wells, or stole one; and just as likely that while in the DNC on June 12 he removed whatever bugs McCord had placed there. If McCord had shown him the location on a diagram, the removal of a bug would have taken Baldwin only a few seconds.

Baldwin left the DNC. Several days later, the burglars came to town.

On June 15, 1972, Phil Bailey and his attorney Edwin C. Brown, along with assistant United States attorneys John Rudy and Vincent Alto, appeared before U.S. District Court Judge Charles R. Richey in the federal courthouse in downtown Washington, D.C., for Bailey's arraignment. What occurred during this arraignment, and how it was altered in later proceedings, was so highly unusual that it bears some close scrutiny. It started out in a normal fashion, with Rudy presenting the twenty-two-count indictment and the defendant being asked how he pleaded. As expected, Bailley pleaded not guilty to all counts, and a date was set, fifteen days hence, for a trial status conference. Rudy informed Judge Richey that the government had "no objection to Mr. Bailley's release on personal recognizance," meaning that Bailley would not be required to post any bond and would be allowed to be free and responsible himself for showing up in court at such later time when a trial or any other judicial proceedings would begin. So far, so standard.

Judge Richey was a presidential appointee who owed his recently acquired lifetime seat on the federal bench to Vice President Spiro Agnew. He had been assigned the Bailley case by a regular lottery system. We are not certain if he first learned of this case at the arraignment, but as the reader will recall, the *Star* had on June 9 carried a front-page story about the case, characterizing it as a call-girl ring with a White House connection. On June 10, the *Washington Post* had weighed in with its own front-page story, quoting courthouse sources as saying that "the White House had shown a special interest in the case and was exerting pressure on prosecutors not to comment on it." In any event, the June 15 arraignment proceedings before Judge Richey would take an extraordinary turn.

After stating that the prosecution had "no objection to Mr. Bailley's release on personal recognizance," the prosecutor proposed two things at once—first, to advise of an alternative to Bailley being released without bond (or released at all), and second, to disassociate himself and the government from that same alternative. He suggested that Judge Richey might wish to act on his own—the legal phrase is *sua sponte*—and specifically not at the request of the government, to order Bailley to be immediately committed to St. Elizabeth's Hospital for a sixty-day period to determine if he was mentally competent.

What transpired—the commitment of a practicing attorney to a notoriously understaffed mental hospital—was highly unusual. This is so particularly where neither the accused nor his counsel had been afforded prior notice that the issue of his commitment would be raised.

Almost embarrassed, Rudy now suggested that the rest of this discussion be held *in camera*, that is, in the judge's chambers, away from the public and the press, so that Rudy could present "certain objects and facts which we believe might justify this court" in sending Bailley to St. Elizabeth's. In effect, Rudy was asking Richey to view the "objects and facts" privately—while making it clear that if the judge wished to commit Bailley for observation, he'd have to do so on his own, without the prosecution requesting the commitment.

Richey, his clerk, Rudy, two U.S. marshals, a court reporter, and the rather stunned Bailley and his lawyer Brown adjourned immediately to an adjoining, unused jury room, where Richey convened a hearing on whether Bailley should be committed. In it, Rudy showed the judge the "objects and facts," i.e., the same photographs he had displayed to John Dean six days earlier, and argued from these that Bailley engaged in unusual sexual practices. He buttressed the point by graphic descriptions of photographs, sexual aids, and the motion picture films seized from Bailley's apartment.

Rudy told the court that "Mr. Bailley took photographs of females, a wide variety of females, in the nude. Some of these females were asked to engage in various acts such as putting whipped cream on their bodies. . . . This was done at Mr. Bailley's request for the purpose of exciting Mr. Bailley at a later time when he could look at these photographs, giving him a thrill so to speak beyond the normal act of sexual intercourse."

All of these showed, Rudy argued, that there was "something the matter with Mr. Bailley." Rudy suggested that these sexual materials might cause the court to want to determine, "*sua sponte*," whether Bailley "is competent to stand trial, but, more importantly, to see whether he suffered some mental disease or defect [insanity under D.C. law] at the time" of the alleged crimes. How these sexual depictions and paraphernalia had any bearing on whether Bailley was competent to understand the charges against him and aid in his own defense, or was insane, were questions that were not truly addressed. In summation, Rudy added, once again, that any proposed commitment of Bailley to a mental hospital would be *sua sponte*, and not at the government's request.

Attorney Brown attempted to cut through the prosecutorial baloney and to argue that while Bailley might have been quite sexually inventive, these activities had to do with consenting adults, and that none of Rudy's "objects or facts" were "sufficient for a showing to have him committed or to have him examined with reference to some possible defect." He was adamant that Bailley was not even faintly considering a defense of insanity against the pending charges. He vigorously opposed the idea of his client being committed.

Nonetheless, Richey concluded these secret proceedings—where none of the photos, sexual aids, motion pictures, or unmentioned address books made their way into the court file—by ruling that Bailley would be sent to the mental hospital as soon as a bed could be found. And then he added a further *sua sponte* condition on Bailley's freedom: a gag order, restraining "the accused and his counsel, as well as government counsel" from engaging in "any *further* publicity, pre-trial publicity." Richey's words suggest that he may well have known about the press attention to this case.

Richey's ruling was a complete contradiction: On the one hand Richey would commit Bailley to a mental hospital to determine if he was competent, and on the other hand Richey would allow Bailley to remain free and to practice law until a bed became available at St. Elizabeth's. The discussion included the fact that Bailley was going to be able to continue to represent clients and to appear in court on their behalf while waiting for a bed to become available at St. Elizabeth's. Richey evidently believed that Bailley was competent to represent clients, but not himself.

All of this would have been enough to raise plenty of questions, as well as eyebrows. But what happened next was confusion bordering on deception in the official court docket sheets of the case. Rudy had disassociated the government from responsibility for Bailley's commitment. But the docket entry on the file was written to state falsely that Bailley was committed to St. Elizabeth's upon "the oral motion of the government." And a second document on the date of the arraignment, the actual court order committing Bailley, signed by Richey, says in effect that Richey committed Bailley because Bailley and his counsel asked to have Bailley committed! The operative paragraph reads, "Upon consideration of the motion by the Defendant for an examination of the mental competency. . . ." Down on the bottom of the second page, Bailley's attorney Brown signed it with the notation, "seen and approved." But Brown had objected to Bailley's commitment, and so had Bailley.

When Rudy noticed the error in the docket entry that erroneously identified the government as having asked for Bailley's commitment, he became upset. Rudy was so upset that, before the status hearing on June 30, he asked Bailley co-counsel Allan M. Palmer to take the matter up with Judge Richey. Palmer informed Richey, on the record, that the docket sheet was in error, and that the docket sheet should have read *sua sponte*, meaning that Richey acted on his own. Richey made no response on the record to the pointing out of this error, and the documents were not changed nor any addendum made—the docket sheet in the court file still reads that Bailley was committed upon motion of the government, and the court order still reads that Bailley asked to have himself committed.

Consider: Bailley was gagged and committed to a mental hospital on the day of his arraignment. However, the record of who initiated Bailley's commitment procedure was confusing, was in conflict with the facts and with itself—was false. "The only reason Bailley was sent to St. Elizabeth's was to discredit him," John Rudy recently told us. But who would want Bailley discredited? Why would it have to be done right away? Why discredit a presumed innocent defendant in a criminal case, particularly when that defendant was a member in good standing of the bar? And why would an unrequested gag order be issued in this case?

We know that John Dean had an extraordinary interest in the address book; and we have also seen that there is strong evidence linking Dean to the break-ins at the DNC. Not only did Dean express an interest in Bailley's case, he had a girlfriend whose name and Clout nickname were in an address book along with the alias of her friend Heidi Rikan, an address book that might well be introduced into evidence in a Mann Act court case.

Judge Charles Richey would not talk with us directly, but when a third party asked Judge Richey about these matters, he asserted that he had never met or spoken to John Dean at any time about any subject, Bailley or otherwise; that he knew nothing of Dean's meeting with Rudy and Smith; and that he had little memory of the proceeding in which he had ordered Bailley committed to St. Elizabeth's.

While the initial case was pending, a second grand jury was convened by Rudy, in response to the *Star* article, to look into the possibility of a call-girl ring. Rudy told us recently that he had issued subpoenas in this case to the women listed in Bailley's address book— the one he had shown Dean.

Only about 10 percent of those served came to the grand jury to testify, Rudy remembers. If a woman was out of town, the prosecutors went on without her. As for those who did come in, as a way of identifying them Rudy compared the women to those depicted in the photographs found in Bailley's apartment. This unusual procedure etched the entire sequence of events deeply in Rudy's memory.

As Maureen Dean reported in her book, a bit earlier in the year she found herself precipitously dropped because John wanted to enjoy his freedom. Then had come a reconciliation, and even an engagement. Then, she writes, there was a sudden break: "I realized that John was not ready to marry me and would not be for some time. There was only one course for me: to quit my job, return to Los Angeles, and disappear." So that's what she did, disappearing effectively for the entire summer of 1972. Dean's own version of this event, reported in *Blind Ambition*, puts the date of the breakup in late June of 1972. We know from Rudy that the subpoenas were served during that same period.

Rudy's second grand jury called Bailley's parents and some of his seven sisters, and had only one question for them: Where was Jeannine? They all testified that she was backpacking in Europe and could not be reached.

Out of this second grand jury came a second indictment that superseded the first, and again made no mention of any charges relating to any call-girl ring. This new and slightly longer indictment was given an entirely new case number. Usually, such a second indictment that supersedes a pending indictment would retain the number of the first one, in order to prevent confusion and to keep a record of the proceedings that had been amassed in the first case. Here, just the opposite happened: the presence of a new, and seemingly unrelated, case number assigned to the second indictment had the effect of making the first Bailley case, and its paper trail, all but disappear. Any reporter who wanted to find out about the Bailley proceedings would find only a file with the new case number 1718-72, and would not have been able to discern from this file the relevant matters that had occurred in the first case, such as the secret commitment hearing, the confusion about who had proposed the defendant's commitment to the mental asylum, and other matters. And that was good news for anyone seeking to bury Phil Bailley and his address books before they became the focus of intense scrutiny.

We will return to Bailley and the devastating disposition of his case later in this book, in temporal sequence.

We come at last to the second and final Watergate break-in, the one to which most Americans refer as the beginning of the case that resulted in many people going to prison and in the resignation of Richard Nixon. Eight men were involved in the execution, supervision, and observation of the break-in that night of June 16–17: Gordon Liddy, Howard Hunt, James McCord, Alfred Baldwin, Bernard Barker, Frank Sturgis, Rolando Martinez, and Virgilio Gonzalez. The men from Miami were staying at the Watergate hotel, and Liddy agreed to meet everyone in Room 214 at 8:00 P.M., the hour at which guards at the Watergate office building made the last regular inspection of the premises before a midnight check. Liddy arrived late, having had a scare when he jumped a light and was pulled over by a traffic officer. McCord, Martinez, Gonzalez, and Sturgis were eating lobster tails in the Watergate hotel restaurant. Upstairs in 214, Liddy found lights, camera stands, and men practicing rapid-fire photography because they'd have to shoot so many photos during the time they were at the DNC headquarters.

Because of the rush, the ostensible need to change the bugs, and the recent Magruder insistence on photographing everything, many details had not been completed. For instance, only earlier that evening, Baldwin had to be sent out to buy some extra wire and some batteries for a microphone-transmitter that McCord was concealing in a smoke alarm to be placed on a wall; he'd found the batteries but not the wire. McCord told him to solder the batteries together, and Baldwin managed to melt them. Liddy was told by McCord that some of the other battery-operated transceiver units were low and hadn't been recharged; Liddy couldn't believe how sloppy the bugging preparations were— but then, he himself was a perfectionist.

He was not, however, the surreptitious entry expert, and left the particulars of that to McCord and the other ex–CIA men. It was a Friday night, and the expectation had been that the DNC would be vacant, but lights in the Democratic headquarters stayed on and on, and Liddy decided to delay the break-in from a scheduled 10:00 P.M. until after midnight.

Using the pretext of delivering a typewriter, McCord got himself into the office building. According to the logs maintained by the Watergate's private security service, General Security Services, Inc., McCord, under an alias, signed in at 10:50 P.M. He took the elevator up to the eighth floor, his announced destination—where coincidentally the Federal Reserve Board had recently been burglarized. Then he went quickly through the stairwell all the way down to the garage, taping open doors and stuffing latches with bits of paper on the eighth and sixth floors, the B-2 and B-3 levels, and the doors leading into the underground garage. He returned to the Watergate hotel, then went over to Baldwin's observation post, all before 11:30 P.M.

At the office building, security guard Frank Wills arrived, logged in, and began the scheduled midnight tour of the building. Just as soon as he began, he discovered the tampered locks on B-2 and B-3, returned to the lobby, and wrote down that they had been "stuff with paper." He unstuck these locks, making them work again. Although the stuffing could have been a maintenance man's doing, Wills decided he'd better call his superior, but couldn't reach him immediately, as Captain Bobby Jackson was making rounds in a location about twenty minutes away. Wills left a message on the GSS answering service saying there was a problem and requesting Jackson be contacted by beeper to give instructions. Jackson had some difficulty getting to a phone, and while Wills waited for him he called another supervisor, who told him to check the locks on other floors. If those were taped, too, there could be a burglary in progress; if not taped, the first ones could have been a maintenance man's leftover handiwork. As Wills was preparing to check, a young man came downstairs from the DNC headquarters, and Wills went with him across the street to the Howard Johnson's to get something to eat.

The DNC was now dark, and so was the Watergate office building's lobby—but McCord reached Hunt and Liddy by walkie-talkie and told them, in effect, that the coast was not yet clear. The break-in was delayed. Liddy thought little of this; as we have seen, in the first break-in it was he who had let several hours go by, just to be sure there would be no problems.

Wills returned to his guard post just in time to get Captain Jackson's call, which made the same suggestion he'd previously gotten from the other supervisor: check the other locks before hitting the panic button. Before making that inspection, Wills evidently decided to finish his cheeseburger.

Gordon Liddy at the command post was dependent on information from McCord, who wasn't sitting tight. Every few minutes, he seemed to be somewhere else—the HoJo's restaurant, the exterior of the complex, the Baldwin listening post. McCord arrived at Room 214 at 1:05 A.M., claiming he had been across the street in the garage, checking the locks. If he had, he would have discovered that Wills had unstuffed them. It is not clear if McCord was just trying to explain away a delay to a nervous group of men, or if this was a deliberate lie. The burglars set out. Hunt and Liddy were to remain behind in 214, connected to the McCord group and to Baldwin by walkie-talkies. Five minutes later, when the business-suited burglars reached the B-2 door, they found it relocked, and couldn't get in.

From here on, accounts differ. As author Jim Hougan first revealed in his 1984 book *Secret Agenda*, based on conversations with a number of the participants in the burglary, after finding the way blocked, McCord, Barker, and Martinez went back to confer with Hunt and Liddy while Gonzalez tried to pick the lock and Sturgis acted as his bodyguard. The decision to go back in was made by Liddy, over Hunt's objection. Liddy reasoned that a maintenance man could have undone the lock-stuffing, and that since no alarm had been raised, the coast was actually clear.

The burglary group left the Watergate hotel so quickly that they were incredibly sloppy. Though they carried false identification, on their persons they had many things that would tie them to Hunt, Liddy, the CRP, and the White House—a key to Room 214, $100 bills that had come from the money previously laundered by Barker for Liddy, and a pop-up address book notebook with Howard Hunt's name in it. The Cubans especially felt they had nothing to fear by dashing off for this burglary, for they were intensely loyal to Howard Hunt and knew he wouldn't do anything to harm them. Hunt had given particular instructions to Martinez, but, acting as a good cutout should, hadn't said where the instructions had originated.

To recap: Liddy thought the men were aiming for O'Brien's office. Hunt—according to Martinez—had given Martinez a marked floor plan showing the target in the Oliver/Wells/Governors section of the DNC as well as a key to Maxie Wells's desk. Howard Hunt has denied giving a key or a floor plan to Martinez or any of the burglars, but, as the reader will recall, Hunt did confirm that the target of the first break-in was a phone Hunt said was used by Wells and Oliver.

It was 1:30 A.M., June 17, 1972. Gonzalez had been successful in opening and retaping the door. The burglars were able to enter from the garage to the building, and they went in and up the stairs. After several minutes, McCord reappeared and joined them in the stairwell; then the five men walked up to the sixth floor.

The burglars were trying to get into the DNC offices proper when Frank Wills discovered that the B-2 lock had been retaped. Returning to the lobby, Wills discussed this with the just arrived Federal Reserve Board office's guard Walter Hellams, who wanted to call the police. Wills wasn't ready yet. He telephoned the man who had had the shift before him to find out if there had been any taped locks on that shift; the man said no. Wills called Jackson again and informed him of the new taping, and it was only after this that Wills telephoned the District of Columbia police. At 1:52, the call went out from the dispatcher and was picked up by a unit of plainclothesmen only a block and a half from the Watergate, who said they'd respond. One of the policeman, Carl Shoffler, had hair down to his shoulders.

Meanwhile, McCord, Martinez, Barker, Sturgis, and Gonzalez had with some difficulty removed a door and gotten into the DNC suite and were moving about, though not in Larry O'Brien's office. They were in the offices near Virginia Avenue and the terrace, those belonging to Oliver and Wells and the office of the press secretary on the other side of Oliver's. Martinez was setting up a camera atop Maxie Wells's desk.

After some confabulation in the lobby with Wills and Hellams, the three police officers and two guards went up a stairwell to the eighth floor, the logical place to begin looking for burglars since the Federal Reserve Board office on that floor had been recently hit. Inside the DNC on the sixth floor, Martinez heard noise of their tramping up the stairs. McCord told him it was probably the regular two o'clock inspection round, and advised Barker to turn off his walkie-talkie to prevent the static from being heard. The police and guards had a hard time getting into the FRB on the eighth floor, decided no one was in there, and then headed down, stopping to look at the seventh floor, and then at the sixth.

Now Baldwin in the HoJo's could see the interlopers. Over the walkie-talkie he rather casually asked Liddy in Room 214, "Hey, any of our guys wearin' hippie clothes?" "Negative," Liddy replied. "All our people are in business suits. Why?" Baldwin told him they had "trouble": men with guns on the sixth floor.

Inside the DNC, the burglars deduced that the jig was up. McCord grabbed some papers from the press secretary's desk—application blanks for press credentials at the convention by campus newspapers, a memo on where to get low-cost dormitory rooms in Miami, and a memo on allowable travel expenses. Then the burglars all hid behind desks. "They got us," Barker whispered over the walkie-talkie. Rolando Martinez thought about what was happening and decided that he and his fellow Miamians had been betrayed by James McCord.

Guns drawn, the police and guards entered the DNC offices, discovered the men hiding behind the desks, and ordered them to stand up and "assume the position"—hands against a wall, legs spread—for a pat-down. The burglars complied readily, almost with nonchalance, and offered no resistance. They looked so odd, in business suits and wearing rubber gloves, that the police assumed they were dealing with professionals, probably men from organized crime who might well be armed. No weapons were found. Somebody called for backup units, and from nearby streets squad cars with lights flashing began heading for the building.

Realizing that this was not a crime involving street criminals, Shoffler and the two other plainclothesmen proceeded with care, so as to produce from their searches of the burglars the sort of solid, properly taken evidence that would stand up in court. Shoffler recalls,

> We put them all against the wall and I was going to be the listing officer and [fellow officer John] Barrett was going to be the searching officer. That being the case we only patted them for weapons and then left them on the wall so that Barrett could go one by one to seize items from them.

While under arrest with his hands against the wall, Martinez took a calculated and highly dangerous risk, one that could have cost him his life. He reached inside his coat pocket for something. When Shoffler saw Martinez do this, he immediately slammed and wrestled the Cuban until he was neutralized. "I almost had to break his arm off," Shoffler remembers. Shoffler searched him thoroughly to see what Martinez had been trying so desperately to get rid of: It was a small key, taped to the back of a notebook. Martinez has acknowledged to us that he was trying to get rid of the key that he says was given to him by Howard Hunt, and that this action by Shoffler prevented him from doing so.

Shoffler asked Martinez what the key was for, but got no answer. He decided not to remove it from the notebook and try it on any of the desks, realizing that to do so might compromise the evidence. The burglars had lots of loose keys, mostly blanks, and lock-picking equipment. Of more immediate concern was the smoke alarm device—the police thought it might be a bomb.

The function of Martinez's key would not become apparent until ten days later, when the FBI by trial and error discovered that it fit the desk of Maxie Wells. When interviewed about this by the FBI, both Wells and Barbara Kennedy—to whom Wells had given the spare key to her desk—were able to produce their keys. But, according to the available FBI reports, neither woman was asked the obvious follow-up questions: *Why* would a Watergate burglar have a key to Wells's desk in his possession, and what items of possible interest to a Watergate burglar were maintained in Wells's locked desk drawer? Although another DNC employee told us that Wells was interviewed by the FBI "four or five times," no reports of additional Wells/Martinez key interviews are to be found in the official Watergate files at the National Archives or at the J. Edgar Hoover Building in Washington, D.C. And curiously, two years later, when testifying about the break-in before the Senate Watergate committee, Wells would avoid disclosing her knowledge that Martinez had in his possession a key to her desk. Howard S. Liebengood, assistant counsel to the minority staff of the committee, confirmed to us that the information Maxie Wells kept to herself, if known to the minority staff, could have significantly altered the focus of the investigation.

In the Watergate hotel, Hunt knew it was all over, and told Liddy they'd have to get out quickly, because Barker had the key to the hotel room. Soon, the cops would come there. They exited so rapidly that they didn't have time to clean out the second room, and so left behind electronic equipment, $100 bills that matched sequentially with those in the burglars' pockets, a Barker address book that also contained Hunt's White House telephone number, and a check made out by Hunt to a local country club. Liddy got in his jeep and prepared to go home, as Hunt said he'd take care of Baldwin and the observation post. Hunt went into the HoJo's and found Baldwin calmly looking over the scene across the avenue, observing the squad cars with lights, and McCord and the other burglars being led out of the building and into a paddy wagon. Hunt wanted Baldwin out of town, but Baldwin complained that he had a lot of stuff to load. By his own account, Hunt then told him to load it up in McCord's van and get away. Baldwin took everything out of the room, but then drove the van and the electronic equipment, including the walkie-talkies that matched the one taken from Barker in the DNC, to McCord's home in a Maryland suburb. Then he got out of town, heading for Connecticut.

Gordon Liddy reached his own home about three in the morning, thinking about all the files and the evidence linking this burglary to higher-ups that he'd have to destroy when he got to the office the next morning. He knew that McCord's fingerprints were on file, since McCord had been in government service, which meant he would be "made" within twenty-four hours and his employment easily traced to the CRP. That, of course, would place Liddy himself in jeopardy, even if all the burglars kept their mouths shut. His wife stirred in bed and asked him if anything was wrong.

"There was trouble. Some people got caught. I'll probably be going to jail," he told her, then climbed into bed and tried to get some sleep.

10

LOS ANGELES AND MANILA: THE COVER-UP BEGINS

THE story of the arrests at the Watergate came too late for most of the newspapers in the United States to print it in their Saturday editions, so many Americans first learned from their Sunday newspapers on June 18, 1972, that five men had been arrested at gunpoint inside the headquarters of the Democratic National Committee on the sixth floor of the Watergate office building in Washington. Richard Nixon chose in his autobiography to chronicle his first reaction as a response to the front-page story in that Sunday's *Miami Herald*, sentiments that reflected the views of most who read similar stories that day:

It sounded preposterous: Cubans in surgical gloves bugging the DNC! I dismissed it as some sort of prank. . . . The whole thing made so little sense. *Why?* I wondered. Why then? Why in such a blundering way? And why, of all places, the Democratic National Committee? Anyone who knew anything about politics would know that a national committee headquarters was a useless place to go for inside information on a

161

presidential campaign. The whole thing was so senseless and bungled that it almost looked like some kind of a setup.

Insiders to the events reacted with considerably more intensity. To Jeb Magruder, deputy director of the reelection committee, news of the arrests brought an attack of panic. On June 17, the morning of the break-in, Magruder was in Los Angeles traveling with John Mitchell, Fred LaRue, and Robert C. Mardian, political coordinator of the CRP. Political meetings were scheduled for that day, and a Bel Air party with entertainment industry celebrities for the coming evening. Magruder, several other campaign officials, and their wives were having breakfast in the Polo Lounge of the Beverly Hills Hotel when Jeb was paged and a telephone brought to his table. It was 8:00 A.M., and Gordon Liddy was on the line. Liddy had first tried to reach Magruder at 7:00 A.M. Washington, D.C., time, only to learn that Magruder was in California, where it was 4:00 A.M., and decided that it was too early to call. Liddy spent the intervening hours at CRP, shredding documents associated with the break-in and other campaign activities, and when CRP Deputy Press Director Powell A. Moore arrived Liddy told him of McCord's arrest. Moore informed Liddy that Mitchell was to hold a news conference in California that afternoon, and would undoubtedly be asked about the break-in. Liddy headed to the Situation Room at the White House to call Magruder on an absolutely secure phone. He still had a pass, thanks to John Dean's intervention with the Secret Service, who had tried to revoke it.

From the White House, Liddy reached Magruder at the Polo Lounge, but wouldn't tell him the news. He insisted that Magruder rush to the nearest military base and call him back from a similarly secure phone. Magruder protested and went instead to a nearby pay phone, whence he called the White House. Liddy told him of the botched break-in and that McCord and the burglars had been caught. Of course they had all given aliases, but these would soon be seen through by the police, and it would become evident that McCord, the security chief of the president's reelection committee, had been apprehended in the act of trying to bug the opposition's headquarters.

"What the hell was McCord doing inside the Watergate?" the apoplectic Magruder shouted into the pay phone. "You were supposed to keep this operation removed from us. Have you lost your mind?" Liddy accepted full responsibility for having used McCord inside, but tried to keep Magruder focused on what he saw as the more pressing problem, relaying the information to Mitchell so a statement could be prepared for the press conference.

Magruder remembered the phone calls differently. In Jeb's version, it was not Liddy but himself who raised the urgency of talking to Mitchell. "I've got to talk to Mitchell. Stay by the phone. We'll get back to you," he quoted himself as saying in his memoir, *An American Life*. For most people, including the Senate committee, the investigating reporters, the courts, and the American public, Magruder's transfer of information to Mitchell triggered the Watergate cover-up, an action in which Magruder himself was understood to be only a minor player.

Recently, however, when we confronted him with evidence to the contrary, Magruder began to change his story and to agree that there was far more to what happened that Saturday morning than he had ever previously revealed. This was a painful realization for him, and to understand it we must point out that Magruder has changed considerably in the years since Watergate. When we interviewed him, he had become the Presbyterian Reverend Jeb Magruder, assistant pastor of the First Community Church of Columbus, Ohio, and the head of that city's ethics commission, and he recognized that what he was doing, in coming to these new realizations, was admitting that his testimony to the Senate and to the Watergate juries had been untrue.

Why did Magruder originally finger Mitchell? As is now apparent, much of what Magruder said about the events of Watergate—and specifically about John Mitchell—was untrue. But in judging Magruder it is necessary to understand the situation in which he found himself in 1973. Dean's story of Watergate had already become the federal prosecutors' and the Senate Watergate committee's accepted version, the benchmark against which anyone else's version was being measured. Everyone we talked to who knew Magruder from the period described him as not a strong person and someone who could not cope with heavy pressure. Magruder described to us his predicament: "The prosecutors were tough and they played real hardball. . . . Their main interest it struck me was not about Dean at all. It was about Mitchell." He said they made it plain to him that "I better cooperate."

Magruder now acknowledges that one of his first actions after being informed of the break-in was to get hold of John Dean. That call to Dean was the real trigger of the Watergate cover-up. That call, and the events it started rolling, have been concealed for many years; in the following pages we will put them all into proper perspective.

In the account that follows, the reader will learn how Magruder and Dean wildly altered time sequences, transposed actions from one person to another, and made allegations that placed the cover-up at the level of Mitchell, Haldeman, Ehrlichman, and, eventually, Nixon.

Magruder's old version of events in the hours following the phone call from Liddy comes from *An American Life*, which Magruder initially told us was his most accurate version of events, compiled from contemporaneous notes. Despite the urgent need to inform Mitchell, Magruder returned to his breakfast and calmly finished eating, in order not to alarm the others. Then he waited almost ninety minutes, until close to 10:00 A.M., to tell anyone else in Los Angeles about the break-in and the arrests. "Breakfast seemed to drag on forever," Magruder wrote in his book, "but when we finally left the Polo Lounge I took Fred LaRue aside and said I had to talk to him in private." To find privacy, they moved upstairs to the third floor, where the campaign entourage was staying, and Mitchell's security director, Stephen B. King, let them into his own room, across the hall from Mitchell's. King's log showed this to be at 9:55 A.M. Mitchell was then in conversation in his suite with Mardian and Thomas Reed, who would later become Secretary of the Air Force. Mitchell was due to leave the hotel at 10:30 and drive with Governor Ronald Reagan to an 11:00 A.M. political meeting across town, so Magruder and LaRue didn't have much time. "Quickly, I told LaRue the facts—McCord and the Cubans had been arrested in Larry O'Brien's office, and Hunt and Liddy might be next," Magruder wrote. LaRue decided that he would go across the hall alone and tell Mitchell, while Magruder waited in King's room. LaRue interrupted the Reed meeting, pulled Mitchell into an adjoining part of the suite, and gave him the bad news. As LaRue later testified to the Senate committee, Mitchell was "very surprised" and exclaimed, "That is incredible."

In Magruder's writing and testimony, after being told of the crisis by LaRue, Mitchell called across the hall for Magruder to come in; then Mitchell, Mardian, LaRue, and Magruder hatched the cover-up. Mitchell, Magruder said, in that rump meeting issued the instruction that began the cover-up, specifically, the attempt to get McCord out of jail before his true identity was discovered. " 'If we could just get [McCord] out of jail before they find out who he is,' " Magruder reported "someone" as suggesting in this meeting, " 'then maybe he could just disappear. . . .' One of us suggested that Mitchell call Dick Kleindienst, his successor as Attorney General, and see if he could help us get McCord out of jail." In Magruder's version, Mitchell then responded that it would be better if Mardian made that call; it was known to them all that Mardian and Kleindienst were friends. Mardian was dispatched to call Kleindienst, who turned out to be then on the golf course. So Mardian next called Liddy and gave him the message to pass to Kleindienst. Then they all went down and joined the Reagan motorcade and were out of telephone touch with anyone for a few hours. On that trip, according to Magruder, security man Steve King asked him why he was brooding, and if he needed help, and Magruder told him it was "just a little p.r. problem back in Washington."

Before proceeding further with the events of that morning, we must point out that Magruder's version of what happened when he first informed Mitchell through LaRue was untrue. "Did Mr. Mitchell give any instructions to anybody after getting that information?" Democratic counsel to the Watergate committee Sam Dash asked Fred LaRue in 1973. "Not at that time," LaRue responded.

According to LaRue, Mardian, King, and Mitchell, after learning the news from LaRue, Mitchell went back into his meeting, finished it, and then went downstairs to meet Reagan. Neither LaRue, Mardian, nor Mitchell, all three have said, issued any instruction that morning to talk to Kleindienst, and never attempted in any way to spring McCord from jail. Furthermore, Mardian, the supposed conveyor of the message to Liddy, hardly knew Liddy, and testified he did not make a call to Liddy.

The fourth witness, Steve King, a former FBI agent who later became chairman of the Wisconsin Republican Party and ran for a U.S. Senate seat in the 1988 Republican primary, remembers the motorcade incident distinctly, because he didn't go on in the cars at all, but, rather, was asked by Mitchell to stay in the hotel and take care of Martha. King told us that Magruder's account of a conversation between them in the car is "absolutely wrong [because] I never made that trip."

But Magruder's previous version has been the accepted one for eighteen years, and its major consequence was to place the launching of the cover-up on John Mitchell's shoulders.

Gordon Liddy's version of what happened in the Watergate affair was not made public until 1980, when he published his memoir, *Will*. In that book, Liddy makes deliberate note of the fact that more than seven years had elapsed since the events of the burglary, and that the statute of limitations on the crimes associated with it had run out; it was one of the reasons why he had waited until then to publish. For the eight years between the burglary and the publication of his book, Liddy maintained silence. He did so, he said, in order to protect the president, to limit the damage to Nixon and his men, and to the political philosophy that Liddy believed he shared with the president. But his silence allowed other people's versions of events to go unchallenged for all those intervening years.

Liddy wrote that the crucial phone call that morning came to him not from Mardian, but from Jeb Magruder, at around noon in Washington, or 9:00 A.M. in Los Angeles—that is, *well before* Magruder reports that he had informed Mitchell of the break-in. Liddy had already talked with Magruder that morning and when Magruder called him this time, "I was set for another bout of sniveling," Liddy wrote, "but it never came: instead he had a message from Mitchell. I was to find Dick Kleindienst, the Attorney General, and ask him to get McCord out of jail immediately." The precise words he was to convey were, "Tell him 'John sent you,' and it's a 'personal request from John.' He'll understand." Liddy thought this was a terrible idea, but, ever the good soldier, he started to carry it out. "I hung up and asked Powell Moore where I'd be likely to find Dick Kleindienst at noon on Saturday." Burning Tree golf course, Moore said, and they discussed the idea for a while.

We spoke recently with Moore, who confirmed his clear impression that the call to Liddy came from Magruder and said he remembers the events distinctly, because he was standing beside Liddy and because he, too, thought that asking Kleindienst to spring McCord was "the dumbest idea I ever heard of." They already had enough problems with a CRP employee being arrested in the DNC headquarters, and "to drag the attorney general into it is stupid." Liddy insisted that he must follow orders, and Moore said he'd go with him to Burning Tree, "because, frankly, I was concerned about Kleindienst."

They found the attorney general at lunch at the golf course at about 12:30 P.M., and convinced him to move into the locker room, where they couldn't be overheard. Kleindienst already knew of the break-in, having learned about it from Assistant Attorney General Henry Petersen earlier in the morning, but Kleindienst had no details. Liddy told him directly that the burglary had been an operation of the intelligence arm of the CRP, and that he himself had been in charge. Liddy then said he had a message from Mitchell to deliver, and Kleindienst interrupted to ask if he'd heard it from Mitchell directly. Liddy told him it had come through Magruder, and proceeded to ask him to spring McCord as a "personal request from John."

Kleindienst was stunned. His reaction, he later told the Watergate committee, was "instantaneous and abrupt. . . . The relationship I had with Mr. Mitchell was such that I do not believe that he would have sent a person like Gordon Liddy to come out and talk to me about anything. He knew where he could find me twenty-four hours a day." Kleindienst told Liddy that he could not and would not do what Liddy asked.

The testimonies, memories, and writings of Liddy, Kleindienst, and Moore all agree on this version of events, and so does the timing. Magruder remains absolutely certain that he didn't convey his message about McCord's arrest to Mitchell (through LaRue) until ten in the morning; Steve King's log puts the time of Magruder's arrival in the room across the hall at precisely 9:55 A.M. If that was the case—and all the evidence substantiates it—then the conversation in the locker room at the Burning Tree golf club could not have legitimately invoked Mitchell's name. Because when Liddy, Moore, and Kleindienst were in the locker room, it was only 9:30 A.M. back in Los Angeles, and Mitchell had not even talked to LaRue.

The Watergate committee and the courts were told of these discrepancies; in fact, Powell Moore was closely questioned about them, and never wavered in his position on the timing of the call and the substance of his discussions with Liddy and the ways in which Kleindienst acted. And there was other evidence that the committee also ignored—the testimonies of Mardian, LaRue, and Kleindienst, for instance—because the committee's focus was on Magruder's roping in of Mitchell and Mitchell's supposed culpability for the beginning of the cover-up. Mardian, for instance, told the committee that if Mitchell had instructed him to get a message to Kleindienst, he "would have instructed me to call Kleindienst myself. I didn't need an intermediary for him. Mr. Kleindienst is a close friend of mine."

So the Watergate committee didn't look to poke holes in Magruder's testimony implicating Mitchell, and neither did the Watergate Special Prosecutor's office, which later indicted Mitchell, Mardian, and five other Nixon aides on charges of conspiracy, obstruction of justice, and other offenses; one of the first "overt acts" with which they were charged was Mitchell's supposed order to Liddy to ask Kleindienst to get McCord out of jail. As readers shall discover as these chapters progress, nearly all of the men charged in that indictment had not actually committed the specific acts with which they were charged, and on which they were later convicted. (Mardian's conviction was reversed on appeal.)

The evidence is overwhelming that Magruder made the call to Liddy and told him to importune Kleindienst without consulting Mitchell or anyone else in the CRP hierarchy, and that he did so even before Mitchell learned that burglars had been caught in the DNC. We confronted Magruder with the evidence, especially with the conflicting time sequences, and Magruder now acknowledges that he, not Mardian, must have called Liddy and said "something to the effect, 'We've got to figure out how to get this thing done.' . . . I must have said something to [Liddy] about that we ought to try to talk to Kleindienst." Later in the interview, Magruder tried to backpedal, emphasizing repeatedly that he could not himself have been responsible for starting the cover-up, but then again conceded, "I could have said something like you ought to try to talk to Kleindienst." Then, in a later interview, Magruder admitted, "I didn't see Mitchell until later." So, Mitchell didn't send you, didn't send Mardian, didn't send anybody? we asked. "Right," said Magruder.

Did Magruder really act on his own in directing Liddy to go to Kleindienst? We have talked to more than a dozen people who knew Magruder at that time, and all describe him in that time frame as a cautious, often indecisive man who was not inclined to take any actions unless those were endorsed by a superior; in Washington parlance, Magruder was not a self-starter. Magruder agrees in part to this characterization of his old self: "The fact is that the way I worked— and anybody would tell you, anybody who knew me—I would never start a cover-up on my own."

In fact, he started it because of a conversation that Saturday morning with John Dean.

On the morning of June 17, White House counsel John Dean was in Manila, where he had traveled with officials from the U.S. Bureau of Narcotics and Dangerous Drugs, an agency of the Justice Department. Dean knew some of the BNDD officials personally, and they had invited him as the representative of the president to present a graduation address at the BNDD training school in Manila. Even Philippine president Ferdinand Marcos would be there to hear him. Dean had received clearance for a four-day trip, from June 14 to June 18.

In evaluating the following events, it is important to remember that during the month of June, Manila is twelve hours ahead of Eastern Daylight Time, and fifteen hours ahead of Pacific Daylight Time. For instance, the arrests of the burglars were made at 2:30 A.M. on June 17, Washington time, but 2:30 P.M. Manila time, the same day. And the Liddy-Magruder calls, made between 8:00 A.M. and 9:00 A.M. Los Angeles time on June 17, were made between eleven o'clock in the evening and midnight Manila time, on the seventeenth.

One of the men of the BNDD on the trip was Assistant Director Perry Rivkind, a friend of Dean's. On the afternoon of June 17, Rivkind and Dean were sitting on a balcony of the Manila Hilton Hotel, overlooking the bay. The ceremony was over and they could relax before they flew out of Manila and headed for home the next morning. "There was this most violet-looking dark cloud coming on towards the Hilton," Rivkind recalled recently for us, and Dean said to him, "Gee, you ought to take a picture of that." He did. A month later, Dean called him and asked about the picture, because Dean thought it had been taken almost precisely when the Watergate burglars had been arrested. Rivkind sent him a copy of the photograph.

Later, in the evening, the friends went to dinner and Rivkind ate some local food while Dean stuck to less exotic fare. Rivkind can't pinpoint the time, but remembers it as being well after dinner when, according to a short conversation he had with Dean about that time, Dean received a call from "somebody in the White House" telling him to "break off the trip" and return to the capital.

Who made that call to Dean? After being told of Rivkind's story, and being reminded of dates, time zones, and the like, Jeb Magruder told us he had deduced that it must have been he who made the call.

Magruder took us through the chain of logic that moved him to arrive at this conclusion. There were three people Magruder said he would have had to call when he first received the news about the capture of the burglars from Liddy. Bob Haldeman was in Florida, but Magruder didn't want to talk to the fearsome Haldeman without having something good to tell him—and there was no good news—so he didn't call Haldeman. Or he would have called Haldeman's assistant, Gordon Strachan. Similarly, Magruder remembers ducking Strachan's calls to him all day, for the same reason: fear of Haldeman's wrath. Haldeman and Strachan, in testimony, said that Magruder had not spoken to them on the morning of the seventeenth; Strachan remembered particularly that he kept trying to get Magruder all during that day, and was only able to reach him on Sunday the eighteenth.

There was a third logical candidate for Magruder to call, and that was John Dean. "He was somebody I would have wanted to call," Magruder allowed. But, we asked, what about Rivkind's sense that the call had come from the White House? "It would have been very easy for me," Magruder pointed out, "to call the White House, get the signal board, and say 'I want to get hold of John Dean.' They could have patched me in to Manila," and he wouldn't even have known where Dean was. That sort of thing happened all the time. Further, Magruder conceded that this call must have happened some time between 8:20 A.M. and 9:00 A.M. California time, or between 11:20 P.M. and midnight in Manila. In that call, Magruder agrees, he and Dean came up with the idea of sending Liddy to talk to Kleindienst, and of using Mitchell's name to spur Kleindienst to action.

We pressed further on this point. "If it's John Dean who is telling you at eight-forty A.M. to get Liddy to find Kleindienst, it could not have been Mitchell who said that," we suggested.

"No," Magruder answered, "because I didn't see him, I didn't see Mitchell until later."

It was then that we asked, "Mitchell didn't send *you*, he didn't send *Mardian*, he didn't send anybody?"

"Right," Magruder said.

"Now, we are talking about the incident that ended up with Liddy out at Burning Tree—that's Dean?" we asked.

"Yes," Magruder agreed, "I'm sure that's Dean."

Magruder's admission is startling, because it identifies John Dean as the originator of the cover-up and controverts Dean's stance that he did not even hear of the break-in until he returned to the United States.

Dean's standard story—given to the Watergate committee, for instance—has been that he learned of the break-in when he landed in San Francisco on the morning of June 18. His hope had been to spend an additional day of relaxation in San Francisco before coming back to Washington, but that hope ended when he called his associate Fred Fielding to check in and Fielding told him of the burglary and urged him to return to Washington. "I recall that at first I resisted," Dean testified, "but Mr. Fielding, who was not explicit at that time, told me I should come back so that he could fill me in."

In later years, Dean embellished this story, in *Blind Ambition* adding some details and even contradicting his earlier stance. Thus Chapter Four of that book begins,

MANILA, PHILIPPINES, June 19, 1972 (Monday). I was heading back to Washington. The four-day round trip, including a day in Tokyo, had been rushed. Pigeon, octopus and turtle delicacies from a native Philippine restaurant challenged my digestion on the flight. Tomorrow, when I crossed the international date line, it would be *yesterday*. I arrived in San Francisco on Sunday, June 18, and decided to stay over. I was tired, and the exotic cuisine was still sending distress signals. I called Fred Fielding to tell him I would not be in the office Monday morning as planned.

One can only relish the brashness of the lie, the way Dean used words with a magician's flair for concealment and misdirection, even appropriating the dinner eaten by Perry Rivkind to give Dean himself reason for his emotional upset. In Dean's story, he flew back to Washington via San Francisco on schedule, called Fielding, and it was only when he got to his townhouse and found Fielding waiting for him that he learned the details of the break-in. Dean's account then goes on to tell of the jokes he made in the office in Washington about having two Mondays in a week, something that no one should have to endure.

The idea of two Mondays was sand in the eyes of anyone trying to follow his trail, and it worked for many years. But Dean didn't have two Mondays, he had *two Sundays*. We have recently obtained a document from the Republic of the Philippines Bureau of Immigration that shows quite clearly that John Dean departed the country on Sunday, June 18, 1972, at 8:15 A.M. on Philippine Airlines flight 428 bound for Tokyo. That is, on the first plane he could get after he had received the phone call near midnight on June 17 from Jeb Magruder.

Why would Dean lie about when he had left Manila? Why fabricate the business about two Mondays? What difference did it make when Dean learned of the break-in? It made all the difference in the world, because Dean desperately wanted to convince everyone that he had had nothing to do with the beginning of the cover-up, which started in Magruder's phone call to him in Manila on the night of the seventeenth. If he started admitting that Magruder had called him quite so early in the game, all sorts of inquiries would be stirred alive, and he would not be able to keep the questioners from probing his story closely, and coming upon such people as Perry Rivkind and his assistant Bob Stutman, whose testimony could have impugned Dean.

We kept following Dean's trail on the way to Washington, and discovered even more evidence to contradict his story. When he landed in Tokyo that Sunday afternoon, he had a one-hour layover before boarding Pan American flight 846, which left Japan at 2:15 P.M. This flight crossed the international dateline in the Pacific Ocean and landed in San Francisco on Dean's second Sunday at 7:25 in the morning. Bob Stutman, another BNDD official who was Rivkind's assistant, traveled with him—and Stutman provided information that helped confirm that Dean's story of that flight was inaccurate.

Stutman recalled that he and Dean had been planning since Manila to spend an extra day in San Francisco, and had hotel reservations and plans for dinner. Upon landing in San Francisco, they went directly to Pan Am's Yankee Clipper lounge, where Dean began making phone calls. It was early Sunday morning, and the logical move would have been to go to the hotel and check in, but, Stutman says, Dean was insistent on using the phone. Stutman waited for Dean in the lounge.

Dean, the consummate actor, returned and told Stutman, "I've got to go back. I apologize. Why don't you stay here?" Stutman remembers Dean's explanation for the summons to Washington: "Some guys got caught breaking into Democratic headquarters and it's causing a problem." Dean said he needed to make more calls, so Stutman left to get a connecting flight to Baltimore. Dean awaited a flight back to Washington.

What Stutman did not know as he left Dean was who else Dean

might be calling in the interim before he could get aboard a flight to Washington.

Scrambling for a lifeline, Dean reached out for his only remaining and uncompromised intelligence asset: Tony Ulasewicz. In an interview, Ulasewicz told us that he was called on the eighteenth and told to fly to Washington immediately; he agreed that it was a "Dean request." In his autobiography, published after the interview was conducted, Ulasewicz added that it was Caulfield who called him on behalf of Dean.

Caulfield denied talking to Dean or Ulasewicz on June 18; in any event, Ulasewicz hopped a plane and took up residence in the capital.

As we have seen in earlier chapters, John Dean's story changed depending on the circumstances in which he told it. He told one set of lies to the Watergate committee, and another in his book, but when he was still employed in the White House and was reporting directly to Nixon, Dean very often came the closest to telling the whole truth of the Watergate affair, always excepting his own integral part in it. He seemed to feel that in briefing the president, he had to be honest and accurate—at least, as honest as he could ever be on these matters. Dean did not know at the time he spoke with Nixon that he was being taped, and so the tape recordings of the Nixon-Dean conversations provide some of the best and most candid evidence available on Dean's actions. To conclude this section on how the cover-up began, here is the relevant section of the Nixon-Dean conversation of March 21, 1973.

Dean said he wanted to tell the president how everything started.

> **D:** The next point in time that I became aware of anything was on June 17th when I got the word that there had been this break in at the DNC and somebody from our Committee had been caught in the DNC. And I said, "Oh, (expletive deleted)," you know, eventually putting the pieces together—
>
> **P:** You knew who it was.
>
> **D:** I knew who it was. So I called Liddy on Monday morning. . . .

There it was: more or less, the true sequence of his learning about the break-in, which he placed on June 17. In later versions, to the Senate and in his book, he said that the date was June 18. And when the tapes were first released, everyone was concerned with the president's actions, and so missed the significance of the date on which Dean told the president that he had first learned about the break-in and that he knew Gordon Liddy was involved.

11

A WALK IN THE PARK

PRESIDENT Richard Nixon was on vacation in Florida when he learned about the break-in. As usual, though he had brought staff members down with him, he had them lodged some distance away so he could have his privacy but still summon them when he needed them. Chief of Staff Bob Haldeman recalled in his autobiography the mood of the staff upon learning the news for the first time on Saturday, June 17. Haldeman was on the terrace of his hotel villa with assistant Larry Higby when a bathing-suited Ron Ziegler approached, waving a wire service sheet with the information that five men had been caught breaking into the DNC with electronic equipment. "The news item was jarring, almost comical to me. Watergate historians have always supposed that the heavens fell when those in the President's party in Florida learned the break-in had been discovered. Quite the reverse is true. My immediate reaction was to smile. Wiretap the Democratic National Committee? For what? The idea was ludicrous."

It took Haldeman until the next morning to get hold of Magruder and learn from a "nervous" Jeb that the break-in had been "sponsored" but not ordered by the CRP, and that the burglars had been operating on their own and "just got carried away." Magruder mentioned the name of the runaway operative, James McCord, and said he worked for Gordon Liddy. Haldeman had no idea who McCord was, and had heard of Liddy but had never met him. It all seemed very remote from the White House, and Haldeman was relieved.

Magruder read him a press release that said McCord had been a freelance operator and that the CRP had "no involvement" in the break-in. Since Haldeman understood this to be technically true, "it sounded okay to me," and he told Magruder that and hurriedly hung up.

Magruder's account differs in a most important respect; he writes that when he spoke to Haldeman, it was "with the assumption that he knew about the break-in plan, and nothing [Haldeman] said indicated he did not." This assumption was based on the chain of command—Magruder knew that Dean was supposed to report to the president through Haldeman, and assumed that Dean had told Haldeman about his activities and was acting with Haldeman's knowledge and authority.

When Haldeman received the news from Magruder, he reached out for John Ehrlichman.

Haldeman's old college buddy had already been at work on the matter. Ehrlichman had received a call from a Secret Service agent who had a copy of a police report saying that when one of the burglars had been arrested he had in his possession a check signed by Howard Hunt and Hunt's White House phone number. Ehrlichman knew Hunt to be Chuck Colson's man, and had immediately seen the danger to Nixon from his connection. So, as Ehrlichman recounts in his memoir, he had done the logical thing, phoned Colson and asked whatever had become of "that fellow Howard Hunt." Colson wanted to know the reason for the question, and Ehrlichman gave him the bad news. Colson assured Ehrlichman that Hunt's White House employment had been "terminated" some time ago, and he was now working for the Bennett firm. "Why does Hunt have a White House phone?" Ehrlichman asked, and Colson said he didn't know.

Ehrlichman couldn't immediately reach Haldeman in Florida, so he left an extended message with Ron Ziegler about his conversations with the Secret Service agent and Colson. He reiterated those once more on Sunday, when he and Haldeman finally connected. Both men commiserated that if Colson was involved—even if, as Colson claimed, Hunt was long gone from the White House—they were in for a lot of problems. Haldeman decided to talk directly to Colson, and received the same denial Colson had given to Ehrlichman: He had last used Hunt two months earlier, on the ITT matter, and even then Hunt had been off the payroll.

"You gotta believe me, Bob," Haldeman quoted the upset Colson as saying. "It wasn't me. Tell the President that. I know he'll be worried." Colson told Haldeman that he understood all of the serious implications, that it could mean his political life, and that "they'll try to tie me into an absolutely idiotic break-in, and it's not right."

Haldeman next called Nixon, who reassured him that it probably wasn't Colson but was "some crazies over at CRP," and it wouldn't matter because "the American people will see it for what it was: a political prank. Hell, they can't take a break-in at the *DNC seriously*." [Italics in original]

Years later, Haldeman would learn that Nixon, too, had frantically phoned Colson, in what Colson later described as a towering rage. Nixon had gone so far during that conversation as to throw an ashtray around the room, but he had shown only a "calm, cool, even amused" face to Bob Haldeman.

On Monday morning, the *Washington Post* had a front-page story linking James McCord to the CRP, and, at about the same time, *Post* police reporter Eugene Bachinski was getting from his police sources the same information previously conveyed by the Secret Service to Ehrlichman, that Hunt was connected to the burglars.

This, then, was the situation on Monday morning, June 19, 1972, when John Dean arrived at his White House office, grumbling that no one should have two Mondays in a week. He knew that McCord had been arrested, and could figure out that Howard Hunt and Gordon Liddy would shortly be connected to the break-in, and that these men could lay the break-in at his doorstep.

In his later testimony and book, John Dean took care to construct a narrative of his activities over these first few days of Watergate whose main point was that he first learned in detail of the burglary on that Monday morning; for instance, he wrote that it was on this Monday (rather than two days earlier) that he had his first conversation with Magruder. In Dean's version, when Jeb announced that the burglars had been arrested and said, "We've got a real problem, John," Dean wrote that he thought, "What do you mean, *we've* got a problem, Jeb? . . . *You've* got a problem, baby!"

Then, according to Dean, Ehrlichman called and Dean told him that Magruder had telephoned to say the whole thing was "Liddy's fault." In Dean's version, Ehrlichman was uncharacteristically mild-mannered when he received this bombshell, and merely asked Dean to obtain more information. This supposed conversation with Ehrlichman prior to Dean's meeting later that morning with Liddy, one of the centerpieces of Dean's narrative, effectively implicated Ehrlichman in a conspiracy to cover up the burglary.

But Ehrlichman says he did not talk to Dean at all that day until noon, which was after Dean's meeting with Liddy.

To go the next step forward, we must take a step backward. As we have demonstrated, Magruder first talked to Dean moments after he learned of the break-in, and by Saturday afternoon Washington time the two of them had already set a cover-up in motion. Although in his own book Magruder omitted their Saturday conversations and followed their cover-up line—that he didn't talk to Dean until Monday—Magruder inadvertently left a hint of what really happened that Monday morning: Seeing Liddy at CRP headquarters, Magruder told him, "Gordon, let's face it, you and I can't work together. Why don't you talk to Dean? He's going to help us on this problem." Liddy said that he would do just that, and that he had already shredded his incriminating records. Magruder nodded, and said he would call Dean "and ask him to call you." Clearly, the "not-a-self-starter" Magruder wouldn't have done so if Dean had not previously agreed to talk to Liddy, or if Dean himself were not so deeply involved in the planning of the break-in that such a suggestion would have been entirely reasonable. Either way, Dean was in, not out of the picture before Liddy even took a walk in the park with him that day.

In *Blind Ambition*, Dean paints a psychologically neat picture of his state of mind leading up to that open-air meeting. He wrote that he called the CRP and left a message, then kicked himself because he realized such a message might implicate him in knowing that "Liddy's all mixed up in this." He found a reason to let himself off the hook—it could have been a legitimate call about campaign finance laws—and steadied himself, "but the fears had already set in." Then he "grimly pictured" what would happen if Liddy came to see him at the White House and there was a record of Liddy entering the EOB to see Dean at 11:15 A.M., for records on entering visitors were routinely kept by the Executive Protection Service.

This tortured reasoning is nonsense, since, as we have noted, Liddy still had a White House pass. Dean had previously intervened to prevent his having to give it up, so Liddy wouldn't have to sign in to the White House.

Indeed, Liddy flashed his pass at the guard, and approached Dean's office with some satisfaction. As he noted in *Will*, "I was pleased because Dean was the man who had recruited me for the intelligence arm of the committee and the logical choice to serve as damage control officer for the White House. Now I'd be getting some decisions and assistance in getting our men out on bail."

Dean was nervously waiting in the hall, and when Liddy approached, said only to him, "Let's go for a walk." Familiar with the conventions of clandestine work, Liddy obliged without objection. They went out through a side door of the EOB and silently walked south on 17th Street until they stopped at a park across the street from the stately Corcoran Art Gallery. According to Dean, Liddy needed a shave, wore a rumpled suit, and was disheveled and tired from a weekend of shredding papers and covering his trail. Dean was dressed in his usual crisp, lawyerly attire that only clashed a bit with the blond hair that hung over his suit collar. According to *Will*, Liddy had been up early, and had changed and shaved before going to CRP.

The difference between the shaved and not-shaved descriptions is just the beginning of the disparity between the two versions of the event. In writing that Liddy was unshaved, Dean tried to nudge his readers in the direction of viewing Liddy as a strange man who was out of control—and who could very easily be blamed for the debacle of the break-in.

When they started to talk, Liddy wanted to know whether Dean would be his "damage control action officer." If so, he would tell Dean everything. Dean agreed that he was that man, and Liddy proceeded to lay it all on the line. According to Liddy's version, he then told Dean, "I was commanding the aircraft carrier when it hit the reef. I accept full responsibility. All of the people arrested are my men. You remember the intelligence operation you recruited me for and those meetings in the AG's office? Well, by the time that damn thing was finally approved we were down to a quarter million." The decrease in funding, Liddy explained, was why he'd had to use McCord instead of an outsider who could not have been linked to the CRP.

Dean was, Liddy wrote, "distinctly uncomfortable" at being reminded that he had recruited Liddy and had been a participant in the first two GEMSTONE meetings. According to both Dean and Liddy versions, Dean then interrupted to ask the crucial question: Was anybody in the White House connected to the break-in?

Of course Dean knew very well that someone in the White House was involved—himself. His question seems to have been designed to learn if Liddy understood that, too, since the actual instruction for the second break-in had been transmitted to Liddy through Magruder without mention of Dean. Liddy pondered for a moment and answered, "Gordon Strachan. . . . I don't know that he knew the exact day we were going back in there, but . . ."

In Dean's published version of this tête-à-tête, this was a moment of great revelation. "I really didn't want to know more," he wrote, "because I had to assume that if Strachan knew, Haldeman knew. And if Haldeman knew, the President knew. It made sickening sense." These lines in Dean's book point the reader toward the ultimate villain, Nixon, and obscure all other possible interpretations. But the mention of Strachan by Liddy would have caused Dean to gulp and pause on quite another account: For Strachan knew that Dean was the Nixon administration focal point for political intelligence—officially in Strachan's view but in reality self-anointed. And Strachan may have known more. At the very least, Dean must have worried that Strachan might identify him as having known in advance about the DNC break-ins. The Strachan name was a dangerous one for Dean, and throughout the coming months he concealed the notion that Liddy had told him on June 19 that he thought Strachan was involved. Dean kept that fact from the Senate Watergate committee in its hearings, and gave the senators and the watching television public a truncated version of this walk in the park. To them, he said that when he'd asked Liddy whether anyone in the White House had been involved, Liddy had answered "no." But Dean hadn't simply forgotten what Liddy said; in his March 13, 1973, conversation with the president, Dean told Nixon—nine months after he had "learned" the fact from Liddy—that Strachan knew about the break-in. We will examine later why Dean told the president of Strachan's involvement at that particular time, and why he did not tell the same thing to the Watergate committee.

But Liddy thought that in telling this to Dean he was, in effect, telling it to the president, whom he very much wanted to protect. "My whole reason for talking to Dean [in the park]," he told us recently, "was I thought I was conveying information to the president of the United States to let him know exactly what the situation was. . . . I wanted him to know what the situation was so that he could deal with it." Liddy had no sense that Dean was operating on his own, and believed Dean was operating with the specific knowledge of such superiors as Mitchell, Haldeman, and/or the president himself, or else he would not have been so forthcoming.

Liddy's complete trust in Dean-as-the-message-carrier was evident in what he said next in the conversation: a plea for assistance to the arrested burglars. He wanted them out of jail, and he wanted financial support for them in the period before their trial.

According to Dean, when Liddy raised the issue of support for the burglars, Dean cut him off, saying, as he later wrote, "I can't do anything about that, and I think you understand why I can't do anything about that."

Liddy's version of Dean's response is as different as night is from day, as culpability is from innocence. According to Liddy, it was Dean himself who promised bail, attorneys' fees, and support for the burglars' families—and he did so, Liddy reports, immediately after Liddy had explained that these same Cubans had been involved in the earlier break-in at the office of Dr. Fielding, Daniel Ellsberg's psychiatrist. Liddy assured Dean that as professionals "they won't talk," but it was "imperative" to get them out on bail because "that D.C. jail's a hellhole, especially in summer, and they expect it. They were promised that kind of support."

Dean made these promises on his own, without having talked to a single senior member of the administration, not Mitchell, nor Ehrlichman, nor Haldeman.

"Everyone'll be taken care of," Liddy quotes Dean as saying. In his book, Liddy notes that Dean later denied promising support money, but Liddy is adamant that Dean specifically did so, and that while doing so, "Dean's tone of voice was confident, but the look on his face was decidedly troubled."

Liddy then sought to assure Dean that, having been captain of the ship, "I'm prepared to go down with it. If someone wants to shoot me . . . just tell me what corner to stand on and I'll be there, O.K.?" Liddy recalled that Dean searched his face to see if he was joking, and discerned that Liddy was not. Liddy evidently believed that this offer to be killed on demand would convince Dean as to the extent of his loyalty to the Nixonian cause.

Since Dean had shown himself to Liddy as a true damage control officer by promising to help the foot soldiers, Liddy now tried to assist Dean. There would be an FBI investigation, former FBI-man Liddy told the young White House counsel, and Dean should make an effort to obtain the raw data, the "FD-302s" that field agents regularly filed and the "airtels" that were sent to them; the former would enable Dean to know what information was coming in to headquarters, and the latter would tell him who the FBI planned to interview next.

Dean must have been grateful for this insider's tip—it would assist him enormously in running the cover-up during the next months—and then introduced his main topic of concern: Howard Hunt. Where was he, these days? Hunt was lying low, Liddy said, trying to dodge reporters, and Dean commented that it would be a good idea, in light of "what you've told me" (which Liddy took as a reference to the Dr. Fielding break-in), for Hunt to take a powder. Hunt's wife and children were in Europe, and Liddy offered to pass the word that Hunt should join them there. "The sooner the better," Liddy quotes Dean as responding. "Today, if possible."

They had begun walking again and Dean was about to go back into the EOB. Hopping impatiently from foot to foot, he told Liddy, "I don't think it's a good idea for me to be talking with you anymore." Liddy asked who the new damage control action officer would be, and Dean told him that that person would "come to you and identify himself." Though mystified, Liddy saluted and left.

First Dean had said he was the action officer, enabling Liddy to tell him everything; once Liddy had spilled all that he knew, and identified the potential trouble spots, Dean then informed Liddy that he was no longer the action officer, and waved him off into limbo. Assured that Liddy would keep silent on Dean's own involvement in the break-in, and that Liddy did not suspect him of any actions in regard to the instigation of the cover-up, Dean could now safely proceed with many other matters.

Haldeman and Ehrlichman agreed to give Dean the task of finding out what had really happened at the break-in. After Dean returned from his park-bench meeting with Liddy, he was summoned to see Ehrlichman at noon and given his orders. Though Dean reported to the Senate that he told Ehrlichman "in full" his conversation with Liddy, he actually gave Ehrlichman very little of the substance, concealing, for instance, 1) Liddy's statement concerning the involvement of Strachan, 2) the request for bail and support money, and 3) his instruction to Liddy to get Hunt out of the country. Dean would later claim that at a meeting around four that afternoon, in the presence of Colson, Ehrlichman told Dean to call Liddy and have Liddy tell Hunt to get out of the country. Dean claims he dutifully made the call, but then, in his version, had second thoughts and returned to tell Ehrlichman and Colson that sending Hunt away was not "very wise." They agreed, whereupon Dean says he got on the horn to Liddy and at the last moment prevented Hunt from leaving the country.

When the Watergate Special Prosecutors indicted the cover-up conspirators, the third "overt act" was a charge that Ehrlichman had ordered Hunt through Dean and Liddy to flee the country.

Dean's version is untrue, say Liddy, Colson, Ehrlichman, and the facts. As we have seen, Liddy reports that Dean ordered Hunt out of the country even before the counsel saw Ehrlichman. Ehrlichman denies attempting to send Hunt away, and points out that shortly before Dean was to leave the White House in April 1973, Dean tried to inveigle him into remembering that he, Ehrlichman, had sent Hunt out of the country. The reader will recall that Dean had successfully played the same trick on Haldeman, "reminding" him of a meeting at which Haldeman supposedly "turned off" any Liddy-sponsored bugging operation. But Ehrlichman didn't buy Dean's ploy; he told Dean then that it was untrue, and went to Colson to check his memory. Colson recalled the event vividly, and verified Ehrlichman's own memory. Recently, in an interview with us, Colson expanded on what had actually happened. Earlier in the day of June 19, Dean had advised Colson that he'd already ordered Hunt to flee, and Colson had then told him that was "the dumbest thing I ever heard. . . . You better get him back," whereupon Dean went to the phone and called Liddy for the last-minute retrieval.

Even more damaging for Dean, Howard Hunt recalled the incident just that way, too, in his 1974 memoir, *Undercover*, saying that he had received the first call from Liddy around 11:30 in the morning to meet him on yet another park bench, this one on 18th Street. There, Hunt was startled to learn that "they" wanted him out of town, and he protested that "What I *do* need is a lawyer." Liddy agreed to find him one if Hunt would prepare to leave the country. He went home to pack, and "half an hour later" Liddy called to say that the orders had been changed. The time sequence tallies well with Colson's remembrance of the event. In sum, the 4:00 P.M. meeting in Ehrlichman's office had nothing to do with getting Hunt out of the country; yet Dean later used that meeting in his sworn testimony to place blame for the incident on his superior.

Who would have benefited if Hunt had gone out of the country? Not Colson, to whom Hunt seemed most closely tied, for Colson had vetoed the idea, knowing that if Hunt did vanish, the finger of suspicion would point even more strongly at himself. Ehrlichman didn't want Hunt to leave, and neither did Gordon Liddy, for much the same reasons—for Hunt to take a powder would heap suspicion on Colson, who was known far and wide as Nixon's wild man, which wouldn't be good for the boss. The only man in the power structure who had a reason for wanting E. Howard Hunt out of the country was John Wesley Dean, because the longer Dean could keep Hunt from saying anything to the authorities, the better off Dean would be.

The order to send Hunt away had been reversed, and Hunt was to remain in the country. Two questions about him continued to bother the participants that Monday afternoon. Was Hunt still on the White

House payroll? And what was inside the safe he still kept in the White House?

Dean handled the second of these matters several hours before he met with Ehrlichman and Colson at 4:00 P.M. Early that afternoon, he asked Bruce A. Kehrli, another one of Haldeman's assistants and the man who dealt with White House personnel matters, to enter Hunt's office and, as Kehrli later testified in a civil suit, "see if there were any materials or papers left and clean them out." Kehrli found only stationery in the desk, but located a locked safe, and removed the safe to a storage room.

In that safe were several kinds of political explosives, ranging from powder caps to dynamite to plastique, and Hunt knew it. Even earlier in the day, he had visited his old office for the last time, browsing about in the hours before he received his first call of the day from Gordon Liddy. He tidied up a bit, and then, on his way out, told Colson's secretary, "I just want you to know that the safe is loaded."

It sure was. In that safe were: a .25 caliber automatic revolver with a live clip of ammunition; McCord's attaché case, which contained tear gas canisters and electronic gear; the CIA psychological profile of Daniel Ellsberg and other material on Ellsberg; classified material on the Pentagon Papers; a folder on Hunt's investigations of Ted Kennedy; fabricated State Department cables created by Hunt to link President John Kennedy to the 1963 assassination of South Vietnamese President Ngo Dinh Diem; a pop-up address book; and—last but not least, as we shall see in later chapters—two black, cloth-bound notebooks made by the Hermès firm.

Kehrli and Deputy Press Secretary Ken W. Clawson joined Colson, Dean, and Ehrlichman at 4:00 P.M. Colson had been insisting that Hunt had left his staff on March 31, 1972, but Ehrlichman wasn't going to take his word for that and so had ordered Kehrli to bring Hunt's employment records to the meeting. Clawson would handle expected press inquiries about Hunt because Ziegler was still in Florida with the president. There was consternation because although a Colson assistant had sent a memo asking payroll to drop Hunt by the first of April, there was no reflection in the personnel files that this had actually been done.

Well, that would have to be pursued. Fortunately, the safe had been removed from the Hunt office, and the conferees discussed what to do with it. Most of the people in the room didn't know what was in the safe; they had no idea, for example, that it contained a gun. Colson had some suspicions that the Dr. Fielding stuff might be in there, but he didn't know what else. Dean didn't know the precise contents yet either, but must have suspected there might be material in the safe that could link him with Hunt more strongly than the others in the room understood. That was why he'd already begun to act as if he owned it.

"I suggested to Dean that he take custody of the safe," Colson later testified to the Senate committee in a closed-door session about that 4:00 P.M. conference. "It was my view that the White House counsel had a responsibility to secure the safe and any other evidence." Ehrlichman agreed, and said that Kehrli and Dean should be present when the safe was drilled open by technicians, so that, as Ehrlichman later testified, "there ought to be people who could, one day, tell what had happened." In legal parlance, this would preserve what Ehrlichman (a lawyer, as were Colson and Dean) correctly labeled, "the chain of evidence."

But that chain of evidence was now in the hands of the person who had sent the men into the DNC in the first—and in the second—place, John Dean.

By the evening of June 19, 1972, confusion reigned in both the White House and the CRP about the burglary and the arrested men. Dean and Magruder had set certain cover-up events in motion, but in the cadres of people in high places in the Nixon power centers, only they knew about them. Compounding the confusion were personal rivalries among Nixon's top men, a tension the president understood and even fostered at times. Two damage control/investigative teams were at work, one in each headquarters. In the White House, Haldeman had given the assignment to Ehrlichman, who had charged Dean with the work; at the Committee to Re-elect, Mitchell (still in California) had assigned Bob Mardian the task of digging up the facts. Since each camp harbored quite a bit of distrust for the other, neither was inclined to share information.

The information gap opened partly because John Mitchell believed the break-in had been engineered by the White House, most probably by Chuck Colson, who had been Hunt's superior. Jeb Magruder continued to conceal from Mitchell (as he had from Haldeman) the fact that he had personally instructed Liddy to go into the DNC.

On the White House side, though Dean knew precisely what was going on, no one else had a clue. Neither Ehrlichman nor Haldeman could make any sense out of what they had been told was Liddy's personal decision to go into the DNC. In any event, it seemed a CRP problem, especially after McCord had been implicated. Colson was backing away as fast as he could go, and was thankful that although his former employee Hunt was up to his neck in it, the other people of the break-in all seemed to be from the Mitchell camp.

Neither camp was particularly interested in dealing with the other, and both were content to leave matters to the one man who seemed easily able to talk to both sides, John Dean. That was why, when John Mitchell finally reached Washington on the evening of June 19, and called a meeting in his apartment in the Watergate complex among his top aides—Mardian, LaRue, and Magruder—he also invited John Dean to stop by.

The mood was despondent in the well-appointed apartment only yards away from where the burglary had taken place. What was needed, agreed the men with drinks in their hands, was a public relations strategy to deal with the crisis. Mitchell was frequently called to the telephone to calm his wife, Martha, who had remained in California and whose behavior bordered on hysteria. "More drinks were passed around," Jeb Magruder recalled of this meeting in his book, "and I could see a long evening of booze and self-pity shaping up. The prospect was not an inviting one."

Magruder, like Dean, was saying very little in this meeting, and nothing of substance. Both men had too much to hide—the orders to Liddy to break into the DNC, the attempt to get Kleindienst to spring McCord from jail, the attempt to get Hunt out of the country, and all the information that Dean had learned from Liddy that morning, just to name a few key pieces of information kept from Mardian, LaRue, and Mitchell. In later testimony, Mitchell was caustic about Dean's silence in that meeting, particularly because Dean did not reveal his talks earlier in the day with Liddy. Had Dean told the group what Liddy had to say, Mitchell would have taken some strong actions and possibly ended the cover-up very quickly.

Before the commiseration party ended, Magruder got up to leave; he had received an unexpected invitation to round out a tennis foursome with Vice President Spiro Agnew. Magruder wrote in his book, "Before I left, however, I addressed a final question to Mitchell. 'I have the GEMSTONE file,' I said. 'What do you want me to do with it?' 'Maybe you ought to have a little fire at your house tonight,' Mitchell replied. I nodded and left."

Later in the evening—but not until after trading lobs with the vice president—Magruder claims he did burn those files. And when federal prosecutors brought their case against the cover-up conspirators, they relied on this Magruder allegation. The prosecutors contended that this meeting confirmed Mitchell's prior knowledge of Liddy's activities, and listed Mitchell's order to "have a little fire" as the fifth overt act of the cover-up. But the evidence suggests that Mitchell did not give that order. Mitchell and Mardian deny it and, as we shall see, even Dean's version of the meeting supports Mitchell and Mardian.

Mitchell testified that he had no recollection of a discussion of the GEMSTONE files or wiretap logs, or of instructing anyone to burn anything. Mardian testified that he had been there for the entire meeting and that "no such discussion took place in my presence. I think I would have recalled such a discussion had it taken place in my presence."

LaRue initially upheld Magruder's allegation. He testified that "there was a reference to files pertaining to electronic surveillance," and that he recalled Mitchell saying, "it might be a good idea if he [Magruder] had a good fire in his house." LaRue even pleaded guilty to being a party to the destruction of those files and was sent to jail for that. Today, however, LaRue is troubled about what precisely went on in that meeting. He pointed out in an interview with us that Mitchell was distracted by the repeated phone calls from Martha, and that when Magruder spoke of files, he did not make a clear reference to the GEMSTONE papers. "If Magruder said, 'I have some sensitive papers, and what's wrong with burning the sons-of-bitches?', that doesn't mean it has anything to do with the Watergate break-in." Therefore, he believes, it was possible for Mitchell to have assented to Magruder's destruction of files without knowing what files Magruder meant. After all, Mitchell believed then, and believed to his dying day, that he had never approved any break-ins and had never seen any fruits of the wiretaps, so he would not have known what Magruder was referring to.

Curiously, John Dean's testimony supported Mitchell's and Mardian's. Since at so many other points Dean tried hard to bring Mitchell into the conspiracy, and used his name so many times without permission, it is interesting that Dean did not agree that Mitchell had ordered the destruction of evidence in Jeb Magruder's fireplace.

President Richard M. Nixon was angry on Tuesday morning, June 20. A front-page story in the *Washington Post* by a young reporter named Bob Woodward assaulted his eyes. In it was the information that Howard Hunt's name appeared in the burglars' address books, that one of Hunt's signed checks had been found on the person of one of the Cubans, and that Hunt had been a consultant to White House Special Counsel Charles Colson. Haldeman had already convened a senior meeting on the whole affair for ten that morning, and Nixon hoped it would yield some answers. Though Colson had denied to Haldeman,

Ehrlichman, and Nixon any continuing connection to Hunt, the news-papers were on to that connection, and that was bad for the White House. Moreover, the Democratic Party had already filed a $1 million civil suit against the CRP for invasion of privacy and violation of civil rights.

The 10:00 A.M., June 20, meeting was held in Ehrlichman's office—the one in which he'd produced Admiral Welander's confession six months earlier—and was attended by Haldeman, Mitchell, Klein-dienst, and Dean. The first subject, as always, was leaks. How had the information about McCord and Hunt gotten out? Kleindienst assured the men that it had not come from Justice, but from the Metropolitan Police Department.

Dean maintained a deep silence, and the other men were completely in the dark about the events, so there wasn't much to discuss. Halde-man and Ehrlichman harbored doubts about Mitchell's role in the break-in, but, according to Haldeman's memoir, though the meeting produced no new information he was glad to see that Mitchell "looked better than I had seen him in days. He puffed on his pipe with that humorous glint in his eye that we all knew so well. I felt that was a good sign because Mitchell was now the Chairman of CRP, and should have been worried if there was a major crisis impending. Instead, he said, 'I don't know anything about that foolishness at the DNC. I do know *I* didn't approve the stupid thing.' We believed him—and that lightened our mood considerably."

Dean left that meeting in the company of Kleindienst, and returned to Justice with the attorney general. Kleindienst was furious about the break-in and about Liddy's approach to him at Burning Tree. Dean said nothing about his role in those events. When they reached the Justice building and the two men were joined by Henry Petersen, the assistant attorney general in charge of the criminal division, Dean's motive for making the trip became clear: He wanted the FBI 302s, the investigative reports prepared by the field agents. Dean invoked Nix-on's name to get them.

"The representation that he [Dean] made to me and to Mr. Petersen throughout was that he was doing this for the President of the United States and that he was reporting directly to the President," Kleindienst later testified. Kleindienst and Petersen quite properly refused to give up the 302s, which were raw data, and said they would only supply summaries of the data. The attorney general added that if the president wanted to see the reports, he would take them to Nixon himself. Dean left, empty-handed.

Meanwhile, back at the White House, Haldeman was reporting to

Nixon what had happened in the ten o'clock meeting—but the exact particulars of that conversation will never be known, because that's the tape in which there is the infamous eighteen-and-a-half-minute gap. A new notion on how that gap came into being will be offered in a later chapter, but at this point in the narrative we can suggest some of what was covered in the meeting, based on the memoirs of both participants. According to both men, Nixon's main interest was in the Hunt-Colson connection. He had learned from Colson that Hunt had been involved in the Bay of Pigs operation, and that gave him an idea. As he remembered in *RN*, Nixon told Haldeman that the way to play the break-in was to say it had been a Cuban operation, perhaps designed to learn how the Democrats were going to view Castro in the coming election; that would stir the anti-Castro community in Miami "to start a public bail fund for their arrested countrymen and make a big media issue out of it." This would damage the Democrats and at the same time turn the Watergate affair into something favorable to the White House.

This reaction was vintage Richard Nixon. Watergate would become simply another battle in his lifelong war with the Democrats. Floundering in ignorance as to how the affair had begun, and instead of attempting to solve the crime, Nixon was busy calculating how he might use it to strike at his enemies. Among the hallmarks of Nixon's personality were a penchant for turning away from facts and continual attempts to transform problems for himself into problems for his opposition.

While the president was constructing his fantasy scenario, John Mitchell's men were trying to ascertain facts. Bob Mardian was in charge, and he decided to talk to Liddy directly on the afternoon of the twentieth, at Fred LaRue's apartment (near Mitchell's) in the Watergate complex. Liddy was nearly as direct with them as he had been with Dean. He spoke convincingly of his supervision of the failed break-in and of his other operations with Hunt, including the burglary at Dr. Fielding's office in Beverly Hills and the ITT affair, in which Hunt attempted to get lobbyist Dita Beard to deny a news report of a secret money deal between the White House and ITT that involved the Republican convention.

Mardian and LaRue tried to follow the implications of what Liddy was saying. McCord, Hunt, and the Cubans all had ties to the CIA, ties that also were evident in the Dr. Fielding break-in and in the trip Hunt made to see Dita Beard in a hospital bedroom in Denver—for instance, Hunt had worn a CIA-made wig to disguise himself on that venture. Nothing in this explanation squared with their already-formed view that the break-in had been a White House operation spawned by Colson.

Liddy informed Mardian and LaRue that neither the Cubans nor McCord would talk; then he added the absolutely vital fact that the previous day a person at the White House had assured him that, as he wrote in his memoir, "they'd all be receiving the usual family support and legal fees. I stressed that they should be bailed out as soon as possible." In Liddy's version, he said he told the men that the man who promised the money was Dean.

Mardian disagrees on this important point, and says Liddy only suggested that the promise had come from some White House person. Because of his set of mind, Mardian assumed that person had to have been Chuck Colson.

Liddy also told the men that Magruder had pushed him to go back into the DNC.

Magruder? Mardian and LaRue wondered how Magruder could be involved if this were a CIA or a Colson operation, but Liddy was quite definite about it, and they had to accept the statement at face value. Liddy left the meeting, and Mardian and LaRue took the substance of what they had heard to Mitchell, including the idea that support be paid to the burglars.

As Mardian later testified, "Mr. Mitchell told me that under no circumstances would bail money be forthcoming, and for me to call Mr. Liddy and tell him. And I did so." In other words, when Mitchell heard for the first time of the requests for support money, he issued an emphatic no on behalf of the employer of record, the CRP. "Mitchell appeared to be as sincerely shocked as I was when I got this information." LaRue too testified that Liddy had told them of his and Hunt's escapades, and of the promises made to him and the burglars, and they had conveyed all this to their chief.

Mitchell seems not to have taken the accusation about Magruder at face value. As he later testified when asked if Magruder had been involved in the break-in, "We had people such as Mr. Liddy and so forth say yes, that Magruder was involved, Magruder was saying no at one time and maybe yes the other time, and so forth," and Mitchell seemed convinced that whoever pushed the button, the whole affair was a derivative of a Colson-directed dirty tricks campaign orchestrated by Liddy and Hunt. As with the other senior officials, Mitchell knew Magruder wasn't a self-starter, and had to have been acting on orders from someone else. Mitchell's mistake was to assume that the person who started Magruder's battery was Colson, rather than Dean.

Mardian, Mitchell, and LaRue chewed on the substance of these shocking notions all during the afternoon and on into the evening. All three men had apartments either in or near the Watergate complex, and were close companions, near-bachelor buddies in the days when Martha Mitchell was sliding into alcoholism, despair, and rage. Often, they'd move from the CRP offices in the late afternoon to Mitchell's apartment in the early evening, have a few drinks, order in Chinese food, and continue their discussions of the day until they all felt it was time to turn in. The discussion of the afternoon-evening of June 20 followed this pattern, except that LaRue and Mardian spent that afternoon interviewing Gordon Liddy, and joined Mitchell in the evening.

In any event, after learning the news from Mardian and LaRue, Mitchell did not immediately call Richard Nixon with the information and in no way tried to confront his close friend. "I believed at that particular time, and maybe in retrospect it was wrong, but it occurred to me that the best thing to do was just to keep the lid on through the election . . . we wanted to keep the lid on. We were not volunteering everything," he testified. He added that if he had, the president "would have lowered the boom" on his subordinates and the resulting publicity would have hurt his reelection. In essence, Mitchell argued, by keeping the president uninformed, he had saved Nixon from himself.

This was Mitchell's cardinal mistake in the entire Watergate affair. As we have seen, he tried to turn off GEMSTONE on three occasions, and believed he had never agreed to fund any illegal entries. Moreover, he did not send Kleindienst any illegal message to spring McCord from jail, and also refused to pay bail for the burglars. He acted entirely within the law on those occasions. But when apprised of quite a few facts about the affair, Mitchell decided not to go to Nixon, for he feared that if Colson were exposed as the mastermind and fired, public reaction would be so negative that Nixon's reelection campaign would be damaged.

John Dean had promised Kleindienst and Petersen at Justice that when he returned to the White House he would directly brief the president about Watergate, but he didn't do that. Dean had a more personally important task to accomplish—namely, to examine the contents of Hunt's safe. While the Mardian meetings with Liddy and then Mitchell were taking place, Dean was finally studying those contents, in conjunction with Fred Fielding. The previous evening, while Dean had been at the Mitchell apartment, Kehrli and the technicians had opened Hunt's safe, found the gun, and had immediately tried to get hold of Dean. Failing to reach him, they had found his associate and trusted friend Fred Fielding, who had helped Kehrli and the technicians pack the contents of the safe into cardboard boxes to be secured overnight.

Dean later testified what while he and Fielding only glanced at the documents, they were concerned about "the public impact some of these documents might have." He told Fielding to segregate the most politically sensitive papers, while he placed McCord's briefcase in a locked closet in his office and hid Hunt's personal papers in his safe. The remaining Hunt materials, he testified, were left in cartons on the floor of the office.

Dean did *not* tell the Senate that the Hunt papers he placed in his safe were the two Hermès notebooks and the pop-up address book, which he placed beneath the documents that dealt with President Nixon's personal estate plan. As Hunt later testified himself, these notebooks contained what he knew about GEMSTONE; in his book, Hunt wrote that they contained specific references to Dean's own role as one of Liddy's "principals" on GEMSTONE. And that was information Dean absolutely had to hide—or destroy.

In *Blind Ambition*, Dean relates two conversations he had on the afternoon and evening of June 20, 1972. Both, we now know, were complete fabrications designed to keep readers from discovering the holes in Dean's own tale of noninvolvement.

The first story was one that, if it had actually happened, would have been essential for him to tell to the Senate, because it implicated Mitchell. Here's the Dean version: Toward the end of the afternoon, Jeb Magruder came to see Dean, and they walked together back toward the CRP offices. Magruder wanted to speak of events in early February; he related a story of how Colson had been pushing him "like mad" to get the Liddy-Hunt program going, and that as a consequence he had brought up the GEMSTONE plan again to Mitchell in Key Biscayne. Dean quotes Magruder as saying that Colson "kept calling me and asking what's going on. So I went to Mitchell and I told him. I said, 'Listen, if we don't take care of this Colson's going to take it over!' "

At that instant, Dean writes, he and Magruder were crossing Pennsylvania Avenue, and he was so thunderstruck by Magruder's admission that he was nearly hit by a bus rounding the corner. In Dean's version, it was then that he experienced the great revelation of how the Watergate affair had begun: Magruder, knowing that "Mitchell was jealous and leery of Colson," had "pushed Mitchell's 'Colson button.' "

Poppycock, Magruder says of this Dean story. "If Colson had told me to go into the Watergate, I would have ignored it," he told us recently. The conversation never happened. If it had, Magruder would have testified to it as he testified to many other matters that implicated Mitchell. But he never had that talk with Dean on June 20.

Dean's second story involves Bob Mardian. In the Dean version, after he had finished with Magruder at the CRP headquarters, he saw Mardian, and he and Mardian talked through the afternoon and "into the night" about Liddy's expectation that certain commitments to the arrested men would be honored. Supposedly Mardian said he didn't like the implications of Liddy's idea, and Dean told him that he didn't like them either, a stance that neatly exculpated Dean himself from that very commitment.

Mardian denies being with Dean on June 20, or that the long conversation that Dean describes ever took place. Among the reasons to believe that the Dean version is a complete fabrication is that Mardian spent the afternoon interviewing Liddy in company of Fred LaRue, and the evening with Mitchell and LaRue, rather than talking "into the night" with John Dean. Liddy's book also upholds Mardian's version; in LaRue's apartment that afternoon, Liddy said a lot to Mardian because Mardian agreed that he was the new "damage control action officer."

Dean was so busy on the twentieth that he appears to have forgotten all about Tony Ulasewicz, who had been cooling his heels in a Washington hotel room since Sunday. Near the end of the day on that Tuesday, Tony decided he'd had enough of sitting around, and flew home to New York to await any further calls from Caulfield or Dean.

On Wednesday, June 21, Dean turned his full attention to the FBI investigation. Liddy had told him he needed the raw data, but Kleindienst and Petersen had refused to provide it. However, Dean's instruction from Ehrlichman to stay on top of Watergate provided a perfect vehicle for approaching a man very amenable to suggestions from the White House—Acting FBI Director L. Patrick Gray. In the first of several meetings that the two men would have during the next few days, on June 21 Gray passed to Dean some hot new information that the FBI had uncovered but still didn't understand, that $114,000 in cashier's checks had been discovered in a Miami account belonging to burglar Bernard Barker. These were the campaign contributions that Hugh Sloan had handed to Gordon Liddy in April for laundering. One of these, for $25,000, had been made payable to a man named Kenneth Dahlberg, and the other four, totaling $89,000, were drawn on a Mexican bank and made payable to a man named Manuel Ogarrio. The

FBI wasn't certain, Gray told Dean, but thought these were somehow connected to the break-in.

Dean wanted to sit in on all FBI interviews of White House employees. This was a rather unusual request, and Gray asked Dean if he was going to report directly to the president on this matter or through Haldeman or Ehrlichman. As Gray later testified to the Senate, "Mr. Dean stated he would be there in his official capacity as counsel to the President. . . . He informed me that he would be reporting directly to the President."

Dean had no intention of carrying the information to the president, but Gray had been told precisely the opposite, and so said he'd allow Dean to attend FBI interviews of White House employees. As we will see, this put Dean in the catbird's seat: He would not only control the White House investigation of the crime he had initiated, but would also be in a position to influence strongly the FBI investigation.

The president alternated between bouts of sulking and imagined vengeance. On Wednesday, June 21, Bob Haldeman came to see him with the news—evidently learned from someone at CRP—that "Gordon Liddy was 'the guy who did this,' " as Nixon recalled in his memoir.

Nixon's mind seemed always to have organizational charts in view. Hearing Liddy's name, he leaped from Liddy to Liddy's employer, John Mitchell. Could this have been Mitchell's fault? He and Haldeman kicked that around a bit but came to no definite conclusions. Instead, they focused on what Liddy, Hunt, and the Cubans could reveal that would be far more damaging than the DNC break-in—the Dr. Fielding break-in and Hunt's red-wigged trip to Dita Beard's hospital bedside. As Nixon explained in *RN*, "Haldeman said . . . the real problem for the White House had nothing to do with the Watergate break-in itself, but concerned what he called 'other involvements'—things that an investigative fishing expedition into the break-in could uncover and exploit politically. That was what made the Democrats' civil suit the biggest problem for the White House [because] a lot of unrelated things . . . could be uncovered in the kind of freewheeling legal depositions the Democrats clearly had in mind."

He was afraid that once again he would be the victim of a conspiracy to get him by Democratic and liberal media enemies. "I told Haldeman that it seemed that the Democrats had been doing this kind of thing [bugging] to us for years, and *they* never got caught. Haldeman agreed that the Democrats always seemed to get off easier. He said the press just never went after them the way they went after us. Later in the day

I said that every time the Democrats accused us of bugging we should charge that we were being bugged and maybe even plant a bug and find it ourselves!"

The next day, Thursday, June 22, Nixon got two pieces of good news. The Democrats' civil suit had been assigned to the court of Charles Richey, whom Nixon had appointed. He was also pleased that the FBI still did not know that Hunt and Liddy had actually been involved in the break-in. Nixon knew, but made no attempt to pass on the information to the FBI; this was one of his first acts in covering up a crime in which he did not participate and which he did not understand.

He held a press conference that afternoon, and was also delighted to take only one question about Watergate, which he easily deflected with a reference to an earlier denial issued by his press secretary: "As Mr. Ziegler has stated, the White House had no involvement whatever in this particular incident."

Meanwhile, the FBI and the CIA were holding separate meetings about Watergate. The crime was now almost six days old, and the FBI was beginning to develop some theories about it. Pat Gray met that day with Charles W. Bates, the head of the investigative division, who laid out the main theory for him. All signs seemed to point to the CIA. McCord and the Cubans had long-standing ties to the Agency, and the cashier's checks in Barker's account seemed to be laundered funds, possibly having to do with some international intelligence operation.

On learning this, Gray called CIA Director Richard Helms to warn that the FBI might be poking into one of the Agency's operations. As Gray later testified, he asked Helms to confirm or deny that, and Helms told Gray he "had been meeting on this every day with his men," and while they couldn't figure out the case, Helms was sure "there was no CIA involvement."

At 6:30 P.M. that evening, Gray met again with John Dean to discuss the scheduling of interviews with White House staffers. Gray later testified that he also discussed with Dean "our very early theories of the case; namely that the episode was either a CIA covert operation . . . or a CIA money chain, or a political money chain, or a pure political operation, or a Cuban right wing operation, or a combination of any of these." The FBI couldn't yet choose among these explanations, and couldn't figure out the motive for the burglary or the "attempted intercept of communications operation."

John Dean had been doing very well in his attempts to cover all the bases so far. He had offered money to Liddy and through Liddy to the burglars; he had kept his superiors in the dark while at the same time he had been able to turn a suggestion that he investigate the case into a crowbar to pry information on the real ongoing investigation out of the FBI. He had many of the bases covered. But what Gray suggested to him as one of the FBI's theories about the case—that it was a CIA operation—offered Dean a way to kill the official investigation.

"I remember telling Mr. Dean in one of these early telephone calls or meetings," Pat Gray later testified, "that the FBI was going to pursue all leads aggressively unless we were told by the CIA that there was a CIA interest or involvement in this case."

There was the idea for Dean: If the FBI could be convinced that its agents had indeed stumbled onto a CIA operation, and told to go no further, it was likely that the probe could be contained and restricted to the five men already arrested. Hunt wouldn't be dragged in, and maybe not even Liddy. That meant Dean himself couldn't be touched.

It was an exciting idea for Dean, and he tried to figure out how to set it in motion. He couldn't accomplish the task by himself; he would need help from much higher up, and planned to get it in the morning.

12

"THE SMOKING GUN"

IN the previously accepted version of Watergate history, June 23, 1972, is the day on which the event occurred that would eventually sink the Nixon presidency, an event chronicled on a White House tape known as "the smoking gun." This tape was concealed by the White House for some time after many other taped conversations in the Oval Office and Nixon's EOB office had been released in written form to Congress and the press, and was only forced out by a decision of the Supreme Court in the summer of 1974; shortly after it had become public knowledge, Nixon resigned. The reason for the long concealment seemed immediately obvious: On this tape, the president is heard directing the obstruction of justice by instructing Haldeman to have the CIA impede the FBI's investigation into the Watergate burglary. Since the tape contains the discussion of the problem, the acknowledgment that there is no reason to deter the investigation other than political expediency, and the issuance of the order, the tape is a "smoking gun," that is, in police and prosecutorial slang, direct evidence of criminal guilt.

What has not been understood until now is that the Nixon remarks on the smoking gun tape are the products of John Dean's deceptions that *tricked* Haldeman and Nixon into joining a conspiracy to obstruct justice.

As we have seen in earlier chapters, by June 22 Dean had already constructed his big lie to conceal his instigation of the Watergate burglary, and had begun to cover all traces of his involvement in events prior to June 17. At 8:15 A.M. on Friday, June 23, the phone on Bob Haldeman's desk rang, startling him a bit, since he generally expected no calls before a regular, early morning meeting with the president. John Dean was on the line.

As Haldeman recounted in his book *The Ends of Power*, in that conversation Dean told him that the FBI was "out of control," and that Acting Director Gray "doesn't know what the hell to do, as usual," because one check in Bernard Barker's account bore the signature of Kenneth Dahlberg and others had come from a Mexican bank that the FBI already had found. "They'll know who the depositors are today," Dean warned Haldeman, who responded sarcastically that this was "great news." Haldeman made notes on a pad (which he later used to reconstruct this conversation) as Dean continued on to tell him that "our problem now is to stop the FBI from opening up a whole lot of other things," especially the names of contributors who had been guaranteed anonymity. Mitchell and Stans, Dean said, "are really worried about that," and "they say we have to turn off that investigation of the Mexican bank fast, before they [the FBI] open up everything and spread this mess a lot wider than it is."

Having softened up Haldeman with the bad news—and, indeed, it was alarming news that could adversely affect the outcome of the president's bid for reelection—Dean now offered Haldeman a lifeline, telling him, Haldeman wrote in his book, that the FBI "is convinced" that the people behind the break-in were the CIA, and that "Gray has been looking for a way out of this mess. *I spoke to Mitchell, and he and I agree the thing to do* is for you to tell Walters [Deputy Director of the CIA General Vernon Walters] that we don't know where the Mexican investigation is going to lead. Have him talk to Gray—and maybe the CIA can turn off the FBI down there in Mexico." (Italics added for emphasis.)

In an interview, Haldeman recalled that conversation, in which Dean not only said he had spoken with Mitchell but that "*Mitchell had suggested*" calling in the CIA, and that Dean had simply "concurred on it." (Italics added for emphasis.)

Thus was the idea planted in Haldeman's mind and the responsibility for the suggestion affixed to John Mitchell. The chain of logic was most powerful: use the CIA to block the FBI so that the FBI would not stumble upon and publicize the politically explosive fact that the burglary had been committed with money given to the CRP that had been laundered.

Dean was able to sell Haldeman on the idea principally because he lied on two most important points. First, he embellished what Gray had told him on the twenty-second, picking out of a grab bag of theories being developed by the FBI the one that could be best used to shut down or at least to hinder seriously its investigation. Second, and more important, he invoked "John Mitchell" to mask a desperate need to cover his own misdeeds.

John Dean was able to use Mitchell's name with impunity because he understood the president's confidence in the former attorney general, and because Dean himself was believed at the White House to be a Mitchell man. Since Dean had worked at Justice, he was thought to be in Mitchell's own confidence, even a Mitchell protégé—which he was not.

In fact, Dean did not even speak to Mitchell on the twenty-second, nor on the morning of the twenty-third.

Before going into the events of the twenty-third, and the tape itself, let's examine this crucial point. In Dean's own later testimony to the Senate Watergate committee, he dated his supposed conversation with Mitchell as having taken place on the afternoon of the twenty-third or the twenty-fourth, well after the conversation recorded on the "smoking gun" tape had occurred.

But Dean testified to the committee before the White House's taping system itself had become known to the committee, and a year before the "smoking gun" tape was made public, and thus could not have known that evidence on the tape could ever be used to refute his story of having been uninvolved. When that evidence became available, after Dean had finished his jail sentence and was writing *Blind Ambition*, he sidestepped the whole issue, lest it come back to haunt him. In that book, Dean did not even mention the all-important conversation with Mitchell to which he had testified, or the conception and transmittal of an idea that had such a devastating effect on the presidency.

In a recent interview after the death of John Mitchell, we asked Dean four times to explain the inconsistency between his testimony and the "smoking gun" tape. He could not. First, he tried to tell us it was a matter of dates, on which "it could well be that my memory is wrong. I don't know. I don't want to go back and try to figure this out; it doesn't affect my life a second." When we pointed out that there was no discussion of the supposed Mitchell conversation or the tape of the twenty-third in his book, he responded, "I'm sure there's a lot of things that are not in the book," and pleaded that he was no longer able to fix his mind on what had happened in those days. On a third try, Dean did acknowledge that the issue of CIA involvement in Watergate and a meeting with Mitchell had been raised by the Watergate prosecutors, but that he had said then, "Guys, this is the way I remember it and, you know, that's all I can tell you." When asked a fourth time if he recognized the seriousness of having accused Mitchell of counseling that the CIA obstruct the FBI, Dean was unable to address the point at all, suggesting only that we not rely on his current memory, which was spotty, and instead go back to his testimony and book. "People can pick at it," he said, referring to the testimony, but he still stood by it.

We recently asked Haldeman about the contradictions between the tape and Dean's statements. After reviewing our evidence, Haldeman told us, "I don't know how he [Dean] can deny that he fabricated Mitchell's involvement in his conversation with me on the morning of the twenty-third. . . . The implications are grave for everything he said about Watergate." Wasn't Dean taking an incredible chance that Haldeman would not check with Mitchell before seeing the president? "He knew I wasn't checking with Mitchell on any of this stuff. It wasn't an incredible chance, really," Haldeman allowed. Dean knew, Haldeman added, that "Whatever reports I got [on Watergate] I got from Dean."

As for Mitchell himself, the former attorney general told us that "Dean's whole gambit" was "to drop my name wherever he found it could work." Mitchell has always denied any conversation with Dean in which he counseled or condoned the use of the CIA to deter an FBI investigation. Mitchell's logs of meetings and phone conversations confirm this. On the twenty-second, he had called Dean at 11:15 in the morning, but had not connected with him. That evening Mitchell left his office at 7:05 P.M., went home to his apartment accompanied by LaRue, and had no telephone conversations before an early bedtime. Next morning at 8:15, when Dean was selling the idea to Haldeman and invoking Mitchell's name, Mitchell was at the White House for his first meeting of the day, and had had no opportunity to speak to Dean before it. Not until 6:10 that evening of the twenty-third, Mitchell's logs report, did Dean return Mitchell's call of the twenty-second and speak with him. Mitchell did see Dean at 12:30 on Saturday the twenty-fourth, nearly twenty-seven hours after the "smoking gun" tape was made, when Dean joined a meeting already in progress between Mitchell, Mardian, and Magruder. We'll get into what actually happened in that meeting in the next chapter.

At 8:15 A.M., then, Dean planted in Haldeman's mind that it was Mitchell's recommendation to use the CIA to block the FBI. At 10:04, Haldeman began to brief President Nixon, and the conversation soon turned to Watergate. We've used italics to emphasize Dean's invoking of Mitchell's name:

> **H:** Now on the investigation, you know, the Democratic break-in thing, we're back to the—in the, the problem area because the FBI is not under control, because Gray doesn't exactly know how to control them, and they have, their investigation is now leading into some productive areas, because they've been able to trace the money, not through the money itself, but through the bank, you know, sources—the banker himself. And, it goes in some directions we don't want it to go. . . . *Mitchell came up with yesterday, and John Dean analyzed very carefully last night and concludes, concurs now with Mitchell's recommendation that the only way to solve this,* and we're set up beautifully to do it, ah, in that and that . . . the only network that paid any attention to it last night was NBC . . . they did a massive story on the Cuban—
>
> **P:** That's right . . .
>
> **H:** —thing.
>
> **P:** Right.
>
> **H:** That the way to handle this now is for us to have Walters call Pat Gray and just say, "Stay the hell out of this . . . this is, ah, business here we don't want you to go any further on it." That's not an unusual development. . . . Ah, he [Pat Gray] will call [Assistant Director of the FBI Mark Felt] in and say, "We've got the signal from across the river to, to put the hold on this." And that will fit rather well because the FBI agents who are working this case, at this point, feel that's what it is. This is CIA.

Haldeman then told Nixon that the FBI examination of the checks might lead to Dahlberg and some Texan contributors. Nixon had no idea who Dahlberg was; in fact, the entire conversation is shot through with presidential exclamations of astonishment and exasperation at the break-in and what had been found out about it to date, strongly supporting the notion that Nixon had no knowledge whatsoever of the event prior to learning about it on the morning of June 17.

However, at this important juncture, when his aide first suggested to him the magnitude of Watergate, that it entailed not only out-of-control employees of the CRP (the explanation believed by the upper echelon just then) but now also money that could be traced to the campaign, Nixon's reaction was strikingly similar to the one he had displayed precisely six months earlier, on December 22, 1971, when presented with the fact that Admiral Welander had confirmed the essence of Yeoman Radford's admissions about a military spy ring: The president sought to limit the investigations and to prevent political damage. In December, he had acted on his own initiative; in June of 1972, he grasped at the device presented to him by John Dean, though he did not know it was Dean's. There seems to have been no hesitancy on the part of Haldeman, either, to embrace this line of action.

Learning of Dahlberg and the others, Nixon's immediate response was to suggest that these people be instructed to say that they had given the money directly to the Cubans. Haldeman knew this was an unrealistic approach, and steered Nixon back to the CIA. Nixon liked the idea, reminding Haldeman, "We protected Helms from one hell of a lot of things," taking the CIA-connection line of thinking and running with it. Hunt, he suggested, was the lever:

> P: . . . Hunt . . . that will uncover a lot of things. You open that scab there's a hell of a lot of things and that we just feel it would be very detrimental to have this thing go any further. This involves these Cubans, Hunt, and a lot of hanky-panky that we have nothing to do with ourselves. Well, what the hell, did Mitchell know about this thing to any much of a degree?

> H: I think so. I don't think he knew the details, but I think he knew.

Nixon asked if the problem could be traced to Liddy—who the president said was "a little nuts"—and Haldeman said yes, but that Liddy had been under pressure to get more information.

> P: Pressure from Mitchell?

> H: Apparently. . . .

> P: All right, fine, I understand it all. We won't second-guess Mitchell and the rest. Thank God it wasn't Colson.

Now it was settled in the president's mind: The break-in seemed to have been a CRP operation that had Mitchell's tacit approval but had gone amuck. He was happy and satisfied that it could not be laid where he had thought for the past few days it had actually belonged, at the feet of Chuck Colson—that is to say, responsibility could not be placed in the White House. Colson had denied any connection to the break-in to Haldeman, Ehrlichman, and the president himself, in separate conversations during the past week. Now, here was confirmation of Colson's uninvolvement, seeming to come from Mitchell.

Nixon and Haldeman returned to the CIA-FBI theme. Nixon said he was "not sure" of what was being described to him as the FBI's analysis—that the break-in was "a CIA thing"—but "I'm not going to get that involved." Nonetheless, Nixon bought Dean's package, and left it to Haldeman to wrap it properly. Haldeman should call in the CIA and lean on the agency. However, the president couldn't leave the matter without coaching Haldeman on how to "play it tough" in that meeting because "that's the way they play it and that's the way we are going to play it" with the CIA:

> When you get these [CIA] people in, say, "Look the problem is that this will open up whole, the whole Bay of Pigs thing, and the President just feels that"—ah, without going into the details . . . don't, don't lie to them to the extent to say there is no involvement, but just say this is sort of a comedy of errors, bizarre, without getting into it, [say] "The President believes that it is going to open the whole Bay of Pigs thing up again. And, ah, because these people are plugging for, for keeps, and that they should call the FBI in and say, 'That we wish for the good of the country don't go any further into this case.' " Period.

Note that the president apparently *never considered* summoning Mitchell, Gray, or anyone else, and asking them what had gone on. To do so would have been confrontational, and Nixon's style was to avoid confrontation. Even more astounding, Nixon accepted without further question the involvement of his closest friend in the administration, John Mitchell, in the break-in and in the suggestion to obstruct justice, by using one agency to hamper another.

Nixon clung to that belief throughout Watergate, complaining to press secretary Ron Ziegler a year later in a June 4, 1973, taped conversation that "the key to this thing, Ron, is Mitchell. Always been the key. . . . Mitchell would never step up to this. Well, I suppose, would you? No. No. Former attorney general step up and say you bugged? Shit, I wouldn't."

Mitchell had helped Nixon's fortunes through the law firm in which they had been partners, and then helped engineer Nixon's election victory in 1968. Yet Nixon couldn't even pick up the phone and check on the veracity of what Mitchell was reported to him (through two intermediaries, Dean and Haldeman) as saying or doing. Now, without full cognizance of the facts, and badly misled, the president was springing into action, taking the very step that would eventually seal his own fate. "I never personally confronted Mitchell" on the matter, Nixon wrote in *RN,* because "if there was something he thought I needed to know, he would have told me." But Nixon added another reason: If he asked and Mitchell said, " 'Yes, I did it.' Then what do we say?"

Haldeman's June 23 meeting with the president ended at 11:39 A.M., and he immediately arranged a meeting between Walters, Helms, himself, and Ehrlichman for 1:30 P.M. Moments before that meeting, Haldeman poked his head in again to the Oval Office, and Nixon reemphasized the way to get the CIA to cooperate. Tell the CIA officials, Nixon instructed, "it's going to make the . . . CIA look bad, it's going to make Hunt look bad, and it's likely to blow the whole Bay of Pigs thing, which we think would be very unfortunate for the CIA and for the country at this time, and for American foreign policy. . . . I don't want them to get any ideas we're doing it because our concern is political." Haldeman answered that he understood that instruction.

Haldeman was once again impressed, he writes, by Nixon's brilliant instincts. "Dean had suggested a blatant political move by calling in the CIA—now Nixon showed how much more astute he was by throwing a national security blanket over the same suggestion."

At 1:30, in Ehrlichman's office, the four men sat down. All the participants knew that Helms disliked Nixon and the feeling was mutual. But now Nixon had been maneuvered into believing he had a need to use Helms and his agency. The director began the conversation by surprising Haldeman with the news that he had already spoken to Gray at the FBI and had told him that there was no CIA involvement in the break-in and none of the suspects had worked for the Agency in the last two years. After Helms's surprise, Haldeman then played what he called "Nixon's trump card," telling the CIA men that the entire affair might be linked to the Bay of Pigs.

"Turmoil in the room," Haldeman reported later in his book. "Helms gripping the arms of his chair, leaning forward and shouting, 'The Bay of Pigs had nothing to do with this. I have no concern about the Bay of Pigs.' "

Haldeman understood that Nixon had been right about mentioning the old disaster, for Helms immediately calmed down and voiced no further objections to having Walters tell Gray to back off. Ehrlichman's remembrance of the meeting closely parallels Haldeman's. Just as important is the fact that neither man mentioned in his memoir telling the CIA chiefs that the reason for asking them to block the FBI was political; following Nixon's rather precise instructions, that notion was specifically kept out of the conversation.

At 2:20 P.M. Haldeman went back to the Oval Office and informed Nixon that "Helms kind of got the picture" and had promised, " 'We'll be happy to be helpful, to ah—you know—and we'll handle everything you want.' " Haldeman then added: "Walters is gonna make the call to Gray." The CIA men agreed to help, Helms would later testify, only because they figured the president was privy to a CIA operation in Mexico that even the CIA director did not know about. "This possibility always had to exist," Helms said. "Nobody knows everything about everything."

Dean apparently had an idea about what was going on, for at 1:35 that afternoon—before Haldeman actually had had a chance to brief the president on the Helms meeting—Pat Gray got a call from Dean apprising him that Walters would be phoning for an appointment, and that Gray should see him that afternoon. Walters' secretary called Gray twenty minutes later and scheduled a 2:30 P.M. meeting. Dean phoned Gray again at 2:19 P.M. to see if it was on, learned that it was, and asked Gray to call him when he'd seen Walters.

Once again, John Dean's testimony on these events is strikingly at odds with that of others. In his testimony to the Senate Watergate committee, before the committee was to hear from Gray about the Gray-Dean telephone conversations of June 23, Dean would first avoid revealing any knowledge of the Helms-Walters meeting. Then, when pressed by Senator Inouye, Dean claimed that he had "had no idea that Mr. Haldeman and Mr. Ehrlichman were going to meet with Mr. Helms and General Walters, that was unknown to me until I subsequently was so informed by Mr. Ehrlichman but not as to the substance of the meeting they had held."

Gray and Walters met at 2:34 P.M. at FBI headquarters, and, according to Gray's testimony before Congress, Walters "informed me that we were likely to uncover some CIA assets or sources if we continued our investigation into the Mexican money chain. . . . He also discussed with me the agency agreement under which the FBI and CIA have agreed not to uncover and expose each other's sources." Acting Director Gray had never read that agreement, but considered it logical, and told Walters that the matter would be handled "in a manner that would not hamper the CIA."

By the time Gray testified in 1973, two Walters memcons had been given to the investigating committee by the CIA, and Gray was at pains to answer certain points raised by these memcons, such as the notion that he, Gray, had mentioned to Walters the fact that this was an election year and that there were political considerations above and beyond the interagency ones. Gray admitted he might have said that; certainly, it was on both men's minds.

After Walters left, Gray telephoned Dean to tell him of the meeting—even before Gray phoned his own assistant director in charge of the Watergate investigation to tell him not to schedule interviews of Ogarrio or Dahlberg. Twice more during the afternoon Gray phoned Dean, at 3:24 and at 3:47, to report that the CIA and FBI had both been properly instructed about impeding the ongoing investigation.

The deed was done. Dean had succeeded beyond his expectations. He had deceived the president of the United States into joining a conspiracy to obstruct justice in order to cover up a crime that Nixon had not committed, and to conceal Dean's own crimes. And the president, once again reacting to a crisis without gathering the facts, willingly slipped the noose Dean had handed him around his own neck.

Two years from that time, the revelations of the smoking gun tape would force an end to the Nixon presidency. And in 1991, the words on that astounding tape, and contradictions it pointed up in Dean's sworn testimony, would put an end to John Dean's claim of being only an innocent message-carrier in the cover-up. It is completely ironic that the famous smoking gun tape had as its two most important casualties the president of the United States, Richard Nixon, and his principal accuser, John Dean.

The White House inner circle: Henry Kissinger, John Ehrlichman, President Richard
Nixon, and H. R. Haldeman. *(Official White House photo)*

Nixon and Kissinger often conducted their diplomacy through private rather than official channels. *(Official White House photo)*

The president, Alexander Haig, and Kissinger were engaged in an intricate dance of egos and ambitions that frequently placed the two advisers at odds. *(Official White House photo)*

John Mitchell was Nixon's closest friend in the administration, but their failure to communicate about the Watergate break-in had catastrophic consequences. *(Official White House photo)*

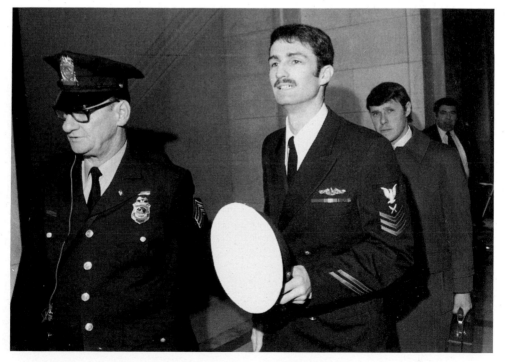

Navy Yeoman Charles Radford. *(AP/Wide World Photos)*

Vice-Admiral Thomas H. Moorer, upon his appointment as the new chairman of the Joint Chiefs of Staff on April 14, 1970. *(Gene Forte/Pictorial Parade)*

Admiral Robert O. Welander (right), arriving for a closed 1974 hearing of the Senate Armed Services Committee in regard to the Moorer-Radford affair. *(AP/Wide World Photos)*

Don Stewart, the Pentagon investigator who helped uncover the Moorer-Radford affair, receiving the Pentagon's second-highest civilian award in recognition of his work. Six months later the White House would campaign to have Stewart indicted for blackmailing the president.

A meeting of the National Security Council, May 1, 1972. At left are Alexander Haig, Henry Kissinger, Admiral Thomas Moorer, an unidentified man, and CIA Director Richard Helms. At right are Secretary of Defense Melvin Laird, President Richard Nixon, Secretary of State William Rogers, and an unidentified man. (*Official White House photo*)

Bob Woodward and Carl Bernstein, at their desk at the *Washington Post.*
(UPI/Bettmann)

USS *Wright*, the aircraft carrier–turned–floating national command post, on which Bob Woodward served his first Navy assignment. As the circuit control officer from 1965 to 1967, Woodward helped operate the ship's massive communications system. *(National Archives)*

From 1967 to 1969, Woodward served as communications officer aboard the USS *Fox*, a guided-missile frigate that helped direct air strikes in Vietnam. His first commanding officer on the ship was Robert O. Welander. *(National Archives)*

John Wesley Dean III, counsel to the president. *(Official White House photo)*

Maureen Elizabeth Kane Owen Biner Dean. Before she became John Dean's wife, she roomed with close friend Heidi Rikan, a.k.a. "Cathy Dieter," who ran a ring of call girls with the help of attorney Phillip Mackin Bailley. (Sygma)

Phillip Mackin Bailley, after his arrest on charges of Mann Act violations. (Copyright Washington Post)

Dean's four major operatives in his intelligence-gathering efforts: *(above)* John "Jack" Caulfield *(Sygma)*; *(above right)* Tony Ulasewicz, the ex–New York City detective who became a private eye in service of the White House *(Sygma)*; *(below)* G. Gordon Liddy, "a weapon waiting to be aimed and fired" *(UPI/Bettmann)*; *(below right)* E. Howard Hunt, Liddy's cohort and an ex–CIA employee *(UPI/Bettmann)*.

Jeb Stuart Magruder, the Committee to Re-elect the President official who worked most closely with Dean. *(Official White House photo)*

Closeup of notebook and key confiscated from Martinez by police. The key fit the desk of Maxie Wells, secretary to Democratic National Committee official Spencer Oliver; Martinez says he was given the key by E. Howard Hunt, but Hunt denies it.

Watergate burglar Eugenio R. Martinez. *(UPI/Bettmann)*

Alexander Haig, newly appointed White House chief of staff, greets newsmen in
H. R. Haldeman's former office on May 4, 1973. *(UPI/Bettmann)*

J. Fred Buzhardt (right, with aides) worked with Haig to keep the Moorer-Radford spy ring—and its implications—under wraps. *(Official White House photo)*

Alexander Butterfield, Haig's longtime friend, revealed the White House taping system. *(Dennis Brack/Black Star)*

Leonard Garment worked with Buzhardt in counseling the beleaguered president as Watergate began to overwhelm him. *(Official White House photo)*

Richard Nixon, departing Bethesda Air Force Base and the presidency, on August 9, 1974. *(Official White House photo)*

President Gerald Ford, Phil Buchen, Alexander Haig, and Benton Becker on September 26, 1974, discussing the subjects of the Nixon pardon and the transfer of the president's records, papers, and tapes. Shortly thereafter, Becker would fly to San Clemente on behalf of President Ford to negotiate these issues—neither man knowing that Haig had already been negotiating on his own. *(Official White House photo / permission of Benton L. Becker)*

13

HUSH MONEY— FOR HUNT

DEAN has long admitted participating in obtaining support money for the burglars, but has said that he did so in an attempt to keep the terrible tar baby of Watergate from sticking to the president. But Dean's desperate search to find money and pay it had nothing to do with protecting Nixon, and everything to do with protecting Dean himself. It also had nothing to do with the burglars, and was not money collected for their support. Among the best testaments to that notion is the fact that almost all of the "support" money raised for the burglars' legal and personal expenses eventually became hush money given to Howard Hunt.

At 6:10 in the evening of June 23, after his long series of phone calls with Pat Gray, Dean phoned Mitchell and arranged to take part in a meeting on Saturday, June 24, at the CRP offices. The next day, at 12:30 P.M., he joined a meeting that was already in progress with Mitchell, Mardian, and LaRue, while Magruder came in and out.

Dean later painted a brief picture for the investigating committee of this meeting that he thought had taken place either Friday afternoon or Saturday morning:

205

I reported to [these men] Gray's theories of the case as he had related them to me. . . . During this meeting there were wide ranging discussions of the many problems then confronting the reelection committee including such matters as the problem the civil lawsuit filed by the Democratic National Committee could cause, the problem of the Dahlberg and Mexican checks, and to the best of my recollection this was the first time I had heard any discussion of the need for money to take care of those who were involved in the break-in of June 17.

Dean told the Senate that a discussion of the CIA involvement hypothesis "prompted Mr. Mardian, as I recall, to suggest that the CIA might be of some assistance in providing us support, and he also raised the question that the CIA might have a very proper reason to do so because of the fact that these were former CIA operatives." In this version, Dean claimed that Mitchell and Mardian then told him to explore that very idea with Haldeman and Ehrlichman.

Dean's testimony about this meeting is a tissue of lies and half-truths. First, this was not when Dean first learned of the need to pay support for the burglars—Dean had heard the request of Gordon Liddy on this matter, and acceded to it, during their walk in the park on June 19. Second, Mardian denied being the first to bring up the idea of support at this meeting, and neither Mitchell nor Mardian told Dean to take up the support issue with Haldeman and Ehrlichman. Mardian told us that they went into the subjects that Dean lists, but that the issue of paying money for the burglars was first brought up by Dean. Mardian testified that it was Dean's mention of the CIA that pushed Mardian to exclaim that if these were CIA people, the agency could "take care of its own people," because it was "a CIA problem and not a committee [to Re-elect] problem." Here Mardian, the lieutenant, was echoing the party line already laid down by his general, Mitchell, that any payment of support was not a CRP problem, and even making light of it. Such conversational patterns were common in the close-knit group of Mardian, LaRue, and Mitchell, but the position that the CRP would not pay support money was real.

As Dean had taken a theory of Pat Gray's and turned it into the notion to trick Haldeman (and, ultimately, Nixon) into using the CIA to block the FBI's investigation, Dean now took Mardian's flip remark that the CIA ought to pay for its own people and made it into an attempt to extort from the intelligence agency the funds to keep the burglars quiet. On Monday, June 26, Dean phoned Ehrlichman. Dean's testimony and Ehrlichman's account of what was said during this phone call are completely at odds. We find Ehrlichman's account credible. Ehrlichman told us that Dean said that it was necessary for him, Dean, to liaise with the CIA, and asked for permission to call Walters. He did not say his purpose was to try squeezing money from the burglars' old employer, and so Ehrlichman didn't know he was condoning such a course of action when he told Dean that he could call Walters.

That call came at 10:00 A.M., Walters remembered in a memcon to the CIA files that he wrote a few days later. In the conversation, according to Walters, he was asked to meet with Dean "about the matter that John Ehrlichman and Bob Haldeman had discussed with me on the 23rd of June," and was invited to check this out with the two men before doing so. Walters dutifully phoned Ehrlichman and was told to "talk freely to Dean."

So far, Dean had managed to trick both Walters and Ehrlichman about this matter of the money. But he didn't reckon on opposition from the formidable Walters. When the general arrived in Dean's White House office at 11:45 A.M., they fenced a bit: Dean said the "bugging" case was becoming "awkward," and that one of the FBI's theories was that it was done by the CIA, which Walters denied vehemently. To quote the memcon, "Dean then said that some of the accused were getting scared and 'wobbling'. I said that even so they could not implicate the Agency."

In fact, it was not the burglars who were scared and wobbling, but Dean. We can see that in retrospect, for instance, because his intimate knowledge of the burglary and its objectives was belied by his use of the word *bugging*, which Walters even put in quotes in his memcon. Next, in the conversation, Dean misrepresented to Walters his authorization from Ehrlichman and Haldeman. As Walters later wrote, Dean asked, ostensibly on behalf of the White House, "whether there was not some way that the Agency could pay bail for [the burglars]. . . . He added that it was not just bail, that if these men went to prison, could we (CIA) find some way to pay their salaries while they were in jail out of covert action funds."

Walters became grim after this request, and turned it off quite decisively. The value of the CIA to the nation, he pointed out, was that it was apolitical; if the Agency were to pay bail and salaries to the burglars it would "become known sooner or later" and would then escalate the scandal to ten times its original size. "The Agency would be completely discredited with the public and the Congress and would lose all value to the President and the Administration," the general reported himself in the memcon as telling Dean. Paying bail for the burglars "could only be done upon direction at the 'highest level.'" In this, Walters was clearly making reference to the president without naming him. And Walters in effect warned Dean not to go to the president by saying that if such payments were made, they would inevitably hurt those who ordered or condoned them.

Dean seemed taken aback, Walters noted with some satisfaction, but asked again if there was anything the CIA could do. Walters agreed to carry the request to Helms, even though Walters told Dean he was sure he knew what Helms would say.

Next day, Walters was again summoned to Dean's office at eleven in the morning, and reported that in the interim he had spoken with Helms, who, as Walters had suspected, also did not want to pay the burglars. In his memcon of this second day Walters recalled raising the metaphorical ante of his warning to Dean: "Involving the Agency would transform what was now a medium-sized conventional explosive into a multi-megaton explosion and simply was not worth the risk." Dean, Walters reports, looked "glum" but "said he agreed with my judgment in all of these matters." On Wednesday the twenty-eighth, the two men met for a third time. Dean asked for ideas about how to handle the whole Watergate affair, and Walters gave him a beauty:

I said that this affair already had a strong Cuban flavor and everyone knew the Cubans were conspiratorial and anxious to know what the policies of both parties would be towards Castro. They, therefore, had a plausible motive for attempting this amateurish job.

It was just after this third conversation, on June 28, that Walters (whose photographic memory is the stuff of legends) sat down and wrote the first of the memcons of the meetings, which were later given to several senatorial committees investigating Watergate. The committees were quite interested in them, but did not question Dean intensively about their validity.

Recently, we asked Dean for his memories of these conversations with Walters, and the memcons of them that place him at the heart of the cover-up in its earliest stages. He had made no mention of talking to Walters in *Blind Ambition*. With us, he remembered only one meeting, not three, and said that Walters had pompously taken a "Young man, you're playing with fire" approach. He characterized Walters' memories of a request from him, Dean, for bail and support money as "Horseshit; I mean, it just never ever happened the way he portrayed it."

*   *   *

A moment for an aside on another memcon written by Walters at about the same time—this one about his and Helms's June 23 meeting with Haldeman and Ehrlichman. The four memcons were written starting on the afternoon of June 28, and the timing is of note. That afternoon, Walters' boss, Richard Helms, was dictating a memo of his own, an internal one. In it, he told his deputy that his meeting with Pat Gray had just been canceled, but that he had told Gray on the telephone to call off scheduled interviews with CIA officers Karl Wagner and John Caswell. Gray agreed to do so. Helms was going to be out of town for the next several days, and wanted Walters to know this in case Walters had to do further business with Gray.

We believe that the Helms memo of June 28 and the Walters memcon of the same date that refers to the meeting of the twenty-third are intimately related. In his version of the June 23 meeting, Walters wrote right at the top of his description of the four-way meeting with Helms, himself, Ehrlichman, and Haldeman that the White House men were upset about the DNC break-in and they contended that "the Democrats are trying to maximize it." Moreover, "the investigation was leading to a lot of important people and this could get worse. . . . The whole affair was getting embarrassing and it was the President's wish" that Walters call Gray.

This account differs from those of Haldeman and Ehrlichman in one important particular: It brings in politics—the one subject, as we can read from the tape transcript quoted above, that the president expressly forbade Haldeman to mention as the reason for the blocking request. Since Haldeman was very good at following precise orders, it is likely that he did so on this occasion, and that Walters' account is somewhat suspect. The Helms memo, written on the same afternoon as Walters', also supports this thesis, for the Helms memo is a real statement of the CIA's desire to brush over tracks that the CIA itself, for its own reasons, did not want uncovered. The Walters memo can then be seen as an attempt to use the cover of a White House "political" request to do what was in the CIA's interest anyway.

The Walters memcon was designed to cover the CIA's rear, to sit in the files awaiting a future investigation that might want to examine some documentary evidence. Walters had to have realized after speaking with John Dean that the CIA would sooner or later be dragged into any inquiry on Watergate, and despite official CIA denials, the Agency's fingerprints were all over the people involved in the Watergate burglary—the Cubans and Hunt and McCord had all worked for the Agency. Martinez was still on the payroll, and Hunt worked for the

Mullen Company, a known CIA front. There were many reasons the CIA would have wanted to keep such ties quiet.

As Jim Hougan first noted in his 1984 book *Secret Agenda*, the CIA traces surrounding Watergate are intriguing. Unraveling the mystery of these traces as well as the questions raised by the behavior of McCord, who seemed to be running a totally separate agenda from those of Liddy and Hunt during the break-ins, is best left to future historians; these questions do not impact on the story we tell, to which we now return.

On June 28, when it became clear to Dean (after three rebuffs by Walters) that the CIA wasn't going to pay bail and salaries to anyone, he tried a different source. Knowing that Herb Kalmbach had access to some old campaign money, Dean met with John Ehrlichman at 2:10 P.M. on the twenty-eighth and used Mitchell's name a third time. On this go-round, the "idea thief" married the misuse of Mitchell's name to a notion suggested by Walters' Cuban connection reference during their June 28 meeting. Dean told Ehrlichman that Mitchell counseled that Dean should contact the president's personal attorney to help set up a defense fund for the Cuban burglars. Hearing the magic name of Mitchell attached to the proposal, Ehrlichman okayed the idea, and Dean then trotted it to Haldeman, who said Dean could indeed call Kalmbach. That call was made at 3:00 P.M., and was a demand that Herb meet him in Washington the very next day. He even told Kalmbach to call Ulasewicz and have him in town, too, and ready for action. Kalmbach did as requested, made the call and hopped the red-eye for the capital.

In Dean's testimony to the Senate committee, he described an important meeting he said he'd attended on that same day of the twenty-eighth, at which Mitchell supposedly approved the use of Kalmbach to raise money and asked Dean to get similar approvals from Ehrlichman and Haldeman. In Dean's recollection, Mardian and LaRue were also at the meeting, but Mitchell pulled Dean aside to whisper directly in his ear that Ehrlichman in particular should "be very interested and anxious to accommodate" the burglars because of the Cubans' past involvement with the Dr. Fielding break-in.

This supposed meeting with Mitchell was a complete fabrication. There was never any whispering in the ear, for Mitchell's logs and a newspaper article reveal that he was in New York that day, trying to deal with his disintegrating wife, who accompanied him back on the plane, which arrived in Washington at 5:30 that evening. In fact, as the *Washington Post* story of June 29 revealed, Mitchell had been away from the capital for three days. In that article, reporter Dorothy McCardle recounts that she spoke to various members of the CRP and quoted them as saying that Mitchell and Martha had been in her eighth-floor suite at the Westchester Country Club in Rye, New York, for the past two days, "talking over their problems." McCardle quoted a committee official who said that "Various doctors were called in to try to help Mrs. Mitchell. . . . Her husband has been trying to get help for her."

Mitchell himself did not know at the time he testified before the Senate committee that this newspaper story would have helped him deny Dean's accusations, or else he would have provided it as evidence, along with his log. And the committee never sought verification for Mitchell's version of events, because they were intent on believing John Dean.

In Dean's testimony, June 28 was a crucial and very long day—the talk with Walters, the (fabricated) meeting with Mitchell, and so on. Dean was in Ehrlichman's office at 6:30 in the evening when Pat Gray walked in. As the reader will recall, a week earlier Dean had had Howard Hunt's safe opened. Dean and Fred Fielding had divided the material into three piles, one of which Dean had handed over to the FBI, and another—containing the Hermès notebooks and the pop-up address book—he had placed in his safe. One pile remained. It consisted of two files, and Dean had it at this meeting. According to Dean, when he'd told Ehrlichman about this material, Ehrlichman had told him to "deep six" it.

Pat Gray agreed that there had been a meeting in the Ehrlichman office that evening, and he testified that during it, Ehrlichman told him, "John has something that he wants to turn over to you." It was two legal-sized folders containing what Dean described to Gray as "sensitive and classified papers of a political nature" on which Hunt had worked, and which had nothing to do with Watergate. Gray asked if these should become part of the FBI's Watergate file, and Dean responded that he wanted to be able to say that he'd turned them over to the FBI, but asked Gray to keep them away from the others because they were "political dynamite" and "clearly should not see the light of day." As Gray testified, many months later,

It is true that neither Mr. Ehrlichman nor Mr. Dean expressly instructed me to destroy the files. But there was, and is, no doubt in my mind that destruction was intended. . . . The clear implication of the substance and tone of their remarks was that these two files were to be destroyed and I interpreted this to be an order from the counsel to the President of the United States issued in the presence of one of the two top assistants to the President of the United States.

Gray took the files home, stashed them under his clean shirts, and found various other places to keep them. He did not immediately destroy them, though he intended to do so and eventually did burn them; we shall see in a later chapter how these files, and Gray's acceptance of them, would be brought to the fore again by John Dean at a time when he desperately needed to distract prosecutors from his own trail. And the most important papers from Hunt's safe—the Hermès notebooks that contained Hunt's chronology of the events and people involved in the two break-ins—which Dean did *not* give to the FBI or to Gray, remained in Dean's possession, carefully hidden under the president's estate plan.

The long day of June 28, 1972, had drawn to a close for John Dean. There remained a last set of men to be tricked in order for Dean's payment scheme to be established: lawyer Herb Kalmbach and gumshoe Tony Ulasewicz.

In using these two men, Dean relied on his few remaining assets. He had used them in his original intelligence operation. They already knew him, believed him to be acting for the president, and were generally willing to go along with his requests for speed and secrecy. Dean was getting to like park benches these days, and on June 29 he met Kalmbach on one in Lafayette Park, across from the White House, and advised him of a "very important assignment," namely that "We would like to have you raise funds" for the burglars. Dean told Kalmbach that he wanted him to use Ulasewicz for the deliveries of the money, so that this could all be kept away from the door of the White House.

Kalmbach called Maurice Stans, who had charge of that old money, and asked him to bring it over to the Statler-Hilton Hotel from the CRP headquarters. Stans brought the cash over himself and asked no questions about its disposition. After Stans left, Kalmbach called Ulasewicz to come to Washington. Upon Ulasewicz's arrival on the next day, Kalmbach handed him what Tony remembered was a laundry bag that contained $75,000 in cash, plus "a yard," that is, a $100 bill. As Ulasewicz later wrote,

It was through Kalmbach that I learned, for the first time, that others were involved in the burglary at the Democratic National Committee who hadn't yet been arrested. Kalmbach explained that a man named Hunt and his wife were exerting a lot of pressure to come up with enough money to cover the bail, attorneys' fees, and living expenses for the Watergate burglars and their families.

No other names were told to Ulasewicz by Kalmbach—no Gordon Liddy, no James McCord, no Barker, Martinez, or any of the other men from Miami, only Hunt. Dean later testified that Kalmbach had suggested the use of Ulasewicz as a bag man, but both Kalmbach and Ulasewicz said it was Dean's idea. That day in the hotel, Kalmbach told the querulous Tony that he had checked Dean's request with Ehrlichman, who had said that in paying money for the burglars' defense, "the White House was responding to a moral obligation."

Clearly, the idea-chief was at work again, using Ehrlichman's moral willingness to pay support money for small fish caught in a net, and turning that sentiment into a way to get silence money to the man Dean had, in a panic, already tried and failed to get out of the country, Howard Hunt. The moral tone of the payments didn't make Tony Ulasewicz feel any better about the possibility of this operation being contained for very long, but it seems to have sanctified it enough in his mind so that he agreed to go ahead. Kalmbach and Ulasewicz used code names: Mitchell was "the pipe," Hunt was "the writer," and the entire code had to do with "players" following the "script." There were no code names for Liddy, McCord, or the Cubans, because no payments were destined for them, though Ulasewicz didn't yet know that. Prospective payees would easily understand the code, Ulasewicz was told. He took the money home to New York and waited for instruction on where, when, and to whom to deliver it.

As any attorney knew, whoever made the payoff decisions—determining to whom Ulasewicz should deliver silence money, and in what amounts—could be violating the federal criminal statute of obstruction of justice. Ulasewicz states that he received his instructions from Kalmbach, and Kalmbach tells us that he received his instructions from John Dean, the first one on June 29.

When Dean later testified, he kept an eye on that obstruction of justice statute and constructed his version of the meeting with Kalmbach in Lafayette Park so he could avoid being charged with it. He said that after Kalmbach had obtained the funds for the payoff, Kalmbach visited Dean in the EOB accompanied by Fred LaRue, so that Dean could give them the details of who was to get how much. "I recall that such a meeting did occur in my office," Dean testified, "but I was on and off the telephone while LaRue and Kalmbach were going over the figures and I have absolutely no recollection of the details of their discussion. . . . I have no further knowledge of how or when or to whom delivery was made." But Kalmbach was quite clear to us that he received instructions from Dean. Moreover, Watergate committee records show that of the $219,000 in money disbursed by Ulasewicz, $154,000 went to Hunt or his wife, and $25,000 more to Hunt's lawyer, William C. Bittman. Hunt was one of the few people who could testify to Dean's involvement prior to the break-ins, the only person who knew that Dean had cut Liddy out of knowledge of the break-ins' real target and knew that Dean was responsible for the order to target the Olivers/Wells/Governors' area instead of O'Brien's office. Hunt also knew of Dean's continuing involvement in post–break-in acts.

On Friday, June 30, John Mitchell was summoned to a private lunch with the president. He had very little inkling as to what it would be about, but he knew that his difficulties with his wife Martha had been spread all over the newspapers.

That family situation became the overt text of the president's conversation at the luncheon. But there was an unstated subtext, and it had to do with Nixon's beliefs as to Mitchell's involvement in Watergate. Taking his information from Haldeman, who had it from Dean, Nixon had come around to the belief that Mitchell had sanctioned the break-in. That belief had been bolstered by the attribution to Mitchell of the suggestion that the CIA be used to stop the FBI— which, we now know, was a lie planted by Dean. Nixon may also have been informed of a third Dean lie—that Mitchell had approved the payment of support money to the burglars. In any event, believing that Mitchell had a role in the break-in and understanding that the Watergate trail would soon lead to the CRP employee Liddy, Nixon wanted to put distance between himself and the head of the reelection committee.

Citing Mitchell's family situation, Nixon asked him to resign as head of the CRP but to continue on in a private capacity as the leader of the campaign. Mitchell was taken aback by this suggestion, and had had no intention of resigning when he had entered the White House for lunch, but felt he had to bow to his chief's wishes in this matter. Shortly, he resigned. Thus did Dean's tricking of the president into the cover-up claim as its first palpable victim the man whose name Dean had so often invoked without permission, John Mitchell.

14

DAMAGE CONTROL ACTION OFFICER

IN *Blind Ambition*, John Dean sets out succinctly his version of the cover-up:

I began my role in the cover-up as a fact-finder and worked my way up to idea man, and finally to desk officer. At the outset, I sensed no personal danger from what I was doing. In fact, I took considerable satisfaction from knowing I had no criminal liability, and I consistently sought to keep it that way. I wanted to preserve my function as an "agent" of my superiors, taking no initiatives, always acting on orders. . . . I sustained the image of myself as a "counsel" rather than as an active participant for as long as I could, but the line blurred and finally vanished. I was too central a figure, and there was too much hasty activity required as the cover-up proceeded speedily along its two main themes—containing the Justice Department investigation, and paying the hush money to the defendants. I am still not sure when I crossed the line into criminal culpability. . . .

This *mea culpa* is strong psychologically, but bears very little relationship to the truth. Dean had crossed the line between legitimate actions and criminal culpability long before the payment of hush money to the Hunts.

Gordon Liddy had spilled the beans to Dean after Dean agreed that he was what Liddy insisted on calling his "damage control action officer." As the summer of 1972 wore on, John Dean became just that, and more. He orchestrated the cover-up that he had already set in motion and sold it (on the supposed basis that it was John Mitchell's idea) to Haldeman, Ehrlichman, Nixon, the FBI, the CIA, and nearly every other participant in the obstruction of justice. He was able to do so because his own expansion into a power vacuum and the reluctance of superiors to get involved superbly situated him for the task. For instance, Ehrlichman and Haldeman accepted him as the White House point man on Watergate, even encouraged him to take on the work, and allowed Dean to deal directly with Walters and Gray.

How Dean appeared to many different people depended on where they were on the spectrum of involvement in the Watergate affair and in earlier, clandestine matters undertaken on behalf of the White House. To the men who knew of his deep involvement in Watergate prior to the break-ins, Dean was a co-conspirator who had apparently been charged by the president with the responsibility of keeping their own participation minimized. To Haldeman and Ehrlichman, Dean was a subordinate working aggressively on their behalf to contain the law enforcement investigation by restricting it to the burglars only, and therefore to prevent the investigation from reaching the White House; they knew, for instance, that Dean was acting to conceal the Hunt-Liddy activities such as the break-in to Dr. Fielding's office. To President Nixon and to John Mitchell, Dean was a bright young man throwing his energy into keeping the scandal from lapping at their doors. To the law enforcement community—principally the prosecutors and Pat Gray of the FBI—Dean was the president's counsel, a man who appeared to have had no involvement in the break-in, and who was charged with looking after the president's interests.

Dean must have been grateful to be at the center of everything and to be regarded by the others in these benevolent ways, for he had a great deal to hide. To conceal what he had done, in the summer and fall of 1972 Dean spent his days arranging hush money payments to the Hunts, keeping himself apprised of and in fact influencing the FBI investigations, coaching witnesses to the grand jury, and staying abreast of the developments in the various criminal and civil cases being brought as a result of the Watergate break-in. We are going to examine each of these tasks separately, but want the reader to recognize that they were being pursued simultaneously during the several months prior to Election Day of November 1972.

At first, Tony Ulasewicz's efforts to deliver money to people were a comedy of errors. Neither Douglas Caddy, the initial lawyer for the burglars, nor Paul O'Brien, CRP's lawyer, would take any of the money—they didn't want to be a part of the "script"—and Tony was only able to make one $25,000 payment to Hunt's attorney, William C. Bittman, before he, too, refused to take any further part in the payoffs. The proposed drops involved lockers in transportation centers, brown paper bags, staged rendezvous and fallback strategies, and a whole array of devices to avoid having the person being paid learn the true identity of the money carrier. Ulasewicz made so many telephone calls from public phone booths that he needed a hefty supply of nickels and dimes, so, as he later wrote, "To save my pants, avoid heavy bulging pockets, and an increasing dose of irritation, I bought myself a busman's money changer and hooked it on my belt." His deliveries hit their stride only after Kalmbach (acting on instructions from Dean) connected Tony to the "writer's wife," Dorothy Hunt.

Dean had a special reason to take care of Hunt, since Hunt had information on Dean's role in the DNC break-ins. To neutralize Hunt, Dean had already emptied Hunt's White House safe, given some of the sensitive files in it to Pat Gray, telling him that the files "clearly should not see the light of day," and had retained and concealed the Hermès notebooks that could link him to Hunt.

In the summer and fall of 1972, the deliveries to Dorothy Hunt went far beyond the money Tony had originally been given for the purpose of supplying the burglars' needs, and so Ulasewicz had to meet Kalmbach three more times to get more cash: $40,000 passed into Tony's care at the Regency Hotel in New York, $28,900 at the Statler-Hilton in Washington, and $75,000 at the Airporter Motel near the Orange County Airport in California. Mrs. Hunt told Tony that they had to get some money to Gordon Liddy, but "the way she spoke about him, however, made me feel that she was looking for a way to deal him out of the game as quickly as she could."

In short order, Ulasewicz delivered to Dorothy Hunt installments of $40,000, $43,000, $18,000 and $53,000, all in cash. These payments were ostensibly for the Cubans as well as for Hunt, but the Cubans saw very little of it. Two years later, after serving his prison sentence, Hunt admitted to Richard Ben-Veniste of the Special Prosecutor's office that, as Ben-Veniste later wrote, "the cash received from CRP and the White House *was* a quid pro quo for silence." We find interesting an exchange that took place at the trial of the defendants on the cover-up charges. When Hunt was asked whether his demands were really blackmail, Hunt replied, "No, sir."

"What did you consider it, investment planning?" the cross-examining lawyer sarcastically asked.

"I considered it, if you will, in the tradition of a bill collector, attempting to get others who made a prior contract to live up to it."

Gordon Liddy believed he had made a contract of a different sort, and had vowed to live up to it. On the twenty-eighth of June, in the CRP offices, he had taken the first action in his campaign of silence. He had refused to be interviewed by the FBI and had been summarily fired for refusing to cooperate. He arranged to go back to Poughkeepsie and work on some legal matters, but knew that sooner or later the Watergate trail would lead to him and he would be indicted and arrested. He believed he had made errors and was willing to take full responsibility for them; more importantly, he had determined never to allow the investigation to reach higher than himself. He had personally assured both Magruder and Dean that he would never talk, and made it the central point of his life to adhere to that promise. During this period between the burglary and his indictment, Liddy received a phone call suggesting that he was going to be paid for his "manuscript" in the form of money left in a locker at National Airport in Washington. Ulasewicz writes that he was insistent that money for Liddy "should go directly to him and not pass through the Hunts' hands. I did this not to keep Liddy quiet, but to keep him from getting screwed."

Liddy retrieved the money from the drop site and gave it all to his lawyer. Then he had a strange conversation with the Hunts, who said that if their "principals" wanted Liddy and Hunt out of the country, the Hunts would arrange for both families to be transported to Nicaragua, where they could live like kings under the protection of Hunt's friend Somoza. Later on in the summer, still before he was indicted, Liddy received $19,000 directly from Mrs. Hunt. She later told him that it really came from herself and Howard, not from their "principals," who didn't really care about Liddy. Liddy was furious but accepted this freeze-out with a stoic shrug, and went on remaining silent. Not until many years later did Liddy learn of the huge amounts that had been paid to Hunt as hush money.

That summer of 1972 was hectic. The FBI was interviewing lots of people, and Dean managed to insert himself into this process in two ways. First, in an extraordinary move, he convinced both the FBI and various White House employees that he should sit in on the interviews the FBI was conducting of them—because he was counsel to the president. Actually, had he been functioning in a correct manner as counsel to the president, he would have refused to have anything to do with those interviews, on the grounds that they might interfere with his duty to his actual client, the president. It was not to the benefit of those being interviewed or to Nixon for Dean to sit in on the interviews, for his presence showed prejudicial conduct on behalf of the president, which could only reflect badly on Nixon should it become known. And, according to several FBI agents, Dean did not merely sit in on the interviews; he actively influenced them, always ready and eager to demonstrate his authority. Dean's arrogance and abrasiveness were sore spots for the agents, who complained among themselves of the counsel's involvement in and knowledge of an FBI matter. During the interviews, Dean would constantly interject himself, often chiding the agent for pursuing a "fishing expedition" with the witness, or abruptly terminating the interview with a wave of his hand, announcing "Time's up." One agent who met with Dean "more than a dozen times" during such interviews told us that "each time I wanted to punch him in the face." Sitting in on the interviews was solely of benefit to Dean, who did so in order to learn what people in the White House might have to say that could be dangerous or helpful to him, and, by his very presence, to coerce possible witnesses into silence.

Second, Dean convinced Pat Gray that he, Dean, ought to receive copies of all the FBI's raw investigative reports on the Watergate matter. When he requested these reports, Dean did not tell Gray that he had previously requested them from Kleindienst and Petersen, who had turned him down. In Hoover's time, as a matter of policy, the FBI always refused to give out such things as the 302s and the airtels, because they contained undigested material, some of it only allegations that were often disproved by further investigative work. The only FBI materials usually let out of the house were summary-type reports in which field investigations were at least weighed and put into context. Gray acquiesced in the demand for the raw data because he believed Dean to be acting for the president, who, as chief executive, had the right to any documents produced by an executive branch department. The president didn't want these raw reports and would have had little use for them; but they were of great benefit to Dean because they allowed him to learn what the investigators knew almost as soon as they did, so he could take actions to counter or head off the FBI's excursions into territory that might be dangerous to him.

Dean began receiving FBI reports from Gray in late June 1972. None of the White House tapes and no written record of the Nixon White House shows that Dean reported any of the substance of the investigative information to the president, either himself or through Haldeman or Ehrlichman. It was information he kept to himself, though in witness interviews, we were told, Dean would openly read copies of the 302s and "remind" the FBI agent conducting the interview about relevant material contained in the reports. For the FBI to give raw files to Dean was tantamount to giving a match to a pyromaniac.

In early August, Jeb Magruder learned from the prosecutors that he was a target of the grand jury probe. Magruder had said very little to the FBI or to the grand jury in his one brief appearance, but was worried about what could happen to him if he was asked to testify at length. During this period, he wrote in *An American Life*, both Mitchell and Dean gave him assurances that he wouldn't be hung out to dry. He recalled standing in his CRP office, looking out the window at Pennsylvania Avenue one hot summer afternoon, when Dean told him, "Jeb, the President is very pleased with the way you've handled things. You can be sure that if you're indicted you'll be taken care of." And, Magruder says Dean added, "executive clemency would be exercised in my behalf." Magruder was scheduled to appear a second time before the grand jury on August 16, and to see the prosecutors one day earlier, without a lawyer present. It had only just become publicly known that the burglars had been paid with money from the CRP, and Magruder, as a high campaign official, could expect rough treatment this time around. Magruder wrote that he discussed his forthcoming appearance with Mitchell—Mitchell denied that—but that specific coaching on it came from John Dean at the Executive Office Building on the morning of the fifteenth:

> I paced nervously around the large office while Dean sat at his desk firing questions at me, the toughest ones he could come up with, particularly on the money and Liddy's role at CRP. We discussed in great detail how I should speak of Liddy. On the one hand, we wanted to suggest that Liddy was the sort of erratic individual who was capable of having planned and carried out the Watergate burglary on his own. . . . On the other hand, Dean and I agreed that I should not be too harsh on Liddy in any personal way, lest he learn of it and become angry and decide to speak out instead of remaining silent. . . . Dean was at his best that morning . . . and the advice he gave me was excellent. As it turned out, he had a very good fix on what the prosecutors would ask me, and his two-hour interrogation of me was time well spent.

We have become so inured to scenes like this arising out of the Watergate affair that it is important to pause for a moment and consider the spectacle of a lawyer, the counsel to the president, illegally coaching a co-conspirator on how to perjure himself before the grand jury, with the "dress rehearsal" taking place in an official executive branch office. Neither Magruder nor Dean ever considered telling the truth to the grand jury just then. Also, remark how good Dean's information was: Dean was better briefed than the prosecutors, probably from his viewing of the FBI's raw investigative files. Indeed, a frustrated agent told us that "the Watergate investigation was being run out of the White House," and that "the one man who knew everything about the investigation was John Dean. Dean knew more about the Watergate investigation than Earl Silbert." In their coaching session, Dean told Magruder that he knew Chief Prosecutor Earl Silbert personally, and that Silbert would be tough; this was the ostensible reason for Dean's coaching.

Dean's grilling of Magruder lasted two hours. The prosecutors' own questioning lasted three, and Jeb felt the tension lift after the first hour, when he discerned that the prosecutors had begun to believe his fabrications. His actual grand jury appearance the next day was "anti-climactic," and, Magruder concluded with relief, "apparently I had sold them our story. To do so seemed all-important at the time, for selling our story seemed crucial to the reelection of the President."

It was also crucial to keeping Magruder himself out of jail, and even more crucial to protecting John Dean. That's why Dean spent so much time preparing Magruder, for if Jeb "strayed off the reservation"—the phrase that came to be used in the Nixon inner circle to mean refusing to adhere to the approved story of the burglary and the cover-up—Dean could not have remained at liberty himself.

Magruder was even more astounded at Dean the day after the grand jury appearance, when Dean phoned to say that his sources reported that Jeb would *not* be indicted, and neither would anyone else other than the four Cubans, McCord, Liddy, and Hunt. Since those actual indictments would not be announced for another entire month, Dean's sources had to be very good indeed.

They were. As we will document later, in chronological sequence, Dean was receiving information on the grand jury proceedings from a variety of well-placed sources.

In the two weeks following Magruder's grand jury appearance and Dean's apparent learning of the limits of the indictments, problems for the White House began arising on several fronts even as Nixon was renominated by the Republicans at their Miami convention. Democratic Representative Wright Patman, chairman of the House Banking and Currency Committee, ordered a staff investigation into the money-laundering aspects of the Watergate affair; lawyers for the DNC began taking depositions in their civil suit against the CRP; in a Florida suit against Bernard Barker, Kenneth Dahlberg said that he personally gave to Maurice Stans the $25,000 check that had shown up in Barker's account; and the General Accounting Office released a report citing Stans's finance committee for eleven "apparent and possible violations" of the new federal election law, involving up to $350,000 and including the $114,000 in Dahlberg and Mexican checks in Barker's account. The GAO referred these possible violations to the Justice Department for investigation, and, on August 28, Attorney General Richard Kleindienst promised that his department would undertake the most comprehensive investigation "since the assassination of President Kennedy."

It was against this background of mounting pressure to do something about Watergate that President Nixon held a news conference on August 29, 1972, on his lawn at San Clemente, and announced that there was no need for a special prosecutor to be appointed to deal with Watergate because there were five investigations already under way. In addition, Nixon said,

> Within our own staff, under my direction, the counsel to the president, Mr. Dean, has conducted a complete investigation of all leads which might involve any present members of the White House staff or anybody in the government. I can state categorically that his investigation indicates that no one in the White House staff, no one in this Administration, presently employed was involved in this very bizarre incident.

No one was more surprised by this statement of an ongoing investigation, John Dean reported, than he was himself. He was sitting in a motel bedroom elsewhere in San Clemente when he saw the president on television, and he reports he almost fell off the bed at the announcement. He had not done anything in the way of investigation but, rather, had worked hard to stymie the probes of all the legitimate bodies trying to learn what had happened in the Watergate affair.

Dean was ecstatic that the president had mentioned his name on national television, and was, he later wrote, "basking in the glory of being publicly perceived as the man the President had turned to with a nasty problem like Watergate."

On a more practical level, Dean should well have been happy with Nixon's characterization of his work, for it helped Dean's desperate actions. It announced to his co-conspirators that Dean was actually the man who was, indeed, running the cover-up for the president; now such people as Strachan, Magruder, Liddy, and Hunt would be even more inclined to take direction from Dean. The announcement also said to many others outside the conspiratorial circle that Dean obviously had the president's ear, and that when Dean spoke, it was a command from the commander-in-chief.

On August 29, the day of the news conference at which Nixon said that Dean had been investigating Watergate, Phil Bailley was answering to a second indictment returned by a second Washington grand jury looking into his affairs. This was when Bailley's second case number, 1718-72, was begun, and the first indictment was superseded. The first entry on the docket sheet of case number 1718-72 soon read that on August 29 Bailley had been arraigned and pleaded not guilty, and that "all pending motions and all orders physically transferred from Cr 1190-72 to this case." The new docket sheet made no reference to any of the events that had occurred prior to the second August 29 arraignment, including the June 15 order committing Bailley. In addition, the new docket sheet stated that all pending motions and orders had been "physically transferred" from the prior file into the new file. This docket entry suggested that all documents from the prior case file could in fact be found in the new case file, and there would therefore be no reason for anyone to request to examine the prior file.

In fact, Judge Richey's order committing Bailley was *not* transferred into the new file and could not be discovered from that file or the new docket sheet; that business had now effectively been hidden from the sight of anyone who did not already know what had happened in the older, first case. (The first case file was retrieved during the preparation of this book.)

In the interim between the old case and the new, Bailley's attorneys had been in court arguing vigorously to quash Judge Richey's order committing Bailley to St. Elizabeth's—or, at the very least, to hold the order in abeyance pending the outcome of Bailley's ongoing outpatient examinations. Bailley's attorneys had secured the services of a psychiatrist and a psychologist who were prepared to examine Bailley as an outpatient. In addition, counsel had informed Judge Richey that Bailley was currently a patient of Dr. Harold Kaufman, a supervising psychiatrist in private practice in Washington who was also a professor of Georgetown University Law School, where he taught a course in law and psychiatry. Kaufman, the court was told, had "indicated [Bailley] does not act out hostility toward the public . . . and there is no danger presently to the community." Despite these arguments, on

June 30 Richey denied Bailley's motion to quash his commitment order and denied counsel's request to hold the order in abeyance.

Bailley's attorneys then filed a "motion to suppress" that argued that the original FBI search was invalid and that it and its fruits—Bailley's address books, photos, et cetera—should be thrown out of the case. The basis for this argument was that the affidavit had stated that the photos and address books had last been seen in Bailley's home and apartment seven months before the search; normally, a federal magistrate considering the issuance of a search warrant for items described as being at a certain location must consider the question of "staleness of information," that is, whether too much time has elapsed between the date of the viewing of those items described in the warrant's accompanying affidavit, and the date of the warrant. If a suppression hearing was held to resolve Bailley's suppression motion, and if the motion was addressed properly and granted—and there were good grounds to grant it on the basis of the Fourth Amendment's provision against unreasonable searches and seizures—it could have blown the government's case right out of the water. As important, all of the seized evidence, including Bailley's address books, would have been introduced into the public record during the suppression hearing.

Faced with this motion to suppress brought to the court's attention by Bailley's attorneys on August 29, Richey refused to even schedule the motions for hearings or to set a trial date. He said,

I am not going to set any motions at this time until I have received the psychiatric reports. I am not going to set any motions down for a hearing such as those I told you I would give leave to file today, there is a suppression motion, until such time as I have had the benefit of your psychiatric reports.

And so the suppression motion was itself suppressed. Today, no one can find that original search warrant, or the government's written answer to Bailley's motion to suppress. These documents have completely vanished from the available court files. The entire file of the Bailley matter maintained by the U.S. Attorney's office is also missing and cannot be located.

A week after this second arraignment, Bailley entered St. Elizabeth's and began two weeks of exposure to the horrors of mass psychiatric treatment in an understaffed and overpopulated government mental hospital.

*   *   *

On September 15, the indictments in the Watergate burglary were announced. Hunt, Liddy, McCord, Martinez, Sturgis, Barker, and Gonzalez were charged with eight counts that included tapping phones and stealing documents. The Justice Department said that these indictments had ended the investigation, since "We have absolutely no evidence to indicate that any others should be charged."

Later in the day, Dean was ushered into the Oval Office and the presence of the president, who was sitting with Bob Haldeman, and they took part in the first of what would become a series of conversations about Watergate that were taped and are thus available for us to examine in detail. As Dean later testified and wrote in his book, this conversation became etched into his mind, since before this time, as a midlevel official in the White House, he had not had much personal contact with the president. Indeed, the president's first words, uttered even before Dean had a chance to sit down, were remarkable:

P: Hi, how are you? You had quite a day today, didn't you? You got Watergate on the way, didn't you?

D: We tried.

H: How did it all end up?

D: Ah, I think we can say "well" at this point. The press is playing it just as we expect. . . .

After an exchange about how well Clark MacGregor was handling this—he was the new CRP chairman—the conversation turned to a bug that had recently been found on Spencer Oliver's telephone, nearly three months after the break-in. This was news to the president.

P: What bug? . . . You don't think it was left over from the other time?

D: Absolutely not. The Bureau has checked and re-checked the whole place after that night. The man had specifically checked and re-checked the telephone and it was not there.

P: What the hell do you think was involved?

D: I think DNC was planted.

P: You think *they* did it?

D: Uh-huh.

P: (Expletive deleted)

Dean's knowledge of what the FBI had found two days earlier on September 13 was exceedingly accurate, indicating he was current on the FBI's every move. Dean even knew and told the president what the FBI would do next—try to trace the bug through its original manufacturer. As the reader will recall, sweeps in the aftermath of the burglary (and even one conducted a day or two before it) had found no bugs. What had now been discovered was an ancient bug on Oliver's phone that had either been missed in those sweeps, or lately planted, either as a joke or to shore up the Democrats' civil suit, which could have floundered on the basis that no in-place bugs had been located at the DNC and therefore there might never have been any actual bugging. Prosecutor Silbert and the FBI were at odds over this late find, for, as we have noted in an earlier chapter, Silbert was then pursuing the path of trying to prove that the bugging had been done to record sexual information and with an intent to use that information for blackmail.

Dean next distracted the president by reminding him that Barry Goldwater had recently said in public that everybody bugs everybody else. Nixon agreed, offering the information that he had been bugged in 1962 and 1968, and his inner circle had considered using the fact that President Johnson bugged people as a way of deflecting heat from Watergate. After more banter about this, the president returned to the main subject, telling Dean, "We want to get to the bottom of it. If anybody is guilty over here we want to know."

The president was specifically asking if anyone in the White House other than those already indicted was connected to the burglary, and Dean deflected the question by turning the discussion to some of the collateral cases associated with Watergate, in particular the Democrats' civil suit and a libel suit against Stans by Larry O'Brien.

D: You might be interested in some of the allocations we got. The Stans libel action was assigned to Judge Richey.

P: (Expletive deleted)

D: Well, now, that is good and bad. Judge Richey is not known to be one of the (inaudible) on the bench, that is considered by me. He is fairly candid in dealing with people about the question. He has made several entrees off the bench—one to Kleindienst and one to Roemer McPhee [by then counsel to the Republican National Committee] to keep Roemer abreast of what his thinking is. He told Roemer he thought Maury [Stans] ought to file a [counter] libel action.

So Dean was telling Nixon that Judge Richey was having *ex parte* conversations with the attorney general and a lawyer in a major case against the CRP. *Ex parte* conversations, should they become known, are highly improper and could result in the overturning of verdicts. How could Dean have known about these conversations? McPhee, or someone in McPhee's office, is a possibilty, but Dean seemed to have a source in Richey's chambers, as can be discerned from what he next told the president—that Richey had halted depositions in the civil case at the request of Earl Silbert, thus enabling Stans to file a countersuit and also effectively delaying the Democrats' suit until after the November election. Some of these decisions would not become known for another week, so they must have been told to Dean by Richey or someone close to his court who knew Richey's thinking. Later on in the conversation, Dean predicted with accuracy what actions Richey would take the following week in another case, down to legal grounds Richey would cite for his decision, a decision quite favorable to the Republicans.

We have learned of at least two other instances in which Judge Richey initiated *ex parte* conversations with lawyers representing Republican Party interests, conversations that had to do with ascertaining how the Republican Party wished him to rule in a particular case. We have had confirmation on one of these from John Mitchell and Bob Mardian; and on the other from an attorney who knew about the conversation.

At this point in the forty-minute conversation, Nixon took a call from John Mitchell and joked with his old friend, saying "Get a good night's sleep, and don't bug anybody without asking me? O.K.?" Having sent Mitchell into exile, the president could now afford emotionally to kid him about it.

As Nixon hung up the phone, Dean came to his summary point: "Three months ago I would have had trouble predicting there would be a day when this would be forgotten, but I think I can say that fifty-four days from now [date of the election] nothing is going to come crashing down to our surprise."

Nixon complimented Dean on being "skillful" in putting his fingers in the leaks, and it was obvious to everyone in the room that this meeting was of the sort that the Nixon White House labeled a stroking session. But Dean was stroking Nixon, too. He took the occasion to steer Nixon through a laundry list of other political matters on which he had been acting, including that he was putting together "notes on a lot of people who are emerging as less than our friends." This was a hot button of Nixon's that Dean seemed to know, and he was rewarded when Nixon instantly escalated the idea to a command to Haldeman that "the most comprehensive notes" of this sort be kept, and a discussion about how these people would suffer in Nixon's second term, when he began to use the full powers of the presidency against them. "What an exciting prospect," echoed Nixon's new acolyte.

There was some discussion of how to head off Wright Patman's investigation through the use of various congressmen who were assumed to be disposed toward doing what Nixon asked. Dean seemed to be up to date on what all of them were doing and how they could be persuaded to go along.

The meeting was almost over when Dean brought up something that the president must have thought came from left field. He told the president that he had seen the Cubans' attorney, Henry Rothblatt, laughing at the start of a symposium that had to do with some of the overlapping cases. "He is quite a character," Dean identified Rothblatt for the president, and then went on to tell Nixon,

> **D:** He [Rothblatt] has been getting into the sex life of some of the members of the DNC.
>
> **P:** Why? What is the justification?
>
> **D:** Well, he is working on the entrapment theory, that they [the Democrats] were hiding something, that they had secret information of theirs to hide. . . . It is a way-out theory that no one had caught.

It was not a way-out theory, nor was it true that no one had "caught" it. Shortly after the indictment, Rothblatt told Peter Maroulis, Liddy's attorney, that "the Democrats were using call girls." Maroulis let the remark pass, not thinking that it was related to the break-in. Moreover, as Dean had to know, Earl Silbert was then pursuing the sexual-blackmail angle based on Alfred Baldwin's relevations, and was trying to get enough evidence to show that the burglary had been committed to obtain information for sexual blackmail. But since neither Nixon nor Haldeman had even a glimmer of what Dean might be referring to, they let it pass.

When the meeting was over, Nixon reflected briefly in his diary on his young counsel:

> I had a good talk with John Dean and was enormously impressed with him. I later told Haldeman, who said that he brought him into the White House, that he had the kind of steel and really mean instinct that we needed to clean house after the election in various departments and to put the IRS and the Justice Department on the kind of basis that it should be on.

* * *

On September 21, fifteen days after he had been committed to St. Elizabeth's mental hospital, Phil Bailley emerged. He had not stayed the full sixty days to which Judge Richey had consigned him, but he had been subject to two weeks of horror. In those fifteen days he had had a total of only forty-five minutes of psychiatric consultation. The rest of his time was spent confined to wards used to contain psychotic criminals who had been judged too insane for prison. When Bailley left St. Elizabeth's he was a broken and frightened man, haunted by his experiences—but a man certified by the superintendent of the institution as having "sufficient present ability to consult with his counsel with a reasonable degree of rational understanding and has a rational as well as a factual understanding of the proceedings against him."

Bailley's attorneys brought him into Richey's court on September 22. There, the government had no objection to his being continued on personal recognizance bond pending trial. But before a trial date was set, Richey raised the possibility of a "disposition" in the case, that is, some sort of plea bargain. The judge said it several times:

> I would also inquire as to whether or not there is a possibility of disposition in this case? . . . Have you had any discussion along these lines? . . . Well, gentlemen, I think it is not over everybody's head that when I say if there is a possibility of a disposition this would be a good thing. The government must have thought about it and moreover, the defense has thought about it I am sure. I know that you [government attorney] and Mr. Palmer [Bailley's second attorney] are both able lawyers and Mr. Bailley himself is no neophyte in this field, either. . . .
> If there is any way to resolve this I think it would be in everyone's interest.

In whose interest? Surely not in Bailley's, but possibly in the interest of certain outside parties. For at a trial or before it Bailley's attorneys would certainly have pushed the suppression motion, demanded to see the seized evidence and to make it part of the public record, inquired if it had ever been out of the prosecution's hands, and demanded the identity of the five unnamed women ("victims") in the indictment. Rudy would then have been required to tell of his visit to the Executive Office Building and of John Dean's interest in and copying of Bailley's address book. Dean's interest in that address book would have piqued the press's interest, too. At trial, the defense would have called Dean—and we can imagine what chaos would then have ensued for Dean.

In the status conference of September 29, the judge again pushed to have the case resolved without trial, even going so far as to advise one of the prosecutors to confer "with his superiors, Mr. Collins in particular, this morning, before you leave the courthouse." Returning to the theme he had struck at the earlier hearing, early in this one Richey said, "You know, if there is any way that a case like this can be resolved in the interests of everyone, I think it ought to be done." Palmer responded that it was premature to discuss the guilty plea while the motion to suppress was pending. Since the government's opposition to that motion to suppress wasn't in the file jacket, Richey scheduled a hearing on it for October 2, but again urged the lawyers to explore a plea bargain that day, September 29, in order to avoid "a lot of unnecessary legalistics." Confer they did. Bailley, emotionally exhausted, had decided not to fight anymore. When the parties reconvened that afternoon of September 29, Palmer announced to the court that Bailley had agreed to plead guilty to Count 11 of the indictment.

Count 11 of the original indictment carried a penalty of two years, while most of the other charges carried a five-year penalty. It made sense to plead to the two-year Count 11 charge of the original indictment, and perhaps Bailley—and his attorney—thought this was what he was doing. However, in the second series of indictments the sequence had been rearranged, so that the original Count 11 had become Count 14, and the present Count 11 bore a five-year charge. Rudy read into the record the full basis for that charge to which Bailley pleaded— that he'd transported a female into the offices of a D.C. lawyer named Levine so that she could have sex with that lawyer for a fee of twenty-five dollars.

As required in court, the precise charge was read to Bailley along with the underlying basis for it, that is, that it involved Levine and the woman. The prosecutors were asked to provide a factual basis for the charge and said the basis was Levine's testimony at the first grand jury. As it would turn out, if there was the required factual basis for this charge, there wasn't much of one.

After entering a guilty plea, Bailley was allowed to remain on bond for a month, until sentencing. At the October 25 sentencing, Bailley's lawyer made a motion to withdraw the guilty plea based on Levine having told Bailley and his lawyer that Levine had recanted before the second grand jury the testimony that he gave the first. Rudy argued that Levine's testimony at the two grand jury appearances could be interpreted as consistent. Judge Richey read the first and second grand jury transcripts quickly, and immediately pronounced them to be essentially the same; the defense was not permitted to read the transcripts on the grounds that grand jury testimony is secret. Later, when Bailley would pursue an appeal, his new appellate counsel would obtain the two grand jury transcripts of the Levine testimony. Appellate counsel would vigorously argue that there was a "serious conflict" between the two transcripts insofar as they dealt with the reason Levine paid Bailley twenty-five dollars. But in any event, on that day, Richey proceeded to sentence Bailley to the maximum term of five years. This was quite a harsh sentence considering that it was a first offense and that the transaction involved twenty-five dollars. Phil Bailley was taken immediately to prison.

The resolution of this case through a guilty plea guaranteed that the evidence seized from Bailley's home and office back in April of 1972 would never again see the light of day. And the way in which the case was handled, from beginning to end, ensured that any attempt to discover what had happened to Bailley would be frustrated by tricks and roadblocks. Last, Bailley's unwarranted and unnecessary commitment to St. Elizabeth's made it a virtual certainty that Bailley would be permanently discredited, and his guilty plea and sentencing ensured that he would be disbarred.

When Tony Ulasewicz had picked up a last batch of cash from Herb Kalmbach at the Airporter Motel near the Orange County airport, the two men had had a long talk. Ulasewicz advised Kalmbach that the demands of the Hunts had grown far out of proportion and had gone on too long to be continued, and that both Tony and Herb ought to get out of the game now. Kalmbach agreed, and after the indictment of the burglars they both opted out. Then, Tony reported in his book, Dean and Fred LaRue insisted that Kalmbach raise more money; Kalmbach refused, and, on September 19, 1972, Ulasewicz flew to Washington and stashed the remaining money that he did have in an airport locker and watched as LaRue came and picked it up. From then on, and still at the direction of Dean, LaRue handled disbursements to the Hunts. Though LaRue was close to Mitchell, and Mitchell had nixed paying support money to the burglars, Mitchell had by this time left Nixon's campaign altogether; so, still with CRP, LaRue looked to the White House—specifically John Dean—for direction.

There was one more item for John Dean to take care of, now that he had the confidence of the president and had assured himself and Nixon that things would not come crashing down, now that he had seen Phil Bailley and his address books consigned to oblivion, and now that he had managed to continue the flow of hush money to keep Hunt quiet. At the beginning of October, and without prior hint that this might happen, Dean announced to Haldeman that he had decided to marry Maureen Biner—immediately.

The upper echelon White House executives were in the midst of a reelection campaign whose payoff was less than a month away. Most loyal staffers would have put off major surgery, let alone marriage, until after November 7, but Dean was insistent on marrying what he called his "lovely California girl" on Friday, October 13, as he told Haldeman in a cute memo of October 5, routed through "The Society of Single White House Secretaries," a memo which had a place for Haldeman to indicate yea or nay. (Haldeman's only comment on the memo was the single word "Reconsider.")

Dean was so much in a hurry to get married that he helped himself to $4,850 from a White House slush fund kept in his safe. He later avowed that he put his own personal check in to cover that amount, but the dating of that check has been questioned; in any event, the taking of the money indicates the rush toward matrimony.

With this marriage, of course, Dean effectively made it more difficult for Maureen to be a witness against him, since Dean would be entitled under the law to prevent her from revealing marital confidences. And, being married to Dean, Maureen's interests would be tied to the progress of her husband's career—a career that could be ruined if an unmarried "Mo Biner" explained to a jury or congressional committee why her nickname "Clout" appeared in Phil Bailley's address books, or what her nickname meant, or what knowledge or interest John Dean had of Heidi Rikan/Cathy Dieter. So marrying Maureen immediately was an essential career move for John Dean.

15

THE PRESSURE
MOUNTS

THE Key Biscayne honeymoon of John and Maureen Dean was interrupted two days after it began by a call from Larry Higby, Haldeman's assistant, summoning Dean back to Washington.

Dean had fantasized that his conversation with the president on September 15 would be just the beginning of a new life among the elite who were close to the Oval Office; Maureen even believed rumors that in the second Nixon administration John would be rewarded for his work on Watergate with an ambassadorship, perhaps to France. Shortly, however, it would become apparent to Dean that his conversation with the president of September 15, 1972, was the zenith of his high-wire act, the moment when it seemed entirely possible that Dean could prevent Watergate from ever touching him, and that from there it was down all the way. A month after that summit, with the summons to cut short his honeymoon and come back to the White House, Dean started on a long slide into desperation and panic.

Confronting him were two matters for which he had not planned. Donald Segretti's dirty tricks to disrupt the Democrats' campaigns had become known to the press, who had labeled White House appointments secretary Dwight Chapin the mastermind for Segretti's "campaign dirty tricks and sabotage." This was the first time a serious charge had been traced into the White House, and the president's men were upset about it. Actually, Segretti had begun as a Haldeman operation, reporting through Chapin, but within a few months Liddy and Hunt had taken him over. At a meeting in Florida, Liddy told Segretti that Hunt would break his knees if he didn't cooperate, and Segretti agreed in effect to be taken away from Chapin and made a part of Liddy's apparatus. Since Liddy had reported to Dean, that made Segretti a Dean problem. Returning from his honeymoon, Dean quickly determined the extent of the damage Segretti could cause, met with him, taped Segretti's confession (which made no mention of Dean himself), and told the prankster to stay out of sight until after the election. Segretti did so, traversing the country by train and bus to avoid reporters who he thought might be lurking at the airports, watching for him.

Dean had less success handling a second wild card. By mid-October 1972 the White House had become the target of stories by *Washington Post* reporters Bob Woodward and Carl Bernstein about an unreported $350,000 fund that had been used for political purposes. Since September, the reporters had been writing about the fund and its links to the CRP, but now they were focusing on Haldeman's control of the fund. Haldeman had asked deputy presidential assistant Alexander Butterfield in April to find a place for this large amount of cash because he didn't want it in the White House during the election, at a time when people were snooping around. Butterfield contacted a friend in Virginia who stashed the money in a safe-deposit box.

The fund stories made headlines; their importance for our chronicle is that they alerted John Dean that there were other players in the Watergate game—confidential sources for the *Post* reporters, players he could not control. The fund stories were the first that used as a source what Woodward and Bernstein would come to refer to as Deep Throat.

The Watergate scandal did not seem to raise the hackles of the American people or in any way deter the electorate on November 7, 1972, from rejecting Democratic candidate George McGovern and choosing Richard Nixon by more than 60 percent of the popular votes and 97 percent of the electoral college votes. Nixon's was a landslide of the proportions not seen in American politics since the heyday of Franklin Roosevelt. At a post-election meeting at Camp David, the president, Haldeman, and Ehrlichman met to plan the second administration. They believed Watergate was firmly behind them. Among other actions the trio planned at this time was to have every appointed official tender an undated resignation, so that they could reappoint only those people who were unquestionably loyal to the president and willing to do his bidding.

The prosecutors were having a hard time with E. Howard Hunt, and this, too, became something for John Dean to handle. On October 11, Hunt's lawyer filed a motion to force the government to turn over to Hunt's defense, or cause to be turned over, the Hermès notebooks that Hunt said had been in his safe at the time of his arrest. This motion deeply troubled the prosecutors, for if the Hermès notebooks could not be produced, Hunt might very well claim that evidence critical to his defense had been withheld, and the prosecution's case against Hunt might collapse.

Pursuing these notebooks, in December prosecutor Earl Silbert called Bruce Kehrli, Fred Fielding, and John Dean to come in and talk to them about the disposition of the contents of Howard Hunt's safe. It was the first time that Dean had been questioned by any law enforcement agency or officer of the court—and Silbert, as Dean had once told Magruder, was tough. Dean kept saying he couldn't recall what had happened to every single thing in Hunt's safe, and kept to the story that he had given it all to the FBI. After an hour of interrogation on this subject, with no end in sight, Dean caught sight of a familiar person. It was Henry Petersen; Dean put his arm around him and took him aside for a chat in which Dean made one of his most bold-faced lies.

"Henry, I've got to talk to you," Dean reports that he said in the version printed in *Blind Ambition*. He then told Petersen, "Listen, the only thing I can figure out about why there are some documents missing is that not all the stuff we found was turned over directly to the FBI agents. . . . Some of the documents were politically very embarrassing, and we sent them straight to Pat Gray. If there are missing documents, he's got them."

"Oh, shit!" Petersen exclaimed. "You're not serious!"

"Yeah, I'm afraid so, and I don't have any idea how to handle that if I get called to testify. I don't really want to get on that stand. . . ."

It was as smooth a performance as the one Dean had given to the president in September, and as Dean had intended, the information stunned Petersen and immediately stopped Silbert's grilling. "I heard nothing more about being called as a witness," Dean concluded of the matter in his book.

Indeed, the matter then became Petersen's dilemma of what to do about Gray, the acting director of the FBI, who Petersen had been led to believe had evidently taken possession of potentially important evidence, Hunt's notebooks, and failed to report his initial or continuing possession of this evidence. Moreover, Dean had just told him that Gray's silence on the matter had been going on for six months. While Petersen explored that dilemma, Dean remained off the hook. So: At the first sign of impending trouble John Dean had thrown Pat Gray overboard in an attempt to save himself; before his slide was finished, he would have to throw over many other people in his attempts to protect himself from prosecution.

Even though the Hermès notebooks question had been pushed aside for the moment, Hunt himself was still a problem for Dean because he was demanding money, more and more of it. Dean's difficulties with Hunt were made all the more acute by a plane crash on December 8, 1972, in which Dorothy Hunt was killed. (Ten thousand dollars in cash was found in her purse, but it was impossible to prove a connection between this money and the payments ordered by Dean that had been made to her by Kalmbach.) After his wife's death, Hunt was distraught, and asked Dean through his lawyer if the government could find a friendly psychiatrist who would certify Hunt as unfit to stand trial. Dean tried to get Henry Petersen to go along with this request, but could not.

The trial of the Watergate defendants was scheduled to begin in January of 1973. As that date grew ever closer, Hunt and McCord—two of the men whom Dean feared most—raised increasingly loud noises about having been abandoned. As the noises swelled in volume, Dean began to take actions that left him more and more exposed.

For instance, he had learned that the CIA had given to the prosecutors a packet of photographs relating to the Dr. Fielding break-in, one of which showed Gordon Liddy in front of a building whose sign clearly identified it as the doctor's office; now, in December of 1972, he tried to induce the CIA to request that Justice return the packet of photos, so that Liddy's illegal actions prior to the Watergate break-ins would not be brought to the fore. The CIA refused to ask for the photos back, and Dean's ham-handed attempt to obtain the photos left a paper trail with his name emblazoned on it.

When Ehrlichman returned to the White House following a vacation, on January 3, 1973, Dean and Chuck Colson met with him to discuss Howard Hunt and the requests of Hunt's lawyer, Bittman, to obtain clemency for Hunt. In *Witness to Power*, Ehrlichman described how he handled the situation: "I said as plainly as I could that Colson could not say anything to Bittman that even hinted at clemency. I said the President had decided that right after the burglary." He later learned that Colson had gone behind his back to get Nixon's consent to talk about clemency to his old friend Hunt. (Hunt denied that he had sought clemency at all, and said that the $154,000 paid to him had all gone to his lawyers. But, as we have shown, in 1974 he acknowledged that the cash he and his wife had received was for his silence.)

The day after their meeting with Colson, Dean and Ehrlichman had lunch with Attorney General Richard Kleindienst to learn what sort of sentences the burglars would get; Kleindienst didn't know—the trial hadn't even begun—but later reported back to Dean that Judge Sirica, whose nickname was "Maximum John," was likely to hand out heavy sentences.

This worried Dean even more.

On Saturday, January 6, 1973, two days before the trial was to begin, Gordon Liddy received a call. "Gordon, I think you'll recognize my voice," the caller said, as Liddy reported in *Will*. It was Dean, and Liddy did recognize the voice, even though he had not heard from Dean since June 19, 1972, at which time Dean had promised support for the burglars, support that had become hush money for Hunt. The ostensible reason behind Dean's call to Liddy now had to do with Bud Krogh, and not with Liddy's own trial. Krogh, the former Plumber and the man who had recruited Liddy for the White House, was about to enter confirmation hearings for a post as undersecretary of transportation, and Liddy had been called to testify. He didn't want to testify for Krogh, even though Liddy could have exonerated him from Watergate. Liddy felt that if he appeared, he'd also have to testify for many others, and Liddy had tried to reach Krogh to tell him the reason for refusing to testify. Krogh wouldn't take his call. Now here was Dean, telling Liddy that it was impossible for Krogh to talk to Liddy now, since Bud wanted to be able to say he hadn't talked to Liddy in the past year. Then Dean shifted to an entirely unexpected point: "I want to assure you; everyone's going to be taken care of—everyone. . . . Absolutely. First, you'll receive living expenses of thirty thousand per annum. Second, you'll have a pardon within two years. Three, we'll see to it you're sent to Danbury Prison; and fourth, your legal fees will be paid."

Liddy tried to pin Dean down further, asking if he understood the difference between a commutation and a pardon—Dean said he did— and telling Dean that legal fees were his real concern. "I want it understood there's no *quid pro quo* here. I'll keep quiet no matter what," Liddy concluded, and he was sure Dean knew it. But the promises Dean had made were so unusual that Liddy took a felt-tipped pen and wrote down the substance of the conversation on a piece of paper that he shortly gave to his lawyer, Peter Maroulis.

This call reinforced Dean's belief that Liddy would remain silent, a silence Dean counted on. Liddy's steadfast refusal to talk, which Liddy imagined as an unbreakable line of defense for the president of the United States against knowledge of Watergate, was shamelessly used by John Dean to protect himself. It would not be until 1980, when the statute of limitations had expired, that Liddy would reveal that Dean had made an illegal inducement of money and a presidential pardon in order to keep Liddy quiet, even though there had been no indication that he would break.

At about the same time as Dean's call to Liddy, Tony Ulasewicz received a plea from Jack Caulfield, who "once again asked me to play courier for the delivery of a message from Dean to McCord." Tony was to tell McCord, "A year is a long time, your wife and family will be taken care of, you will be rehabilitated with employment when this is all over." Tony didn't want to do the job, but Caulfield begged him, based on their long friendship and because Caulfield was on assignment in California and couldn't do it himself. The call was to be the response to a letter McCord had sent to Dean via Caulfield, that said if the White House tried to blame the CIA for Watergate, "every tree in the forest would fall." When Tony recited the message, McCord asked him if it meant that he was to plead guilty. "I told him that all I was delivering was a message, not a promise," Ulasewicz writes, "and that it was up to him to draw the inferences. But it didn't take a genius to read between the lines."

The trial began. On January 12, after it had commenced, Caulfield met McCord at night at an overlook on the George Washington Parkway and offered the wire-man clemency "from the highest levels of the White House." McCord was evidently not convinced of the seriousness of this offer, for whoever made it insisted that the pair meet in a clandestine manner twice more during the course of the trial. At one of these rendezvous, Caulfield told McCord that "the president's ability to govern is at stake. . . . Everybody else is on track but you." Caulfield later testified that he reported back about these meetings to John Dean.

It seems most probable that none of the illegal promises made by Dean himself or through Caulfield or Ulasewicz were reported to his superiors and especially to the president during this period, for if they had been, they would have shown up in the discussions that involved Ehrlichman and Haldeman recorded on the White House tapes. The absence from those tapes of any report of Dean's frantic activity to ensure the silence of Hunt, Liddy, and McCord is particularly striking, and buttresses the idea that Dean made those promises entirely on his own.

As the trial began, Howard Hunt pleaded guilty, and testified that to his "personal knowledge . . . no higher ups" were involved in Watergate crimes. That statement was what $179,000 in payoffs made to that time had bought.

It was just after Hunt's guilty plea, John Dean wrote, that he destroyed Hunt's Hermès notebooks. Hunt had sought them as evidence to clear him, and had repeatedly claimed they would reveal the names and actions of his principals in the White House. In *Blind Ambition*, Dean makes a joke of the destruction, saying his shredder had a hard time digesting the books and that he feared the noise might set off a delicate sensor he'd had installed. He rationalized their destruction, saying the notebooks were "no longer relevant to the trial after Hunt's guilty plea," but this is specious. Hunt's guilty plea was irrelevant to the evidentiary value of the notebooks in other, ongoing, Watergate-related cases, or in clearing Pat Gray of Dean's false charge of having secret possession of the notebooks. As a lawyer, Dean knew full well that destruction of evidence at any time was itself a criminal violation—obstruction of justice—and that he had a distinct and continuing obligation to turn over this evidence to the prosecutors and to Hunt. By destroying the notebooks, Dean shredded forever any documentary evidence that could link him to Hunt and his order to go into the headquarters of the Democratic National Committee.

Dean's own account of this episode belies his claim that he had not really looked at the notebooks since he'd taken possession of them. If Dean had not read the notebooks, or had not learned from them that Hunt had chronicled Dean's role in the two break-ins, it would have been logical for Dean to have turned the notebooks over to the FBI with the other records from Dean's safe. But Dean hadn't done that, he'd kept them for a time and then destroyed them. Dean says the notebooks were under the president's estate papers—but we know from Haldeman and Ehrlichman of frequent demands for those estate papers in the second half of 1972, so Dean would have had to take them out of the safe many times, and could hardly have missed seeing the Hunt notebooks. In his later Senate testimony, Dean made no mention at all of what he styles "this direct, concrete and sweaty act" of destroying the notebooks. In fact, he never revealed his possession of the notebooks to the prosecutors who would have been most interested in them, Earl Silbert and Henry Petersen. When Dean testified before Congress one more time, in 1974 at the House Judiciary Committee hearings, he told the House that the fact of his destruction of the notebooks had simply

"slipped his mind" when he'd testified to the Senate, and then admitted
not only that he had destroyed the notebooks, but that he had examined
their contents prior to shredding them. When he made the disclosure
it was only to a new set of lawyers, those from the Special Prosecutor's
office, who had not participated in his December 1972 grilling by
Silbert. And Dean waited to reveal the destruction (1) until he had
cemented his deal for a light sentence, (2) until he had pleaded guilty
to one count of obstructing justice, and (3) until he had allowed the
Special Prosecutor's office to build criminal cases against John Mitchell
and others based on Dean's own testimony.

During the Watergate burglars trial, Hunt, Barker, Sturgis, Martinez,
and Gonzalez all pleaded guilty. Alfred Baldwin got on the stand, and
Silbert began to ask him whose voices he had overheard on the wiretaps
and to describe the contents of the overheard conversations.

This was the moment we have described earlier, when Charles
Morgan, Jr., the lawyer for Spencer Oliver and the DNC, halted the
proceedings with an objection. Sirica overruled the objection and
momentarily suspended the trial to allow Morgan to obtain a ruling
from the appeals court. In Judge Bazelon's appeals court, Baldwin's
testimony was ruled inadmissible. By this ruling, Silbert was compelled to abandon the sexual blackmail motive of the burglary, and to
proceed with a different tack for the burglars' motive: that the break-in
target was Larry O'Brien's office. That was shaky, but it didn't matter,
because the prosecution did not need to prove a motive for the burglary,
only that the burglars had been caught red-handed, and that there
were traceable links to their superiors. It seemed an open-and-shut
case, and on January 30, 1973, after deliberating only ninety minutes,
the jurors found Liddy and McCord guilty. Sentencing for all the
defendants, those convicted and those who had previously pleaded
guilty, would come in February, Sirica announced.

Also looming in February for John Dean were the formation of the
Senate Watergate investigating committee under the chairmanship of
Democrat Sam Ervin, and Senate Judiciary Committee hearings to
confirm L. Patrick Gray as director of the FBI. Both sets of committee
hearings could be dangerous to Dean, Ervin's because Dean would
have to carefully control what such men as Jeb Magruder and Gordon
Strachan might have to say in a public forum, and the Senate Judiciary
Committee's because Gray might well be asked about Dean having
handed him part of the contents of Hunt's safe.

On February 9, just after the Senate overwhelmingly approved the
establishment of the Ervin committee, President Nixon closely ques-

tioned Haldeman and Ehrlichman about preparations to deal with the committee. He wanted to know who in his administration was in charge of readying the White House's response to this political challenge. Ehrlichman told him it was Dean and Richard Moore, special presidential counsel, if it was anyone.

"Well, what do they say?" Ehrlichman remembers Nixon as asking, and that he also asked who was going to be on the committee and its staff, what the committee's rules would be and how far its subpoena powers were to extend. Ehrlichman and Haldeman didn't know. In his book, Ehrlichman recounted what happened next:

> For months I'd been comfortable with Nixon's injunction to "stay out of Watergate." Now he was demanding that Bob Haldeman and I get into it all the way. Nixon said we should spend the weekend with Moore and Dean and learn everything we could about the Senate's plans. . . . We sent for Moore and Dean and spent parts of two days with them at the La Costa resort where the staff stayed when the President was at San Clemente. In that series of meetings I heard enough to trouble me deeply.

The "enough" that he heard was Dean's description of the support money payments and the things the Senate could expect to find that linked "Hunt to Colson, and Liddy to Jeb Magruder to Gordon Strachan." Of course, Dean omitted his own name and connections to the burglary and the cover-up. After the sessions, Ehrlichman reported, Nixon wanted to know everything that Moore and Dean had said, "and typically, he asked a hundred questions we'd not thought to ask Moore and Dean. I finally said, in exasperation, that the President ought to be talking to Dean directly."

Thus was the stage set for the intimate, taped series of Oval Office conversations held between John Dean and President Richard Nixon in February and March of 1973.

When John Dean walked into the Oval Office at 9:12 A.M. on the morning of February 28, 1973, for his first meeting alone with the president, he brought with him quite a load of baggage. He had touched too many people and investigations, and his cover-up was beginning to come apart. Heavy sentences were expected from Judge Sirica, heavy enough to force the defendants in the burglary trial to talk in order to lessen the sentences. Hunt wanted more money, and the CRP and other sources had now been exhausted. Dean could not be certain how long such men as Magruder and Strachan would hold up before questioning by Congress, by the prosecutors, and by lawyers for the Democrats in their civil suits. Kalmbach, Ulasewicz, and Caulfield knew of Dean's earlier illegal activities and his recent, unsanctioned offers of clemency; there was the possibility they would be called to testify, as well. Nor could Dean be certain how long the prosecutors would continue to stay away from him.

To successfully keep all the wolves at bay, Dean needed to gain the president's confidence.

For his part, President Nixon seems to have decided just before this meeting to finally deal with Watergate, now that it had become a political liability hampering his plans for his second administration. Having been in politics a lot longer than Haldeman or Ehrlichman, he knew far better than they how much focus would be placed by the public on the open, televised hearings of the Ervin-led Watergate committee. In order to deal effectively with that committee, he had to know what they might discover about Watergate—and he had been told that Dean had all the information. So Nixon needed to listen carefully to Dean, and to assure himself of Dean's loyalty.

Nixon came on strong and direct. He wanted to know what sort of line Dick Kleindienst was going to take in his dealings with senators Ervin and Baker, who were the senior members of the investigative committee, and how far Kleindienst would go in insisting that witnesses from the White House would be able to cite executive privilege as a way to avoid testifying on sensitive matters. Nixon wanted Dean to firm up Kleindienst's resolve not to make any deals on executive privilege. There was still some hope that the committee would agree to accept from the president's men only written responses to written interrogatories; Dean agreed this would be a good strategy, because "publicly you are not withholding any information and you are not using the shield of the Presidency." Nixon referred him to the first chapter of his book *Six Crises*, and rambled a bit about how he had handled the Hiss case as a congressman on the Hill, even in the absence of cooperation from the FBI and Justice.

"Funny, when the shoe is on the other foot how they look at things, isn't it?" Dean responded, fawning a bit and drawing the president out on the old matter. He brought up the notion, mentioned previously to Nixon by Haldeman, of having Maurice Stans as a stalking horse before another committee investigating financier Robert Vesco, to see how such a forum would deal with executive privilege questions—and when Nixon said it was a good idea but didn't know where it came from, Dean acknowledged the stalking horse notion as his own suggestion.

Dean busily took the president through some of the related cases and committees, lightly provoking Nixon to monologues about the press and its antipathy to him. The president's counsel lost no opportunity to mouth derogatory phrases about such well-known "enemies" of Nixon's as the press, and then, with Nixon's enemies as a theme, got around to the committee.

> D: I am convinced that [Sam Ervin] has shown that he is merely a puppet for Kennedy in this whole thing. The fine hand of the Kennedys is behind this whole hearing. There is no doubt about it. . . . [Ted Kennedy] has kept his quiet and constant pressure on this thing. I think this fellow Sam Dash, who has been selected Counsel, is a Kennedy choice.

Perhaps, Dean offered, that notion of the fine hand of the Kennedys could be leaked and so sabotage the hearings. Dean reported that he'd been told that Bobby Kennedy had had Lyndon Johnson bugged, and that support might be found within the FBI's files for the idea that the Democrats had done just as much bugging as the Republicans, and that this information could further damage the hearings. Former FBI assistant director William Sullivan was the key to this, Dean said, but, "I haven't probed Sullivan to the depths on this thing because I want to treat him at arm's length until he is safe, because he has a world of information that may be available."

The president didn't understand how Sullivan knew about the bugging, and asked, "Who told what to whom again?"

Dean related a wild story about information that Nixon had been bugged in 1968 having gone from Hoover to Patrick Coyne to Nelson Rockefeller to Henry Kissinger, and that maybe FBI Assistant Director Mark Felt could go public with it even if there were no records. This led Nixon into a discussion of the fate of men who go public with sordid stories, such as Whittaker Chambers in the Hiss case—and Dean had the president hooked. Minutes flew by on these immaterial side discussions before the president tried once more to take charge of the meeting.

> P: What is the situation anyway with regard to the situation of the sentencing of the seven? When in the hell is that going to occur?
>
> D: That is likely to occur, I would say, as early as late this week, but more likely sometime next week.
>
> P: Why has it been delayed so long? . . . He [Sirica] is trying to work on them to see who will break them down?

Nixon was incredulous at the idea of thirty-year sentences for the burglars, citing the facts that there had been no weapons found on them, no injuries to anyone, and that the burglary had not succeeded.

P: I feel for those poor guys in jail, particularly for Hunt with his wife dead.

D: Well, there is every indication they are hanging in tough right now.

P: What the hell do they expect, though? Do they expect clemency in a reasonable time? What would you advise on that?

Dean was not about to tell Nixon that—without permission—he had already promised clemency to several men. So he agreed with Nixon's premise that clemency couldn't be offered, even six months into the future. The president became adamant that nothing should be said publicly about any of the burglars while the cases were on appeal.

P: Maybe we will have to change our policy. But the President should not become involved in any part of the case. Do you agree with that?

D: I agree totally, sir. Absolutely.

Nixon then began to grumble that the people who were really worked up over the supposed White House horrors were the congressional Republicans, rather than the Democrats, who had in the past done some shenanigans of their own. Dean countered with the suggestion that the White House offer Segretti as a sacrificial lamb, admit to his pranks and nothing more. But Nixon was angry:

P: What in (characterization deleted) did [Segretti] do? Shouldn't we be trying to get intelligence? Weren't they trying to get intelligence from us? . . . Don't you try to disrupt their meetings? Didn't they try to disrupt ours? (Expletive deleted) They threw rocks, ran demonstrations, shouted, cut the sound system, and let the tear gas in at night. What the hell is that all about? Did we do that? . . . What did Segretti do that came off? . . . Pranks! [Dick] Tuck did all those things [for the Democrats] in 1960.

Dean then mentioned a name as a difficulty, and it was one for which the president seemed completely unprepared: Herb Kalmbach. Dean told Nixon that Kalmbach's bank records were being subpoenaed. Nixon thought this had something to do with the only matter that touched him in which Kalmbach regularly figured, Nixon's personal transactions for income taxes, the house at San Clemente, and so on. Had they asked for the San Clemente records?

"No," Dean said.

"Kalmbach is a decent fellow," the president went on, still mystified as to why anyone would want to grill Kalmbach. Nixon even thought that the calling of Kalmbach had to do with the CRP finance committee and the contributions that had been traced into Mexico.

"Oh, well, all that can be explained," Dean said, and didn't illuminate the president on the difference between Kalmbach's money-gathering and that of the reelection committee. The president had absolutely no idea that Dean was concerned about Kalmbach, nor that Dean had called for Kalmbach to come to the White House the following week for a detailed coaching before his committee appearance. As we know, Dean had used Kalmbach to raise and deliver hush money. Kalmbach's records—those records Dean mentioned to the president without explaining their real significance—would contain many references to Kalmbach's paying of Tony Ulasewicz, and both Tony and Herb could testify to Dean's own deep involvement in illegal payoffs and promises of clemency, both of which were obstructions of justice. Dean mentioned Kalmbach so that if he showed up next week and ran into Nixon, the president would think he knew why his "personal attorney" was at the White House.

The president returned to his own agenda with an interesting suggestion that the Senate committee be forced to set rules for testimony that would exclude hearsay and innuendo, just as these would be excluded in a courtroom trial; Kleindienst should take that very line with Ervin, the president insisted. Dean tried to wrap up the conversation with the suggestion that Watergate would end up in the "funny pages of the history books."

Nixon said the most important thing was that at least he had been completely isolated from the incident and hadn't known about it. His anger surfaced again as he summarized,

P: Of course, I am not dumb and I will never forget when I heard about this (adjective deleted) forced entry and bugging. I thought, What in the hell is this? What is the matter with these people? Are they crazy? I thought they were nuts! A prank! But it wasn't! It wasn't very funny. I think that our Democratic friends know that, too. They know what the hell it was. They don't think . . . I'd be involved in such stuff. They think I have people capable of it—and they are correct, in that Colson would do anything. Well, OK—have a little fun. And now I will not talk to you again until you have something to report to me.

D: All right, sir.

P: But I think it is very important that you have these talks with our good friend Kleindienst. . . . Let's remember this [burglary] was not done by the White House, this was done by the Committee to Re-Elect, and Mitchell was the Chairman, correct?

D: That's correct!

P: And Kleindienst owes Mitchell everything.

The president mused that Kleindienst would behave properly to help Mitchell, and imagined that Mitchell himself would have to testify and that it might ruin him, even though Mitchell would "put on his big stone face" and admit to nothing. As he wrapped up the conversation with his young counsel, Nixon seemed almost willing to have Mitchell thrown to the wolves just then, but he thought he knew what the senatorial committee was really after:

P: Somebody at the White House. They would like to get Haldeman or Colson, Ehrlichman.

D: Or possibly Dean. You know, I am a small fish.

P: Anybody at the White House, they would—but in your case I think they realize you are the lawyer and they know you didn't have a (adjective deleted) thing to do with the campaign.

D: That's right.

P: That's what I think. Well, we'll see you.

D: Alright, sir—Goodbye.

In his diary, Nixon wrote that Dean was "an enormously capable man," and cited Dean's "amazing" knowledge of how Lyndon Johnson had used the FBI to do intelligence work. Dean, he noted, had already read *Six Crises* and a speech about the Hiss case that Nixon had made when in Congress, made reference to them in the conversation, and Nixon was "very impressed. He has shown enormous strength, great intelligence and great subtlety. . . . I am glad I am talking to Dean now rather than going through Haldeman or Ehrlichman. I think I may have made a mistake in going through others, when there is a man with the capability of Dean I can talk to directly."

As for Dean, the president's lawyer closed the door to the Oval Office knowing that he had talked to the president for over an hour, had not told him anything of substance, and had kept him away from Dean's own culpability in criminal actions. But he also knew he would have to see the president again, and soon, and that he might not be able to hold the facts from Nixon for very much longer.

16

CONFESSION TIME

L. Patrick Gray's confirmation hearings had begun as Dean and the president were talking on February 28, and almost immediately Gray acknowledged that he had shown FBI files on Watergate to Dean. To soften the admission, Gray offered to show these same files to any senator who wished to view them. It was clear that the Judiciary Committee would now have to call Dean to testify about this, and for the first time public attention came to be focused on John Wesley Dean III. Who was this young White House counsel to the president, and why would the acting director of the FBI report to him? At an impromptu news conference on March 2, the president took some care to defend and protect the "enormously capable man" he was coming to like.

Dean, Nixon said, would not testify because he was covered by executive privilege. The president didn't leave it at that, however, and with a further assertion began to dig a hole under Dean, perhaps without meaning to. Nixon stated flatly that "No one on the White House staff at the time he [Dean] conducted the investigation—that was last July and August—was involved or had knowledge of the

Watergate matter." As could have been expected by the White House, reporters then asked for the documentary proof of the president's assertion, in the form of some written report by Dean to the president of the sort that the president had mentioned back in September 1972. Of course there had been no Dean investigation and no report, but the president's statement stoked the fire for one to be produced.

Gray continued to testify, and each time he did he raised the ante on John Dean. On March 7, Gray told the Judiciary Committee that he had given Dean eighty-two FBI reports and was "unalterably convinced" that Dean had concealed nothing from him about the contents of Hunt's safe. In this same session, Gray also provided testimony that for the first time linked Haldeman aide Dwight Chapin and Herb Kalmbach to campaign dirty trickster Donald Segretti. At Dean's instigation, the White House issued a statement saying that Dean had turned over to the FBI all the contents of Hunt's safe, but the matter did not die. Gray next testified that he had met with Dean or talked to him by telephone thirty-three times between June and September of 1972.

While the Gray hearings held the spotlight, behind the scenes Magruder was coming under increasing pressure from the prosecutors to admit a pre–break-in role. And, awaiting sentencing, James McCord was feeling more and more abandoned.

On March 12, the president issued a long statement about executive privilege (vetted by Dean and possibly prepared by him as well) saying that present and former members of the president's staff would "normally . . . decline a request for a formal appearance before a committee of the Congress," even though "executive privilege will not be used as a shield to prevent embarrassing information from being made available." In immediate response, the Senate Watergate committee voted unanimously to "invite" Dean to testify.

Who could and who could not testify was in the air as John Dean walked into the Oval Office at 12:42 P.M. on March 13, to find Bob Haldeman sitting with the president, and became immediately involved in a discussion of whether Chuck Colson could be billed as an unpaid consultant to the White House, and thus covered by executive privilege not only for the previously concluded period of his actual employment in the White House, but for the current, unpaid period; Haldeman even suggested backdating the papers on this so Colson's employment would be continuous. Nixon cut off this discussion by introducing his own agenda:

P: Apparently you haven't been able to do anything on my project of getting on the offensive?

D: But I have, sir. To the contrary!

P: Based on Sullivan, have you kicked a few butts around?

Dean said he had done just that, taken information from Bill Sullivan about FBI bugging in the past and given it to a speechwriter to prepare a letter to be signed by Senator Barry Goldwater and sent by Goldwater to Senator Ervin. The president and Haldeman were delighted, the president even offering to dig into Internal Revenue Service material to add to the derogatory information. "There is no need at this hour for anything from IRS," Dean said, and then, in effect, told the president the smallest part of the reason why two weeks ago he had raised the issue of Kalmbach. It had been "substantiated" in the press that "Chapin directed Kalmbach to pay Segretti." In a rush to get out bad news in a single breath, Dean referred to an "absolutely inaccurate" story in that morning's *Washington Post* saying that Dean had turned over information about grand jury proceedings to people at the CRP so they could confront CRP employees who had not adhered to the proper line during testimony. That story, said Dean, had been based on an affidavit from a CRP secretary who had been, of all things, a "registered Democrat." Continuing the blast of bad news, Dean prophesied that there would be lots of press questions that week, questions that did not have "easy answers. For example, did Haldeman know that there was a Don Segretti out there? That question is likely."

Since on the transcript Haldeman did not respond to this intensely red flag, and was not heard from throughout the next hour of the conversation, we must assume he had left the room by the time Dean brought up his name. Dean answered his own question: "Yes, he [Haldeman] had knowledge that there was somebody in the field doing prankster-type activities."

Nixon's response was, "I don't know anything about that"; he then asked Dean if it would be possible to duck such questions behind a claim that he couldn't go into such matters while they were being investigated by a congressional committee. Dean and the president then rehearsed what Nixon or press secretary Ron Ziegler would say in response to hard questions.

D: "But if you have nothing to hide, Mr. President, here at the White House, why aren't you willing to spread on the record everything you know about it? Why doesn't the Dean Report be made public? Why does Ziegler stand up there and bob and weave, and [say] 'No comment'?" That's the bottom line.

P: All right. What do you say to that? . . . "We are furnishing information. We will . . ."

D: "We have cooperated with the FBI in the investigation of the Watergate. We will cooperate with the investigation of, the proper investigation by the Senate."

P: "We will make statements."

D: "And, indeed, we have nothing to hide."

Abbott and Costello couldn't have thrown the ball back and forth with more gusto or better timing. The president now practically begged for coaching. What should he say about Segretti? Haldeman? Chapin? Dean began to grill Nixon as he had grilled Magruder prior to Jeb's appearance before the grand jury.

D: "Will Mr. Haldeman and Mr. Ehrlichman and Mr. Dean go up to the Committee and testify?"

P: "No, absolutely not."

D: "Mr. Colson?"

P: "No, absolutely not. . . . We said we will furnish information, but we are not going to be called to testify." That is the position. "Dean and all the rest will grant you information." Won't you?

D: Yes, indeed I will!

Nixon was convinced that "they" hoped to compel an admission that "Haldeman did it" and that, one day, someone would be forced to say that Nixon himself had done it, but his mind was at ease on the subject because "they might question his [Haldeman's] political savvy, but not mine! Not on a matter like that!" Not even his enemies, Nixon clearly thought, would believe he had been dumb enough to have initiated, condoned, or had personal knowledge of the Watergate break-in.

This was a dangerous area for Dean, and he found an immediate escape hatch by bringing the conversation back to Bill Sullivan for five minutes, and then jumping to the subject of how he, Dean, would answer the request to testify at the Gray confirmation hearings; Dean said he would offer to respond fully under oath, but only in a letter. After the committee got his written response, friendly Democratic

Senator James Eastland could ask for an immediate vote of confirmation on Gray, foreclosing further discussion.

The president attempted to get out from under this subject by saying that Gray wouldn't be a good FBI director "after going through the hell of the hearings," and Dean jumped on the bandwagon, agreeing that Gray would be a "suspect Director." Gray overboard, the pair next turned to the committee hearings, and it was at this point in the conversation that Dean began a great confession to the president.

In this confession to the president, Dean laid out the dimensions of the Watergate problem in detail, though he concealed the most important fact, his own central involvement. In all of Dean's thousands of pages of writings and sworn testimony, this is the closest he ever came to telling the truth; he seems to have held simultaneously in his mind both a belief that the president must be told about Watergate, and a certainty that the president must not be allowed to learn of Dean's own culpability. The confession began as the president tried to understand what damage would be done to the White House as people started to testify on the Hill.

P: Who is going to be the first witness up there?

D: Sloan.

P: Unfortunate.

D: No doubt about it. . . . He's scared, he's weak. He has a compulsion to cleanse his soul by confession. We are giving him a lot of stroking. . . . The person who will have a greater problem as a result of Sloan's testimony is Kalmbach. . . .

The mention of Sloan's weakness was indication that Sloan had something to hide; the president evidently understood that already. But here was that name Kalmbach; again, the president was mystified, and bristled at the idea of the press calling Kalmbach his personal attorney when Nixon only saw him once a year, to sign his income tax returns. What Kalmbach really did, the president said, was handle the payroll at San Clemente. Dean didn't acknowledge the real problem, that Kalmbach had paid Ulasewicz; that would have been too close to Dean.

The president wanted to know how others would testify. Those Dean listed in the column of potentially good witnesses were the ones whom Dean had coached: Kalmbach and Magruder.

Nixon wanted the hearings over with, and quickly, because the press was viewing this as a "grave crisis in the confidency of the Presidency," and that could not be allowed to go on for very long. Although he believed only the "upper intellectual types . . . , the soft heads" were interested in Watergate, there would be "new revelations" at the hearings, and "Let's face it, I think they are really after Haldeman."

"Haldeman and *Mitchell*," Dean said, emphasizing the cover-up line designed to protect his own agenda. (As we will see, a few moments later Dean would come close to contradicting himself and almost tell the truth about Mitchell's noninvolvement.) The president began to probe in the style that his chief aides had come to know so well, the asking of many questions to bring out information. Nixon's focus was intense and direct.

P: Haldeman's problem is Chapin, isn't it?

D: Bob's problem is circumstantial.

P: Why is that? Let's look at the circumstantial . . . Bob didn't know any of those people like the Hunts and all that bunch. Colson did, but Bob didn't, OK?

D: That's right.

P: Now where the hell, or how much Chapin knew I will be (expletive deleted) if I know.

D: Chapin didn't know anything about the Watergate.

P: Don't you think so?

D: Absolutely not.

P: Strachan?

D: Yes.

P: He knew?

D: Yes.

P: About the Watergate?

D: Yes.

P: Well, then, he probably told Bob.

Dean had just informed Nixon, nine months after the break-in, that Strachan had known about it all along. At one stroke, Dean told the president that everything Dean or Haldeman or Ehrlichman—reflecting Dean—had told the president of "no White House involvement" was a lie and had been a lie from the beginning. Testament to how close Dean was coming to spilling the truth is that he told this to the president at all. Before the Senate, later in 1973, he would deny Strachan's involvement, and it was only after he had served his four-month sentence that he would admit, in *Blind Ambition*, to having known of Strachan's role since his walk in the park with Gordon Liddy on June 19, 1972.

In the conversation in the Oval Office, he tried to tell the president that Strachan would not break on the witness stand, but Nixon knew an alarm bell when he heard one.

P: I will be damned! Well, that is the problem in Bob's case. Not Chapin, then, but Strachan. Strachan worked for him, didn't he?

D: Yes. They would have one hell of a time proving that Strachan had knowledge of it, though.

P: Who knew better—Magruder?

D: Magruder and Liddy.

P: Oh, I see. The other weak link for Bob is Magruder. He hired him, et cetera.

D: That applies to Mitchell, too.

The president continued to press, leaping in his mind from Mitchell to Magruder to Colson and Hunt, remembering a faint impression of a time when Haldeman had mentioned to him "something about the Convention . . . problems they were planning. . . . I assume that must have been . . . Segretti."

No, Dean said rather definitively, Segretti wasn't involved in intelligence gathering. This was new to Nixon. If not Segretti, the president wanted to know, then who had done it?

D: That was Liddy and his outfit. . . . Well, you see Watergate was part of intelligence gathering, and this was their first thing. What happened is—

P: That was such a stupid thing!

D: It was incredible, that's right. That was Hunt.

P: To think of Mitchell and Bob would have allowed—would have allowed—this kind of operation to be in the campaign committee!

D: I don't think he [Haldeman] knew it was there.

P: I don't think that Mitchell knew about this sort of thing.

D: Oh, no, no! Don't misunderstand me. I don't think that he knew the people. I think he knew that Liddy was out intelligence gathering. I don't think he knew that Liddy would use a fellow like McCord, (expletive deleted), who worked for the Committee. . . . I don't think Mitchell knew about Hunt, either. . . .

The president mused on what Mitchell would say, hoped it would be precisely what Dean had just told him, and leaped to the idea that Mitchell's deputy Magruder would back up Mitchell. Here was a danger signal for Dean, for as he then told the president, under recent questioning by the prosecutors Magruder had named Dean as the man who had sponsored Liddy to the CRP. Nixon asked directly whether Liddy had ever worked for Dean, and Dean denied it completely, and immediately segued into the same defense of Liddy as he had given for Strachan—that Liddy would not crack under questioning.

Nixon, realizing at least in part the ramifications of what Dean had been telling him, cut short Dean's paean to Liddy's strength, and asked a key question. "Is it too late to go the hang-out road?"

Here was a terrifying idea for Dean, made all the more so by the president's noting that Ehrlichman was recommending that the president do just that—lay out on the table precisely what had happened, admit responsibility, fire whomever was responsible, and let Congress, the courts, and the American public judge how small a matter Watergate had been in relation to Nixon's more significant achievements. But a complete "hang-out road" would mean that Dean's central role in both the break-ins and the cover-up would be revealed. In response to this suggestion, Dean suddenly became almost inarticulate.

D: There is a certain domino situation here. If some things start going, a lot of other things are going to start going, and there can be a lot of problems if everything starts falling. So there are dangers, Mr. President. I would be less than candid if I didn't tell you there are.

The president backed off a bit, saying he hadn't meant that everyone should go up on the Hill and testify, but, rather, the true story should come from the "PR people." Dean gratefully took the ball and ran with it, admitting to the president that the cover-up line, to the effect that technically no one at the White House knew about the break-in, could be sustained even though "there are some people who saw the fruits of it, but that is another story. I am talking about the criminal conspiracy to go in there." Nixon understood this to be (he later wrote) "a lawyer's distinction," but one that would allow him to continue to maintain that the White House had not planned the break-ins.

That was only momentary respite for the president, however, because his young counsel was seeing and identifying incoming missile fire from all directions. Dean segued to Segretti and noted that the president's enemies would have to twist Segretti's story in order to paint it as "more sinister, more involved, part of a general plan." The president shook a metaphorical fist at the sky, ranting about those enemies, saying that "the establishment is dying" and that the fuss over Watergate was their last gasp before his ultimate triumph.

"That is why I keep coming back to this fellow Sullivan," Dean said. "It could change the picture."

The president wasn't buying that as he had in past meetings. How could Sullivan help? Perhaps only if the former FBI assistant director "would get Kennedy into it."

Having deflected Nixon, and using the totemic Kennedy name, Dean now tried to frighten the president away from the "hang-out road" by informing him that if people went after Segretti they would find Kalmbach, and if they found Kalmbach they would find Caulfield and the fact that a man working for Caulfield had spent two years investigating Chappaquiddick on the president's nickel.

Again, the president wasn't buying. So what if he'd had a potential opponent's biggest calamity investigated? "Why don't we get it out anyway?"

"We don't want to surface him [the Chappaquiddick investigator—Ulasewicz] right now," Dean said quickly, and came close to admitting his real reason for saying so, that people were asking for Kalmbach's bank records.

Still mystified, and perhaps needing to digest all that he had been told in this confession that shattered all his previous understandings and beliefs about no White House involvement in Watergate, Nixon grasped at the Sullivan straw and stirred it about for the last minutes of the conversation.

But Dean now tried to suggest that trotting Sullivan out wouldn't be entirely positive for Nixon either, because though Sullivan wouldn't "give up the White House," he did have "knowledge of the earlier (unintelligible) that occurred here."

"That we did?" Nixon asked.

"That we did," Dean affirmed.

Nixon argued that Sullivan could conceal this if he had to, and then ushered Dean out at 2:00 P.M. with a rhetorical question, "It is never dull, is it?"

"Never," Dean agreed.

On March 15, at a press conference, the questions to Nixon centered on Dean and Watergate, and the president still defended Dean and said he was doubly covered from testifying by executive privilege and his position as the president's lawyer. But the questioning worried Nixon. "With the doggedness of one who suddenly finds himself surrounded by a raging storm" he wrote in *RN*, "I clung to my one landmark— even though it was now apparently anchored upon a technicality: that no one in the White House had been involved in the Watergate break-in. I had been told that Strachan had known about the bugging after the fact—but he had not been part of the decision to do it."

That wasn't quite so. Dean had actually told Nixon that Strachan knew of the break-ins before they happened, but the president chose to interpret Dean's admission otherwise. In any event, after this confessional conversation, the president resolved to press more firmly for a written statement from Dean that would repeat what Dean had been telling the upper echelon for nine months, and that would show, in Nixon's words, "there was no evidence against Colson, Chapin, or Haldeman on Watergate."

He conveyed that idea in those words to Dean on the sixteenth, and repeated the need for a Dean Report on the seventeenth, in another conversation recorded in the Oval Office. Although portions of this tape that should have been made public in 1974 were withheld at the time, some additionally relevant portions were included in Nixon's autobiography, written later; they refer to John Mitchell and Bob Haldeman.

Having exonerated both men in his own confession of March 13, Dean on the seventeenth tried to clarify the matter for the president, and to protect himself at the same time. Dean said he had attended meetings in Mitchell's office where Liddy's plans were laid out. They included bugging, but, Dean said, neither he nor Mitchell had agreed to the bugging. Nixon later wrote that he could visualize the scene "and Mitchell's inscrutability," saying nothing and puffing on his pipe, "the manner he always adopted when having to tolerate amateurs."

Dean reported as fact his fabricated meeting with Haldeman, the one in which he claimed to have come back to the White House and told Haldeman about the Mitchell-Liddy meeting and the GEM-STONE plan. He and Bob, Dean reported to the president, had agreed that the White House had to stay "ten miles away from it—because it is just not right and we can't have any part of it." According to Dean this was when he and Haldeman thought they had "turned off" any bugging actions.

As we have seen, Haldeman later wrote that he couldn't remember this supposed incident, but that Dean kept referring to it and insisting that it had happened, until Haldeman for a time convinced himself that it had. It wasn't until Haldeman consulted his logs and extensive meeting notes that he discovered that the Dean disclaimer session with him had never happened.

Nonetheless, on March 17 the president was glad to hear about that disclaimer session, and suggested that Dean wouldn't have to write about the meeting with Mitchell in the Dean Report since everyone had said no to the bugging! Then the president went on to tick off the administration's vulnerabilities, as he now understood them: Mitchell, Colson, Haldeman, and Chapin. Dean responded that he would add his own name because he had been "all over this thing like a blanket." Nixon agreed, but said that was post–break-in, and suggested that, unlike the others, Dean had no problem of criminal liability.

"That's right," Dean said.

The president pressed Dean on Magruder and Strachan and why anybody would have gone into, of all places, the DNC.

"That absolutely mystifies me," Dean said.

The president was concerned about Magruder, who, Woodward and Bernstein reported in the *Washington Post*, was telling prosecutors that Colson, Haldeman, and Dean had known about the break-ins in advance. "I did not believe the accusation," Nixon later wrote, "but I thought that, as Dean observed, if Magruder ever saw himself sinking he would reach out to grab anyone he could get hold of." The president could see no alternative but to admit that Liddy had done the job.

Dean now said this would be a problem—though he didn't say it was a problem for himself. Instead, he substituted Ehrlichman as the new target, telling the president that Hunt and Liddy had worked for Ehrlichman, specifically in the break-in at the office of Dr. Fielding.

"What in the world—?" Nixon exclaimed. "What in the name of God was Ehrlichman having something (unintelligible) in the Ellsberg (unintelligible)? . . . This is the first I ever heard of this! . . . I can't see that getting into, into this hearing."

It wasn't the first Nixon had heard of it, according to Ehrlichman's memoir; he remembers distinctly telling Nixon about that break-in during the summer of 1972, as they walked together on the sand south of San Clemente. The event came up because Nixon was discussing the possibility of pardons, and Ehrlichman—who objected to the idea— brought up the point that Liddy and Hunt might want especially broad pardons to exonerate them from just such escapades as the Dr. Fielding break-in. Nixon has denied ordering the Dr. Fielding break-in or knowing of it before Dean told him. When Ehrlichman reminded him in 1973 of their 1972 conversation, Nixon shrugged it off with the observation, "Well . . . it evidently didn't make any impression on me." In any event, during his conversation with Dean, Nixon's real concern was not whether the burglary had occurred; it was that the whole affair was in danger of being brought to light.

Dean then told him about the picture of Liddy in the CIA files, and how the date of the burglary was contemporaneous with Liddy's employment at the White House. Nixon reiterated his main point, the hope that the Dr. Fielding burglary was irrelevant to the Ervin hearings, and that it could be concealed.

Three days later, in an evening phone call, John Dean said that he wanted to come to the president and lay out everything, "so that you operate from the same facts that everybody else has." Nixon sounded grateful for this, asked rhetorically if he wanted anyone else there, then acknowledged, "It is better with nobody else there, isn't it? . . . Anybody else, they are all partisan interest, virtually."

"That's right," Dean agreed.

They set a date for ten the next morning, March 21, 1973, for the time when John Dean implied he would let the president know all that he knew, in a tape that has become famous for Dean's warning to the president that there was a cancer growing within Nixon's presidency.

17

THE CANCER WITHIN THE PRESIDENCY

THE "cancer within the presidency" tape of March 21, 1973, has previously been understood as the time when John Dean warned Nixon of the grave danger to his presidency and ended the cover-up. But that interpretation of the March 21 tape is based almost entirely on the perception of a credible and truthful John Dean, and, as we have shown, Dean lied repeatedly before the Senate committee and to every other forum in which he testified.

As Dean and the president prepared to meet on the morning of March 21, James McCord was off the reservation, and Howard Hunt seemed likely to follow. McCord had written a letter to Judge Sirica saying that he and other defendants had been under heavy pressure to plead guilty and remain silent, that higher-ups were indeed involved, and that perjury was committed at the trial. Shortly, Sirica would release this letter and McCord would begin to spill some of what he knew. Howard Hunt had left five clearly desperate messages at the White House indicating that he, too, might want to sing rather than to spend a long time in jail; it was these latest Hunt demands, Dean wrote in his book, that drove him to end the cover-up. As if McCord and

Hunt were not enough to worry Dean, Senator Ervin had threatened to cite for contempt of Congress any executive branch official who refused to testify before the Watergate committee on the challenged grounds of executive privilege—and Dean was the official they wanted most to hear.

After initial discussion about how stupid Pat Gray had been in offering to show senators raw FBI files—an offer Kleindienst had now rescinded, with Nixon's approval—the conversation came directly to the point.

D: I think there is no doubt about the seriousness of the problem we've got. We have a cancer within, close to the Presidency, that is growing. It is growing daily. It's compounded, growing geometrically now, because it compounds itself. That will be clear if I, you know, explain some of the details of why it is. Basically it is because 1) we are being blackmailed; 2) people are going to start perjuring themselves very quickly that have not had to perjure themselves to protect other people in the line. And there is no assurance—

P: That that won't bust?

D: That that won't bust.

Dean said he wanted to take the president over how the whole thing got started, and insisted that it had done so "with an instruction to me from Bob Haldeman to see if we couldn't set up a perfectly legitimate campaign intelligence operation" at the CRP. This was false, as it was Dean rather than Haldeman who had pushed Liddy and the revised Sandwedge Plan on the CRP for Dean's own purposes. But Nixon didn't know that, and kept listening as Dean went on, describing almost precisely what happened but at every turn ascribing the initiator as someone other than himself. At times the culprit was Haldeman, Ehrlichman, Colson, Strachan, Magruder, Mitchell, or Liddy, depending on whom Dean needed to cover his own tracks. For instance, he attributed the desire to use Hunt and Liddy to Colson, who, Dean told the president, had issued an ultimatum to the CRP to "fish or cut bait" in regard to these valuable resources.

Every time the president tried to pin Dean down as to a particular person's culpability, Dean would shift the focus to yet another person. Nixon thought he had Strachan firmly in his sights, but Dean said that Strachan had merely been the tickler to Magruder, who had issued orders to Liddy. So was it Magruder? Dean said yes, but immediately shifted the conversation to the startling statement,

D: I don't know if Mitchell has perjured himself in the Grand Jury or not.

P: Who?

D: Mitchell. I don't know how much knowledge he actually had. I know that Magruder has perjured himself in the Grand Jury. I know that Porter has perjured himself in the Grand Jury.

P: Who is Porter?

The president might as well have asked, "Who's on first?", the tag line to the old comedy routine. Befuddled by Dean's verbal quick-change act, he was softened up for Dean's real point, his flat-out statement, "I know that as God is my maker, I had no knowledge that they were going to do this [go back into the DNC]." Since no contradiction or even an insightful question came from the president after that bald-faced lie, Dean shifted and told the president some things that were true: "I was totally aware of what the Bureau was doing at all times. I was totally aware of what the Grand Jury was doing. I knew what witnesses were going to be called. I knew what they were asked, and I had to." What Dean did not tell the president was his true motive for being so "totally aware."

Now Dean hit the heavy stuff, "the most troublesome post-thing." He said that "1) Bob [Haldeman] is involved in that; 2) John [Ehrlichman] is involved in that; 3) I am involved in that; 4) Mitchell is involved in that. And that is an obstruction of justice."

This was a lot for Nixon to digest, the idea of his two top aides, his closest friend, and his counsel all accused of obstructing justice. He wanted to go over the names one by one. Dean started to explain Haldeman's involvement, but soon shifted back to his real theme, the "continual blackmail operation by Hunt and Liddy and the Cubans." This was a problem because "the blackmail is continuing," again, not telling Nixon that only Dean himself was being "blackmailed" by Hunt. The president told Dean that he had had a discussion about a possible commutation of Hunt's sentence on the grounds of compassion for Hunt's wife's death, but hadn't agreed to it.

Now Dean hit his stride and revealed his true agenda for the meeting—not, as he had promised, to tell the president everything Nixon needed to know, but to ask Nixon for money with which to continue to keep certain lips sealed. "There is a real problem in raising money," Dean asserted, and told of the difficulties that even John Mitchell had in finding money for this purpose.

P: How much money do you need?

D: I would say these people are going to cost a million dollars over the next two years.

The president said that could be obtained, in cash if necessary. "I know where it could be gotten. It is not easy, but it could be done." There was some discussion of who would handle the task.

Since this tape was made public in 1974, people have argued whether or not the president really agreed to pay hush money to the burglars in this tape. Some say he did, others claim that he simply explored the matter with Dean at this point on the tape—"I'm just thinking out loud, here, for a moment," Nixon actually said—since later in the conversation Nixon also said that the money could be obtained, "but it would be wrong." The clearest indication of support for the latter notion is that the president did not direct anyone to find or pay money in the next days and weeks, so even if he had tacitly agreed to pay in this meeting, he didn't take action to do so. And when the president wanted action, he usually got it. Contrast this nonpayment of further hush money with the quick action taken to have the CIA obstruct the FBI's investigation in June 1972, within hours of the president's having agreed to that notion.

In this conversation, the president tried again to play Dean's guessing game. Who, precisely, had to be kept under control—Bud Krogh, who had just perjured himself? Mitchell and Magruder, who Nixon was told were about to? Liddy? Hunt? Kalmbach?

Here was that odd name again. But this third time Dean brought up Kalmbach's name, Dean finally spilled the beans—a bit. "He has maintained a man who I only know by the name of "Tony; who is the fellow who did the Chappaquiddick study." But Kalmbach disappeared as quickly as Dean had made him appear: "Herb's problems are politically embarrassing, but not criminal." A half-minute earlier, Dean had been saying that Kalmbach was about to commit perjury. No wonder the president seemed befuddled. Was Dean's argument that a cancer was growing, but could be ameliorated by the application of hush money, which should now be spread around more magnanimously to assuage the problems of those who were perjuring themselves as well as those who were maintaining silence? That seemed to be the message coming through such impenetrable lines as these:

D: What really bothers me is this growing situation. As I say, it is growing because of the continued need to provide support for the

Watergate people who are going to hold us up for everything we've got, and the need for some people to perjure themselves as they go down the road here. If this thing ever blows, then we are in a cover-up situation.

Nixon thought the way out would be to fire some of the men involved, and Dean seemed to agree, though he said the real problem was "the person who will be hurt by it most will be you and the Presidency." The president understood that threat, but had reached the point of believing that some disclosure, perhaps even complete disclosure, had to be made.

Dean could not withstand full disclosure. He raised an idea that the president had already heard from Ehrlichman. They would ask for a new grand jury and then send many White House and CRP witnesses before it. Dean embraced this notion but was careful to agree that one of the few men who could really hurt him, Jeb Magruder, ought to be granted immunity before testifying. "Some people are going to have to go to jail," Dean said flatly. "That is the long and the short of it."

Then Dean completed the last bit of his own selective confession, telling the president that he, Dean, could go to jail for obstruction of justice. Nixon scoffed at this, but Dean lectured as if Nixon were a first-year law student: "I have been a conduit for information on taking care of people out there who are guilty of crimes." The president thought that could be glossed over with a little luck; of course, the president did not know all of what Dean had done, nor for how long Dean had been involved in criminal acts.

Dean pleaded for the chance to bring Haldeman, Ehrlichman, Mitchell, and himself together in a single room and get everyone's story straight so that if called to testify they could have a coherent line that would clear them all. The president wasn't opposed to that, but vowed that should Haldeman and Ehrlichman be indicted, he was prepared to "tough it through." Nixon asked his young counsel to come and brief the cabinet on what he had found out about all the people involved, and tell the cabinet not what he knew, but what he had been told— "Haldeman is not involved, Ehrlichman is not involved," the president told Dean to say to the cabinet. "Sir, I can give them a show. We can sell them just like we were selling Wheaties on our position," Dean said. Clearly, neither the president nor Dean considered admitting to the cabinet the whole truth and nothing but the truth.

Since Dean had agreed to his scheme, Nixon would now agree to Dean's, and called in Haldeman to see if the four-way meeting could be arranged. Mitchell and Ehrlichman were away, but by Thursday it could be done. The bulk of the next half-hour was spent discussing the culpabilities of the president's men with Haldeman and Dean. The president's position was clear: Even if certain people were criminally liable, the White House and CRP people were to check their stories with one another, then find and adhere to a single line to keep the investigation away from the first and second ranks—away from Haldeman, Ehrlichman, Chapin, Strachan, Magruder. Well, maybe they would let Magruder perjure himself and be sent to jail.

Nixon told Bob Haldeman of Dean's idea of covering over sins with money, but Nixon acknowledged that payment of $1 million in continued hush money would be fruitless, because eventually people would talk anyway. That point cleared up, Nixon returned to the suggestion of a new grand jury at which his men would testify, "and that gives you a reason not to have to go before the Ervin and Baker Committee," because the witnesses could then argue that they had already testified in secret, and that their testimony was sealed. Better a private forum than a public one.

In the time since Dean had last heard the suggestion, a half-hour earlier, he had evidently decided that appearing before the grand jury was not without its perils—for him. "Once we start down any route that involves the criminal justice system," he warned, "we've got to have full appreciation that there is really no control over that."

Haldeman, however, wanted to have everyone go to the grand jury, and Ehrlichman had been the original sponsor of the idea, and they were going to bring in Mitchell and have him reflect on it, too. Trapped for the moment, Dean said little more. He was way ahead of the others in his understanding of the position they might shortly assume: that everyone must testify without immunity, even Dean. That, of course, would be devastating for Dean, so he kept his mouth uncharacteristically shut toward the later part of the conversation. The president was willing to meet with the foursome or not, he left it to their discretion, but on one point he was specific: At the end of their deliberations, Dean should report to him on how it came out. As the meeting ended, Nixon seemed resigned to some losses. The Watergate monster had been contained before the election, but he told Haldeman and Dean that he couldn't allow it to eat at his administration for the next four years. The public furor over Watergate must be brought to an end. "Delaying is the great danger to the White House," the president summed up before ushering his aides out.

At a late afternoon meeting that same day, Dean, Haldeman, and Ehrlichman met with the president, and the immediate subject was "John's Grand Jury package," which included immunity for some witnesses. Ehrlichman, White House counsel before Dean, advised that this "can't be carried off," and pushed for a document that would review the facts as the White House saw them, "and that would have the effect of turning the scope . . . becoming the battle ground on a reduced scope." The Dean Report would be "a basic document" on "a limited subject that would rather conspicuously hit the target."

They discussed clemency; the president had said in the morning that it couldn't be done for at least two years, but Dean repeated Hunt's demand that he be out of jail by Christmas of 1973. Dean was clearly worried about more and more people possibly "blowing."

> **D:** It is not only . . . within this circle of people, that have tidbits of knowledge. There are a lot of weak individuals and it could be one of those who crosses up: the secretary to Liddy, the secretary to Jeb Magruder, Chuck Colson's secretary, among others, will be called before the Senate Committee.

The real problem, Dean maintained—and, although he did not say so, this was the crucial problem for Dean himself—was that depositions and testimonies would be checked one against another for "inconsistencies."

Nixon said he wasn't "going to worry about that," and was concerned for "these young people . . . [who thought] they were doing things for the best interests of their country." Haldeman echoed this thought, saying that no one had done anything for money, as had been the case in the Eisenhower administration.

Dean had a new idea, a "super-Presidential board" to hear the witnesses, thus bypassing both the Senate and the grand jury. Haldeman thought that was a terrible notion, for the public would see through it; Ehrlichman came back to "another way," a Dean Report.

> **E:** The President then makes a bold disclosure of everything which he then has. And is in a position if it does collapse at a later time to say, "I had the FBI and the Grand Jury, and I had my own Counsel, I turned over every document I could find. I placed in my confidence young people and as is obvious now . . ."

The Dean Report: The president complained that he had asked for it and did not yet have it. As the men discussed it, the report grew in importance and size. It would have appendices listing the FBI data Dean had seen, and his interviews with Kalmbach, Segretti, Magruder, Chapin, and Ehrlichman. "The President is in a stronger position later, if he can be shown to have justifiably relied on you [Dean] at this point in time," Ehrlichman concluded. Dean was alarmed at the thought:

> **D:** Well, there is the argument now that Dean's credibility is in question. Maybe I shouldn't do it. Maybe someone else—
>
> **H:** This will rehabilitate you, though. Your credibility—
>
> **P:** As a matter of fact, John, I don't think your credibility has been much injured.

There'd be a report, and perhaps they'd publish it, perhaps only show it to Sam Ervin, or only to the Justice Department. But Magruder was now at the Commerce Department, and portions relating to him would have to be shown there. Who else would be vulnerable that way?

> **D:** Draw numbers with names out of a hat to see who gets hurt and who doesn't. That sounds about as fair as you can be, because anyone can get hurt. . . . The thing that I would like to happen, if it is possible to do it, is—Hunt has now sent a blackmail request directly to the White House.

But they were no longer interested in Hunt, because a Dean Report would put the White House way out in front of whatever damage Haldeman, Ehrlichman, and the president thought Hunt could do to them, say, insofar as impugning Colson. The others in the room didn't for a moment realize the danger Hunt posed to Dean. Nixon quoted Dean back to him, suggesting that cutting out the cancer would eliminate such small problems as Hunt. Dean backed off: "You see, it is a temporary cancer."

What Dean could not say, and what those in the room never completely understood, was that the true cancer within the presidency was John Dean himself. That cancer had metastasized now, had reproduced itself in so many places in the administration that even radical surgery to remove the original tumor could no longer save the patient. The Nixon presidency was mortally infected, and Nixon did not know it.

Dean was so slippery and well informed that it was hard to accept that he was the problem. For instance, Dean began to suggest to his audience precisely what Sirica would do and say from the bench two days hence when he sentenced the burglars. "He will charge that he doesn't believe that . . . the lawyers for the government presented a legitimate case and that he is not convinced that the case represents the full situation." How did Dean know? His sources must be truly amazing, the listeners had to conclude; he was a man to whom, in their state of ignorance, they had to pay close attention. A week after sentencing, Dean went on to prophesy, all the burglars would go before a new grand jury, with Sirica promising to give lighter sentences to those who talked.

How to get out in front of that? Maybe it could all be resolved the next day, when the sagacious, stone-faced John Mitchell gave them the benefit of his thoughts. The meeting was thus adjourned until March 22, at 1:57 P.M., when Mitchell, Haldeman, Ehrlichman, and Dean met—with the president present—in Nixon's office in the EOB.

In the interim between Wednesday evening and Thursday afternoon, Pat Gray had told the Judiciary Committee that Dean had probably lied when he first told the FBI that he didn't know whether or not Howard Hunt had a White House office. This became the first topic of the meeting in Nixon's EOB office. Haldeman summed it up succinctly, "The headline for tonight will be GRAY SAYS DEAN LIES."

As Dean was beginning to realize, even a man long since chucked overboard could come back to haunt you.

The Dean Report: Even Mitchell thought that a good idea; the young counsel could go to Camp David over the weekend and write it. Trying to seem cooperative, Dean said that he already had the Segretti section done, but "I really can't say until I [write the Watergate sections] where we are and I certainly think it is something that should be done, though." And the president fantasized how it would read:

> **P:** "I have reviewed the record, Mr. President, and without at all compromising the right of defendants and so forth, some of whom are on appeal, here are the facts with regard to members of the White House staff *et cetera, et cetera,* that you have asked me about. I have checked the FBI records; I have read the Grand Jury transcripts—*et cetera, et cetera.*"

They went around the room about the Dean Report for some minutes, and then came to the heart of the discussion, the plan for all the president's men to go before a grand jury.

Mitchell was all for it; indeed, his suggestion was almost breathtaking in its simplicity, ingenuity, and political savvy: everyone, without exception and including himself, Haldeman, Ehrlichman, and Dean, would testify before the grand jury, without immunity. They would open themselves to possible criminal liabilities, but must be willing to pay such a price to allow the president to then say that none of his people would testify on the Hill, because they had already done so to the more proper forum, the grand jury. Politically, they would have had full disclosure, but since the grand jury hearings were supposed to be kept secret, they would be protected.

A moment of reflection. Haldeman, Ehrlichman, and Mitchell were not fools, nor were they intent on going to jail to save the chief. They firmly believed they had done nothing wrong, and that while grand jury appearances would put them in danger, they would not be indicted nor convicted on the basis of their appearances. None of these three men had approved the break-ins, and for that reason they thought they were pretty much in the clear.

There was some banter that perhaps Dean could be "negotiated out" of the arrangement by claiming the lawyer-client privilege with the president, but the other "big fish" would have to go. (As Dean feared they would, a few days later Haldeman and Ehrlichman came to the conclusion that Dean ought to testify without immunity before the grand jury; of course there would be areas that touched the president on which he could legitimately refuse to testify, but before the grand jury Dean would have a chance to defend himself.)

Haldeman was all for the grand jury appearances of the "big fish," telling the president that while on constitutional grounds he was correct in preventing his aides on the basis of claiming executive privilege from testifying before the Senate,

> **H:** To the guy who is sitting at home who watches John Chancellor who says that "The president is covering this up by this historic review blanket of the widest exercise of executive privilege in American history and all that," [the guy at home] says, "What the hell's he covering up? If he's got no problem, why doesn't he let them go talk?"

Mitchell emphatically agreed, saying that the matter related to a domestic affair, not to something truly important such as foreign affairs or Henry Kissinger's next mission. Full disclosure, that was Mitchell's message.

In the meantime, they would talk to the Senate committee and try to establish some general procedural rules on executive privilege— Kleindienst was to be point man on that with Baker and Ervin—but all the while, they'd be trying to circumvent the committee through mounting a grand jury show. And Dean was to go to Camp David and write a document that would allow the individual players to know what they should say to that grand jury.

P: Do you think we want to go this route now? Let it hang out, so to speak?

D: Well, it isn't really that—

H: It's a limited hang out.

D: It is a limited hang out. It's not an absolute hang out.

P: But some of the questions look big hanging out publicly or privately.

D: What it is doing, Mr. President, is getting you up above and away from it. That is the most important thing.

P: Oh, I know. I suggested that the other day, and they all came down negative on it. Now, what has changed their minds?

D: Lack of candidate or a body.

Everyone in the room laughed at Dean's reference to their not having a person handy who could properly take the fall. The meeting cascaded to a close, and Dean headed toward Camp David.

In Dean's version of what happened to him when he was sent to Camp David to write the Dean Report, everything was a surprise—the idea of the report, his sudden conversion to truthfulness, and so on. He brought Mo along, and confessed everything to her; she told him to be honest and tell the world what he knew. Troubled, he went walking in the woods until a guard asked him if he was lost. No, he replied, he had just found the way. In his moment of finding grace, he understood that Haldeman, Ehrlichman, and Nixon really did have "a candidate or a body," that the fall guy was to be John Mitchell, and that he, Dean, must not take part in the savaging of such a wonderful man. Therefore, there could be no Dean Report. It was then, in Dean's version, that he decided to tell the truth to the prosecutors, in hope that justice would be kind as well as blind.

Nonsense. Or, perhaps, the sort of judiciously couched psychological explanation of events that convinces for a time in the absence of facts.

Dean could not write a Dean Report for several reasons. If he wrote a truthful one, it would incriminate himself; if he wrote one that was false, that would also put him at risk because of the criminal implications of submitting a false report. Last, if he submitted any sort of report that was detailed enough to be believed, others would be able to read it and deduce its history of deception. Moreover, the facts controvert Dean's version of a sudden lurch toward truth. From his own account and from collateral ones, we know that at Camp David Dean did not write a report but made three crucial telephone calls, none of which were even faintly connected to ascertaining or relating the truth.

The press had reported what had happened in Sirica's courtroom: Sirica had made public James McCord's letter saying that higher-ups in the White House were involved in the break-ins. Dean's first call was in relation to these press reports, and it was to Jeb Magruder, who knew and could testify to Dean's central role in both the break-ins and the cover-up. To get out of this tight spot, Dean needed to neutralize Magruder. Dean had managed to procure a tape recorder and sought to get Jeb on tape exonerating him from pre–break-in knowledge.

He telephoned and found Magruder frantic because both of their pictures and McCord's damning letter were splashed over the front page of the Los Angeles *Times*. The opening paragraph of that story stated clearly that McCord had said that both Magruder and Dean had "prior knowledge of the bugging" before the break-in. So Magruder said, "We've got to figure—John, I think we gotta just figure out how we can handle this. I don't know what we—I mean I don't know what we can do right now. I don't know if there is anything that we can do right now." Beyond that, Magruder wanted to believe that McCord had no evidence connecting him to the break-ins—"McCord never met with either myself or anyone else at our committee"—and wanted Dean's help on corroborating that. He told his coach that McCord, whom they deprecated as a name-dropper, would probably say Dean, Mitchell, Haldeman, and Strachan were "all behind it."

But Dean had another agenda: He wanted Jeb to say on the tape that he, Dean, had nothing to do with it at all. Unfortunately, Jeb wasn't biting. He told Dean, "I'm going to have to rely on you or whatever when we have to go down to the grand jury."

Unable to get Jeb to say the magic words, Dean tried stating his own case, to see if Magruder would agree or disagree. "I know that I'd told Haldeman after that meeting that it had to be turned off. Now what happened in the interim I don't have any idea, I don't want to know, I can only opine and speculate."

Magruder answered, "I would hope so, John, of course on that meeting, that—I have testified that that meeting that we had with Liddy and Mitchell was simply on the general counsel's job and so on. . . . That we just went over the general framework of the job and the new [election] law and those kind of problems."

That was as far as Dean could get Jeb to go. Nevertheless, Dean would later argue to the Watergate committee—who were evidently convinced by his argument and this tape—that Magruder had admitted that Dean had no advance knowledge of the break-ins.

Now that he had a piece of evidence, Magruder on tape supposedly exonerating him, Dean made his other two critical calls.

The second was to Peter Maroulis, Liddy's lawyer. Dean tried to tape that one, as well, but didn't do very well. However, Maroulis did assure Dean of the one thing he really wanted to know—that Liddy wasn't going to talk, no matter what pressure was applied to him by Sirica or Congress. This was good news, for if Liddy kept his mouth shut, Dean could promulgate his version of a whole spectrum of events that could have been incriminating to Dean—from Sandwedge to GEMSTONE to the entries into the DNC to the walk in the park of June 19. With Liddy unwilling even to deny Dean's accusations, Dean was safe from assault from that quarter. He would still have Hunt and McCord to fend off, but Dean could ascribe all the evil doings to the man who was going to keep his lips sealed.

Liddy and Magruder in hand, Dean made the third call. In it, he sought and retained counsel for himself, and convinced that counsel to call the prosecutors and tell them the single thing the prosecutors most wanted to hear: that Dean could "deliver the P," that he could implicate the president as a co-conspirator in the sorry mess of Watergate. In other words, Dean wanted his counsel to tell the prosecutors that the lawyer for the president of the United States could and would now throw overboard the last and most important of all the men on the ship, its captain, Dean's client, Richard Nixon.

What Dean did not tell his own counsel, nor the prosecutors, nor the Senate, nor the House Judiciary Committee, nor his fellow co-conspirators when they sat down in jail together, nor the public in his book, nor the avid listeners at the hundreds of forums to which Dean has lectured in the years since Watergate, was that he threw over Richard Nixon to prevent his own deep criminality from becoming known.

It was almost complete, now, the journey of this amazingly capable young man from the ambitious, fawning midlevel official to the man who set off the astounding series of crimes that we know as Watergate, to the depths of treachery involved in sabotaging fatally the presidency of Richard Nixon.

After Dean came down from the mountain with no report in hand, he began talking to Silbert and his associates on April 2. The initial conversations were enough to convince Silbert that Dean would have major revelations, but Silbert and Dean's counsel disagreed on how much Dean would reveal in exchange for various degrees of immunity from prosecution. Initially, the prosecutors wanted no immunity for Dean, and he refused to say much without some sort of protection.

By April 14, it had become known in the White House that Dean had retained counsel and the president's inner circle believed that Dean was singing to the prosecutors. Dean was just warming up, though, while his counsel was playing off the prosecutors against the Senate committee, trying to see which group would give his client more immunity from prosecution. Both groups were willing to invest so heavily in Dean and his purported credibility, however, that their entire edifices of allegations actually rested on his proposed testimony. Though Sirica initially rejected the prosecutors' request for immunity for Dean, the Senate embraced the idea.

Dean's plan for his testimony was as brilliant as his manipulation of the president and the president's men had been. Dean would say that he had been complicitous, and paint a picture of how he had been enmeshed in the conspiracy because he was so ambitious and eager to please. Dean may actually have agreed to take a small fall in the belief that if people knew he was going to go to jail anyway, that would render his story more credible than if he was able to walk away from his crimes.

While Dean's deliberations with the Senate committee and the prosecutors were going on, the president was sinking ever deeper into actions that would hurt him, for instance, his clandestine offer of the directorship of the FBI to Judge Matthew Byrne, who was then presiding over the trial of Daniel Ellsberg. The offer was rejected, but it made a mess of that trial.

Ehrlichman had been conducting his own, hurried investigation of Watergate, and on April 14 laid out a body of facts for the president, facts that in Ehrlichman's mind implicated Mitchell, Magruder, and Dean. He urged the president to act, because "you can't just sit here."

Dean couldn't just sit there, either, and on April 15—a Sunday— played one of his best cards. He told Silbert of the Liddy-Hunt supervision of the burglary of Dr. Fielding's office, information that he knew would totally disrupt the government's case against Ellsberg.

It was a busy Sunday. That day, based on their interviews with Dean and Magruder, government prosecutors gave Kleindienst and Petersen a report that implicated Haldeman and Ehrlichman in the cover-up along with the others that Dean had named. Both Kleindienst and Petersen informed Nixon of these matters, with Petersen recommending the firing of Haldeman and Ehrlichman, but the retention of Dean, since Dean was now cooperating with the prosecutors.

Shortly after nine that evening Dean met the president in his EOB office and said that while he had, indeed, gone to the prosecutors, he had discussed only the roles of various people in the cover-up, including himself, and that no national security matters had been discussed. Since Nixon felt that the Dr. Fielding burglary was definitely related to national security, and Dean knew that, his statement was a lie.

Next morning, Silbert sent a memo about the Hunt-Liddy supervision of the Dr. Fielding burglary to Henry Petersen, who phoned the president about it as soon as he had received the piece of paper. Nixon bluntly told Petersen to "stay out" of the matter since it involved "national security," and Petersen didn't really respond. (Since the Silbert memo didn't mention that the allegation had come from Dean, no one in the White House yet knew that he was the source of the information.)

But when the president met briefly with Dean, alone, on April 16, they fenced about. This was not a discussion, but, rather, two men telling one another that this was the parting of the ways; from now on, each would know the other principally as an enemy. Dean told Nixon he had retained counsel, and Nixon proffered him letters of resignation to sign. Dean refused to sign ones that had been prepared and said he'd write his own. It wasn't clear that the resignation would be made public right away, though Haldeman and Ehrlichman were already on record as requesting indefinite leaves of absence and had themselves retained counsel. The thought then current in the White House was that if Dean were to stay on staff, the president could claim the lawyer-client privilege and thereby prevent Dean from squealing. As with so much of the legal thinking done in the White House at the time, this was inaccurate, but no one seemed to understand that, or to suggest that it might be so. Dean told Nixon he would resign only if Haldeman and Ehrlichman also did so. Nixon may have misunderstood this as Dean's attempt to lift himself to the level of importance of those two aides. It had an entirely different meaning for Dean; he wanted Haldeman and Ehrlichman to go at the same time because that would provide support for his claim that they were his principals. He told Nixon, and later told the press, that he would not be a "scapegoat" for Watergate.

Nixon and Dean never again met face to face.

On the seventeenth Nixon told the press that after "serious charges" about Watergate were first made known to him on March 21, he had ordered another investigation; and Ziegler told the press that all previous White House statements on Watergate were "inoperative" because they had been based on the earlier investigation, which everyone now knew referred to Dean's work. In the next fortnight McCord filed suit charging he had been entrapped into his activities, Henry Petersen told the president that the break-in at Dr. Fielding's office had become known to the grand jury, Magruder resigned from Commerce, Gray resigned as acting director of the FBI after admitting that he had destroyed files from Hunt's safe—Nixon pronounced himself shocked that Gray would have done such a thing—and Ehrlichman admitted to the FBI his knowledge of the Plumbers' activity. In the midst of all this, the president called Dean at home on April 22 to wish him a happy Easter and to both praise Dean and threaten him with the information that the president still considered him his counsel.

Henry Petersen was still bothered by the Silbert memo about Hunt, Liddy, and the Dr. Fielding break-in, and told Attorney General Kleindienst about it. Kleindienst agreed with Petersen and called Nixon on April 25; he threatened to resign if he were not allowed to send to Judge Byrne the Silbert memo and other documents telling what the government knew about the Dr. Fielding break-in. Nixon agreed, and when Judge Byrne got the documents he held a conference with the prosecutors about them; they wanted him to deal with the documents only *in camera*. Enraged, Byrne read the documents aloud in court on April 27, and made headlines.

That day, Nixon asked Ehrlichman "to make up a list for me of all the national-security-related activities that he thought Dean might be able to expose." According to Nixon's autobiography, that list read, "Ellsberg, the 1969 wiretaps, and the yeoman episode during the Indo-Pakistan war." By the end of the day, Nixon knew that the "Ellsberg" material had already reached public consciousness. It was the last straw.

Judge Byrne, on behalf of the defendants, who believed they had been wiretapped years earlier, had been asking the prosecution for any information concerning "electronic surveillance" on Ellsberg and his associate, Anthony J. Russo, for some time. The government had said it knew nothing of such wiretaps. On Monday, April 30, 1973, in the wake of the revelation of the Hunt-Liddy burglary, Judge Byrne reissued his earlier demand that the government produce any information concerning "electronic surveillance." Shortly, the "1969 wiretaps" would be out of the bag.

Later that evening, President Nixon went before national television to announce that he was accepting the resignations of Haldeman and Ehrlichman, "two of the finest public servants it has been my privilege to know." He had received new information on Watergate in March, he reported, and was now pursuing it vigorously. Toward that end, he was relieving Kleindienst of his responsibilities as attorney general, since he wanted someone who had no previous connection to Halde-man, Ehrlichman, Mitchell, or anyone else in the adminstration; that new attorney general, Elliot Richardson, would be empowered to appoint a special prosecutor for Watergate-related matters. So Nixon said he was accepting the resignation of Kleindienst, and announced in the next breath that "the counsel to the President, John Dean, has also resigned."

Nixon had played one last time into Dean's hands, giving Dean fuel for asserting that Haldeman and Ehrlichman were involved in the conspiracy.

After announcing that Dean had resigned, Nixon hastened to point out that he was meeting in the next few days on momentous matters having to do with the future of Europe, and that he would shortly have to deal with the enormous problems of Southeast Asia and the "poten-tially explosive Middle East." To do so would take all of his energy and commitment, and that was why he was going to put Watergate behind him and call on the leaders of both political parties to run better campaigns, and call on the American people to write rules to free future campaigns of the abuses of the past one. Winding up, in his valedictory Nixon pointed out that there were exactly 1,361 days remaining in his term, and that "I want these to be the best days in American history."

BOOK THREE

EXIT
THE PRESIDENT

18

THE RETURN OF ALEXANDER HAIG

THE espionage and conspiracy trial of Daniel Ellsberg and his associate Anthony Russo in the Pentagon Papers case was in its closing days on April 25, 1973, when a surprise prosecution witness entered, took a front-row seat in the Los Angeles courtroom, and created quite a stir. He wore a crisp Army uniform with a chest full of medals and four polished stars on his shoulder boards. It was Alexander Haig, vice chief of staff of the Army. "Many of the jurors seemed to stare" at those stars and "a nearly full chest of decorations," the next day's story in the *Washington Post* reported, and *The New York Times* suggested that "court observers felt that he had been called more for the dazzle of his appearance and background than for the substance of his testimony."

Haig took the stand briefly as a government rebuttal witness whose role was to attack the credentials of two defense witnesses, his former NSC colleague Morton Halperin and University of Michigan professor Allen S. Whiting, a former State Department intelligence analyst. In Haig's testimony, writes biographer Roger Morris, he "misrepresented significantly Halperin's role" at the NSC, going so far as to deny that

Halperin had been a key Kissinger aide in the early months of the first Nixon administration.

Haig also did not testify that he had known that Halperin was among those wiretapped after the publication of the Pentagon Papers, nor that he had seen the fruits of the wiretap on Halperin's phone that had yielded fifteen of Halperin's conversations with Daniel Ellsberg. To reveal that information would have blown the case sky-high, and damaged himself in the process. Haig also denied under oath that he had any evidence that was material to the trial, though it must be pointed out that he was not specifically asked about an Ellsberg-Halperin tap. As we have shown, such taps were suspected, but Federal Judge Matthew Byrne would not reissue his demand for such evidence until April 30, and that demand would not be answered and the existence of the tap on Halperin revealed until May 8. So when Haig left the courtroom after his thirty-five-minute appearance on April 25, that secret and his role in the wiretapping remained safely hidden.

On April 30, 1973, after the departure of Haldeman, Ehrlichman, and Dean, the White House was in an uproar. Haldeman convinced a reluctant Nixon that he would need a new chief of staff, and recommended Alexander Haig, someone Nixon already knew and could trust, someone with a penchant for making order out of chaos, a strong man who knew how to shield a boss from unwanted intrusions into his privacy. On May 3 Haig came in for an interview.

The *Washington Post* of May 3 had a story by reporters Bob Woodward and Carl Bernstein that had the effect of shielding Haig from the wiretap scandal, just at the moment when the participants in the wiretapping knew it was about to be publicly exposed, and just as Haig was about to return to considerable power in the White House. The timing of the *Post* story and its contents demand examination. The immediate roots of the story went back to late February 1973, when *Time* magazine broke the news that between 1969 and 1971, "six or seven reporters and an undisclosed number of White House officials" had had their phones wiretapped. In response to the *Time* story, denials of the wiretapping were immediately issued by the White House and by Pat Gray, whose confirmation hearings on his promotion to permanent director of the FBI were to open that week.

The idea of domestic wiretapping was a notion to make any reporter's editor sit up and take notice. The team of Woodward and Bernstein had been writing on Watergate since the summer of 1972, had kept in close touch with the prosecutors and the FBI, and had developed many other sources. Their most important source was an old and trusted friend of Woodward's, a highly placed government official whom Woodward would later dub "Deep Throat" in his and Bernstein's bestseller, *All the President's Men*. Woodward had consulted Deep Throat often in September and October of 1972, but after that their meetings had slackened. In late January of 1973 the reporter met his source once again, and this time, according to *All the President's Men*, Deep Throat told Woodward that "[Charles] Colson and [John] Mitchell were behind the Watergate operation," and were the "sponsors" of burglars Hunt and Liddy. Unable to corroborate Deep Throat's story, Woodward and Bernstein did not publish it. But with the *Time* wiretap story in late February, the *Post* had been scooped, and Woodward immediately contacted Deep Throat.

According to *All the President's Men*, Woodward and Deep Throat met, at Deep Throat's request, in "an old wooden house which had been converted into a saloon for truckers and construction workers." Over scotch, Deep Throat described Nixon's "rampage about news leaks on Watergate. . . . Nixon was wild, shouting and hollering that 'we can't have it and we're going to stop it, I don't care how much it costs.'" The discussion moved into the matter of the just-published *Time* report. Deep Throat confirmed that there had been wiretapping, but characterized it as having been conducted by an "out-of-channels vigilante squad," and said that the targets had included taps on Hedrick Smith and Neil Sheehan of *The New York Times* in the wake of that newspaper's publication of the Pentagon Papers. The records had been "destroyed," Deep Throat assured Woodward, but said that the "out-of-channels" people had included "ex–FBI and ex–CIA agents" and had been supervised at Justice by Robert Mardian.

Deep Throat's description of the 1969–1971 wiretapping was a mixture of partial truths and of information so distorted that it smacked of deliberate misdirection. Throat was correct in implying that Hunt and Liddy had been involved in buggings—their names and biographies were public knowledge from their just-concluded trial, and their identities could be easily deduced from Throat's description of "ex–FBI and ex–CIA agents." But they had had nothing to do with the 1969–1971 wiretaps. Throat was also wrong in regard to Mardian's supervision, in saying Sheehan had been tapped, and in his characterization of the operation as a rogue escapade. It has been shown that the wiretapping was initiated at the highest levels by Nixon, Kissinger, and J. Edgar Hoover, supervised by Haig and William Sullivan at the FBI, and condoned by Attorney General Mitchell.

In the tavern session with Woodward, Deep Throat alleged that Haldeman had spurred a "reluctant" Mitchell to "move part of the vigilante operation from the White House to the campaign," and stressed the roles of the ex–FBI man Liddy and the ex–CIA man Hunt in everything that went before that transfer and that came after it. This allegation distracts the reporter by focusing his attention on Liddy and Hunt, and suggests that they, rather than the actual perpetrators, had organized the wiretapping operation. Deep Throat summarized it all for Woodward:

> "In 1969, the first targets of aggressive wiretapping were the reporters and those in the administration who were suspected of disloyalty," Deep Throat said. "Then the emphasis was shifted to the radical political opposition during the anti-war protests. When it got near election time, it was only natural to tap the Democrats. The arrests in the Watergate sent everybody off the edge because the break-in could uncover the whole program."

In one grand statement, Deep Throat married the "national security" wiretapping to the campaign intelligence operation, and attributed it all to Liddy and Hunt, thereby effectively covering over the traces of NSC involvement in the early wiretapping.

Returning from his tavern rendezvous, Woodward talked with Bernstein the next morning. They wanted to print the information from Deep Throat, but, unable to find a second source, they did not publish it just then. Nine weeks later, when the Ellsberg trial revelations were at their height, they published on the morning of May 3—when Haig was on the threshold of the president's door.

In Haig's interview with Nixon, he accepted the position of chief of staff in the White House. He would start the very next day, May 4. Haig would now wield power in a way that had not been possible when he had been an NSC deputy. Now Haig could eclipse Kissinger and become that "new breed" of soldier and that single presidential adviser whose appearance on the horizon he had foreseen and recommended in his master's thesis eleven years before.

Many people have tried to pinpoint the identity of Deep Throat in the reporters' earlier book, *All the President's Men*, and in pursuing Throat's identity have been led astray from the real story, that of the joint involvement of Bob Woodward, the Navy briefer-turned-reporter, and Alexander Haig, the man he often briefed at the White House, in the complex tragicomedy we have come to know as Watergate. Our philosophy in the following pages and chapters will be not to chase Deep Throat through the dramatizations in *All the President's Men*—the flowerpot and marked-up newspapers that Woodward and Deep Throat supposedly used to signal one another, and the darkened parking garage where Woodward claims he and his source met. Rather, we will trace the activities of Bob Woodward and Alexander Haig, and see what relevance those had to the removal of Richard Nixon from the presidency of the United States, and thereby understand why the Deep Throat cover has shielded both men for nearly two decades.

The fortunes of Deep Throat, of Alexander Haig, and of Bob Woodward had been intertwined since hours after the break-in of June 17, 1972.

When the five burglars were arrested at DNC headquarters that morning, word of the foiled burglary quickly reached the *Washington Post*. Joe Califano, who had become general counsel of the Democratic National Committee, as well as one of the lawyers for the *Post*, called the managing editor, who phoned the metropolitan editor. Both editors agreed this was more than a routine police story, and that day nine reporters were at work on various aspects of the case, including neophyte Bob Woodward.

At the time, former Navy officer Woodward had been at the *Post* only nine months, following a year at the weekly paper, the *Montgomery County Sentinel*, in suburban Maryland. He was a staff reporter assigned to metropolitan Washington stories—that is, matters not considered of national importance—but Woodward had worked extremely hard and had earned praise for some enterprising local reporting. When Woodward arrived at the newsroom that morning after the break-in, it was buzzing with activity. There Carl Bernstein, who usually covered Virginia politics, had photocopied the notes of other reporters at the scene and was working the telephones, trying to dig up more information.

Woodward and Bernstein were young at the time—Woodward was twenty-nine, Bernstein, twenty-eight. According to *All the President's Men*, when they first started working together, Woodward and Bernstein didn't like one another. Bernstein thought the former Yale and Navy man hadn't covered "enough pavement for him to be good at investigative reporting." Moreover, "Bernstein knew that Woodward couldn't write very well. One office rumor had it that English was not Woodward's native language." Conversely, the book declared that Bernstein, a college dropout who had begun at the *Washington Star* as a copyboy and had been a reporter at the *Post* since 1966, "looked like one of those counterculture journalists that Woodward despised."

On Sunday, June 18, the Associated Press wire service named James McCord as "security coordinator" for the Nixon reelection committee, and there was a statement from John Mitchell acknowledging that link but denying that the burglars had acted on behalf of the CRP. That same day, Woodward and Bernstein wrote their first joint byline story, which appeared on Monday, that combined this wire service information with some more personal details about McCord's background.

In the early hours of Monday, June 19, 1972, *Washington Post* night police reporter Eugene Bachinski was allowed by one of his police sources to inspect address books seized from burglars Barker and Martinez, found the cryptic notation of Howard Hunt and his "W.H." link in those books, and was told about the check from Hunt in Barker's belongings. An assistant editor told Bachinski to pass the information to Bob Woodward.

According to *All the President's Men*, Woodward, searching for information on Hunt, "called an old friend and sometimes source who worked for the federal government" and did not like to be called at his office. "His friend said hurriedly that the break-in case was going to 'heat up,' but he couldn't explain and hung up." Later in the game, Woodward would label this "old friend" Deep Throat, and rely on him almost exclusively for investigative leads. He would describe Deep Throat in *All the President's Men* as a "source in the Executive Branch who had access to information at CRP as well as the White House," whose position was "extremely sensitive," and that what he knew "represented an aggregate of hard information flowing in and out of many stations." Woodward boasted that his friendship with Deep Throat was "genuine, not cultivated," and went on to explain it:

> Long before Watergate, they had spent many evenings talking about Washington, the government, power. On evenings such as those, Deep Throat had talked about how politics had infiltrated every corner of government—a strong-arm takeover of the agencies by the Nixon White House. Junior White House aides were giving orders on the highest levels of the bureaucracy. He had once called it the "switchblade mentality"—and had referred to the willingness of the President's men to fight dirty and for keeps, regardless of what effect the slashing might have on the government and the nation.

Woodward considered Deep Throat "a wise teacher," but one who "distrusted the press" and "detested" newspapers. Woodward wrote that his old friend had his own "weaknesses," among them that he was an "incurable gossip" who was "fascinated" by rumor and who was "not good at concealing his feelings, hardly ideal for a man in his position."

As an official in a highly sensitive position, Deep Throat would not have talked to the neophyte reporter Woodward unless he trusted him implicitly, and their conversations of "*long before*" (italics added) had apparently assured him about Woodward. Woodward had held three jobs in his adult life—five years as a Navy officer, one year on a suburban weekly newspaper, and nine months at the *Washington Post* assigned to the metropolitan desk. Given the trust displayed by Deep Throat in his dealings with Woodward, it is virtually inconceivable that the relationship could have developed anywhere but the Navy. It was in the Navy that Woodward had held the trusted role of briefer and in that capacity had briefed, among others, Alexander Haig. The subject of the old conversations between Deep Throat and Woodward, and Woodward's descriptions of his friend, echo experiences Haig had been through in the White House, and, perhaps more important, they echo some of the phrases and concerns about the overwhelming civilian influence in national affairs detailed in the master's thesis that became Haig's own blueprint for achieving and understanding power.

On June 19, Woodward received a virtual confirmation from his source that Hunt was, indeed, connected to the White House—this was the implied message of Woodward's "friend" in the warning that the case was going to heat up. Woodward then did some good spade work. Calling the White House directly, he learned that Hunt was on Colson's staff, but could be reached at the public relations firm Robert R. Mullen & Company. Woodward dialed the Mullen firm and when Hunt picked up his phone, Woodward identified himself as a reporter and asked Hunt why his name was in the address books of two Watergate burglars. "Good God!" Hunt exclaimed, then told Woodward he would say nothing more, and hung up. A call to Robert Bennett, Hunt's boss at Mullen, obtained the admission, "I guess it's no secret that Howard was with the CIA"; and a call to CIA headquarters confirmed Hunt's employment there from 1949 to 1970.

Having received all this information, "Woodward didn't know what to think," the reporters' book narrated, and so he "placed another call to his government friend and asked for advice." Deep Throat told Woodward that the FBI regarded Hunt as a prime suspect "for many reasons aside from the address-book entries and unmailed check," and assured Woodward that there would be "nothing unfair" about a story that reported the address book and the check. Woodward and Bachinski put some but not all of this information into a story with both their bylines, published on June 20.

It was good stuff, a veritable scoop; moreover, it impressed people within the *Post* hierarchy by announcing that junior reporter Woodward unexpectedly had a well and highly placed source willing to tell him inside material about a major political development. That raised Woodward's stock within the newspaper enough to obtain for him an assignment to continue covering the Watergate case. The junior reporter became the *Post*'s day-to-day Watergate man—somewhat of a promotion from "metro" matters, to be sure—but in the next few weeks his reportage yielded only straight news accounts or summaries of legal and political developments of the case. On his own, he found no revelatory information. After the initial calls, Deep Throat had been petulant with Woodward, according to *All the President's Men*, and the source remained silent for some time.

By July, David Halberstam wrote in his media study, *The Powers That Be*, the *Post* "seemed to be slowing down on the story." Bernstein had been sent back to his beat and Woodward was assigned to other stories besides Watergate—the Nixon administration's antidrug effort, for instance. When Executive Editor Ben Bradlee was on vacation, and Howard Simons, the managing editor, was in charge, Simons, according to Halberstam, "was bothered by what was *not* happening on the Watergate story . . . [while] Woodward alone was assigned to it." The *Post* was being scooped by its rivals, including *The New York Times*. Simons decided the paper needed a two-man team, and that the reporters should be Woodward and Carl Bernstein. Over the summer, Bernstein doggedly pursued leads and came up with important information tying CRP funds to the burglars.

On September 7, 1972, Nixon awarded Alexander Haig his fourth star and nominated him to become a full general and vice chief of staff of the Army, the number-two job in that service. Haig was to be vaulted entirely over the three-star rank and over 240 more-senior officers to cap his meteoric rise through the officer corps. However, as a condition to Haig's promotion, Nixon required Haig to stay at the White House until after the election, and after the next round of negotiations on ending the war in Vietnam. As it turned out, Haig would end up staying in the White House and continuing to play a prominent role, nominally as Kissinger's deputy, until he left for the Pentagon in early January of 1973. The weeks immediately following Haig's award of his fourth star were among the most fruitful in the Deep Throat–Woodward relationship.

Haig had been Kissinger's deputy for four years. By the fall of 1972, Kissinger and he were full-fledged rivals, and Haig could rise no further in the White House hierarchy. Once elevated to the rank of full general, though, Haig was in position to be considered for the post of chairman of the Joint Chiefs. In nine months, Admiral Moorer was scheduled to retire, and Nixon would be able to appoint his successor. Haig would be a prime candidate—if the military would accept him. That might be difficult, because there was no doubt in the minds of Haig's high-ranking military peers that Haig had risen to four stars because he was a favorite of the civilian politician who happened to be the president. Haig needed to deal with this perception.

Haig knew many of the most closely held secrets of the Nixon White House—the 1969–1971 wiretaps, the formation of the Plumbers, the details of Moorer-Radford, and the foreign policy initiatives made through the military backchannel.

Deep Throat had sat on the sidelines for three months, saying nothing about Watergate during the summer, Woodward and Bernstein wrote in *All the President's Men*, when in mid-September of 1972 he suddenly became a major player. Bernstein had been able to find a CRP bookkeeper who provided the first details—but no documentary proof—that CRP money had been used to finance the Watergate bugging. Bernstein also managed to crack Stans's deputy Hugh Sloan, who divulged more clues. On September 16, the day after the indictments of Hunt, Liddy, and the burglars were announced, Woodward telephoned Deep Throat and told him what Bernstein had uncovered. Deep Throat confirmed that the secret campaign fund had not only financed the Watergate bugging but also *"other intelligence-gathering activities."* (Emphasis in original.) He further volunteered that wiretap logs from the bugging had gone to some of the same John Mitchell aides who had disbursed the funds. This confirmation and its confidential, anonymous source became the meat of the Woodward and Bernstein story, published on Sunday, September 17, that revealed the use of campaign funds to bug the DNC.

As we can see in retrospect, this story also revealed that Deep Throat was not tied directly to the CRP, for his information about who saw what in the committee was fuzzy and reflective of the thinking in the White House camp at that time. That thinking was also tipped in a story that Woodward checked with Deep Throat the following day, one that implicated Bart Porter, another CRP employee; Throat told Woodward that Porter and Magruder were "deeply involved," and Throat was "explicit in saying the withdrawals [of campaign funds] financed the Watergate bugging." Actually, Porter was only peripherally involved in funding Liddy, but a source at the White House wouldn't know that.

According to Woodward his next conversation with Deep Throat came several weeks later, on October 9. This was four days after John

Dean had sent Bob Haldeman his lighthearted memo about his impending marriage to Maureen Biner. Woodward and Deep Throat were no longer conversing by telephone; in the fall of 1972, according to *All the President's Men*, they had arranged dramatic 2:00 A.M. trysts in an underground parking garage. It Woodward wanted a meeting, says the book, he would signal Deep Throat by moving a flowerpot on his apartment balcony, and if Deep Throat wanted a meeting he would scribble a message inside the morning newspaper at Woodward's front door.

Bernstein had developed material about the dirty tricks activities of Donald Segretti that Woodward wanted to confirm. Barely stopping for drags on his cigarette, Deep Throat told Woodward in the garage more of what he had alluded to in September, the extent of the Nixon campaign's intelligence-gathering activities. Throat said that "fifty people worked for the White House and CRP to play games and spy and sabotage and gather intelligence," that the November Group which had handled campaign advertising was involved in the dirty tricks, and that the targets included Republican contributors as well as Democratic candidates. He also said that Mitchell was behind the Watergate break-in and other illegal activities, and that for ten days after the break-in, Howard Hunt had been assigned to help Mitchell conduct an investigation of Watergate.

This information was wildly inaccurate in many particulars, for instance, the number of people in campaign intelligence, and Hunt's role in the cover-up. But Deep Throat's disclosures reflected White House thinking in the fall of 1972, insofar as it related to Mitchell's role in the break-in.

If Deep Throat was Haig, why would he release a flood of information—some of it clearly inaccurate—at this time? In the fall of 1972, Nixon was riding high as a result of major success in his foreign policy and arms control initiatives, including the antiballistic missile and SALT treaties with the Soviet Union and the China opening. These initiatives had been opposed by the military as giving too much away to the Russians and the Chinese. At the time of the October 10 *Post* article, Haig was scheduled to leave the White House to assume the position of vice chief of staff of the Army and Nixon was on his way to an unprecedented landslide reelection victory that would give him even more power in the foreign policy arena. Revelations of the dirty practices of the Nixon campaign as reported in the *Post* would have the effect of weakening Nixon's postelection influence, a desirable outcome to someone seeking a greater role for the military and a dampening of Nixon's secret diplomacy. Whether or not Deep Throat knew that some of the information given to Woodward was inaccurate, the inaccuracies did serve to cover the trail that could identify him as Woodward's source. Most important to Deep Throat, however, was that his purpose had been served—tarring Nixon before the election.

Woodward had a great need for Deep Throat's information. Deep Throat's revelations were Woodward's way to vault to the forefront of investigative reporters by having a confidential source who divulged information to him and to him alone. For Woodward, Deep Throat was key to the realization of journalistic ambitions. If Deep Throat was Haig, he and Woodward were engaged in a high-stakes game in which confidentiality was essential—to Haig especially, for if Nixon knew that his trusted general was leaking damaging stories to a man who had briefed Haig in the basement of the White House in 1969–1970, even that fourth star would not be enough to protect the general from the president's well-known wrath.

To secure the post of vice chief of the Army, Haig had to go through October 1972 Senate confirmation hearings, and for these Fred Buzhardt served as his personal counsel. No hard questions were asked, and Haig was confirmed. However, as explained earlier, he did not immediately take up his new post, for Nixon asked him to remain in the White House to participate in the last round of discussions with the North Vietnamese. This was when Henry Kissinger made his oft-quoted remark that "peace is at hand," a prophesy that helped carry the election for Nixon, but that soon was transmuted into a mocking cry because no peace treaty was then signed.

Haig accompanied Kissinger to the Paris negotiations, but on his return to the White House he privately warned Nixon of a "murderous bloodbath" that would ensue if a ceasefire was forced on the South Vietnamese. Admiral Zumwalt records in his memoir that Haig, reflecting the sentiment of the JCS, told Nixon that Kissinger "was going too far and giving up too much." According to Zumwalt's notes, Haig "got himself alone with the President—Kissinger doesn't know this," and succeeded in getting Nixon to slow down the troop withdrawals. By Christmas, when Nixon bombed Hanoi, he did so with the open advocacy of Haig, who was now in clear revolt against Kissinger on that and other matters.

Haig did not transfer his office to the Pentagon until January 4, 1973. Afterward, Nixon continued to beckon him to the Oval Office for discussions about foreign policy. In February, the president sent Haig on yet another private mission to Vietnam and to Cambodia. Around that time the *Time* magazine story about the 1969–1971 wiretapping broke, leading to Woodward and Deep Throat's rendezvous in the truckers' tavern. As we have seen, the fruits of that meeting were not printed until the morning of May 3, 1973.

The Woodward and Bernstein article said that *two* highly placed sources in the executive branch confirmed that the telephones of "at least two newspaper reporters" were tapped in the Nixon administration's investigation of the publication of the Pentagon Papers, and that these taps were "supervised by Watergate conspirators E. Howard Hunt, Jr., and Gordon Liddy," whose "vigilante squad" was not part of the FBI (the agency usually charged with legal wiretapping responsibilities) but "was authorized" by Mitchell. It said that all records of that wiretapping had been destroyed, repeated that this wiretapping was essentially different from the one reported earlier by *Time*, in that it was expressly *not* run by the FBI, and that "the only wiretapping of reporters and White House aides known to the *Post*'s sources" was done by vigilantes Hunt and Liddy, who "were regularly routed information obtained from national security wiretaps."

In their book, Woodward and Bernstein were deliberately vague about their second source for this information, and all signs point to the notion that it came solely from Deep Throat, for any other source would have challenged the details that we know to have been false. Recently, Gordon Liddy reread that May 3 story, and states unequivocally that it is "a total fraud. There is not a word of truth to it."

A third clue as to the source of the information comes from a seemingly inconsequential sentence in *All the President's Men* that deals with why the reporters "decided to go" with the story in May, after holding it since February. They had not printed the story because they had been unable to confirm from any other source the names of the *New York Times* reporters as subjects of the wiretaps. But, by the beginning of May, "They did find, however, that there was a possibility that Ellsberg had been overheard on a tap."

This fact was not included in the May 3 story itself; indeed, if it had been, there would have been quite an uproar, for it was just this confirmation of Ellsberg as a subject of the taps that William D. Ruckelshaus, who had replaced Pat Gray as acting director of the FBI, was frantically searching for in the days after Judge Matthew Byrne's April 30 directive that the government search its files for evidence of wiretaps of Daniel Ellsberg. That evidence was not found until May 8.

But Woodward and Bernstein wrote that they knew of it before May 3, which means that someone in the know must have told them— most likely, Deep Throat. Those who had actually seen the Morton Halperin tap logs on which Ellsberg was overheard included Kissinger, Sullivan, and Haig, and it was possible that Nixon, Haldeman, Ehrlichman, Mitchell, and Mardian could have known about them, along with Bernard Wells, a supervisor for the FBI's domestic intelligence division, and those FBI agents who had actually monitored the taps. In other sections of their book, the reporters freely acknowledged their particular FBI sources, and that they do not attribute this information on the overhearing of Ellsberg to the FBI suggests that Wells and the field agents did not leak it. Actually, Sullivan, who had left the FBI, helped Ruckelshaus locate the logs. Sullivan would not have known intimately the "switchblade mentality" of the White House that Deep Throat described to Woodward. If Woodward and Bernstein are to be believed, Sullivan could not have been Deep Throat because he died in the 1970s, and the reporters say Deep Throat is still alive. Mardian, Mitchell, Nixon, Haldeman, and Ehrlichman would not have given the information to the reporters because it was damaging to them. But Kissinger or Haig could have volunteered it, especially packaged in a way so as to lead the reporters away from the NSC. However, Kissinger did not know Woodward, and it can safely be presumed that on May 2, 1973, two days after the firestorm in which Haldeman and Ehrlichman had just resigned and Dean and Kleindienst had been fired, Henry Kissinger would not take a call from a reporter he didn't know or trust to blithely confirm one of the darkest secrets of the Nixon years.

By a process of elimination, the most logical candidate to have delivered the knowledge of the Halperin-Ellsberg tap to Woodward at that moment in time was Alexander Haig.

On May 4, 1973, Haig settled into the job of White House chief of staff as if he were a commander taking charge of a besieged military outpost—he even continued to wear his general's uniform for a while. During that week, the wiretap scandal broke wide open. William Ruckelshaus spurred his men and they finally located the wiretap logs in the White House safe that had belonged to John Ehrlichman. The existence of those logs was conveyed to Judge Byrne, who used them as the basis for dismissing the case against Ellsberg and Russo, and on May 14, Ruckelshaus was able to tell the public that some seventeen persons in and out of the government had been wiretapped over a period of twenty-two months during 1969–1971. But Haig's role in the wiretapping remained hidden.

During that week, Haig flew to Florida to join Nixon and his friends Bebe Rebozo and Robert Abplanalp as well as the visiting John Connally. Nixon held in high regard the former Texas governor, who had recently switched his party affiliation from Democrat to Republican, and asked Connally to serve as a general adviser in the White House. Connally accepted, but didn't stay long.

In 1969, Haig had successfully pushed out all his rivals in the Kissinger NSC; in 1973, he used the same tactics—vanquishing and freezing out rivals, confiscating bureaucratic power—to stake out a position as the guardian to Nixon's door that made Haldeman's earlier lock-out techniques look tame by comparison. Ron Ziegler had told the press that in the future cabinet members would not have to go through Haig to see the president, as they had done when Haldeman was in charge; that sop to liberalization soon went by the boards.

On returning from Florida to Washington on May 8, Haig made a move that helped ensure his success as chief of staff: He asked Fred Buzhardt to come into the White House to assist Nixon's former law partner Leonard Garment in handling the president's defense.

Buzhardt and Haig had been associated for a quarter-century, and were bound together by shared secrets. Both knew of the buried Moorer-Radford reports and the two Admiral Welander confessions; the second one, elicited by Buzhardt, eliminated significant references to Haig from a confession by a major participant in the spying conducted by Yeoman Radford. Nixon knew that Haig and Buzhardt were old friends. He did not know about the second Welander confession, or that the two men had a real need to conceal the significant remarks about Haig in Welander's first confession.

After sacking Haldeman and Ehrlichman, Nixon biographer Roger Morris told us, the president was "so confused and generally at sea I think it [was] mentally and psychologically impossible for him to do what's necessary." Thus impaired, the president was putty in the hands of those he trusted and who he hoped would save him from the accusations of John Dean, which he expected would be lobbed at him shortly in front of Sam Ervin's Senate committee and a television audience of millions.

Haig and Buzhardt sat down with Nixon on May 9, and it was agreed that Buzhardt would maintain his current position as general counsel to the Department of Defense while he moonlighted at the White House, helping to direct the president's legal defense together with Len Garment.

As general counsel to the Defense Department, Buzhardt retained control of his confidential Pentagon files, which included both Welander confessions as well as various reports on the Moorer-Radford matter by Don Stewart, David Young, and by Buzhardt himself. Thus, in tying Buzhardt ever more closely to himself in the Nixon White House, Haig kept his old friend and those crucial files within his effective reach. The final person with knowledge dangerous to Haig was also brought under Haig's control in June, when former defense secretary Mel Laird was hired by the White House as a counselor. Laird had resigned at the close of Nixon's first term, and had never gotten along very well with the president, but Buzhardt and Haig wanted Laird around. Laird, too, knew of the two Welander interviews and of Haig's relationship with Robinson and Welander at the time their yeoman was spying for the military. By having him nearby, Haig neutralized Laird. White House logs show that after Laird's appointment he rarely met with Nixon, and when he did it was almost always in the presence of Haig.

The same thing happened with Garment. Buzhardt's arrival resulted in Garment's eclipse. Once Buzhardt arrived, Garment did not see Nixon for an entire month, and afterward only saw him about once a month, generally in concert with other lawyers. Garment recalls that he "wanted to go in" and see the president alone, but "the door was blocked. . . . Haig trusted Buzhardt and not me. . . . My access [to Nixon] was basically, I went in and talked to Haig. . . . There were times I just couldn't go in to see [Nixon]." Garment thinks that Nixon believed that Buzhardt was better equipped to defend him because Buzhardt "knew everybody in Congress," and also because Nixon felt "he was tougher than I was."

Under Haig, Larry Higby recalls, the day-to-day operation of the White House changed dramatically from what it had been under Higby's former boss, Haldeman. Higby told us that "The changes were fundamentally that Al controlled everything—everybody and everything." Whereas Haldeman had acted as a "general manager and coordinator as well as a personal adviser," Higby contends that Haldeman never blocked people from seeing the president, particularly Kissinger or Ehrlichman, and actually interceded to urge the president to see these men. "Bob [Haldeman] would often just glance at the stuff Henry was putting in or John was putting in or anybody else. Whereas Al tightly controlled each and every thing. I mean Al got much heavier involved in policy. . . . Al was trying to manage the whole thing personally."

Haig's heavy hand meshed with the increasingly difficult times to heighten Nixon's isolation. Often the president would sit alone in his office, with a fire roaring and the air-conditioner running, a yellow tablet and pencil in hand, unwilling to see anyone. Stephen B. Bull, who served as a scheduler and later as a special assistant to Nixon during his entire presidency and also after his resignation, says that "The irony of Richard Nixon is that he had little trust in a lot of people, and he put too much trust in too few people. . . . When the world started closing in . . . it was quite convenient for [Nixon] to deal with Haig on a lot of matters and a lot of areas in which Haig really wasn't qualified." Bull remains angry at Haig, not because they were rivals, but because he viewed Haig as looking out for himself over Nixon.

The second Woodward and Bernstein book, *The Final Days*, paints a picture of a Haig who did not want to be everything to the president, and did not want to get Nixon into trouble. Bull saw precisely the opposite behavior on Haig's part during Bull's tenure as the day-to-day administrator of the president's office from February 1973 through the August 1974 Nixon resignation. He watched with dismay as Haig "allowed the president to be isolated and indeed perhaps encouraged it." White House logs of the president's last fifteen months in office show Haig and Ziegler as the aides most often let into the inner sanctum with the president. To Bull, in those fifteen months, Haig seemed "duplicitous . . . motivated by self-aggrandizement, rather than ideology or principle."

When Haig learned at a staff meeting of a decision that had been made without consulting him, Bull recalls that Haig "began pounding the table with his fist . . . and said two or three times, 'I am the chief of staff. I make all the decisions in the White House.' We thought he was crazy." Such outbursts would characterize Haig's responses even to decisions made on nonpolicy matters such as the president's daily schedule. According to Bull, Haig at one point said, "If you think that this president can run the country without Al Haig . . . you are mistaken."

Haig's arrogance masked his insecurity. On one working trip to San Clemente, he complained to Bull about the quarters he had been given, and snapped that Haldeman would not have been so badly treated. Colonel Jack Brennan, another military aide to Nixon who had also been a colleague and a friend of Haig's at the NSC, said, "there wasn't really the respect for him" among the White House staffers that there had been for Haldeman. "Haig did not have the capability or the confidence to run the White House the way Haldeman did, yet he tried to," Brennan says.

Moreover, Haig kept deprecating Nixon to the staff. Brennan recalls that Haig would say to the staff, " 'We're in trouble, we're really in trouble,' and would cast some disparaging remarks about the president. It was like he was saying, 'I'm the hero around here. And this guy [Nixon] doesn't know what he's doing.' It was that kind of attitude." It was not a new attitude, either, for Haig had evidenced it while working as Kissinger's deputy—he would deprecate Nixon to Kissinger, and Kissinger to Nixon. According to Woodward and Bernstein in *The Final Days*, published long after Nixon's resignation, "Haig sometimes referred to the President as an inherently weak man who lacked guts. He joked that Nixon and Bebe Rebozo had a homosexual relationship, imitating what he called the President's limp-wrist manner."

Among those who worked with Haig under Nixon, some remain Haig's admirers. Press Secretary Ron Ziegler is one. "There was nothing in my frequent dealings with Al that would have ever led me to feel that he was anything but dealing with President Nixon in an honorable fashion." Ziegler's comment deserves considerable weight because he knew that shortly after Haig's arrival, Haig had tried to dump him as press secretary in order to restore the credibility of the press office that had been damaged by being forced many times that spring to retract earlier statements about Watergate as "inoperative." Few volunteers could be found; staying on after surviving the intended purge, Ziegler nonetheless felt "comfortable" in the belief that Haig was "leveling with me and with the president." He reminds us that those were difficult times in which "you're not thinking about distrusting someone even though you are surrounded by distrust."

Nixon clearly trusted Haig and became dependent on him. But Haig did not trust Nixon, certainly not enough to tell him of the relationship Haig still enjoyed with the principal Watergate reporter, Bob Woodward, and not enough to even apprise the president that he had known Woodward since the young lieutenant had come over from Admiral Moorer's office to brief Haig in the White House basement in 1969–70.

To have given Nixon knowledge of even the smallest part of that particular Haig connection to the press would have meant curtains for Haig as Nixon's chief of staff—for precisely the reasons Ziegler cites, the need to be able to trust your close companions in time of battle.

According to such men as Haldeman, Ehrlichman, Ziegler, and Mitchell, there is no question that Nixon was deeply bothered by Woodward's and Bernstein's reporting. Through Ron Ziegler and through another press aide, David Gergen (a former Yale classmate of Woodward's), Nixon had sent warnings to Woodward and Bernstein as recently as April 27, 1973, that—as the White House tape of the Nixon-Ziegler conversation put it—"they better watch their damned cotton-picking faces" about what they said regarding the current state of mind at the White House. And there is no question, either, that Nixon was not aware of Woodward's background. Before John Mitchell's death, when we informed him of Woodward's Navy career and that he had been a briefer to Haig in 1969–1970, Mitchell took that information to Nixon, and reported back to us that "Nixon had no idea" of this and was "quite surprised" to hear it.

Through the former attorney general, we requested interviews with Nixon repeatedly over a three-year period and were refused, on the basis that Nixon did not want to discuss anything having to do with Alexander Haig. That refusal strained Nixon's relationship with Mitchell, and strengthened Mitchell's belief that Nixon was refusing to face what had actually happened during the Watergate crisis.

A second Haig alliance also was unknown to the president: Haig's ties to Joe Califano, who had been Haig's patron ten years earlier in the civilian hierarchy of the Pentagon. Califano was now a power in Democratic circles because of his status as a senior official in the Kennedy and Johnson administrations, his current employment as counsel to both the DNC and the *Washington Post*, and his partnership in the Washington law firm headed by Edward Bennett Williams. Williams had personal friendships with *Post* Executive Editor Ben Bradlee and owner Katharine Graham, and was one of the "enemies" specifically named in several of the White House tapes whom Nixon planned to "fix" after he had been reelected. Haig stayed in touch with Califano during the tense months at the close of the Nixon presidency, according to Woodward and Bernstein in *The Final Days*, for instance, having dinner with Califano for advice about Haig's prospective testimony before the Senate Watergate committee. Equally important, Califano helped to recommend Leon Jaworski to Haig as Special Prosecutor, and sometimes acted as an intermediary between them. We will provide an additional perspective on the Haig-Jaworski relationship in a later chapter.

When Haig and Buzhardt took command of Nixon's defense in early May 1973, the president had one Watergate preoccupation: John Dean, who the president knew was about to become his principal accuser. On May 4, in a highly publicized action, Dean's attorney Charles Schaffer handed to Judge John Sirica the keys to a safe-deposit box in which Dean claimed to have placed classified documents that he had spirited out of the White House before his forced resignation of April 30. Press speculation was that the documents implicated the president and his top aides in criminal activities. Nixon's anxiety increased as he wondered what Dean might have in that safe-deposit box.

One of the documents in the box was described to be forty-three pages long, and this enabled Buzhardt, with his extensive contacts in the departments of Defense and Justice, to quickly figure out that Dean had taken the 1970 Huston Plan. Nixon later wrote that though this document would undoubtedly prove sensational and politically damaging, he was "almost relieved that this was Dean's bombshell document," because although he had initially approved it, that approval had been rescinded five days later (at the urging of John Mitchell), and so "I was certain that we could completely defend and explain it in a way that people would understand." The most important thing in Nixon's mind was that this document had nothing to do with his series of private discussions with Dean about Watergate.

While this tempest in a teapot was alternately heating up and cooling, the search for the 1969–1971 wiretap logs was continuing, a hunt that was coming toward the White House and Ehrlichman's safe, in which the documents resided. As we have shown earlier, those documents were very bad news for Al Haig, and he must have been concerned as the search for them drew ever closer.

It was in this atmosphere that Haig's old friend Lieutenant General Vernon Walters, deputy director of the CIA, arrived at the White House on May 12, 1973, with one more document that could prove dangerous to the White House, this one drawn from the CIA's files.

May 10, 1973, had been a tumultuous day at CIA headquarters at Langley, Virginia. Dr. James R. Schlesinger, director of the Agency for only four months, who had replaced Richard Helms in January, was about to leave his post. As part of an overall shake-up of the administration announced by the White House, Schlesinger had been nominated as the new secretary of defense. The previous day Schlesinger had cabled his deputy, Walters, to fly home immediately from Taiwan, and on May 10 Walters walked into the office. Even though the Watergate committee hearings had not yet begun, two other senatorial inquiries that touched upon the CIA's possible involvement in Watergate were in full swing. The CIA was concerned about questions being asked by the Senate Armed Services Committee and a Senate appropriations subcommittee. Walters and Helms were going to be called to testify to at least one of these forums.

According to Walters' memoir, on his return Schlesinger asked him to prepare an affidavit about Watergate—and Walters knew he had just the materials at hand, his four "memcons" written the previous June after his discussions with John Dean, the first of which included notes of the four-way meeting on June 23, 1972, among himself, Helms, Ehrlichman, and Haldeman. That was when the Bay of Pigs flag was waved by the White House men in Helms's face in order to induce him to have Walters instruct Pat Gray of the FBI to go no further into certain Mexican monies, lest the FBI compromise CIA operations.

As we have suggested earlier in the book, Walters' first memcon, written five days after the June 23 meeting, seems to have been part of a deliberate attempt by the CIA to identify the Nixon-requested blocking action as politically motivated. Whereas Haldeman recalled that they had transmitted Nixon's instructions precisely, and had not mentioned a political basis for the blocking action (a position that the June 23 tape supports), the Walters memcon composed on June 28 strongly construed the White House instruction of June 23 as political, and omitted any mention of the touchy Bay of Pigs project.

On the basis of the four memcons, Walters prepared a six-page affidavit, "recounting my whole connection" with Watergate. The next day, he received a call summoning him to the White House on the following day, May 12. Walters, Haig, and Buzhardt had known one another for years. Haig and Walters were both Army generals. Haig had been instrumental, Roger Morris reports, in obtaining for Walters the job of translator for the secret Paris talks between Kissinger and the North Vietnamese—Walters included French among the seven languages he spoke, and that was the language used with Le Duc Tho. Evidently in preparation for his White House meeting, Walters took his affidavit to a suburban Virginia notary and had it notarized, and then went to see his old friends. He left them a copy of the affidavit, and asked them to call him if the White House felt that anything in it was covered by executive privilege or other restrictions, so that he could say so and withhold those parts when called to testify.

About what happened next, there are three versions—Walters' own, given in his memoir, *Silent Missions*; Nixon's, in *RN*; and that reported by Woodward and Bernstein in *The Final Days*.

According to Walters, he heard nothing from the White House about the affidavit, so when he first testified on the Hill on May 14, in a closed-door session of the Armed Services Committee, he held little back. He evidently used the affidavit as the basis for what he said, because Acting Chairman Stuart Symington, Democrat of Missouri, afterward asked Walters to provide the memcons themselves. Walters remembered that the attitude of the committee had been "curious and interested, but not hostile." For his part, Symington had obviously heard some echo of the CIA's memos of the June 23 meeting behind those closed doors, for when he emerged he told newsmen "it was very clear . . . that there was an attempt [on the part of the White House] to unload major responsibility for the Watergate bugging and coverup on the CIA." That was why Symington wanted the actual memcons—to check the original documents rather than one man's recollections.

After his testimony on May 14, Walters wrote, Haig and Buzhardt still showed no concern, and when he went to see them, "they said that there were no parts of my affidavit on which they wished to claim privilege." Walters was quite adamant in his memoir that in this second meeting, as well as in the first one he had had at the White House, he had showed Haig and Buzhardt only the affidavit, not the memcons themselves.

Nixon remembered the affair differently. He writes that Walters definitely did bring the memcons to the White House, and "the minute we saw them we knew we had a problem." It was the first Walters memcon (about June 23) that contained most of the problems. Nixon had been clear to Haldeman that Richard Helms, whom Nixon disliked and distrusted, should not be allowed to think that the instruction to impede the FBI was political—and here was a memcon that strongly implied that the CIA had involved itself in a crime (obstruction of justice) precisely in order to protect the president from political damage. And it was coming from a man whom Nixon considered "one of my old friends," Vernon Walters.

Nixon wrote that he and Buzhardt tried to puzzle out what had happened. According to this version, Haig was not involved in that discussion, and a lateral glance at the headlines of May 14 suggests why: That morning, Acting FBI Director Ruckelshaus announced the discovery of the 1969–1971 wiretap records in Ehrlichman's safe, records that implicated Haig in the electronic eavesdropping of his former colleagues. Haig was not named in Ruckelshaus' announcement, but Haig must have been concerned by the discovery of the records and perhaps his attention was diverted from the Walters matter. Moreover, Buzhardt was a lawyer, and Haig was not, so it was logical for Nixon to consult Buzhardt on this matter.

The only explanation Buzhardt could offer to Nixon was that when Walters wrote of the June 23 conversation on June 28 his memory had been colored by three days of butting heads with John Dean, who had tried three mornings in a row to convince Walters that the CIA should pay bail for the burglars. "Buzhardt postulated," Nixon wrote, that Walters "had unconsciously reconstructed the conversation from the perspective of what he felt Dean was trying to do, rather than from what Haldeman and Ehrlichman had actually said." A few days later, Haldeman came to visit Nixon, and the president took up the matter with him; Haldeman was quite certain that he hadn't given the CIA any grounds for thinking that the request had been political, and Nixon was "relieved by Haldeman's certainty." So Nixon decided that Walters had merely been confused, stopped worrying about that incoming missile, and turned his attention to others. Buzhardt made no further attempt to get in touch with Walters, to straighten out Nixon's old friend on the misconstrued June 23 meeting or to prevent the memcons themselves from surfacing.

That was Nixon's version of events.

Woodward and Bernstein, apparently reflecting interviews with Buzhardt, wrote that Buzhardt did indeed see the memcon of the June 23 four-way meeting, and was "worried" because it "tied the President to an order that seemed intended to throw the FBI off the track." In Buzhardt's view, Walters was an unfortunate person to impugn the president, because he was not John Dean and "had neither an ax to grind nor an ass to save." Troubled, Buzhardt then went to see the president, expecting that Nixon would tell him either "that Walters was mistaken, or that Haldeman was so accustomed to doing things in the President's name that he had acted on his own authority." But—in this version—Buzhardt found Nixon unconcerned, defiant, and adamant that there had been nothing political behind the four-way June 23 meeting. When Buzhardt inquired if Walters should be allowed to turn the papers over to the Senate, Nixon was indifferent, and said, "Take them up and give them to the committee."

The only version that exonerates Buzhardt (and Haig) from failing to warn Nixon that the Walters memcons could seriously undermine Nixon's position of having acted within the law is that of Woodward and Bernstein, which reconstructed Buzhardt's private talk with Nixon and thus reflected interviews with Buzhardt, and, possibly, Haig.

Equally important is what happened as a result of the president not being moved to try and stop Walters from turning over the damaging documents. First, the memcons did go to various Senate committees, and were quickly released by them to the newspapers, who had a field day. Headlines charged that the president's men had used the CIA to block the FBI's investigation of Watergate for reasons that were overtly political.

The second consequence was the generating by the Haig-Buzhardt team of a crucial public statement by Nixon. Taken together with other matters then in the news—John Dean's safe-deposit box copy of the Huston Plan, the revelation of the Dr. Fielding break-in and the Plumbers' activities, as well as the locating of the logs of the 1969–1971 wiretaps—the release of the Walters memcons made five incoming missiles aimed at the White House, all of which had to do with "national security" matters. With these matters in the air, and the Watergate committee about to start public sessions within a few days, Buzhardt and Haig pressed Nixon to draft a blanket denial, one *The Final Days* suggested would have to be "a final definitive statement that dealt with the major allegations, both direct and implied." It was going to be a statement that would have to "stand for all time" and be "consistent with *anything* that might surface." (Emphasis in original.) According to the book, Nixon agreed to let Haig and Buzhardt "give it a try," and they recruited as cowriters Garment and the president's two chief speechwriters, Raymond K. Price, Jr., and Patrick J. Buchanan.

The statement would attempt to deal with all the incoming missiles, and with one that had not yet made its appearance on Nixon's radar screen but was already fully known to Haig and Buzhardt: the Moorer-Radford affair. That may have been the crucial reason for a statement that could be a shield against "*anything* that might surface."

Haig and Buzhardt began a series of private strategy sessions with the president late in the afternoon of May 15 that lasted through that day and the next, well into the evening. The statement would be revelatory because it would admit responsibility for many of the matters then in the news, such as the Dr. Fielding break-in and the Plumbers' other activities, the Huston Plan, even the domestic wiretapping. Nixon would meet these missiles head on, and so defuse them.

The statement would also make headlines because in it the president was going to reduce drastically his reliance on claims of executive privilege. It would say that executive privilege could not be claimed by any of the president's former aides in talking about matters directly connected with possible criminal conduct in the matters then under investigation, including Watergate, though the claim could still be legitimately raised in regard to matters of national security. That, of course, would protect several other matters as well as Moorer-Radford, but since the president was going out of his way to leave unprotected such things as the Plumbers' activities and the Dr. Fielding break-in, which he had theretofore refused to discuss under a claim of national security, the new, reduced-size claim of executive privilege would have the effect of protecting only Moorer-Radford. We will see how precise the protection actually became in the next few chapters.

The section of the statement on which Nixon fixated most intensely dealt with the June 23, 1972, meeting and the instruction to the CIA to block the FBI. Early drafts of this section followed the Walters memcon line that politics was involved. Nixon adamantly insisted that the reason had been national security, and the statement eventually reflected that view—but in a way that intermingled his stopping of the FBI operations with a defense of the Plumbers: "I wanted justice done with regard to Watergate, but in the scale of national priorities with which I had to deal—and not at the time having any idea of the extent of political abuse which Watergate reflected—I also had to be deeply concerned with ensuring that neither the covert operations of the CIA nor the operations of the Special Investigations Unit [the Plumbers] should be compromised. It was certainly not my intent, nor my wish, that the investigation of Watergate be impeded in any way."

That wasn't what Nixon had told Haldeman on June 23, nor what Haldeman and Ehrlichman had told Walters and Helms. It was a statement that tried to put the one remaining undisclosed Plumber activity—Moorer-Radford—under the national security shield.

Around 11:00 P.M. on May 16, according to *All the President's Men*, Woodward had another meeting with Deep Throat, an ultradramatic one in the underground garage. When Woodward arrived, his source "was pacing around nervously. His lower jaw seemed to quiver. Deep Throat began talking, almost in a monologue. He had only a few minutes, he raced through a series of statements. Woodward listened obediently. It was clear a transformation had come over his friend." Deep Throat would answer no questions about his statements or anything else, but did add that Woodward should "be cautious."

In this rendering, Woodward called Bernstein, who arrived at Woodward's apartment to find his reportorial twin refusing to talk and masking the silence with classical music while he tapped out on his typewriter a warning that electronic surveillance was going on and that they had "better watch it." Who was doing the monitoring? "Woodward mouthed C-I-A." Both men then feared for their lives, and went around for some days looking for spooks behind every tree.

Later in the book, Woodward and Bernstein describe the doings of that night as "rather foolish and melodramatic." Actually, the dramatic elements of the scene draw the reader away from the material that Deep Throat presented to Woodward that night, which concerned the precise matters that Nixon had been discussing with Haig and Buzhardt—those incoming missiles, and Dean's allegations of a cover-up. Some of the leads that Deep Throat gave to Woodward that night were outlandishly wrong, such as the claim that some of the people involved in Watergate had been in it to make money, that Dean had regular talks with Senator Baker, and that the covert national and international schemes had been supervised by Mitchell. The matters about which Deep Throat spoke that were later proved correct—discussions of executive clemency, Hunt's demands for money, Dean's activities with both the White House and the CRP officials, Dean's talk with Liddy— were the ones Nixon had earlier that evening discussed with Buzhardt and Haig.

* * *

On May 22, 1973, President Nixon issued a major statement of four thousand words in which he released information about the 1969–1971 wiretaps, the activities of the Plumbers, and the Huston Plan, and justified them all as necessary reactions to the rampant leaks, campus unrest, antiwar violence, and other threats to the nation's security. In the major passage quoted above, he also assured the nation that he had not tried to impede the FBI or to obstruct justice when he had directed Haldeman and Ehrlichman to sit down with Helms and Walters on June 23, 1972.

This statement provided a very public, seemingly very definitive explanation of events, and was meant to establish a benchmark against which all future allegations, documents, and as-yet-hidden evidence could be measured. Pressed on the president by Haig and Buzhardt as their first real action in "protecting" the president, it had precisely the opposite effect. It put the president very far out on a limb, and challenged the world to try and saw off that limb.

19

STEWART SHAKES UP THE WHITE HOUSE

ON May 14, 1973, the Pentagon's top civilian investigator, Don Stewart, reached out for help in finding a new assignment in the government. Six months earlier Stewart had been elevated to the post of inspector general of the Defense Investigative Service, but now he wanted to get out of the Department of Defense.

Recent events had disturbed Stewart, the man who, while investigating the military spying at the White House, had pulled the initial confession from Chuck Radford and had stayed on top of that case as best he could. In his career as an investigator in the Pentagon, he had frequently been at odds with Defense Department general counsel Fred Buzhardt, for example over such cases as the leak of the Pentagon Papers and the flap over Jack Anderson's columns. Buzhardt, a former military officer turned lawyer, viewed each investigation as a political problem to be managed; Stewart, a former FBI agent, approached each one as a case to be solved, with wrongdoers to be punished and national security secrets protected at all costs. "When I was in the Pentagon," Stewart told us, Buzhardt "was the only guy who actually tried to thwart me from doing my job. He was the one who tried to obstruct my investigations." On one report prepared about leaks of classified information to Congress, Stewart said that Buzhardt had told him to alter the findings so as to remove the most politically sensitive items; Stewart did so on all copies of the report except the one sent to the Defense Intelligence Agency. In other cases that Stewart had investigated, government officials who had leaked classified materials to the press had not been punished, and neither were the reporters, who, Stewart argued, should have been prosecuted for printing what they knew to be classified information.

Most important, Stewart and Buzhardt had clashed over Moorer-Radford. Buzhardt had ordered Stewart to turn over to him all the files and reports on the case, ostensibly so Buzhardt could prepare his report for Laird, and it was Buzhardt who had summoned Stewart back from vacation in Florida in January 1972 to sit in on the Welander reinterview.

Seeking a route out of Defense and into a new assignment, Stewart called the White House and asked for David Young. Young was gone, he was told, and his call was shunted to an aide to Len Garment named Richard Tufaro, whom Stewart had never met. In his conversation with Tufaro, Stewart was bitter about several matters. He expressed anger at the way the Pentagon handled national security investigations involving DoD personnel, but he was also annoyed about the overtly political handling that the White House was giving his old agency, the FBI. Former police chief of Kansas City Clarence Kelley had recently been named acting director of the FBI, and Stewart thought that was wrong and that the bureau needed a seasoned investigator as its chief. Stewart told Tufaro that several congressional committees had approached him about work, but because of his contempt for the way Congress leaked he didn't want to go to Capitol Hill. However, he said, he might have to go to the Hill if he couldn't find another job in the executive branch. He was forty-eight, and two more years of government service would allow him to retire at age fifty with a good pension.

In the remainder of the conversation, Stewart told Tufaro some details about several investigations he'd conducted that hadn't resulted in punishment for leakers. In 1970, then-Undersecretary of State Elliot L. Richardson had authorized access for Daniel Ellsberg, then a Rand employee, to classified records about an opponent of the South Vietnamese government, information that Ellsberg had leaked to the press. In the past few weeks, Richardson had become the new attorney general, the charges against Ellsberg had been dismissed, and one of the chief leak-recipients in the press, William Beecher of *The New York Times*, had been selected as assistant secretary of defense for public affairs. Beyond that, Buzhardt's elevation to the White House as a special counsel really burned Stewart, because on the Ellsberg investigation Buzhardt had been entirely uncooperative in supporting the FBI and the Justice Department's case; in fact, Stewart claimed, he had had to go around Buzhardt in order to get information on the case to Justice.

Stewart was truly irked that none of the people involved in the Moorer-Radford affair had been punished. Moorer had been reappointed for a second term as chairman of the Joint Chiefs, Welander and Robinson had been awarded new commands, and even Chuck Radford was still at work for the Navy.

Stewart made insistent requests. Tufaro heard threats. He hung up on Stewart and immediately started to sound the alarm in the White House. He got out a memo to Len Garment, who had replaced John Dean as counsel to the president. "Stewart clearly is in a position to damage the Administration because of his direct involvement in White House investigations of national security leaks," Tufaro said in his May 14 memo. Tufaro did not understand all of what Stewart had said to him, especially about the Yeoman Radford matter—Tufaro had not known of it, and Stewart's references had been veiled—but Tufaro used the reference as a buttressing for his own concern in relation to the recent elevation of Buzhardt. In closing his memo to Garment, Tufaro wrote that Stewart's "appearance [on the scene] does underline my warning to Doug Parker [another White House aide] on Friday about the risk of putting Buzhardt in such a sensitive position."

The first indication Stewart got about what the White House's response would be was the seizure of all his files. "Buzhardt . . . came over and ordered them seized," Stewart told us, "and they almost flipped out when they discovered the top-secret stuff I had." Then, Stewart reports, his secretary was approached and asked to keep tabs on him and report his movements. She declined to cooperate. After these forays, Stewart found that he had very little work to do.

In June 1973, not long after these events, Admiral Robert Welander received a phone call from his former subordinate Bob Woodward. Welander had recently returned to the Pentagon after a year at sea, following the discovery of Chuck Radford's activities and the closing of the military liaison office. Woodward wanted to see him immediately, and he agreed.

"We met at a Marriott hotel in Virginia, across the river from D.C.," Welander remembers. "Woodward started right out by saying that the Radford story was 'bubbling around,' and that it was going to break sooner or later." Woodward clearly knew about the story. Welander says, "He just kept pressing me for information on what I knew, but I told him I wouldn't give him anything," and the meeting ended on an inconclusive note. Welander then returned to the Pentagon and informed both Chairman Moorer and Admiral Zumwalt of his meeting with Woodward.

According to *All the President's Men*, Woodward had had a meeting in a garage on May 16 with Deep Throat, two days after Stewart's call to Tufaro. And, as we know, immediately after Haig and Buzhardt took up positions at the White House, they were clearly concerned about the possible revival of Moorer-Radford. Was Woodward sent to see Welander? Was he trying to dig up information on Moorer-Radford, or was he really seeking to confirm that information on it would not be revealed by Welander, not even to a reporter who had once been his subordinate? Such an assurance would have eased Haig's mind. After this meeting, Woodward did not write anything about Moorer-Radford for many months, and evidently made no other attempts to pursue the story.

Stewart continued to wait for a call from Tufaro, and in late June, when he'd gotten no word back, wrote to another White House aide, W. J. "Bill" Baroody, with whom he shared a mutual friend. In his letter, Stewart sought "guidance and assistance" on how to get out of the Defense Department; he stressed that he needed only two more years of employment toward a good retirement, and said that he might have to take one of the Capitol Hill positions. If he did so, he told Baroody, it was certainly possible that details of some of his investigations might come out during the job interviews, and he wanted to assure Baroody that he would not disclose details of any case that had a national security interest. However, Stewart wrote, he had no such compunction about the cases involving Daniel Ellsberg or Jack Anderson because "I don't feel Fred's [Buzhardt's] interest in the Ellsberg or Anderson case was for security interest but rather totally for political considerations. . . . I knew professionally he [Buzhardt] was running the [Ellsberg] case for politics and not security." He also added that the "Anderson case," by which he meant the investigation of Radford, "speaks for itself. All the culprits are still on board. . . . As you can see, the foregoing is enough to upset an honest investigator and I just want to get the hell out of DoD."

Stewart softened his stance somewhat by pointing out he had become a target. "You may or may not realize that I was put here to be buried which is quite humiliating and to add insult to injury I'm sure

Fred had the files that were in my custody seized about a month ago. How stupid. There wasn't anything in those files I needed."

In his letter to Baroody, Stewart again cited Clarence Kelley's appointment as FBI director. The phone call to Tufaro had merely made reference to Kelley, for Stewart had learned that his own name had been on a list for consideration as director of the FBI. He had not (as Haig and Buzhardt would later charge) demanded the directorship—Stewart knew enough about Washington politics not to do that. His aims were a rung lower. His first choice, Stewart wrote Baroody, was to be appointed as Clarence Kelley's deputy, but if he got no help from the White House, he would go for employment to Republican senators Barry Goldwater and Hugh Scott, or, as a last resort, to Democratic conservative Senator Henry Jackson. Stewart feared that the Democrats would try to "enlist me for political reasons and damn it, that's what I don't want and is why the hell I want to get out of DOD—for politics." Stewart ended his letter to Baroody by reemphasizing the role he had played in forcing Radford to confess to spying for the military.

Buzhardt and Garment believed Stewart's letter to be an attempt at blackmail. They decided to go after Stewart directly. According to Garment, he was influenced by Chief of Staff Haig's desire to keep Moorer-Radford under wraps. On June 28, 1973, Buzhardt phoned Attorney General Elliot Richardson—who himself had a reason for keeping Stewart under wraps—about prosecuting Stewart. Next day, Garment sent Richardson an EYES ONLY letter, together with the Tufaro memo and Stewart's letter to Baroody; Garment wrote that "Stewart is using the threat of disclosure . . . in an effort to induce a high-level appointment for himself." Garment's letter concluded by urging Richardson to investigate the matter and determine if Stewart should be prosecuted for criminal conduct.

Years later, when interviewed by us, Garment remained clearly uncomfortable discussing the Stewart matter. He refused to review the documents in the case, including his own EYES ONLY letter to Richardson, but did take full responsibility for sending it. In our first interview, he insisted, "I took his [Stewart's] letter as a threat," and that neither Buzhardt nor Haig had anything to do with the suggestion that Stewart be prosecuted. "Nobody said any such thing to me," he asserted in our interview, and added, "Boy Scout's honor!" In a second interview, two years later, he admitted the probable involvement of Haig and Buzhardt, recalling that Buzhardt might well have said to him words to the effect that "This guy [Stewart] is a troublemaker and we should do something." In the next sentence of the interview,

Garment got to the heart of the matter: "Fred believed that it would be calamitous for the country to have this [Moorer-Radford] come out. Haig also felt this way . . . [and] I accepted that the disclosure of Moorer-Radford would be hurtful." The fear, Garment reported, was that Congress might use the information in a vendetta against the JCS that would result in undue interference in military affairs that were better left to the president and his advisers.

At the time, Garment's memo regarding Stewart was routed by Richardson down to Henry Petersen, head of the criminal division, who took a close look at it. Petersen wrote back to the attorney general on July 10 and stated in unequivocal terms, "We do not believe that the materials furnished you by Mr. Garment warrant a criminal investigation of Stewart," and added that it "is not at all clear" that Stewart had made a "threat" to disclose classified information. Neither the federal espionage statutes dealing with disclosure of classified material nor any other federal criminal law statutes applied to the particulars furnished by Garment, Petersen explained; in other words, there was no case to be made against Stewart.

Richardson all but rejected the Petersen memo, and on the day he received it scribbled a note to an aide asking whether Stewart could possibly be charged with extortion or blackmail. Richardson's note ended up with a midlevel official in Petersen's criminal division, Carl W. Belcher, chief of the general crimes section.

Stewart had heard nothing from Baroody, and didn't know that this process was going on at Justice. But he still wanted another job, and wrote another letter to senior Defense Department aide Martin Hoffman, on July 16. In this one, he held nothing back in his condemnation of how Moorer-Radford had been buried. After telling Hoffman of his desire to find a job outside Defense, Stewart wrote of his role in breaking the case of "a rear admiral and a Navy enlisted man engaged in a plot of spying on the President of the U.S. with the purpose of furnishing the results to Adm. Moorer." The whole matter, he wrote, had been hushed up "to spare OSD [Office of the Secretary of Defense], the military and the President political embarrassment." Stewart said that the story could not remain a secret forever and recommended that Secretary of Defense Schlesinger obtain a briefing "before he finds himself in an embarrassing position."

Back at Justice, Belcher's first move was to have Justice's own files checked, and he learned that Richardson had indeed been a party to the 1970 Ellsberg leak in the ways in which Stewart had outlined. He then passed this information and all the materials to his own deputy, Alfred L. Hantman, and had him look into the entire matter. On

August 2, Hantman wrote back to Belcher that the effort to go after Stewart was "foolishness," that the Tufaro-Stewart session had been "low-key," and that Tufaro had gone overboard in placing a "sinister cast" on Stewart's request. What Stewart had written to Baroody, Hantman said, was nothing more than a request for assistance to an old soldier from the ranks, and its nature was underscored by Stewart's telling Baroody that he didn't want to go to work for Senator Jackson because he feared political exploitation. "It certainly strains credulity," Hantman wrote, "to believe that if a former FBI agent, such as Stewart, intended to 'commit or attempt an act of extortion,' he would reduce such intention to physical proof in the form of a writing. . . . My own view is that the present Administration may be buying more trouble than the matter is worth if they seriously desire some concocted theory of prosecution be developed on these facts." If the government tried to prosecute any government employee who asked a friend for help in getting a job because he does not like "what is going on," Hantman added, the result would be chaos; "to merely articulate such a proposition is to realize its foolishness." This remarkably forthright and insightful analysis of the situation was sent upstairs by Belcher to Petersen, who sent it on to Richardson, writing him that no federal charges likely could be pressed, and suggesting that the Stewart matter be referred to the Department of Defense for possible administrative action.

Richardson now certainly had enough ammunition to say no to pressure from the White House—but he didn't do so. He gave the matter to his personal special assistant, John T. Smith. On September 6, 1973, in an EYES ONLY memo, Smith apologized for a delay on the matter, writing that it had gotten "lost in the shuffle, which is probably where it belongs." Smith echoed Petersen and Hantman in suggesting that criminal prosecution was unwarranted and would engender precisely what everyone hoped to avoid, by making the matter public.

With this, and only after several attempts to pursue prosecution of Stewart, did the effort to go after Stewart come to an end.

In the meantime, Haig was trying to recruit Solicitor General Robert H. Bork for the job of counsel to Richard Nixon on Watergate matters. Bork had joined the Justice Department only weeks earlier, after years of private practice. Bork later told us that Haig made an emotional appeal to Bork's patriotism in asking him to handle the president's defense, which was in disarray.

"Haig was pointing out that all kinds of crazy things were going on and he wanted to get things back under control. . . . He was just lamenting what was happening at the White House," Bork told us.

Haig mentioned specifically three tough issues. The first was Watergate, the second was that Vice President Spiro Agnew was "in trouble," and the third issue had to do with what Haig referred to, Bork says, as the "military penetration" of the White House—in other words, the Moorer-Radford affair.

Bork, of course, had no idea what Haig was talking about on the third issue, although Haig portrayed it to him as a horrible episode. "He just seemed shocked by it and said, 'My God, this happened!' He was deploring it," recalls Bork.

Apparently Haig had calculated that if Bork did come to the White House, he would eventually trip over Moorer-Radford, and Haig wanted to launch a preemptive strike that would position him as being outraged over the military penetration. But Bork declined to come to the White House, and stayed on at Justice.

Despite the attempts at pursuing Stewart and misleading Bork, Moorer-Radford wouldn't stay buried.

Jack Anderson got back into the act in a big way, through an article in *Parade* magazine of July 22, 1973, entitled "My Journal on Watergate." The article was published when the nation's attention was firmly fixed on the televised Senate hearings about Watergate, with their revelations about a White House taping system, the "White House horrors," the Plumbers, and everything else. In the article, Anderson boasted that the Nixon administration had for years been trying to discover his sources, but couldn't do so, and that arms of the government had flailed out in all directions when he broke news stories the administration hadn't liked. For instance, he wrote that "Inside the Pentagon, suspected sources were grilled behind the forbidding doors of Room 3E993." His piece on the tilt to Pakistan, Anderson noted, had been investigated by the notorious White House Plumbers, who "concluded mistakenly that the source was located on Henry Kissinger's staff. Innocent staffers were yanked from behind their desks and dragged to polygraph machines, although it was the White House, not my sources, doing the lying about Pakistan. Eventually, an entire section of Kissinger's staff was scattered around the world, and Admiral Robert Welander who headed it was exiled to the Atlantic fleet."

If Anderson had wanted to start a fire, he could not have chosen better fuel than to mention such particulars as the room in which Radford had been interrogated by Stewart, and the name of Welander.

First to pick up the burning kindling was Donald G. Sanders, deputy minority counsel of the Senate Watergate committee. Sanders and Don Stewart had worked together in the FBI, and stayed in touch afterward, so Sanders recognized the room mentioned by Anderson as the one in which Stewart conducted investigations. Sanders conveyed this knowledge to two other men on the minority staff, Howard Liebengood and Fred Thompson, both of whom reported to Senator Howard Baker, vice chairman of the panel. On July 24, Sanders called the Pentagon, and within hours, Stewart showed up to talk to Sanders and Liebengood. He was very much inclined to do so because Anderson's article had angered him, too: Here was the leak recipient, flaunting his triumph in the face of the authorities.

Stewart readily told them that the India-Pakistan leak was much bigger than what Anderson had described, and said it involved an episode whose implications were grave. He outlined to them the dimensions of Moorer-Radford. (Again, we must emphasize that Stewart knew nothing about the Ehrlichman-Young-Welander interview, and had participated only in the Buzhardt-Welander reinterview, during which the significant references to Al Haig were omitted.)

Sanders and Liebengood immediately wrote a memo on the interview for Thompson, who showed it to Baker. Upon being apprised of the military espionage, Howard Baker sensed that it could be an important piece of the Watergate puzzle. The whole affair bothered Baker. He was somewhat aware that the White House regarded him as being in their pocket, and as the ranking Republican on the Democratic-controlled committee he did feel a deep responsibility to the Republican president—but he was saddened by the revelations of White House wrongdoing and could not understand them. John Ehrlichman was one of the next scheduled witnesses, and the vice chairman of the Senate committee determined to put some questions about Moorer-Radford to Ehrlichman when he testified under oath.

John Ehrlichman arrived for his inquisition on July 26 accompanied by lawyer John Wilson, who was also currently representing Bob Haldeman before the committee.

Baker had in front of him the August 11, 1971, memo to Ehrlichman from Bud Krogh and David Young that outlined the pending Ellsberg–Pentagon Papers probe and suggested, among other things, an operation to obtain Ellsberg's medical facts. Why, Baker wanted to know, was one and only one paragraph deleted from his copy of the memo? He asked Ehrlichman, "Does it have to do with the national security matters that the President refers to repeatedly in his statement of May 22 as being interwoven?" Ehrlichman agreed that it did, and that it was "one of the items exempted from the executive privilege exceptions, so to speak," and that he would "probably be violating two or three statutes if I disclosed [it] at this point."

A bit later Ehrlichman allowed that if it came out in public, "that would be interesting and titillating and whatnot, but it would cause more mischief than the good [that] would be produced from the disclosure."

Baker believed he knew full well what Ehrlichman was referring to, because two days earlier Don Stewart had briefed his staff about Moorer-Radford. In fact, as someone who has read the unexpurgated original told us, that fifth paragraph related to a report from British intelligence service MI-5 that a copy of the Pentagon Papers had found its way to the USSR.

Baker proceeded carefully. What had the president meant, Baker asked Ehrlichman, when he told the nation on May 22, 1973, that the Plumbers had been involved in "important national security operations which themselves had no connection to Watergate?" Ehrlichman could see that he was entering dangerous territory, but he made a veiled reference to Moorer-Radford, allowing that in the Nixon statement the president had been referring less to the Pentagon Papers and Ellsberg than to "other problems" handled by the Special Investigations Unit.

"What?" Baker asked, almost pleading.

Ehrlichman said that "that is as far as I can go," and when Baker pressed on he ran up against a stone wall in the form of a White House letter that Ehrlichman's counsel John Wilson insisted on reading to Baker and inserting into the public record.

Three days earlier, in the wake of the Anderson article's publication, Wilson had received the letter from Fred Buzhardt. It expressly forbade either of Wilson's clients from discussing one particular matter during their appearances on the Hill: Moorer-Radford. Of course the military espionage was not so named in the letter, but the reference was unmistakable. Buzhardt opened by saying that the letter was in answer to Wilson's request to clarify the extent of executive privilege. The recently appointed counsel to the president pointed out that the president's May 22 statement had waived the executive privilege claim in regard to matters pertaining to Watergate, but "The 1971 investigation about which you inquired" was not related to Watergate, and "does involve most sensitive national security matters, the public disclosure of which would cause damage to the national security."

Baker asked Wilson if the claim of executive privilege "adverts only to the 1971 investigation." Wilson said that it did, and "I have no idea what that is."

Howard Baker was circumspect, but pursued the matter. Did that 1971 investigation have to do with what Baker referred to in veiled terms as "anything related to, say, the Indo-Pakistan War?"

Ehrlichman had to phrase his answer very carefully: "Well, you see, whether I answer yes or no, Senator, I have added to it coming into the public domain, and I think I am precluded from making a fair response to your question because we could sit here and by 'Twenty Questions' eliminate a number of alternatives so that it would be—it would become more readily apparent. . . ." Ehrlichman said he'd be willing to answer "any proper question," but "certain subjects of this kind of a sensitive national security nature are simply not mine to give."

It wasn't "certain subjects," it was this *one* subject, Moorer-Radford. The Buzhardt letter to Wilson expressly forbade discussion of this matter, and of no others. Eighteen months after the espionage had ceased, Buzhardt—speaking, ostensibly, for Nixon and presumably with the permission of his direct boss and close friend Al Haig—would let John Ehrlichman talk about the Plumbers, about the Dr. Fielding break-in, about the wiretap logs recently discovered in his safe, but not about what Haig had described to Bork as the "military penetration."

Only under one circumstance, Ehrlichman told Baker, would he talk: If Baker could find "someone in the executive branch to sit down on a confidential basis and talk through this one particular matter, or if they will tell you that I can do it, I would be happy to do it on that basis." Wilson added that he had no knowledge of the matter but would go to Buzhardt and try to set up a private briefing for Baker and other senators, if they so desired, and if they could promise in front of the television public that there would be no leaks.

They promised. The following day, July 27, Buzhardt and Garment met secretly with Ervin, Baker, and their top aides, Sam Dash and Fred Thompson. There was no discussion of the omitted paragraph five, and no interest in it on either side of the table. The subject was Moorer-Radford. In this meeting Garment and Buzhardt said very little about it except to strongly importune Ervin not to pursue it because it was too explosive. Someone must have mentioned Don Stewart in relation to Moorer-Radford, because press reports indicate that Garment and Buzhardt also attacked Don Stewart in this meeting, raising what they said was his alleged attempt at blackmail. The senators apparently did not know that Henry Petersen at Justice had looked into that alleged attempt and had already advised that it was not criminal, and Buzhardt and Garment didn't tell them. Ervin ruled that the matter was not relevant to the Watergate investigation and promised that the committee would not go into it. Baker, who disagreed, continued to pursue it.

In his meeting with Liebengood and Sanders, Stewart had urged that someone speak with David Young, who, Stewart knew, had prepared a lengthy report on Moorer-Radford. Young met with Baker and some aides after Baker had had his meeting with Ervin, Buzhardt, and Garment, but Young only agreed to talk off the record. Baker laid out for Young what he knew, which was incomplete. According to one participant in the meeting, during Baker's monologue, "Young threw his head back, closed his eyes and remained that way." Once Baker was finished, Young said distinctly, "That is the one thing that the president told me not to discuss at all, and I won't." He urged Baker to go to the president directly. Our source, a former Baker aide, noted that Young did talk about the Dr. Fielding break-in, which had already become public, and gave what he knew about the "White House horrors," but "he wouldn't discuss Moorer-Radford."

Baker did not then see Nixon but he did go directly to Haig and asked him for an explanation. The former Baker aide remembered the outcome: "Haig wouldn't give up the Pentagon report on Moorer-Radford."

20

FIVE DAYS IN JULY

BACK in the first few months of 1973, when the Senate Watergate committee was getting started, Chief Counsel Sam Dash invited to lunch one of the reporters who had done the most to break the multiple stories of Watergate. "I was starting from scratch and I really thought Woodward had a lot of information," Dash told us. "I couldn't promise him any leaks or anything, but since I thought he wanted to get this thing exposed as much as I did, could he at least point me in the right direction?" Woodward "really didn't have any facts other than telling us to talk to certain secretaries and other little people around the White House." Later, Dash offered Woodward a job working for the committee; Woodward declined, but suggested a "great investigator and a guy with integrity," Scott Armstrong. Dash interviewed Armstrong, was impressed, and sought to hire him.

Armstrong was a childhood friend of Woodward's from Wheaton, Illinois, and his hiring was somewhat controversial, as members of the Republican minority considered it tantamount to placing a direct line from the committee to the *Washington Post*. "There was considerable discussion about the wisdom of having him [Armstrong] on the committee in the first place, because of the relationship," Republican staffer

Michael Madigan told us. Senior minority counsel Fred Thompson later wrote in his own Watergate memoir, *At That Point In Time*, that while he agreed with Sam Dash that Armstrong had been "very capable," and had done good work, he believed that Armstrong should never have been on the staff because of the close relationship with Woodward. "More than once," Thompson wrote, "I accused Armstrong of being Woodward's source."

More important for our story, Armstrong seems to have been a conduit *to* the committee for information Woodward wanted the senators to know, information that sometimes came directly from Deep Throat. "I was designated as Woodward's point of contact on the committee," Armstrong told us.

"By May 17, 1973, when the Senate hearings opened, Bernstein and Woodward had gotten lazy," they reported in *All the President's Men*.

> Their nighttime visits were scarcer, and, increasingly, they had begun to rely on a relatively easy access to the Senate committee's staff investigators and attorneys. There was, however, one unchecked entry on both lists, presidential aide Alexander P. Butterfield. Both Deep Throat and Hugh Sloan had mentioned him, and Sloan had said, almost in passing, that he was in charge of "internal security." In January, Woodward had gone by Butterfield's house in a Virginia suburb. No one had come to the door. In May, Woodward asked a committee staff member if Butterfield had been interviewed. "No, we're too busy."

Woodward twice pushed Butterfield on the committee—and his explanation of why he did so requires some examination. He wrote that Deep Throat mentioned Butterfield's name first in a conversation in October 1972. When Woodward asked Hugh Sloan in December of 1972 if he knew the name, Sloan responded "almost in passing" that Butterfield "supervised internal security and the paper flow" to Nixon. Woodward wrote that he knew that at Justice, the internal security division, which had been under the direction of Robert Mardian before he went to work for the Nixon campaign, was in charge of government wiretapping, and therefore suspected that the same terminology in the White House might have to do with monitoring private conversations. Woodward underlined the Sloan reference in his notes and in March mentioned it to the Watergate committee investigators.

But the "internal security" label is oddly attributed to Sloan, who had been a scheduling assistant at the White House. Hugh Sloan knew of Butterfield but could not have regarded Butterfield as an "internal security" man because Butterfield's position was overseer of White

House administration and Sloan was not in a position to know about Butterfield's covert duties involving President Nixon's taping system. However, Alexander Haig was, because he was a long-term friend of Butterfield's and also knew quite a bit about "internal security" wiretapping. It is more likely that Deep Throat, not Sloan, urged Butterfield on Woodward.

In March, Butterfield had left the White House to become administrator of the Federal Aviation Administration. It was a reward for four years of arduous service to the president. It was in May that Woodward first mentioned Butterfield to the committee investigators.

Several weeks after the first contact, Woodward again raised Butterfield's name with a committee staff member, this time stressing Butterfield's "internal security" duties at the White House. For the moment, though, the committee had more important work to do, on the John Dean testimony that held the nation's attention for several weeks.

We have earlier drawn many sections from Dean's testimony to demonstrate what was true and what was false about it, so we will not recapitulate here those five days of Dean that gripped the television audience near the end of June 1973. However, some comments on the testimony are needed.

Dean's testimony was extremely detailed because it had to be; his picture had to be complete to be thoroughly convincing. And Dean was in perfect position to draw that picture because he had known all of what had gone on during the planning for the break-in and the cover-up; he alone had all the information.

Dean had cut his hair, donned glasses, and wore only conservative attire when he testified. Behind him sat Maureen, often the subject of photographers and of the television cameras as she sat, in conservative clothing, poised, good-looking, blond, her hair piled atop her head. As her husband of eight months poured out his story she appeared to pay attention but not to betray any emotion.

In his testimony Dean implicated Mitchell—reluctantly, it seemed—and more readily aimed allegations at Ehrlichman, Haldeman, and at the president. He went easy on Magruder and Strachan, only bringing them in when he had to, and all the while being careful lest he anger them unduly and provoke them to the sorts of detailed recollections of what had happened that would have revealed to the Senate committee Dean's own complicity and role as central instigator, and given his interlocutors reason to doubt his story.

The committee bought Dean, lock, stock, and barrel, precisely because he was an arrow that pointed upward, in the direction they chose to look, some members reluctantly, some eagerly, but all firmly casting their eyes toward a single destination: the president. "What did the President know, and when did he know it?" Senator Howard Baker asked. Baker did not inquire as to the president's sources of information, or if those sources lied to Nixon or tricked him into undertaking illegal cover-up actions. Later on, in their own testimony, all that Haldeman, Ehrlichman, and Mitchell seemed to be able to offer to the committee were denials that rang hollow because they were not as densely detailed as Dean's accusations. They did have documents, but Mitchell's logs were ignored, and the notes of Haldeman and Ehrlichman seemed self-serving. Moreover, the committee apparently ignored Strachan's offer of documents that showed that Dean handled political intelligence at the White House.

There were many holes in Dean's story, and logical inconsistencies. Few of these holes and inconsistencies were closely scrutinized, because it seemed inconceivable to the senators and their staff that the arrow should possibly be pointing at Dean and not away from him. In effect, Dean had a free ride.

But toward the end of June 1973, Leonard Garment prepared a memo about Dean, which bore the in-house name of the "Golden Boy" memo, as the Nixon camp's response to Dean's devastating accusations. The Golden Boy memo was transmitted to the Senate by Fred Buzhardt. The memo noted many of the instances wherein Dean's story was contradicted by sworn testimony, documents, and logic, and pointed the arrow at Dean.

As we look at that memo in retrospect, we see that its main contentions were correct, but that the memo was flawed by the assertion that Mitchell as well as Dean was culpable.

Senator Daniel Inouye, Democrat of Hawaii, announced his intention on June 27 to ask Dean questions based on this memo, as "a substitute for cross-examination of Mr. Dean by the President of the United States." That afternoon and on into the next morning of testimony, he read Dean portions of the memo and asked him to comment on the accusations. At every turn, Dean denied the charges, raising an obfuscatory fog of changed dates, switched attributions and outright lies that themselves went unchallenged. For instance, when Inouye read something about the GEMSTONE meetings and Dean's presence at them, Dean replied,

> First of all, after I returned from the second meeting in Mr. Mitchell's office, and reported to Mr. Haldeman what had occurred and told him of my feelings about what was occurring, and that I wanted to have no part in it and told him I thought no one in the White House should have any part in it, he agreed and told me to have no part in it and I have no

knowledge that there was going to be a meeting in Key Biscayne and did not learn about that meeting until long after June 17, 1972.

This denial was full of holes. As we have pointed out earlier, Dean's supposed "no-part-in-it" conversation with Haldeman had never taken place. Furthermore, as Jeb Magruder had tried to tell the prosecutors, if not the Senate, Dean had certainly had knowledge of GEMSTONE after it had been funded and well before June 17, 1972. Inouye, however, did not explore the denial, and merely moved on to other charges made by the memo, for instance, that Dean had known of the break-in since the seventeenth, and, according to Magruder, Dean had had meetings on June 19, at which "the cover-up plan was hatched." To these charges, Dean responded:

> I believe that the policy regarding the cover-up was set long before I returned from the Far East over the weekend of the break-in and when I came into the office and talked to Mr. Strachan I realized that the White House already decided initially that it was going to start destroying incriminating documents and certainly was not going to step forward as to what its knowledge of the matter was at that point in time.

As we have demonstrated, Dean actually began the cover-up from Manila in telephone instructions to Magruder before Dean returned to Washington. But the senators did not know they could have proved that in 1973, when Inouye read to Dean the nearly correct attacks of the Golden Boy memo.

One important passage from the memo deserved a wider audience, for it struck to the heart of the matter.

> Dean's activity in the coverup also made him, perhaps unwittingly, the principal author of the political and constitutional crisis that Watergate now epitomizes. It would have been embarrassing for the President if the true facts had become known shortly after June 17th, but it is the kind of embarrassment that an immensely popular President could easily have weathered. The political problem has been magnified one thousand-fold because the truth is coming to light so belatedly. . . .

The comment was dismissed at the time as self-serving for the White House. Nixon's willingness to enter into the cover-up is unquestioned, but a distinct possibility is correctly raised by the paragraph: If the full facts and culpability had become known to the president at an early stage, he might well have been able to "weather" the "embarrassment" by placing the accurate story in the public's hands and dismissing Watergate as an action taken by misguided aides without his personal knowledge or sanction. But Dean's successful masking of his own criminal actions, which depended in large part on being able to attribute those actions to Mitchell, had the effect of denying that option to Nixon.

The Golden Boy assault on Dean's credibility soon faded, reduced in the press and in the senators' minds to the status of an attempt to throw mud on the witness. Following Dean at the witness table was a parade of current and former Nixon administration officials. But they stonewalled and their stories conflicted with one another and did not lead the committee any further toward solving what had happened during Watergate. The television ratings of the hearings started to decline. After July 4, the hearings were beginning to bog down, and some committee members were concerned that at the end of testimony they might be left with a series of charges but no clear proof of culpability on the part of the president or his chief aides.

On July 5, they talked to Larry Higby, formerly chief aide to Haldeman, who knew about the taping system in the White House. Higby told us in an interview that prior to going to see the committee staff, he had received advice from Haldeman that if the question of the tapes came up, he was to claim that the subject was covered by executive privilege and that he could not talk about it. Haldeman had already listened to some of the tapes at the president's request. The committee staff asked Higby about tapes, and he tried to deflect the question by telling them that the president at the end of the day dictated notes to himself on tape. The staffers were not interested in dictabelt recordings, and asked, "Are there any other tapes that you are aware of?" Higby whispered to his lawyer that he had been told to claim executive privilege on that question, and then proceeded to finesse the question and not mention that claim. He completed his interview with the staff without spilling the secret.

"I went the next day to Haig," Higby recalls. "I told him, 'Al, they're eventually going to get to the taping system.' " Haig responded that the committee already knew about the dictabelts, and Higby informed him that the committee staff were zeroing in on the secret taping system. Haig seemed surprised to learn of this taping system, and Higby laid out its dimensions, after which Haig "looked at me astonished and said, 'I'll get back to you.' And I said, 'Fine. I've got to have guidance before I go up there.' Higby hadn't been told yet that he would definitely be called to testify, but he believed it likely that he would be called.

Higby fully expected Haig to tell him, as Haldeman had, that if asked about the taping system he was to say it was covered by executive privilege and that he could not talk about it. But the advice he received from Haig was not what Higby expected. "He got back to me the next day and he said, 'Tell the truth,' meaning, tell the committee about the tapes." Higby was shocked, but believed that the instruction had come from Nixon, and so was prepared to testify fully if asked the right question.

A week after Higby's appearance, committee investigators called Alexander Butterfield. Assistant Chief Counsel James Hamilton confirms that "Woodward was of the opinion" Butterfield should be called, but insists (as does Scott Armstrong) that the committee already had Butterfield on a list of prospective witnesses and would have summoned him anyway.

At 2:15 P.M. on the afternoon of Friday, July 13, Butterfield sat down with investigators Scott Armstrong, Gene Boyce, and Donald Sanders in room G334 of the Dirksen Senate Office Building. As any reader familiar with the Watergate affair knows, it was at this meeting that Butterfield revealed the existence of the White House taping system, the fruits of which eventually led to the end of the Nixon administration. So, in the history of Watergate, Butterfield's appearance was mightily important.

What has not been known until now are the circumstances surrounding Butterfield's disclosure. During five days in July of 1973, the fortunes of Richard Nixon in regard to Watergate changed dramatically, and the reasons can be found in the actions of Al Haig and Fred Buzhardt, with the apparently unwitting assistance of Len Garment.

Born into a Navy family, Alexander Butterfield had wanted to attend the Naval Academy, but failed the physical exam and instead went to UCLA. There he met fellow undergraduate Bob Haldeman; although the two men were not close friends, they were more than acquaintances because their wives were sorority sisters who remained in touch with one another. After his second year at UCLA, in 1948, Butterfield entered an Air Force cadet program, and graduated the following year as a second lieutenant. He stayed in the Air Force and rose through the ranks; his tours of duty included two years in Vietnam on a special intelligence assignment before he landed at the Pentagon in 1964, where he worked on counterinsurgency planning and other tasks that called on his considerable experience with clandestine operations. In 1965 he was assigned to the staff of Joe Califano, and there met Haig. "We were very, very close when we were in the Johnson administration," Butterfield recalled to us of his relationship with Haig. After some months of working together, he took over from Haig on two key assignments. The first was the resettlement of the Cuban veterans of the Bay of Pigs. The second was as a liaison for Robert McNamara with the White House. He had what he described as a "strange role" that involved "a lot of undercover stuff." Replacing Haig in the job, he spent what he told us was "twenty hours a week minimum [at the White House] . . . in private little meetings with [McGeorge] Bundy and [Dean] Rusk because I was McNamara's chart man and I kept all those Vietnam figures. And I was like a fly on the wall in all these meetings up in the president's bedroom at one A.M."

By 1968, Butterfield was about as far away from the White House and the Pentagon as he could be, in Canberra, Australia, as the senior American military officer in Australia. Headquartered in the American embassy, he monitored nearly two dozen Defense Department activities in Australia, and also had another mission: "I was the principal point of contact [in the military] for the CIA in Australia," he told us. "I traveled around and I had my own airplane and crew. I was the [military's] CIA liaison there."

About what happened next there are two versions.

When Butterfield testified before the House Judiciary Committee in 1974 he asserted that Haldeman had called him, out of the blue, when he was in Australia and had asked him to take the post in the White House as "a sort of personal assistant to the President," but "if I wanted to accept I would have to leave the military altogether, retire, which I was eligible to do at that time, and come on to the staff as a civilian." Butterfield reported that he had always considered himself the sort that wouldn't retire before his thirty to thirty-five years were up, but Haldeman pressed him, so he did retire and went to the White House.

Haldeman has always denied that version of the hiring, and said that the impetus came from Butterfield, from whom he had not heard in twenty years, in a letter written to Haldeman from Australia. Haldeman looked into Butterfield's background and decided he would be a good assistant for the president; however, Haldeman added in his memoir, "he insisted that he would have to resign from the Air Force to take the job. I assured him this was not the case, and urged that he stay in the service and just let us have him assigned to the White House—a procedure with more than ample precedent." But Butterfield wanted to retire, Haldeman said, and so Haldeman went along with that idea. Writing in 1978, Haldeman said he had been told that Rose Mary Woods believed that Butterfield had been a plant placed inside the White House by some other agency, probably the CIA, and, "I have to agree she may have a point." Haldeman rhetorically asked,

"Was the White House filled with plants from other agencies, most particularly the CIA? The overwhelming evidence is that it was. But was Butterfield one of them? It's hard for me to believe it." He said that he still considered Butterfield a friend, but wondered, "Why does he distort the facts now, unless he has something to hide?"

We confronted Butterfield with Haldeman's version and with the fact that Larry Higby remembers seeing Butterfield's original letter to Haldeman, and Butterfield now agrees that Haldeman is correct in the matter of how he was hired. "Yes, I brought myself to his attention," Butterfield tells us. "I certainly did write to him."

Alex Butterfield began his career at the White House on the day Nixon entered it, and from the outset had nearly daily contact with the president. He took notes in meetings and handled the paperwork coming into and going out of Nixon's work basket. He ensured an orderly flow of staff and executive agency memos. During that time, he later testified, "I got a feel for the likes and dislikes of the President, a good feel for his moods, his temperament." In his first year, Butterfield's office was upstairs of the president's. In his second year, when Haldeman sloughed off some of the day-to-day business of running the White House staff, Butterfield inherited the small office Haldeman had used, separated from the Oval Office by a hallway of twenty feet, and took over the task of responding on a "minute-to-minute basis to the President as Haldeman had done that first year."

As he had been to McNamara, he was "a fly on the wall" in many meetings with Nixon. Butterfield told us in an interview, "I was not a functionary, although Haldeman and Nixon would like to pretend that I was. I was on the senior staff. My office adjoined the Oval Office, I was in and out more times than anyone. I was the first guy to see the president every morning and the last guy to see him at night. . . . I was in a position to know relationships of one aide to another and each to the president." He was in charge of Nixon's papers and the files that would eventually go to the Nixon library. He was secretary to the cabinet, and the liaison between the president and the Secret Service, the Executive Protection Service, the office of the military assistants, the office of White House visitors, and the First Lady's staff.

Finally, as part of Butterfield's duties as overseer of White House administration, Butterfield supervised the White House Office of Security—not "internal security" (as was suggested by Deep Throat to Woodward)—which was nothing more than a repository for the files from the FBI background checks on White House staff members and prospective presidential appointees.

In February of 1971, after Butterfield had been in the White House two years, Larry Higby approached him with an instruction from the president. Nixon wanted to tape his conversations and meetings. Butterfield understood that the president wished to do so for historical purposes, for use after Nixon left office and when a Nixon presidential library would be established. Higby told Butterfield that the president had a specific prohibition in regard to this taping system. In his Judiciary Committee testimony, Butterfield recalled that Higby said, " 'be sure that you don't go to the military people on this.' I wasn't sure to whom I would go at that moment, but he said to be sure you don't go to the military people on this. He used the term 'Signal.' Signal denotes the military communications people stationed at the White House and part of the organization known as the White House Communications Agency." It was for that reason, Butterfield said, that he turned to the technical security division of the Secret Service and its chief, Albert Wong, who then brought in two or three of his electronics experts to install the system.

The technicians soon placed tiny microphones inside the Oval Office, five embedded in Nixon's desk and two more on either side of the fireplace. Similar voice-activated microphones were placed in the president's hideaway office in the EOB, on the telephones in the Oval Office, in the Lincoln sitting room in the residential part of the White House, and in the president's personal cabin at Camp David. Another listening device in the cabinet room could be activated manually by Butterfield through buttons on his desk telephone. Though the microphones could pick up even the softest conversations, the tape recorders were of medium, single-track quality, and when two or more persons spoke at once, the sound sequences were often garbled.

The taping system was also tied into another system that let the Secret Service know precisely where the president was at all hours of the day. As he moved from spot to spot, agents would signal Nixon's location to a central office, and the appropriate light in a wall box would be illuminated. When the light for the Oval Office or EOB office was lit, the corresponding taping system for that office would also be put on alert. As Nixon or someone else in the room or on the telephone spoke, in the basement of the White House spools of tape would begin turning on the recording machines. Secret Service agents changed the tapes as the ends of reels were reached, and removed, labeled, and stored completed tapes in a tiny EOB room equipped with an alarm.

According to Butterfield, those who knew of the system when it was first established included himself, the president, Haldeman, Higby, Al Wong, and four or five Secret Service agents. Later,

Butterfield told his secretary, and in March of 1973, when Butterfield was appointed to the FAA, Butterfield informed his replacement at the White House, Steve Bull, about the taping system.

In April of 1973 Butterfield—according to his own account, later given to the Senate Watergate committee investigators—volunteered to appear before the Watergate grand jury about the briefcase stuffed with $350,000 in cash that he had stored in a friend's safe-deposit box at Haldeman's request in April of 1972. He went to Earl Silbert and his associate, Seymour Glanzer, with "everything he knew," and they put him briefly on the stand. The story of that leftover campaign money had become the first of Deep Throat's revelations to Bob Woodward in the fall of 1972. Nothing happened to Butterfield as a result of that go-around with the grand jury, and he proceeded to delve into the exciting job of administrator of the FAA. But he also called his "good friend" Len Garment, who had taken over as White House counsel from John Dean, and told him "what had transpired" in the meeting with Silbert and Glanzer.

When Al Haig moved to the White House as chief of staff in May 1973, old friends Haig and Butterfield spoke. Butterfield later told the Watergate committee staffers that it had been at that moment that he'd told Haig about the taping system "since he had Haldeman's functions. And he [Haig] said, 'I know, I know about that.' " This raises questions about Haig's "astonishment" when Higby later told Haig of the taping system in July.

Shortly after the May conversation between Haig and Butterfield, according to Woodward and Bernstein, Deep Throat told Woodward to look into Alexander Butterfield, and Woodward got that word to the Senate committee staff.

On Friday, July 13, when Butterfield sat in the room with the three committee staffers, he told us that he had assumed he had been summoned because "of the position I had and the place where I sat and the things that I knew. To give light and perspective as to what was going on" in the Nixon White House. And so he calmly answered questions about his four-plus years there, his handling of the paper-work and schedules, the roles and personalities of the other people on the staff, and so on, down to the affair of the cash-stuffed briefcase and his recital of the particulars of that to the grand jury and to Len Garment.

Once again in this strange history, investigators sat in a closed room with a man and asked standard questions, as they had done in the quiet of the polygraph room at the Pentagon suite commanded by Don Stewart at the close of 1971. And once again, a question prompted an answer that had not been foreseen by those who asked the question.

In the Senate committee staff room, Don Sanders, the former FBI colleague and friend of Don Stewart, had become annoyed as Alexander Butterfield calmly took the investigators on a scenic tour of his years as a fly on the wall of the Nixon White House. They were under a mandate from the senators to come up with some real evidence on which Nixon could be pinned to the mat or exonerated. They had struck out with Higby, but Sanders had remembered a document already in their hands, and had brought it to this interview. Weeks earlier, Buzhardt had called Minority Counsel Fred Thompson and related to him Nixon's quite detailed versions of his February, March, and April 1973 meetings with John Dean. Thompson had prepared a memo of his conversation with Buzhardt, and Sanders asked Butterfield to read it.

As Butterfield read the Thompson memo that afternoon, Butterfield later told us, he immediately suspected that Buzhardt had lifted the information from Nixon's tapes. For months, as he had watched the Watergate story unfold in the press, he later told us, "I'd think to myself, Jesus, it's all there on tape. Someday those tapes will come out. I knew I was one of the very few people who knew about them." But when he first saw the document, he was not asked a direct question about a taping system, and so finessed the matter. Later in the interview, though, Sanders pressed on just this point: How could the White House have such a detailed account of the conversations? Butterfield first fudged and said that after meetings Nixon often recorded his recollections on a dictabelt, but did admit that what Buzhardt told Thompson was certainly quite detailed. Sanders pushed on, reminding Butterfield of what John Dean had said when he had testified—that during one meeting with the president Dean had gotten the feeling that the conversation was being taped because Nixon had turned away from him and had talked almost in a whisper about a most important subject, executive clemency.

Did Dean have any reason to believe that he was being taped? Sanders asked.

At a crossroads, Butterfield—like Radford—decided to give the complete answer; this time, he'd been asked a direct question about the tapes. No, he responded, Dean did not know about the taping system, but all of the president's conversations in the Oval Office were recorded. Gushing on, he described in quite a bit of detail the establishment and operation of the taping system. Reaching the end of his description, he told his stunned audience, as they recorded in their own notes, "This is all something I know the President did not want revealed, but you asked me, and I feel it is something you ought to know about in your investigations. I was told no one was to know about the information I have told you."

At that very moment, President Nixon was in Bethesda Naval Hospital in suburban Maryland, suffering from viral pneumonia. He had awakened in the early hours of the previous morning with a high fever and complaining of severe chest pains. That day he spent in bed. He had one tense conversation with Sam Ervin in regard to the committee's request for all White House papers that might relate to the Senate's investigation. Nixon had refused to turn over the papers, citing executive privilege. When his condition worsened and a chest X ray showed that he had viral pneumonia, the decision was made to move him to the hospital.

Nixon continued to work from his sickbed because, as he wrote in his autobiography,

> I was determined to show that even in the hospital I was able to carry out my duties as President. As I received inhalation therapy and underwent tests and X-rays, I continued to take calls and see Ziegler and Haig. I phoned Kissinger and reviewed the plans for Phase IV of our economic policy with [Treasury Secretary George] Schultz. The worst thing about the pneumonia was the inability to sleep because the discomfort was so great. During the nights I lay awake counting the minutes. I ended up staying on the phone until late at night, checking on the day's events.

Nixon may well have believed that he was on top of the day's events, but during that weekend the president remained completely unaware that his political fate was being seriously undermined by the prospective testimony before the Watergate committee of Alexander Butterfield.

That Nixon remained ignorant of Butterfield's doings during the weekend of July 14 and 15 has been regarded by Watergate historians and journalists as little more than an oddity to be briefly noted. It was much more than that.

After showing Butterfield to the door, Democratic staffers Armstrong and Boyce rushed to find Sam Dash at his office, while Republican counsel Sanders went on a similar mission to locate Fred Thompson. When Armstrong and Boyce came into his office, Sam Dash later wrote in his book *Chief Counsel*, "they both looked wild-eyed. Scott was sweating and in a state of great excitement. As soon as he had closed the door the words tumbled out of his mouth as he told me about Butterfield's astounding revelation. . . . [We] became overwhelmed with the explosive meaning of the existence of such tapes. We now knew there had been a secret, irrefutable 'witness' in the Oval Office each time Dean met with Nixon, and if we could get the tapes we could now do what we had thought would be impossible—establish the truth or falsity of Dean's accusations against the President."

Thompson was at the bar at the Carroll Arms hotel, having a drink with a reporter, when Sanders dragged him outside to a small park, checked to see if they could be overheard, and blurted out the news.

There were two problems with any proposed Butterfield testimony. The first was that he did not want to testify and had suggested that the committee get Higby or Haldeman to testify in public about the taping system. Second, he was scheduled to leave on Tuesday, July 17, for the Soviet Union to help negotiate a new aviation treaty.

Learning this, Dash found Sam Ervin and they agreed that Butterfield should be compelled to testify on Monday, and Ervin authorized Dash to prepare a subpoena for Butterfield.

For his part, Fred Thompson and Assistant Minority Counsel Howard Liebengood met with Howard Baker on Saturday morning. As Thompson later wrote, "Baker thought it inconceivable that Nixon would have taped his conversations if they contained anything incriminating. I agreed. . . . The more I thought about what had occurred, the more I considered the possibility that Butterfield had been sent to us as part of a strategy: the president was orchestrating the whole affair and had intended that the tapes be discovered." For that reason, the Republicans came to the same conclusion already reached by Dash and Ervin, that Butterfield should give his testimony in public as soon as possible.

Thompson may well have been correct that Butterfield had been sent to the committee as part of a strategy—but if he was, it was not the president's strategy.

That Saturday morning, as Baker met with his aides, Butterfield flew to New Hampshire to dedicate a new air traffic control facility in Nashua County, and he told us he was so unconcerned about his possible testimony to the Senate that he didn't even prepare for an appearance before the Senate.

"I didn't have the slightest clue" that the committee would call him to testify on Monday, he told us. "No, no—why would I ever do that? I didn't give it one goddamn thought. [Meeting with the Senate staffers] was just another session to me. I know for a fact that I never did anticipate being called by the committee. So I never would have written out any statements, or answers or comments or anything like that having to do with me testifying."

The evidence, however, shows that all through the weekend Butterfield was deeply concerned about what he had told the Senate staffers.
In the records of the Watergate committee, now located in the National
Archives, are thirty-one pages of Butterfield's handwritten notes,
inscribed over that weekend. They show a man not only concerned
about testifying, but even more worried about being forced to resign
from the FAA because of his involvement in the handling of the
$350,000 campaign fund. We know these notes are authentic and
contemporary because they were subpoenaed immediately after Butterfield's appearance, and the transmittal note from Butterfield's secretary
says that "this material represents a series of his own initial drafts of
possible statements (short and long) that he might use when testifying
before your Committee. It includes, too, some anticipated questions
and the approximate answers he would give to such questions."

In a long preamble, Butterfield denied any involvement in or
knowledge of the Watergate operation of the misuse of funds, and notes
that he appeared voluntarily before the grand jury. He said he had
worked for his country and its Presidents "with honor and integrity"
for a quarter century, and would continue to do so. He worried that
his testimony might be taken out of context in news reports, and
pointed out that he had worked in close physical proximity to the
president for most of Nixon's first term and that he was now the FAA
administrator. He wrote that it would be a "gross" and "unconsciona-
ble" injustice to distort in any way his statements, "to me personally"
as well as to the president and to the FAA.

Butterfield's most revealing words were saved for the issue of a
possible resignation. If that were to be brought up, his notes show, he
intended to use as a lifeline his friendship with Alexander Haig. If
asked to resign, he would not, and would say that he had no reason to
resign because

> My record is similar to that of General Haig. . . . The President knows
> this. He knows of . . . my long and close association with General Haig.
> Would it not seem very odd to you then—just to use this one example—
> that the President would ask me to resign . . . in almost the same breath
> that he asks General Haig [into the White House to become chief of
> staff]?

Most of the notes Butterfield made that weekend centered on the
$350,000 fund, and only in the last two pages did he prepare testimony
on the tapes. He had assumed that Higby and Haldeman had also been
asked about the tapes in their interviews with the committee staff, that

they had talked about the taping system, and that he was being asked "so that the fact could be corroborated."

We told Butterfield about his handwritten notes, and he says that he must have forgotten that he wrote them and pronounced himself "amazed" that he didn't remember them.

The notes show that Butterfield considered his friendship with Haig essential to his defense, should he need a defense. We asked Butterfield if he had talked to Haig that weekend. "No," he told us. "I just have to chalk that up with my preoccupation with the other things I was doing." Yes, he agreed, in retrospect it "seems like a terribly big deal" for him not to have warned the White House, but at the time it didn't seem so important.

It was important because a warning to the president that weekend would have allowed him to mount a defense, namely, a written directive saying that the taping system was covered by executive privilege and that executive branch employee Butterfield would have to consider himself constrained from testifying about it. But Nixon was not informed about Butterfield's forthcoming revelations until there were very few hours left in which to act to restrain the damaging testimony.

As Butterfield's handwritten notes for the testimony also show, he considered himself an intensely loyal man. It strains credulity that he did not call Haig, a man to whom he was loyal. We can't prove that he did. But someone did inform the general, possibly on Saturday but certainly by Sunday, that there would be testimony about the taping system in the coming week. Garment told us that he was called to the White House for a meeting on Sunday evening, July 15, with Haig and Buzhardt, at which the two men told Garment they were expecting testimony about the taping system before the Senate committee the next day.

Fred Thompson wrote that he talked to Buzhardt at the White House on Sunday afternoon. He reported in his memoir that he told Buzhardt that the committee was aware that "every conversation in the White House is on tape. I know you realize the significance of that. It's not my place to give you advice, but I think that if I were you I'd start making plans immediately to get those tapes together and get them up here as soon as possible. There was a short pause, then Buzhardt said, 'Well I think that is significant, *if it is true*. We'll get on it tomorrow.' "

Sam Dash claims that Thompson made the call even earlier, on Friday evening, but Thompson says that Dash is mistaken.

Steve Bull, also at home that weekend, received a call from Scott Armstrong telling him to be ready to testify on Monday, and not telling him why. Bull believed that the committee was zeroing in on the taping system, and immediately called Buzhardt to say so. Buzhardt brushed off the warning, telling Bull, "No, they couldn't know about that [the taping system]." On Monday, Buzhardt called Bull back to say he wouldn't have to testify because Butterfield was going to do so.

Buzhardt's reported laconic attitude toward Bull and Thompson on what was clearly a bombshell seems to reflect Haig's earlier colloquy with Larry Higby. Haig already knew that the committee was hot on the trail of the taping system, and had told Higby, more than a week earlier, to testify truthfully about it if asked. The information that someone was going to testify about it on Monday, then, would have come as no surprise. Without informing Nixon, or even asking the president's opinion, Buzhardt and Haig had decided to allow this great and dangerous secret to become public knowledge, and take the consequences.

Woodward also reports that he learned of Nixon's taping system in a phone call at home on Saturday, from someone *All the President's Men* identifies as "a senior member of the committee's investigative staff," who congratulated Woodward on having suggested they question Butterfield and told him that Butterfield had spilled "a story which would disturb the presidential universe as none other would." To Fred Thompson, this was one of the passages in the Woodward-Bernstein book that proved Scott Armstrong was a conduit for information to Woodward. But Armstrong denies he leaked any information to his friend at the *Post*, insisting he and Woodward were "scrupulous" in their dealings. "My conscience is clear," he says.

After learning of this universe-disturbing potential testimony, Woodward conveyed the information to Bernstein, and then they both sat on their hands all day. Inexplicably, they ceased to behave as reporters in possession of an enormous scoop, and fell silent. The supposed reasoning behind their silence lies in the following passage of their book.

> The reporters were again concerned about a White House set-up. A taping system could be disclosed, they reasoned, and then the President could serve up doctored or manufactured tapes to exculpate himself and his men. Or, having known the tapes were rolling, the President might have induced Dean—or anyone else—to say incriminating things and then feign ignorance himself. They decided not to pursue the story for the moment.

This reasoning is absurd. Legitimate reporters in pursuit of a story generally do not worry whether a newly uncovered piece of evidence is incriminating or exculpatory; the fact that it has been uncovered must be presented to the public.

Moreover, there were clear dangers for Woodward and Bernstein in holding back what they knew. How could they be certain that some other reporter, one with different motivations, would not be informed by the same or another staff member and would not beat them into print on the story?

In a second passage of their book that relates to Butterfield, there are some clues that Woodward spoke to someone else that weekend who also was privy to Butterfield's revelation. Butterfield is reported as having told the investigators that Ehrlichman and Kissinger were unaware of the taping system, and Woodward broods on what this might mean: that Kissinger "wouldn't like the idea of secret taping systems plucking his sober words and advice out of the air—whether for posterity or for some grand jury."

According to committee staff notes of the July 13 interview, however, Butterfield hadn't said a word about Kissinger knowing or not knowing about the taping system in his session with the Senate investigators. It seems likely that Woodward had talked to someone not on the committee staff that weekend, someone who knew quite a bit about the taping system, enough to assert baldly that Kissinger had not known about it. The most logical candidate is Haig.

According to their book, Woodward and Bernstein didn't tell anyone at the *Post* about Butterfield's revelation until 9:30 P.M. on Saturday evening, when Woodward spoke with a sleepy Ben Bradlee, who supposedly rated the story only a B-plus and suggested that the reporters not go all out to "see what more you can find out."

The *Post*'s decision to hold back the story had the same effect as the actions of Haig and Buzhardt—it prevented Nixon from learning about Butterfield's potential disclosures in time for him to take action to head off those disclosures.

On Sunday afternoon, after his return from ribbon-cutting, Butterfield received a call from Investigator Armstrong, who informed Butterfield that he would be called to testify the next morning, July 16. Quite upset, Butterfield went personally to see Howard Baker at his home in hopes of having the appearance canceled or postponed. According to Butterfield, Baker was sympathetic but not encouraging, and suggested that Butterfield call the White House for help. Butterfield turned to Len Garment, but he was out of town and Butterfield left a message for Garment to call. As the reader will recall, when Butterfield had testified before the grand jury in April, he had phoned Garment immediately afterward with a summary of his testimony.

When Garment landed at Washington's National Airport on Sunday he was paged to proceed immediately to the White House. Arriving at his office, he found Haig and Buzhardt waiting for him, along with the phone message from Butterfield. Buzhardt and Haig wanted Garment to find out if Butterfield was the person who had talked to the committee about the tapes. Garment called Butterfield, who confirmed that he was going to testify the next day, and Garment so informed Buzhardt and Haig.

They still didn't tell the president.

Garment offered us four explanations why Haig decided not to tell Nixon. First, they didn't yet have all the facts. Second, Nixon was ill, and "why send the president up the wall?" Third, "We always thought that it [the revelation of the taping system] would be protected by executive privilege." And fourth, it was too late to do anything to halt the Butterfield testimony. These suggestions do not adequately explain Haig's decision. The inner circle did have all the facts, and the president had continued to work though he was ill. Nixon actually had time to delay or stop the testimony, as the events of the following day would shortly make clear. Moreover, when the White House wanted to act quickly, it could.

White House logs show that Haig met with Nixon in the hospital between 10:15 A.M. and noon on Saturday, and twice on Sunday between one and two in the afternoon. Haig hadn't told Nixon about the colloquy with Higby earlier, he didn't tell him that Buzhardt had learned from Fred Thompson that someone was to testify about the taping system the next day, and he didn't tell him about Garment's Sunday conversation with Butterfield. Haig finally got around to informing the president about the potentially explosive Butterfield testimony on Monday morning, and he also told the president that there was no way to stop Butterfield's public revelation. As we have seen, there was plenty of time—and plenty of precedent—for the president to sign a letter to the committee and to Butterfield saying that his proposed testimony was prevented on the grounds of executive privilege.

When Nixon learned on Monday morning of Butterfield's proposed testimony, he writes in his autobiography, "I was shocked. . . . I had believed that the existence of the White House taping system would never be revealed. I thought that at least executive privilege would have been raised by any staff member before verifying its existence."

And Press Secretary Ron Ziegler, one of the few people other than doctors and Haig who saw the president that weekend, says that he did not learn of Butterfield's impending testimony until Monday morning, either, and that if Haig, Buzhardt, or Garment knew earlier, none of them told him. What would he have done, we asked Ziegler, if he had known? "I would have told the president. . . . I certainly would not have withheld from him. I can't conceive of that information being withheld from the president for an entire weekend." And Ziegler added that if the inner circle "had discussed not telling him because we didn't want to bother him I certainly would have remembered that, and it didn't happen."

Monday morning at 11:15, Butterfield, who had not been issued a subpoena, was at the barber shop at the Sheraton Carlton Hotel having a trim when he received a phone call from Assistant Chief Counsel Jim Hamilton, who had tracked Butterfield down through his FAA secretary. Hamilton told him he must appear that afternoon, and Butterfield refused. "I was very, very upset and profane," he told us, "and sitting in the barber's chair I said, 'I will not do that. I'm not going up there and you can tell the committee chairman that.' " The television set was on in the barber shop, and Butterfield rather helplessly watched his fate unfold on the screen. He saw Hamilton approach Ervin's chair and whisper something to the chairman, and saw Ervin's characteristic eyebrows move rapidly up and down before he whispered something in Hamilton's ear. The television then showed Hamilton walking deliberately out of the hearing room, and a few moments later, the phone rang again for Butterfield in the barber chair. According to Butterfield, Hamilton told him that Ervin said, "If you're not in his office by one o'clock we will have federal marshals pick you up on the street."

Hamilton told us that the threat was a "bluff" by Ervin, who would have needed the full vote of the Senate in order to proceed with the arrest of Butterfield. But Butterfield believed the threat. In a panic, he called Len Garment again at the White House and told Garment that he had to testify—within two hours. Butterfield recalled for us that Garment "sort of lashed out at me. I always thought Garment was my pal. He said, 'Don't call us for help. Go get your own lawyer.' "

In other words, a last chance for the White House to claim executive privilege on the tapes was not seized. The effect of his conversation with Garment was to render Butterfield contrite and ready to testify— so ready that even when the subpoena was not fully prepared at the time Butterfield arrived at Ervin's office at 1:00 P.M., he waited patiently until it was finished and Ervin signed it at 1:45, and then entered the hearing room for his few minutes in front of the television cameras. Television viewers throughout the country were astonished to hear about a secret taping system in the White House, one that foreign visitors and even most people in the administration did not know had been in existence. Clearly, intimate conversations had been taped without participants' knowledge. The Oval Office was revealed as a place in which supposedly private conversations with the president were clandestinely recorded. In a flash, millions of viewers gained new understanding of the dark side of the personality of Richard Nixon.

The moment Butterfield completed his electrifying testimony, a Capitol policeman handed an envelope to Sam Dash that had just arrived from the White House, and Dash gave it to Ervin. Inside was a letter from Fred Buzhardt confirming "the facts stated to your Committee today by Mr. Alexander Butterfield that the President's meetings and conversations in the White House had been recorded since the spring of 1971." The letter further stated that the system was still in use.

Secret Service Technical Security Division Chief Al Wong arrived at 12:30 P.M. the next day for an executive session with the Senate committee, accompanied by an attorney from the Treasury Department, and armed with a letter from the president that directed Wong and all Secret Service personnel to give no testimony to the Ervin committee. Such matters, the president wrote, were indeed covered by executive privilege.

If someone had been trying to injure the president, they could not have engineered a more deleterious chain of events than these five days in July that surrounded Alex Butterfield's revelation about the White House taping system. As we shall see in later chapters, on several more occasions during Nixon's final year in office, similar patterns of seemingly inadvertent failures to correctly inform the president can be discerned and again it was Chief of Staff Haig who failed to inform the president. Errors of omission or commission?

The senators accepted the letter from Al Wong, dismissed him, and then discussed the matter. They could proceed with contempt proceedings against Wong and other Secret Service agents for refusing to answer questions, but, Sam Dash later wrote, Senator Ervin "expressed the view that this would not be fair to these minor public officials who were caught in the middle between an order from the President of the United States and a subpoena from a Senate committee. He said the committee's dispute was with the President and not with the Secret Service men."

Shortly thereafter, the senators decided to subpoena the actual tapes, the White House refused to turn them over, and the year-long, ultimately decisive final battle of the Nixon administration began.

21

THE SATURDAY NIGHT MASSACRE

FRIDAY, July 20, 1973, President Richard Nixon was released from Bethesda Naval Hospital after his bout with viral pneumonia. He returned to the White House, where the staff greeted him in the Rose Garden and he made a speech. "What we were elected to do, we are going to do, and let others wallow in Watergate," he told the crowd, which included the press corps. Nixon stayed only briefly, then went to Camp David accompanied by his friend Bebe Rebozo, his wife, Pat, his secretary, Rose Mary Woods, and Mamie Eisenhower, widow of President Dwight D. Eisenhower.

He also took with him two matters that demanded immediate attention, a letter from Special Prosecutor Archibald Cox to Fred Buzhardt, and another letter addressed to the president from the Ervin committee. Each demanded some of the tapes. Two days earlier, in the wake of Butterfield's testimony, Alexander Haig had ordered the White House secret taping system shut down, had taken control of two and a half years worth of accumulated tapes, and had designated his deputy, retired Major General John C. Bennett, as the new custodian of the tapes.

Special Prosecutor Archibald Cox had been a thorn in the president's side ever since Elliot Richardson's confirmation hearings. To ensure confirmation as attorney general, Richardson had promised the Senate that he would appoint an independent prosecutor to oversee the Watergate case, one whom he pledged to remove only for "extraordinary impropriety." Richardson was confirmed, and then had to make good on his promise. On May 18, the day after the Senate Watergate hearings began, he announced Cox's appointment. Cox had been one of Richardson's professors at Harvard Law School, and was considered a leading scholar.

Cox was also a man Nixon almost had to hate, a card-carrying member of the Eastern liberal establishment, a former solicitor general under John Kennedy who had written legislation for Kennedy in the Senate and speeches for him in the 1960 presidential campaign. But when Cox's name was announced by Richardson, the atmosphere in the country was such that Nixon could not object. Richardson and Cox both took office on the same day, in separate swearing-in ceremonies. Among those watching Cox repeat the oath were two longtime friends, Senator Ted Kennedy and his sister-in-law Ethel Kennedy, widow of Senator Robert F. Kennedy. As J. Anthony Lukas reports in his book *Nightmare*, "The President's suspicions were exacerbated still further by the staff Cox selected. Of the thirty-seven lawyers he ultimately recruited, all but one were Ivy Leaguers, eighteen from Harvard; most were Democrats; many had worked in the Justice Department under Robert Kennedy or Nicholas deB. Katzenbach."

Nixon was alarmed by Cox's credentials and cohorts; Alexander Haig must have been alarmed by Cox's almost immediate attempts to widen his investigation beyond the Watergate break-in and cover-up to include the Huston Plan, the 1969–1971 wiretaps, and the Plumbers. These last two touched Haig personally. When Cox asked Buzhardt in writing for detailed records and logs on the Plumbers, Buzhardt refused. Cox then threatened to bring indictments against those who had conducted and supervised the Dr. Fielding office burglary, and was warned by Buzhardt that such prosecutions would threaten national security because the Plumbers had been involved in other highly classified matters. Nixon himself became incensed at news reports that Cox was looking into the financing of his home in San Clemente. Cox issued a statement saying he wasn't conducting such an inquiry, but would not entirely rule one out if evidence of wrongdoing was brought to the fore.

Cox's July 18 letter to Buzhardt—the one Nixon had to consider at Camp David—requested eight presidential recordings, "material and important evidence" in the criminal investigation of former presidential aides. Most were tapes of dates on which John Dean had testified that he met with Nixon. Sam Ervin's letter had a broader compass, requesting "all relevant documents and tapes under control of the White House that relate to the matters the Select Committee is authorized to investigate." During the weekend, Nixon and Haig discussed these letters and the president made up his mind what to do.

On Monday morning, the White House's reply to the two letters was released. One missive was written by Charles Alan Wright, a constitutional scholar from the University of Texas who had just been retained as a member of the Nixon defense team. Wright told Cox that:

> It is for the President, and only for the President, to weigh whether the incremental advantage that these tapes would give you in criminal proceedings justifies the serious and lasting hurt that disclosure of them would do to the confidentiality that is imperative to the effective functioning of the Presidency. In this instance the President has concluded that it would not serve the public interest to make the tapes available.

Wright further reminded Cox that while he might consider his post "an office of the court," he was principally an employee of the executive branch, and therefore "subject to the instructions of your superiors, up to and including the President, and can have access to Presidential papers only as and if the President sees fit to make them available to you."

At the same time, Nixon wrote a personal letter to Sam Ervin that cited the principles of "separation of powers" and executive privilege to turn down the request for tapes. The president also explained that the tapes

> would not settle the central issues before your Committee. Before their existence became publicly known, I personally listened to a number of them. The tapes are entirely consistent with what I know to be the truth and what I have stated to be the truth. However, as in any verbatim recording of informal conversations, they contain comments that persons with different perspectives and motivations would inevitably interpret in different ways.

As these two letters went out, Haig called Richardson, Cox's boss, to complain about a questionnaire the Special Prosecutor had sent to government agencies seeking information about "electronic surveillance." Richardson later said in a sworn statement to the House

Judiciary Committee that Haig said the "boss" was very "uptight" about Cox's questions, and bluntly warned Richardson that "if we have to have a confrontation, we will have it." Nixon wanted "a tight line drawn with no further mistakes," and "if Cox does not agree, we will get rid of Cox." Richardson attempted to get Cox to back away from the various inquiries that Haig had told him the "boss" wanted to say were under the umbrella of national security, but Cox resisted the effort to limit his jurisdiction.

Ervin was caustic that Monday as he commented on the letter at an open session of the committee: "The president says that [the tapes] are susceptible of, the way I construe it, two different interpretations, one favorable to his aides, and one not favorable to his aides." There was laughter in the room. There was none as the committee voted to subpoena the tapes and papers from the president. And Archibald Cox showed just what he thought of Haig's attempt to brush him aside by issuing a subpoena in the name of the grand jury, now for nine tapes and other materials, a subpoena whose receipt in the early evening by Fred Buzhardt made the tapes potential evidence in a criminal proceeding.

Two days later, in a letter to Judge Sirica, Nixon wrote that the president was not subject to "compulsory process" from the courts and that it would be "inconsistent with the public interest and with the Constitutional position of the Presidency to make available" the nine recordings. However, Nixon volunteered to turn over the papers listed on the subpoena, two political memoranda; by offering these voluntarily, Nixon avoided complying with any part of the subpoena.

Next day, Sirica issued a "show cause" order requiring Nixon to explain why he should not be forced to comply with the grand jury subpoena. Thus the issue was joined and started on its way toward an ultimate showdown in the Supreme Court.

At the end of July the issue was complicated as Haldeman appeared before the Ervin committee and testified that under instructions from the president he had listened to two of the subpoenaed Nixon-Dean conversations in which he had also been a participant, and that he had done so well after he had resigned from the White House. He had even been allowed to take one of the tapes home overnight. The admission seemed to strengthen Cox's case. How could the president shield his tapes behind a claim of executive privilege if a private citizen could listen to one at home?

On August 7, the president's lawyers responded with Sirica's show cause order, contending that if Cox was able to compel Nixon to turn over the tapes, "the damage to the institution of the Presidency will be severe and irreparable." Cox struck back on August 13, stating that the president was not exempt "from the guiding principle that the public, in pursuit of justice, has a right to every man's evidence." These positions were reargued in person in front of Sirica on August 22, and a week later, Sirica called everyone into his courtroom to issue his decision.

The judge declared that Nixon must surrender the tapes, agreeing with Cox that "simply because it is the President of the United States who holds the evidence," the courts were not constrained from obtaining that evidence. However, also agreeing with Nixon's need to keep some materials shielded, Sirica ruled that the tape recordings would not go directly to the grand jury, but that he would review them *in camera*, and then turn over to the grand jury just those portions of the tapes that he thought were not covered by executive privilege.

"No court had ever before in our history compelled a President to produce documents that he had determined not to surrender," Nixon wrote of this decision in his 1978 memoir. "Because of the principle of separation of powers, a court can issue an order, but a President has a right—and some scholars would argue, a responsibility—not to obey that order if it infringes on the prerogatives of his independent branch of government. I felt then . . . that it was fully within my power to refuse to obey Sirica's ruling." It was only because of the "political reality of the Watergate situation" that he did not do so. Instead, he appealed.

Both Cox and Nixon appealed the decision. It took two weeks for the U.S. Court of Appeals for the District of Columbia to ask that the parties compromise. Perhaps lawyers for both sides could review the tapes and decide what would be forwarded to the grand jury. Despite three days of negotiations between Cox and the White House—during which Cox suggested that an outside, third party verify the tapes before they were submitted to the grand jury—no compromise could be reached, and the court was so informed on September 20. Shortly, the appellate court would issue a decision.

Nixon anticipated that the appellate decision would go against him, and decided it was time to start transcribing the tapes. Rose Mary Woods agreed to do it, and he sent her to Camp David with several machines and tapes. Nixon's plan, he later recalled in *RN*, was to offer typed summaries of the tapes "after national security discussions and other matters irrelevant to Watergate had been deleted." What happened during the attempts to transcribe the tapes will be discussed in detail in the following chapter.

As the president waited for the appellate court decision, he was occupied with other serious matters. He was aware that lawyers for Vice President Spiro Agnew were locked in a battle with Elliot Richardson and other Justice Department officials that would soon lead to Agnew's resignation. Back in August, when Nixon had first learned the nature and severity of the charges against Agnew—tax evasion, bribery, and extortion—the president had sent Haig to see Agnew, and Haig had suggested that the vice president resign. Agnew refused. In September, at Nixon's request, Assistant Attorney General Henry Petersen examined the evidence against Agnew and declared it airtight. Since Nixon was very poor at confronting people, he sent Haig and Buzhardt to convey Petersen's bad news to Agnew, and the vice president's lawyers responded by beginning a plea-bargaining process with Richardson. On October 10, Agnew had his resignation letter delivered, as required, to Secretary of State Henry Kissinger, while he himself stood in a Baltimore court and pleaded no contest to one charge of tax evasion.

A second serious matter for Nixon was the Yom Kippur War, which embroiled Israel and its Arab enemies during the second week of October 1973.

A third matter only lightly touched Nixon that week, but must have disturbed Haig. When Cox tried to pursue the Plumbers, an investigation that would inevitably trip over Moorer-Radford, Buzhardt complained to Richardson that Cox was edging into national security matters and must be constrained. Responding to the White House, Richardson went to Cox and forged an agreement: The Special Prosecutor would not move on any case involving national security without first consulting the attorney general.

Cox's interest in the Plumbers centered on what he saw as the complicity of three former presidential aides, Ehrlichman, Krogh, and Colson, in the Dr. Fielding office break-in. The prosecutors did not have Moorer-Radford in their sights, and there is no evidence that they even knew about it—but indictment of these three men on a matter having to do with the Plumbers might allow the prosecutors to peek through a keyhole and see things that might lead them to the military espionage. Moreover, since these three men were not expected to go down without a fight, they could be expected to raise as a defense the idea that what they had done was in the interests of national security, and in attempts to prove their point, might bring Moorer-Radford to the surface.

On October 11, the day after Agnew's resignation and amid the turmoil over the Arab-Israeli war, Cox announced that Egil Krogh had been indicted for perjury in the Dr. Fielding break-in. Krogh had told the grand jury he had known nothing about Hunt's and Liddy's travels to California.

"The Krogh indictment took Richardson completely by surprise and signaled the possible onset of a new crisis with the White House," James Doyle wrote in his memoir, *Not Above the Law*. Doyle, a newspaperman, was spokesman for the Special Prosecutor's office during the Watergate investigations. "Richardson thought he had a specific agreement with Cox that none of those cases involving the national security question would be moved to the indictment stage without prior notice to him. . . . Now Buzhardt was on the phone demanding an explanation."

In his office the next day, according to Doyle, Richardson admonished Cox for "a serious lapse," insisting that the Krogh indictment violated their understanding on national security cases. Cox, in turn, was "surprised and defensive," reminding his former student that their agreement did not include perjury cases. While national security might be a factor in the Dr. Fielding break-in, Cox said, it was not relevant to Krogh's having testified falsely to the grand jury. Richardson grew more philosophical, accepted Cox's explanation, and warned him that "we are heading into a difficult period." According to Doyle, Richardson mentioned to Cox the possibility that they might both be fired.

Later, in a newspaper story that discussed the events leading up to the Saturday Night Massacre—the firing of Cox and the resignation of Richardson—Woodward and Bernstein would cite unnamed sources as saying that Buzhardt had gone to the Justice Department and met with Cox and Richardson "to buttress his argument that national security interests were more important than bringing prosecution against Ehrlichman, Colson and Krogh in certain cases." Cox and Richardson were reported as "less than responsive" even though Buzhardt made "partial disclosure of the activities in question." In a small paragraph in that story, the reporters gave a clue as to what the Saturday Night Massacre had really been all about: "The sources said that Richardson's and Cox's unwillingness to take White House direction on these indictments *helped precipitate the confrontation*" that led to the Massacre. (Italics added for emphasis.)

On October 12, the same day that Cox and Richardson commiserated over the likelihood that both would be fired, the appellate court ruled that Nixon must turn over the tapes to Sirica because the president "is not above the law's commands." The 5–2 decision pointed out that Nixon had not invoked executive privilege when he let aides testify about the disputed conversations before the Ervin committee, and that, as Cox had argued, the tapes had become important evidence in grand jury proceedings concerning those aides. The president was given one week to appeal to the Supreme Court before he would have to hand over the tapes.

Later that day, Nixon had Haig inform House Minority Leader Gerald R. Ford that he was Nixon's choice to become the new vice president. Ford was willing to accept, and around six that evening the White House made the public announcement of Ford's nomination. The timing was a deliberate attempt to soften headlines about the appellate ruling. The following day, October 13, Nixon retreated to Camp David with his wife, his daughter Julie, and her husband, David Eisenhower.

It had been an incredible week for Nixon, who now had six days left in which to make an appeal to the Supreme Court or be forced to turn over the tapes to Sirica. In the seclusion of his mountain retreat, Nixon and his associates decided on a new strategy.

Nixon recalled in his memoir that "Fred Buzhardt suggested Senator John Stennis of Mississippi" as an outside, third party who could listen to the subpoenaed conversations, compare them to the actual recordings, and then submit a verified version of transcripts to Sirica. Here was a compromise that might satisfy everyone and avoid a confrontation in the Supreme Court. The choice of Stennis was attractive to Nixon, and even more so to Buzhardt and Haig. Stennis was seventy-two, a diehard Dixiecrat and the chairman of the Armed Services Committee. He often voted with the Republicans but was accorded respect by the Democrats because of his seniority. Buzhardt had been a protégé of Stennis' friend and fellow Dixiecrat, Senator Strom Thurmond, and Buzhardt knew Stennis well. In 1970, when Buzhardt had been nominated as general counsel of the Department of Defense, Stennis had swiftly moved the nomination through his committee and had lavished praise on Buzhardt. Haig had also worked closely with Stennis in recent years when the executive branch had sought to keep the legislative branch informed about military matters. The previous October, after Haig had been nominated by Nixon to become a full general, Stennis' committee had quickly approved the nomination.

James Doyle wrote in his memoir that

> Stennis had rigged many a committee hearing by stacking the witnesses in his favor, and he saw no harm in this. He would not deliberately rig this [tapes] case for Nixon, but he would be understanding and was likely to take Buzhardt's word on any doubts. . . . Stennis was a man with a well-deserved reputation for righteousness. Nobody in the Sen-

ate, and few in Washington public life would find it practical to oppose his choice. Yet he was seventy-two years old, and not well. . . . He had been shot in a mugging on January 30, had been near death, and did not return to his desk until September 5. He would rely on Buzhardt to handle the tedious and exhausting job of transcribing and was unlikely to demand that tapes be played over and over until he was sure of their contents.

Moreover, as critics would shortly point out, Stennis was partially deaf and therefore physically unsuited to the task of listening carefully to the tapes, four of which had been recorded in Nixon's EOB office, where a less sophisticated set of microphones produced sound quality that was noticeably muddier than recordings done of conversations in the Oval Office.

The proposition was personally put to Stennis by Nixon—no confrontation in this meeting—on Sunday, October 14, in a ten-minute chat at the White House. "He felt he could handle the job," Nixon wrote in *RN*, and Stennis agreed to verify the accuracy of some tape summaries.

Richardson was called to the White House on Monday and told by Haig and Buzhardt that the president would not go to the Supreme Court. Instead he would prepare his own transcripts, authenticate them, and then exercise his executive authority and fire Cox outright, thus mooting the case and ending the legal dispute over the tapes. A contemporary magazine article by Yale Law School Professor Alexander Bikel contended that Cox's actions amounted to the president suing himself, and thus Cox's suit had no legal standing and the president could fire him at any time. That "Bikel option" was offered Richardson as the rationale for firing Cox. But Elliot Richardson warned Haig and Buzhardt of what he had promised the Senate, and that if pressured to fire Cox, he would probably have to resign.

In this meeting, Buzhardt and Haig did not tell Richardson that the president wasn't going to "authenticate" the tapes himself or that Stennis would do it. All they did during the course of a tense two and a half hours was push for the firing of Cox. Only after Richardson returned to Justice around noon did Haig call to say that he had a compromise he was willing to run by the president if it was okay with Richardson. Haig would try to persuade Nixon to let Stennis review the tapes, and if Nixon agreed, maybe they wouldn't have to fire Cox after all.

Since the Stennis business had already been proposed and accepted by the president and the senator over the weekend, Haig's proposal,

James Doyle writes, "raises the possibility—considered a strong one by those who watched this process during the fateful week—that Alexander Haig deliberately misled Richardson, threatening the cataclysm, then seeming to back away to a far more moderate position as an 'accommodation' with Richardson."

Haig's stratagem worked, for Richardson leapt at a compromise that would allow both Cox and himself to continue in office. Once Haig learned that Richardson would bite at the bait, he closed the trap. There was a catch, he advised the attorney general in another call. The president had reluctantly agreed to allow Stennis to review the tapes, but in order for Cox to keep his job, the Special Prosecutor must promise not to seek any further tapes and documents from the White House beyond the recordings that Stennis would verify. If Cox refused to go along, Haig added, Richardson must agree to fire him.

Richardson couldn't say yes to that without some thought, and told Haig he'd get back to him. It was around two in the afternoon. Buzhardt and Haig drove to Capitol Hill to see Stennis, who told them that listening to all the tapes wasn't possible. Buzhardt assured Stennis that he would lift some of that burden, and, given that assurance, the senator now formally consented to the compromise.

Nixon had not given Stennis all the details and Haig and Buzhardt let the senator believe he was going to authenticate tapes for the Ervin committee. Neither Haig nor Buzhardt told him the dispute involved the Special Prosecutor and that the transcripts would go to Sirica. Stennis, a former judge, later claimed he wouldn't have agreed if he'd known the transcripts were for the federal court.

Attorney General Richardson, after conferring with his aides, told Haig in a 3:20 P.M. phone call that Stennis was acceptable, but that it was a mistake to try and prevent Cox from getting future tapes and that he could not agree to fire him if Cox asked for more tapes. Haig decided at that point not to press that demand, and told Richardson to come over and work out the details. Richardson did so, and tried to defuse the situation by focusing only on Stennis and putting aside the other issues. At that 4:00 P.M. meeting, Richardson later testified to the Senate, he made it clear to Haig that he would resign rather than fire Cox; he told Haig "there was no need to provoke that confrontation," and that there should be no linkage between what Richardson considered a reasonable compromise, the Stennis proposal, and Cox's right to ask for materials in the future.

The only thing Nixon heard from Haig that afternoon, he later wrote, was that "Richardson felt that the plan was good and reasonable . . . that Richardson was confident there would be no problem and that

Cox . . . would agree to the [Stennis] compromise." But Haig had distorted Richardson's position: The president wrote that Haig reported "Richardson's assurance that if Cox refused to accept the Stennis compromise, Richardson would support me in the controversy that was bound to ensue." And, Nixon added, "Richardson's resignation was something we wanted to avoid at all costs."

Richardson, of course, had *not* told Haig that he would support the president in any such controversy.

At six, Richardson met with Cox, who was skeptical about the Stennis idea. Richardson took the night to put it in written form, and produced a document that went to Buzhardt on Wednesday afternoon, October 17. Its most important phrase referred not to the tapes that Stennis would authenticate, but to the future. Any request by the Special Prosecutor "covering other tapes," the document said, "would be the subject of subsequent negotiation" between the White House and Cox. Buzhardt objected to the entire section that dealt with future requests on the grounds that it was irrelevant to the nine tapes subpoenaed by the grand jury. Richardson wasn't looking for a fight, and was looking for a way to narrow the issues and deal with them one at a time, so he agreed. By consenting to the removal from Richardson's proposal of any acknowledgment that the issue of further tapes and documents had been postponed, Richardson played into Haig's and Buzhardt's hands.

Concurrently that afternoon, Judge Sirica ruled that the Senate Watergate committee did not have legal standing to subpoena the tapes. That meant the lone battle for the tapes was now the confrontation between Cox and the White House.

Next day, Cox responded to the Richardson proposal. He didn't want an unnecessary confrontation with the president, but, he wrote, there were substantive problems. He rejected the idea of having Stennis or anyone else verify the president's transcripts, because "The public cannot be fairly asked to confide so difficult and responsible a task to any *one* man operating in secrecy, consulting only with the White House." Moreover, the proposal's "narrow scope" was a grave defect; unlike a court decision, it did not serve the function of "establishing the Special Prosecutor's entitlement to other evidence." Cox was determined to preserve his right to ask for more evidence later—just what Buzhardt and Haig wanted to quash.

In later testimony Cox recounted that he had asked Richardson why the White House was pressing so hard to make a Friday deadline. The negotiations were "far too important and far too serious for us to do it overnight." Surely if both parties asked for an extension the court would grant one, so that the president would have more time to file an appeal to the Supreme Court. Richardson responded that the White House was determined to settle the matter right then and there.

Richardson took Cox's written answer back to the White House at six on Thursday evening and took it up with Haig, Garment, Buzhardt, and Charles Alan Wright. All five men considered the response an outright rejection of the Stennis plan. According to Woodward and Bernstein in *The Final Days*, Haig said that if Cox refused to go along with the Stennis plan, he should be fired. Buzhardt, Garment, Wright, and Haig "were confident that the President could persuade the public of the reasonableness of such an action," Woodward and Bernstein wrote.

Richardson wasn't so confident. He saw large problems looming if Cox were to be fired, and objected to the suggestion that he and Henry Petersen could take over the investigation of Watergate once Cox was gone. Since Wright had been the most vocal proponent of the Stennis plan during this meeting, Richardson told him to try personally to sell it to Cox. Later that evening, Wright and Cox had a tense conversation. According to Cox's book, Wright presented him with a four-point ultimatum. One of the points was that Cox must agree not to subpoena any additional tapes or documents from the president. Wright's four points, Cox later declared, were intended for no other purpose than to "elicit rejection." According to Wright, there was no ultimatum and no demand that Cox give up the right to ask for other materials.

While Wright and Cox were maneuvering over the telephone, a grim Elliot Richardson was at home, writing out on a yellow legal pad a "Summary of Reasons Why I Must Resign." He wrote that while Cox had turned down a reasonable proposal, it could not be regarded as grounds for his dismissal, because the prosecutor was being asked to accept less than he had won from two courts. There was an absolute need for an independent prosecutor, but he himself would not have the requisite independence vis-à-vis "Buzhardt *et al.*" Richardson wrote that he was fundamentally loyal to the president and was by temperament a team player. He didn't understand the need for this confrontation, since, in his view, more cooperation with Cox could have reduced the problems. So, he summarized, because he had appointed Cox on the understanding that he would remove him only for "extraordinary improprieties," and since, Richardson wrote, Cox was not guilty of any wrongdoing, he could not remain in office if Cox was fired.

Next morning, Richardson shared his yellow-pad notes with his aides, who agreed with his stance, and gave the notes to his secretary to type up. He called Haig for a progress report on the Cox-Wright negotiations, and Haig said they were continuing. Should things break down, Richardson responded, he wanted to see the president. There could not have been a clearer signal to Haig that the attorney general was set to resign.

The letter Wright delivered to Cox that morning supported Cox's view of their previous night's tense conversation; it said the White House "could not accede . . . in any form" to Cox's demand that some method be devised for dealing with additional requests for evidence. Reading it, Cox immediately wrote back to Wright that he had promised the Senate to pursue all legal avenues to secure whatever evidence was required to do his job; that meant he could never accept an agreement that barred him from seeking further tapes and documents. "I cannot break my promise now," Cox concluded.

Haig must have realized when he read this letter that Cox was as good as gone, but he still tried to keep Richardson on board so long as it would not require retaining Cox. Since Richardson had agreed to the Stennis plan, Haig tried to see if he had a little wiggle room in which to get rid of Cox while retaining Richardson. He summoned Richardson to the White House by telling him that Cox had rejected Wright's offer and that the president was now ready to meet with Richardson.

The attorney general prepared to hand in his resignation, but when he arrived at the White House he was not ushered into the Oval Office. Rather, he was met by Haig, who suggested a completely new approach: They'd sidestep Cox and proceed with the Stennis plan, presenting it directly to Sirica and to the Ervin committee. The committee would want to agree because it had already lost its own court battle and was in no position to refuse an offer that gave it at least "verified" transcripts. If Elliot would only agree to this, Haig said, he'd try to convince the president not to fire Cox.

Richardson clung to this ray of hope only until he had read Cox's letter to Wright. It saddened and confused him—saddened, because he recognized that it would not be easy to convince Cox to go along with the Stennis plan; confused, because he didn't understand why the matter of future tape and document requests was even being discussed. Hadn't they taken that out of the picture earlier in the week? Richardson was not told that Wright had put it back into the picture in an attempt to force Cox to agree to something that would hamper him, or to resign.

Despite his confusion, Richardson continued his discussions with Buzhardt, Garment, and Wright while Haig supposedly went to try to convince the president not to fire Cox. The attorney general suggested that Wright send Cox yet another letter stating that the future access provision wasn't part of the Stennis proposal deal.

A missive from Wright did arrive at Cox's office a few hours later, but, as Richardson later testified, it was "not in the form I thought it was going to be written." In fact, Wright's letter did not separate the issues and suggest they'd deal with the troublesome one later; rather, it harshly stated an inflexible position: "The differences between us remain so great that no purpose would be served by further discussion."

Meanwhile, Haig was tricking Nixon. Rather than inform the president that Richardson would quit if Cox was barred from later being able to seek additional tapes or documents, Haig told Nixon that Richardson supported the prohibition against Cox getting free access to further material. He also manipulated Nixon into the belief that Richardson would stand by the White House in a showdown with Cox. In other words, Haig led Nixon to believe that the tapes request could be limited to just this first batch, that the issue of the tapes could then be disposed of entirely by firing Cox, all without Nixon's attorney general resigning.

To induce the president to believe this, Haig put responsibility for the proposal on Richardson. "Haig told me that Richardson had suggested as an alternative to firing Cox, putting what he called 'parameters' around him," Nixon later wrote. Those parameters "could include an instruction that he was forbidden to sue for any further presidential documents."

What was the purpose of all this chicanery? If Haig had informed the president that Richardson would quit if Cox was barred from later being able to seek additional tapes or documents, Haig would have run the risk of Nixon's leaving Cox in place, rather than facing the political consequences of Richardson's resignation. With Cox in place, the Special Prosecutor would have been free to pursue the leads that pointed to Haig's role in the NSC wiretapping and, more importantly, to Moorer-Radford.

Here was Nixon, once again about to enter on a disastrous course of action on the basis of an aide telling him that the attorney general of the United States had recommended that very course. And once again, it wasn't true. Of course, citing the name of Elliot Richardson did not have the same power with Nixon as the citing of John Mitchell, but Haig, no less than Dean, understood how to maneuver Richard Nixon into action.

Haig then went to work on selling the Stennis plan to Richardson, misleading Richardson into believing that the Stennis proposal would not automatically be linked to any limitation on future access to tapes and documents. A key element in keeping Richardson at bay was to bring Ervin and Baker on board by means of the Stennis proposal. The two senators were approached with the idea; each was out of town when reached, and flew back to confer with the president, Haig, and Wright in the Oval Office at 5:30 P.M. on Friday, October 19.

Ervin had not been told that Cox had essentially rejected the Stennis proposal, and said later that in the meeting, when he tried to inquire about Cox's position, the subject had been changed. Ervin also asserted that in the meeting he was promised verbatim transcripts, not the third-person summaries that the White House later said would be issued. In what was becoming a recognizable tactic of wrapping the flag around certain notions in order to conceal them, Haig told the senators that it was important to agree to this compromise and relieve the president of the matter of the tapes so that he could have a "strong hand" in dealing with the crisis in the Middle East. Ervin and Baker agreed to recommend the Stennis plan to the full Watergate committee.

Their agreement in hand, Haig revealed the real White House position to Richardson. He telephoned the attorney general to read him a letter from the president that was already on its way. In it, Nixon mentioned that Baker and Ervin had consented to the Stennis compromise as a prelude to telling the attorney general that Nixon was taking actions "to bring to an end the controversy over the so-called Watergate tapes." Nixon would allow "a limited breach of Presidential confidentiality" in the Stennis compromise. However, "as part of these actions, I am instructing you to direct Special Prosecutor Archibald Cox . . . that he is to make no further attempts by judicial process to obtain tapes, notes, or memoranda of Presidential conversations. I regret the necessity of intruding, to this very limited extent, on the independence that I promised you with regard to Watergate when I announced your appointment."

Richardson was stunned and angry, because this was a direct order and he had thought that everything was still under discussion. He said testily, "Al, given the history of our relationship on this, I would have thought that you would have consulted me prior to sending any letter." Haig said that he'd twice tried to convince the president of Richardson's objections, but that the president wouldn't budge, and that the letter was all the president's doing. According to Nixon's memoir, Haig walked into the Oval Office and told the president that Richardson had made a "tepid" complaint about some of the terms of the deal, but also assured Nixon, "it's no big problem."

Haig had perfected a double switch reminiscent of the lies of John

Dean: He had used the name of Richardson to sell his own bad idea to Nixon, and then used the name of Nixon to sell it back to Richardson.

The real story of the Saturday Night Massacre is not yet through, but mention must be made of the version of the event painted in *The Final Days*, the book that so clearly reflects the viewpoints of Buzhardt and Haig.

In that version, an embattled Haig is portrayed as merely the messenger to an unyielding Nixon. There is a crucial scene that purports to take place at the White House while on October 18 Elliot Richardson is at home pouring his conscience onto a yellow legal pad. Buzhardt and Haig were conferring with Nixon, "late that night." They were sure that Cox would resign rather than accept the compromise, and that Richardson would accept the compromise, but "Nixon again bore down on the question of access to the other tapes. The line had to be clearly drawn. The matter had to be settled. Now."

"Buzhardt suggested that the White House remain silent on the issue," and when Buzhardt continued to press, Nixon "blew up." He wanted the access to the tapes issue settled forever, and Buzhardt was chagrined because "by asserting that the special prosecutor could not subpoena additional evidence, they were playing into Cox's hands, laying credible grounds for his defiance—instead of his resignation. And they were probably throwing Richardson into Cox's arms."

No such meeting ever took place, according to the official presidential log of October 18, 1973. Nixon spoke briefly by phone with Haig three times that evening, the last conversation at 8:00 P.M., but did not meet with him. Moreover, the presidential logs do not show Nixon meeting with Buzhardt at all during that entire day or evening. The meeting was probably fabricated to cover Haig's and Buzhardt's roles in pushing Cox and Richardson toward the ultimate confrontation with the White House. This meeting was even used in the Woodward and Bernstein book as a handy way to explain to Richardson on the following morning why the prohibition against future tapes had again crept into the proposed agreement with Cox: "Buzhardt said [to Richardson] that it had been added Thursday night at the direction of the President. They [Haig and Buzhardt] had no choice."

Having received the president's letter, Richardson read it to Cox over the phone. The attorney general made it clear to his former law professor that he was not personally issuing the instructions covered in the letter, merely informing him of the contents.

Cox, Richardson, and the White House all got ready to issue

statements. Richardson's was going to say that he endorsed the Stennis plan but disclaimed any responsibility for the prohibition on future access to tapes and documents.

Haig, who had no reason to want Richardson—as opposed to Cox—out of office, then engineered one last attempt to see if Richardson would stay without Cox. Haig apparently gambled that if Nixon announced the Stennis compromise first, and said that it had Baker's and Ervin's endorsement, then Richardson's desire to keep his job might lead him to stay on board. So at 8:15 P.M. on Friday night, reporters were handed a statement issued over the president's name. Because the prolonged crisis of the tapes could tempt foreign adversaries to take advantage of the political turmoil in the United States, the statement said, the president had decided to take action "to bring the issue of Watergate tapes to an end." It went on to say that Cox had rejected a reasonable compromise, that the Stennis proposal had the endorsement of Baker and Ervin, and that "there would be no further attempt" by Cox to obtain more tapes or documents.

In a sense the statement worked, because Richardson didn't release his own. One more attempt to stiff-arm him occurred at 8:30 P.M., when White House counselor Bryce Harlow called Richardson, saying that at Haig's instruction he had been informing all cabinet members of the Stennis compromise. Richardson complained to Harlow that Haig had treated him shabbily. Harlow didn't tell Richardson that the president had issued a statement, but Richardson found out from Cox when they spoke at around 9:00 P.M. It was then that Richardson decided to scrap his own statement, evidently on the grounds that since the president hadn't mentioned in his statement any orders given to Richardson, there was no need for it.

An hour later, at home, Richardson received a call from Haig, who said he'd been told that Richardson felt he'd been shabbily treated. Richardson responded, "Well, I'm home now. I've had a drink. Things look a little better and we'll see where we go from here." That was quite a reasonable thing to say under the circumstances, but Haig would later use it against Richardson.

In the morning, Richardson still hoped to find a way to keep his job. He sent a letter to Nixon stating that while he'd consented to try his best to get Cox to adopt the Stennis compromise, he had not agreed at any time to accept a prohibition on Cox's access to additional materials. "Any future situation," Richardson wrote, should be "approached on the basis of the precedent established" by the Stennis plan.

Cox's own press statement was now ready, and he delivered it at a news conference held in the National Press Club at one on Saturday afternoon, followed by a long question and answer session with reporters. He said he would not follow the president's order. He maintained that he was not trying to be defiant and that he was "certainly not out to get the President of the United States," but, he added, "it is my duty as special prosecutor, as an officer of the court, and as the representative of the grand jury, to bring to the court's attention what seems to me to be noncompliance with the court's order."

The conference was televised, and at 2:07 P.M., when it was over, Len Garment telephoned Richardson from Haig's office. They'd been watching the news conference, and Garment explained that the president was deeply involved in trying to defuse the crisis in the Middle East, and that Kissinger was in Moscow and ought not to be forced into delicate discussions with the Soviets just as the political situation was exploding back home. Would Richardson agree to first fire Cox and then to resign if he felt he had to do so? No, Richardson told Garment. He would not fire Cox.

Haig's game was up. Richardson would not stay on board—as Haig had assured the president that he would, an assurance Haig knew to be false. Haig called Richardson himself at 2:20. The conversation was brief. Cox was in defiance of a presidential order and must be dismissed.

"Well, I can't do that," Richardson responded. "I guess I had better come over and resign." At 4:30 P.M., Richardson was escorted into the Oval Office and found an angry Nixon, accompanied by Haig. Nixon implored Richardson to hold his own resignation until the Middle East crisis had passed, but Richardson told him he felt he had no choice but to resign now. According to Nixon's memoirs, at this moment Richardson thanked the president "for being such a good friend and for having honored him with so many high appointments," including the cabinet secretaryships of Health, Education and Welfare, Defense, and Justice. Richardson and Nixon parted cordially.

"The deed is done," Richardson told his aides when he returned to the Justice Department. Moments later, a call came from Haig to William Ruckelshaus, Richardson's first deputy, and Haig used the same reference to the Middle East crisis and the same suggestion that Ruckelshaus fire Cox and then wait a week before resigning, if he felt resignation was necessary.

Ruckelshaus told Haig that if things were that bad, why didn't the White House wait a week to get rid of Cox.

"Your commander-in-chief has given you an order," Haig snapped. "You have no alternative."

Ruckelshaus refused, and handed the phone to Robert Bork, the solicitor general who by the abdications of the two men above him had just become the acting attorney general. Haig said he was sending a limousine to bring Bork to the White House.

When it arrived at Justice, the government limousine contained Garment and Buzhardt, as well as a driver. Bork rode the few blocks to the White House and went in to see Haig. When the general started to give his now-standard speech about the international crisis, Bork interrupted and said, "You need not go on. I have made up my mind to carry out the directive." After a brief meeting with Nixon, Bork signed a letter to Cox announcing his dismissal. Later, Bork would say he did this because he believed the president had a right to discharge any executive branch employee if he wanted to do so, and to prevent "mass departures" by other Justice officials that would have left the department "in a chaotic condition and badly crippled."

At 8:22 P.M. Ron Ziegler appeared in the White House press room to make the announcement of what would shortly be dubbed the Saturday Night Massacre: He said that Cox had been fired, Richardson and Ruckelshaus had resigned, and that the office of the Watergate Special Prosecution Force had been abolished. The investigation of Watergate, Ziegler said, would revert back to the Justice Department.

As Ziegler was reading the announcement, Haig ordered the FBI to seal the downtown Washington offices of the Watergate Special Prosecution Force as well as the Justice Department offices of Richardson and Ruckelshaus. By 9:05 P.M., the first agents were in place to guard the doors and prevent anything from being removed from these offices.

Members of Cox's staff converged on their offices late Saturday night to learn that they were not even allowed to remove personal belongings. When James Doyle tried to leave with pictures of his family and other items that had hung on his wall, he was detained by the lead agent, with whom he had become friendly because the agent was the liaison between the FBI and Cox's office. Doyle was stopped near the door with a pile of photos in his arms; atop the pile was a copy of the Declaration of Independence. Doyle told his friend the agent, "Just stamp it 'VOID' and let me take it home."

As news of the firing and resignations spread through print and television reports over the weekend, tens of thousands of letters, telegrams, and phone calls expressing outrage at the president's actions poured into the White House and into offices on Capitol Hill. Republicans as well as Democrats in Congress condemned Nixon's handling of the entire matter, and on Tuesday, October 23, more than twenty bills calling for impeachment inquiries into Nixon's conduct were introduced into the House of Representatives. Shortly, the House approved a $1 million allocation to pursue the matter of impeachment.

In one single maneuver, Watergate had been escalated from a political crisis to a matter in which the president was perceived as actively and continually attempting to subvert the Constitution, to the detriment of the American people. Many of those who had been willing to give Nixon some slack on Watergate, who had seen him as a president submerged in a political mess because of bad advice, now judged him as inept, disdainful of the public, and unfit to rule.

Nixon was shocked. In his memoir, he wrote that he "had been prepared for a major and adverse reaction," but was surprised by the "ferocious intensity" of the public condemnation. Privately, he railed against the wrong target—what he saw as the perfidy of Elliot Richardson. The public quickly lionized the former attorney general for having refused to dishonor his commitment to Congress, which incensed both Nixon and the man who had actually engineered the disaster, Alexander Haig. The general would shortly leak stories to the press that Richardson was a drunkard, a man who had deserted while under fire, a spineless man who had misled Nixon into a debacle.

On Tuesday the twenty-third, as the twenty bills of inquiry about impeachment were being introduced into the House, Nixon met with Haig, Buzhardt, and Garment. At two that afternoon Wright was scheduled to appear in Sirica's courtroom and make arguments for the Stennis proposal. Could they still go ahead with that plan now that the country seemed in virtual revolt against the White House? Nixon and his advisers decided they had no choice but to relent.

Nixon did much more than relent—he made a virtual capitulation. That afternoon Wright informed a startled Sirica and a hushed courtroom that the president would comply after all. The tapes would be delivered to Sirica *in camera*. "This president does not defy the law," Wright declared.

Had Nixon complied earlier, he might have been praised as a president who upheld the law even when it wasn't working in his favor, a cooperative president who had fearlessly allowed a member of his own executive branch, the Special Prosecutor, to sue him in court. The matter of the request for the tapes might have burnished Nixon's image, not tarnished it, at this stage of the drama—but manipulations by Haig had obviated that possibility. He had fed the president wrong information, especially regarding the consequences of potential courses of action, so that even if the final decision can be argued to have been

Nixon's alone, it can equally be argued that he did not have all the facts and possible ensuing scenarios properly before him when he made it.

Did Haig, who after all was a military man and not a seasoned political advisor, simply not understand in his haste to be rid of Cox the political consequences of the Saturday Night Massacre? Was Haig's desire to be rid of Cox so great that he did not care? Or, is it possible that Haig knew exactly what he was doing?

Nixon consoled himself, as he later wrote, with the thought that "at least these tapes might finally prove that Dean had lied in his testimony against me."

Three days later he made another concession. Even though the press statement of Saturday night had said the Special Prosecutor's office would be abolished, public sentiment had now made it imperative to eat those words, too, and find another man for the job. In a new statement, Nixon said that Acting Attorney General Bork would appoint a new prosecutor, who would have "independence" and would enjoy "total cooperation from the executive branch" because "it is time for those who are guilty to be prosecuted, and for those who are innocent to be cleared."

Bork would make the appointment, but Haig would find and instruct the man. Working from a list of names prepared by his friend Morris Liebman, a well-connected Chicago lawyer whom he knew from his years in the Johnson Administration, Haig quickly focused on a Houston attorney who seemed to embody the qualities Haig wanted the new prosecutor to have. Leon Jaworski was a nominal Democrat who had participated in some matters that smacked of liberalism but who was solidly conservative on national security issues. After the war, Jaworski had worked with the government on war crimes trials, for which he had obtained a high security clearance that was never rescinded. Jaworski had successfully defended Vice President Lyndon Johnson in 1960 against a legal challenge that Johnson had been improperly on the Texas ballot as both a candidate for the Senate and for the vice presidency. In 1962 he'd been appointed by Attorney General Robert Kennedy to prosecute Mississippi Governor Ross Barnett, who had blocked black student James Meredith from admission to the University of Mississippi. Later, when Johnson became president, he had appointed Jaworski to several federal commissions.

In 1973 Jaworski was a senior partner in a huge Houston law firm and was a recent past president of the American Bar Association. Cox had been a legal scholar; Jaworski was a top-flight trial lawyer, a man accustomed to making practical decisions. When he had prosecuted Ross Barnett he had received hate mail and abuse from some of his associates, and had endured both because, he later said, he considered the assignment "a call to duty."

Haig used the same appeal to Jaworski's sense of duty when he telephoned the lawyer on October 30. Jaworski initially said no, and allowed that he'd already turned down the job when sounded out by an assistant to Richardson the previous May.

There are two versions of what happened between Haig and Jaworski, one expressed by Jaworski himself in his memoir, *The Right and the Power*, and a second, which can be considered Haig's version, from *The Final Days*. Jaworski recalled that in the conversation Haig had said, "we can give you independence. . . . We'll find a way to get you what you want." Upon hearing this, Jaworski commented, "I had felt the urgency in his voice at the beginning of our conversation. Now I sensed what might be desperation." So Jaworski agreed to fly to Washington to see Haig, but made no promises. Haig sent an Air Force plane and brought him to the capital the next day. They met in Haig's office, and the general turned on the charm; almost as an afterthought, Jaworski remembered, Haig informed him that he was high on the list for appointment to the Supreme Court. Jaworski punctured that balloon by saying such a position had been discussed with him during the Johnson administration, and he hadn't been interested in it then and wasn't now.

" 'I'm putting the patriotic monkey on your back,' " Jaworski remembered Haig as saying. " 'The situation in this country is almost revolutionary. Things are about to come apart. The only hope of stabilizing the situation is for the President to be able to announce that someone in whom the country has confidence has agreed to serve.' "

The Woodward and Bernstein version of the event is pretty much the same, except for one key sentence in which the authors, too, tried to convey what Haig had said to Jaworski: "Only Jaworski had the personal and professional stature; he was tough, independent-minded and not politically ambitious; he knew and understood the presidency, and he understood what national security and state secrets were."

In other words, Haig wanted to have a man who would answer properly to an appeal not to look into certain matters too deeply—for instance, the Plumbers and the still secret Moorer-Radford affair. As a man who had had high security clearances, Jaworski understood what they meant, why they were employed, and could be expected to be sympathetic to appeals based on national security.

The Woodward and Bernstein reconstruction of this concern of Haig's is echoed in the words Nixon later wrote about the Jaworski appointment in his own memoir: Haig had assured Nixon that Jaworski "would see to it that the staff [of the Special Prosecutor's office] limited its activity to relevant and proper areas."

After promising Jaworski that he could not be dismissed without a supporting consensus of House and Senate leaders from both parties, including the ranking members of the House and Senate Judiciary committees, and telling him that he would be allowed to sue the president in court, and receiving assurance from Jaworski that under those circumstances he would seriously consider the job, Haig went in to tell the president.

A few moments later he came back out, looking, as Jaworski later wrote, "like a salesman on the verge of 'closing a deal.'" Haig, accompanied by Bork and Attorney General Designate William B. Saxbe, along with Buzhardt, Garment, Laird, and Harlow, urged Jaworski to accept.

When Jaworski accepted, and the announcement was made the following day, November 1, Haig was both relieved and what Woodward and Bernstein later described as "exultant." Now he had a Special Prosecutor who would pursue Nixon with no less vigor than Cox had done, and with a great deal more latitude—but he also had a Special Prosecutor who, when approached by a properly couched appeal to patriotism, could be pushed to stay out of areas that were problems for Alexander Haig.

22

THE EIGHTEEN-AND-A-HALF-MINUTE GAP

AS Haig called Jaworski on October 30, his associate Fred Buzhardt appeared in Judge Sirica's chambers, together with lawyers from the Special Prosecutor's office who were now working directly for Justice. The court meeting was to establish procedures for the transfer of the tapes. Buzhardt informed Sirica and the prosecutors that two of the nine subpoenaed recordings did not exist. One was a four-minute telephone call between Nixon and Mitchell that took place on the evening of June 20, 1972, three days after the break-in. The second was Nixon's fifty-five-minute meeting with John Dean on Sunday night, April 15, 1973, that took place just after Nixon had learned that Dean was talking to federal prosecutors.

Sirica scheduled a meeting in open court for the next day to deal with this alarming matter. In testimony from a series of witnesses over the next several days, the inquiry revealed that the taping system had been run in a cavalier fashion. It was not clear when certain tapes had been removed and then returned to storage; a Secret Service agent, asked on the stand how the recordings were logged, produced a brown piece of paper seemingly torn from a paper bag, with markings on it.

360

Each spool of tape lasted for six hours, and sometimes on weekends a reel ran out and was not immediately replaced. That, evidently, was what had happened to the April 15 recording; the tape had run out when Nixon and Dean met at 9:17 P.M., and since that happened to have been a Sunday night, there had been no Secret Service agent on duty to change the reel. As for the June 20 call, Buzhardt explained to the court that it had been made from a telephone in the residence quarters of the White House that had not been connected to the recording system.

Steve Bull disclosed to the court on November 2 that he had learned that the April 15 tape did not exist a month earlier, on September 29, when he had looked for it in order to give it to Rose Mary Woods to transcribe at Camp David. Bull also testified that he had obtained twenty-six of the tapes for Nixon in early June, and that the president had reviewed some of them in preparation for Dean's Senate testimony. On June 25, Nixon had even ordered one of the tapes to be flown to him in San Clemente; when no courier flight was available, Bull testified, Buzhardt had listened to it at Haig's request.

These revelations became the headlines of Saturday, November 3, just two days after the announcement of the selection of Jaworski to be the new Special Prosecutor.

It was November of 1973. A year earlier, Nixon had won reelection in a landslide, carrying every state except Massachusetts as well as more than 60 percent of the popular vote. Now, polls showed that 60 percent of the American people felt he was not capably handling the presidency. Nixon escaped the headlines by sailing with his friends Abplanalp and Rebozo aboard Rebozo's yacht. Back on land, *The New York Times*, *Time* magazine, and even the longtime Nixon loyalist *Detroit News* ran editorials urging that, as a public service, Nixon resign. "That weekend in Florida," Nixon later wrote, "was a new low point for me personally."

A strange thing happened that weekend. Buzhardt and Garment flew down to Florida, checked into a hotel near the president's estate, and went to see the boss. Nixon was firming his resolve and looking for ways to rehabilitate his image. The two lawyers had another notion in mind.

The Final Days opens with a scene of Buzhardt and Garment flying to Key Biscayne, convinced that after six months of losing battles with the Congress, the courts, and the Special Prosecutor, Nixon must resign, and they must advise him to do just that. Woodward and Bernstein write that this trip was one Al Haig did not endorse.

There is a factual error in the Woodward and Bernstein account, but beyond that, the issue is the motivation of Buzhardt and Garment. Since May, the two lawyers had cleared their every move with Haig, and it defies logic that they would have made this trip without his permission or cognizance. In the Woodward-Bernstein version, the lawyers arrived and made their recommendation to a stunned Haig. Fighting his friends tooth and nail, Haig insisted that Nixon couldn't quit because Gerald Ford hadn't yet been confirmed. And Haig wouldn't even let the lawyers see the president in person, because, according to Woodward and Bernstein, he "knew that Nixon would reject the suggestion out of hand." Rather, on Sunday, he told Nixon only that the lawyers had come to Florida and why they wanted to see them. "He reassured the President that the lawyers were not doubting his innocence—only his chances to survive," and he assured Nixon that the recommendation belonged to Buzhardt and Garment, that he himself did not concur in it, and "did not wish his own position to be misunderstood." Then Haig conveyed to the lawyers that Nixon would not see them at all.

The factual error in this account is an assertion that Buzhardt had not yet listened to any of the tapes. Two witnesses, Bull and a Secret Service agent, had just recently testified in court that at Haig's request Buzhardt on June 25 had listened to the tape that no courier plane could be found to transport to San Clemente, and in a week, Buzhardt would verify that to the court. But the Woodward-Bernstein account is written in such a way as to insist that Buzhardt didn't hear any of the tapes until a much later date. We will see later in the chapter the reason for making this appear to be so.

Nixon told his press secretary, Ron Ziegler, that having reached the low point he was now prepared for the ascent. It was going to be "a turning point for our approach to dealing with Watergate," he later wrote. " 'We will take some desperate and strong measure,' I told Ziegler, 'and this time there is no margin for error.' " He planned a televised speech for November 7, precisely one year after he'd been reelected, to launch Operation Candor. He would display not the wounded president but the man who had come back from many previous political defeats and who would once more rise from the ashes. The speech would be followed by ten days of "bridge-building" breakfast meetings and private chats with hundreds of Democrats and Republicans in Congress, and a swing through the South to trumpet the message that the president was still on the job and fighting for the country.

* * *

This, then, was the setting for one of the more curious episodes in the history of Watergate, the eighteen-and-a-half-minute gap in a taped conversation. The gap has usually been attributed to a mistake on the part of Nixon's personal secretary Rose Mary Woods, and/or to a deliberate attempt by a mechanically clumsy president to erase information detrimental to him. But there was a more sinister aspect to the affair than has previously been understood, and it involves Haig and Buzhardt and an especially well-timed and dramatic revelation by Deep Throat.

Back on September 28, anticipating that the appellate court would rule that the tapes must be turned over, Nixon had asked Haig to arrange for Rose Mary Woods to go to Camp David and transcribe the subpoenaed conversations. Woods was a particularly good choice for this task because she knew intimately the president's patterns of speech, and also knew most of the voices on the recordings—those of Haldeman, Ehrlichman, and other counselors. Fiercely loyal to Nixon, she could be counted on to delete the expletives and the scatological characterizations that sometimes dotted their chatter, not to be shocked by the conversations, and to keep silent about their contents. To help with the technical arrangements, Haig turned to John Bennett, the deputy presidential assistant whom Haig had appointed custodian of the recordings in July.

The next day, Woods and Steve Bull drove to Camp David carrying eight tapes and three Sony tape recorders provided by Bennett. In the privacy of rustic Dogwood Cabin, Woods began what she soon discovered would be a long and painstaking weekend of listening and typing. She spent twenty-nine hours just on the first item listed on the Special Prosecutor's subpoena, the June 20, 1972, meeting in the president's EOB office attended at various times by Nixon, Ehrlichman, and Haldeman, a meeting that lasted from 10:30 A.M. to nearly noon. As pointed out earlier, the quality of the recordings taken from the EOB office was less satisfactory than those recorded in the Oval Office.

The president was at Camp David that weekend and came in to check on his secretary's progress. She told him it was slow going because she had to replay sections of the tape over and over to get an accurate account. Nixon himself put on the headphones and listened for about five minutes. "At first all I could hear was a complete jumble," he recalled in his memoir. "Gradually I could make out a few words, but at times the rattling of a cup or the thump of a hand on the desk would obliterate whole passages." The Oval Office tapes that he had personally listened to back in June had been much easier to understand, he told Woods, and then left the cabin after sympathizing about her arduous task.

Bull had a problem, too, that weekend. He was to locate the conversations called for in Cox's subpoena on the correct six-hour tape reels, and cue them to the proper beginning spots to ready them for Woods. He found the June 20 EOB tape, but could not match up the conversation on the reel with the subpoena list. The list asked for one conversation among the participants, and there had been two on the morning of June 20, one between Nixon and Ehrlichman, and a second immediately thereafter between Nixon and Haldeman.

Haig phoned the cabin on the morning of September 29 to see how the work was going, and Bull told him he simply could not find the one long conversation referred to on the subpoena. Haig called Buzhardt, who had remained in Washington, and explained the situation. Buzhardt made a judgment, which Haig then passed to Woods, who typed a note that she gave to Bull. The note later became part of the documentary evidence assembled by the House Judiciary Committee. It reads, in full: "Cox was a little bit confused in his request re the meeting on June 20th. It says Ehrlichman Haldeman meeting—what he wants is the segment on June 20 from 10:25 to 11:20 with John Ehrlichman alone. Al Haig."

Bull promptly went back to his search, and it was then that he discovered that two of the other subpoenaed conversations were missing; he passed the information to Haig.

The entire crew returned to the White House on Monday, October 1. Woods had still not finished transcribing the first conversation, but back at her White House office she now had a more convenient mechanical setup. The Secret Service had supplied her with a Uher 5000 recorder that included a foot pedal for easy operation.

Just after two that afternoon, she rushed into Nixon's EOB office, visibly upset and saying, "I have made a terrible mistake." After completing her work on the Ehrlichman conversation, she told Nixon, she had forwarded the tape to make sure that she had indeed transcribed all of that section. As she was doing so, a call came in on her office phone and she had a conversation of four or five minutes. When she hung up and went back to work on the tape, she was rudely greeted by a shrill buzzing sound. A section of the Haldeman conversation had been wiped out.

Later, Woods would reconstruct her mistake for a court hearing. She stated that she must have pushed the "record" button on the machine rather than the "stop" button, while unintentionally resting her foot on the pedal throughout her phone call, an action that kept the machine running and, in effect, recording noise over the previously recorded conversation.

Nixon calmed Woods and told her the mistake was not of consequence because Buzhardt had told him that the Haldeman portion was not among the subpoenaed tapes. Haig called Buzhardt, who reconfirmed that the Haldeman conversation was not on Cox's list, and Nixon was relieved.

He should not have rested easy, because Buzhardt was at the very least plain wrong. The counsel had been in continuous touch with Cox since the subpoena had been served, and was in possession of a memo from Cox, dated August 13, that clarified the grand jury subpoena and made it plain that what he expected was Nixon's conversation with "John D. Ehrlichman and H.R. Haldeman in his Old Executive Office Building [OEOB] office on June 20, 1972 from 10:30 a.m. until approximately 12:45 p.m." Any lingering doubt that both conversations were sought was removed by the additional statement in Cox's memo that "Ehrlichman and *then* Haldeman went to see the President" that morning (italics added for emphasis). Moreover, Buzhardt had also had his alarm bells rung on the matter of the subpoenaed tapes by the news from Steve Bull that two of the conversations couldn't be located. That he reassured Nixon a second time as to the Haldeman conversation's irrelevance suggests that Buzhardt either didn't look at Cox's explanatory August 13 memo, or that he deliberately ignored it. Error of omission or commission?

When Bennett took the stand in Sirica's courtroom on November 6 and described his custodianship of the recordings, his role in providing the tapes to Bull for the trip to Camp David, and so on, the issue was the missing two conversations. The next day, November 7, when Bennett returned to the stand, he told the court that he'd had a talk the previous evening with Rose Mary Woods during which she complained of an unexpected "gap" in one of the tapes she was reviewing for the president.

But this wasn't the gap in the June 20 conversation that she had inadvertently caused. It was a different tape, which as it would turn out had no gap. Woods hadn't mentioned the gap in the June 20 tape to Bennett, but had told Bennett that she'd been reviewing a tape that hadn't even been subpoenaed, an April 16, 1973, Nixon-Dean meeting. "I think she was puzzled," Bennett testified. "The tape was on the machine. She said, 'I've got a gap in this.' " Two days earlier, Bennett told the court, he'd given Woods a new batch of six tapes and had said that the president wanted her to listen to that particular Nixon-Dean conversation and that it was among those reels somewhere.

Rose Mary Woods was called to the stand the next day. She said she had checked the tape and had been mistaken and that there was no gap in that tape. When cross-examined, she made clear that all she had meant by the word "gap" was a missing conversation. With that, the inquiry into this particular gap was settled, and the hearing went on to consider other matters. But by raising the specter of one gap, Bennett had opened up the possibility that the still-secret four-to-five-minute erasure on the June 20 Haldeman tape would shortly be uncovered in the court hearing. That, of course, would be damaging both to Woods and to Nixon.

Meanwhile, Bennett's testimony was the occasion for some curious doings at the *Washington Post*.

There were two stories on the front page of the *Post* on November 8, 1973, the day on which Woods testified. Under the headline TAPES HAVE PUZZLING "GAP" were two articles. One, under the subhead NIXON AIDE TESTIFIES, was the straight news account of Bennett's court testimony on the previous day, in which he had quoted Rose Mary Woods about a gap that puzzled her. The second, situated next to the first, was under the subhead PARTS "INAUDIBLE."

This second story was written by Bernstein and Woodward, and said that "portions of the seven White House tapes" that Nixon was to turn over to Sirica "are 'inaudible' and thus will probably fail to definitively answer questions about Mr. Nixon's role" in Watergate. Quoting "White House sources" to whom the reporters had talked over the past three days, the story said the tapes were marred by " 'gaps in conversations,' 'unevenness,' 'excessive background noise,' 'periods of silence,' and 'cut-ins and cut-outs during conversation.' " The article stated flatly that "there is serious concern among the President's aides and advisers that the latest problems regarding the tapes will further strain the credibility of the White House." For instance, the reporters quoted a "high-ranking presidential adviser" as saying, "This town is in such a state that everybody will say, 'They've doctored the tapes.' " This same official had "made clear he rejected that notion."

Two paragraphs down, the reporters quoted a source who clearly did anything but reject the doctoring notion:

Of five sources who confirmed that difficulties have risen concerning the quality of the tapes, one said the problems "are of a suspicious nature" and "could lead someone to conclude that the tapes have been tampered with." According to this source, conversation on some of the tapes appears to have been erased—either inadvertently or otherwise—or obliterated by the injection of background noise. Such background noise could be the result of either poorly functioning equipment, erasure or purposeful injection, the same source said. The four other sources disputed that there is anything suspicious about the deficiencies and insisted the tapes are marred only by technical problems that can be satisfactorily explained in court.

Who was the one source who believed that an effort might be under way to destroy evidence? Later, in *All the President's Men*, the authors of the article revealed that it was Deep Throat. Sometime in the first week of November 1973, Woodward initiated a meeting with his source in the underground garage, and received startling information: "Deep Throat's message was short and simple: One or more of the tapes contained deliberate erasures."

Deliberate erasures?

At the time of the *Post*'s two articles, as the later admission in *All the President's Men* makes clear, Woodward was apprised of erasures at least a week ahead of the moment at which an eighteen-and-a-half-minute gap in a tape would be discovered at the White House. Concurrently with the publication of the article, Judge Sirica had Rose Mary Woods on the stand and was investigating a tape gap. And Sirica could be expected to read the paper, especially if an article about problems with the tapes was on the front page under the byline of the reporters who had the best sources about Watergate. The hope may have been that Sirica would go more forcefully into the tape gap with Woods, and uncover the real gap, or perhaps that by focusing on the issue of tape gaps Sirica would be pushed to order that more tapes be turned over to the court, thereby further damaging Nixon.

At the point in time when Deep Throat told Woodward about "deliberate erasures," the first week of November 1973, five or at the most six people in the White House knew or could have known about a possible gap in a tape. They were: Nixon, Woods, Bull, Haig, Buzhardt, and perhaps Bennett. Those who knew about a gap also knew that Woods had not made a deliberate erasure. In their book, Woodward and Bernstein say that following Deep Throat's tip they called four sources in the White House who said there was nothing suspicious about the deficiencies on the tape—and then the reporters added some information that had not been in their earlier article: The four Bernstein sources knew nothing at all about any erasure. The article also had made clear that Bernstein's other four sources disagreed with the one who labeled the erasures "suspicious." Woodward and Bernstein's sources had heard through the grapevine that the tapes were of poor quality. The book also confirmed that the source of the remark about the gaps being of "a suspicious nature" and possibly leading "someone to conclude that the tapes had been tampered with" was the same Deep Throat.

Their article had not said their source had called the erasures deliberate, just "suspicious"—but the book, published the following year, asserted that Deep Throat had said so. Use of the term *deliberate* implies that the source knew someone had destroyed evidence, a criminal act. How could Deep Throat have known this? There are three possibilities. Someone could have told him, he could have listened to the tapes and deduced it—or he could have made the erasures himself.

Of those who listened to the tapes (and therefore had the opportunity to alter them), two would not have talked to Woodward about them under any circumstances—Nixon and Woods. Woodward has said that Deep Throat was a single source, not a composite, and Steve Bull was never in a position to know many of the other secrets that Deep Throat passed to Woodward during the course of Watergate. The same can be said of John Bennett, who only had access to some but not all of the information conveyed by Deep Throat to Woodward in that era. Fred Buzhardt died in 1978, and Woodward has said in more recent interviews that Deep Throat is alive and that Woodward will tell all about him if he dies. That leaves Haig.

In a tenth anniversary program about the Watergate burglary, on June 17, 1982, "Nightline" moderator Ted Koppel asked Woodward and Bernstein to describe their famous source. Bernstein responded, "This is a person who occupied a sensitive position in the executive branch of the government, who, although he was unwilling to give us primary information about the story, he would confirm or steer us in the right direction on information we had obtained elsewhere."

Woodward added, "Carl is right is describing this person as an indirect source, somebody who would say 'Look in this direction.' He would confirm things. He was not the person coming in with a wheelbarrow and dumping the entire story and saying, 'All right now. Now print it.' "

Yet that is precisely what Deep Throat did, allegedly in the garage meeting, in the first week of November 1973: He dumped a story on Woodward, who promptly printed it at the precise moment when it could do the most damage to Nixon's credibility.

We asked Woodward in our interview about the apparent contradiction among his various explanations of Deep Throat's role as his source. Did he only confirm information, as Woodward and Bernstein have stated on "Nightline" and elsewhere, or was he a primary source, as is clear from the story of early November 1973? Woodward answered, "Just like any relationship you may have with somebody, a source or otherwise, it's evolving. . . . The book makes it clear." Reminded that he and Bernstein had said something quite different on "Nightline," Woodward said, "Okay, but . . . as you see from the story [of November 8] we said we had five sources, right?" Wrong. Woodward ignored the fact that the article had made clear that while there were five sources, the other four had contradicted Deep Throat. Woodward then added, "Now, I would have to go back to notes and the book and the stories and the sequence and so forth, and I'm not sure I'm saying in there that he was the first source at all. So you're leaping to a conclusion."

In several telephone calls we attempted to put these and other questions about Deep Throat, and questions about his and Woodward's Watergate reporting, to Carl Bernstein. He first told us he would not answer any questions until he had spoken with Woodward, and later requested a letter containing some of our questions. A letter was sent, but he did not respond.

It may be that the inconsistencies in Woodward's and Bernstein's characterization of Deep Throat as a source are only the result of Woodward's attempt to hide his source and to lend appropriate literary drama to his book. Despite Woodward's demurrer, Deep Throat may have been a composite of several sources, as some historians and journalists have concluded. Despite Woodward's other demurrer about the source still being alive, Deep Throat may have had more than a touch of Buzhardt in him. *The identity of Deep Throat is a phantom that it is no longer of any importance to chase. It was always a cover story designed to lead detectives in the wrong direction, and has now outlived its usefulness. What is apparent is that in November of 1973, Chief of Staff Alexander Haig played a key role in feeding damaging information about the White House tapes to his former Navy briefer, Bob Woodward, on the eve of Nixon's Operation Candor, on which the president had pinned such high hopes.*

Nixon was into the sixth of the ten sessions he had scheduled with Congressional leaders on November 14, 1973, when Fred Buzhardt sat down at the White House with Miami trial attorney Samuel Powers. Haig had gotten his name from Morris Liebman (who had also recommended Jaworski) during the weekend he had accompanied the president to Key Biscayne. "I was brought in like a surgeon to do an appendectomy," Powers told us. He came in to represent the White House in the tapes hearing in Sirica's court. On November 14 he was sitting with Buzhardt to review the seven conversations—nine subpoenaed minus the two that couldn't be found—due to be turned over to

Sirica, and to catalogue those portions for which the White House planned to claim executive privilege.

In *The Final Days*, Woodward and Bernstein claim that November 14, 1973, was the first time Buzhardt listened to any of the White House tapes. This claim is interesting since Buzhardt had first listened to a presidential tape recording on June 25, and would shortly testify so in open court.

Of greater importance is something Buzhardt actually did on November 14. That day, he and Powers began work on the June 20 tape, the first one listed on the subpoena, and the tape in which there was a gap that had so alarmed Rose Mary Woods. Buzhardt had twice assured the president that that gap was of no consequence. Now, he and Powers sat down to listen to the tape with stopwatch in hand. "Fred told me we could expect to find a four-to-five-minute gap on either Ehrlichman or Haldeman," Powers recalls. The Ehrlichman section was clear. The gap approached and started. Five minutes went by, and the gap did not cease, but continued on until nearly eighteen-and-a-half-minutes had passed. As if that wasn't enough, Powers now looked at Cox's August 13 clarification memo and saw that the gap was squarely in the area that Cox had subpoenaed. He said so to Buzhardt—who disagreed. Powers was adamant: They were going to have to produce that tape. He recalls insisting that when one reviewed the subpoena and the clarification memo together, "there was no way you couldn't conclude" that the Haldeman conversation was part of the subpoena. Powers also says that when he had demonstrated that, Buzhardt made no further argument against bringing the tape and its gap to the court.

June 20: Haldeman and Nixon speaking together. At that point in time, John Dean knew everything, and Nixon and Haldeman knew very little. It was still three days before Dean would slip to Haldeman the idea that the CIA should be used to block the FBI. If Nixon or someone who wanted to protect him was going to erase any tape, that person would choose the June 23 tape, the one that later became the smoking gun. *There was nothing on the June 20 tape that was crucial to the president's defense, or that could incriminate him in the eyes of the public. The deliberate erasure had not been made to protect the president, but to embarrass him.*

The Final Days portrays Haig as shocked and angry when Buzhardt tells him of the big gap. They go around on the subpoena and the explanatory Cox memo until Haig finally says, "I must share your judgement. . . . How the hell could we have been confused on this, Fred?"

Surely he was not confused. He had first looked into the matter of whether this tape was covered by the subpoena in September, and in early November Deep Throat had leaked information about possible "suspicious" tampering with the tapes.

Buzhardt was not able to find and inform Haig until later in the evening of November 14, Powers recalls. But "the president, as I understood it, was entertaining some senators, some of the leadership of the Senate, in the East Room of the White House, and Haig didn't want to interrupt him." The night passed, and Nixon remained uninformed, as he did during most of the following day, when he made a televised speech to the convention of the National Association of Realtors.

In *The Final Days*, Haig's silence is described as the act of a man who has compassion for the president and who doesn't want to give him bad news when he's in a crowd. "Haig worried about the effect of the news on the Old Man. The constant public exposure throughout the week would be a strain. This news, coming so soon after the disclosure that two of the subpoenaed conversations were not on tape, would be devastating to the president's position. The additional pressure would take its toll."

Nixon recounts in his own memoir that the news did, indeed, take a toll on him. "It was a nightmare," Nixon wrote of the moment when Haig and Buzhardt finally informed him of the gap, late in the afternoon of the fifteenth. "How in hell, I asked, could we have made a mistake about something as fundamental as whether or not a particular conversation was covered by a subpoena?" Moreover, on the other bad news, the gap that ran for so long, "No one could explain how or why it had happened or account for the shrill buzzing sounds that punctuated the otherwise blank portion."

Despite his rage, Nixon determined to press on with his public relations offensive. Two days later, on November 17, in a session before the Associated Press Managing Editors Association convention at Disney World, the president uttered a memorable phrase. "People have a right to know whether or not their president is a crook. Well, I am not a crook." In a less well-reported section of that speech, Nixon also spoke about the essential need to shield certain matters under the claim of national security. To buttress his point that this was not simply a ploy to keep investigators away from illegal activities, he cited the fact that the shield was being used "not only in Ellsberg but also in another matter so sensitive that even Senator Ervin and Senator Baker have decided that they should not delve into it."

On November 20, when asked at the Republican Governors Conference, "Are we going to be blindsided by any more bombshells?" Nixon replied, "If there are any more bombs, I'm not aware of them." He made that reply, Nixon recalled in his memoir, because he still hadn't heard from Buzhardt whether or not the erased conversation could somehow be recovered, and "I knew that if I indicated even the remotest possibility of a new bombshell, I would have to say what it was—and I still was not sure of the answer to that myself."

The Butterfield revelation that had been withheld from Nixon; the handling of the battle with Cox and the resultant Saturday Night Massacre; the foray to Key Biscayne to raise the specter of resignation; the continuing attempt to keep everyone away from Moorer-Radford; the "deliberate erasures" events and leak to Woodward—since Haig and Buzhardt had come to the White House in early May to save the president, all these things had happened, and each one was a body blow to Nixon's hold on the presidency. The sheer number of accumulated errors now make moot the question of whether these were deliberate or innocent mistakes. The pattern was there, if anybody had been able to read it at the time.

On November 21, 1973, the next bombshell, that of the eighteen-and-a-half-minute gap, exploded in Judge Sirica's courtroom as the counsel to the president approached the judge and the prosecution lawyers in Sirica's chambers, and began by saying, "Judge, we have a problem."

23

MOORER-RADFORD DISINTERRED

ARCHIBALD Cox had been fired, in part, for pursuing the probe of the Plumbers and indicting Bud Krogh, matters that threatened to expose the Moorer-Radford affair and the connections of Haig to the participants in it. Cox's departure did not end the problem.

On October 31, as Jaworski was being cajoled by Haig into accepting the job as Special Prosecutor, Bud Krogh's lawyers filed a broad discovery motion in federal court. This motion made clear how they planned to pursue Krogh's defense: on the basis that he had been told that his investigations had come under the umbrella of national security. They requested in support of that defense a variety of White House tapes and other materials involving the Plumbers. One specific request took direct aim at Moorer-Radford. Krogh's defense team asked for "certain tape recordings of conversations" between Ehrlichman, Young, and Nixon "in December, 1971, and January through February, 1972, in which the work of the Special Investigations Unit [Plumbers] was discussed, the India-Pakistan leaks were discussed, and/or instructions were given on the necessity for absolute secrecy regarding the activities" of the Plumbers. Backing up that request was another for "all files of the Special Investigations Unit . . . presently held in the White House as Presidential documents." (No wonder that Haig and Buzhardt had adamantly refused to allow Cox to ask for more tapes and papers.)

Krogh knew perfectly well that the requested materials included the transcript of the Welander interrogation, the notes of Ehrlichman and Young, as well as Young's overall report on the Moorer-Radford matter. He probably didn't want to bring these to light either, and asked for them only because they would show clearly that his work had been done for national security reasons, and that for those same reasons he had been told by superiors to lie to the grand jury on the matter of knowledge of the Liddy-Hunt California trip. He may even have hoped that the White House would refuse to provide the documents, an act that would allow Krogh's lawyers to move for a dismissal on the grounds that they were denied evidence essential to Krogh's defense.

After Jaworski took over on November 5, one of his first acts was to sign the prosecution's reply to Krogh's brief. James Doyle recalled in his memoir of the prosecutor's office during Watergate that this reply had been drafted by Assistant Prosecutor Philip A. Lacovara and others who had worked on the matter during Cox's tenure, but that Jaworski endorsed its strong language and signed it. The reply stated:

> In the recent past, national security has become a kind of talisman, invoked by officials at widely disparate levels of government service to justify a wide range of apparently illegal activities. No government office, not even the highest office in the land, carries with it the right to ignore the law's command any more than the orders of a superior can be used by government officers to justify illegal behavior.

This reply brief was front-page news, and Doyle writes that it "sent shudders through White House aides." Here was Jaworski, taking the same position for which Cox had been fired. Haig, who had been "exultant" when Jaworski had accepted the Special Prosecutor assignment only a week earlier, now realized that he hadn't properly told Jaworski why he had been so insistent on retaining "national security" as a shield for certain matters.

On November 13, Jaworski was summoned to the White House for a late afternoon meeting with Haig and Buzhardt. According to Jaworski's handwritten notes of the meeting, now in the National Archives, the Special Prosecutor was told that "Krogh's demands" were "trouble," and threatened to expose a sensitive national security case. The notes continue: "Yeoman used as secretary by Haig . . . tremendously sensitive conversations and agreements with heads of state . . . dictated memos . . . copy to Chm. Joint C. . . ." Further, the yeoman had been "recommended by Haig" to travel with Kissinger, whose papers had also been copied and passed to the JCS chairman. Jaworski was told that a January 10, 1972, report had been written and contained logs of the investigation. This was the report that Buzhardt had prepared for Melvin Laird.

The notes also reveal that in telling Jaworski about Moorer-Radford, Haig and Buzhardt gave him not only the outline of the case, but also enough information to make Jaworski understand that Haig himself had a personal stake in it.

Upon Jaworski's return to his office, Doyle wrote in his memoir, the Special Prosecutor downplayed what had happened and told his staff that what Haig had said was "so much bullshit. I didn't pay any attention to it and you don't have to, either."

That may or may not have been true. In his memoir, Jaworski wrote that he went to the White House on his own initiative, "to jog Haig's memory about his promises of cooperation . . . and . . . to satisfy myself about the 'grave national security matters' the Plumbers had handled. . . . The national security matters [Haig] described didn't appear to be very grave to me. I concluded that if most of them were made public at that very moment the country would not be endangered." So: Jaworski claimed he didn't take the matters seriously.

At that meeting with Haig, also attended by Buzhardt, the Special Prosecutor discussed the Dr. Fielding break-in, and later wrote that the two aides agreed to surrender the material they had previously refused to give to Cox. Jaworski later testified that "there was no resistance from Haig and Buzhardt when I indicated that some indictments could be brought and that I was going to pursue them" in regard to the Dr. Fielding break-in. Subsequently, he filed charges against Ehrlichman and Colson on the matter.

Since Haig and Buzhardt so easily gave to Jaworski materials they had vehemently denied to Cox only a short time earlier, it seems likely that during their meeting in the White House a deal was made: Jaworski received Plumbers documents pertinent to the Dr. Fielding matter, but in return probably agreed to stay away from Moorer-Radford. Buttressing this supposition is the fact that among the Plumbers documents eventually turned over to Jaworski's office, none mentioned the JCS spying probe.

In mid-November U.S. District Judge Gerhard Gesell denied Krogh's motion to dismiss his indictment, and in the process also denied the discovery motion that requested the December 1971 and early 1972 tapes and document. That was a relief to Haig and Buz-hardt. Krogh's major line of defense gone, he was pushed toward a plea bargain. On November 30, Krogh plead guilty to conspiracy to violate Daniel Ellsberg's civil rights; in exchange, Jaworski dropped the perjury charge.

During Cox's tenure, LaRue, Magruder, and Dean had all pleaded guilty and started serving sentences that were relatively short, mea-sured in months. Krogh was the first official of the former administra-tion to plead guilty in the Jaworski era, and Krogh received an effective sentence of six months. With his guilty plea, the threat to Haig receded significantly.

Moorer-Radford wouldn't stay buried. Back in July, when Ehrlichman and Baker had had their public exchanges about the JCS spying without naming it, many people had been intrigued by what Ehrlich-man said and what he had been obviously constrained from saying. Listening at the press tables were two enterprising reporters. Dan Thomasson was a Washington bureau man for the Scripps-Howard chain of newspapers, and Jim Squires was a Washington correspondent for the *Chicago Tribune*. Though they worked for different news organ-izations, their separate bosses allowed them to collaborate in their reporting. Intrigued by the exchanges, the two reporters began dig-ging, and tried to learn about the mysterious Plumbers investigation cited by Ehrlichman and his lawyer, John Wilson.

On October 10, 1973, the Watergate reporting team Woodward and Bernstein entered the ranks of investigators chasing Moorer-Radford with a story buried on page A27 of the *Washington Post* that said "a low-level assistant to the National Security Council had his phone tapped in an investigation of news leaks in late 1971." An unnamed source suggested that the tap was "in connection with a 1971 probe of the leak of secret documents to syndicated columnist Jack Anderson about U.S. policy in the India-Pakistan war." The unidentified "low level assistant" was Yeoman Charles Radford.

Woodward had been sitting on the Moorer-Radford story since June. This October 10 story has the earmarks of a trial balloon, or of a deliberate leak sent out to see if Thomasson and Squires—who were known to be chasing the military espionage matter—could be forced into print with what they had, and before their investigation was complete.

Thomasson and Squires weren't pushed any faster into print, but did note as they continued to get closer to the story that Nixon was beginning to refer in speeches to an investigation that Baker and Ervin had "wisely declined" to make public. Senator Baker, too, kept on the matter, perhaps annoyed that Nixon was now using as part of his own defense the idea that Baker and Ervin had agreed to keep certain matters under wraps. Baker could do little more than hint to the public that the national security issue might be the "missing link" that could explain the entire Watergate story. Behind the scenes, Buzhardt and Haig would tell him nothing.

On November 29, Thomasson and Squires hit print with a story that in 1971 the Plumbers had tried to stop a leak of highly sensitive information about the Soviet Union. They had few details, only that it involved the Russians. Those in the know could guess that what they were referring to was an investigation of Jack Anderson for a 1971 column that discussed the capacity of the United States to listen in on conversations in certain Soviet limousines. "Some who know about the matter," Thomasson wrote, "believe disclosure of its details ultimately would endanger the life of a U.S. intelligence source close to the highest Russian official circles." The two reporters now thought they'd pinned down the 1971 secret investigation that had been guarded so tenaciously in Ehrlichman's testimony.

They soon discovered that the secret was something larger. A big hint came when Fred Buzhardt asked them to come to the White House in late 1973. Thomasson recently told us that Buzhardt seemed to have assumed that the reporters had learned quite a bit about Moorer-Radford. During this meeting, Buzhardt made cryptic statements and tried to learn what the reporters knew. "I think he was trying to play poker with us, and I think sometimes we played a better game than he did. I really believe that he thought we knew at that juncture one hell of a lot more than we did know." Thomasson reports that Buzhardt made reference to "babysitting people," a reference the reporters did not understand at the time. Later it became clear to them that Buzhardt had been referring to the tap placed on Radford's home phone in Washington, and, after he was transferred, on his phone in the Pacific Northwest, the same tap Woodward and Bernstein wrote of in their October 10 story.

December 21, 1973, was a snowy day in Washington. Leon Jaworski, the Special Prosecutor, was scheduled to fly home to Texas in a few hours, but before he did, he was to have a private meeting with Al Haig.

"The two men had been cultivating their relationship," James Doyle wrote. "Jaworski believed he could use Haig, Haig believed he could use Jaworski. Haig would tell Nixon and Buzhardt and others that

Jaworski was sympathetic to the President's problems but was a captive of the old Cox staff of zealots." Doyle reports that one member of the Special Prosecutor's staff told Jaworski to his face that he was "too cozy with Al Haig," but that Jaworski had "rejected the criticism."

Jaworski and Haig had worked out a way to keep their meetings from the public eye—the Special Prosecutor made his way into and out of the White House complex through the Diplomatic Entrance, one that had been established to shield diplomats who did not want their visits to be known. The two men met in an historic setting, the first-floor Map Room, a parlor to which Franklin Roosevelt had often retired to study battle maps during World War II. The subject of this discussion was the March 21, 1973, tape, that of "the cancer within the presidency." Sirica had recently turned it over to Jaworski's office. The prosecutor and his assistants had listened to it and considered it devastating to the president. That conclusion had been conveyed to Haig, and Haig had summoned Jaworski to hear the White House's position in response.

According to Jaworski's memoir, the conversation was pleasant but adversarial. The White House lawyers, Haig said, had decided that the tape did not show criminal conduct by the president. Hearing this, Jaworski said, "Al, I want to tell you something. I think you should get the finest criminal lawyer you can find—someone not concerned with the White House in any way—and let him study the tapes."

That was the entire message of the conversation. Jaworski was clearly implying that the White House's current analysis was dead wrong, and that a good independent lawyer would tell Haig just that, an opinion that could only hasten Nixon's resignation. As the two men walked to the Diplomatic Entrance, Haig was "silent, thoughtful," Jaworski later wrote. And then the chief of staff "looked up at me and tears were glistening in his fine eyes. I left him that way, and went to my car."

After his trip to Texas for Christmas, Jaworski returned to the Map Room with Haig on December 27, and learned that Haig had been in touch with James St. Clair, a highly regarded Boston trial attorney, whose name he had gotten—as he had Jaworski's—from Morris Liebman. Among the particulars that recommended St. Clair was that he had defended the Army at the infamous hearings held by Senator Joseph McCarthy in the 1950s; Haig liked defenders of the Army.

On January 4, 1974, James St. Clair came aboard. As he did, two other shifts on the White House staff were announced. Buzhardt was appointed sole counsel to the president, and it was announced that he was giving up his other hat, that of counsel to the Department of

Defense. Moving over from the job of counsel to the president to the position of special assistant to the president on domestic affairs was Len Garment.

Two explanations for the shifts were put out by the White House. Nixon was reported as angered at Buzhardt's performance in the matter of the missing and erased tapes, and so had hired St. Clair. That made little sense, if Buzhardt was being elevated to sole counsel to the president, but no one remarked on it. The other explanation was that Buzhardt and Garment had simply become fed up with defending Nixon, and were making way for a more vigorous defense.

Neither explanation held much water. The greater likelihood had to do with Moorer-Radford. Reporters were getting closer and closer to the real story, and there was some agitation for congressional hearings on the matter. For instance, at the turn of the year on a televised interview, Senator Baker urged Nixon "to provide some security information which he has been withholding and to more or less take the repercussions it would have domestically and let it be done and over." The real reason Buzhardt moved out of his Defense Department job entirely was so he could concentrate on containing Moorer-Radford while at the same time appearing to have no further connection to the Defense Department position he had held in 1971–72, when he had done his best to conceal the affair. In the weeks ahead, there would be some comment that Buzhardt had quite precipitously dropped from public view.

It took Thomasson and Squires the remainder of December and the first week in January to nail down the Moorer-Radford story. "Finally it all came together. . . . There was no hesitancy on our part when we found the missing pieces," Thomasson says. Before going to print, they wanted a comment from Haig, and sent Aldo Beckman, White House correspondent for the *Chicago Tribune*, to see the chief of staff. As Thomasson recalls the event, "He goes to Haig and says, 'Thomasson and Squires have this story saying thus and such.' And Haig said, 'Oh, shit, I knew it was going to get out,' and he turned white and said, 'I'll get back to you.' And he came back and said, 'There's not a word of truth in it.' "

Around January 7, Bob Woodward called Yeoman Chuck Radford in Oregon and told him that the story of his 1971 ordeal was no longer going to continue to be a secret, that newspapers would shortly be revealing it. Radford was shocked to learn this. "When I realized it was all going to come out in the newspaper, I was sick to my stomach," he recalls. Woodward "asked me questions but I told him it was something I would not discuss."

That same day, Don Stewart was at the Pentagon when Bob Woodward telephoned him and asked, "What do you know about a telephone tap on Charles Edward Radford?" Stewart referred Woodward to the Pentagon press office for an answer, but he started taking notes because the questions kept coming. Woodward next wanted to know what Stewart knew about "information being leaked from cables on the India-Pakistan War," and about "Radford feeding information from the White House to the Joint Chiefs of Staff and also to them from Kissinger and General Haig." Woodward also asked Stewart if he had been interviewed by the Senate Armed Services and Watergate committees, and "What do you know about Admiral Welander?" Stewart then referred him again to the Pentagon press office, hung up, and wrote his memo of the conversation for his bosses. Stewart concluded in that memo that Woodward had gotten his information thus far from Capitol Hill, and that "My personal feeling is that Democrats are trying to shoot the Republicans down."

Woodward also called Admiral Welander that week. Back in June 1973, the two had had a conversation in which Woodward had tried to learn what Welander might say about Moorer-Radford, and had found out that Welander wouldn't say anything. In January 1974, Welander recalls, Woodward got him on the phone. "He said the story is going to break and I have to write it, and what can you tell me about it?" Welander says he told Woodward very little, and denied any wrongdoing.

While Welander declines to say what he actually told Woodward, he does exhibit a sense of having been betrayed by his former subordinate. "I thought he was a friend," Welander says. The reason for Welander's distress will shortly become clear. At the moment it is necessary to note that before Thomasson and Squires published on January 11, Woodward had information on Moorer-Radford that other reporters did not. But he and Bernstein did not publish until after Thomasson's and Squires's stories broke.

Thomasson's and Squires's stories were each printed on January 11, 1974. Thomasson's began: "A secret White House investigation of leaks of classified information in late 1971 produced evidence that high Pentagon officials were spying on the office of Henry A. Kissinger." The outline of the espionage was brief, but included mention of Moorer and the JCS as recipients of the information, and included a denial by Moorer, through a spokesman. However, the article said, "at least four sources independently confirmed that the military tried to get from Kissinger's office information that had been denied it."

A similar Squires account, published the same day under a banner headline across the *Chicago Tribune*'s front page, also reported Haig's assertion to Beckman that the story was false—and something more. Haig, quoted only as a senior White House official, mentioned the possibility of "lawsuits" and said that any newspaper that printed the story "would have to be responsible for it."

Thomasson and Squires did not yet know the names of those who had been passing material to Moorer—but the names Welander and Radford came out the next day, January 12, in an article by Woodward and Bernstein.

What upset Welander was immediately apparent: The *Post* story prominently displayed his picture next to the text of the article, "Pentagon Got Secret Data of Kissinger's." The article itself was curious in what it said and did not say. It began by saying flatly that "Military liaison aides in the White House passed information" to the Pentagon in 1971, but avoided mention that the material had gone to Moorer or to the Joint Chiefs. The information from Kissinger's files, the article said, "was sought by high Pentagon officers who were uncertain about radically shifting U.S. foreign policy toward Russia, China, and other countries." Beyond this lead, however, the bulk of the article concerned Chuck Radford, the tap on his phone, and the India-Pakistan leak to Jack Anderson. Radford was characterized as "the central figure in the matter," and the article said that Welander had been transferred "only because Radford had worked for him." In a clue about the sources Woodward and Bernstein had tapped, the article stated that the investigation of the leak of Anderson had been "directed by J. Fred Buzhardt," and that Buzhardt's investigation "never established that Welander or Radford did anything wrong." No mention was made in the article of the Ehrlichman or Young probes.

The effect of the Woodward and Bernstein article was to knock down what Thomasson and Squires had revealed—namely, that Moorer and the JCS had been involved. For instance, the Woodward and Bernstein article asserts that four of their sources insisted "that news accounts characterizing this information distribution as spying on or surveillance of Kissinger are wrong," and went on to assert that their sources said, "It was never clear who in the Pentagon set up or benefitted from the unauthorized pipeline of information." The military liaison office had been closed, Woodward and Bernstein quoted some sources as saying, because Kissinger had wanted it closed for some time, and the leak to Jack Anderson "gave him a reason." Finally, Welander's current post, assistant deputy chief of naval operations, was "an important job in the Navy hierarchy that Pentagon officials said would not have been given to anyone suspected of unauthorized distribution of classified material."

The Woodward and Bernstein story, heavily favorable to the White House, suggested that the espionage had done no harm, that it was all Radford's fault, and that the purloined material had never been important and was of no interest to the JCS. Moorer was not named as a recipient, although he was quoted through a spokesman as denying any involvement in the matter, Welander was rehabilitated, and no mention was made of investigations by Ehrlichman or Young—the investigations that turned up the name of Alexander Haig. Just how far off the mark and slanted the *Post* story was could be seen from a competing story by Seymour Hersh in that morning's *New York Times*.

Hersh's reporting focused on David Young and the Plumbers' discovery in late 1971 "that a 'ring' of military officers was attempting to relay highly classified information on the China talks and other matters to officials in the Pentagon," and that while Young's investigation had first focused on leaks to Anderson, it "quickly spread into a broad investigation of possible widespread military spying." Both Kissinger and Young, Hersh wrote, "suspected that reports on the White House's negotiations with China, North Vietnam and the Soviet Union were being leaked to Secretary of Defense Melvin R. Laird and Adm. Thomas Moorer, chairman of the Joint Chiefs of Staff." Hersh's sources all agreed that Kissinger "shared Young's belief that Pentagon officials were eager to obtain—by covert methods if necessary—details of . . . secret deliberations with nations usually considered America's enemies by military men." Moreover, other sources said that the Young investigation "really did uncover a ring of some sort inside the NSC." Hersh reported that Welander had been reassigned after the investigation, but the *Times* reporter apparently had not yet learned about Radford's role.

Hersh cut much closer to the bone than Woodward and Bernstein on the White House's effort to suppress Moorer-Radford, and commented on the meeting at the White House in which Ervin had agreed to keep the Watergate committee away from this matter. He wrote that though within the White House some people had pressed for disclosure in the hope of bolstering the argument that the Plumbers had indeed investigated serious national security matters, "the advocates of disclosure were overruled by a faction headed by J. Fred Buzhardt." There were still unanswered questions, Hersh reported a source as saying; that source added that if there had been misconduct by the military, "then we had the rudiments of the kind of thing that leads to a military takeover."

Woodward tells us that he cannot remember any contact with Welander in the spring of 1973, but asserts, "As you know and as a matter of record, I think Carl and I wrote the first story identifying [Welander] as the Kissinger aide who was fired, or relieved or transferred, depending on how you look at it." How did he feel writing such a story about his former commanding officer? "I guess I would cite it as an example of the newspaper's and my independence. He was a former skipper and somebody I knew, but names were being taken and we went ahead and did it."

The day following their big Moorer-Radford story, Woodward and Bernstein wrote one more article that mentioned Moorer-Radford, again naming Radford as "the central figure" and quoting a White House source complaining that "someone is trying to make the Pentagon-Kissinger affair look like *Seven Days in May*. It's nothing of the kind." After that, responsibility for this important story was handed to Michael Getler, the *Post*'s beat reporter at the Pentagon, and to Laurence Stern. "Frankly," Getler tells us, "I don't remember the details, [but] it may have gone from an investigative story to a running story in which the beat reporter takes it over." Did Getler, now the *Post*'s assistant managing editor for foreign news, know of Woodward's past relationships with Welander and Moorer, two key figures in the affair? "I honestly don't remember that. It's quite possible, maybe that's why he [Woodward] bowed out of the story. I just don't remember. It's not inconceivable that he told me."

Hersh continued to pursue the story, but made a mistake in an article published on January 13. He said that an unidentified government official involved in the spying probe had tried to "blackmail" President Nixon into giving him a more important job by threatening to expose the secret investigation. Moreover, the "White House told the Senate Watergate committee last summer" of the blackmail threat, as part of the conference between Baker, Ervin, and the White House.

This was a reference to what we now know—but Hersh did not then know—to have been Don Stewart's job request to the White House and the Buzhardt-Haig-Richardson attempt to prosecute Stewart. Hersh wrote that Baker had continued to investigate the espionage on his own, and had recently met with Young. The article also quoted some sources as saying that what Moorer had done was "not in the operational manual for his office," and other sources who labeled the pilfering as reasonable under the circumstances. These latter sources argued that because Kissinger had not shared his information with the military, it was "not so impossible to understand that a liaison man in the Security Council would do what he could to get information back to his boss."

In the *Chicago Tribune* and *The New York Times* that weekend, the competing reporters continued to point at Moorer. Squires's sources had told him that when Nixon had found out about the espionage he'd been so angry that he had considered firing Moorer; Hersh wrote that his sources "wondered why, in the face of the reported evidence amassed by Mr. Young, Mr. Nixon reappointed the admiral [Moorer] to a second two-year term" in mid–1972. The White House continued to deny that Moorer had been involved, but those denials no longer held water. Secretary of Defense James Schlesinger said through a spokesman that he had interviewed Moorer, who had denied any involvement in the spying. A later statement issued by Schlesinger put the blame for the espionage on the "overzealousness" of people in the liaison office.

That weekend, there was one headline that was good news for Haig and Buzhardt. Senator Stennis announced that the Armed Services Committee, which he chaired, would hold hearings on the espionage next month, and that "As far as the published implications that Admiral Moorer was spying on Kissinger, it'd take hard substantial facts to prove it."

Curiously, Jaworski's office had very little to say on the subject, issuing to reporters only a terse "no comment." And, reflecting Sam Ervin's viewpoint, Watergate Committee Chief Counsel Dash flatly ruled out any inquiry into the spying charges. This isolated Senator Baker even more, and forced him to continue his inquiries behind the scenes.

On January 18, the *Post* got into the military espionage matter in a story that deprecated the way others were pursuing it. Under Stern's byline was an analysis designed to bury, not to disinter, Moorer-Radford: "The tale of the alleged Pentagon spy ring opened with dark overtones of 'Seven Days in May.' But as the story evolved it was veering toward 'Catch-22' with accents of 'M*A*S*H.' " Citing the confusion surrounding the story, Stern asked, "Was the file-snitching operation the handiwork of a full-fledged 'military spy network' (New York Times) or of principally two officers (Washington Post)?" He crowed that the *Times* had eventually reached the same conclusion as the *Post* when it quoted sources on January 16 as saying "the spying episode had been blown out of proportion."

That was not the entire truth. Hersh also had written that while some officials disparaged Young's work, others took Young's findings very, very seriously. Later, Hersh clarified this by writing that the "high White House officials" who attacked the Young inquiry reflected the thinking of presidential counsel J. Fred Buzhardt.

Jack Anderson weighed into the reportorial battle with a new detail—that Moorer's assistant, Captain Arthur K. Knoizen, had received some of the purloined papers from Welander. Now Moorer decided it was time for him to say something in public. In an interview on NBC's "Today" show on January 18, the day of the *Post*'s analysis debunking the seriousness of the espionage charges, Moorer made a categorical denial: "The mere thought that the Joint Chiefs of Staff were cut off from sources of information and then set about to establish a system of acquiring this information in an unauthorized way is ludicrous, ridiculous and a lie." He did acknowledge that Welander had shown him "a file" of documents improperly obtained by Radford, but contended the papers were "essentially useless" and that he had told Welander to put them back when he learned that they had been taken without permission.

At that very moment, the materials that controverted Moorer's assertions, the transcript of the Ehrlichman-Young interview with Welander of December 22, 1971, and the transcript of the Buzhardt-Stewart interview with Welander of January 7, 1972, both sat in the White House files under the control of Haig and Buzhardt. But nobody else could then get at those buried documents.

On the basis of Moorer's public denial, Secretary of Defense Schlesinger announced on Monday, January 21, that he was effectively ending the Pentagon's investigation of the alleged espionage. Four days later, Schlesinger told reporters that Moorer had been exonerated even though there were "clearly improprieties" in the way documents had been funneled from the White House to the Pentagon. What improprieties? Schlesinger admitted they had included breaking into Kissinger's briefcase and the pilfering of documents that were to have been burned.

Even more important for our concerns, Schlesinger admitted to reporters that Buzhardt had refused to turn over to one of his aides the Ehrlichman-Young taped interrogation of Welander. He appeared to accept with equanimity the remarkable spectacle of a man who had been one of his nominal subordinates—counsel to the department—refusing to turn over something to his office. But he did attack the David Young investigation of the matter. Schlesinger said he had never been allowed to read Young's report, but he asserted he had no confidence that it was correct.

The one question on everyone's mind during the period just after the matter broke through to public consciousness was what Kissinger would have to say about it. The secretary of state was on a ten-day mission to the Middle East at the moment the headlines began. When Kissinger came back from that trip, he agreed to comment.

On January 22, Kissinger went before the press and said, "I have no reason to question the argument that has been made by Admiral Moorer, that this incident of the unauthorized transfer of papers from my office to his office reflected overzealousness on the part of subordinates and in any case gave him no information that he did not already possess."

Gone was Kissinger's "mood indigo" and his rage after learning of the espionage, a rage that included the demand that Moorer be fired as JCS chief. Now secretary of state, secure in his Foggy Bottom perch and keeping himself aloof from Watergate, Kissinger said he had known about the pilfering, but that it had been inconsequential. Yes, he told reporters, Ehrlichman had allowed him to listen to the Welander interview, and he had known that David Young was involved in Welander's interrogation—but he had not known that Young had been involved in his capacity as a member of the Plumbers. In fact, he pointed out, Nixon had ordered that he, Kissinger, be kept away from those matters.

With Kissinger joining Schlesinger, Moorer, Haig, and Buzhardt in a cover-up, the defenders of the secret of Moorer-Radford made quite a formidable array of guardians.

During one of their December 1973 meetings, Haig allowed Jaworski to listen to presidential tapes that had not been subpoenaed and to read some files. According to the Special Prosecutor's memoir, he found nothing relevant in what he listened to at that time. In January, Jaworski asked Haig for what was known as the "tape of tapes"—a June 4, 1973, recording of Nixon listening to some of his conversations with Dean, and which included Nixon's discussions that day with Haig and Ziegler about what he'd heard.

That "tape of tapes" was far from innocuous. It was a road map that showed what other tapes might be germane to any criminal inquiry—as Haig must have clearly understood. In Nixon's memoirs, he said that Haig came to him only once, in December 1973, with a Jaworski request for a group of additional tapes, and that Nixon granted the request based on Haig's report that "Jaworski had assured him [Haig] that this would be his [Jaworski's] last request for tapes."

That was the situation when Jaworski, in early January 1974, approached Haig with his request for the "tape of tapes." Jaworski told Haig that if he could listen to the tape, he might be able to judge which additional tapes, if any, he would need. In *The Final Days*, the authors claimed that despite Jaworski's plain statement that he intended to seek additional tapes, Haig went to Nixon for permission to turn the tape over on the grounds that "this would probably be the last request from Jaworski." In this account, Nixon told Haig to have Buzhardt listen to the tape and Buzhardt then recommended that it not be turned over. But Haig "persuaded" Nixon to release it in order to "bring the special prosecutor's investigation to an end."

However inexplicable Haig's actions as depicted in *The Final Days* may appear, the reality may have been worse. There is a possibility that Haig himself made the decision to release the tape without asking Nixon for permission. Nixon's account of Jaworski's requests for tapes during this period and his reaction to these requests omits entirely any reference to a request by Haig for the "tape of tapes." Moreover, Jaworski wrote that when he asked Haig for the June 4 "tape of tapes," Haig responded "there would be no problem." Jaworski did report a subsequent problem with Buzhardt, but said this problem was resolved a short time later when Buzhardt phoned Haig.

In any event, the result was predictably disastrous. The day after Jaworski listened to the "tape of tapes," he submitted a letter to the White House seeking twenty-five additional Watergate tapes. That request Haig had to take to Nixon, whereupon, according to *The Final Days*, "Nixon ridiculed Haig for his trust in Jaworski."

An official letter from St. Clair to Jaworski turned down the request, and it was clear that the matter was heading for a court battle. Nonetheless, Haig and Jaworski continued to talk through their private backchannel.

Shortly, the Moorer-Radford inquiry would move into the hands of Senator Stennis, on whom Buzhardt and Haig believed they could rely for a quick series of closed-door hearings that would reseal the tomb. With Rear Admiral Rembrandt Robinson dead since the May 1972 helicopter accident, and Moorer, Schlesinger, Welander, and Kissinger all guarding the gates, those hearings should have presented very few difficulties for Haig and Buzhardt. Two problems still remained, however: Young and Stewart.

Young was not really a threat because in May 1973 he had been granted immunity by federal prosecutors in exchange for his own testimony and the release of some documents. Stewart was another matter, and to neutralize him Haig and Buzhardt sprang into action in the latter part of January. On the twenty-fourth, Stewart was on sick leave, at home and in bed, when his secretary telephoned with the news that Bob Woodward had been trying to reach him to discuss a matter "of vital concern," the phrase Stewart later used in a memorandum on the incident. Stewart called back and, according to the memorandum, Woodward "informed me that I was being accused of blackmailing The White House into giving me the job of Director of the FBI, and that failing, Deputy Director." Woodward mentioned to Stewart his June 25, 1973, letter to Baroody, and told him that Woodward's source had passed on the notion that Stewart had sought to use his knowledge of the Moorer-Radford case to secure the FBI post. Stewart denied pressuring the White House, and said that he felt he was qualified for a high post at the FBI and that the letter had only put forward his qualifications and ensured that he be considered as a candidate.

Clearly, Woodward had gotten this information from the White House. But so had Seymour Hersh. On January 25, both the *Washington Post* and *The New York Times* published stories saying that Stewart had tried to pressure his way into a high-ranking FBI job by threatening to disclose what he knew about Moorer-Radford. Hersh's article said that Haig had intercepted a Stewart threat intended for Nixon and had subsequently told Stewart personally to "go to hell. General Haig subsequently confirmed the incident without naming Mr. Stewart and said that he had not been discharged from the Pentagon post for fear that he would make the facts known publicly. Mr. Stewart could not be reached for comment. His telephone is unlisted."

Stewart denies Haig's claim, saying he and Haig had never talked about the matter. But there is one further interesting aspect to the story: by confirming to Hersh the report that he told Stewart to go to hell, Haig in essence corroborated that he had been part of the effort to discredit Stewart, though the article did not make that point.

Under the Woodward-Bernstein byline, the story of Stewart's attempted blackmail had quite a different slant. The *Post* reported the charge within the broader context of a story about additional FBI telephone taps on the phones of Radford and his friends in late 1971 and early 1972. Another revelation in this article said that Stewart's letter to Baroody had been forwarded to Justice by Buzhardt—something that very few people knew. The article did contain the fact that Justice had determined that Stewart had not violated the law, and included the denial that Stewart had given over the phone to Woodward.

Don Stewart was shaken by these twin front-page allegations, and about 10:30 A.M. on January 25 he reached Seymour Hersh and denied any attempt at blackmail. He told Hersh—as the story was printed on the following day—"I was looking for a job, no question about it. But

I wasn't trying to put the muscle on them. I don't have a damn thing to hide and I didn't shake anybody down." In that follow-up article, Hersh went on to report that "Stewart suggested that some officials in the White House or elsewhere might have acted improperly in their handling of the snooping investigation," and that Stewart said he would be "tickled to death" to testify before any congressional inquiry into the subject. Hersh also reported that Pentagon spokesman Jerry Friedheim had confirmed that Stewart still retained the top investigator's job at the Pentagon, and that Friedheim had commented, "The general feeling here is that he's a good investigator."

Hersh later admitted that he had not made a diligent enough effort to get in touch with Stewart for the original story. "It's my fault for not checking it farther," he now says, and recalls that he was pressed by a deadline and concerned about getting beat on the story by a competing newspaper. "There's no question I should have gone to him [Stewart] and got a comment and been balanced." The two men subsequently smoothed over their differences. Stewart was further bolstered on January 29, when one of Schlesinger's special assistants, Martin Hoffman, called Stewart to his office and shared with him all of the Justice documents that showed Stewart had been cleared of potential blackmail charges more than six months earlier. Stewart wrote a memorandum after he had looked at these documents, and noted that Garment and Buzhardt had told Baker and Ervin that Stewart was blackmailing the White House on July 27, when the White House lawyers had been informed on July 10 that there was no evidence for making a prosecution of Stewart on that claim.

In an important revelation buried deep in Hersh's follow-up story, one small paragraph suggested that Stewart had disclosed to Senator Baker's staff that the December 1971 investigation "had determined that many National Security Council documents had, in fact, been provided to Admiral Moorer." This was the first indication to those who were not members of the inner circle that Stewart could be a crucial witness about Moorer-Radford if asked to give sworn testimony.

On January 31, 1974, Don Stewart went to a meeting of former FBI agents accompanied by a large poster that he had prepared. He propped it up on an easel just outside the meeting room. It read:

In recent articles in newspapers, I have been maligned—White House attorneys called me a "blackmailer" and stated I tried to pressure them for the FBI director and deputy director job. Not true! . . . . Senator Baker allegedly referred to me as a "crook or a nut." Believe me— breaking a good domestic espionage case has its problems when high people are involved. I would welcome a congressional hearing.

24

SENATOR STENNIS HOLDS A HEARING

IN late January 1974, Senator John Stennis met privately and individually with Moorer, Welander, Kissinger, Schlesinger, and Haig, and then decided on his strategy for the forthcoming hearings about Moorer-Radford. It would be a one-day, closed-door hearing.

One of the fifteen members of Stennis' Armed Services Committee strongly disagreed. Harold Hughes of Iowa, a liberal Democrat, had been a crucial player in a previous investigation of the secret bombing campaign against Cambodia. Then, in Hughes's opinion, the committee had produced a whitewash. Now, he was insistent: "No once-over-lightly in executive session with Admiral Moorer or Kissinger is going to suffice," he told *The New York Times*. Radford and Young should be called as witnesses, and the much-debated Young report should be turned over to the committee, because "the stakes are very high here. . . . This involves the ability of the chief executive and his advisers to be in command of an operation and to keep to themselves whatever information they have."

Hughes's comments were offered on the same day that Hersh published major new information on the story, February 3. He wrote

390

that the espionage had started in September 1970, when Radford had started at the liaison office, and continued until it was discovered at the end of 1971; and he reported that documents had been handed to Robinson, Welander, Knoizen, and Train. Hersh also made clear that Radford's pilfering had taken place almost daily and that it had been regarded as especially important during the Haig and Kissinger overseas trips.

These were major revelations, and demanded to be examined by the proper authorities, for instance, the Armed Services Committee, which had an oversight responsibility. Unfortunately for the cause of the unearthing of the truth, those hearings were in the crafty hands of John Stennis, the man who, in James Doyle's phrase, "had rigged many a congressional hearing."

Senator John Stennis banged down the gavel to begin the hearing on February 6 in Room 212 of the Russell Senate Office Building. Eight of fifteen senators, plus various aides, were present to hear the first witness, Admiral Thomas Moorer, the chairman of the Joint Chiefs.

There was some press interest in this hearing, but major attention was focused on another action taking place in the Congress that day: By a vote of 410 to 4, the House of Representatives authorized the Judiciary Committee to investigate President Nixon and determine if he should be impeached. The committee was granted broad subpoena powers.

In front of Stennis' committee, Moorer insisted that he had excellent relations with Kissinger; that was why the charges "sicken me as a man, concern me as a military officer, and deeply disturb me as the nation's senior uniformed official." He testified: "I gave no orders, issued no instructions, gave no encouragement—either direct or implied—to anyone to collect or retain in any irregular or unauthorized manner any information, papers, or documents from the NSC." He'd never learned of the contents of Welander's interview with Ehrlichman and Young, and never read any of the investigative reports. Everything he knew came from a briefing given to him by Fred Buzhardt on January 5, 1972. When he found out what had happened, he told Welander to return any bootlegged papers to the White House. Yes, he'd seen documents from the Kissinger and Haig trips, but in both cases, these had told him nothing he hadn't already known, and he therefore had regarded the documents as insignificant.

The committee did not have the evidence before it to challenge Moorer. For one thing, Mel Laird had not been called to testify, even though he was sitting in the White House, packing up his belongings preparatory to leaving for a job with *Reader's Digest*, and he fully expected such a call. He even expected Stennis to ask for the Buzhardt report, but "Stennis never asked me," he recalls. According to Laird, Stennis "thought it would serve no useful purpose" to conduct a full inquiry.

Senator Thomas J. McIntyre, Democrat of New Hampshire, asked Moorer a good question. If, as Moorer had testified, he usually had his aides screen the voluminous material that was routed to him, why would his close aide Welander hand-deliver supposedly insignificant papers? Moorer quickly started to change his story. "I did not term the papers unimportant . . . the papers were important, but I had already acquired the information."

Evidence that would have raised serious questions about those assertions could have been found in the Welander interviews or in the meeting notes of the NSC, but the committee didn't have such documents.

Moorer concluded two hours of testimony by saying that not "one word" about the espionage matter had ever been mentioned to him by Nixon, even though they were in frequent personal contact. "He has never indicated anything but complete satisfaction with the way I handle my job."

The next witness was Henry Kissinger, who conceded that "extremely sensitive" papers, such as his personal memos to Nixon, had not been designed to be shared outside the White House. Nevertheless, he testified, it was "absurd to argue that there was any subject of any major significance that was kept from the Joint Chiefs of Staff." Kissinger artfully avoided denying that there had been any spying— but he did say that if the military had really objected to any of his or Nixon's policies, "that opposition was never made explicit at any of the many meetings" of the NSC. "On the contrary, all of those policies were supported by Admiral Moorer. . . . I was never conscious of any disagreement between myself and Admiral Moorer."

The Kissinger-Moorer love fest continued. Moorer knew all of his positions, the secretary of state said, for instance in regard to talks with the North Vietnamese; perhaps "he [Moorer] might have thought that we would surface those positions in the open sessions in Paris, when in fact they surfaced at secret meetings." That was not such a big deal. Yes, he had been "enraged" when he had listened to a portion of the Welander-Ehrlichman-Young interview and thereby learned that his briefcase had been broken into, but later he had "calmed down" and concluded that there really could not have been very much military spying, "considering the confidential relationship that existed before, the close association, and the total absence of any friction" between himself and the Joint Chiefs. He had abolished the liaison office "in a fit of pique." He sloughed off questions from Symington and others, and by late afternoon Stennis declared that the "cross-examination" of Moorer and Kissinger had convinced him that the two men were clean. Stennis came outside and told reporters that "I don't see them [Moorer and Kissinger] as the root of any conspiracy," but did announce that the committee would call Welander and Buzhardt, and bring Radford from the Pacific Northwest. Moorer told reporters that he had twice recommended that court-martial proceedings be initiated against Radford, but "civilian authorities" had overruled him.

Michael Getler of the *Post* reported that "Moorer's apparent willingness to court-martial Radford to determine his 'guilt or innocence' would appear to contradict allegations that it was Moorer who was secretly behind the alleged plan to spy on Kissinger's operation." That was the message Moorer was trying to convey by his disingenuous remark that other people had decided against going after Radford.

Radford was now the center of the controversy, and the committee moved to bring him to Washington for a private meeting with Stennis.

The yeoman had learned a few things in the past three years. Before leaving the Naval Reserve Center in Salem, Oregon, for Washington, he decided to consent to an interview with CBS correspondent Mike Wallace, who had convinced Radford to appear on camera on that coming Sunday's edition of "60 Minutes." Thursday evening, February 7, Wallace broadcast over the CBS radio network part of a voice-only interview with Radford, in which Radford said he had done his work for Robinson and Welander, who had created the climate and strongly encouraged him to do so.

Sy Hersh of *The New York Times* had learned of Radford's trip to Washington, and cornered him at the airport concourse in Denver, where Radford was changing planes on February 8. "The yeoman acknowledged that he had pilfered hundreds of documents [that] were funnelled to the office of Adm. Thomas H. Moorer," said a dispatch Hersh sent from the airport.

When Radford arrived in Washington, Stennis convinced him to stop talking to the public and to cancel the interview with "60 Minutes," previously scheduled for Sunday. "Stennis had me under wraps in Washington for three days," Radford says. Accompanied by a lawyer he had retained, Radford met Stennis and his aides in the senator's office on Saturday, February 9, and "told them everything." Afterward, Stennis told waiting newsmen that Radford "was cooperative fully and I have no complaints about him."

Congress was in the midst of a ten-day recess, and Radford was scheduled to testify when Congress reconvened. Meanwhile, Senator Baker was continuing his own inquiry. According to one of his aides at the time, Senator Baker and his staff believed that Stennis' hearings were "a farce," a judgment concurred in by Mel Laird.

Stennis had Radford; Baker wanted to grab Don Stewart. At nine in the evening of February 7, Stewart received a phone call from his old FBI buddy Don Sanders, who was on Baker's staff. Would Stewart come to another meeting to discuss Moorer-Radford with Baker aide George Murphy? Stewart was tired. He'd already sat with Sanders, Liebengood, and Thompson in July and again in November—what more could he tell Murphy, he asked Sanders. If such a meeting were really necessary, Stewart said, Sanders should clear it with Martin Hoffman, special assistant to Schlesinger.

Next morning, Stewart himself wrote Hoffman a memo describing the previous evening's phone call from Sanders. Stewart was playing by the rules, making it clear to the civilian command at the Pentagon that he wasn't dealing secretly with Baker. The memo was addressed to Hoffman, who just ten days earlier had shared with Stewart the Justice file in which Stewart had first been accused and then cleared by Petersen and others. In the memo, Stewart said that he had advised Sanders that he thought the Watergate committee was "out of the action" on this matter, and that he did not want "to prejudice or preempt any testimony I may later have to give before Senator Stennis' committee should I be called."

Just hours after he had fired off his memo to Hoffman, around one in the afternoon, Stewart received a call from Woodward. Getler had been handling the reporting of the military espionage in the *Post* for some weeks, yet Woodward wanted to talk to Stewart about the accuracy of various charges being leveled in the hearings. Woodward mentioned something that Stewart felt the reporter should not have known—that Radford and Jack Anderson had dined together two days before the publication of the tilt-to-Pakistan article. "This surprised me," Stewart later wrote of this phone call, "because this particular date had to come from the file," that is, from the file Stewart himself had compiled after his own interrogation of Radford. Not a hint of that Radford-Anderson meeting had surfaced in the press, and Stewart was convinced that someone with access to this report had leaked the information to Woodward. In his memo of the phone call, Stewart said, "This [fact about the Anderson-Radford dinner] and the general questioning Woodward put to me makes me believe that he, too, is being provided info from the White House." Two hours later, Woodward called back and asked Stewart about Fred Buzhardt. While the earlier conversation had been marked, Stewart wrote, by "five to ten minutes of sparring," Woodward was more blunt this second time around. Stewart took down Woodward's main question verbatim, jotting it down at the bottom of his memo of the earlier call: "If Buzhardt told what he knew, could he contradict Adm. Moorer and bring about Moorer's court-martial?" Stewart told Woodward that he didn't know what Buzhardt knew, and hung up.

Five minutes later, Martin Hoffman called Stewart about the still-unresolved request from Baker's staff for Stewart to meet with them, and Stewart recounted his recent conversation with Woodward.

Woodward's two calls to Stewart were reminiscent of his call to Welander in May 1973: They were attempts to find out information that was not particularly of interest to the reporter, but was of great interest to certain men close to the president. Would Stewart testify? What did he know? How much did Stewart understand of what Buzhardt knew? Putting the best face on these phone calls, Woodward seemed to be trading information with his White House sources; putting a less good face on the phone calls, he seemed to be doing his White House sources' dirty work for them. In the ensuing days Woodward wrote nothing about Moorer-Radford or his conversation with Stewart.

On Monday, February 11, Hoffman called Stewart with the news that the Watergate committee was about to serve a subpoena requiring Stewart's testimony at 10:00 A.M. the next day, and that Hoffman was going to get in touch with the Armed Services Committee and advise them of the Watergate committee's interest. The subpoena came in the afternoon, and it said the appearance was for the nineteenth, after Congress' recess, when Ervin was due to return to the capital.

It was Baker, not Ervin, however, who met Stewart on the nineteenth, in the same room in which Alexander Butterfield had revealed his great secret seven months earlier. Baker was accompanied by his aides Sanders and Murphy, and by chief counsel Sam Dash. In two hours of sworn testimony, Stewart laid out for the men the entire dimensions of Moorer-Radford, excepting Welander's references to Haig in his confession, which he did not know about.

As the questioning proceeded, it became obvious to Stewart that Baker and the staff had not seen any of the White House or Pentagon reports and memoranda on Moorer-Radford. For instance, the questioners wanted to know if Moorer had personal knowledge of Radford's activities. When Stewart described his reports, such as the fourteen-page transcript of his own interview of Welander, Baker asked, "Could you tell us where we could locate them?" Stewart told Baker that his own files had been seized the previous May, and described the timing, three days after he'd spoken to Tufaro about getting a job. "I think Fred Buzhardt had them taken away," he said, and suggested attempting to obtain similar documents through Hoffman at Schlesinger's office.

Baker wanted to know, "What is the big national security issue involved here?" The one that would cause Radford to be moved out of town overnight, and the White House to pressure Ervin and Baker not to investigate the matter? "As a taxpayer, if I found out that the military was spying on a president of the United States, it would worry the hell out of me," Stewart responded. "Me, too," Baker said.

Moreover, Baker told Stewart, what troubled him was that the White House was now downplaying the entire episode and claiming that the allegations and news stories were overblown. That White House position is "inconsistent with the idea that it [Moorer-Radford] is of such huge national security importance. So what I'm after is, what is there in this that's of such huge national security importance?"

No one in the room could answer that question.

The following day, the Armed Services Committee met behind closed doors to hear Yeoman Radford. Waiting reporters were handed transcripts of the Moorer and Kissinger testimony of two weeks earlier, and Radford's twenty-three-page opening statement. As that statement made clear, Radford was sticking to what he had told Stewart more than two years earlier: Robinson and Welander had encouraged him, and Chairman Moorer had received hundreds, perhaps thousands of pages of highly sensitive documents that he would otherwise not have seen. Radford denied having leaked anything to Jack Anderson, and declared that he would not be the fall guy even for the senior Navy brass.

In front of ten senators, Radford gave chapter and verse about his part in the military espionage—what he had taken, who had seen it and praised him for his pilfering, and so on. He testified that during his time in the liaison office he had passed to his superiors at least twenty-five to thirty EYES ONLY messages addressed to Nixon from Kissinger and/or from Haig. Accompanied by an attorney and no longer contrite, as he had been when he first confessed to Stewart, Radford was no less straightforward: "All the time I was following the directions and advice of my superiors. I felt like I was doing what I did for the good of the service. At no time did I feel the decision as to whether or not to do as I was told or asked to do was mine to make."

Under questioning, he said that Robinson had told him to collect papers from White House desks.

Stennis and several of the Republicans hammered at Radford and tried to shake his story. Strom Thurmond, Buzhardt's old boss, asserted that Radford had no proof that Moorer knew of the clandestine operation. Asked by Hughes if he would "welcome a court-martial inquiry," Radford responded, "I have no qualms whatsoever about facing" Moorer or Welander "in public session. . . . I will be glad to."

Senator Sam Nunn made a rare inquiry about Haig's possible knowledge of the liaison office's clandestine operations. It was specula-tion to "examine someone else's mind," Nunn said, but did Haig know "that your whole job and the job of that outfit was to keep Admiral Moorer informed, or was this some kind of a very secretive operation . . . ?"

"No," Radford responded. "I assumed that he [Haig] would know why Admiral Robinson was there. Admiral Robinson was reporting not only to Admiral Moorer in the morning at the Pentagon, but he would also report to General Haig. He sent memos to General Haig the same way we sent memos to Admiral Moorer."

If Haig was "conscious of his activity and conscious of this being your job," Nunn asked, why would Haig "ask for or agree to your going on the trip with him?"

"I have no idea," Radford responded, and veered off into another subject.

The next day was Welander's turn before the committee, and he went to some lengths to refute all that Radford had said. Contrary to the confessions he had made, Welander put all the onus on Radford. He had "never ordered or directed" Radford to do any of the things Radford had charged, and moreover asserted that Radford had told him that he'd acquired "the documents on these trips in the regular course of his clerical duties." Had he learned the true source, Welander testified, "I can assure this committee I would have reacted. . . . I would have put an immediate end to such activity." His predecessor Robinson, Welander asserted, had never talked to him about Radford's activities. Welander also accused Radford of being the source of the leaks to Jack Anderson.

There is a strong indication that Stennis had been able to see Buzhardt's January 7, 1972, Welander reinterview report—the one that was silent on the connection of Haig to the members of the spy ring—and that he shared it with close aides but not with his fellow senators. When committee lawyer W. Clark McFadden II cross-examined Welan-der, he asked a series of questions that could only have been derived from that reinterview report. For instance, in that reinterview Welander cited troop withdrawals from Vietnam, and the negotiations to base a carrier group in Greece as examples of documents that Radford had obtained for him; McFadden asked about these in virtually the same words used in the reinterview report.

Welander's denials were full and ringing in the early part of the day of questioning, but toward the end he began to make revealing statements, and he eventually acknowledged that he had retained about 25 percent of the contents of the bulging envelopes Radford brought back from the Kissinger trip, and that among these papers were a half-dozen key documents, including NSC documents calling for faster troop withdrawals from Vietnam than the JCS thought was warranted, as well as memoranda of Kissinger's private conversations with various people in Vietnam. But, Welander said, he only looked at these as reminders to go and talk to the NSC staff about these matters.

An incredulous Sam Nunn asked why Radford would have given him such important papers if Welander could have obtained the information through regular channels. Concluding his testimony, Welander responded, "Senator, I do not know. . . . I never asked him to do this, sir. He did it. And, again, I guess I should have told him not to."

Having heard from Moorer, Kissinger, Radford, and Welander, the committee's next logical step would have been to obtain testimony from Ehrlichman, Young, and Stewart. Several senators on the panel expected to do so, and to press for the documentary evidence. Chairman Stennis had a different idea. He told reporters that the hearings would continue at some point in the future, but didn't know when, because the committee had important budget business to handle.

Meanwhile, the revelations continued in the press. Seymour Hersh wrote an article published by *The New York Times* on February 24 in which he reported that "sources close to the inquiry" told him that Nixon "personally ordered" that there be no prosecutions of any military figures even though Nixon had been "extremely angry about the pilfering of high-level documents that were not intended for the Pentagon." Nixon, Hersh wrote, had "decided to cancel the inquiry after consultation" with Mitchell. The article stated that Nixon feared exposing the secret negotiations then in process, including the opening to China, the SALT negotiations, and the Vietnam peace talks; these, the article said, would have been seriously threatened had the president tried to punish the Joint Chiefs. "You could call this a brutally realistic exercise in Presidential judgment," a White House source was quoted as observing.

The following day the *Washington Post* weighed in with a long editorial suggesting that the evidence presented to date showed that Moorer had been running an espionage operation, and that after it was discovered, "a rather shabby deal was then struck between the White House and the Pentagon to keep the whole thing quiet. . . . President Nixon—for reasons it would be interesting to learn—was evidently unwilling to take on the Pentagon." The *Post* noted that Kissinger "now echoes Adm. Moorer," and that Schlesinger did, too, and concluded, "it smacks, in a word, of coverup." Curiously, this editorial is at odds with the *Post*'s rather casual reporting on Moorer-Radford, and instead echoes the seriousness with which Hersh and *The New York Times* handled the story.

During January and February, Haig talked to Nixon about what he said was going on in the Special Prosecutor's office. Haig painted a favorable picture of Jaworski, telling Nixon that Jaworski "was being very expansive and cooperative in evaluating the situation . . . that the staff inherited from Cox had a number of 'fanatics' " that Jaworski was having difficulty keeping under control, and that "Sirica was really a friend of the president," who would not take kindly to the idea that Cox's leftover staff was "more interested in 'getting the President' than in getting the facts."

Indeed, the Special Prosecutor's staff was restive about Jaworski's private dealings with Haig. According to James Doyle, "Nobody in the office was quite sure what was in Jaworski's mind because he chose not to confide in us, at least not completely." There was also no evidence that Sirica was in any way disposed against the leftover staff for their supposed zealousness, as the judge continued to press vigorously to get to the bottom of the affair, as he had done for the entire year that the matter had been before him in the court.

On March 1, 1974, the grand jury handed up indictments that named Mitchell, Haldeman, Ehrlichman, Colson, Mardian, Strachan, and Kenneth W. Parkinson (a CRP attorney) in the Watergate cover-up. That day the prosecutors also handed to Judge Sirica a sealed envelope and a briefcase. These contained the grand jury's still-secret report naming Nixon as an unindicted co-conspirator, and materials that had been sought—unsuccessfully so far—by the House Judiciary Committee, which had been charged with the responsibility for the impeachment inquiry. Negotiations began for those materials between the Judiciary Committee, the court, and the Special Prosecutor's office.

This indictment exposed much of what Haig had been telling Nixon about Jaworski's behavior as nonsense. There was no way to consider the indictments of Nixon's former attorney general and his former chief of staff as anything other than devastating to the president. If, by tidbits from the Jaworski backchannel, Haig had been shielding Nixon from the imminence of this blow, when it came on March 1, it must have fallen all the harder.

When full transcripts of the Radford and Welander testimonies before the Stennis committee were released on March 3, *Post* reporter Michael Getler picked up a new lead from something Welander had said in his own defense—that he was carrying stuff to the White House, out of normal distribution channels—and wrote this up as a story about the Pentagon going around Secretary of Defense Mel Laird. This second operation was "authorized but highly 'unorthodox,' " Getler wrote; he had learned that Laird and his deputy David Packard became aware that they were being cut out when at certain government meetings they noticed that Kissinger was working with material related to Vietnam that Defense had specifically not provided to the NSC adviser.

A few days later, on March 7, Stennis called his final witness— Buzhardt. The man who was counsel to the president (and who had also been counsel to the Department of Defense until two months ago) brought a copy of his January 10, 1972, report to the hearings—but no copies were given to the senators. Stennis told his colleagues they could only read the document at the committee offices, since it was from "the bosom of the executive branch," and strictly confidential. It could not be removed from the premises or released or even disclosed to anyone else. Senator Hughes was skeptical, and said that if he found that the report had nothing in it that threatened national security, he was determined to have it released. Buzhardt claimed it could not be released because it had been prepared for Laird, and that he had obtained it from Laird only on the condition that its contents be kept secret. "No one else saw this report," Buzhardt told the senators. "No other copy was kept of it."

"Stennis never asked me for the report," Laird told us, and firmly believes that the full Senate "did not want to get into this [Moorer-Radford]."

Buzhardt testified very carefully. He had relied on Stewart's infor-mation to conclude that Radford "was most probably" Jack Anderson's source, but the case had been "entirely circumstantial," and that was why it had not been pursued for prosecution. He admitted that Welander had told him of the pilfering and that the admiral had seen the product and passed it onward—testimony that refuted both that of

Welander and Moorer. But he carefully stopped short of saying that Moorer had seen anything important.

He also minimized the importance of Don Stewart—"I think I did have Mr. Stewart present to take notes" at the Welander reinterview— and of the two other major documents that would have skewered his own testimony, the Ehrlichman interview of Welander, and Young's hefty investigative report. There was "no material substantive difference," Buzhardt testified, between that January 7, 1972, reinterview and the taped interview of Welander on December 22, 1971, further burying the single piece of evidence that contained the significant references to Haig. Finally, he asserted that Young's report "had available almost precisely the same information from which I prepared my report," and therefore the senators had no need to consult it.

Symington, in a written question, threw Buzhardt what should have been a curve. Why had Buzhardt refused to provide the tape of his interview with Welander to Schlesinger in mid-January? In his written answer, Buzhardt batted the question away neatly, saying that he had resigned as counsel to the Pentagon on January 4, and thus Schlesinger had no authority over Buzhardt at the time the secretary's request was made! It was the complete explanation of the peculiar timing of his resignation from that particular post.

In the hearing, under questioning Buzhardt did an astounding thing. He chucked overboard the entire line of defense that had been taken for years by Nixon and everyone else: "I do not believe [my report] contains material which would be—endanger the national security if released."

So: the claim of national security had all been a sham. While the senators were reeling from that revelation, Buzhardt told them that— unfortunately—he did have another problem with releasing the report, though, a new difficulty: The report contained "private pieces of correspondence, memorandums" between Laird and other Defense officials and the White House. These papers were "quite sensitive. They deal with the actual workings of the NSC." Moreover, it wasn't fair to release the report because it contained only "summary conclusions" and relied in part on polygraph examinations that were not admissible in court and could possibly be construed as "libelous" to Charles Radford.

This surprising defense of why the report could not be released was hotly debated among the senators. McIntyre, Goldwater, Symington, and Hughes all stated during Buzhardt's testimony that they wanted to see both his report and that of David Young—obviously to compare them.

Senatorial push then came to senatorial shove. Stennis told his colleagues that he was still "negotiating" with Buzhardt over both those reports and there was a fifty-fifty chance the committee would eventually get both of them. Hughes weighed in with the observation that the investigation was far from complete, and that two or three other witnesses should be called, principal among them, Ehrlichman. With this demand, Stennis exploded. He began openly to advise Buzhardt not to let the committee see the document he had waved about, after all. "So this report that you had with you, just take it back. I don't want to see a line of it."

By this point in the hearings, the other senators had left the room and only Stennis and Hughes remained. Hughes pointed out that Stennis had promised them the report in the morning, and that he, Hughes, had a "moral obligation to read the report that you said is available to us." Stennis then closed a parliamentary trap by telling Hughes that since there were only two senators in the room, no action could be taken. Hughes continued to assert that he would ask Buzhardt if he could see the report privately, and Stennis warned him that this would not do, and if Hughes went to the press, that would "just kill every chance" that the committee had of ever getting the report from Buzhardt.

The hearing was over, and would not call any further witnesses. Nor would it ever obtain the document from Buzhardt, and it would not even issue a final report on the matter until six months after Nixon had left office. On March 7, 1974, the disinterment had not discovered the major evidence, but the second funeral was declared over, and the gates of the cemetery were then closed.

Shortly, in June, Admiral Moorer retired at the end of his second term as chairman of the Joint Chiefs, after forty-one years of service to his country. Welander, identified as one of the major culprits in the committee's late report, was pressured to retire in 1975, after thirty years in the Navy. "My name had been spread all over the goddamned press," he told us bitterly, "and the Navy doesn't take something like that lightly."

Since May 1973, Haig and Buzhardt, and unwittingly and to a lesser extent Len Garment, had labored mightily to keep Moorer-Radford from surfacing. They had lost many skirmishes, because much of the information had now been made public, but with the conclusion of the Stennis hearings it was clear that they had won the decisive battle to keep Haig's name away from the issue of the military spy ring. In the hands of a determined and thorough investigative body, the tape of the

Ehrlichman-Young-Welander interview, with its references to the admiral's dealings with Haig, could have led to questions about the "very, very sticky relationships" that Welander had mentioned to Ehrlichman and Young.

Len Garment today says he didn't know what battle he was really fighting at the time. He did not then know the dimensions of Moorer-Radford. Asked by us recently whether Haig had a conflict of interest when he came back into the White House as the new chief of staff in May 1973, Garment replied, "Conflict of interest, capital C, capital O, capital I."

Why did Buzhardt conduct his reinterview of Welander, an interview that carefully avoided the significant references to Haig that had appeared in Welander's earlier confession to Ehrlichman and Young? Since neither Laird nor Nixon had ordered the reinterview, Buzhardt must have done it on his own, or at the request of the only man who had benefited from that reinterview, Alexander Haig—who, as the reader will recall, had listened to the Ehrlichman-Young tape about two weeks before the Buzhardt reinterview. Had Buzhardt and Haig, schooled in the ways of Washington, arranged for Welander to be questioned again with the express purpose of using it as a last line of defense in the event that someday an inquiry might find its way to Haig's door?

25

THE REAL FINAL DAYS

TWO weeks after Buzhardt reappeared in public as the last witness at the Stennis hearings, he took his place at the head table as James St. Clair held a two-hour meeting with Nixon about his defense, a meeting also attended by Haig and Ziegler. It was the first time in three months that Buzhardt had joined such a discussion, but with Moorer-Radford back in its grave he could rejoin the inner circle, and in the ensuing months of April and May, Buzhardt continued to sit in on all such sessions with Nixon, as well as to meet with the president and Haig without St. Clair present. During those months, St. Clair virtually never saw the president without Haig or Buzhardt being present, though Haig had said when he initially hired St. Clair that he himself was too swamped with other duties to devote enough attention to the president's legal defense.

Shortly, there were reports in the press that St. Clair was not being allowed to review the tapes—the very evidence over which the White House was battling the Special Prosecutor and Congress. Buzhardt was reviewing the tapes for St. Clair because, as *Congressional Quarterly* noted, the White House "was not willing to allow St. Clair to make his

404

own judgement" on how many tapes should be turned over. Nor was the Boston trial attorney being allowed to deal with Jaworski directly. Woodward and Bernstein wrote in *The Final Days:*

> Even with James St. Clair on the scene, Haig thought he ought to maintain the personal relationship he had so carefully nurtured with Jaworski. He informed St. Clair that he would continue to act as the pipeline to the special prosecutor's office. That would allow St. Clair to focus totally on the impeachment inquiry. . . . At all costs, Haig wanted to avoid a court battle with Jaworski over additional tapes, the very question of future access which had figured in Cox's firing.

Woodward's and Bernstein's account was precisely wrong—or, perhaps, just badly influenced by the writers' sources, Haig and Buzhardt. For, as we have seen, Haig was doing all he could to provoke and intensify the court battle: Toward that end, Haig had facilitated Jaworski's efforts to obtain additional tapes, perhaps authorized him personally, and without referring the matter to Nixon, to listen to the "tape of tapes," and played a scene of stunned surprise when Jaworski had come back with a demand for twenty-five additional tapes.

In mid-March 1974 Sirica ruled that the House Judiciary Committee ought to have the evidence that Jaworski had turned over to the court on March 1, the evidence supporting the grand jury's designation of Nixon as an unindicted co-conspirator in the cover-up. Sirica turned over the briefcase full of evidence to the committee's chief counsel, John Doar.

On April 3, a joint congressional committee released a report that Nixon owed nearly a half-million dollars in back taxes and interest because he had improperly deducted his gift of vice-presidential papers to the National Archives. Rather than contest the matter, the president agreed to pay $467,000 to the IRS.

On April 11, the Judiciary Committee issued a subpoena for forty-two tapes. The committee vote was 33–3, indicating that Nixon's Republican support had eroded. One week later, responding to a request from Jaworski, Sirica issued a subpoena to Nixon to hand over sixty-four recordings to the Special Prosecutor; the second of the items listed contained the Haldeman-Nixon conversations of June 23, 1972, that would later become known as the "smoking gun" tape.

Nixon figured that the most urgent challenge was the House impeachment inquiry, and decided that a stunning public relations move might throw the Judiciary Committee off stride. On the evening of April 29, Nixon appeared on national television, seated beside a stack of green loose-leaf books. He announced that these were transcripts of the forty-two recordings subpoenaed by the Judiciary Committee, and that he was turning over these 1,308 pages of transcripts in lieu of the tapes. He asserted that these would prove that he had not been involved in a cover-up, and that these were all that was needed to "get Watergate behind us."

They were not. Public reaction to the transcripts was quite negative; the expletives had been deleted, but not the thought behind them. People objected to the bald language, the discussions of hush payments and stonewalling, and the atmosphere of suspicion and hostility that pervaded the Nixon White House and that the transcripts laid bare. For the first time in American history, Americans had been taken directly into the Oval Office and made privy to hours upon hours of the conversations that went on in that inner sanctum; what they learned appalled them. Even stalwart Nixon defenders like Senate Minority Leader Hugh Scott declared that the transcripts were "deplorable, disgusting, shabby, immoral." More to the point, on the day after the transcripts were officially released, May 1, the Judiciary Committee rejected them and informed Nixon that he had failed to comply with the subpoena.

Overlooked in the reaction to the release of the transcripts was any close comparison of them to John Dean's testimony, an examination that would have revealed Dean's repeated lies under oath about his conversations with the president, and that also would have shown how Dean had misled Nixon. The focus was on the president, and he could not shake it. Just days after the release of the transcripts, the Judiciary Committee began impeachment hearings; highlights from those hearings illuminated the nightly news broadcasts.

Jaworski was on a collision course with the president over the tapes, but wanted to avoid a confrontation. He called Haig, and when Haig returned from out of town on Sunday, May 5, the two men met alone in the Map Room. While two of Jaworski's aides waited nearby in the White House library with Haig's aide Major George Joulwan, the Special Prosecutor played his high card. He told Haig that the grand jury had voted 19–0 to name Nixon as an unindicted co-conspirator; this information was still secret, and Jaworski was willing to keep it that way. His price was eighteen of the sixty-four tapes, one of which was the June 23, 1972, recording. If those tapes were handed over, Jaworski told Haig, he'd keep the co-conspirator designation secret, and drop his fight for the rest of the tapes, thereby ending the court case. But if the president refused the deal and there was a court fight,

Jaworski would be forced to reveal the grand jury's action as part of his legal strategy to obtain the tapes.

Haig agreed to explore the idea, and brought into the room Jaworski's two assistants and James St. Clair. The Boston lawyer was opposed to the deal. Haig was inclined to compromise, and went to Camp David to relay it to Nixon.

"A form of blackmail," Nixon characterized the offer in his memoirs, but "the thought of actually ending the courtroom battle over the tapes was like a siren song. Haig felt it too." Nixon quoted Haig as saying, "We're at the point that we can see the barbed wire at the end of the street. What we have to do is mobilize everything to cut through it." (Nixon liked it when Haig talked military.) Haig urged Nixon to listen to those tapes and not to reject the offer "out of hand." Nixon agreed to put on the earphones.

During the past several months, the Special Prosecutor had been able to obtain many of the tapes that had been identified as being the most potentially incriminating. Nixon had been forced into a corner. Presented with Jaworski's latest demand, Haig told Nixon that the choice of how to handle the situation was up to him, but in reality Nixon's options had been so drastically reduced that he could now choose only the timing of his political suicide. The instrument lay in wait in the midst of the batch of tapes.

Closeted in his EOB office, Nixon began to listen to the eighteen conversations on the evening of May 5, and some time the following afternoon he reached the June 23 recording of his conversations with Haldeman. Almost immediately, he wrote in *RN*, his spirits fell. "I had indicated in all my public statements that the sole motive for calling in the CIA had been national security. But there was no doubt now that we had been talking about political implications that morning."

He found his thoughts immediately forced back to the previous May, when the damaging Vernon Walters memcons had first surfaced, the first one of which concerned the meeting Walters and Helms had held with Haldeman and Ehrlichman, following Nixon's instructions to Haldeman on June 23, 1972. In May 1973, Nixon had discussed the matter with Buzhardt, who declared that Walters must have been confused when he wrote the memcon on June 28. "I should have asked Buzhardt to listen" to the June 23 tape then, Nixon thought; it could have been made public in May 1973 and that "would have been damaging, but far less so than being forced" to disclose it by the court a year later. Nixon also remembered his discussions in the summer of 1973 with Haldeman about the Walters memcons and the June 23 conversations, when Haldeman had visited the White House. Haldeman, too, had distinctly remembered that the reason for calling in the CIA had been national security, not politics—but they had both been wrong in their memories of June 23, 1972. Listening to the tape made that clear, Nixon thought.

Worst of all, Nixon wrote, the existence of that tape made a mockery of his May 22, 1973, statement, especially of the portion that addressed why the CIA had gotten into the act. Well, he would not turn over these tapes to Jaworski, and would take his chances on a court fight. He consoled himself with the idea that he had survived many another political disaster, and would survive this one, too. If, eventually, this tape was forced from his hand, maybe other people would have the same trouble interpreting it as he and Haldeman had.

As had happened so often before to Nixon, in this situation he failed to pose the real questions. Why hadn't Buzhardt warned him of the danger of the Walters memcons in time? Why had Walters not been prevented from releasing the documents to Congress? Why had Jaworski been led to believe he could successfully ask for more and more tapes?

Jaworski was informed that there would be no deal. Two weeks later, on May 20, 1974, Sirica upheld Jaworski's sixty-four-tape subpoena and ordered Nixon to turn over the recordings. The president appealed, and Jaworski countered with a risky and bold maneuver. He leaped over the heads of the appeals judges and petitioned the Supreme Court. On May 31, the Supreme Court agreed to hear the case.

In preparation for his own trial on the Dr. Fielding break-in, in late May 1974 John Ehrlichman hit the White House with a broad subpoena for his notes and files. Ehrlichman was going to base his defense on the fact that in late 1971 Nixon forbade any disclosure of the Plumbers' activities on the grounds of national security. When Ehrlichman had learned after the fact about the Dr. Fielding burglary he had remained silent because of the national security blanket. He subpoenaed the Welander interview tape and other documents of the Moorer-Radford investigation in order to argue that they proved the extreme sensitivity of the national security secrets and the reason for Nixon's unequivocal gag order.

The thrust for the Welander tape was as potentially damaging to Haig as Jaworski's thrust for the June 23 "smoking gun" tape was for Nixon. But while Haig had been willing to compromise on Nixon's behalf, he was not willing to bend on material that was so clearly threatening to him. Seven months earlier, when Bud Krogh had tried to force the Moorer-Radford material out, Haig and Buzhardt had told

Jaworski that there were grave national security issues at stake in them; that danger had passed when Krogh agreed to a plea-bargain.

When Ehrlichman demanded the Welander tape, Buzhardt and Haig took the opposite tack. National security wasn't the issue, they said, but executive privilege was—Buzhardt moved to quash the subpoena on the latter grounds. Expecting this, Ehrlichman's lawyers then moved for the case to be dismissed, saying there would be no way for them to prepare a proper defense without the material. Judge Gerhard Gesell initially sided with Ehrlichman and indicated he would approve the defense motion to dismiss the case if the White House continued to stonewall.

On June 6, St. Clair filed more papers on Nixon's motion to quash the subpoena. His motion was accompanied by motions of Buzhardt and Haig to quash the subpoenas against them. The two aides had been identified by Ehrlichman as retaining control over the material in his files. Haig and Buzhardt filed supporting affidavits in which they denied "custody or control of any document or object" described in Ehrlichman's subpoena.

In fact, the tape and the transcript of the Welander interview were hidden at the White House along with the detailed David Young report and other papers from the Moorer-Radford investigation. Haig was, of course, chief of staff and had been so for over a year.

Ehrlichman showed up at the White House to try to review his files. He was forced to sit in a waiting area outside the presidential counsel's office that had once been his own, and wait for Buzhardt. "I never saw him," Ehrlichman says of that day, but "I was sitting in his outer office and I could hear through the door that Buzhardt was listening to the Welander tape" of the December 22, 1971, confession. "I could hear it through the door because it was turned up loud. I went back to my attorney, William Frates, and told him what had happened. He said, 'We have to get our hands on that tape.' "

Shortly afterward, Buzhardt submitted a second affidavit asserting that there was nothing in the Ehrlichman files that was relevant to his defense—in other words, no material covered by "national security." That flag had been of use in November, against Krogh, but it was taken down and "executive privilege" run up the flagpole when Ehrlichman wanted the Welander tape. Ehrlichman tried to argue this, but Gesell accepted the Buzhardt representation. "With that ruling, much of the steam went out of our defense," Ehrlichman later wrote.

He continued to fight. A week later, his attorney submitted another motion asking for a subpoena, a motion that specifically discussed the JCS espionage inquiry and the backchannel. The motion asserted that during the secret negotiations with the North Vietnamese, Nixon had ordered bombing strikes against Hanoi to add to the pressure at the bargaining table, that these strikes had been ordered directly through the Joint Chiefs, and that Moorer had been at the center of this bombing backchannel. It was for this reason that Nixon had put a lid on the military spying episode—because disclosure "would have seriously impaired the direct chain of command to the Joint Chiefs of Staff," Ehrlichman's attorney wrote. Therefore, they needed, among other items, Ehrlichman's notes from the meeting at which he had advised Nixon of Welander's confession, as well as the notes of Nixon instructing him that "any testimony" on the Plumbers unit "is affected by national security and their activities were not to be disclosed."

This second subpoena of Ehrlichman's was still in the air on June 10, and the impeachment inquiry was into its second month of hearings, when Nixon flew to the Mideast. On the agenda were a week of talks in four Arab countries and in Israel. Only recently, after a month of exhausting shuttle diplomacy, Henry Kissinger had won acceptance from Syria and Israel for an American-sponsored accord to disengage their troops after the October 1973 war between the two nations. Nixon appeared at the height of his powers in Cairo on June 12: Hundreds of thousands of people shouted greetings and waved American flags as Nixon and Egyptian President Anwar Sadat passed by them in open cars.

In his diary, Nixon comforted himself with the idea that the Mideast trip "put the whole Watergate business into perspective—to make us realize that all the terrible battering we have taken is really pygmy-sized when compared to what we have done and what we can do in the future not only for peace in the world but, indirectly, to effect the well-being of people everywhere."

But that wasn't what was really happening. Kissinger wrote in his memoirs that "at every press conference I was asked about the impact of Watergate on foreign policy. I consistently denied any relationship. Though everybody knew it to be untrue, only a show of imperviousness would enable us to salvage anything." According to Kissinger, both the Chinese and the Soviets were profoundly confused by Nixon's domestic political crisis. When he met with Mao Tse-tung in November 1973, Kissinger wrote, the Chinese leader's "principal concern was not our Soviet policy, but our domestic situation, specifically Watergate. . . . He contemptuously dismissed the whole affair as a form of "breaking wind.' " However, Kissinger reported, China began to "hedge its bets," waiting to join the U.S. in a policy of containing the Soviet Union until Watergate "had played itself out."

As for the Soviet Union, according to Kissinger's book *Years of Upheaval*, General Secretary Leonid Brezhnev told the United States ambassador to Moscow in 1974 of his "amazement that the United States had reached the point that the President would be bothered about his taxes," and ultimately, Kissinger wrote, Nixon "became less and less interesting to the Soviets as a negotiating partner."

Nixon was also less and less interesting to Kissinger for the same reasons. Roger Morris, who has written biographics of Haig, Kissinger, and Nixon, told us, "It was Kissinger's view all through the latter part of 1973 and the spring of 1974 that Richard Nixon, really sooner rather than later, ought to go for the sake of the stability of the [NATO] alliance, the prospects of any kind of SALT II treaty, et cetera. There were grandiose calculations made about sacrificing this president, who, after all, had become a cripple." Morris recalled dining at the home of Kissinger's aide Larry Eagleburger in late 1973 and early 1974, when Watergate was "an obsessive topic of conversation" as to the effect it was having on U.S. foreign policy, "not just to Kissinger's initiatives in the Middle East, but to the great tenor of American relations abroad." Kissinger's "great dilemma," said Morris, was that Nixon had elevated him to secretary of state, yet in Kissinger's view "had to be gotten rid of."

Returning to Washington from the Mideast on June 19, Nixon realized the extent to which his weakened position had emboldened his conservative opponents, the anti-détente forces within the government. In his foreign policy, Nixon had steadfastly tried to adhere to initiatives for a rapprochement with the Soviets, an embrace of former enemy Communist China, and for limitations on nuclear and conventional arms. By early 1974, Nixon wrote, his own "military establishment and its many friends in the Congress and the country were up in arms over the prospect" that there might actually be a breakthrough on limiting offensive nuclear weapons. Five days after his return from the Mideast, Nixon was due to fly abroad again, this time to Moscow, for the third U.S.-Soviet summit since the signing of the SALT accords two years earlier. He had learned from Kissinger, Nixon wrote in his memoirs, that Brezhnev was complaining to the secretary of state about "confronting the same problems as we were of military opposition to a permanent agreement to limit offensive nuclear weapons." No major new proposals had been offered by either side.

The NSC took up the subject of what should be done in this summit the day after Nixon returned from the Mideast. Defense Secretary Schlesinger had recently demonstrated his distance from Nixon by backing a position held by the leading anti-détente senator,

Henry "Scoop" Jackson, the Democrat from Washington; it had been an extraordinary public rebuff to the president. In the June 20 meeting Schlesinger presented a Pentagon proposal that, Nixon wrote, took "an unyielding hard line against any SALT agreement that did not ensure an overwhelming American advantage. It was a proposal the Soviets were sure to reject out of hand."

Nixon said just that, and—as Kissinger and Nixon both reported in their memoirs—Schlesinger made a sharp, condescending reply: "But, Mr. President, everyone knows how impressed Khrushchev was with your forensic ability in the kitchen debate [when Nixon was vice president]. I'm sure that if you applied your skills to it you could get them to accept this proposal." The Schlesinger slap, Nixon wrote in his diary that night, was "a real shocker . . . an insult to everybody's intelligence and particularly mine. . . . Many of the Defense people don't want any agreement because they want to go ahead willy-nilly with all the defense programs they possibly can and they do not want constraints."

On June 25 Nixon flew to Russia aboard *Air Force One;* the talks with Brezhnev that lasted until July 3 were cordial but brought no major breakthroughs, a result hardly surprising to the participants. According to Kissinger, the Soviet hosts were "uncharacteristically sensitive to Nixon's human predicament." They could have "harassed . . . the old Communist-baiter" Nixon, but instead treated him with "respect and courtesy." Even so, the TASS statement reporting Nixon's opening toast to Brezhnev removed the president's reference to a "personal relationship" with the Soviet leader and substituted a phrase saying that the two countries had a good relationship. "The Soviets were cutting their losses," writes Kissinger in citing this TASS statement, and they were doing so because they "had an interest in not tying a major policy to the fate of an individual."

Petty spats among the Nixon entourage had marred the Mideast visit, and did so to an even greater degree in Moscow. "There was an unworthy dispute between Al Haig and me about whose suite in the Kremlin palace would be closest to Nixon's," Kissinger wrote, and noted that Haig had won that battle, though Kissinger lessened its importance by likening it to fighting "over seats at the captain's table on the *Titanic* after it had struck the iceberg."

Upon his return to Washington on July 3, Nixon did not stay in the capital but instead flew to Key Biscayne for the weekend. In the headlines for that day were notations that a new phase of the House Judiciary Committee's inquiry into Watergate had begun. For two months, the committee had been hearing evidence gathered by its staff, including that given to them by the Special Prosecutor's office. On July 2, they began to hear from a parade of former and current Nixon administration and campaign officials about the inner workings of the White House.

Alexander Butterfield was the first witness. He was questioned about his four years in the White House, and his role in Nixon's taping system; but during his testimony he pointed a finger at Alexander Haig's role in the 1969–1971 wiretapping program.

It had all begun in the first year of the administration, Butterfield told the congressmen; December 29, 1969. The tap on Morton Halperin's phone had turned up some information on Clark Clifford, and FBI Director Hoover had written a letter to Nixon about it, being careful not to mention the phrase wiretapping, but using instead the standard cover language, "extremely sensitive source." Clifford was the former secretary of defense, a prominent attorney, and an important man in the Democratic Party. An unidentified male voice had been heard on the tap, and from it Hoover had concluded that Clifford was preparing an article, possibly for publication in *Life* magazine, that would attack Nixon's Vietnam policies. More important, the unidentified voice said he was scheduled to meet with Kissinger that same day.

Hoover's letter was routed to Magruder, then on Haldeman's staff, with the instruction to work up a counterattack to the forthcoming Clifford article. Magruder asked Butterfield for advice, and on January 8, 1970, Butterfield wrote Magruder that "You should go—first of all—to Al Haig" to find out who had met with Kissinger on December 29, and see if the caller could be identified. There were three other suggestions, and then a final one: "Al Haig can get you squared away on at least a preliminary scheme" for dealing with Clifford. A bit later, Magruder wrote a memo to Haldeman suggesting that Dean Acheson write an article for *Look* magazine to compete with Clifford's, and that he had asked "Al Haig to see if this could be done."

These two documents, of course, might have led investigators to uncover Haig's prominent role in the 1969–1971 wiretaps—but that fact had meant nothing to the Watergate investigation until those wiretaps had been revealed in the spring of 1973. These documents also exposed the truth about the wiretaps—that they had been used to spy on political opponents and not to protect national security secrets.

In amassing documents, the Special Prosecutor's office had at that time been given a memo written by Butterfield regarding Clark Clifford—but the date on it was January 8, 1969, not January 8, 1970. When Butterfield had been called in to look at it, in the spring of 1973, he had immediately recognized it as a fake.

There were several things wrong with it. First, the memo was clean and seemed freshly typed; it wasn't dog-eared and didn't appear to be four years old. Second, the introductory wording to Magruder that Butterfield remembered, "in response to your query," had been excised. Third, the date was wrong. It was a date that preceded the wiretaps and even Nixon's inauguration. Fourth, the second to last paragraph, the one about Haig, was also gone. The net effect of this altered memo was to imply that Butterfield had sent unsolicited comments to Magruder, that he knew about the Halperin wiretap, and that he was trying to get Magruder to undertake an anti-Clifford project.

Convinced that the memo had been doctored by the White House—who had given it to the Special Prosecutor's office—Butterfield managed to search the White House central files. He found that his records for January of 1970 had been rifled and were missing.

It took him many months to find a copy of the real memo that he had written, the one with the proper date in January of 1970, the words that showed it was in response to Magruder's query, and the paragraph suggesting that "Al Haig can get you squared away on at least a preliminary scheme. We can build from there." But by the time Butterfield appeared for questioning on July 2, 1974, the House Judiciary Committee had published both the fake memo and the true one, side by side, in one of its volumes of evidence—and yet failed to deal with the implications of the memos.

Butterfield says today he is convinced that his old friend Alexander Haig, whom he considered a close friend but now regards as "a world-class manipulator," fabricated this memo, because Haig was the only person protected by the fake memo. It was designed, Butterfield thinks, to throw the prosecutors off Haig's trail and onto his own. He recalls that the Special Prosecutor's office agreed with that suspicion because, among other reasons, it was Haig who had given them the memo: "the memo came from Haig. He was then chief of staff. . . . He was the chief suspect" to have written it.

In the game of chess, the king is not killed. The game is won by forcing the opposing player to resign while his king is still on the board. Making sure there is no stalemate or draw is the great skill necessary to the correct play of what is known as the endgame. In the period between Nixon's return from Russia in early July, and his resignation on August 9, 1974, the endgame tactics of Haig and Buzhardt were especially brilliant. They have remained hidden or obscured in the intervening years, and we will reveal them in the following pages.

Before we begin, it is worthwhile to give Haig's and Buzhardt's version of events, a version best encapsulated in the Woodward and Bernstein book *The Final Days*. As noted earlier, Haig says he is currently writing his memoirs, and perhaps those will provide more about his version of that last month, but for the present, we have *The Final Days*.

It was July 23. Nixon had been chasing the sun almost every day since he had returned from Russia—a long weekend at Key Biscayne, a dozen days at San Clemente—anything to stay out of Washington while the Judiciary Committee hearings were in process, and while the Supreme Court was deliberating about Jaworski's demand for the tapes. On the afternoon of the twenty-third, Nixon received word that all three Dixiecrats on the Judiciary Committee were now ready to vote against him, which meant certain defeat and the passage of an impeachment resolution. Nixon telephoned his old opponent, Alabama Governor George Wallace, to ask if he would pressure his fellow Alabamian, Representative Walter Flowers, and prevail upon him not to help remove a president from office. Wallace said no, and Nixon turned to Haig and said, "Well, Al, there goes the presidency."

The next morning brought word to Nixon that the Supreme Court had ruled, 8–0, in the tapes case. Rejecting Nixon's claim of executive privilege, the Supreme Court reaffirmed the lower court's ruling that the president would have to hand over to Sirica the sixty-four recordings that included the June 23, 1972, tape. When Haig in San Clemente called Buzhardt in Washington to discuss the decision, Nixon took the phone and asked Buzhardt personally to listen to the June 23 tape.

In the Woodward-Bernstein version of events, that morning of July 24, 1974, was the first time that Buzhardt had listened to the June 23, 1972, tape, and he became immediately convinced that the evidence was fatal. Buzhardt promptly phoned Haig and told him they had now found the smoking gun they had all feared had been in existence. Nixon could survive no longer, Buzhardt told Haig. But Haig disagreed—even though he had never listened to the tape. As late as July 27, Woodward and Bernstein wrote, Buzhardt "couldn't get any support" for his conviction "that the June 23 tape completely undermined the President's position. . . . Haig wasn't sure."

After this, the account continues:

> The general had expressed grave doubt that it was his and Buzhardt's job to force a President to resign. . . . He and the lawyers had access to the President, they really had undue influence over him. They were only staff men, after all. Nobody had elected them. The President was

elected by the people. Suppose an ex-President were to accuse his aides and their congressional allies of forcing him out of office? Were they brushing perilously close to *coup d'état?* . . . Haig now put forth the notion that Nixon must make the decision. It must be perceived that way—by the President, by the country, by the historians. "It has to be a willing act on his part," Haig insisted. "We can't force him."

So, in this version, in the ensuing days the heroic, selfless Haig merely gave the president all the facts and the options, and let him make the decision to resign on his own. For instance, the Woodward-Bernstein book quotes Haig as telling White House aide David Gergen that Nixon was "guilty as hell," but that they all had to see it through to the end.

Actually, in the days following the Supreme Court decision, Haig's behavior toward Nixon was an act, part of a "good cop, bad cop" routine he and Buzhardt were playing. Buzhardt was insisting that the president had no way out, while the general was bucking up the president and encouraging him to believe he could pull through.

The Final Days version is incredible on its face. If we accept the notion that Haig, who had custody of the tapes for over a year, never was curious enough to listen to at least those Jaworski had expressed a strong interest in—even accepting that notion, a fundamental flaw in the account remains. Is it credible that Haig would not accept the characterization of the "smoking gun" tape as the end of "the ballgame" by White House counsel and Haig's good friend Fred Buzhardt without taking the trouble to listen to that tape and make his own judgment?

Nixon was "standing in the beach trailer" at Red Beach, near San Clemente, he later wrote, "barefoot, wearing old trousers, a Banlon shirt, and a blue windbreaker emblazoned with the Presidential Seal," when he learned from a Ron Ziegler telephone call that the Judiciary Committee had approved Article I of an impeachment resolution, 27–11. It was July 27, the charge was obstruction of justice—just the matter covered in the June 23 recording—and "the vote went exactly the way I had feared," Nixon wrote. He would be the first president in 106 years to be recommended for impeachment. Two days later, the committee approved Article II by a 28-10 vote; it charged Nixon with systematic abuse of power and violations of citizens' constitutional rights, for instance in the 1969–1971 wiretapping program. In the following days, a third article would be also approved, while a fourth and fifth were rejected. A full vote in the House was set for August 19.

* * *

On July 30, Haig was called to testify at a closed-door hearing of the Senate Foreign Relations Committee regarding those wiretaps. It was a moment he had long been trying to avoid. The impetus for the hearings had come during an emotional news conference in June when Kissinger and Nixon were on their triumphant tour. Kissinger had denied new allegations that he had personally ordered wiretaps on his NSC aides. He had testified during his confirmation hearings to be secretary of state that he had had nothing to do with the matter, and the implication now was that he had lied during those hearings. At that press conference, Kissinger demanded an investigation to clear his name. On July 30, Haig appeared before Congress to answer questions about his own role in that wiretapping.

Haig knew that a great deal was at stake here, and that his fate could be intertwined with Nixon's—because the House Judiciary Committee had the FBI files on the wiretaps, files that showed Haig's involvement. Should Nixon go on trial in the Senate, it was extremely likely that Haig's role in the wiretaps would be made public and debated. It was just as likely that a Senate trial would involve the Plumbers, and with it expose the Welander interview, the Young report, and the other Moorer-Radford evidence that endangered Haig but had been twice buried. So Haig had a reason to want Nixon to resign rather than to let him be impeached. Actual impeachment was several weeks away, Haig knew, but on July 30 he had to deal with the Senate Foreign Relations Committee.

By Haig's side, at these hearings, was Fred Buzhardt. Back at the White House, St. Clair and his staff were working frantically to prepare for an appearance in Sirica's courtroom where they were to hand over the first batch of twenty tapes. Buzhardt was the person most familiar with the recordings, and St. Clair's people needed his help—but, as Woodward and Bernstein wrote, Buzhardt had dropped everything having to do with the president in order to serve "as unofficial personal counsel to Haig" during the general's three hours of closed-door testimony on the taps.

It was all Kissinger's doing, Haig testified. Before Haig had submitted names to the FBI, he had received general instructions "that they [targeted individuals] be surveilled," and he figured that had included wiretapping, so he sent the names to the appropriate authority, the FBI. Haig testified that he "never viewed myself as anything but an extension of Dr. Kissinger." He was asked if it was true that Kissinger had never been involved in an instruction to tap a specific person. "I do not know that I can say that categorically," Haig responded, and undermined a presumption of Kissinger innocence even further when he responded to another question by saying, "I never would have submitted a name that I did not get from Dr. Kissinger, or from the president with Dr. Kissinger's knowledge."

The committee couldn't resolve the testimony of Kissinger and Haig; in a report issued two months later, the committee stated that it could not conclude who had initiated or terminated the taps. The report cleared Kissinger, though, at least of the allegation that he had been untruthful during his confirmation hearings. At the point that the committee's report was issued, however, Ford had become president, Kissinger was viewed as the stable rock that enabled the continuity of foreign policy in a time of chaos, and Haig was about to become supreme commander of NATO. To have impugned either Haig or Kissinger at that moment in time might have submerged the Ford presidency into even greater difficulties.

The Final Days picks up Haig's story after the hearings. In this version, Haig returned to the White House to find that St. Clair had now listened to the tape and had come to the same conclusion as Buzhardt— that the president must resign. On July 31, when Buzhardt and St. Clair lobbied Haig to press for Nixon's resignation, Haig reportedly asked, "Should I listen to the tape?"

And Buzhardt supposedly said to him, "No, don't listen to any tapes," and instead suggested that a transcript be prepared. Haig then had to go to Nixon for permission to make a transcript. The president initially said no, but Haig argued him into having the transcript made. Next day, August 1, Haig first read a transcript of the June 23 "smoking gun" tape.

In this version, it took Haig *eight days* from the time he learned of the decisive evidence until the moment he bothered to study that evidence himself. That is unlikely, for the reasons discussed earlier. How could Haig during those eight days strongly disagree with Buzhardt's gloomy assessment of the tape itself if Haig himself had refused to look at the evidence? What the eight-day gap did do, however, was support two linked contentions of *The Final Days:* that Haig had never listened to the tape at any earlier point in time, and that Haig was not trying to force Nixon out of office.

For many years the Woodward-Bernstein book stood as the accepted version of what happened at the end of the Watergate affair. In the following pages, we have amassed evidence to support a more factual version from the memoirs of Nixon, Kissinger, Gerald Ford, Ford counselor Robert T. Hartmann, and other members of Ford's inner circle, from our interviews with Ron Ziegler and other Nixon aides, and from the work of journalists such as J. Anthony Lukas, James Doyle, and Seymour Hersh, who interviewed still other people close to the White House at the time.

Nixon was torn between resignation and continuing the fight. He soon realized, however, that if he lost an impeachment trial, "I would be defeated and dishonored, the first President in history to be impeached and convicted on criminal charges." When both Haig and Ziegler separately advised him that the situation was hopeless, he believed he had to quit, and on August 1 told Haig that he had decided on resignation, and "asked Haig to see Jerry Ford and tell him that I was thinking of resigning, without indicating when."

Haig saw Ford, all right, but told him something completely different.

It is evident that Haig realized Nixon would not call Ford directly, and that Ford, for reasons of propriety, would not call Nixon either—a stance vice presidents had been taking since 1919, when Vice President Thomas Marshall would not even visit the White House to inquire as to the health of ailing President Woodrow Wilson, for fear of being seen as suggesting that he had any interest in whether Wilson died or recovered. Knowing that there would be no direct communications between Nixon and Ford, Haig played the go-between, and in the coming days withheld information from both men in order to further his own agenda.

Vice President Gerald Ford's chief of staff at that time was Robert T. Hartmann, former Washington bureau chief of the *Los Angeles Times*. Hartmann writes in his memoir, *Palace Politics*, that he received a call at home from Haig shortly after 5:30 P.M. on the thirty-first (one day before Nixon told Haig to see Ford). Haig wanted to visit Ford the next morning, and Hartmann said he'd arrange it. Hartmann apprised Ford, but also suggested to the vice president that he come along as a witness, and Ford consented.

Haig arrived at Ford's office early on August 1, 1974, and, Ford recounted in his own memoir, *A Time to Heal*, "seemed surprised" by Hartmann's presence, "and I had the impression that [Haig] didn't feel he could be as forthright as he might normally have been." Hartmann echoed this thought in his book, saying "it was equally obvious that [Haig] wished I would go away." (Interestingly, the Woodward-Bernstein account agrees that this was the case but has Haig disparaging both Hartmann and Ford, in this incident and throughout the remainder of the book. Ford is painted as naïve, and Hartmann is dismissed as a drinker.)

In this August 1 meeting, Haig told Ford that he hadn't seen the evidence, but had been told by others that it contained the smoking gun. When Ford asked for details, Haig said he couldn't offer more because the tapes were being transcribed.

Strikingly, Haig's claim to Ford that he hadn't seen the "evidence" is belied by his own statements to Nixon. Nixon reports in his memoirs that Haig told him he had read the transcript of the "smoking gun" tape on July 31. Nixon wrote that Haig had come to him on the thirty-first, said that he'd reviewed the transcript and had to agree with Buzhardt and St. Clair, and had said, "I just don't see how we can survive this one."

Later in the day on August 1, Haig called Ford directly, and asked for another meeting—specifically without Hartmann present. Haig returned to the vice president's offices at 3:30 P.M. Ford got the impression that by that time Haig had either seen the transcript or had been briefed about it in considerable detail, because Haig outlined the several options available to Nixon: riding out the impeachment process, resigning, or pardoning himself along with the other Watergate defendants. (Nixon had told Haig to say to Ford that he was probably going to resign at some unspecified time in the future.)

Finally, Haig raised the possibility that Nixon's inevitable successor, Ford, could pardon Nixon, in return for Nixon's agreement to leave. "Haig emphasized that these weren't *his* suggestions," Ford wrote of this meeting, "and he made it very clear that he wasn't recommending any one option over another." (Italics in original.) Haig wanted to know if Ford's assessment of the situation agreed with his, and if Ford had any recommendations to make to the president. Ford writes that he told Haig it would not be proper to make any recommendations; and as Haig left, he told Ford, "We've got to keep in contact. . . . Don't hesitate to call me, and I won't hesitate to call you."

This meeting was very important, so we must note that Ford repeated this story, under oath, in sworn testimony to the House Judiciary Committee in October of 1974. In Haig's own testimony in 1981 at confirmation hearings to be secretary of state, Haig denied that he had ever discussed any agreement with Ford in which Nixon would resign in exchange for a pardon.

But Haig had taken steps to conceal his second meeting with Ford. An aide to the then–vice president later told reporter Seymour Hersh how the deception had been accomplished. On the afternoon of August 1, Ford was scheduled to meet his wife Betty, and when Ford was late, this aide went to find him. The aide asked the receptionist at the vice president's office if there was a problem, and demanded a look at the appointment book. It said that Secretary of the Interior Rogers Morton was inside, meeting with Ford. "What's he doing here? It wasn't scheduled," the aide asked, and the receptionist told the aide that the person inside was "General Haig, and he made me write Morton in the appointment book." The aide waited. Thirty minutes later, Haig burst out of the room, seemed startled, and asked the aide, "What are you doing here?" Then Haig quickly departed. Hersh later managed to confirm that the appointment book did list Rogers Morton for that time.

There was no doubt in Hartmann's mind as to why Haig held the 3:30 P.M. Ford meeting without him. Hartmann waited a long time in his office for the Haig-Ford meeting to end, and when the vice president called Hartmann in, he gave Hartmann a report, including Haig's options, the last of which was the suggestion that Ford could pardon Nixon. Hartmann later wrote that he was appalled that such a discussion had occurred: " 'Jesus!' I said aloud. To myself: So that's the pitch Haig wouldn't make with me present!"

That night, Ford recalled in his memoir, his wife Betty told him that he "shouldn't get involved in making any recommendations at all. Not to Haig, not to Nixon, not to anybody." On the afternoon of August 2, Ford, in the presence of his aides Hartmann, John O. Marsh, Jr., and Bryce Harlow, called Haig and told him, "I have no intention of recommending what the President should do about resigning or not resigning, and that nothing we talked about yesterday afternoon should be given any consideration" by Nixon in making his decision. In his memoir, Ford quoted Haig's reply to this instruction: "You're right."

August 2 was a Friday, and that night Nixon met with his family, who urged him to keep fighting—that is, not to resign. This bolstered the response Nixon had previously suggested in a note to himself: "End career as a fighter." Nixon decided he would hold off resigning. Instead, on Monday, August 5, he would release the June 23 transcript together with a statement that would put the best face on a bleak situation. He would wait and gauge the public reaction, then, he recalled of his state of mind, "if by some miracle that reaction was not so bad," he might consider hanging on through an impeachment trial.

At Camp David that weekend, Haig, Buzhardt, St. Clair, and Pat Buchanan insisted to Nixon that resignation was the only option. St. Clair was angered by learning that Nixon had listened to that June 23 tape on May 6 but had failed to inform him; St. Clair threatened to quit if Nixon did not resign.

On Monday morning, before the transcript and an accompanying statement were to be released, Haig located Jaworski, who was in Texas on personal business. With St. Clair also on the line, the general told

Jaworski of the impending release of the June 23 tape, which showed that the president had had political motives in asking the CIA to block the FBI investigation of the break-in.

"We didn't know it, Leon," Jaworski later quoted Haig as telling him. "He [Nixon] didn't tell us about it." After St. Clair had explained his threat to quit, Haig continued to assert his nonknowledge: "I'm particularly anxious that you believe me, Leon. . . . I didn't know what was in those conversations." Jaworski writes that he accepted the explanation. The reason why Haig wanted Jaworski to "believe" him would come into play a few days later.

The statement put out by the president on Monday, accompanying the transcript of the June 23, 1972, conversations, showed him still fighting. Nixon admitted that the new evidence "may further damage my case," but reminded the public that he had always insisted on a full investigation of Watergate, and that "I am firmly convinced that the record, in its entirety, does not justify the extreme step of impeachment and removal of a President."

There was an eruption of anger over the transcript. Most people concluded that it was, indeed, the smoking gun, and public opinion moved even more into the column of wanting Richard Nixon out of office. Nixon still wouldn't quit, though. On August 6 and 7 he met with his cabinet and with congressional leaders. He indicated to them that he knew he would be impeached in the House, but believed he had a chance to prevail in the Senate, as had President Andrew Johnson, a century earlier.

Prevailing in the Senate was the subject of a private meeting Nixon held with three leading Republicans, Senator Barry Goldwater, Senate Minority Leader Hugh Scott, and House Minority Leader John Rhodes. Nixon reported the meeting in his autobiography. "It's pretty grim," Scott told Nixon, estimating that the president could count on only about fifteen solid votes for him in the Senate. "I don't have many alternatives, do I," Nixon responded. He realized that he would have to resign.

Nixon went to break the news to his shaken family—and Al Haig rushed to his backchannel. He telephoned Jaworski.

The standard account of the Haig-Jaworski meeting that was the result of this call has Haig trying to avoid prosecution of the disgraced president, and shaking hands with Jaworski at the end of a long ordeal for both of them. There was a handshake, but it was not the whole story.

Haig had learned from Nixon that he would resign. That meant the threat of a Senate trial was gone, and with it, the possibility that

Moorer-Radford would surface in such a trial. But Haig had to make sure that Moorer-Radford also would not be brought into the picture during a criminal trial of Nixon. Such a trial was unlikely, but even so, Haig had many reasons to see to it that the White House's papers and tapes—including the Welander confession, David Young's report, the documents relating to the 1969–1971 wiretaps, and so on—were whisked out of Washington instantly, and taken to a place where the Special Prosecutor could not indiscriminately comb them over.

Before Jaworski met with Haig on the morning of August 8, the Special Prosecutor talked with three of his senior assistants, all of whom told him there should be no deals. Around 11:30 A.M., Haig's aide, Major George Joulwan, picked up Jaworski at his Jefferson Hotel quarters and drove him to Haig's home in a residential section of northwest Washington. Back at the White House, Nixon was gathering himself with his family. That night, he told them, he would announce to the nation his intention to resign on the following day.

The chief of staff on whom he had relied for so much during the past fifteen months was not at his side that August 8 morning. He was at home, meeting with Leon Jaworski. Over coffee, according to Jaworski's memoir, the Special Prosecutor told Haig that he was not going to reach an agreement right then on prosecuting Nixon. Haig indicated that he understood this, and informed Jaworski about the resignation speech scheduled for that evening. Haig then said, "Now, he's going to be taking his tapes and papers with him, Leon. There's no hanky-panky involved. Your office will have access to them if you need them. He's going to San Clemente tomorrow and the tapes and papers will be shipped out later." (*The Final Days* does not report this part of the Haig-Jaworski conversation.)

Jaworski reports that he did not protest, but that he did say the materials must be made available as needed. Haig spoke of Nixon's deteriorating mental and physical condition, and said a congressional resolution would likely urge Jaworski not to indict the deposed president. There would also be no pardons for any Watergate defendants, Haig said.

Then, like two battle-weary comrades, the men said good-bye. "I want you to know how much I appreciate your taking on the Special Prosecutor's job," Haig said, and Jaworski responded that it had been "strenuous," but that he recognized that Haig's job had been "even worse." The two had a "strong handshake" that belied the "sadness in our parting. Both of us had been knee-deep in an unparalleled tragedy, and it had forged a strange kinship."

So strange was it that Jaworski's staff immediately and suspiciously importuned him when he returned to the office. He assured them that there had been no deal, and a press statement was issued saying that there "has been no agreement or understanding of any sort" between Nixon and the prosecutor's office.

The statement went unchallenged by the press and public, but not by the Special Prosecutor's staff. James Doyle wrote that "there were many staff members who did not believe that Alexander Haig, as an act of courtesy, would take two hours out of such a climactic day to go to his suburban home simply to inform Leon Jaworski of events about to transpire." So dubious was the staff that in the final report of the Watergate Special Prosecution Force, published in October 1975, this meeting was handled with especial emphasis placed on the fact that the only report of it was Jaworski's. Doyle interpreted this in his memoir: "Nowhere else in the report is any meeting in which the special prosecutor was a party reported with the qualification that this was what the special prosecutor *said* happened at the meeting, as opposed to a flat statement of what transpired." (Italics in original.)

According to Nixon, when Haig returned from his meeting with Jaworski, Haig said that "he got the impression that I had nothing further to fear from the Special Prosecutor." Nixon wrote that he was not comforted, because, as he told Haig, "considering the way his [Jaworski's] office had acted in the past, I had little reason to feel assured."

In the afternoon hours of August 8, Ford staff members learned of frantic housecleaning under way at the White House, of files and records being destroyed or prepared for shipment. William E. Casselman II, a member of Ford's staff, came to Hartmann with a copy of a White House memo that directed Nixon staffers to decide for themselves what to remove and what to leave behind. "The document read as if a Democratic Administration was about to take over, not ours," Hartmann later wrote. Casselman told him that "people have been hauling suitcases and boxes out of here all this week. If we don't have any records, how can we carry on the government?"

Concerned, Hartmann got in touch with Benton L. Becker, a former Justice Department lawyer who had represented Ford during his vice-presidential confirmation hearings in Congress. Hartmann asked Becker to "snoop around" and find out what was going on. That, of course, Becker could not do effectively until Ford actually took over.

At nine on the evening of August 8, 1974, the thirty-seventh president of the United States spoke to the nation from the Oval Office for the thirty-seventh time. Alternately defiant and contrite, Nixon said he felt "it was my duty to persevere" and finish his term, but that it had "become evident that I no longer have a strong enough political base in the Congress to justify continuing that effort." Nixon then returned to the theme of the note he had made, days ago: "I have never been a quitter. To leave office before my term is completed is opposed to every instinct in my body. But as President I must put the interests of America first. . . . Therefore, I shall resign the Presidency effective at noon tomorrow." The bombshell having been dropped, Nixon added, "I regret deeply any injuries that may have been done," but "if some of my judgements were wrong—and some were wrong—they were made in what I believed at the time to be in the best interest of the nation."

The next morning, August 9, Nixon made a final, emotional speech to the White House staff. Awaiting him outside was a helicopter. The plan was for him to take this to an airfield where he and his family would transfer to *Air Force One*. The plane would then take off for California. While he was in the air, a statement would be released saying that he had resigned the presidency as of that hour. Nixon would leave the White House as president but would alight in California as the ex-president.

Nixon's speech to the White House staff was more than emotional, it was heartrending, a deep mining of his soul centered around a paean to his mother—people would write no books about his mother, Nixon said, though she had been a good and important woman. Many in the audience wept.

The speech rambled on and then Nixon decided he had said enough, shook some hands, and walked outside. He had a brief conversation with Ford in which he suggested that Ford keep Haig, "at least during the transition period. Haig, I assured him, was always loyal to the commander he served, and he would be an invaluable source of advice and experience" during "the scramble for power within both the Cabinet and the White House staff."

Nixon then walked to the waiting helicopter accompanied by his family. At the door of the helicopter, Nixon turned and raised both hands above his head, his fingers forming a V in each one, as if in triumph.

Epilogue

...AND THROW AWAY THE KEY

MOMENTS after Nixon departed and Ford was sworn in, Robert Hartmann entered the White House and found an office next to the Oval Office "heavy with the acrid smell of paper recently burned in the fireplace." Meanwhile, the new president was instructing lawyer Benton Becker to look into the disposition of tapes and papers that Nixon had left behind at the White House. One of the first orders issued by Ford was to retain all the Nixon records and tapes at the White House, permitting none to be sent to the former president. Becker soon received a tip from a Secret Service agent that ongoing record destruction was so furious that the White House chemical paper shredders were being pushed beyond their limits. Hartmann and Becker went to Ford, who authorized his aides to intervene and ensure that only the most highly classified papers were shredded.

A transition team had advised Ford to replace nearly every Nixon staffer, the one exception being Haig. "Al has done yeoman service for the country," the transition memo said, and advised that Haig should help in the transition. But, as Hartmann reported in his book, the memo added, Haig's power should be immediately reined in, and "He

426

should not be expected, asked, or be given the option to become your [Ford's] chief of staff. We share your view that there should be no chief of staff, especially at the outset."

Haig was not to be outdone. A separate, anonymous memo was slipped to Ford in advance of his 1:00 P.M. staff meeting of August 9, his first as president. Its first recommendation was to "reassure the staff of your respect, your need for their help, and your regard for President Nixon." In doing so, the memo recommended, Ford should emphasize "The special and heroic role of Al Haig," and tell everyone that Haig would be actively involved in the transition efforts. A special section had the heading of DO NOTS, and stated, "At this time, do not commit yourself to dealing directly with anyone but Al Haig." Under the heading of DO, it said, "Ask each staff member to be alert to problems and to make suggestions to Al Haig or to Transition Team members." As Hartmann noted, "This memo is unsigned; its origin can only be surmised from its content."

Steve Bull had gone with the Nixons to San Clemente. On August 11, Bull recalls, the distraught ex-president tried to reach his former chief of staff at the White House. "Two days earlier Haig had been the loyalist," says Bull. "And now he was too busy even to take Nixon's call from California . . . too busy currying favor with Gerald Ford. We were told that Haig was changing into his tuxedo for his first social event at the Ford White House and he didn't have time to talk to Nixon."

At about this time, Jaworski received a call from Senator James Eastland, chairman of the Senate Judiciary Committee, who had just spoken with Nixon by telephone. In his book, Jaworski quoted Eastland as saying that Nixon "was crying" and pleading, "Jim, don't let Jaworski put me in that trial with Haldeman and Ehrlichman. I can't take any more." Eastland told Jaworski, "He's in bad shape, Leon." The ongoing battle in the Special Prosecutor's office was over this very point: The staff wanted to consider prosecuting Nixon, and Jaworski argued to the staff that Nixon could never get a fair trial. The issue was left unresolved—hence, Nixon's anxiety.

Ford hoped that public attention would move quickly from Watergate. But Nixon's legal status and the matter of the disposition of his tapes and papers dominated press questioning. On August 14, press secretary Jerry F. terHorst told reporters that the tapes and papers had been "ruled to be the personal property of former President Nixon." TerHorst referred to the decision as a "collective one," and in response to a reporter's question, stated that he presumed that a judgment had been made with the concurrence of the Special Prosecutor's office that the tapes were not relevant to the ongoing investigation.

The Special Prosecutor's office promptly issued a press statement saying it had been informed that Nixon claimed the papers as his own, but did not concur with the Justice Department's conclusion. Jaworski was out of town, but the acting head of the Special Prosecutor's office, James Vorenberg, received assurance from Ford counsel Philip Buchen that none of the disputed material would be removed from the White House.

Public reaction to terHorst's statement was encapsulated in headlines that suggested, in Hartmann's words, that Ford was "trying to pull a fast one in the interests" of Nixon. In a morning Oval Office staff meeting, terHorst started to explain that he had been had by Fred Buzhardt, who had supplied the information for the press conference. Ford immediately replaced Buzhardt as counsel to the president with Phil Buchen. TerHorst announced this change at a press conference, and afterward, Haig and terHorst nearly came to blows, Haig claiming that terHorst was responsible for "firing a sick man at a press conference." Buzhardt had suffered a heart attack in June.

Haig was particularly irate at Hartmann, and the loathing came to be mutual. Hartmann saw Haig as a dangerous manipulator seeking to protect himself at the expense of everyone, including Ford. According to an account by Seymour Hersh, Haig's ire was so intense that he once grabbed a Hartmann aide by the lapels and fumed, "If you have any influence over that fat Kraut, you tell him to knock it off or he's going to be the first stretcher case coming out of the West Wing." In earlier years, Haig had directed this sort of schoolyard bully behavior at Henry Kissinger.

One day shortly after the press flap, Becker discovered a huge number of files, boxes, and other materials being removed from the White House, destined for San Clemente. Outside in the parking lot, an Air Force colonel was supervising the loading of the material onto a truck. "I told him to halt the loading immediately," Becker recalls, "at which point he told me he was acting under instructions from General Haig." The two men proceeded indoors and found Haig, who was in his office. Haig "claimed he was totally unaware that it was happening," Becker says. The shipment was unloaded and returned to the White House. Hartmann reported that in a separate incident, "Haig had successfully removed all of his own files from the White House. . . . When it was discovered, Haig agreed to bring them back."

On August 22, Ford's Justice Department published its legal opinion on the Nixon documents: Attorney General William Saxbe had concluded that since the founding of the country, every president had retained the right to his papers as personal property, and therefore, Nixon's papers and tapes were the personal property of the former president.

On August 28, Ford held his first news conference. At it, he was barraged with questions on the tapes and papers, and on a possible pardon. Following the news conference, Ford and his staff concentrated their efforts on resolving the question of a pardon. After several days of legal research, Becker determined that Ford had the constitutional authority to grant a pardon to the former president, even though Nixon had not been formally charged with any crime or convicted of one, and even though a pardon, if issued, would not recite the specific acts or offenses for which Nixon was being pardoned. Becker reported this to Ford, who, Becker points out, "had not yet decided to grant or to decline to grant a pardon to the former president." On August 30, Ford wrote, he "broached the possibility of a pardon with five key aides: Buchen, Haig, Kissinger, Hartmann and Marsh. I swore each of them to secrecy, emphasizing that there simply could not be any leaks until I had reached a decision."

Buchen spoke privately with Jaworski, trying to learn what the Special Prosecutor would do in regard to Nixon. Jaworski recounted the division in his office about prosecuting Nixon, reiterated his position that Nixon could not get a fair trial now, and that passage of as much as two years might be necessary before any trial of Richard Nixon could commence. The issue of the papers and tapes also remained unresolved, but, according to his memoirs, Ford did not "want to condition the pardon" on Nixon's "making an agreement on the papers and tapes."

Becker was particularly adamant that the Ford White House should retain the Nixon material, even though the Justice Department had issued the opinion that the materials were the personal property of the former president. There was an enormous amount of it, 950 reels of tape and 46 million pieces of paper—so much that the Secret Service had warned Ford that the fourth-floor storage area in the EOB was in danger of collapsing from it. To allow the files to go to San Clemente prematurely, Hartmann and Becker argued, was to flirt with disaster. The files might be needed in such forthcoming criminal cases as that of John Mitchell, or in the many civil suits still in the dockets; moreover, if something happened to those files later, it might look bad for the Ford White House.

While Ford deliberated, Haig continually importuned him to grant the pardon and to transfer all of the Nixon records and tapes to San

Clemente, advancing the argument that those records were Nixon's problem, not Ford's. The new president, Haig argued, had a country to run—let Nixon's lawyers deal with the records problem. Becker recalls one meeting with Ford at which Haig was present: "I told the president that if he allowed the papers and tapes to be removed from the White House and sent to San Clemente, history would record this as being the final act in the Watergate cover-up. Ford listened, and Haig did not argue."

Becker had determined that one way to keep the papers and tapes from being shipped to San Clemente was to have the Special Prosecutor issue a blanket subpoena for them. "I communicated to Phil Buchen that color of authority [over the material] would go to the Ford White House if Jaworski would issue the subpoena," Becker recalls. "Phil talked to the prosecutors and he told me, 'They won't do it.' " Jaworski apparently said that he couldn't establish the legal basis for such an action—even though, as others pointed out, the president had left office with the threat of criminal proceedings dangling over his head.

Citing the Justice Department opinion that the materials belonged to the former president, Nixon was demanding that the papers and tapes be shipped to San Clemente. The issue had to be resolved.

On September 5, Becker flew to California accompanied by Nixon's new attorney, Herbert J. Miller, Jr. Becker carried a draft pardon, but was instructed not to open substantive discussions on the subject of a grant of a pardon until the issue of the papers and tapes was substantially resolved. If the pardon question was reached, Becker was to inform Nixon that President Ford was considering the grant of a pardon to Nixon. Becker was told to try to obtain a statement of contrition from Nixon; he remembers Haig's reaction to that idea: "There's no way Richard Nixon will ever make such a statement or give up his papers."

While Becker was on his way to California, Ford called a staff meeting attended by Hartmann, Haig, Buchen, and another senior aide. Hartmann reported in *Palace Politics* that Ford announced at that meeting that he had decided to pardon Nixon.

Ford had told his staff—including Haig—that all dealings with Nixon on these issues were to be handled by lawyers Buchen and Becker. But, when Becker arrived in San Clemente later that day, he was greeted by a surly Ron Ziegler, who declared, "Let's get one thing straight immediately. President Nixon is not issuing any statement whatsoever regarding Watergate, whether Jerry Ford pardons him or not."

Becker was shocked that Ziegler was obviously privy to the private discussions of Ford and his staff, and he threatened to go right back to Washington. "I was not there to negotiate a grant of a pardon and I made that clear," Becker recalls. "I said, 'If Nixon does not resolve the issue of the records and tapes, it will be viewed with great disappointment back at the White House.' . . . It was the carrot that I was bearing." Miller calmed the two men, and they began the process.

During the next two days Becker negotiated with Miller and Ziegler. He would make progress on what could be done about the papers, and give a draft deed proposal to them; they would discuss it, take it to Nixon, and come back with comments. The parties came up with a deed of trust plan that called for Nixon to transfer all of his ownership interest in the papers to the General Services Administration. Nixon would retain the right to object to the release of certain items under a claim of privacy, and if a request was pursued after such a claim, the question would be resolved by the courts. But, under the plan, the former president would have access only to copies, not originals, because "we wanted to be sure that nothing would be destroyed," Becker recalls.

By the second day, Becker had enough indication that this deed of trust matter was going to be resolved in a manner that would relieve the White House's concerns, and so, after consulting with Ford and Buchen, indicated that the other matter—that of the pardon—could be addressed. Ziegler began preparing drafts of a statement of acceptance of the pardon that Nixon would issue. Becker made notes on it, and it went back and forth several times.

In the first drafts, there was no admission of guilt. Becker pushed for one, but could only get so far. Citing an important 1921 Supreme Court case, which ruled that in order for the pardon to be binding, it had to be accepted, and, moreover, that acceptance of a pardon was acknowledgment of guilt, Becker explained that Ford would not grant a pardon unless he knew that Nixon would accept it and thereby acknowledge guilt.

Nixon finally agreed to say, in a statement of acceptance of the pardon, that he "was wrong in not acting more decisively and more forthrightly in dealing with Watergate, particularly when it reached the stage of judicial proceedings." This reference to his own behavior during the cover-up was the closest that Nixon ever came to acknowledging his participation in an obstruction of justice. The statement continued: "That the way I tried to deal with Watergate was the wrong way is a burden I shall bear for every day of the life that is left to me."

On September 6, Becker met briefly with Nixon. The former president appeared physically and mentally exhausted, and had difficulty carrying on a substantive conversation. Becker explained to him from the 1921 case that acceptance of the pardon was acknowledgment of guilt, but Nixon didn't want to talk about that, and asked Becker where he lived. Washington, Becker responded, and the former president asked about the chances for the Washington Redskins during the next football season. Becker tried to return to the subject at hand, and eventually Nixon agreed to accept the pardon if it was offered by Ford, and executed the deed of trust for his documents, tapes, and papers. Becker left the room unsure whether or not the former president would survive more than a few months.

While by this action most of Nixon's papers had been made available to the public, as an inevitable consequence of allowing Nixon to deny access to certain of his papers if he chose to do so, the action had also closed certain internal doors within that treasure trove. For instance, it shuttered the one containing such documents as the Welander interview tape and David Young's book-length investigation of Moorer-Radford—and had the further effect of throwing away the key, precisely the result that Alexander Haig had worked so long to achieve. Coupled with an expected pardon of Nixon that would end the specter of a public trial, this was just what Haig needed to bury his past and leave no barriers to his future.

Later, Congress enacted legislation that placed all presidential materials, including Nixon's, under the control of the National Archives. This act superseded and nullified the Nixon deed of trust to the GSA, but nonetheless Nixon retained the right to withhold some materials under privacy, national security, and other provisions.

Becker flew back to Washington on September 7. He had a deep suspicion that Ziegler—and thus Nixon—had a backchannel source in the Ford White House, and that throughout the San Clemente negotiations, they had known in advance that President Ford had decided to pardon Nixon. Becker believed that Haig had somehow communicated with Nixon or his staff, advising that a Nixon statement of contrition was not needed to secure a pardon and urging the former president not to give up too much in the negotiations over the records and tapes.

Becker met with Ford that evening, at which time Ford gave his final approval for the pardon. On September 8, President Ford announced his decision to grant Nixon a "full, free, and absolute pardon." Many months or years might pass, the president said, before Nixon could get a fair trial, causing a delay during which "ugly passions would again be roused," and leading a challenge of the government's credibility at home and abroad. To heal the nation in earnest, the pardon was essential, Ford argued.

* * *

In the weeks after the pardon, Ford later wrote, staff infighting and jockeying for position took quite a toll, and despite his belief that Haig was loyal, "I began to look at the broader picture." Both liberal and conservative columnists, as well as members of Congress, were calling for Ford to get Haig out of the White House. Haig wished to return to the Pentagon as Army chief of staff, replacing General Creighton Abrams, who had died on September 4. Both Haig and Ford recognized that Haig might not be able to weather the required Senate confirmation so soon after the debacle of Watergate. "That would not have been the best thing to happen to the Ford administration," Ford told us.

In late September, Haig agreed to take the job of Supreme Allied Commander of the North Atlantic Treaty Organization, a position that did not require Senate confirmation. Not everyone was pleased with the prospect of Haig as NATO commander. According to Roger Morris, when Secretary of State Kissinger received word about the potential appointment, he "threatened to veto the posting with his own enormous cachet." Haig then " 'stormed into Henry's office and had a little talk about what could come out' in a Senate hearing or a series of leaks," Morris reported, quoting Kissinger assistants. "Looming over that conversation with his old boss were all the shadows they had cast together, yet so far publicly escaped"—the wiretaps, the Plumbers, and the "long trail of sordid policies not yet exposed." There were no further objections from Kissinger, and in November Haig left for his new command.

In early 1975, a frustrated Howard Baker continued to press for the truth about Moorer-Radford. On March 7, the senator and his aide Howard Liebengood had lunch with Don Stewart in the Senate Dining Room. According to Stewart's notes on the meeting, Baker said that he had been repeatedly "shut out" by the White House. Blocked by Haig from obtaining any evidence, the senator had gone to Nixon in 1974, but the president told him "not to push the Pentagon spy ring investigation" and then "bitterly denounced" Stewart. Later, Henry Kissinger "had Senator Baker called off the Senate floor to request him not to push the investigation . . . Senator Baker intends to push this matter until he gets to the bottom of it."

Baker was not able to get to the bottom of it because the evidence remains in the archival records under Nixon's control; the papers of Haig and Buzhardt are similarly sealed. Baker, now out of elective office and an influential Washington attorney, will not comment for the record, but close associates say that today, nearly twenty years after the Moorer-Radford investigation, he still wants to know why the case was buried.

Woodward and Bernstein's book *All the President's Men* was published in 1974, and their second book, *The Final Days*, in 1976. By the time the second book was published, all of the Watergate burglars and cover-up defendants had finished serving their time, except Gordon Liddy. Phil Bailley was out on parole. Fred Buzhardt died in December 1978, one year after an article published in the *Federal Times* that quoted the director of the Justice Department's office of privacy and information appeals about Justice documents from 1973 pertaining to Don Stewart, recently released under the Freedom of Information Act. The director, Quinlan J. Shea, Jr., said that these documents "seemed to support" Stewart's claim that there had been "a high-level attempt to do a hatchet job on him."

Gordon Liddy came out of prison and began to write *Will*, first published in 1980. After that publication, an understanding of John Dean's true role in Watergate became feasible.

In early January 1981, Alexander Haig was under consideration by the Senate to be President-elect Reagan's secretary of state. (One of Haig's biggest supporters was Richard Nixon, who in a personal memo to Reagan strongly recommended Haig and added, "He would be personally loyal to you and would not backbite you on or off the record.") The Senate Foreign Relations Committee, under the chairmanship of Senator Charles Percy, Republican of Illinois, was locked in a heated debate as to whether it should try to obtain any of the Nixon White House tapes that included conversations between the ex-president and his former chief of staff. Haig was represented this time by Joseph Califano, and both men objected vigorously to the release of any of those conversations.

Leon Jaworski sent a letter to Major General Julius Klein, a constituent of Senator Percy, the committee chairman, who entered that letter in the hearing record. It said, in part, "I dealt with General Haig for almost a year. There was hardly a week that we were not in contact with each other and sometimes several times a week." Jaworski was effusive in his praise, but went even further than that, attacking Haig's critics as people who "are naturally vindictive and have little regard for ascertaining the facts." During Watergate, Haig was "only being loyal to his commander in chief . . . General Haig is a great soldier who performed in the highest and noblest tradition." Jaworski died in 1982, and never commented on the questions raised by his relationship with Haig. Neither has Haig, although he possibly will do so in his forthcoming book.

As this battle raged in the Foreign Relations Committee—a battle that could possibly disclose Haig's undue influence on Nixon during his last year, and that might even lead to Moorer-Radford—Bob Woodward went to bat for the man he had once briefed and on whom he had relied as a source since that time, though few people knew of their connection. The *Washington Post*'s Op-Ed page for January 15 contained a column written by Woodward that was remarkable. It said, in part:

> The U.S. Senate should probably forget about obtaining any of the notorious Nixon tapes as part of the confirmation hearings of Alexander M. Haig, the secretary of state–designate. The subpoena for the logs of the 1973 Haig meetings with President Nixon should also be abandoned. It is a senseless chase. The subpoena is quite possibly illegal and, if challenged in court, is an almost sure loser for the Senate; the search is itself unfair and has not precedent in any other confirmation hearing.

Woodward went on to argue that the historic 1974 Supreme Court ruling that forced Nixon to release his recordings had also stated expressly that the confidentiality of presidential records was protected. The language and tone of the decision, Woodward wrote, made it clear that such recordings could only be made public if there was a presentation of sworn testimony that the taped discussions might be criminal in nature. "The Haig-Nixon conversations of 1973 do not come close to meeting such a standard," Woodward continued. "The senators in fact have said exactly the *opposite* and have fallen all over themselves praising Haig, saying that there is no evidence to suggest improper conduct on his part."

Woodward claimed that Haig had been "unofficially cleared" by the Watergate Special Prosecutor's office. Beyond this, he argued, the tapes were of poor quality and so vague that the senators probably could not figure out what was on them. But even if there were statements on those tapes that incriminated Haig, Woodward suggested that Haig didn't mean them. Haig was in a "tough spot," Woodward argued, so it would not mean much "if Haig, in an effort to console Nixon," had said something that "would look bad" now.

In the conclusion of the article, Woodward wrote that Haig was "probably a shameless self-promoter, and carried situation ethics to the point of making it a personal character flaw. Haig, nonetheless, did keep a rickety and criminal ship of state afloat and helped ease Nixon out of office." Woodward said that Haig should be held accountable, but "let it happen without the tapes."

Given the evidence we have amassed, we find the opinion piece to be stunning, all the more so because it reads as if it were a brief prepared by Haig's legal team. Asked why he wrote the column, Woodward says, "It speaks for itself." And he adds that Meg Greenfield, the *Post*'s editorial page editor, had urged him to write the piece after he told her his views on the matter. Woodward says Greenfield thought readers would find it unusual for the Watergate reporter to take such a position defending Haig and arguing against the disclosure of President Nixon's notorious tape recordings.

Woodward's column carried some weight, and Haig pressed the senators hard to abandon their quest for the tapes. Shortly, Alexander Haig was confirmed as secretary of state.

On March 30, 1981, President Reagan and his press secretary James Brady were wounded by a gunman. While Reagan underwent surgery and Vice President George Bush was en route to Washington by airplane, cabinet members gathered in the Situation Room in the White House basement and monitored the chaotic situation. Secretary of State Haig was among them. Upstairs, Assistant Press Secretary Larry Speakes told assembled reporters that he could not answer many of their questions. Haig saw this on television in the basement, and, without getting permission from the other cabinet members, sprinted up the stairs to the press room, and commandeered the microphone. The press conference was being broadcast live to millions of television sets. Breathing heavily from his exertion and visibly shaking, Haig reported that the president was in stable condition and that the government was functioning.

A reporter asked, "Who is making the decisions for the government, right now?"

Haig's response was this: "Constitutionally, gentlemen, you have the President, the Vice President, and the Secretary of State, in that order, and should the President decide he wants to transfer the helm, he will do so. He has not done that. As of now, I am in control here, in the White House, pending return of the Vice President and in close touch with him. If something came up, I would check with him, of course."

A bit later, when calm returned, Haig was roundly criticized for misrepresenting the chain of succession. He had placed himself as secretary of state above the speaker of the House of Representatives and the president *pro tem* of the Senate. In fact, four people would have had to be seriously incapacitated before Haig would have been permitted to say legally that he was "in control."

This episode did more than any other to show Haig's odd response to crises and his faulty understanding of the laws of the land. It also contributed significantly to his already strained relationship with key aides to President Reagan.

Haig's differences with the White House inner circle deepened throughout Reagan's first year in office. In February 1982, Woodward published what purported to be excerpts of notes from Secretary of State Haig's staff meetings. The story was trumpeted by a front-page *Washington Post* headline as the "unvarnished Haig," portraying the tough-talking secretary as he bravely tackled world problems while fighting a White House that would undermine him. The story included Haig's defense of his own actions on the day Reagan was shot and complained that the negative story about his performance had been "fed from the White House." The day the story was published, Haig claimed he was distressed by the leak to Woodward.

But a source familiar with the Woodward-Haig relationship and who was involved in the staff meetings told us the notes were fed to Woodward by Haig through one of his top aides. We asked Woodward for a response, and he exclaimed, "Bullshit! Again you're wrong." He said "a lot of people" told him that "the story helped Haig," but he insisted that Haig was not the source "directly or indirectly." Haig refused to talk with us, but his former aide David Korn said the story was "a blessing in disguise" because it was favorable to Haig, although he argued that Haig was not Woodward's source.

After eighteen months of internal battles in the administration, in June of 1982 Haig resigned his post as secretary of state and returned to private life.

Research on this book began in 1985, and some time passed before we came to understand the dimensions of Moorer-Radford and the extent to which Haig and Buzhardt had worked to conceal the scandal and Haig's connection to it. Learning of Benton Becker's old suspicions about the conditions surrounding the transfer of Nixon's papers— suspicions that the intervening years had done nothing to quell—the authors spoke to Becker, and then to Ron Ziegler about early September of 1974, when Becker had arrived in San Clemente to deal with the papers and documents.

Ziegler immediately confirmed that he had been in constant touch with Alexander Haig at the White House from late August until the moment of the announcement of the pardon of Nixon. "Al Haig and I had discussions relevant to the pardon as Ford moved through the decision and approached the decision," says Ziegler. "Primarily they were to a great extent mechanical, you know, . . . what President

Nixon would say in a statement, those type of things. In other words, Al was [Ford's] chief of staff, and me as Nixon's chief of staff had exchanges about . . . what President Nixon would be prepared to say." The Haig-Ziegler discussions also touched frequently on the disposition of the papers and documents.

Told of Ziegler's comments, Becker responded that it was now clear that Haig's backchannel had undermined Becker's negotiations in San Clemente. The people in the ex-president's camp "had been led to believe that a pardon was a *fait accompli*. . . . While I was out there Al Haig was on the phone to Ron Ziegler negotiating the terms of a pardon, the terms of Nixon's acceptance statement, the words that Nixon was going to use, and advising, 'Hang on to the papers. You don't have to give up the papers.' "

President Gerald Ford, in a recent interview for this book, attended also by Becker, was visibly dismayed when informed of Haig's dealings with Ziegler during that period. He had always believed that there had been no private channel to Nixon from the Ford White House. "The sole responsibility of dealing with Nixon was with Phil Buchen and Benton Becker," Ford told us. "No one else ever had any authority to deal with Nixon other than through Buchen and Becker—across the board, no discussion with anybody. Haig could have acted this way, but I never knew it."

After serving four months of a one-to-four-year prison term for his role in the Watergate cover-up, John Dean returned to private life. His 1976 book *Blind Ambition* remains his final word on the subject of Watergate; today, he says, those years are "too painful" to relive. In 1982 he wrote a second book, *Lost Honor*. He and his wife Maureen live in Los Angeles where, Dean says, he works in investment banking.

Alexander Haig served as Supreme Allied Commander of NATO until resigning in 1979 and publicly blasting the defense and foreign policies of President Jimmy Carter. He returned to private life and served as chief operating officer of United Technologies Corporation. After eighteen months as secretary of state under President Ronald Reagan, Haig again became a private citizen in 1982. In 1988 he campaigned against George Bush and others for the Republican nomination to the presidency, but gathered little public support. Haig remains a public figure and frequently comments on political and military affairs.

Bob Woodward stayed at the *Washington Post* and in 1979 became its assistant managing editor for metropolitan news. His tenure was marked by controversy when in 1981 one of his staff reporters was found to have written a fraudulent story that forced the *Post* to return a Pulitzer Prize. Woodward is now the *Post*'s assistant managing editor in charge of an investigative reporting team. Since Watergate, he has published several controversial, best-selling books—about the Supreme Court (with his friend Scott Armstrong), about the late comedian John Belushi (the subject of a lawsuit against Woodward by Belushi's widow, Judy), and about the late CIA Director William Casey (that included a much-disputed passage in which Woodward said he interviewed Casey on his deathbed). His new book, to be published in 1991, will focus on the Pentagon.

After a period of self-imposed exile, Richard Nixon gradually returned to public life, as the author of memoirs and books on foreign policy, and as an informal adviser to President Ronald Reagan and President George Bush. The pinnacle of his personal comeback came in 1990 with the opening of the Richard Nixon Library in Yorba Linda, California. His most recent book, *In the Arena*, makes a tantalizing reference to White House aides whose personal agendas may have been behind the Watergate break-in. Referring to his June 23, 1972, order to have the CIA intervene with the FBI, Nixon said, "I made the inexcusable error of following the recommendation from some members of my staff—some of whom, I later learned, had a personal stake in covering up the facts—and requesting that the CIA intervene." Other than that remark, the former president has given no indication of what knowledge—if any—he has of the actions and motives that led to his removal from the nation's highest office.

Appendix A

LIST OF INTERVIEWEES

More than 150 persons talked to us on the record. Less than ten others spoke on background, meaning we could use what they said, but we could not identify them. Following is the list of those interviewed on the record. Titles generally reflect that person's position during the time frame of this book, 1968–1974.

Spiro Agnew, vice president

Vincent Alto, assistant U.S. attorney

Myles Ambrose, Drug Enforcement Administration official

Jack Anderson, columnist

Scott Armstrong, investigator, Watergate committee

Dr. William Bader, former Navy officer and briefer

Jeannine Bailley, sister of and secretary to Phillip Bailley

Phillip Mackin Bailley, attorney

Francie Barnard, Bob Woodward's second wife

Richard Bast, private investigator

Benton L. Becker, attorney for President Gerald Ford

David Beckwith, correspondent, *Time* magazine

Robert H. Bork, solicitor general, U.S. Department of Justice

Col. Jack Brennan, Nixon military aide

Edwin C. Brown, attorney for
  Phillip Bailley
Stephen Bull, Nixon aide
Alexander Butterfield, Nixon aide
John Campbell, aide to John
  Ehrlichman
Jim Cannon, Ford aide
Dick Capin, aide to Defense
  Secretary Melvin Laird
Rear Adm. Eugene J. Carroll, U.S.
  Navy
Sophia Casey, wife of William
  Casey, former director of the CIA
John Caulfield, aide to John Dean
  and Ehrlichman
Dwight Chapin, Nixon
  appointment secretary
Col. Vernon Coffey, Nixon military
  aide
Charles Colson, special counsel to
  Nixon
Capt. Andrew Combe, U.S. Navy,
  Yale classmate of Bob Woodward
William Corson, author
Candace L. Cowan, attorney for
  Bureau of Narcotics and
  Dangerous Drugs
Sam Dash, chief counsel, Watergate
  committee
Col. Bennie L. Davis, U.S. Air
  Force
John Dean, counsel to the president
John Ehrlichman, counsel and
  assistant to the president for
  domestic affairs
Roy Elson, chief of staff for Sen.
  Carl Hayden
Roger Farquhar, editor, *Montgomery
  County Sentinel* (Maryland)
Bud Fensterwald, attorney for James
  McCord
Robert Finch, Nixon aide
Rear Adm. Francis Fitzpatrick, U.S.
  Navy, assistant chief of naval
  operations

Peter Flanigan, Nixon aide
Harry Flemming, aide to John
  Mitchell
President Gerald R. Ford
Jerry Friedheim, Defense
  Department spokesman
Leonard Garment, counsel to the
  president
Payton George, FBI agent
Peter George, clerk to U.S. District
  Judge Charles R. Richey
Michael Getler, reporter, *Washington
  Post*
Roy Goodearle, Colson aide
Hays Gorey, correspondent, *Time*
  magazine
Larry Gregg, attorney, Department
  of Justice
Winston Groom, reporter,
  Washington Star
Sen. Edward Gurney, member,
  Watergate committee
H. R. Haldeman, White House
  chief of staff
Andrew Hall, attorney for
  Ehrlichman
James Hamilton, assistant chief
  counsel, Watergate committee
Robert Hartmann, Ford aide
Susan Hedling, reporter,
  Montgomery Journal (Maryland)
Seymour Hersh, reporter, *The New
  York Times*
Lawrence M. Higby, chief aide to
  Haldeman
Jim Hougan, author
Dick Howard, aide to Colson
Lt. Gen. James D. Hughes, Nixon
  military aide
William Hundley, attorney
Charles Hunnicut, Navy
  communications specialist
E. Howard Hunt, member of White
  House Plumbers
Jerry Jones, Nixon aide

Herbert Kalmbach, Nixon personal attorney

Robert Kephart, publisher, *Human Events* magazine

Stephen B. King, FBI agent and aide to Mitchell

Cmdr. John Kingston, U.S. Navy

Richard Kleindienst, attorney general

David Korn, aide to Alexander Haig

Egil Krogh, Jr., aide to Ehrlichman

Melvin Laird, Secretary of Defense

Anthony Lake, member, National Security Council staff

Rear Adm. Gene LaRocque, U.S. Navy

Fred LaRue, aide to Mitchell

Victor Lasky, author

Sgt. Paul Leeper, Washington, D.C., police, arresting officer at Watergate

Jerris Leonard, assistant attorney general

G. Gordon Liddy, general counsel, Committee to Re-elect the President, member Plumbers unit

Howard Liebengood, aide to Sen. Howard Baker

Stephen Linger, Army communications specialist

Robert Loomis, editor, Random House

J. Anthony Lukas, author

John McAllister, Yale NROTC graduate

Michael Madigan, Republican staff member, Watergate committee

Jeb Magruder, deputy director, Committee to Re-elect the President

Victor Marchetti, former CIA agent and author

Robert C. Mardian, assistant attorney general, aide to Mitchell

Peter Maroulis, defense attorney for Liddy

Robert Martin, Navy communications specialist

Eugenio R. Martinez, Watergate burglar

Rudy Maxa, writer, *The Washingtonian* magazine

Alice Mayhew, editor, Simon and Schuster

John Mitchell, attorney general

Dan E. Moldea, author

Powell Moore, spokesman, Committee to Re-elect the President

Richard Moore, Nixon aide

Adm. Thomas Moorer, Chairman, Joint Chiefs of Staff

Charles Morgan, ACLU attorney for R. Spencer Oliver, Maxie Wells, and others

Roger Morris, member, National Security Council staff, author

Adm. Dan Murphy, U.S. Navy and aide to Laird

Ryan Murphy, reporter, Knight-Ridder Newspapers

Robert Odle, director of administration, Committee to Re-elect the President

Jeremiah O'Leary, reporter, *Washington Star*

Bruce Oudes, author

Allan M. Palmer, attorney for Phillip Bailley

Sandy Perk, secretary to Mitchell

Henry Petersen, assistant attorney general

Herbert Porter, scheduling director, Committee to Re-elect the President

Samuel Powers, special counsel for Nixon on Watergate matters

Raymond Price, Nixon speechwriter

Col. L. Fletcher Prouty, U.S. Air Force, author

Gen. Robert Pursley, military aide to Laird

Yeoman Charles Radford, U.S. Navy

Robert Reisner, aide to Magruder, Committee to Re-elect the President

Charles R. Richey, U.S. district court judge (interviewed by Benton Becker)

Perry Rivkind, Bureau of Narcotics and Dangerous Drugs official

Harry Rosenfeld, metropolitan editor, *Washington Post*

John Rudy, assistant U.S. attorney

Neille Russell, secretary to Mardian

Daniel Schorr, journalist

Geoff Shepard, assistant to Ehrlichman

Robert Sherrill, author

Carl Shoffler, Washington, D.C., police, arresting officer at Watergate

Robert Silverstein, assistant minority counsel, Watergate committee

Howard Simons, managing editor, *Washington Post*

Sandy Smith, correspondent, *Time* magazine

Phil Stanford, columnist, *The Oregonian* (Portland, Oregon)

Maurice H. Stans, finance chairman, Committee to Re-elect the President

Shelby Stanton, U.S. Army Green Beret, author

W. Donald Stewart, investigator, Department of Defense

Gordon Strachan, aide to Haldeman

Frank Sturgis, Watergate burglar (interviewed by Benton Becker)

Robert Stutman, Bureau of Narcotics and Dangerous Drugs official

Col. Harry G. Summers, Jr., U.S. Army

Jane Thomas, secretary to Dean

Dan Thomasson, reporter, Scripps-Howard newspapers

Fred D. Thompson, minority counsel, Watergate committee

Adm. William Thompson, U.S. Navy

Loretta Tofani, reporter, *Washington Post*

Darrell Trent, deputy director, U.S. Office of Emergency Preparedness

Joe Trento, author

Lee (Jablonski) Uhre, secretary to Mitchell

Anthony Ulasewicz, private investigator

Gerald Warren, deputy White House press secretary

William Watts, member, National Security Council staff

Adm. Robert Welander, U.S. Navy

Woody West, reporter, *Washington Star*

Tom Wicker, reporter, *The New York Times*

Prof. Robin Winks, professor, Yale University, author

Alfred Woodward, Bob Woodward's father

Bob Woodward, reporter, *Washington Post*

Kathleen Woodward, Bob Woodward's first wife

Ron Ziegler, White House press secretary

Adm. Elmo R. Zumwalt, Jr., U.S. Navy

Appendix B

WELANDER CONFESSIONS

Note to reader: The ellipses throughout this document represent breaks in speech patterns and do not indicate deletions.

THE WHITE HOUSE
WASHINGTON
DECEMBER 23, 1971

MEMORANDUM FOR THE RECORD

SUBJECT:	Transcription of Tape Recorded Interview
PARTICIPANTS:	ADMIRAL ROBERT O. WELANDER, JOHN D. EHRLICHMAN AND DAVID R. YOUNG
TIME & DATE:	1:00–2:12 p.m., December 22, 1971
PLACE:	John D. Ehrlichman's Office, White House, West Wing

E: I don't know if you realize, but since I came here I've been sort of the house detective.

W: Yes.

E: I started out as counsel and have sort of had this responsibility, and when Al Haig called me about this first Anderson story I got into it. Of course, David has been doing all the work, but I have been following it for the President while he was gone. I really need an opportunity to visit with you about this and to get a feel for this man Radford. I just don't have the familiarity that David does with the procedure and I'd like to get a little feel for that, because we're sort of coming to a decision point on what to do about this. So if you don't mind, I'm going to tape this just so that I . . . . .

W: No hesitation.

E: It's alright with you. First of all, I need to understand a little bit about the Joint Chiefs of Staff liaison operation and how that works. Now, you're regular Navy.

W: That's correct.

E: And you're technically assigned to the Joint Chiefs of Staff, I gather.

W: Technically.

E: By the Bureau of Personnel of the Navy.

W: Right.

E: Okay. And your role there is as a kind of a bridge or a liaison?

W: This position's been occupied for something like ten years. Now with the change of Administration, the character of the job has changed somewhat. Bob Ginsburg who had been here during the end of the Johnson Administration, of course, did much the same thing with Walt Rostow that Al does now for Henry.

E: I see.

W: But there's been a succession of people and Bob Ginsburg was the first flag or general officer that had the job. At that time actually there were two officers. There was a Lt. Colonel assigned with him, young Lemnitzer. With the change of Administration, when Al came on and everything else, Ginsburg was relieved by my predecessor, Rembrandt Robinson, but after a short time, Lemnitzer left and it was down to a one-man job. So I'd say, with this Administration that job has changed rather significantly.

E: I see.

W: Instead of being of a primary military advisor or assistant, specifically to the Assistant for National Security Affairs, now it has taken on more of a liaison function.

E: I see.

W: I am regarded as a Senior National Security Council Staff member. I think Robbie established that function quite well. Technically, I'm a member of the Chairman's Staff group. I have the title of Assistant for National Security Affairs to the Chairman of the JCS.

E: You have two hats.

W: I have two hats and two offices.

E: I see. And Robinson was a Navy Captain also.

W: But he was selected for Admiral in the job.

E: So he's an Admiral now.

W: Yes.

E: I see, I see, because I had always called him Captain.

W: He had been 27 months in the job, and during most of that time he was a flag officer.

Y: And Lemnitzer was with him most of the time?

W: No. I think about the first six months. I don't recall. If it is very significant I could get those.

E: Basically, what do you do?

W: I'm a two-way avenue of communications. I try and explain things to the staff. I mean some of the formal military positions, things of that sort. I'm an in-house military expert; if they need some things done quickly, I can go ahead and punch into the organization over there much more quickly and hopefully effectively, than if we go down through the formal mechanism.

E: Henry to the Secretary and all down through the . . .

W: Things of that sort.

E: I see.

W: I think you ought to talk to Al Haig really about some of the things I do specifically for Henry, but many times there are things which he wants to come to the attention of the Chairman and things of that sort. I am an avenue for him to make his thoughts known and everything else directly to the Chairman, and vice versa. I do substantive work, often times I do get action on some of the formal NSC papers when they have problems and things of that sort. I have been assigned to several of those, and there I act strictly as an NSC member.

E: Now, at your office over here.

W: That's correct. The EOB.

E: Of what does your office consist?

W: Of myself and one clerical type. Robinson initially had a girl, and then that didn't seem to work out too well, because there were problems of her getting home late at night. Problems of that sort.

E: Was she a civilian?

W: She had been a civilian. GS7 or 8, something of that sort. So shortly after, no it wasn't shortly, it was last November, I guess, she had not worked out well so we decided to go to a Navy enlisted man—Radford was the first that had been assigned.

Y: A year ago last November.

W: Yeah.

E: That would be about thirteen months.

W: Thirteen months, something of that sort.

E: Were you in the Joint Chiefs operation at that time?

W: I had been, yes. The first of January 1971, I went on down and I had one of the divisions in the Plans and Policy Directorate. And I worked closely with Admiral Moorer over a number of years and then with Admiral Zumwalt while I was on the Navy staff. And then when Robinson was anxious to leave, he wanted to go to sea, it was a question as to who was to take his place and everything else. The various nominations were made back and forth and both Admiral Moorer and Admiral Zumwalt settled on nominating me and my nomination was made to Henry and he approved it. And the 1st of May I moved in with Robinson, we had about a month turnover period.

E: That was about the Cambodia time, wasn't it?

W: Right after it. . . .
No, this was this past May.

Y: When we had Laos.

E: Oh, that's a year ago.

W: When we had Lam Son 719.

E: Well now, you then didn't select Radford. He was selected by your predecessor.

W: That's correct.

E: And is that a process of interview and selection, or does the Bureau of Personnel just assign somebody to you?

W: No, the Bureau of Personnel screens and for any of those clerical positions, either as an Admiral's writer or specifically in the Chairman's office or in Zumwalt's office anything of that sort, they're extremely selective. This is a record check, and often times they call people with whom the individual has worked. Then a number of people are nominated for the job, and they are interviewed and looked at and some judgment made as to who the best candidate might be. I don't know specifically what went into that.

E: Yeah, you weren't engaged in that process with regard to Radford. He was in place when you got there and was introduced to you I suppose, by Robinson, as a good man and so on. Then, tell me a little about him as you observed him. What sort of a person is he?

W: An unusual young man. Until last week, I mean. I think I told Dave and everybody that I just thought he was one of the finest young fellows that I'd been associated with. I mean, he was extremely conscientious, he would work any length of time, he'd do anything and was always right on the job and seemed to be completely selfless in the whole thing.

We didn't have too much of a personal relationship. We have not seen him outside of office hours, but we drive back and forth when we have any free time together, and we chat about things. He impressed me as a very bright young guy, he had a wide range of interests and everything else. He spoke well; he seemed to be current with what was going on with things. He had a great facility for meeting people and he used to tell me about some house guest he was having, which kind of surprised me, a young guy, you know, having people who had been in the embassy or New Delhi stop by as house guests. You know, people of considerable consequence.

I've never met his wife but I talked to her on the telephone a number of times.

E: How would you happen to talk to her?

W: Oh, when she called the office or something of that sort. She did quite frequently.

Y: She called quite a bit, John.

E: Would it just be a perfunctory chat—how are you?

W: Yeah, something of that sort, or how are things going.

E: Dave's indicated that this fellow actually had some home problems. Were you aware of that?

W: It came to my attention about a month or so ago, about the time when he had his formal request for a transfer of duty and when I got that, we sat down and had a long talk. I said well alright, just let me wait for about a week or so before I take any formal action on this. You think about this thing a little bit, and if you still wish to formally request it, I would do so. At that time my initial feeling was that I just couldn't spare him at this time until I'd been in the job a little bit longer and I felt that I would recommend that his request not be approved.

E: What did he want to do?

W: Well, to be assigned to some other duty that had less demanding hours.

E: I see.

W: He indicated that he was having problems at home with his family. He'd get up in the morning and leave before he had a chance to see his children. He'd be getting home at night . . .

E: Oh, he has kids. I didn't realize that.

W: Yes, yes.

Y: They were born in India too.

W: His wife doesn't drive and they just moved to a military housing here at Bolling field, so when they want to take the children to the family dentist over in Arlington, that was a major problem, and with his schedule he couldn't get time off to drive her over there. When she had to go to the commissary or things of that sort, I mean, he wasn't there to help. So, on Saturdays he was hard put to take care of all his chores and there had been a great deal of discussion.

Apparently his wife has indicated that she was going to take the children and go home to her family on the West Coast or something. So we tried to liberalize the schedule a little bit. I'd previously had another man cleared for duty here on the staff at the White House on the basis that we needed somebody in case Radford were sick, or we gave him leave or something of that sort, that was generally familiar with the operation here and who could come over and pinch-hit rather than I bring somebody over who hadn't been cleared or exposed to the thing.

E: Now you've gone through this procedure in getting that man, as you described.

W: Yes, some months ago.

E: Who's he?

W: Chief Sessoms, he's a Chief Yeoman.

E: Sessoms?

W: S-E-S-S-O-M-S, Sessoms.

Well, what I've tried to do was liberalize his schedule so Radford could have a morning off when his wife has domestic things.

E: Did that satisfy him then?

W: It seemed to, and when I took formal action on it and forwarded it with my comments and recommended that it not be approved at this time, but perhaps six months in the future. He seemed to be fairly relieved and he said, "Okay—well, really, you know, now I've kept faith with my wife. She's been after me to get a change. At least now I can tell her that I have tried and show her the copy and that you recommended disapproval, and I think this will put a cap on it."

E: But he was not nursing a grievance.

W: Outwardly, no. He felt that, okay this would relieve some of the pressure.

E: In retrospect, do you think he was? Would that account for any of his conduct?

W: After I had formally recommended disapproval on his request, it went up through the chain over to BUPERS and nowadays, I mean all these things are looked at in the Bureau, rather than being settled locally, and the formal BUPERS action came out what, the Thursday or the Friday before this whole thing triggered off.

Looking at the time sequence when he knew that, you know, the final recourse of the Bureau where they had supported my position and regretfully that they couldn't transfer him at this time, there were no jobs available, etc. That may have had some impact on him.

E: Although, when you recommended against it and told him so, he must have known that the die was cast at that point.

W: Yes. There was only one in a million chance that that would be overturned.

Y: Just let me add one thing on the same subject. One of the other fellows that works in the office was asked about his wife and the transfer and I said do you think he was that disappointed and he said the exact same thing. He was relieved, mainly, and said that at least now he could go home and tell his wife he had tried. One other thing that goes into this, John, is the fact that even though he did get the time off, he would go to work someplace else.

W: Well this is something that disturbed me. Over Thanksgiving, he had asked for four days of leave, and I said fine, things will be fairly quiet and everything else. And he was supposed to be going up to Philadelphia to spend the time with some old friends of theirs—some old marine who was now out. So I said this was fine and I approved it and everything else, and again Chief Sessoms was supposed to pick up his part of the job Friday if anything was going on that we had to come on over here.

But Friday morning when I came into the office I was surprised to see Chuck there. I said, "Chuck, what the hell are you doing?" He said, "Oh well, I decided not to take the leave. The people came down from Philadelphia and are staying with us." About three days later Chief Sessoms came in and said, "Admiral, I feel I ought to tell you, you know, after you approved Chuck's leave chit and all, I found out that Chuck has a part-time job and he has planned to work all that weekend. I guess Thursday, Friday and Saturday, and get overtime. And apparently the Chief had braced him with this because he, as his Chief Petty Officer, has to approve such requests. And, as a consequence, Chuck had decided to withdraw his request.

I was a little bit provoked because, you know, I'd already made these other arrangements to go ahead and try and liberalize his time and give him time off and meet every, you know, request for time off that he had because I was aware of his family situation. That disappointed me a little bit. It didn't sit very well. We don't like to be taken on something of that sort.

E: Well now, aside from those two men, then, you as the liaison officer have no other staff.

W: That is correct. I do not.

E: Or do you have staff over at the Pentagon?

W: No, Radford and I have been kind of a portable team. We both get over there in the morning, I go through my Pentagon things and everything else and the two of us jump in the car and come over here and open up the office. At the end of the day we go back over to the Pentagon. . . . . .

E: You're the taxi squad. . . . . . Laughter.

W: Yes, indeed.

Y: I know Robinson wanted to get back to the sea, but is this job generally considered a good assignment in the Navy?

W: Yes it is. It is very much in demand. It is supposed to be the finest job for a flag officer.

E: Career enhancing?

W: Yes, indeed.

E: And you're Academy, are you?

W: That's correct, yes.

Y: Are you a submariner, surface or what?

W:　I'm a destroyer officer.

E:　Well, let me get back to Radford. Now you're [*sic*] job is to keep both ends of your conduit informed of what is going on at the other end. And his job, I take it, is to develop in writing anything which you feel has to be transmitted. . . . .

W:　When I dictate or hand draft or anything else, he is the guy that writes for me, he maintains my files. I have a set of files over here in the Executive Office Building with things I most frequently am asked about over here, so I can go back and research and do a quick paper or something like that to satisfy the immediate need. I have a set of files over on the other side which again more or less relates to ongoing JCS actions so if I again have to do a little paper, like where do we stand on so and so, I've got most of the references.

E:　He keeps that file.

W:　He keeps both sets of them.

E:　Okay, now you don't have an administrative assistant or anything of that kind. Does he perform any of those kinds of functions? Do you put him in a car and send him over there to. . . . .

W:　Frequently, yes, to pick up stuff or chase things around. He kind of acts like a junior aide . . . . he also takes care of a few personal things and what have you.

E:　Okay, now in your role, I think it, you report to what, four men, five men, or do you report to the Chairman? Just to Admiral Moorer?

W:　There's nobody between me and Admiral Moorer. I mean it's a direct personal liaison.

E:　I see. And so your job is to keep him informed and then if he wants to share that with the rest of the Joint Chiefs that's up to him.

W:　That's his decision.

E:　uh-huh, I see.

W:　To the point where this has caused, I must say, a good bit of anguish. Because obviously a lot of the information I have is very sensitive and given to me many times as a personal privilege of the Chairman. And when he is out of town, people who are generally aware of my function, you know the Acting Chairman, feels he should have this information, and I've had some knock-down-and-drag-out fights.

E:　It's a hard and fast rule where that's concerned. Nobody has access to your material except the Admiral.

Y:　But as an Acting Chairman, you don't, unless it's so pertinent and relevant that he has to have it . . .

W:　That he has to have it. And then I very carefully paraphrase it or just give him exactly what he needs to have to act as chairman.

Y:　During the week actually that the meeting that was reported by Anderson, there was a sort of musical chairs. There were about three or four days in a row that there was somebody else there.

W: That's right. Westmoreland, Ryan, and, I think, on one occasion, Bud Zumwalt.

Y: Does it go one day each? 24 hours per . . .

W: No, it depends upon their mutual schedules. All these people are fairly heavily committed well in advance to things they can't get out of. So then there is an intricate little schedule worked out from a certain hour of a certain day. The senior man has it and as soon as he flies off on some commitment then whoever else is around picks it up. It works on a seniority basis.

Y: It does go on seniority?

W: Yes. The Senior Chief.

E: Now, is there a comparable arrangement at this end of your conduit? That you report to one man, or a set of people, or . . . ?

W: I report to Al Haig and Henry.

E: And nobody else?

W: Nobody else.

E: Okay.

W: I mean, the things that I do are outside of the correspondence system unless it's a formal NSC staff action given to me. Nine-tenths of the things that I do I give to Al, and then it's a matter of his judgment whether or not it goes to Henry. On some occasions where I know there's other interest, Dick Kennedy gets copies of things, John Holdridge, or other principal staff officers, and we know over the course of time that the things that I'm giving them come from the essentially privileged sources. That is, things that have been held very, very closely within the military, private communications to the Chairman. Things of that sort.

Everybody knows the basis on which I give them these things, it's essential background that they have to know, so that they can fill out their part of the picture over here.

E: Well then as your alter ego, this Yeoman was at a very critical crossroad, so to speak, in the transmission of information in the national security apparatus.

W: I have access to everything the Chairman sees.

E: And he has access to virtually everything there is, I take it.

W: And I don't specialize in one area. I cover the whole waterfront so I have an unusual accumulation of things.

E: You see CIA memoranda and cables and you see State Department stuff and the whole gamet [*sic*].

W: I see things from the Office of the Secretary of Defense, everything from the Joint Staff . . . . . .

E: Yeah, yeah, okay. Now, I take it from what you said about his leave, that you more or less set this man's schedule for him, Radford, as to when he comes to work, when he goes home, what he does while he's there, is all by assignment.

W: Yes, he works exclusively for me.

E: Is he the kind of a fellow that's a self-starter, or is he an enlisted man who waits for orders before he does something, or what kind of a person is he?

W: We've established a routine. I mean, we process a hell of a lot of paper you know, and we're in a hurry. He'll get in early and will try to sort things out, you know. I'll give him some broad guidance, like Laos is of primary concern now, and anything we've got to see immediately so that I'm ready to respond, etc. He uses his judgment and initiative in this regard, to try to keep the things that are important in front of me. The maintenance of my files—we kind of set that up—and I indicate the things I want to keep and what files I want to go to [unintelligible] as he gets time, he puts those things [unintelligible]. That is about the extent of any necessity for individual judgement or actions.

E: Otherwise, his initiative is a plus, I take it. If he's doing those things that you've assigned to him and taking dictation.

W: Yes, and within the broad guidance he takes care of all those kinds of things. He kind of runs my little porthole office as set up in the two places.

E: Yeah, yeah, I see. Aside from the family problems that you told me about, does he have any other emotional problems or hang-ups that you've noticed, or any prejudices or quirks that sort of define his personality for you?

W: Not really. My impression is that he is a very serious young guy. We've not philosophized a great deal in our discussions on anything. I know on one occasion, I forget what we were talking about, either the war in Vietnam or something, I know he kind of closed things with a statement "Well I'm a man of principles, too." And this came to mind the other day.

E: Is he hung-up on India?

W: Not to my knowledge. We never discussed the pros and cons of the current situation. We've just been running too fast to sit down and think about it. He's never volunteered anything to me one way or the other and we have not discussed how things are going nor have I asked him how do you see things.

E: You've had a chance to think a lot about this whole episode on this Anderson stuff. Can you account for it in any way?

W: Well, I mean I've constructed a theory.

E: Alright.

W: And I did as of last Tuesday when I first saw Al and subsequently you, Dave and everyone else. And to my mind as I read this whole series of things, I know it all comes from my files.

E: There's no question in your mind?

W: I'm morally certain about it. And yesterday I gave Stewart over on the other side another piece of information.

Y: Yes, he called me yesterday.

W: Chuck had typed it for me. It was a little think piece I had just kind of done on scratch paper for a conversation I was going to have with Al.

Y: That's on the sequence of leaks—planned leaks—as the ships came through. And that's what is in yesterday's article.

W: And, again, that is something unique. Nothing else was out in the formal bureaucracy.

E: Didn't go to the Pentagon, didn't really. . . . .

W: It was an original and one copy, both of which I have had to the best of my knowledge in my personal possession. I never gave one to Al. We talked about some of these things and a lot of other decisions had been made which . . .

Y: How was that sent out? When Al took that thing, then how did you get word out to leak it out at particular places.

W: We didn't, we didn't, this was my own think piece.

Y: It never was done?

W: No.

Y: I didn't realize that.

W: The decision was pending on which ships we were to send and we talked about a generalized game plan on this whole thing and everything, so I sat down at home at night and got some random thoughts down. You know, how do you want to play this thing? What the possibilities are . . . then to see what the full game plan was and what was to be developed the next day and everything. And looking at how we could manage for some weeks and how we could get the signal across that we seemed to be wanting to send at that time and yet do it in a way that would not be overt or anything else. So these were just top-of-my-head thoughts.

E: Did you hand that paper to anybody?

W: The next morning I gave it to Radford to type up my scratchings and he made an original, I say, and xeroxed a copy. And I was going to leave a copy with Al, but by the time I got to see him later on that afternoon, the decisions had been made after the meeting that day to send *Enterprise* and a few other things, and the rest was to be held in abeyance. So, I said, you know, there are other ways we could do this whole thing with P3 surveillance and a number of other things which would be immediate and send immediate signals. Well, we just never got into it in any detail because, you know, other things were going.

Y: Don't you think he would have known that it was not discussed and that it was not transmitted?

W: No.

E: Did you bring both copies back with you?

W: That's correct, the original and the one copy. And, I say, they have been in my personal possession in a sealed envelope in my briefcase ever since.

E: In a sealed envelope?

W: Yes.

E: The only way he could have gotten a copy then would be to make two xeroxes, I take it.

W: Or have kept my hand-scratched original.

E: Yeah, yeah. Because you had the two work copies in your possession ever since—as far as you know.

W: Yes.

Y: One thing, John, that we did go into on the hand-scratched notes—we thought that perhaps—do you write secret on your hand-scratched notes or do you figure he automatically is going to know enough to put the classification on it?

W: No, usually I indicate what it is.

Y: You do. Okay.

W: In a similar case I didn't.

Y: Yeah, alright, good. It really wouldn't matter except that it would be easier on his conscience if he got the hand-written note and it doesn't say what classification. In any event, he then takes it, supposedly tears it up, because, he says, he usually tears it in fours, and puts it in the burn bag. We went all through this the other day in trying to find out if the one that involved "Tartar Sam" was in the burn bag, and we tried in the interrogation to draw him out on that and to say we were in the process of checking all the burn bags and we had not been able to find that memo. He wasn't phased too much, but he said, "Well, I'm sure, you know, as best I can remember I'm sure I put it in there. I always put them in the burn bag." Now I don't know if that is a. . . . . .

E: Is he pretty methodical about that?

W: Yes, we keep the burn bag there and everything else.

Y: Do you see him ever doing it?

W: Well, we work in adjacent offices.

Y: That's right, and he would go out and the burn bag would be in his section.

W: The burn bag is in his section, and as I cull through traffic and everything else, I put a green mark across the front that I don't want to keep it or anything and he would pick it up periodically from my outgoing basket. I can hear them tearing it up out there. And the last thing we do before we close up the office over here at night; I ring for the elevator and he runs across to the other office and puts our burn bag in the big pick-up thing over there in I and L.

E: Well, let me ask you to go back now to your theory of the case, so to speak. Why did he do this?

W: I knew he had some amount of money problems. I mean just living here and everything else, and I really thought that he had some kind of Ellsberg syndrome about the Indian thing. I know he has had Indian friends visit with him and everything else. I know he always regarded that as the finest tour of duty he had ever had. He was delighted when he had a chance to go back there with

Henry on this last trip and to see old friends there in New Delhi and all the rest of the business. Money, that and I thought there was some disappointment about having to stay on in the job.

E: Is that the sum and substance of what you've come up with?

W: Yes.

E: When he would go on a trip like that with Henry, for instance, you were not along.

W: No, I was not.

E: And then I take it what you've done is turned him over to your . . . principal.

W: I just made him available and in the first case when he went with Henry, I did not have Chief Sessoms cleared. I brought one of our temporary office girls over to the office. That just didn't work out. Then I got Sessoms cleared by a telephone call to come on over and be with me in the office. And it was at that time that I decided that I would formally get a backup man cleared and ready for occasions like this.

Y: Admiral, what did Robinson do when he let him go with Al a couple of times? The same thing. Did he get a backup girl . . . ?

W: A backup girl, yeah. We had access to the temporary pool over there if one of the men is sick or anything else—these girls are all security cleared and everything else.

E: Now when he would come back from a trip like that there would be a lot of writing up to do I suppose for Henry, and would he move out of your office to do that or . . . .

W: Depending upon where it was being done. In the instance of when Henry came back from his trip, I think there was about a day's clean-up stuff that Radford had done, but everything else was being done by the gals. You recall we were all out in San Clemente and everything else—the operation was going there.

E: Yeah, I see.

W: With Al's most recent trip on out there, Al had a temporary aide that the Navy had provided him before the trip. A youngster Bud Zumwalt had recommended to me and to make available to Al. And then Radford and he worked, I guess, for about a day cleaning up some of the hang-over things. But after that I guess Al's gals finished up the other stuff.

E: Well, no, no. When he comes off a trip like that, does he visit with you about the trip?

W: Yes.

E: Does he kind of fill you in on what all went on and everything? Does he show you the work he's done on the trip?

W: I was a little bit surprised the first trip he came back from with Henry. Before he went out he said what are you interested in? I said obviously we'd be interested in whatever Henry's observations are of the situation in South Vietnam and things of that sort. So anything you hear about that, why, we'd be very much interested in.

The chairman and I flew out to the NSC meeting out in San Clemente and that was the day that the announcement was made about Henry's first trip to Peking. So I only had a chance to talk with Radford very briefly. He stayed out there another day or two and flew on back. And when he came back he had an envelope full of things, and he said perhaps you might care to go through some of these things. They may be of interest to you; and I started to go through them and I was very much startled.

E: What was it?

W: I said, "Chuck, where did you get these things?" He said, "Well, I used to take the burn bags out for disposal and things of that sort, and I'd kind of go through them and as far as typing I'd keep a flimsy or whatever."

E: On the trip?

W: On the trip.

E: Hmmmmmm.

W: And there were portions of MFR's uh. . . .

E: What does that mean?

W: Memos For the Record.

E: Oh.

W: Memcons, things of that nature. Spare copies of incoming messages and what have you. And I spent a night culling through this and 90 percent of it I just had burned. There were a few things that gave some fairly significant insights on some things that were going on, which I assembled and made some comments on a cover sheet and I showed to Admiral Moorer. And when he had read them we discussed them. Then he gave them all back to me and I have them all locked in my personal safe over at the Pentagon.

I then asked Radford, "Just how did you get all these things?" He said, "Well I just kind of came across them and I thought maybe they might be of interest so I kept them for you."

When Al was going out on his trip, he said, "Is there anything of particular interest?" I said, "Look we're concerned about the troop withdrawal rate and anything else in any discussions Al may have with General Abrams or Ambassador Bunker or President Thieu." I said, "Chuck, I don't know what you're doing on this thing, but come on now, you know, there's a confidence here and everything else. I don't want you to, you know, go peeking, but if you hear of anything, fine."

When he came back he again had a couple of memcons and some of the messages and what have you which he made available. Of those there was only one significant. Which was Al's discussion with President Thieu about some forthcoming plans. That I made available to the Chairman on the same basis and he back to me.

E: Has he ever done that before with anything that he'd come up with that had not been generated in your office?

W: Every now and then he runs a messenger service, when he comes over to deliver something over here (White House). I guess the gals give him some stuff to drop off at I and L, and he would say, "Admiral, is this of any interest to you?" And I would scan it and say no.

E: If it were something of interest, did you take it out?

W: I would look at it and occasionally I'd say, "Okay, Chuck, would you make a xerox of this one portion of it?" Or something of that sort.

E: And send it over to the chairman?

W: (Nodded yes.)

E: So he has had some access that is outside of your ordinary channels. . . . So he would be bird-dogging occasionally and bring you things?

W: I'm obviously not happy about having to relate that.

E: I understand. But he, of course, has gone into this in his testimony and he testified that he had actually delved into people's briefcases and come up with material which he had duplicated and turned over to Captain Robinson in some cases.

W: I never delved into it, you know, to find out specifics on anything. And as I say, the first time he went out with Henry he asked me what I was particularly interested in. And I was aghast, you know, that it was this kind of stuff. I thought it would be, you know, all oral . . . what went on and everything, what he had seen and what have you.

E: Did he have stuff in Henry's handwriting?

W: I don't know. There were annotated first drafts of things and things of that sort. But he assured me that he got this out of burn bags and everything and this seemed to be consistent since there would only be portions of things—hand-scratched drafts of portions of memcons.

E: To your knowledge has any of the stuff that he has ever brought you here, other than his trip proceeds, come from briefcases or people's offices or anything of that kind?

W: No, I mean, I heard, you know, since this investigation had started that he had penetrated Henry's briefcase.

E: Does that jibe now with anything that you may have seen that he has brought you? That conceivably could have come from a source like that?

W: Not from Henry's briefcase.

E: Anybody else?

W: Maybe some of the things. I had complete copies of memcons from Al's recent trip. Some of these things he himself had typed.

E: Al?

W: No. Radford for Al. Where, you know, he had made a flimsy copy or something else. But that would have come directly from busting into somebody's luggage or something? No, I can't think of anything in that regard.

E: But there isn't any question in your mind, though, that he has brought you stuff from time to time that has been obtained from . . .

W: Surreptitiously and everything else.

E: Now, does Admiral Moorer know that this kind of source has been available to the JCS?

W: I have shown him, as I say, some of the most significant things that I felt that he had to know.

E: Sure, but again he is aware that the source is irregular.

W: He knows that Radford picked this up on a trip.

E: Now, as far as you know, Radford is in possession of recollections of a tremendous amount of Top Secret material?

W: That's correct.

E: Knowing him and knowing his frame of mind and the makeup of his personality, do you have any recommendations as to what the disposition of his case should be?

W: I don't see where he has any further utility to me, regardless of what the ultimate findings are of this whole investigation. It's a complete loss of confidence and everyone else in the office has kind of surmised what's going on in view of the fact of all of their interrogations and everything else.

I could not in good conscience in view of the conclusions I've drawn, recommend that he go to any kind of sensitive position in the Navy.

Personally, I can't understand people who would, either for money or some other reason, divulge things of this sort. I frankly think the man ought to be prosecuted if there's a case against him.

E: Are you concerned if he is prosecuted that he might divulge secrets that he knows?

W: I'm more concerned that if he's not prosecuted, that all the stuff can dribble on out.

Y: Is his memory such or have you ever seen an example of where he could sit down after reading something and then quote it or come up with a very accurate recounting. I'm just wondering how, you know, whether his mind would . . .

W: Have instant recall? No, I've not seen any evidence of that.

But what does concern me is that I've got stuff up in my safes which is of ten times more consequence than anything that's been leaked out in the Anderson articles right now.

E: And he's had access to it?

W: He's had access to it and when we go back to the Pentagon at night. . . .

E: Can you give me a rough idea of the kind of things that you're talking about?

W: I've got everything about SALT; I've got everything about an operation which is currently planned which has been deferred due to weather. I don't know whether you're a part of that or not.

E: You don't have to say anymore about that.

W: No, but that has, you know, lives to be lost if this kind of stuff is leaked. I've got a full recount on our involvement in Cambodia from Day One which would make the Pentagon Papers pale by comparison; the full recount of almost our complete involvement in Southeast Asia. You name any other sensitive area. . . . . .

Y: How about any of the secret negotiations or secret channels that Henry has. Do you have any of that?

W: No, I've not been a party to any of that . . . except for one piece of paper which came back when he was with Henry on the trip.

E: That this fellow produced for you?

W: (Nodded yes.)

E: So he advised you of something that you were not privy to, I take it.

W: That's right. Nor to the best of my knowledge had the Chairman been privy to it.

E: So Radford developed superior knowledge of that by reason of his contact with Henry on the trip. Have you ever had any occasion to instruct Radford to obtain information for you that you wouldn't ordinarily be on the distribution list for?

W: On one recent occasion. There was a staff action going on and I knew the Navy was highly interested in it. I had talked to Phil Odeen on what their position was going to be because I had been routed info on the staff action sheet. He indicated that at the present time we were going to play it low key. I mean it was between State and DOD on the basing of some of our ships in Greece.

And as time went on I just got buried in some other stuff. I said, "Chuck, would you go on over to the IL and find out if the staff has completed action on this thing, because I would be interested in finding out what if anything they're recommending to Henry on it."

He came back in about five minutes with a copy of Phil's memo to Henry which essentially was what Phil had told me orally, but I knew that action had been completed so I just set it aside.

Y: Who decides the distribution?

W: On?

Y: On paper coming out of IL.

W: Jack Murphy.

Y: Does Jack Murphy do all of it?

W: Jeanne Davis would do some of the highly sensitive things.

Y: Jeanne would act on the most sensitive things?

W: Yeah.

Y: Because for instance in Monday's article you remember there were two cables that made that one up, and I called up to get copies and each has a stamp on the side with the line drawn through the names of the distributees and I just wondered who actually does draw the lines on that.

W: That would be the people in the cable room.

Y: Fairly low level.

W: Fairly low level.

Y: Simply on the basis of area.

W: Pretty much so.

Y: Not to cut people out of stuff.

W: Robbie had pretty much set it up so that people knew his areas of interest, and I just kind of inherited those. And the groundrule is that I get anything up to Exdis over there at the NSC side.

E: Now when you took over from Robbie, did he say in effect about Radford that this guy's a pretty good bird dog, or something to that effect?

W: No . . . Oh . . . he said occasionally you're going to get a request from Al to go on a trip or something else, and I've found it worthwhile to go ahead make him available to them and everything else. He does a fine job, he's a good image for the Navy and everything else. Sometimes he could be very helpful to you.

E: And by that he implied that you could get some information back.

W: Yeah, I didn't press for details, you know, especially. . . . . .

E: But you understood that's what he meant. . . .

W: Yeah, you know, I figured he'd keep his ears open, his eyes open, being a fairly bright young guy and everything else. He would obviously be exposed to things which would be of interest.

E: Do you have anything else, David?

Y: I was wondering whether anyone else might be aware of Radford operating sort of this way. To some degree, you know, from what you say, it seems like it's a rather a regular thing. I've tried to put in my own mind after listening and talking with him and the polygraph operator—especially after he broke down that night and I called you and he went into this particular part of it—what sort of quantity or flow he is talking about. I haven't the foggiest idea whether he's talking about one paper every two months when he goes on a trip or whether he was able to get things almost at will.

Did he make a practice, so that you could say every day or two he might drop by and say I just picked this up. Is he exaggerating or is he . . .

W: Well, he's made the two trips. I would say that on about four occasions he played

messenger bringing the stuff back here for IL when he's shown me folders and so on that are going back to files.

E: What do those initials stand for?

Y: Information and liaison. I & L.

E: I see.

W: It's their correspondence center. It's right across the hall from my office over there in the EOB. Dick Kennedy makes available to me the books which are prepared for the various meetings over here so I can go ahead and make sure the Chairman is prepared to talk at the various meetings and what have you. If it is a particularly complex subject or something of that sort, I will have Chuck xerox a copy of the staff comments and Henry's talker. So that we can go ahead and generate the answers to the questions which have been posed for the Chairman. This is fairly frequent. I mean, whenever we have a meeting, Dick will call. . . .

E: I think Henry knows that and that would be assumed.

W: Yes, certainly.

Y: In any event, Kennedy is the one who is responsible for it in terms of overseeing preparation and I think by the same token often coming back the other way they say this is going to be their talker—their plan . . .

W: I have provided JCS papers which is contrary to all JCS instructions simply because these staff people have to have the God damn things. Rather than getting part of the picture in the working groups. The thing is of consequence and they have to know what the JCS rational is and what their thinking is, what their position is. And I have shown it to them on a privileged basis.

E: But on David's point, these things other than the whole file that he might give you to flip through, do you find things in your reading or does he bring you things from time to time that he's abstracted here and there?

W: No, no. I get things in my regular distribution from the NSC staff and everything else. Seventy-five percent of it is duplicated, I mean, from what I get over at my Pentagon distribution. . . . . .

E: So basically his operation would be on trips—that's where he's most effective.

W: Right.

Y: Do you think Al is in any way aware that when he was on a trip with him that he might come back and bootleg a copy and give it to you?

W: You can only ask Al, I've never discussed it with him. Obviously, if to take a man along on a trip like Al makes out in the boon docks, it's a lot easier and Radford does a lot of other chores and everything else which are very helpful on the trip, that one of the girls couldn't do. Were I in the same case and having borrowed a Yeoman, I think I would have concluded that most of the things the yeoman might have been exposed to would in turn be exposed to the guy he normally works for. But, as I say, that's something you'll have to talk with Al about. I don't know. I've never discussed any of these things with Al or anything else.

E: You've been fair with us and I appreciate it.

W: Well, I agonized a hell of a lot over this thing. I agonized mostly last Tuesday, you know, when I first saw this whole thing laid out and it is very personally embarrassing to me, and I think it could be potentially embarrassing to Admiral Moorer, whom I think the world of.

E: Well, it's simply a question of what the facts are at this point.

W: But as I saw it there is no choice in the matter. I mean, too much else is at stake.

E: In anticipation, we have developed a statement, largely based on the testimony of the yeoman, but I wonder if you'd look at that and tell me whether that's a correct statement of fact.

W: "Internal White House political dealings". . . . I can't think of anything that would . . . Well, maybe I don't understand what you mean by political dealings.

E: Well, that's taken out of his testimony, he says that he has, and this covers not only your period of time, but Robinson's as well, and that at some point in time and not fixed by the testimony apparently, some of the material which he produced involved non-factual data relating to political decisions and political discussions or inner–White House meetings or conversations, the kind of thing that typically could be involved would be Henry's notes of a meeting with the President where the President was noted in the notes as saying Israel should not have jets or that kind of thing. Now that's a guess or a hypothetical on my part.

W: Well, I don't know from my personal knowledge about any of those kinds of things. I know the inter-play between Secretary Laird and Henry and the President and the Chairman and everything else I've been deeply involved in and anything I find out about this is of course of interest to Admiral Moorer, but that has been the extent of it. But, I mean, any other what I would have termed political . . . .

E: Now how would that be evidenced? Would that be evidenced by memos between say Haig and Kissinger, or Kissinger and the President, or . . . .

W: Well, my conversations with Al . . . my point is that I've relayed these things often times . . . you know. . . .

E: But of the things that this fellow produced out of the I & L files or otherwise. . . . .

W: To my recollection, there has never been anything of that sort.

E: Or from trips.

W: But what I was going to say though is that often times based on my discussions and sense of things, if I can't get to see the Chairman to make an oral report, I will dictate something, a little memo with information and so on. . . . . . .

E: Which then Radford types.

W: Yeah.

E: Now I'm directing your attention specifically to documents that he might have had appropriated from some source outside of your office and brought you.

W: None to my recollection in that particular area.

(Reading from statement) . . .
"Memcons of private top-level meetings"—Yes, from his trips.

"Internal White House political dealings"—not aware of.

"Secret negotiations with foreign governments"—from his trips.

"Contingency plans"—I'm not aware of any that he has brought me.

I mean, Al Haig has cut me in on what we've been thinking about on the most recent thing, and given me a copy of game plans and so on.

E: Sure. Sure.

Y: Most contingency plans originate with you anyway.

W: Yeah.

E: You see that is right out of his testimony again.

Y: He does seem or tend to exaggerate, and this has been one of our problems in his whole testimony.

E: Well, bear in mind he is talking about service to two different officers here too. That might not relate to the Admiral.

Y: That's right. That's true.

W: "Political agreements" . . . in the international sense—You mean Al's most recent trip and his discussions with Thieu?

E: Exactly.

W: "Troop movements"—

Y: Or I suppose you could say movements or withdrawals—withdrawal rates . . .

W: Nothing very significant came up that I saw from Al's last trip. We knew pretty much what the game plan was going to be. Al related to me orally his discussions and some observations that the staff people had made—that he had turned around about the most recent troop announcements.

"Telcons"—I can't think of any unless there were from the trip or something of that sort. I think on one occasion there was some reference made in a message to a telephone conversation with the White House and Ambassador Smith with regard to the SALT negotiations.

E: That wouldn't have been on the trip though, would it?

W: Yeah. Apparently the cable had been sent to Henry.

Y: Yes, when Henry's away a lot of the cable traffic is forwarded to him.

E: Oh, I see.

W: But not a copy of a telecon from Henry's office.

Y: You know how they transcribe calls down there.

W: Yeah.

Y: It would be very easy for somebody to pick those up out of the in boxes.

W: I've never seen one of those.

Y: Maybe he's picking them up and reading them himself.

W: "Secret channel papers"—I don't know what you mean by that.

E: Well, I don't know what he meant by that.

Y: Well, the only thing I can think of is that Henry does meet without the knowledge of Defense or State with particular ambassadors of major countries and they are done in a very, very quiet way with only Al, Henry, Coleman and possibly Jon Howe knowing. And I would think there is a tremendous volume of stuff generated from these talking points. . . .

E: Have you ever run across any memoranda of such meetings outside of the normal distribution?

W: Well, I say, Haig's with Thieu. Again, there's one indication of a meeting Henry was to have had in Paris when he came back from his recent swing out there.

E: That was generated off the trip?

W: Well, as I understood the situation—this had been set . . .

E: I mean your man Radford generated it on the trip.

W: Yes. And as I say the significance was that this was the first indication we had that this avenue was open . . . over in Paris.

"Secret channel information"—I think what he could be talking about there is that much of the information which I provide over here comes out of what we call SPECAT Exclusive message category which is eyes only between the military originator and the Chairman and a few other people and I make these available to people over here. As I did yesterday and as I did this morning.

Y: I was thinking more in the sense of talking points for meeting with Dobrynin and things like that. . . .

W: Like I said, I've never seen any of these.

Y: And I think a lot with the (unintelligible) this last year.

W: "Defense budget papers."

Y: Who's going to get what . . . stuff like that.

W: We have done some work for Al and Henry last year in that regard—which you will have to talk to them about. I did some work for them this July and August . . .

E: This would be information moving the other way—from here over to the Pentagon.

W: No, I've again dictated memoranda based on my conversations with Al and some other things which I've picked up in the normal course of my talking with people on the staff.

E: Do you have any sources in the Office of Management and Budget that this fellow might have exploited?

W: No. I personally know Ken Damn who I would have sat down and tried to talk with. But I sit in the staff meetings down there and knew that things are being generated and that there is going to be meeting "umptee ump" but I don't know the particular subject. So often times I relate what I surmise to Admiral Moorer and I dictate it—and kind of (unintelligible) on actions I see shaping up—what have you.

(Reading from statement)

I have in fact either shown or discussed these papers with Admiral Moorer, as I say, not with the Acting Chairman at the time. I might orally brief, or I will go through these things and dictate a little memo usually based on my conversations with the NSC staff. I believe you will be asked the following questions at the (unintelligible) meeting this afternoon. And then I may paraphrase the questions. . . .

E: That would be to an Acting Chairman.

W: That's to an Acting Chairman.

Y: Yeah.

W: The literal papers and everything else I show only to Admiral Moorer.

E: Well I don't think a statement of this kind is necessary. . . . I'm not going to retype that and submit it to you but I thought it would be a useful reference in comparing his testimony.

Anything else?

Y: I have only a couple of other things. If it came to the point where they didn't prosecute him on the outside in a criminal trial but they could possibly go after him on a Court Martial, I'm just wondering what's your reaction to that?

W: I think the man has to get out of the service. As a yeoman and everything else, I mean he's almost useless unless he's cleared for security.

E: Unless you put him to work counting socks someplace.

W: And I do feel that some punitive action ought to be taken if in fact there is a substantial case against him.

Y: My point is that if punitive action is taken, to what extent do you want to risk his turning around and saying I did all this other stuff?

W: Well, he can say these sorts of things. But what really concerns me is how much else has he xeroxed . . . and have stashed away.

E: Think about this though. Supposing he says I didn't feel too badly about turning this stuff over to Anderson because I was a spy for the Joint Chiefs. I used to turn stuff over to them all the time. And the morals involved in one is about the same as the other as far as I'm concerned.

W: He could rationalize it that way.

E: That would obviously create an impairment of relationships that would be very difficult to live with in the future. Do you have qualms about that? (Laughter) That's a leading question, isn't it? We have qualms about that.

W: I've had qualms about it ever since last Tuesday morning. I really mean it. And I know that Mr. Laird is going to take a very dim view of this. I'm sure he has seen the transcripts of the investigation and things of that sort . . .

E: Not (unintelligible)

W: Well, his people are investigating it. I mean, it exposes some very, very sticky relationships and the function here that has been going on.

E: Could the function go on without the liaison office existing?

W: Not really.

E: Some substitute would have to be developed.

W: Really, I think you ought to talk to Al Haig on this. It's been a two-way street. It's been valuable both ways. You always have another guy sitting at the other side that you can call up on the telephone. Many times you have to have a long discussion and I'd go back and have a long discussion with Admiral Moorer.

Y: I think that a lot of this explains your making the distinction at least with the polygraph guy between "uncleared" and "unauthorized."

W: That's correct.

E: What's that?

Y: Like . . . well, in the series of questions when he was asked did you receive any material or give material to unauthorized persons. Bob said, "I don't want to say unauthorized because maybe somebody wasn't on a distribution list. Because obviously when he brought back the thing on Henry's secret negotiations that was unauthorized, though I think everyone would agree that if the chairman isn't "cleared" then . . .

E: Then there isn't anybody. Yes, I follow.

Y: That's the only thing. The one final thing, Bob . . . remember we hit on this over there (the Pentagon) and I think also when we first talked—and after I met this guy (name omitted)—who's apparently his best friend down there and is quite effeminate—(name omitted) is—whether or not there was any grounds for suspecting that Anderson might have a handle on him in any way like that.

E: You mean sexual deviation?

Y: Yeah.

E: Have you seen any indication of that?

W: Chuck is not the big manly type or anything else, you know, . . .—but 9/10th of the Navy yeomen are that way.

E: Really.

W: Who else wants to be a typist. So I would not consider him unusual—he's married—has children. He's not my kind of guy, you know. Our relationship, ideas and whole personality are different. But, I don't like to point a finger and say he's a possible homosexual or anything else.

E: No evidence of that to speak of.

W: No evidence.

Y: You know it's just so hard . . . I mean. I agree with you, Bob. We put together the motives—maybe he needed the money, a feeling toward India, family. But if it does turn out and he really is the guy and he could have had access to everything for the past year.

W: What the heck could be the common thread between the releasing a letter from King Hussein and seeing that the Indians look good, or whatever else came out in this last year. You know part of it may be that there's a handle on him that defies any common thread. And that could be money—it could be something in the church—and it could possibly be something he's blackmailing him with.

E: Or it could be just a sense of inadequacy if his wife is putting him down. . . . I mean, it's sort of an Ellsberg syndrome.

Y: Yes, that's right.

W: That would be a real. . . .

Y: Yeah.

I suppose also just antagonism to the President. Remember I asked—or maybe we talked a little about his attitude toward Henry, and you said, well Henry introduced him to his girlfriend one day when he was walking through and they had a passing relationship, but you never got into a long discussion on it.

I asked him, you know, what he thought about Henry and he gave me a very interesting answer in that there was a long pause, and then he said, "I have mixed feelings. I think he's a brilliant professor, but I've seen him throw temper tantrums which I thought were unnecessary." And he went into quite a bit of detail describing Henry's personality. And it was an either/or, 50/50, six of one, half a dozen of the other answer. And I wonder if you've seen any indication at all that he really might not just be 50/50 but really down on him.

E: Harboring a resentment or something?

Y: Yeah.

W: I just can't recall anything.

Y: You see the problem. I wonder if he got close enough and was disillusioned. I think that's all I have.

W: I don't know. But as to where to go with him . . . boy . . . I don't know.

E: Thanks a lot Admiral.

W: Yes, indeed.

Re-Interview with Rear Admiral Robert O. Welander, USN, Assistant for National Security Affairs to the Chairman's Staff Group, Joint Chiefs of Staff, and Senior Member of the National Security Council Staff

On January 7, 1972, Rear Admiral Welander was re-interviewed by Mr. J. Fred Buzhardt, General Counsel, OSD, and by Mr. W. Donald Stewart.

Admiral Welander advised that he had been assigned to Admiral Moorer's office on May 3, 1971, and assumed his present position on June 1, 1971. He had no familiarity with his present position prior to taking the job and had the opportunity to be given some guidance by his predecessor, Rear Admiral Rembrandt C. Robinson, from the period of May 3 to June 1, 1971.

In regard to his duties in his present assignment, Admiral Welander stated he handles staff papers and prepares comments for those papers requiring action by the Chairman. Additionally, prior to December 23, he handled National Security Council (NSC) affairs matters relative to the Chairman's office and also served as liaison between the Chairman's office and NSC and the State Department.

Admiral Welander stated that his particular position does not actually have a job description per se and his basic guidance came from Admiral Robinson during their overlap period. In the matter of assistance, Admiral Welander advised that YN1 Charles E. Radford had been assigned to him. Radford was a carry over from Admiral Robinson's office. One of the problems that Admiral Robinson had was that because of the heavy work load he (Admiral Robinson) was unable to get any leave for approximately 7 months prior to June 1. The same condition existed for Radford. Therefore, Admiral Welander on or about July 1 had Chief Yeoman Sessoms cleared for the same access that he and Radford had so Radford could have leave occasionally.

Admiral Welander advised that he has office space in the Chairman's Staff Group suite and is supported somewhat by approximately 6 other officers who have individual geographic areas of responsibility. Each of these officers has a young military enlisted man assigned for clerical purposes. Colonel Bennie L. Davis, USAF, has the specific responsibility for the Southeast Asia area and is supported by SF5 Floyd G. Hagar, USA. Normally, if a problem in that area develops, Admiral Welander looks toward Colonel Davis for "expert" guidance and also provides Colonel Davis with information relative to his area so that Colonel Davis can assess and assemble the information and brief the Chairman accordingly as the "expert".

Admiral Welander further advised that he has an office located in the Executive Office Building (EOB). His duties there require him to provide background data for Dr. Kissinger or the President relative to matters concerning the JCS. He stated that he has never been given any formal job description by Dr. Kissinger or General Haig relative to his duties there, but developed guidance relative to his duties from his predecessor, Admiral Robinson.

In regard to Radford, Admiral Welander stated that Radford has no job description per se but he too received his guidance from Admiral Robinson. Admiral Robinson advised Admiral Welander in general detail what Radford's duties were. Admiral Welander stated that when Radford became assigned to him, Admiral Robinson did not tell him (Admiral Welander) what specifically he could expect of Radford in the way of obtaining information which was not normally routed to them. Admiral Welander, of course, was aware that Radford travelled with General Haig on trips to Southeast Asia, but Robinson had never specifically informed Admiral Welander of any information Radford brought back.

In regard to a question concerning office files, Admiral Welander stated that he maintained files in his office in the Pentagon and also in his office in the EOB. These files, according to Admiral Welander, overlapped to some extent. For the most part, they contained information pertinent to his business in the particular office that they are kept. Occasionally, the overlap results from the fact that he has a problem with which he is dealing with both in the Pentagon and at the White House. Admiral Welander stated that since he has assumed these files he has become thoroughly familiar with them out of necessity. Radford is entirely familiar with the files because he was the individual who set them up.

Admiral Welander stated that only himself, Radford and Chief Sessoms had the combinations to his White House safes. In regard to his safes in the Chairman's suite, all of the officers and their enlisted aides have the combinations to these safes.

Admiral Welander said that on December 23, 1971, he was instructed to close his office at the EOB. In the course of doing so, Mr. Russell Ash, the NSC Security Officer, assisted him in separating the NSC materials from the JCS materials. The latter he brought back to the Pentagon and the former Mr. Ash took control of. The material that Admiral Welander returned with to the Pentagon was reviewed by him (some 10 cartons) and some of the old operational material was destroyed while other material deemed of pertinence was integrated into his Pentagon files. Admiral Welander stated it took approximately 3 or 4 days to handle the reorganization of these files and the destruction of the unwanted material. During this period, he was assisted by Chief Sessoms.

In regard to a question relative to his access, Admiral Welander stated that both he and Radford had virtually unlimited access in the Chairman's office with the exception of one or two intelligence matters. At the White House office they also had very broad access. In particular, he received numerous matters as an NSC staff member.

Concerning "Talking Papers" Admiral Welander advised that he had seen numerous such papers prepared for Dr. Kissinger because of a specific interest he (Admiral Welander) might have. This particular interest would stem from information he may later be called upon to furnish or a question which may be put to Admiral Moorer. Frequently, Admiral Welander would get copies of drafts of memoranda to Dr. Kissinger or General Haig and, according to Admiral Welander, he would xerox some of these papers if the matter therein was too complicated to orally digest and inform Admiral Moorer. He reiterated it was his job to alert Admiral Moorer as to questions he may be asked and as to topics which might be discussed in future meetings so that the Admiral could be appropriately prepared. In regard to the particular papers that would be routed to him for his interest, Admiral Welander stated that normally the NSC Administrator would make the determination as to what should be furnished him (Admiral Welander) or on occasion one of the NSC staff officers might furnish him a document to obtain his comments or reactions.

Admiral Welander stated that he had almost complete access to everything in OJCS and, in response to a question, he advised that he would normally have access to proposals from the Chiefs to the Secretary of Defense and frequently he would have to provide some comment. When asked whether he submitted these proposals to the White House, Admiral Welander stated he had. This action was generally taken in response to a request from Dr. Kissinger or General Haig as to the Chiefs' position in a particular matter. On some occasions, he would orally provide the information. In other occasions, he would show the Chiefs' proposal to the Secretary of Defense.

Admiral Welander was asked whether or not Radford at any time furnished him a document or information which he (Admiral Welander) did not normally have access. Admiral Welander said "yes". He cited a particular occasion that a memorandum was prepared apprising Dr. Kissinger of facts relative to "home porting a carrier group in Greece". He had seen this particular memorandum because a comment was requested from him. However, he had never been advised of the final action and had a need to follow this matter. Approximately a week later, he asked Radford if he could ascertain what the final action was on that document. Radford was able through some contact unknown to Admiral Welander find out the desired information. As an aside Admiral Welander commented that Radford had great contacts amongst White House people and on one occasion was able to arrange to have a telegram sent from President Nixon to his (Admiral Welander) 105-year-old grandfather.

Admiral Welander cited other occasions which he received material from Radford to which he (Admiral Welander) would not normally have access. He advised that when Radford delivered material from him to General Haig, Radford would ask any of the secretaries in General Haig's office or other offices in the West Wing of the White House whether they had mail which had to be delivered to the EOB. If so, he would volunteer to deliver it. Admiral Welander described this mail as inter-staff NSC memoranda for the secretariat. Radford would show him these memoranda and if he felt they were of interest he would on occasion have the document xeroxed. The specific occasion he recalls doing this was relative to a memorandum concerning "offset negotiations".

In response to a question Admiral Welander stated that he normally would personally brief the Chairman on matters, but on some occasions he would provide information he developed to one of his "area experts" who would later brief the Chairman because the "expert" could provide the greater detail and answer any questions.

Dr. Kissinger's Trip to China—July 1971

Admiral Welander was asked about Dr. Kissinger's trip to China and Radford's related activities. Admiral Welander advised that Radford accompanied Dr. Kissinger throughout this trip. However, he stayed in Pakistan when Dr. Kissinger went to China. Prior to the trip, he recalls Radford asking "What are you interested in?". He informed Radford that he would be interested in any specific observations made by Dr. Kissinger during the trip and also any information relative to troop withdrawals. Admiral Welander informed that Radford was selected for these trips as a result of Admiral Robinson having to fill a request made by General Haig for administration support. General Haig liked Radford and preferred him to a female secretary because Radford was able to provide many more administrative services. As a result, Radford was automatically selected for the Kissinger trip and again for General Haig's September 1971 trip to Southeast Asia.

Admiral Welander was asked what type of material did Radford provide him upon return from Dr. Kissinger's trip. Admiral Welander advised that Radford obtained flimsies of messages, and rough drafts of material he was assigned to type and also drafts of meetings Dr. Kissinger held in Southeast Asia. Admiral Welander stated that none of these drafts appear to be those which would be used for a memorandum from Dr. Kissinger to the President.

In regard to the disposition he made of the material, Admiral Welander stated he reviewed all of the material, absorbed it and analyzed it and later orally discussed some of the data with the Chairman and left some of the material with the Chairman. The particular material which Radford provided is still in Admiral Welander's possession and is maintained in his safe in his office in the Chairman's suite.

In regard to where Radford obtained the material, Admiral Welander stated that Radford had been assigned to the "burn detail" and apparently, while unsupervised, went through the burn bag and extracted material considered of interest. Some of this material Radford had arranged to send back in the diplomatic pouch to Admiral Welander through a friend of his in the American Embassy in New Delhi. The remainder of the material Radford handcarried to him. In response to a question as to whether or not he would normally have access to this material, Admiral Welander said "no". When asked who else in the Chairman's office would have known about this, Admiral Welander stated no one, not even Captain Knoizen, USN, (Executive Aide to Admiral Moorer). Admiral Welander stated that he had an arrangement whereby that he could see Admiral Moorer alone whenever he desired and that the material he provided him on occasion of Dr. Kissinger's trip and later General Haig's trip was so sensitive that the Chairman did not keep it overnight. Therefore, Admiral Welander concluded that no one but he and the Chairman were aware that he was furnishing the Chairman this information.

Admiral Welander was asked whether or not he prepared a memorandum of transmittal to the Chairman for the material. Admiral Welander stated he did not prepare a transmittal memorandum as such. He advised that he organized the material, tabbed it and prepared a hand-written index for it along with hand-written parenthetical comments he had to offer. Admiral Welander was asked if he had complimented Radford for Radford's service in furnishing him this unauthorized material. Admiral Welander said he did not compliment him directly, but probably informed him how important he felt the information was.

General Haig's trip to Southeast Asia—September 1971

In regard to General Haig's trip to Southeast Asia in September 1971, Admiral Welander was asked if he gave Radford any particular guidance. Admiral Welander stated that he had been personally informed by General Haig of General Haig's missions but that he did ask Radford to provide him (Admiral Welander) with any information he might learn concerning "troop withdrawal rates".

In regard to information that Radford furnished him upon return from this trip, Admiral Welander stated that again he was furnished with rough drafts and flimsy copies of memoranda of conversations with various people.

Admiral Welander was asked what sensitive material he was provided and he stated that he received a document relative to General Haig's conversation with President Thieu. He informed that he did not make a copy of this but provided the particular document to the Chairman and after the Chairman read it he took it back and locked it in his safe.

Again Admiral Welander stated that he sorted out all of the material that Radford had furnished him, absorbed it, analyzed it, tabbed it, indexed it, and affixed the hand-written comments and thereafter provided the data to the Chairman.

Again Admiral Welander stated that no one knew Radford was conducting his clandestine operation; that Captain Knoizen was not aware of the content of the material that he (Admiral Welander) was furnishing the Chairman; and that he had not praised Radford directly but had told him that the material he provided was important and significant and made many things understandable.

* * * * * * * * * * * *

After Admiral Welander provided the above information, because of his extreme cooperativeness and candidness throughout the interview, he was asked whether he might provide anything else which could be considered helpful.

Admiral Welander stated that on the morning of December 14 when he read Anderson's column, he felt that possibly Radford might be Anderson's source and, until such time that he had brought it to the attention of higher authority, he realized the personal impact on him that his reporting of the matter might have. He also theorized to himself that if Radford were, in fact, the source to Anderson "what else might Anderson have". He stated that Radford would have a tremendous amount of information because he had tasked Radford to personally review much of the material forwarded him and to analyze it and prepare a brief summary. He felt Radford was a highly intelligent individual and had the necessary capability to comprehend the material he had seen.

Admiral Welander was asked whether or not Radford could be the source for Anderson's exposures in his columns during March, April and May of 1971. Admiral Welander recalled that Mr. Stewart had let him review, during his interview on December 16, 1971, a summary of some 10 or 11 "leaks" Anderson published, and at that time he informed Mr. Stewart that all this material was contained in his files. He could not specifically recall any information relative to the "Rain Maker" leak by Anderson. During the interview with Radford, the same material was reviewed with Radford and he admitted having seen all of the material which appeared in Anderson's disclosures during the March-May period, but he also stated that he did not see anything on "Rain Maker". (It is believed Anderson obtained his information on "Rain Maker" from a member of his Church who is employed in the Department of Agriculture and has been associated with that project.)

In regard to any discussion in which he and Radford may have engaged, Admiral Welander stated that he really never had much time to sit down and discuss political situations with Radford or obtain his impressions in general about activities in Southeast Asia.

Admiral Welander, in retrospect, now has the feeling that perhaps he was "set up" by Radford and that Radford, perhaps with guidance, may have been involved in a very clever operation to obtain information under the guise of doing it for Admiral Welander.

* * * * * * * * * * * *

Prior to terminating the interview, Admiral Welander was asked whether or not he ever provided any document relative to ecology and nuclear ships to Admiral Zumwalt. Admiral Welander stated that approximately 6 weeks ago around December 1st Mike Doolin, an NSC Staff Member, provided him a copy of such a document and wanted his comments. He did not transmit this document anywhere and, in fact, did not even provide comments because the matter was overtaken by events. He had intended to give a copy of the document to the CNO and ascertained the Navy's position, but because he did not have the opportunity to do so nothing was ever done on the matter. He believes that Radford could have easily made a copy of the document and, if he so desired, could have provided it to Anderson.

The above interview commenced at 10:11 a.m. and was terminated at 11:32 a.m.

NOTES

Throughout the book we sought to identify our sources whenever the information appeared in the text. The following notes provide the reader with additional details on sources and evidence for each chapter, listing the principal books, principal on-the-record interviews, congressional and judicial testimony, and documents, both published and unpublished.

Books are listed alphabetically by last name of author, with the first reference in the notes also including the title of the work. (See Bibliography for full citations.) Interviews are listed alphabetically by the last name of the individual. (For more information see List of Interviewees, Appendix A). In regard to testimony, Book I is taken from the 1974 Senate Armed Services Committee hearings on the Moorer-Radford affair, while Books II and III are taken predominantly from the 1973 hearings of the Senate Select Committee on Presidential Campaign Activities, better known as the Watergate committee, and the 1974 House Judiciary Committee hearings and investigation, often referred to as the impeachment inquiry, as well as the 1974 Senate Armed Services Committee hearings. (Congressional hearings are cited in the Bibliography.) The reader should note the following abbreviations: Senate Select Committee—SSC; House Judiciary Committee—HJC. First references to SSC testimony include the Book number in which the testimony appears.

Finally, sources for documents and other materials are listed in the order in which the information appears in the chapter.

1. SPYING ON THE WHITE HOUSE

Books: Ehrlichman, *Witness to Power*; Haldeman, *The Ends of Power*; Hersh, *The Price of Power*; Kissinger, *White House Years*; Morris, *Richard Milhous Nixon*; Nixon, *RN*; Perry, *Four Stars*; Zumwalt, *On Watch*.

Interviews: Anderson; Ehrlichman; Haldeman; Laird; LaRocque; Linger; Moorer; Morris; Radford; Stewart; Welander; Zumwalt.

Testimony: Radford and Welander, Senate Armed Services Committee, February 1974.

Documents and Articles: An abstract of President Nixon's logs of daily activities was provided to us by a former White House official with access to the information. These logs detail the president's schedule during his entire presidency, listing the time and duration of each meeting as well as the participants. The Nixon Presidential Materials Staff of the National Archives has the official White House detailed Daily Diary for each day of the Nixon presidency that also includes times of and participants in the president's phone calls; Stewart's investigative report is unpublished but was provided to us by Stewart; the December 1971 Anderson columns appeared in the *Washington Post*.

2. CARRYING THE CONTRABAND

Books: Hersh; Kissinger; Morris, *The General's Progress;* Zumwalt.

Interviews: Ehrlichman; Radford; Stewart; Welander.

Testimony: Radford; Welander.

Documents: Stewart report as noted above; Polygraph reports also unpublished but provided by Stewart.

3. THE ADMIRAL'S CONFESSION

Books: Ehrlichman; Gulley, *Breaking Cover;* Kissinger.

Interviews: Ehrlichman; Krogh; Moorer; Radford; Welander.

Testimony: Radford; Welander.

Documents: Nixon logs; Welander confession (see Appendix B) and the statement drafted by Young are located in the files of the National Archives, but remain sealed. They were provided to us by a source, not associated with the archives, who had access to the documents.

4. NIXON ORDERS A BURIAL

Books: Ehrlichman; Hersh; Kissinger, *Years of Upheaval;* Lukas, *Nightmare;* Morris; Nixon; Safire, *Before the Fall;* Sullivan, *The Bureau;* Truman, *Memoirs;* Woodward and Bernstein, *The Final Days*.

Interviews: Ehrlichman; Haldeman; Laird; Mitchell; Moorer; Morris; Radford; Stewart; Welander.

Testimony: Buzhardt, Senate Armed Services Committee, March 1974; Kissinger same, February 1974; Welander.

Documents and Articles: Nixon logs; Transcript of December 23, 1971, Ehrlichman-Laird phone conversation also under seal at the Archives but provided to us by a source unaffiliated with the Archives; the document; Ehrlichman's notes of his December 23 and 24 meetings with Nixon are located in his files at the Nixon Presidential Materials Staff; FBI memorandums, relevant testimony, and other documents on the 1969–71 wiretapping program can be found in the House Judiciary Committee Statement of Information, Book VII, Part I, beginning on p. 141; Haig's testimony in wiretap civil suit was reported in Timothy S. Robinson's article "Mistrust of Kissinger Hinted," *Washington Post*, July 10, 1975; Walter Pincus' article "Alexander Haig" in *New Republic*, October 5, 1974, also reported Haig's role in wiretapping program; Ehrlichman made available to us his unpublished diary entries on the Moorer-Radford affair; Young's December 24, 1971, memo to Ehrlichman is under seal at the Archives but provided by a source unaffiliated with the Archives; January 7, 1972, reinterview of Welander (see Appendix B) was provided by Stewart.

5. THE WOODWARD-HAIG CONNECTION

Books: Blackman, *Jane's Fighting Ships;* Downie, *The New Muckrakers;* Halberstam, *The Powers That Be;* Hersh; Hougan, *Secret Agenda;* Mooney, *Dictionary of American Naval Fighting Ships;* Morris; Prouty, *The Secret Team;* Winks, *Cloak and Gown;* Woodward and Bernstein, *The Final Days* and *All the President's Men.*

Interviews: Bader; Carroll; Coombe; Farquhar; Fitzpatrick; Friedheim; Garment; Higby; Hougan; Hunnicut; Kingston; Korn; Laird; LaRocque; McAllister; Moorer; Morris; Murphy; Prouty; Rosenfeld; Stanton; Watts; Welander; Winks; Al Woodward; Bob Woodward; Kathleen Woodward.

Documents and Articles: The National Personnel Records Center provided basic information on Woodward's military career, including duty stations, assignments, dates of rank, decorations, and dates of induction and discharge; When the Navy disbanded Task Force 157 in 1977, *Post* reporter Woodward broke the story. His article "Pentagon to Abolish Secret Spy Unit" in the *Post* of May 18, 1977, made reference to the secret TF 157 channel employed on Kissinger's China trip. Woodward also quoted his old commanding officer, retired Admiral Moorer, who criticized the decision to shut down the spy unit; Wheaton Community High School yearbook of 1961 provided details on Woodward's successes there. We also consulted the Yale Yearbook of 1965; *Playboy* interview was conducted by journalist J. Anthony Lukas and published in February 1989; NROTC guide was obtained from Naval Military Personnel Command; Woodward's citation for the Navy Commendation Medal was provided by National Personnel Records Center; Woodward himself provided us a copy of his 1969 resignation letter and of NAVOP order, also known as an ALLNAV; An excerpt from Haig's 1962 master's thesis was published in the *Washington Post* on January 18, 1981; Lasky letter was published in *AIM Report*, October 1976.

6. THE PRESIDENT'S PRIVATE EYE

Books: Dean, *Blind Ambition;* Ehrlichman; Haldeman; Kissinger, *White House Years;* Kutler, *The Wars of Watergate;* Lukas; Morris, *Richard Milhous Nixon;* Nixon; Ulasewicz; *The President's Private Eye.*

Interviews: Caulfield; Dean; Ehrlichman; Haldeman; Kalmbach; Mitchell; Strachan; Ulasewicz.

Testimony: John Caulfield, Senate Select Committee, Books 1, 21, and 22; John Dean, Books 3 and 4; John Ehrlichman, Books 6 and 7; Herbert Kalmbach, Book 5; John Mitchell, Books 4 and 5; Anthony Ulasewicz, Books 1 and 6.

Documents: Ulasewicz's interviews with Senate investigators and the list of 73 of his White House assignments can be obtained from Center for Legislative Archives, National Archives; Huston Plan and related documents and testimony can be found in House Judiciary Committee, Statement of Information, Book VII, Part I, beginning on p. 437; Dean memo to Mitchell of September 18, 1970, is in Book VII, Part I, p. 493; January 14, 1971, memo from Nixon to Haldeman regarding Larry O'Brien investigation can be found in Oudes's book *From the President*, p. 202, or in Haldeman file at Nixon Presidential Materials Staff; Dean's August 16, 1971, memo on political enemies can be found in SSC hearings, Book 4, Exhibit 48, p. 1689, and HJC, Book VIII, p. 95; Strachan memos to Dean on political enemies are located in SSC, Book 4, Exhibits 52 and 53, pp. 1700–1701; The Sandwedge plan can be found in SSC, Book 21, beginning on p. 9899; Caulfield's report on the Ulasewicz November 18–21, 1971, investigation of McCloskey campaign is in SSC, Book 3, Exhibit 34-11, p. 1134, Dean's December 1, 1971, memo is on p. 1142, and the January 12, 1972, memo is Exhibit 34-12, p. 1149; Strachan's October 27, 1971, memo reporting Sandwedge refunding is in HJC, Appendix IV, with relevant passage on p. 35.

7. SANDWEDGE BECOMES GEMSTONE

Books: Dean; Ehrlichman; Haldeman; Hersh; Hougan; Hunt, *Undercover;* Liddy, *Will;* Lukas; Magruder, *An American Life;* Morris; Nixon; Ulasewicz.

Interviews: Caulfield; Ehrlichman; Haldeman; Hartmann; Krogh; Liddy; Mitchell; Strachan; Ulasewicz.

Testimony: Dean; Ehrlichman; Magruder, SSC, Book 2; Mitchell; Porter, Book 2; Strachan, Book 6.

Documents: Krogh-Young memo of August 11, 1971, to Ehrlichman on Pentagon Papers matters is in SSC, Book 6, Exhibit 90, p. 2643; Agenda for Mitchell-Dean-Liddy meeting of November 24, 1971, is in SSC, Book 3, Exhibit 34-13, p. 1150; Liddy March 15, 1972, memo on Democratic convention with Dean's "Need more info" notation is in SSC, Book 3, Exhibit 34-14, pp. 1152–1153; Ulasewicz assignment list in archives shows assignment Number 21 as "Investigation into Convention Hall in financing in Miami, Florida."

8. THE BAILLEY CONNECTION

Books: Congressional Quarterly Staff, *Watergate: Chronology of a Crisis;* Dean; Dean (Maureen), *"Mo," A Woman's View of Watergate;* Edmondson and Cohen, *The Women of*

Watergate; Haldeman; Hougan; Hunt; Liddy; Lukas; Magruder; Morgan, *One Man, One Voice;* Stans, *The Terrors of Justice.*

Interviews: Jeannine Bailley; Phillip Bailley; John Dean; Ehrlichman; Flemming; Haldeman; Hunt; LaRue; Liddy; Magruder; Martinez; Mitchell; Rudy; Stans; Sturgis.

Testimony: Hunt, SSC, Book 9; LaRue, Book 6; Magruder; Mitchell; Sloan, Book 2.

Documents: The diagram of the DNC was made available to us by Liddy; Bailley's attorney, Allan Palmer, provided an inventory of those items seized from Bailley's home and office in April 1972; Hunt's request for his notebooks and Dean's November 1973 admission to prosecutors that he destroyed them are documented in HJC, Summary of Information, p. 63, and Statement of Information, Book II, pp. 501 and 511–512.

9. THE LAST BREAK-IN

Books: Dean; Dean (Maureen); Hougan; Liddy; Lukas; Magruder.

Interviews: Jeannine Bailley; Phillip Bailley; Brown; Flanigan; Haldeman; Higby; Hunt; Groom; Liebengood; Liddy; Magruder; Martinez; Mitchell; Palmer; Richey; Rudy; West.

Testimony: Magruder; Mitchell.

Documents: All legal and judicial papers from Bailley case are located in National Records Center, Suitland, Md., CR 1190-72 and CR 1718-72; Official White House visitors record of the 4:00 P.M. visit by Rudy and Smith to Dean's office on June 9, 1972, is located in the files of the Nixon Materials Project Staff; FBI and Silbert memoranda on the issue of no bug inside the DNC can be found at FBI's public reading room, listed as in Watergate files as Serials 139-4089-1454 and 139-4089-1455 (see also Hougan for thorough exposition of issue); FBI interviews of Barbara Kennedy and Maxie Wells on issue of key to Wells's desk are FBI Serials WFO 139-166, pp. 135–136; June 15, 1972, transcript of Bailley hearing at National Records Center.

10. LOS ANGELES AND MANILA: THE COVER-UP BEGINS

Books: Dean; Haldeman; Liddy; Magruder; Nixon; Ulasewicz.

Interviews: King; Kleindienst; LaRue; Liddy; Magruder; Mardian; Mitchell; Powell Moore; Rivkind; Stutman; Ulasewicz.

Testimony: Kleindienst; LaRue; Magruder; Mardian; Mitchell, Strachan.

Documents: The indictment of Mitchell, Mardian, and others in the Watergate cover-up case is located in HJC, Appendix II, p. 103, with relevant "overt acts" section on p. 109; Philippine government records of Dean's June 18, 1972, departure from Manila were obtained from the Department of Justice, Bureau of Immigration in Manila. We also obtained official schedules of Philippine Airlines and Pan Am to trace Dean's route back to the U.S.; Transcript of the March 21, 1973, tape can be found in *Submission of Recorded Presidential Conversations to the Committee on the Judiciary of the House of Representatives by President Richard Nixon*, April 30, 1974, with relevant passage on p. 180, also in HJC, Transcript of Eight Recorded Presidential Conversations, p. 79.

11. A WALK IN THE PARK

Books: Dean; Ehrlichman; Haldeman; Hunt; Liddy; Magruder; Nixon.

Interviews: Colson; Ehrlichman; Haldeman; Kleindienst; LaRue; Liddy; Magruder; Mardian; Mitchell.

Testimony: Colson, located in HJC, Statement of Information, Book II, p. 201; Dean; Ehrlichman; Gray, SSC, Book 9; Haldeman; Hunt; Kleindienst; LaRue; Magruder; Mardian; Mitchell; Petersen, SSC, Book 9.

Documents: Nixon logs; Ehrlichman's office log of June 19, 1972, submitted to the Watergate committee, can be found in HJC, Statement of Information, Book II, p. 238; As noted above, "overt acts" listed in Watergate cover-up indictment can be found in HJC, Appendix II; Colson's draft statement to the Watergate committee supports his contention he told Dean not to send Hunt out of the country and is located in HJC, Book II, p. 158; Hunt's executive session testimony to the Senate confirms the 11:30 A.M. meeting with Liddy on June 19 and is located in Book II, pp. 205–206; Kehrli's testimony in the civil suit over the DNC break-in is located in Book II, p. 193; The FBI inventory of Hunt's White House safe is in Book II, pp. 422–423 and in FBI serial WFO 139-166, pp. 39–42.

12. "THE SMOKING GUN"

Books: Dean; Ehrlichman; Haldeman; Nixon.

Interviews: Dean; Ehrlichman; Haldeman; Mitchell.

Testimony: Dean, Ehrlichman; Gray; Haldeman; Helms, SSC, Book 8; Mitchell; Walters, SSC, Book 9.

Documents: Mitchell's office logs were submitted to the Watergate committee and made available to us by the former attorney general; The transcripts of the "smoking gun" tape and subsequent conversations of June 23, 1972, between Nixon and Haldeman were submitted as evidence in the Watergate cover-up trial (*U.S. v. John Mitchell, et al.* CR 74-110), and were provided to us by Nixon Presidential Materials Staff; Transcript of the June 4, 1973, conversation is in HJC, Book IX, Part 1, with relevant passage on p. 225; Walters' memcon on his June 23, 1972, meeting with Gray is in SSC, Book 9, Exhibit 129, p. 3815.

13. HUSH MONEY—FOR HUNT

Books: Dean; Ehrlichman; Haldeman; Hougan; Nixon; Ulasewicz.

Interviews: Dean; Ehrlichman; Haldeman; Kalmbach; LaRue; Mitchell; Ulasewicz.

Testimony: Dean; Ehrlichman; Gray; Kalmbach; Mardian; Mitchell; Ulasewicz; Walters.

Documents: Vernon Walters' memcons of his meetings with Dean from June 26–28, 1972, are located in SSC, Book 9, Exhibits 130–132, pp. 3816–3820; Walters' memcon on the June 23 meeting with Ehrlichman, Haldeman, and Helms is in SSC, Book 7, Exhibit 101, p. 2948; Helms's memo of June 28, 1972, is in HJC, Book II, p. 459; Mitchell's logs were submitted to the Senate committee and made available to us by Mitchell; Ulasewicz's interview with the Watergate committee investigators included his role in the payments and this record can be found in the Ulasewicz file at the Center for Legislative Archives.

14. DAMAGE CONTROL ACTION OFFICER

Books: Ben-Veniste and Frampton, *Stonewall*; Congressional Quarterly; Dean; Lukas; Liddy; Magruder; Nixon; Ulasewicz.

Interviews: Phillip Bailley; Ehrlichman; Haldeman; Kalmbach; Liddy; Mardian; Mitchell; Richey; Ulasewicz.

Testimony: Dean; Gray; Kalmbach; LaRue; Magruder.

Documents: The second indictment of Bailley, docket sheets, motions, and associated papers involving the Bailley case are in the court files at the National Records Center; September 15, 1972, Dean-Nixon conversation can be found in *Submission of Recorded Presidential Conversations* and in HJC transcripts; September and October hearing transcripts in Bailley case in National Records Center; Dean memo of October 13, 1972, on his impending marriage to Maureen can be found at Nixon Presidential Materials Staff.

15. THE PRESSURE MOUNTS

Books: Congressional Quarterly; Dean; Dean (Maureen); Ehrlichman; Liddy; Lukas; Nixon; Woodward and Bernstein, *All the President's Men*; Ulasewicz.

Interviews: Caulfield; Ehrlichman; Liddy; Maroulis; Ulasewicz.

Testimony: Caulfield; Dean, HJC Testimony of Witnesses, Book II, and Petersen, Book III (on Earl Silbert's questioning on whereabout of Hunt's notebooks); Hunt; Ulasewicz.

Documents: Reference to Hunt's October 11, 1972, motion can be found in HJC Summary of Information, p. 63; Nixon-Dean conversation of February 28, 1973, is in *Submission of Recorded Presidential Conversations* and in House Judiciary transcripts, and *New York Times* staff.

16. CONFESSION TIME

Books: Congressional Quarterly; Dean; Ehrlichman; Haldeman; Nixon.

Documents: Transcript of March 13, 1973, Nixon-Dean conversation in same sources cited in previous chapter; March 17 conversation and March 20 phone call located in *Submission* and *New York Times* staff.

17. THE CANCER WITHIN THE PRESIDENCY

Books: Congressional Quarterly; Dean; Ehrlichman; Lukas; Nixon.

Documents: Transcripts of the two March 21, 1973, conversations and March 22 conversation are in *Submission, New York Times* staff, and House Judiciary transcripts; Dean's taped conversation with Magruder from Camp David on March 26, 1973, can be found in SCC, Book 3, Exhibit 34–10, pp. 1258–1260; Memorandum on Maroulis' conversation with Dean can be found in SSC, Book 3, Exhibit 34–42, p. 1262.

18. THE RETURN OF ALEXANDER HAIG

Books: Congressional Quarterly; Dean, *Blind Ambition* and *Lost Honor;* Halberstam; Haldeman; Hersh; Hougan; Hunt; Lukas; Morris; Nixon; Sussman, *The Great Coverup*; U.S. Senate Committee on Armed Services, *Nomination of Major General Alexander Meigs Haig, Jr.*, 1972; Walters; Woodward and Bernstein, both books; Zumwalt.

Interviews: Brennan; Bull; Garment; Haldeman; Higby; Liddy; Mitchell; Morris; Price; Bob Woodward; Ziegler.

Documents and Articles: Additional sources on Haig's role in wiretapping also included Pincus' 1974 *New Republic* article cited above, *Washington Post* story of December 20, 1980, "Haig: Supervising the Nixon Wiretaps," by Pincus, Scott Armstrong, and Robert G. Kaiser, and *New York Times* story of September 29, 1974, "Haig Testimony: He Acted for Kissinger on Wiretaps," by John M. Crewdson; *Time* magazine broke the wiretapping story in its edition released on February 26, 1973; The Woodward-Bernstein story of May 3, 1973, was headlined "Wiretaps Put on Phones of 2 Reporters." *Washington Post* Watergate stories cited are those of June 18 and 19, August 1, September 17 and 18, and October 10, 1972; *Washington Post*, September 8, 1972, "Haig, Kissinger Aide, Jumps to No. 2 Army Job," by Michael Getler; Nixon logs were especially helpful in detailing Nixon's early meetings with Haig and Buzhardt and the freezing out of others, especially Garment; Transcript of the April 27, 1973, tape is in *Submission of Recorded Presidential Conversations*, pp. 1268–1269; Vernon Walters' affidavit on Watergate is reproduced in SSC, Book 9, Exhibit 137, pp. 3828–3833; Nixon's intensive May 15–16, 1973, meetings with Haig and Buzhardt are recorded in presidential logs; May 22 statement can be found in Congressional Quarterly staff, *Watergate: Chronology of a Crisis, Volume 1.*

19. STEWART SHAKES UP THE WHITE HOUSE

Interviews: Bork; Ehrlichman; Garment; Stewart; Welander.

Documents: Tufaro's May 14, 1973, memo to Garment was provided to us by Stewart, who obtained it under a Freedom of Information Act request in the late 1970s. Stewart also provided us his private letter to Baroody of June 25, 1973, and his July 16, 1973, letter to Hoffman; Garment's June 29, 1973, EYES ONLY letter to Richardson and all subsequent Justice Department documents on the Stewart matter cited in the chapter were obtained by Stewart in his FOIA suit. He made them available to us; The Sanders-Liebengood memo on the July 24, 1973, interview of Stewart is reproduced in part at HJC, Statement of Information, Book VII, Part 2, pp. 891–892; Ehrlichman's July 26, 1973, testimony, discussion with Baker, and Buzhardt letter to Wilson can be found in SSC, Book 7, pp. 2701–2710. As noted above, the Krogh-Young memo on the Pentagon Papers is in SSC, Book 6, Exhibit 90, pp. 2643–2645; reference to the four-way July 27, 1973, meeting is in the Watergate committee's Final Report, Appendix to Views of Senator Baker, p. 1119.

20. FIVE DAYS IN JULY

Books: Dash, *Chief Counsel;* Ervin, *The Whole Truth;* Haldeman; Lukas; Nixon; Thompson, *At That Point in Time;* Woodward and Bernstein, both books.

Interviews: Armstrong; Bull; Butterfield; Dash; Haldeman; Hamilton; Higby; Garment; Liebengood; Madigan; Ziegler.

Testimony: Butterfield, SSC, Book 5, and HJC, Testimony of Witnesses, Book 1; Dean, SSC, Book 4; Sloan, SSC, Book 2.

Documents: Two versions of the "Golden Boy" memo were produced by Garment, one in mid-June 1973 prior to Dean's testimony, and a revision about a week later and sent to Senator Inouye on June 27. They can be found in SSC, Book 4, Exhibits 66 and 67, pp. 1754–1782; Notes of Butterfield's interview with the Watergate committee staffers on July 13, 1973, as well as his handwritten notes prepared that weekend are in the files at Center for Legislative Archives; The presidential logs show that Nixon was taking visitors at his hospital bed and was meeting with Haig during the weekend; Transcript of Albert Wong's appearance before an executive session of the Watergate committee on July 17, 1973, is at Center for Legislative Archives.

21. THE SATURDAY NIGHT MASSACRE

Books: Congressional Quarterly; Doyle, *Not Above the Law;* Ervin; Jaworski, *The Right and the Power;* Lukas; Nixon; Woodward and Bernstein, *The Final Days.*

Documents and Other Material: Haig's 1973 Watergate grand jury testimony on his order shutting down the taping system and naming Gen. Bennett as custodian can be found in HJC, Statement of Information, Book IX, Part 1, pp. 385–387; Cox's July 18, 1973, letter to Buzhardt is found in Book IX, Part 1, pp. 390–392; The July 23 letters of Wright to Cox and Nixon to Ervin are in same book, pp. 408–412; Richardson's sworn statement to the House Judiciary Committee is on pp. 404–406; Nixon's July 25, 1973, letter to Sirica is on pp. 426–427; Haldeman's testimony that he had listened to tapes is in Book IX, Part 1, pp. 433–473; Woodward-Bernstein story on Buzhardt's concern about national security, "Halt to Indictment of 3 Sought by White House," was published on November 16, 1973; The events of the week culminating in the Saturday Night Massacre—October 15–20, 1973—are carefully documented in HJC, Statement of Information, Book IX, Part 2, pp. 755–825, including the testimony, letters, office logs, proposals, and public statements of the participants, especially Cox, Richardson, Haig, and Wright; The official presidential log, known as a Daily Diary, for October 18, 1973, was obtained from Nixon Presidential Materials Staff.

22. THE EIGHTEEN-AND-A-HALF-MINUTE GAP

Books: Congressional Quarterly; Ben-Veniste and Frampton; Doyle; Haldeman; Lukas; Nixon; Woodward and Bernstein, both books.

Interviews: Bull; Garment; Haldeman; Powers; Bob Woodward.

Documents and Articles: Testimony of Bull, Woods, Bennett, Secret Service agents, and others in Sirica's courtroom on the disposition of the tapes and the operation of the taping system itself can be found in HJC, Book IX, Part 1, pp. 289–312, and Book IX, Part 2, pp. 607–735; Buzhardt's testimony that he listened to a tape on June 25, 1973, can be found in Book IX, Part 1, pp. 295–299; Woods's September 29, 1973, note to Bull on her conversation with Haig regarding the June 20, 1972, tape can be found in Book IX, Part 2, p. 637; Cox's August 13, 1973, memo clarifying his subpoena is located in Watergate Special Prosecutor files at the textual reference division of the National Archives; "Nightline" quotes taken from ABC NEWS transcript of June 17, 1972, program entitled "Woodward & Bernstein: Watergate Revisited"; Haldeman discusses the contents of eradicated portion of the June 20 tape in his book, pp. 16–19.

23. MOORER-RADFORD DISINTERRED

Books: Congressional Quarterly; Doyle; Jaworski; Lukas; Nixon; Woodward and Bernstein, *The Final Days*.

Interviews: Getler; Hersh; Krogh; Thomasson; Radford; Stewart; Welander; Bob Woodward.

Documents and Articles: Krogh's filings on his discovery motion are in Watergate Special Prosecutor files at Archives textual reference branch, as are Jaworski's November 13, 1973, handwritten notes on meeting with Haig and Buzhardt; A compendium of all indictments, convictions, and sentences involving Watergate defendants can be found in Garza's index of House Judiciary Committee hearings and investigation, pp. vii–ix; Stewart provided us copies of his memos on his telephone calls with Woodward about Moorer-Radford; The *Chicago Tribune*, *New York Times*, and *Washington Post* coverage of the breaking Moorer-Radford story in January and February of 1974 can be reviewed on microfilm at the Library of Congress. Our sources provided us copies of Scripps-Howard and wire service stories; The June 4, 1973, "tape of tapes" can be found, as noted above, in HJC, Statement of Information, Book IX, Part 1, pp. 177–236.

24. SENATOR STENNIS HOLDS A HEARING

Books: Congressional Quarterly; Doyle; Hersh; Jaworski; Nixon.

Interviews: Garment; Laird; Radford; Stewart; Welander.

Testimony: Moorer, Senate Armed Services Committee, February 6, 1974; Kissinger, February 6; Radford, February 20 and 21; Welander, February 20.

Documents: As noted above, February 1974 press coverage of Moorer-Radford can be reviewed at Library of Congress; Again, Stewart provided us his memos to Hoffman and on phone calls with Woodward; The transcript of Baker's executive session interview of Stewart on February 19, 1974, is in the Watergate committee files at the Center for Legislative Archives; See Appendix B for Welander reinterview of January 7, 1972, as well as taped interview of December 22, 1971; As noted above, March 1, 1974, Watergate cover-up indictment is in HJC, Appendix II, p. 101.

25. THE REAL FINAL DAYS

Books: Congressional Quarterly; Doyle; Ehrlichman; Ford, *A Time to Heal*; Hartmann, *Palace Politics*; Jaworski; Kissinger, *Years of Upheaval*; Lukas; Nixon; U.S. Department of Justice, Watergate Special Prosecution Force, *Report*; Woodward and Bernstein, *The Final Days*.

Interviews: Becker; Butterfield; Ehrlichman; Hartmann; Morris; Ziegler.

Testimony: Butterfield, HJC, Testimony of Witnesses, Book I, July 2, 1974.

Documents and Articles: Presidential logs show Buzhardt's reentry to White House inner circle shortly after Stennis concluded the Moorer-Radford hearings; Nixon's 1,308-page book of transcripts, nicknamed the "Blue Book" for its distinctive cover, was titled *Submission of Recorded Presidential Conversations*, as noted above; Ehrlichman provided docket sheets from his legal case that outlined the maneuverings in the case. The textual reference branch at the Archives confirmed the wording of the Buzhardt and Haig motions of June 6, 1974; Regarding Butterfield's Judiciary Committee testimony—Hoover's letter to Nixon on the Halperin tap, the authentic follow-up memo to Magruder as well as the doctored copy can be found in HJC, Statement of Information, Book VII, Part 1, pp. 359–363; For report on Haig's Senate Foreign Relations testimony on the wiretapping, see *The New York Times* article by John M. Crewdson, September 29, 1974, as noted above; We relied greatly on Seymour Hersh's excellent article "The Pardon," published in *The Atlantic*, August 1983.

EPILOGUE: . . . AND THROW AWAY THE KEY

Books: Doyle; Ford; Haig, *Caveat;* Hartmann; Jaworski; Morris; Nixon, *In the Arena.*

Interviews: Becker; Bull; Ford; Hartmann; Korn; Liebengood; Bob Woodward; Ziegler.

Documents and Articles: Hersh, "The Pardon"; Among the many documents in the archives that Nixon has kept sealed under a national security classification are the December 22, 1971, Ehrlichman-Welander-Young interview, Young's December 24, 1971, EYES ONLY memo to Ehrlichman, Young's lengthy investigative report on the military spying, and other papers from the White House investigation of Moorer-Radford; The *Federal Times* story on Stewart's Freedom of Information Act case appeared on December 5, 1977, "Stewart Case Intrigue—Richardson, Clements Roles Confirmed," by Sheila Hershow; The Nixon memo to Reagan can be found in Lou Cannon's book *President Reagan: The Role of a Lifetime*, as excerpted in the *Washington Post* of April 21, 1991; Jaworski's letter to Maj. Gen. Klein was reproduced in Haig's book, *Caveat*, p. 42; Woodward's Op-Ed piece of January 15, 1981, is titled "Don't Subpoena the Tapes"; Haig also recounted in his book his "I am in control" statement of March 30, 1981, on p. 160; Woodward's story on Haig's secretary of state notes was published on February 19, 1982, "Meetings' Notes Show the Unvarnished Haig."

BIBLIOGRAPHY

BOOKS

Ambrose, Stephen E. *Nixon, Volume II: The Triumph of a Politician 1962–1972*. New York: Simon and Schuster, 1989.

Ben-Veniste, Richard, and George Frampton, Jr. *Stonewall: The Real Story of the Watergate Prosecution*. New York: Simon and Schuster, 1977.

Bernstein, Carl, and Bob Woodward. *All the President's Men*. New York: Simon and Schuster, 1974.

Blackman, Raymond V. B. (editor). *Jane's Fighting Ships*. London: Jane's Yearbooks, 1971.

Colson, Charles W. *Born Again*. Lincoln, Virginia: Chosen Books, 1976.

Congressional Quarterly Staff. *Watergate: Chronology of a Crisis*. 2 vols. Washington, D.C.: Congressional Quarterly Inc., 1973 & 1974.

Corson, William R., Susan B. Trento, and Joseph J. Trento. *Widows*. New York: Crown, 1989.

Dash, Samuel. *Chief Counsel: Inside the Ervin Committee—The Untold Story of Watergate*. New York: Random House, 1976.

Davis, Deborah. *Katherine the Great: Katherine Graham and The Washington Post*. Bethesda, Maryland: National Press Inc., 1979.

Dean, John W., III. *Blind Ambition: The White House Years*. New York: Simon and Schuster, 1976.

———. *Lost Honor*. Los Angeles: Stratford Press, 1982.

Dean, Maureen (with Hays Gorey). *"Mo," A Woman's View of Watergate*. New York: Simon and Schuster, 1975.

Downie, Leonard, Jr. *The New Muckrakers*. Washington, D.C.: New Republic Book Company, 1976.

Doyle, James. *Not Above the Law: The Battles of Watergate Prosecutors Cox and Jaworski*. New York: William Morrow and Company, 1977.

Drew, Elizabeth. *Washington Journal: The Events of 1973–1974*. New York: Random House, 1975.

Edmondson, Madeline, and Alden Duer Cohen. *The Women of Watergate*. New York: Stein and Day, 1975.

Ehrlichman, John. *Witness to Power: The Nixon Years*. New York: Simon and Schuster, 1982.

Epstein, Edward Jay. *Between Fact and Fiction: The Problem of Journalism*. New York: Vintage Books, 1975.

Ervin, Sam J., Jr. *The Whole Truth: The Watergate Conspiracy*. New York: Random House, 1980.

Ford, Gerald R. *A Time to Heal: The Autobiography of Gerald R. Ford*. New York: Harper and Row/Reader's Digest Association, Inc., 1979.

Garza, Hedda (compiler). *The Watergate Investigation Index: Senate Select Committee Hearings and Reports on Presidential Campaign Activities*. Wilmington, Delaware: Scholarly Resources Inc., 1982.

———. *The Watergate Investigation Index: House Judiciary Committee Hearings and Report on Impeachment*. Wilmington, Delaware: Scholarly Resources Inc., 1985.

Gulley, Bill (with Mary Ellen Reese). *Breaking Cover*. New York: Simon and Schuster, 1980.

Haig, Alexander M., Jr. *Caveat: Realism, Reagan, and Foreign Policy.* New York: Macmillan, 1984.

Halberstam, David. *The Powers That Be.* New York: Knopf, 1979.

Haldeman, H. R. (with Joseph DiMona). *The Ends of Power.* New York: Times Books, 1978.

Hartmann, Robert T. *Palace Politics: An Inside Account of the Ford Years.* New York: McGraw-Hill Book Company, 1980.

Hersh, Seymour M. *The Price of Power: Kissinger in the Nixon White House.* New York: Summit Books, 1983.

Hougan, Jim. *Secret Agenda: Watergate, Deep Throat and the CIA.* New York: Random House, 1984.

Hunt, E. Howard. *Undercover: Memoirs of an American Secret Agent.* New York: Putnam, 1974.

Jaworski, Leon. *The Right and the Power: The Prosecution of Watergate.* New York: Reader's Digest Press, 1976.

Kissinger, Henry. *White House Years.* Boston: Little, Brown and Company, 1979.

———. *Years of Upheaval.* Boston: Little, Brown and Company, 1982.

Kutler, Stanley I. *The Wars of Watergate.* New York: Knopf, 1990.

Liddy, G. Gordon. *Will: The Autobiography of G. Gordon Liddy.* New York: St. Martin's Press, 1980.

Lukas, J. Anthony. *Nightmare: The Underside of the Nixon Years.* New York: Viking Press, 1976.

Maas, Peter. *Manhunt.* New York: Random House, 1986.

Magruder, Jeb Stuart. *An American Life.* New York: Atheneum, 1974.

Mooney, James L. (editor) *Dictionary of American Naval Fighting Ships. Volume VIII.* Washington, D.C.: U.S. Naval Historical Center, 1981.

Morgan, Charles, Jr. *One Man, One Voice.* New York: Holt, Rinehart and Winston, 1979.

Morris, Roger. *Haig: The General's Progress.* New York: Playboy Press, 1982.

———. *Richard Milhous Nixon: The Rise of an American Politician.* New York: Henry Holt, 1990.

Newhouse, John. *Cold Dawn: The Story of SALT.* New York: Holt, Rinehart and Winston, 1973.

The New York Times staff. *The White House Transcripts.* New York: Bantam, 1974.

Nixon, Richard Milhous. *RN: The Memoirs of Richard Nixon.* New York: Grosset & Dunlap, 1978.

———. *In the Arena.* New York: Simon and Schuster, 1990.

Oudes, Bruce. *From the President: Richard Nixon's Secret Files.* New York: Harper & Row, 1989.

Perry, Mark. *Four Stars.* Boston: Houghton Mifflin Company, 1989.

Powers, Thomas. *The Man Who Kept the Secrets: Richard Helms and the CIA.* New York: Knopf, 1979.

Prouty, L. Fletcher. *The Secret Team: The CIA and Its Allies in Control of the United States and the World.* Englewood Cliffs, N.J.: Prentice-Hall Inc., 1973.

Safire, William. *Before the Fall.* New York: Doubleday & Company, 1975.

Sirica, John J., *To Set the Record Straight: The Break-in, the Tapes, the Conspirators, the Pardon.* New York: W. W. Norton & Co., 1979.

Stans, Maurice H. *The Terrors of Justice.* New York: Everest House, 1978.

Sullivan, William C. (with Bill Brown). *The Bureau: My Thirty Years in Hoover's FBI.* New York: Norton & Company, 1979.

Sussman, Barry. *The Great Coverup: Nixon and the Scandal of Watergate.* New York: Crowell, 1974.

Thompson, Fred D. *At That Point In Time: The Inside Story of the Senate Watergate Committee.* New York: Quadrangle, 1975.

Truman, Harry S. *Memoirs, Volume Two, Years of Trial and Hope.* Garden City, New York: Doubleday & Company, 1956.

Ulasewicz, Tony (with Stuart A. McKeever). *The President's Private Eye: The Journey of Detective Tony U. from the NYPD to the Nixon White House.* Westport, Connecticut: MACSAM Publishing Co., Inc., 1990.

U.S. Department of Justice. Watergate Special Prosecution Force. *Report.* Washington: U.S. Government Printing Office, 1975.

U.S. House of Representatives. Committee on the Judiciary. *The Hearings and Report of the House Judiciary Committee.* 93d Congress, 2d session, 1974.

U.S. Senate. Committee on Armed Services. *Nominations of J. Fred Buzhardt, Jr., and Darrell M. Trent, Hearings.* 91st Congress, 2d session, 1970.

U.S. Senate. Committee on Armed Services. *Nomination of Major General Alexander Meigs Haig, Jr., USA, to the Rank of General, U.S. Army, Hearings.* 92d Congress, 2d session, 1972.

U.S. Senate. Committee on Armed Services. *Transmittal of Documents from the National Security Council to the Chairman of the Joint Chiefs of Staff, Hearings.* 93d Congress, 2d session, 1974.

U.S. Senate. Select Committee on Presidential Campaign Activities. *Watergate Investigation, Hearings. Books 1–9. Hughes-Rebozo Investigation, Executive Session Hearings. Books 21–23.* 93d Congress, 1st and 2d sessions, 1973, 1974.

Walters, Vernon A. *Silent Missions.* New York: Doubleday & Company, 1978.

Woodward, Bob, and Carl Bernstein. *The Final Days.* New York: Simon and Schuster, 1976.

Wyden, Peter. *Bay of Pigs: The Untold Story.* New York: Simon and Schuster, 1979.

Zumwalt, Elmo R., Jr. *On Watch.* New York: Quadrangle, 1976.

PERIODICALS

Chambers, Andrea, and Jack Kelley. "Maureen Dean Makes a Steamy Literary Debut with a Tale of Passion on the Potomac." *People* magazine, November 9, 1987.

Hersh, Seymour M. "The Pardon." *The Atlantic,* August 1983.

Hougan, Jim. "Peeking Under Bob Woodward's Veil." *City Paper,* October 30–November 5, 1987.

Lasky, Victor. "The Woodstein Ripoff." *AIM Report,* October 1976.

Lee, Richard. "Bob Woodward: Is He the Next Ben Bradlee?" *The Washingtonian,* July 1980.

Lukas, J. Anthony (interviewer). "Playboy Interview: Bob Woodward." *Playboy,* February 1989.

Matusow, Barbara. "Woodward Strikes Again." *The Washingtonian,* September 1987.

Moritz, Charles (editor). "Bob Woodward." *Current Biography,* 1976.

Morris, Roger. "Alexander Haig." *Regardie's,* November 1987.

Nixon, Richard M. "Cuba, Castro and John F. Kennedy." *The Reader's Digest,* November 1964.

Pincus, Walter. "A Con Man for Europe? Alexander Haig." *The New Republic,* October 5, 1974.

Stanford, Phil. "Watergate Revisited." *Columbia Journalism Review,* March/April 1986.

Time magazine staff. " 'Deep Throat': Narrowing the Field." *Time,* May 3, 1976.

———. "Deep Throat: John Dean Says It Was Haig." *Time,* November 8, 1982.

Woodward, Bob. "The Admiral of Washington." *Washington Post Magazine,* September 24, 1989.

INDEX

Abplanalp, Robert, 291, 361
Abrams, Creighton W., 37, 433
Acheson, Dean, 413
Agnew, Spiro, 150, 184, 310, 342
Air Force, U.S., 10, 17, 29, 85
Albert, Carl, 95
Allende, Salvador, 28
All the President's Men (Woodward and Bernstein), 89, 281, 282, 284, 286, 287, 288, 290, 317, 332–33, 367, 434
Almond, Edward, 86
Alto, Vincent, 149
American Life, An (Magruder), 163, 164, 219
Anderson, Jack, 304, 307, 377, 384, 396, 397, 400
   Defense Department leaks to, 16, 17
   on high-level source of leaks, 19, 311
   investigation of Welander memo leaked to, 14–24, 41
   Nixon's obsession with, 50–51, 96
   Pakistan "tilt" column of, 14–16, 19, 31, 57, 311, 376, 381, 394
   Pulitzer Prize awarded to, 57
   Radford and, 18–20, 50, 57, 394
Anderson, Libby, 18
antiballistic missile (ABM) systems, 11
Armstrong, Scott, 316–17, 322, 328–29, 439
Army, U.S., 10, 29, 85
Ashbrook, John, 95
Associated Press (AP), 283
At That Point in Time (Thompson), 317

"babysitting," 377
Bachinski, Eugene, 175, 284, 285
backchannel communications, 287
   definition of, 8–9
   Kissinger's use of, 8–9, 12, 17, 70, 85
   Nixon's protection of, 33, 48, 51, 67
   Nixon's use of, 8–9, 12, 17, 70, 85, 409–10
   SR–1, 9, 70
Bader, William, 81–82
Bailley, Jeannine, 127, 128, 132, 153
Bailley, Phillip Mackin, 126–32, 142–47, 149–54, 222–24, 228–31, 434
   address books of, 127, 128, 132, 145–46, 151, 152, 154, 223, 224, 229, 230–31
   arraignment of, 149–52
   background of, 126
   committed to mental hospital, 150–54, 223–24, 228, 231

Bailley, Phillip Mackin, *(cont.)*
   files missing in case of, 154, 224
   indictments of, 129–30, 132, 142–43, 144, 153–54, 222, 230
   Maureen Dean and, 127, 128, 130
   nude photographs taken by, 126, 132, 142, 145, 146, 151, 223
   plea bargaining and sentencing of, 229–31
   Rikan's prostitution ring and, 126–29, 131–32, 143
Baker, Bobby, 126
Baker, Howard H., Jr., 124, 140, 302, 329
   Ehrlichman questioned by, 312–14
   Moorer-Radford inquiry of, 312–14, 376–77, 384, 389, 394–96, 433–34
   as Senate Watergate investigating committee member, 242, 269, 314–15, 319, 333, 350–51, 353, 371
Baldwin, Alfred C., III, 138, 147
   banned testimony of, 139, 240
   DNC Watergate offices visited by, 148–49
   in first Watergate break-in, 135
   in second Watergate break-in, 154–156, 158, 159
Barker, Bernard L.:
   CRP money laundering by, 134, 156, 191, 193, 196, 221
   Dahlberg's lawsuit against, 221
   in first Watergate break-in, 135, 136
   Hunt's recruitment of, 134
   indictment of, 224
   in second Watergate break-in, 154, 156, 157, 158, 159, 284
   trial of, 240
Barnett, Ross, 357
Baroody, W. J. "Bill," 307, 309, 310, 388
Bates, Charles W., 193
Bay of Pigs invasion, 7, 94, 114, 187, 297
Bazelon, David L., 139, 240
Beard, Dita, 187–88, 192
Becker, Benton L., 424, 426, 428–32, 437–38
Beckman, Aldo, 379, 381
Beecher, William, 54, 305
Before the Fall (Safire), 53
Belcher, Carl W., 309
Bennett, John C., 337, 363, 365–66, 367, 368
Bennett, Robert F., 102, 113, 119, 120, 174, 285
Bennett, Wallace F., 102
Ben-Veniste, Richard, 217

Bernstein, Carl, 54, 89, 368–69
  background of, 283
  wiretap story by Woodward and, 280–82, 289–90
  Woodward's initial relationship with, 283
  see also Woodward-Bernstein, coverage of Moorer-Radford by; Woodward-Bernstein Watergate coverage
Bikel, Alexander, 345
Biner, Michael, 129
Biner, Mo, see Dean, Maureen Biner
Bittman, William C., 214, 217, 237
Black Panthers, 98
Blind Ambition (Dean), 98, 101, 105, 153, 170, 176, 190, 208, 215, 235, 239, 254
Book and Snake, 75
Bork, Robert:
  Cox fired by, 354–55
  Haig and, 310–11, 314
  Jaworski appointed by, 357, 359
Boyce, Gene, 322, 328–29
Bradlee, Ben, 286, 296, 333
Brady, James, 436
Breaking Cover (Gulley), 42
Brennan, Jack, 294
Brezhnev, Leonid, 411–12
briefing officers, 70–71, 80–83
Brown, Edwin C., 149, 150, 151, 152
Buchanan, Patrick J., 301, 421
Buchen, Phil, 428, 430, 438
Buckley, John, 116, 119
Bull, Stephen, 293, 294, 326, 332, 361, 363–64, 365, 367, 368, 427
Bureau of Special Services and Investigations (BOSSI), 94
Bush, George, 75, 436, 438, 439
Butterfield, Alexander, 234, 395
  background of, 322–23
  Deep Throat and, 317–18, 324
  Haig and, 87, 318, 326, 330–31, 414
  on Haig's fake memo, 413–14
  Nixon's unspent campaign funds and, 234, 326, 330, 331
  Nixon's White House tapes revealed by, 31, 321–36
Buzhardt, J. Fred, 16, 88, 113, 289, 307, 319, 322, 355, 356, 359, 360, 381, 388, 389, 393, 395, 407–8
  appointed Nixon's counsel, 378–79
  in attempted Stewart prosecution, 308–9, 383
  background and career of, 61
  in battle to limit Cox's investigation, 338, 340, 342, 344, 345–49, 352
  death of, 368, 434
  eighteen-and-a-half-minute tape gap and, 363, 364, 367, 369–70, 371
  firing of, 428
  Haig and, 61, 292–93, 372, 417
  Jaworski's deal with Haig and, 374–75
  Laird briefed by, 61, 62, 63–64
  in Moorer-Radford cover-up, 308, 309, 313–14, 315, 379, 381, 382, 384, 385, 386, 402–3, 433, 437
  Nixon's blanket denial urged by, 300–303
  Nixon's resignation and, 414–16, 420, 421
  Nixon's White House tapes reviewed by, 362, 369–70, 404–5, 415

Buzhardt, J. Fred, (cont.)
  revelation of Nixon's White House tapes and, 327, 331–36
  Robinson primed by, 58
  Senate testimony of, 400–402
  Stewart's files seized by, 306, 307, 396
  Stewart's investigations thwarted by, 304–6
  Thomasson and Squires questioned by, 377
  Walters's memo and, 298–300
  Welander questioned by Stewart and, 62–64, 305, 309, 397–98, 401, 403, 470–74
Byrne, Matthew, 273, 275, 279, 290, 291

Caddy, Douglas, 217
Califano, Joseph A., Jr., 53, 88, 283, 296, 323, 434
Cambodia, secret bombing of, 8, 10, 54, 85, 98, 390
Carroll, Eugene J., 77–78, 79
Casey, William, 439
Casselman, William E., II, 424
Caswell, John, 209
Caulfield, John J., 107–10, 111, 116, 172, 238, 242, 256
  background of, 94
  Dean as boss of, 100–101, 105, 106, 110, 131
  Ehrlichman's hiring of, 94–95, 110
  "Happy Hooker" prostitution ring investigation and, 105–6, 130
  Mitchell's meeting with, 108–9, 117
  in O'Brien investigation, 101–2
  Operation Sandwedge and, 107–10
  Ulasewicz hired by, 95
  as Ulasewicz's boss, 96, 106, 191
  Ulasewicz's Watergate visit and, 106–7
CBS, 393
Central Intelligence Agency (CIA), 8, 9, 28, 80, 82, 85, 86, 102, 182, 236, 324
  Cuban recruits' ties to, 193, 209
  FBI's suspected links between Watergate break-ins and, 193–94, 201, 297
  Hoover's feud with, 98
  Hunt's hush money and, 206–10
  Hunt's ties to, 113, 115, 118, 119, 187–88, 209, 285
  McCord's ties to, 126, 187, 193
  Nixon's view of, 6, 7–8, 94
  in Watergate cover-up, 194, 195–99, 201, 202–4, 209–10, 214, 263, 297, 299, 301–3, 407–8, 422, 439
  Yale recruitment by, 74
Chapin, Dwight, 234, 249, 250, 253, 254, 257, 258, 266
Chicago Tribune, 376, 379, 380, 383
Chief Counsel (Dash), 329
China, People's Republic of, 5, 410, 411
  Nixon and Kissinger in talks with, 7, 13, 29, 30, 44–46, 69
Chou En-lai, 30
Clifford, Clark, 413
Cloak and Gown (Winks), 74
"Clout," see Dean, Maureen Biner
Coco Lobo III, 14
Colson, Charles W., 102, 106, 130, 134, 241, 246, 253, 254, 257, 258, 259, 261
  in Dean's fabricated conversation, 191

Colson, Charles W., *(cont.)*
  on Dean's orders to Hunt, 180–81
  Deep Throat's implication of, 281
  executive privilege and, 249
  Fielding break-in and, 342, 375
  Hunt as employee of, 113, 174, 183–84,
    185–86, 187, 285
  Hunt's clemency request and, 237
  indictment of, 399
  post-break-in phone calls of, 174, 175
  seen as behind Watergate break-ins, 183,
    188–89
  in "smoking gun" tape, 200–201
Committee to Re-elect the President (CRP),
    156, 160, 206, 242, 246, 250, 255, 261,
    265, 284
  distrust between Nixon administration and,
    183–84
  DNC's lawsuit against, 186, 192–93, 221,
    225, 226, 242
  Liddy as counsel to, 115, 117, 119
  Liddy on finance committee of, 121–22,
    123, 125–26
  money laundering for, 134–35, 156, 191–
    92, 193, 196, 197, 198, 199, 221
  as shield for criminal action, 123
  Woodward's linking of Watergate burglars
    and, 286, 287
Connally, John, 291
Conscience of a Conservative, The (Goldwater),
    72
Cooke, D. O., 20
Coombe, Andrew, 74
Court of Appeals, U.S., 139, 341, 343
Cox, Archibald, 364, 365, 370, 375, 377, 399
  appointment of, 338
  battle to limit investigation by, 337–54
  firing of, 343, 345, 348, 349, 354–55, 373,
    374
  guilty pleas in tenure of, 376
Coyne, Patrick, 243
Cuban recruits, of Hunt:
  CIA ties of, 193, 209
  in Fielding break-in, 114–15, 179, 192, 210
  in first Watergate break-in, 134, 135
  hush money not given to, 217
  indictments of, 221, 224
  list of, 135
  in second Watergate break-in, 154–59, 179,
    185

Dahlberg, Kenneth H., 134, 192, 196, 199,
    200, 204
  Barker sued by, 221
Dash, Samuel, 110, 124, 165, 243, 314, 316,
    317, 328–29, 332, 336, 384, 395
Davidson, Daniel I., 55
"Dealing with our Political Enemies" (Dean
    memo), 104
Dean, John Wesley, III, 93–276, 370, 434
  as accepted Watergate chronicler, 163, 211,
    272, 318–19
  antiwar demonstrations investigated by,
    102–3
  background of, 96–97
  Bailley's address book photocopied by,
    145–46
  Bailley's case and, 153, 229, 232

Dean, John Wesley, III, *(cont.)*
  Camp David revelation and phone calls of,
    270–72
  "cancer" warning to Nixon by, 259, 260,
    261, 267, 378
  Caulfield supervised by, 100–101, 105, 106,
    110, 131
  character of, 228
  CIA used in Watergate cover-up by, 194,
    195–98, 201, 202–4, 209–10, 214, 297,
    299, 301–3
  clemency promised by, 237–39, 242, 244,
    245
  as damage control action officer, 176–77,
    179, 216
  Democratic convention operation and, 120
  different perspectives on, 216, 222
  documents given to Sirica by, 296–97
  domestic intelligence plan of, 103–4
  Ehrlichman's and Haldeman's questioning
    of, 241
  enemies list of, 227
  FBI break-in reports sought by, 186
  FBI information passed to, 191–92, 193–
    94, 197, 203–4, 216, 218–19, 225,
    248–49
  Golden Boy memo on, 319, 320, 321
  "golden boy" reputation of, 97–98
  Gray implicated by, 235–36, 239
  Gray's accusation of lying by, 268
  Gray's confirmation hearings and, 248,
    251–52
  Haldeman as Nixon connection for, 174
  Haldeman's fabricated meeting with, 119,
    181, 258, 320
  Haldeman sidestepped by, 120–21
  Haldeman's phone call from, 196–97, 198
  "Happy Hooker" prostitution ring investi-
    gation ordered by, 105–6
  holes and inconsistencies in story of, 100,
    104–5, 108–10, 116, 119, 170–72, 177,
    178, 180–81, 190–91, 197–98, 203,
    206, 210–11, 215–16, 260, 261, 270,
    318–21
  Hunt ordered to leave the country by, 179–
    81, 184
  Hunt's hush money obtained by, 205–10,
    212–14, 216, 217–18, 236
  Hunt's notebooks hidden and destroyed by,
    140–41, 182, 190, 211, 212, 217, 235–
    36, 239–40
  Hunt's safe in possession of, 182–83, 189–
    90, 211, 235
  Huston plan and, 98, 99–100
  as "idea thief," 112, 210, 213
  immunity sought by, 273
  indictment of, 140
  intelligence gathering seen as route to power
    by, 98, 102–4, 111
  Kalmbach coached by, 245, 252
  Liddy's domestic intelligence plans and,
    116–20, 122
  Liddy's meeting with Krogh and, 116–17
  Liddy's meeting with Mitchell and, 117
  Liddy's photograph and, 236
  Liddy's post-break-in meeting with, 175–
    80, 254
  Liddy's promises received from, 237–38

Dean, John Wesley, III, *(cont.)*
  Magruder's Camp David phone call from, 270–72
  Magruder's grand jury coaching by, 219–21, 251, 252
  Magruder's post-break-in phone call to, 163, 168, 169–70, 171, 175, 176, 320
  Maroulis's Camp David phone call from, 272
  marriage of, *see* Dean, Maureen Biner
  McCord's promises from, 238–39
  at Mitchell's apartment meeting, 184–85
  named Nixon's Watergate investigator, 221
  Nixon asked for hush money by, 262–64, 265
  Nixon's hearing of confession from, 252–59, 261–64
  Nixon's taped conversations with, 172, 178, 224–28, 241–47, 249–70, 339, 340, 357, 378, 386–87, 406
  Nixon's view of, 228, 246–47
  in O'Brien investigation, 101–2
  Operation Sandwedge and, 107–10
  others implicated in Watergate cover-up by, 163, 176, 178, 190–91, 196–98, 214, 216, 240, 250, 257, 258, 261–62, 271–74, 318, 321
  political enemies memo of, 104
  post-prison life of, 438
  resignation of, 274, 276, 291
  Rikan's friendship with, 131
  Rudy's and Smith's meeting with, 144–46
  Segretti problem handled by, 233–34
  self-image of, 215
  Senate committees feared by, 240–41
  sentencing deal of, 240, 376
  Silbert and, 272–73
  Sirica's actions known by, 267–68
  source of grand jury information for, 221
  as source of Watergate break-in orders, 133, 140–41, 148, 177, 184
  superiors' names misleadingly used by, 112, 169, 185, 186, 192, 196, 197, 198, 199, 210
  Ulasewicz as underling of, 100–101, 191
  Ulasewicz's contract extension and, 109
  Ulasewicz's post-break-in phone call from, 172
  Ulasewicz's Watergate visit denied by, 107
  Walters's meetings with, 207–8, 210, 299
  Watergate burglars promised support money by, 178–79, 188, 191, 193, 205
  Watergate cover-up, 163, 168–72, 175–84, 193–276
  White House hiring of, 96–97
  written report sought from, 249, 257, 258, 266–67, 268, 269–71
Dean, Maureen Biner, 438
  background of, 129
  in Bailley's address book, 128, 145, 153, 232
  Bailley and, 127, 128, 130
  code name of, 127, 128, 129, 132, 153, 232
  Dean's confession to, 270
  Dean's marriage to, 129, 153, 231–32, 287–88
  physical appearance of, 127, 318
  previous marriages of, 129, 130

Dean, Maureen Biner, *(cont.)*
  Rikan and, 127–30, 132, 145, 153, 232
  subpoena evaded by, 153
De Diego, Felipe, 135
Deep Throat:
  Butterfield urged on Woodward by, 317–18, 324, 326
  coded signals between Woodward and, 288
  Colson and Mitchell implicated by, 281
  on deliberate erasures in Nixon's White House tapes, 367–68
  eighteen-and-a-half-minute tape gap and, 363, 370
  Haig and Woodward protected by story of, 283
  Haig as, 88, 285, 286, 288–91, 302, 333, 363, 367–69
  inaccuracies of, 281–82, 287, 288, 290, 302
  on Nixon, 281
  on Nixon administration, 284, 288, 291
  other possible identities of, 290–91, 367–69
  political motivation of, 288–89
  Woodward-Bernstein's first use of, 234, 280–81, 326
  Woodward-Bernstein wiretap story and, 28–182, 289–90
  Woodward on character of, 284
  Woodward's need for, 289
  see also Woodward-Haig connection
Defense Department, U.S., 4, 7, 70, 82
  Anderson leak investigated by, 14–24
Defense Intelligence Agency (DIA), 98, 305
Democratic National Committee (DNC), 296
  break-ins of, *see* Watergate break-in, first; Watergate break-in, second
  CRP sued by, 186, 192–93, 221, 225, 226, 242
  office layout of, 128
  Rikan's prostitution ring used by, 127–32, 227–28
  Rothblatt's investigation of, 227–28
  sweeps for bugs in offices of, 149, 225
  Ulasewicz's visit to Watergate offices of, 106–7
  as Watergate break-in target, 124–25, 147–48
Democratic party:
  Congress controlled by, 6
  Haig's wiretaps on members of, 55–56
  Nixon administration intelligence activities against, 55–56, 95, 104–5, 115, 16, 117, 120
Detroit News, 361
Diem, Ngo Dinh, 113, 182
Dieter, Cathy "Erika," *see* Rikan, Erika L. "Heidi"
Digital Information Relay Center, 8–9, 17
Dixon, Richard M., 96, 101
Doar, John, 405
Dobrynin, Anatoly, 7
Donohue, Joseph D., 19
Downie, Leonard, Jr., 74, 77, 80, 82, 84
Doyle, James, 343, 344, 345, 355, 374, 375, 377, 391, 399, 419, 424
Dulles, John Foster, 7

Eagleburger, Lawrence, 85, 411
Eastland, James, 251–52, 427

Eastman, Hope, 138
Ehrlichman, John D., 6, 56–57, 60, 63, 69, 106, 131, 191, 202, 208–9, 235, 246, 247, 295, 299, 319, 333, 363, 364–65, 373, 376, 402, 407
  Anderson leak investigation and, 15
  Caulfield hired by, 94–95, 110
  Dean questioned by Haldeman and, 241
  Dean's implication of, 163, 176, 258, 261, 262, 273, 274, 276, 318
  on Dean's lifestyle, 97–98
  on Dean's orders to Hunt, 180–81
  Dean's political enemies memo and, 104
  Dean's possession of Hunt's safe approved by, 183
  Dean written report suggested by, 266–67
  as Deep Throat suspect, 290–91
  and disposition of files from Hunt's safe, 211
  eighteen-and-a-half-minute gap in tape of Nixon and, 187, 362–72
  Fielding break-in approved by, 114, 258–59, 312, 342
  Fielding break-in charges against, 375, 408
  grand jury suggestion of, 264, 265–66
  on Haig-Kissinger-Nixon relationship, 53
  "hang-out road" recommended by, 255
  on Hunt's clemency request, 236–37
  Hunt's hush money and, 206–7, 210, 213
  indictment of, 399
  jail sentence of, 114
  in Moorer-Radford affair cover-up, 312–14
  Moorer-Radford material subpoenaed by, 408–10
  on Nixon's burial of Moorer-Radford affair, 48, 49, 66
  as Nixon's connection to Caulfield and Ulasewicz, 95
  Nixon's instructions to Kissinger through, 52
  on Nixon's vengefulness, 50–51
  Nixon told of Radford's confession by, 32–33
  Nixon told of Welander's confession to, 47–48
  NSC security review by, 67
  post-break-in phone calls of, 174, 175
  on Radford's theft of NSC documents, 24
  resignation of, 274, 275–76, 291
  Robinson questioned by, 58
  Watergate investigation by, 273
  Welander's confession to Young and, 33–46, 61, 66, 292, 293, 374, 382, 384, 386, 391, 401, 403, 408–9, 417, 432, 445–69
  White House Domestic Council appointment of, 96, 100
  wiretap reports given to, 56, 297, 299
Eisenhower, Dwight D., 7
Eisenhower, Julie Nixon, 96, 344
Eisenhower administration, 266
Ellsberg, Daniel J., 182, 307, 309
  Pentagon Papers leaked by, 15, 113–14
  Plumbers' investigation of, 15, 16, 113–14, 275, 290–91, 306, 313, 376
  trial of, 273, 279–80, 282, 305
  see also Fielding, Lewis J., Plumbers' break-in at office of

Ends of Power, The (Haldeman), 7–8, 196
Enterprise, USS, 16, 17
Ervin, Sam, 250, 267, 382, 389
  contempt of Congress charges threatened by, 261
  Dean on, 243
  as Senate Watergate investigating committee chairman, 240, 245, 269, 292, 314–15, 328, 329, 335, 339–40, 350–51, 353, 371, 384
Executive Protection Service, 176, 324

Farquhar, Roger B., 84–85
Federal Bureau of Investigation (FBI), 56, 94, 103, 113, 149, 159, 186, 243, 246, 250, 268, 305, 306, 325, 355
  Bailley's address books seized by, 132, 223
  CIA's rivalry with, 98, 99
  CIA used in blocking Watergate investigation by, 194, 195–99, 201, 202–4, 209–10, 214, 263, 297, 299, 301–3, 407–8, 422, 439
  CIA-Watergate suspicions of, 193–94, 201, 297
  Dean given information by, 191–92, 193–94, 203–4, 216, 218–19, 225, 248
  domestic intelligence operations of, 17, 55
  Haig briefed by, 85
  Liddy's critique of, 115
  Liddy's refusal of interview by, 218
Federal Times, 434
Felt, Mark, 243
Fielding, Fred F., 98, 115, 170, 190, 235
Fielding, Lewis J., Plumbers' break-in at office of, 114–15, 134, 179, 182, 187, 188, 192, 210, 216, 236, 258–59, 273, 274, 275, 300, 301, 312, 315, 338, 342, 343, 374
Final Days, The (Woodward and Bernstein), 54, 89–90, 294, 296, 298, 300, 352, 358, 361, 369, 370, 371, 386, 387, 405, 414–16, 418, 419, 423, 434
Fitzpatrick, Francis J., 70, 76, 80, 83
Flanigan, Peter, 143, 144
Flemming, Harry S., 123, 124
Flowers, Walter, 415
Ford, Betty, 420, 421
Ford, Gerald R., 362, 418
  and disposition of Nixon's White House tapes, 426–32
  Haig retained by, 425, 426–27, 433
  Nixon pardoned by, 421, 429–32, 437–38
  Nixon's resignation and, 419, 425
  vice-presidential nomination of, 344
Fox, Alonzo, 86, 87
Fox, USS, 78
Frates, William, 409
Friedheim, Jerry, 82, 389

Garment, Leonard, 301, 355, 356, 359, 389
  in battle to limit Cox's investigation, 348, 349, 354
  Buzhardt's eclipse of, 292, 293
  Golden Boy memo of, 319–20, 321
  in Moorer-Radford cover-up, 306, 308–9, 314–15, 402–3
  as Nixon's special assistant, 379

Garment, Leonard, *(cont.)*
  revelation of Nixon's White House tapes
    and, 322, 326, 331, 333–34, 335
  on Woodward-Haig connection, 89–90
GEMSTONE plan, 131, 134, 319–20
  budget for, 116–17, 124, 126, 177
  Hunt's destroyed notebooks as record of,
    140, 190, 212, 239
  Liddy's proposals for, 117–18, 123
  Magruder's alleged destruction of files of,
    184–85
  Mitchell's rejection of, 118–19, 121, 124–
    25, 133, 189
  as shield for criminal action, 139
General Accounting Office (GAO), 221
General Security Services, 155
General Services Administration (GSA), 431,
    432
General's Progress, The (Morris), 56
Gergen, David, 295, 416
Gesell, Gerhard, 375, 409
Getler, Michael, 383, 393, 394, 400
Glanzer, Seymour, 326
Glomar Explorer, 113
Goldberg, Woody, 67
Goldwater, Barry M., Jr., 96
Goldwater, Barry M., Sr., 55, 72, 225–26,
    250, 308, 401, 422
Gonzalez, Virgilio R.:
  in first Watergate break-in, 135, 136
  indictment of, 224
  in second Watergate break-in, 154, 156, 157
  trial of, 240
Graham, Katharine, 296
Gray, L. Patrick, 196, 202, 209, 261, 290, 297
  confirmation hearings of, 240–41, 248–49,
    251–52, 268, 280
  Dean accused of lying by, 268
  Dean given FBI information by, 191–92,
    193–94, 197, 203–4, 216, 218–19,
    248–49
  Dean's implication of, 235–36, 239
  files from Hunt's safe given to, 211–12, 217,
    235, 241, 275
  resignation of, 275
Greenfield, Meg, 436
Greenspan, Hank, 119
Gregory, Thomas, 120
Groom, Winston, 143, 144
Gulley, William, 42–43

Haig, Alexander M., Jr., 12, 57, 279–303,
    307, 390, 395, 397, 404, 434–37
  appointed chief of staff, 280, 282
  Army promotions of, 53, 88, 286
  attempted protection of Welander by, 58–
    60, 63
  attempted Stewart prosecution and, 308–9,
    383
  background and Army career of, 86–88
  in battle to limit Cox's investigation, 338,
    339–40, 342, 344, 345–54
  Bork and, 310–11
  briefings received by, 85–86
  Butterfield and, 87, 318, 326, 330–31, 414
  Buzhardt and, 61, 292–93, 372, 417
  Califano and, 296, 323, 434

Haig, Alexander M., Jr., *(cont.)*
  on civilian interference in military decision-
    making, 87
  eighteen-and-a-half-minute tape gap and,
    363, 364, 367, 369, 370
  in fake memo incident, 413–14
  in Ford administration, 425, 426–27, 433
  "I am in control" statement of, 436
  and investigation of Anderson leak, 15, 16
  Jaworski's appointment and, 296, 357–59
  Jaworski's deal with Buzhardt and, 374–75
  Jaworski's friendship with, 377–78, 387,
    399–400, 434
  as JCS-NSC conduit, 34–35, 42–43, 86
  as Kissinger's aide, 53, 88
  on military presidential adviser's role, 87,
    282, 285
  military vs. executive loyalty of, 42–43, 65,
    66
  in Moorer-Radford cover-up, 308–15, 358,
    379, 381, 386, 402–3, 423, 437
  NATO posting of, 433, 438
  Nixon administration secrets known by,
    287
  Nixon influenced by, 289, 291–95, 434
  Nixon misled by, 336, 346–47, 350, 351,
    354, 356, 372, 386–87, 399–400, 419–
    20
  Nixon's blanket denial urged by, 300–303
  Nixon's pardon and, 421, 429–32, 437–38
  Nixon's resignation and, 414–16, 418–25
  Nixon's White House taping stopped by,
    337
  at Paris peace talks, 289
  Pentagon Papers trial testimony of, 279–80
  power balance between Kissinger and, 42,
    52–54, 282, 286, 412, 417–18, 428
  as probable Deep Throat, 88, 285, 286,
    288–91, 302, 333, 363, 367–69
  Radford as aide to, 24–25, 26, 27, 29–30,
    38, 43–44
  as Reagan's secretary of state, 434, 436, 438
  and release of Nixon's White House tapes,
    386–87, 405–7
  resignation of, 437
  and revelation of Nixon's White House
    tapes, 321–22, 331–36
  Robinson and, 23, 45, 293
  St. Clair hired by, 378
  in Vietnam War, 88
  Walters's memo and, 298–300
  Welander and, 37, 58–60, 63
  wiretapping program headed by, 55–56,
    280, 281, 286, 299, 338, 350, 413–14,
    416–18
  see also Woodward-Haig connection
Halberstam, David, 74, 77, 286
Haldeman, H. R. "Bob," 6, 32, 47, 55, 56–
    57, 90, 99, 101, 106, 124, 125, 131,
    208–9, 224, 227, 231, 235, 246, 247,
    249, 250, 258, 268–69, 271, 281–82,
    287, 292, 293, 295, 298, 299, 312, 319,
    321–22, 326, 331, 340, 363, 364–65,
    407
  antiwar demonstration investigations or-
    dered by, 102–3
  Butterfield and, 322, 323–24
  Dean questioned by Ehrlichman and, 241

Haldeman, H. R. "Bob," *(cont.)*
  in Dean's confession to Nixon, 253, 254, 255, 257
  as Dean's connection to Nixon, 174
  Dean's domestic intelligence plan rejected by, 103–4, 111
  Dean's fabricated meeting with, 119, 181, 258, 320
  Dean's hiring and, 97
  Dean's implication of, 163, 178, 250, 261, 262, 273, 274, 276, 318
  on Dean's meeting with Bailley, 146–47
  Dean's phone call to, 196–97, 198
  Dean's sidestepping of, 121
  as Deep Throat suspect, 290–91
  domestic intelligence operation sought by, 115–16
  gap in Nixon's taped conversation with, 187
  Hunt's hush money and, 206
  indictment of, 399
  Magruder's fear of, 169
  Magruder's post-break-in phone call with, 173–74
  on Mitchell's innocence, 186
  in Nixon administration hierarchy, 96
  Nixon and Helms compared by, 7–8
  Nixon as viewed by, 93
  Nixon's surveillance orders and, 94
  in O'Brien investigation, 102
  Operation Sandwedge rejected by, 108
  resignation of, 274, 275–76, 291
  Segretti and, 116, 234
  slush fund and, 234
  in "smoking gun" tape, 195, 198–201, 405
  Watergate break-in reaction of, 173–74
  Watergate complications feared by, 192, 199
Halperin, Morton H., 54–55, 56, 279–80, 290, 413
Hamilton, James, 322, 335
Hantman, Alfred L., 309–10
"Happy Hooker" prostitution ring, 105–6, 130
Harlow, Bryce, 353, 359, 421
Harriman, W. Averell, 55
Hartke, Vance, 95
Hartmann, Robert T., 112, 418, 419, 420, 421, 424, 426, 428, 429, 430
Hellams, Walter, 157
Helms, Richard M., 7–8, 98, 99, 202, 208–9, 297, 299, 407
Hersh, Seymour, 419, 420, 428
  Moorer-Radford stories of, 382, 383, 384, 388–89, 390–91, 393, 398–99
Higby, Lawrence, 90, 146, 173, 233, 293, 321–22, 324, 325, 326, 327, 331, 332, 334
Hoffman, Martin, 309, 389, 394, 395, 396
Hollander, Xaviera, 106
Hoover, J. Edgar, 23, 54, 55, 94, 98, 99, 115, 243, 281, 413
Hougan, Jim, 82, 113, 136, 156, 209
House Banking and Currency Committee, 221
House Judiciary Committee, 339–40, 364, 399, 417, 420
  Dean's testimony to, 240
  Nixon's White House tapes subpoenaed by, 405–6

House of Representatives, U.S., Nixon impeachment procedures in, 355–56, 391, 405, 406, 412–15
Hoyer, Stenny, 126
Hughes, Harold, 390, 400, 401–2
Hughes, Howard, 28, 101–2, 107, 113, 119
Humphrey, Hubert H., 93, 95, 133
Hunnicut, Charles, 80, 82
Hunt, Dorothy, 217, 236, 244
Hunt, E. Howard, 125, 136, 221, 239, 244, 254, 255, 268, 272
  Barker recruited by, 134
  blackmail motive denied by, 138
  CIA ties of, 113, 115, 118, 119, 187–88, 209, 285
  clemency request for, 237, 266
  Colson as employer of, 113, 174, 183–84, 185–86, 187, 285
  confession threatened by, 260
  contents of safe of, 182
  Dean's hiding and destruction of notebooks of, 140–41, 182, 190, 211, 212, 217, 235–236, 239–40
  and Dean's orders to leave the country, 179–81, 184
  Dean's possession of safe of, 182–83, 189–90, 211, 235
  Fielding break-in and, 114–15, 187, 216, 259, 273, 274, 275, 312, 343, 374
  hush money for, 205–10, 212–14, 216, 217–18, 236, 237, 239, 241, 242, 262–63, 267
  indictment of, 221, 224
  ITT affair and, 187–88
  jail sentence served by, 217
  on Liddy's meeting with Dean and Krogh, 116–17
  McGovern headquarters break-in planned by, 135
  Pentagon Papers investigation and, 113–14
  in second Watergate break-in, 154, 156, 157, 159, 284
  Segretti and, 234
  in "smoking gun" tape, 200
  trial of, 218, 239, 240
  Watergate break-in connection of, revealed, 174, 175, 185
  on Watergate break-in purpose, 134, 138, 139, 157
  in Woodward-Bernstein wiretap story, 281–82, 290
  Woodward's first naming of, 185, 285
  see also Cuban recruits, of Hunt
Huston, Tom Charles, 98–99
Huston Plan, 99–100, 104, 296–97, 300, 302, 338

Inman, Bobby Ray, 81
Inouye, Daniel K., 104, 109, 203, 319–20
Internal Revenue Service (IRS), 102, 250, 405
International Telephone and Telegraph (ITT), 124, 174, 187
Intertel, 107
In the Arena (Nixon), 439

Jackson, Bobby, 155, 156
Jackson, Henry, 308, 310, 412
Jane's Fighting Ships, 75

Jaworski, Leon, 369, 384, 427, 430
    appointment of, 296, 357, 361
    background of, 357
    in deal with Haig and Buzhardt, 374–75
    death of, 434
    Haig's friendship with, 377–78, 387, 399–
        400, 434
    Krogh case and, 373–76
    on national security as legal shield, 374, 375
    Nixon's resignation and, 421–24
    Nixon's White House tapes subpoenaed by,
        405, 406–8, 415, 421–22
    "tape of tapes" requested by, 386–87
Johnson, Lyndon B., 76, 98, 126, 226, 243,
    246, 357
Joint Chiefs of Staff (JCS), 29, 30, 69–70, 87,
    308, 410
    Anderson leak and, 17
    Kissinger as viewed by, 10, 28, 41
    Kissinger's secret China mission known by,
        29–30, 44–46
    members of, 10
    Nixon as viewed by, 5, 10–12, 28
    Nixon's and Kissinger's backchannel com-
        munications established by, 8, 25, 48,
        70
    Nixon's and Kissinger's removal as goal of,
        28
    Nixon's manipulations of, 8–10, 26–27
    NSC liaison office with, 4, 5, 12, 43, 51,
        52, 56, 57, 58, 61, 381, 384, 393
    secret peace talks and, 41
    see also Moorer-Radford affair
Joulwan, George, 406, 423
Justice Department, U.S., 103, 113, 221, 224,
    236, 267, 281, 306, 317, 355, 428, 429,
    434

Kalmbach, Herbert W., 242, 266
    Dean's coaching of, 245, 252
    Hunt's hush money obtained through, 210,
        212–14, 217, 231, 236, 245
    Segretti and, 249, 250
    Ulasewicz paid by, 95, 109, 110, 245, 252,
        256, 263
Katzenbach, Nicholas deB., 338
Kaufman, Harold, 223
Kehrli, Bruce A., 182, 183, 190, 235
Kelley, Clarence, 305, 307–8
Kennedy, Barbara, 148, 159
Kennedy, Edward M., 95, 182, 243, 256, 338
Kennedy, John F., 7, 113, 182, 338
Kennedy, Robert F., 126, 128, 243, 357
Kennedy family, 94, 107, 113, 243
Kent State University, student killings at, 98
King, Martin Luther, Jr., 55
King, Stephen B., 164–65, 166
Kingston, John, 82–83
Kissinger, Henry A., 7, 32, 34, 63, 70, 87,
    279, 281, 294, 342, 354, 390, 391, 400,
    418, 429
    Anderson leak and, 14, 16
    backchannel communications used by, 8–9,
        12, 17, 25, 33, 70, 85
    on Cambodian bombing leak, 54–55
    China mission of, 7, 13, 29–30, 44–46, 69
    as Deep Throat suspect, 290–91
    Haig as aide to, 53, 88

Kissinger, Henry A., (cont.)
    on Haig's NATO position, 433
    Haig's wiretap reports and, 56
    JCS manipulated by, 8–10, 25
    JCS-NSC liaison office closed by, 56, 57,
        58
    JCS's dislike of, 10, 28, 41
    on Moorer-Radford affair, 385–86, 392–93,
        396, 399
    Nixon as viewed by, 6, 9, 93
    Nixon's strained relationship with, 56–57,
        60, 67, 411
    Nixon's White House taping system not
        known by, 333
    NSC's power under, 4
    at Paris peace talks, 289
    on Pentagon Papers, 112–13
    power balance between Haig and, 42, 52–
        54, 282, 286, 412, 417–18, 428
    Radford as aide to, 29–30, 37–38, 45, 375
    Radford's espionage against, 12, 13–14, 22–
        31, 40, 45, 52, 62, 375
    in secret peace talks, 7, 11, 41, 298
    talking papers prepared for, 37
    on Watergate's foreign policy effect, 410
    wiretap accusation against, 415–16
    WSAG established by, 14
Klein, Julius, 434
Kleindienst, Richard, 184, 191, 219, 237, 242,
    245, 246, 261, 269, 273
    Liddy's visit with, 166–67, 169–70, 186
    post-break-in contact with, 164, 165, 166–
        67
    resignation of, 275, 276, 291
    Watergate investigation announced by, 221
Knoizen, Arthur K., 28, 36, 384, 391
Koppel, Ted, 368
Korn, David, 89, 437
Krogh, Egil "Bud," Jr., 97, 115, 312, 373–76
    confirmation hearings of, 237
    Fielding break-in and, 342
    on Haig, 43
    Liddy assigned to Plumbers by, 112, 237
    Liddy's meeting with Dean and, 116–17
    Nixon's White House tapes sought by, 373–
        74, 375–76, 408–9
    Pentagon Papers investigation and, 113, 114
    perjury indictment of, 342–43, 373, 376
    as Plumber, 15
Kuhn, Mary Ann, 143, 144

Lacovara, Philip A., 374
Laird, Melvin R., 16, 43, 50, 60, 63, 305, 359,
    382, 391, 394, 400, 401, 403
    Buzhardt's briefing of, 61, 62, 63–64
    on Haig's knowledge of Moorer-Radford af-
        fair, 64
    Haig's neutralization of, 292–93
    Kissinger's circumventing of, 8, 25
    Nixon's appointment of, 7
    Nixon's circumventing of, 7, 9, 17, 48, 51–
        52, 57
    Woodward-Haig connection confirmed by,
        82
Lake, W. Anthony, 56
Laos, 17, 103
LaRocque, Eugene, 13, 77

LaRue, Frederick C.:
  guilty plea and sentence of, 376
  Hunt's hush money passed by, 231
  at March 30, 1972 meeting, 123, 124
  in post-break-in events, 162, 164–65, 166,
    167, 184, 185, 188, 189, 205, 210, 213
Lasky, Victor, 89
Le Duc Tho, 30, 41, 48, 298
Levine (lawyer), 230
Library of Congress, 132
Liddy, G. Gordon, 131, 174, 192, 193, 194,
    206, 210, 214, 221, 241, 257, 434
  background of, 111–12
  as CRP counsel, 115, 117, 119
  CRP finance committee work of, 121–22,
    123, 125–26
  Dean as damage control action officer for,
    176–77, 179, 216
  in Dean's confession to Nixon, 254, 255,
    258, 261
  Dean's meeting with Krogh and, 116–17
  Dean's meeting with Mitchell and, 117
  on Dean's orders to Hunt, 180, 181
  Dean's post-break-in meeting with, 175–80,
    254
  Dean's promises to, 237–38, 239
  Democratic convention understood as
    break-in target by, 125, 133
  documents shredded by, 162, 176
  domestic intelligence plans of, 116–22
  FBI critiqued by, 115
  Fielding break-in and, 114–15, 134, 216,
    236, 259, 273, 274, 275, 312, 343, 374
  in first Watergate break-in, 133, 135–37,
    139
  GEMSTONE proposals of, 117–18, 123–
    26
  hush money for, 217, 218
  indictment of, 221, 224
  intelligence budget received by, 126
  Kleindienst visited by, 166–67, 169–70,
    186
  Magruder's post-break-in phone conversa-
    tions with, 162–63, 165–66, 167, 168
  Magruder threatened by, 121, 125
  Mardian's questioning of, 187–88, 189
  Mitchell shielded from, 120
  money laundering by, 134–35, 156, 191–92
  Nixon's protection sought by, 165, 178, 181
  Pentagon Papers investigation and, 113–14
  in second Watergate break-in, 154–60
  SEDAN CHAIR and, 119–20
  Segretti and, 119, 234
  in "smoking gun" tape, 200
  trial of, 240
  Ulasewicz audited by, 117–18
  vow of silence of, 165, 218, 238, 272
  Watergate break-in purpose unknown to,
    134, 147–48, 157, 214
  White House pass of, 162, 176
  in Woodward-Bernstein wiretap story, 281–
    82, 290
Liebengood, Howard, 159, 312, 314, 329,
    394, 433
Liebman, Morris, 357, 369, 378
Life, 413
Linger, Stephen W., 17–18
Lon Nol, 26

Look, 413
Los Angeles Times, 271
Lugar, Richard, 81
Lukas, J. Anthony, 338, 419

McAllister, John, 73, 74
MacArthur, Douglas, 47–48, 86, 87
McCardle, Dorothy, 211
McCloskey, Paul, 95, 108
McCord, James W., Jr., 174, 187, 193, 209–
    10, 236, 249, 255, 272
  AP's naming of, 283–84
  Baldwin's DNC visit and, 148, 149
  CIA ties of, 126, 187, 193
  CRP connection revealed, 175, 183, 186
  as CRP security chief, 126, 133
  Dean's promises to, 238–39
  entrapment charged by, 275
  in first Watergate break-in, 135, 136–37,
    139, 147
  indictment of, 221, 224
  release from jail sought for, 164, 165, 166,
    184
  in second Watergate break-in, 154–60, 177
  Sirica's letter from, 260, 271
  trial of, 238, 240
McFadden, W. Clark, II, 398
McGovern, George, 117, 133, 134, 135, 147,
    234
MacGregor, Clark, 225
McIntyre, Thomas J., 391, 401
McNamara, Robert S., 53, 87, 88, 323, 324
McPhee, Roemer, 226
Madigan, Michael, 317
Magruder, Jeb Stuart, 115, 118, 131, 134,
    136, 139, 154, 205, 216, 218, 221, 240,
    241, 242, 249, 258, 266–67, 273, 287,
    318, 413
  character of, 163, 168, 189
  Dean-Liddy connection revealed by, 255
  Dean's Camp David phone call to, 271–72
  in Dean's confession to Nixon, 254, 261
  Dean's fabricated conversation with, 190–
    91
  Dean's grand jury coaching of, 219–21,
    251, 252
  Dean's post-break-in phone call from, 163,
    168, 169–70, 171, 175, 176, 320
  discrepancies in account of, 124–25, 147,
    163–65, 167–68
  first Watergate break-in and, 133–34
  GEMSTONE files destroyed by, 184–85
  guilty plea and sentence of, 376
  Haldeman feared by, 169
  Haldeman's post-break-in phone call with,
    173–74
  Liddy's domestic intelligence plans and,
    119–22
  Liddy's post-break-in phone conversations
    with, 162–63, 165–66, 167, 168
  Liddy's threats to, 121, 125
  at March 30, 1972 meeting, 123–25
  Mitchell blamed for Watergate cover-up by,
    163, 164–65
  Operation Sandwedge rejected by, 108
  religious conversion of, 163
  resignation of, 275

Magruder, Jeb Stuart, *(cont.)*
  second Watergate break-in approved by,
    147, 148, 177, 188
  SEDAN CHAIR and, 119
  in Watergate cover-up, 163, 166–67, 169–
    70, 176, 183–84, 219–21, 273
Mao Z Tse-tung, 410
Mardian, Robert C., 210, 227, 281, 317
  as Deep Throat suspect, 290–91
  Hunt's hush money and, 205, 206
  indictment of, 167, 399
  Liddy questioned by, 187–88, 189
  at Mitchell's apartment meeting, 183, 184,
    185
  in post-break-in events, 162, 164, 165, 167
  as Watergate damage control action officer,
    191
Marine Corps, U.S., 10, 74
Maroulis, Peter, 228, 238, 272
Marsh, John O., 421, 429
Marshall, George C., 87
Martinez, Eugenio Rolando, 209
  in first Watergate break-in, 135, 137, 139
  indictment of, 224
  in second Watergate break-in, 149, 154,
    156–59, 284
  trial of, 240
media:
  Nixon's relationship with, 93–94, 361
  reaction to Watergate affair in, 249, 253,
    257, 271
  see also television
Miami Herald, 84, 161
MI-5, 313
Miller, Herbert J., Jr., 430–31
Millhouse, 96
Mitchell, John N., 47, 48, 60, 131, 162, 192,
  219, 227, 246, 258, 273, 281–82, 284,
  290, 302, 319, 350, 360–61, 398
  apartment meeting of, 184–85
  Caulfield's meeting with, 108–9, 117
  Colson's Watergate responsibility and, 183,
    188–89
  CRP resignation of, 214
  Dean's career advice from, 97
  in Dean's confession to Nixon, 253, 254,
    255, 257
  Dean's implication of, 163, 190–91, 196–
    98, 214, 216, 240, 261–62, 270, 318,
    321
  death of, 65
  Deep Throat's implication of, 281, 288
  as Deep Throat suspect, 290–91
  domestic intelligence operation sought by,
    115–16
  GEMSTONE plan rejected by, 118–19,
    121, 124–25, 133, 189
  grand jury disclosure favored by, 268–70
  on Haig, 65
  Hunt's hush money and, 205, 206
  Huston Plan opposed by, 99–100, 104, 297
  indictment of, 125, 167, 399
  Liddy kept away from, 120
  and Magruder's alleged destruction of
    GEMSTONE files, 184–85
  Magruder's implication of, in Watergate
    cover-up, 163, 164–65, 176
  at March 30, 1972 meeting, 123–25

Mitchell, John N., *(cont.)*
  on Moorer, 44–45
  Moorer questioned by, 51, 65
  Nixon interviewed through, 295–96
  Nixon kept uninformed by, 189
  Nixon's avoidance of questioning of, 201–2
  Nixon's dirty work done by, 6, 49
  Nixon's friendship with, 32, 47, 65, 197,
    201
  Nixon's manipulation of, 65
  as Nixon's 1972 campaign chief, 108, 123
  on Nixon's reaction to Moorer-Radford af-
    fair, 48, 49
  Operation Sandwedge and, 108–10
  in "smoking gun" tape, 200–201
  Ulasewicz not known by, 110
  Watergate break-in approval and, 124–25,
    133, 147, 148, 185, 186, 189, 214
  Watergate burglars' support money denied
    by, 188, 189, 231
Mitchell, Martha, 124, 165, 184, 185, 189,
  210–11, 214
"Mo," A Woman's View of Watergate (Dean), 129
Montgomery County Sentinel, 84, 85, 283
Moore, Powell A., 162, 166, 167
Moore, Richard, 241
Moorer, Thomas H., 17, 18, 69, 83, 287, 307,
  390, 410
  Buzhardt on espionage involvement of, 61
  character of, 4, 11
  exoneration of, 385
  innocence claimed by, 64, 391
  JCS appointments of, 11, 51
  JCS-NSC information traded by, 37
  Kissinger's secret China mission known by,
    44–45, 46
  in media's uncovering of Moorer-Radford
    affair, 380, 382, 383–84, 385, 389
  Mitchell's questioning of, 51
  Nixon's backchannel communications pro-
    vided by, 17, 33, 70
  Nixon's retaining of, 48, 60, 187, 306, 383–
    84
  retirement of, 402
  Robinson's passing of Radford's stolen doc-
    uments to, 4–5, 12, 13, 15, 23, 25, 26–
    27, 28, 31, 36
  Senate testimony of, 391–92, 396, 401
  Welander's passing of Radford's stolen doc-
    uments to, 13–14, 15, 23, 28, 31, 35–
    36, 38, 39, 40, 62
  Woodward as subordinate of, 80, 85
  Woodward-Haig connection confirmed by,
    71
  Woodward's Navy briefing duties confirmed
    by, 71, 81
Moorer-Radford affair, 3–67, 287, 292, 342,
  350, 373–403
  Baker's inquiry into, 312–14, 376–77, 384,
    389, 394–96, 433–34
  Buzhardt-Stewart clash over, 305–6
  cover-up of, 308–15, 358, 381, 382, 386,
    399, 423, 433–34, 437
  Ehrlichman's subpoenaing of material from,
    408–10
  executive privilege invoked in, 301–3, 312–
    15, 409–10

Moorer-Radford affair, *(cont.)*
  Hersh's coverage of, 382, 383, 384, 388–89,
    390–91, 398–99
  Jaworski-Haig-Buzhardt deal and, 374–75
  Kissinger on, 385–86, 392–93, 399
  Moorer as recipient of Radford's stolen doc-
    uments in, 4–5, 12, 13–14, 15, 23, 25,
    26–27, 28, 31, 35–36, 38, 39, 40, 62
  Nixon's burial of, 32–33, 47–49, 65–67,
    187, 200, 386, 392, 398–99, 433
  Radford's confession as first news of, 20–24
  Radford's espionage against Nixon and Kis-
    singer in, 12, 13–14, 20, 22–31, 40,
    45, 52, 62
  Stennis's hearing on, 384, 387, 390–98,
    400–403
  Thomasson-Squires coverage of, 376–77,
    379, 380–81, 383
  Welander's confessions in, 33–46, 61, 62–
    64, 66, 292, 293, 309, 374, 382, 384,
    386, 391, 397–98, 401, 403, 408–9,
    417, 432, 445–74
  Woodward-Bernstein coverage of, 306–7,
    376, 379–83, 387–88, 394–95
  Young's report on, 49, 315, 374, 384, 385,
    390, 396, 402, 409, 417, 432
Morgan, Charles, Jr., 138, 139, 240
Morris, Roger, 56, 85–86, 87, 88, 279, 292,
  298, 411, 433
Mullen & Company, 102, 113, 119, 174, 209,
  285
Murphy, George, 394, 395
Murphy, Ryan, 84
Muskie, Edmund S., 133
  Nixon administration espionage against, 55,
    56, 95, 104–5, 116, 117, 119
"My Journal on Watergate" (Anderson), 311

National Archives, 101, 405, 432
National Security Agency (NSA), 8, 16, 80,
  98
National Security Council (NSC), 17, 80, 85,
  291, 411
  JCS liaison office with, 4, 5, 12, 43, 51, 52,
    56, 57, 58, 61, 381, 384, 393
  power of, 4, 6–7
  security review of, 67
Navy, U.S., 10
  briefing officers of, 70–71, 80–83
  civilians feared and distrusted by, 13
  ROTC program of, 71, 73, 74
  SR–1 channel of, 9, 70
  State Department's dispute with, 28–29, 40
  Task Force 157 of, 70
NBC, 384
Nesline, Joe, 130
New Muckrakers, The (Downie), 74
New York Police Department (NYPD),
  BOSSI unit of, 94
New York Times, 54, 112, 113, 279, 281, 286,
  382, 383, 384, 388, 393, 398, 399
Ngo Dinh Diem, 113, 182
Nguyen Van Thieu, 17, 26, 30, 38, 63
"Nightline," 368–69
Nightmare (Lukas), 338
Nixon, Donald, 101
Nixon, Donald, Jr., 95–96
Nixon, Pat, 32, 337, 344

Nixon, Richard M.:
  Anderson as obsession of, 50–51, 96
  Anderson column and, 14, 32
  Anderson-Radford homosexual affair al-
    leged by, 50
  antiwar protest response of, 98
  backchannel communications protected by,
    33, 48, 51, 67, 85
  backchannel communications used by, 8–9,
    12, 17, 32, 48, 70, 85, 409–10
  background of, 7–8
  bitterness and anger of, 6
  blanket denial issued by, 300–303
  Brezhnev's summit meeting with, 411–12
  Byrne offered FBI directorship by, 273
  cabinet appointments by, 7–8
  cabinet ignored and manipulated by, 7–9,
    183
  Cambodia secretly bombed by, 8, 10, 54,
    98
  Connally and, 291
  Cox as seen by, 338
  on Dean as Watergate investigator, 222
  Dean protected by, 248, 257
  Dean's "cancer" warning to, 259, 260, 261,
    267, 378
  on Dean's character, 228, 246–47
  Dean's confession to, 252–59, 261–64
  Dean's hush money request to, 262–64, 265
  Dean's implication of, 163, 178, 272, 318
  Deep Throat on, 281
  Deep Throat identity and, 290–91
  eighteen-and-a-half-minute tape gap and,
    363, 364–65, 367, 368, 370–72
  enemies list of, 104, 227, 243, 296
  executive privilege invoked by, 242, 248,
    249, 257, 261, 269, 301–3, 312–15,
    321–22, 328, 339, 341, 415
  Ford's pardoning of, 421, 429–32, 437–38
  foreign policy of, 5, 48, 276, 288, 411
  government bureaucrats as viewed by, 6
  grand jury immunity discussion and, 264,
    265–66, 268–70
  Haig and Kissinger played off each other
    by, 42, 52–54
  Haig appointed chief of staff by, 280, 282
  Haig's influence on, 289, 291–95, 434
  Haig's misleading of, 336, 346–47, 350,
    351, 354, 356, 372, 386–87, 399–400,
    419–20
  Hoover and, 94
  Huston Plan and, 99, 296–97
  impeachment inquiries against, 355–56,
    391, 405, 406, 412–15
  impending revelation of White House tapes
    kept from, 328, 333–36
  India-Pakistan dispute and, 14, 17, 57
  on Jaworski, 358
  JCS kept unaware of China talks by, 45–46
  JCS manipulated by, 8–10
  JCS's dislike of, 5, 10–12, 28
  Kissinger's strained relationship with, 56–
    57, 60, 67, 411
  Laos invasion ordered by, 103
  Liddy on protection of, 165, 178, 181
  Liddy's FBI critique and, 115
  Liddy's Watergate involvement kept from
    FBI by, 193

Nixon, Richard M., *(cont.)*
media's relationship with, 93–94, 361
Mideast trip of, 410
Mitchell manipulated by, 65
Mitchell not questioned by, 201–2
Mitchell's attempted sheltering of, 189
Mitchell's CRP resignation and, 214
Mitchell's friendship with, 32, 47, 65, 197, 201
Moorer-Radford affair buried by, 32–33, 47–49, 65–67, 187, 200, 386, 392, 398–99, 433
Moorer retained by, 48, 60, 383–84
1960 presidential defeat of, 6, 8, 101
1962 gubernatorial defeat of, 6, 7
1968 election of, 6, 201
1972 election of, 234–35, 288, 361
"not a crook" statement of, 371
NSC security review ordered by, 67
NSC's power under, 4, 6–7
O'Brien investigation ordered by, 101–2
Operation Candor of, 362, 369
Pentagon Papers and, 112–13
personal confrontation avoided by, 6, 49, 187, 201–2, 342
Plumbers defended by, 301–2
post-Watergate life of, 439
private investigator hired by, 94
private nature of, 6, 93
on Radford-Anderson connection, 49–50, 51
Radford's espionage against, 12, 13–14, 20, 22–31
resignation of, 154, 195, 294, 414–16, 418–25
resignations of Ehrlichman, Haldeman and Dean accepted by, 274–76
response to Radford's confession by, 32–33
secret government established by, 6
as Senate Watergate committee target, 319, 327
surveillance targets of, 94, 95–96
taxes owed by, 405
undated resignations demanded by, 235
as unindicted coconspirator, 399, 405, 406
unspent campaign funds of, 95, 210, 234, 287, 326, 330, 331
vengefulness of, 50–51, 93–94, 187, 289
Vietnam War and, 289
on Walters's memo, 298, 299–300
Watergate break-in reaction of, 161–62, 175, 185, 187, 192–93, 199–204, 245–46
in Watergate cover-up, 193, 195–204, 224–28, 241–76, 320–21
wiretapping authorized by, 56, 281, 413
on Woodward-Bernstein Watergate coverage, 295
Woodward-Haig connection and removal of, 283
Woodward-Haig connection not known by, 295
world view of, 5–6
Nixon administration:
cabinet appointments in, 7–8
Deep Throat on, 284
distrust between CRP and, 183–84
Haig's knowledge of secrets in, 287

Nixon administration, *(cont.)*
ITT's secret deal with, 124, 187
Nixon's treatment of appointees in, 7–9, 183
personal rivalries in, 183
undated resignations of, 235
Nixon's White House tapes:
Butterfield's public revelation of, 311, 321–36
Buzhardt's reviewing of, 362, 369–70, 404–5, 415
clemency promises not discussed in, 239
Dean's conversations on, 172, 178, 224–28, 241–47, 249–70, 339, 340, 357, 378, 386–87, 406
disposition of, 426–32
eighteen-and-a-half-minute gap in, 187, 362–72
executive privilege and, 321–22, 331, 334–36, 339, 341
gap in Haldeman's conversation in, 187
House Judiciary Committee's subpoena of, 405–6
installation of, 325
Jaworski's subpoena of, 405, 406–8, 415, 421–22
Krogh's discovery motion and, 373–74, 375–76, 408–9
number of, 429
public reaction to, 406, 422
release of, 356, 406, 417
Sirica's court hearing on, 367, 369, 372
"smoking gun," 195, 198–201, 405, 406–8, 418, 420, 421–22
Stennis's proposed examination of, 344–53
subpoena battle for, 336–54, 356, 439
subpoenaed dates missing from, 360–61, 364, 365
"tape of tapes," 386–87, 405
Woods's transcription of, 341, 361, 363–64
Woodward and Bernstein referred to in, 295
Not Above the Law (Doyle), 343
Nunn, Sam, 397, 398

O'Brien, Lawrence F., 148
Hughes as client of, 101–2, 107
Nixon's order for investigation of, 101–2
roots of Watergate affair and, 102
Stans sued by, 226
as target in Watergate break-ins, 133, 134, 135, 136, 137, 139, 147, 240
Watergate office of, 128, 133, 134, 135, 136, 157
O'Brien, Paul, 217
Ogarrio Daguerre, Manuel, 135, 192, 204
Oliver, R. Spencer, 126, 127–28, 129, 134, 137, 138, 148, 149, 225, 240
Oliver/Wells/Governors' telephone, 134, 137–38, 139, 157
On Watch (Zumwalt), 10, 17
Operation Candor, 362, 369
Operation Sandwedge, 107–10, 111, 116, 261
Owen, George, 129, 130

Packard, David, 400
Palace Politics (Hartmann), 419, 430
Palmer, Allan M., 152, 229
Parade, 311

Parker, Doug, 306
Parkinson, Kenneth W., 399
Patman, Wright, 221, 227
Pentagon, *see* Defense Department, U.S.
Pentagon Papers, 15, 16, 62, 112–13, 182, 279–80, 281, 290, 304, 313
Percy, Charles, 434
Petersen, Henry, 147, 166, 186, 191, 219, 273, 274, 275, 342, 348
    in attempted prosecution of Stewart, 309, 310, 314, 394
    Dean's hoodwinking of, 235–36, 240
Pico, Reinaldo, 135
Playboy, Woodward's interview in, 72, 73
Plumbers (Special Investigations Unit), 311, 313, 338, 377, 382, 417
    Cox's attempted investigation of, 338, 342
    naming of, 15
    Nixon's defense of, 301–2
    see also Krogh, Egil "Bud," Jr.; Liddy, G. Gordon; Young, David R.
Poff, Richard, 101
Porter, Bart, 262, 287
Powers, Samuel, 369, 370, 371
Powers That Be, The (Halberstam), 74, 286
Price, Raymond K., Jr., 301
"Project Jennifer," 113
prostitutes, prostitution:
    DNC's involvement with, 127–32, 227–28
    "Happy Hooker" ring of, 105–6, 130
    Rikan's ring of, 126–32, 143–45, 153, 232
Prouty, L. Fletcher, 81, 82
Proxmire, William, 95
Pursley, Robert E., 55, 86

Radford, Charles Edward, 306, 327, 376, 400
    Anderson's acquaintance with, 18–20, 394
    character of, 12, 27
    childhood and family background of, 5
    confession of, 22–24, 32, 38, 45, 292, 304, 311
    early career of, 3–4
    as Haig's aide, 24–25, 26, 27, 29–30, 38, 43–44
    investigation of Anderson leak and, 14–24, 41
    as Kissinger's aide, 29–30, 37–38, 45, 375
    Kissinger spied on by, 12, 13–14, 22–31, 40, 45, 52, 62, 375
    later career of, 31
    and media's uncovering of Moorer-Radford affair, 376, 379–80, 381, 383, 385, 391
    moonlighting by, 35
    Nixon's allegation of homosexual affair between Anderson and, 50
    Nixon spied on by, 12, 13–14, 20, 22–31
    Oregon transfer of, 57
    range of documents stolen by, 13–14, 27–28, 40–41
    Robinson and Welander compared by, 36
    as Robinson's aide, 4–5, 12–13, 22
    Senate testimony of, 393–94, 396–97, 400
    on spying as JCS self-defense, 31
    stolen documents sanitized by, 27
    on Welander's knowledge of Radford's espionage activities, 37
    wiretap on, 57, 377, 380, 388

Radford, Charles Edward, *(cont.)*
    Woodward's questioning of, 379
    see also Moorer-Radford affair
Radford, Toni, 4, 15, 18
Reagan, Ronald, 164, 165, 436, 438, 439
Rebozo, Bebe, 14, 101, 291, 295, 337, 361
Reed, Thomas, 164
Reisner, Robert, 125
Reserve Officers Training Corps (ROTC), 71, 73, 74
Rhodes, John, 422
Richard Nixon Library, 439
Richardson, Elliot, 305
    appointment of, 276
    in attempted Stewart prosecution, 308–11, 383
    in battle to limit Cox's investigation, 339–40, 342, 343, 345–54
    Cox appointed by, 338
    Haig on, 356
    resignation of, 343, 346–47, 348–55
Richey, Charles R.:
    Bailley case and, 149–53, 223–24, 228–30
    CRP-DNC lawsuit and, 193
    O'Brien-Stans lawsuit and, 226
    Republican party ties of, 150, 193, 226–27
Right and the Power, The (Jaworski), 358
Rikan, Erika L. "Heidi":
    Bailley's connection with, 126–29, 131–32, 143
    John Dean's friendship with, 131
    Maureen Dean's friendship with, 127–30, 132, 145, 153
    prostitution ring of, 126–32, 143–45, 153, 232
    pseudonym of, 126–27
Rivkind, Perry, 168–69, 170, 171
RN (Nixon), 6, 48, 49, 187, 192, 202, 257, 298, 341, 345, 407
Robinson, Rembrandt C., 18, 19–20, 397
    character of, 36
    death of, 58, 387
    Ehrlichman's questioning of, 58
    Haig and, 23, 45, 293
    JCS-NSC information traded by, 37
    Radford as aide to, 4–5, 12–13, 22, 393
    as Radford-Moorer information link, 4–5, 12, 13, 15, 23, 25, 26–27, 28, 31, 36, 391
    sea command promotion of, 13, 15, 29, 306
Rockefeller, Nelson, 243
Rogers, William P., 7, 25, 56
Rosenfeld, Harry, 84
Rothblatt, Henry, 227–28
Ruckelshaus, William D., 290, 291, 299, 354, 355
Rudy, John:
    Bailley case handled by, 142–46, 149–52, 229
    John Dean's meeting with Smith and, 144–46, 153
    Maureen Dean's code name confirmed by, 132
Russo, Anthony J., 275, 279, 291

Sadat, Anwar, 410
Safire, William, 53, 55

St. Clair, James, 387, 407, 409
  Haig's hiring of, 378–79
  Nixon's resignation and, 418, 420, 421–22
  Nixon's White House tapes kept from, 404–5
St. Elizabeth's Mental Hospital, Bailley committed to, 150–54, 223–24, 228, 231
SALT, *see* strategic arms limitation talks
Sanders, Donald G., 311–12, 314, 322, 327, 329, 394, 395
Sandwedge, *see* Operation Sandwedge
sanitization of stolen documents, 27
Santarelli, Donald, 111–12
Saturday Night Massacre, 337–59
  firings and resignations in, 354–55
  prelude to, 337–54
  reaction to, 355–56
Saxbe, William B., 359, 428
Schaffer, Charles, 296
Schlesinger, James R., 297, 309, 384, 385, 386, 390, 399, 401, 411–12
Scott, Hugh, 308, 406, 422
Secret Agenda (Hougan), 82, 113, 156, 209–10
Secret Service, 94, 162, 174, 175, 324, 325, 326, 360–61, 364, 429
secret societies, at Yale, 74–75
Secret Team, The (Prouty), 82
SEDAN CHAIR, 119–20
Segretti, Donald H., 119, 254, 256, 266, 268
  Chapin and Kalmbach linked to, 249, 250
  Dean's hushing of, 234
  dirty tricks campaign of, 116, 233–34, 244, 288
Senate Armed Services Committee, 63, 297, 298
  Moorer-Radford hearing of, 384, 387, 390–98, 400–403
Senate Foreign Relations Committee, 416–18, 434
Senate Judiciary Committee, 240–41, 248–49, 268
Senate Watergate investigating committee, 292, 296
  Armstrong-Woodward connection and, 316–17, 332
  Baldwin's testimony to, 138, 148
  Butterfield's testimony to, 322, 323–36
  Colson's testimony to, 183
  Dean's immunity deal with, 273
  Dean's "invitation" from, 249
  Dean's testimony to, 97, 98, 100–101, 104–5, 108–9, 117, 118, 119, 163, 170, 178, 190, 197, 205–6, 210, 213–14, 239–40, 254, 260, 272, 318–21
  Dean's version accepted by, 163, 211, 272, 318–19
  Ehrlichman's testimony to, 104, 312–14, 319
  formation of, 240
  Gray's testimony to, 203
  Haldeman's testimony to, 319
  Hunt's testimony to, 140, 190
  Kleindienst's testimony to, 166
  LaRue's testimony to, 124, 164
  Magruder's testimony to, 118, 124, 163, 167
  Mitchell's testimony to, 110, 319
  Moorer-Radford affair ignored by, 384

Senate Watergate investigating committee, *(cont.)*
  Nixon as target of, 319, 327
  Nixon's White House tapes subpoenaed by, 336–39, 343–44, 347, 349
  Scott as Woodward's conduit to, 316–17
  Stewart's testimony to, 395–96
  Strachan's testimony to, 120–21, 319
  televised broadcasting of hearings of, 242, 292, 311, 321
  Wells's testimony to, 159
  Yesbeck's testimony to, 148
Shea, Quinlan J., 434
Sheehan, Neil, 281
Shoffler, Carl, 157, 158–59
Silbert, Earl J., 220, 226, 274, 275, 326
  Dean questioned by, 235–36, 240, 272–73
  Watergate break-in investigation by, 138–39, 225, 235–36, 240
Silent Missions (Walters), 298
Simons, Howard, 286
Sirica, John, 100, 139, 360, 378, 399
  Dean refused immunity by, 273
  Dean's foreknowledge of actions of, 267–68
  documents passed from Dean to, 296–97
  McCord's letter to, 260, 271
  nickname of, 237
  Nixon's White House tape hearing and, 367, 369, 372
  in subpoena battle for Nixon's White House tapes, 340–41, 343, 344, 346, 347, 349, 356, 405, 408, 415
  in Watergate burglars' trial, 240, 242, 244
Six Crises (Nixon), 242, 246
Sixth Fleet, 28
"60 Minutes," 393
Skull and Bones, 75
Sloan, Hugh W., Jr., 126, 134–35, 191, 252, 287, 317–18
Smith, Don, 144, 145, 146, 153
Smith, Hedrick, 281
Smith, John T., 310
"smoking gun tape," 195, 198–201, 405, 406–8, 418, 420, 421–22
Sonnenfeldt, Helmut, 55
Soviet Union, 5, 11, 14, 25, 313, 410–11
Speakes, Larry, 436
Special Investigations Unit, *see* Plumbers
Squires, James, 376–77, 379, 380, 381, 383
Stans, Maurice H., 121, 123, 125, 196, 212, 221, 226, 242
Stanton, Shelby, 76
State Department, U.S., 4, 7, 9, 70, 80, 131
  Haig on, 87
  Navy's dispute with, 28–29, 40
  Nixon's view of, 6
Stennis, John, 61
  Moorer-Radford hearing of, 384, 387, 390–98, 400–403
  proposed review of Nixon's White House tapes by, 344–53
Stern, Laurence, 383, 384
Stewart, W. Donald, 50, 58, 61, 113, 292, 304–15, 327–28, 433, 434
  Anderson leak investigation team headed by, 16
  attempted prosecution of, 306–10, 383
  background of, 16

Stewart, W. Donald, *(cont.)*
 blackmail accusation against, 306–10, 383, 387–89
 Buzhardt's thwarting of investigations by, 304–6
 files seized, 306, 307, 396
 Radford questioned by, 19–20, 21, 22, 23–24, 32, 304, 311
 Senate testimony of, 395–96
 Welander questioned by Buzhardt and, 62–64, 305, 309, 397–98, 401, 403, 470–74
 Woodward's questioning of, 379–80, 394–95
Strachan, Gordon C., 124, 147, 148, 169, 216, 221, 240–41, 242, 271, 318, 319
 as CRP liaison, 120–21
 and Dean's confession to Nixon, 253, 254, 255, 257, 258, 261
 on Dean's lifestyle, 97
 Dean-Ulasewicz relationship confirmed by, 101
 domestic political intelligence activities of, 103–5
 indictment of, 399
 Operation Sandwedge rejection by, 108
 as White House connection to Watergate break-in, 177–78
strategic arms limitation talks (SALT), 7, 10, 11, 15, 16, 113, 288, 411–12
"straying off the reservation," 221
Students for a Democratic Society (SDS), 74
Sturgis, Frank A.:
 in first Watergate break-in, 135, 137, 139
 Hunt's recruitment of, 134
 indictment of, 224
 in second Watergate break-in, 154, 157
 trial of, 240
Stutman, Bob, 171
Sullivan, William C., 55, 56, 243, 250, 251, 256–57, 281, 290–91
Supreme Court, U.S., 101
 in subpoena battle for Nixon's White House tapes, 195, 340, 344, 348, 408, 415, 435
Symington, Stuart, 298, 393, 401

talking papers, 37
Tartar SAMs, 16
Task Force 157, 70
Task Group 74, 17
television:
 Senate Watergate hearings on, 242, 292, 311, 321
 see also media
terHorst, Jerry F., 427, 428
Thieu, Nguyen Van, 17, 26, 30, 38, 63
Tho, Le Duc, 30, 41, 48, 298
Thomasson, Dan, 376–77, 379, 380, 381
Thompson, Fred, 312, 314, 317, 327, 328–29, 331–32, 394
Thurmond, Strom, 61, 88, 344, 397
Time, 280, 281, 289, 361
Time to Heal, A (Ford), 419
Titus, Harold, 144
"Today," 384
Train, Harry D., II, 28, 36, 37, 391

Truman, Harry S., 47–48, 87
Tufaro, Richard, 305–6, 307, 308, 310

Ulasewicz, Anthony T., 111, 120, 242, 245
 background of, 95
 Caulfield's hiring of, 95
 contract extension of, 109, 118
 Dean as boss of, 100–101, 191
 Dean's post-break-in phone call to, 172
 DNC's Watergate offices visited by, 106–7, 131
 early investigation assignments of, 95–96, 256, 263
 "Happy Hooker" prostitution ring investigated by, 105–6
 Hunt's hush money passed by, 210, 212–14, 217, 231
 Kalmbach and, 95, 109, 110, 245, 252, 256, 263
 Liddy's hush money passed by, 218
 McCloskey investigation by, 108
 McCord's message from Dean delivered by, 238
 Muskie supporters investigated by, 105
 in O'Brien investigation, 101
 records kept by, 117–18
 source of salary of, 95
Undercover (Hunt), 116, 181
Vance, Cyrus R., 53, 88

Vesco, Robert, 243
Vietnam Veterans Against the War, 96, 101
Vietnam War, 5, 14, 85, 112, 286
 Haig in, 88
 open peace talks in, 289
 secret operations in, 8, 9–10, 11–12
 secret peace talks in, 7, 11, 41, 48, 298, 410
 security leaks in, 26
 U.S. troop withdrawals in, 14, 25, 30
 Vietnamization of, 30
 Woodward in, 73, 77–78, 83
Vorenberg, James, 429

Wagner, Karl, 209
Wallace, George, 95, 415
Wallace, Mike, 393
Walters, Vernon, 196, 202, 203–4, 216
 Dean's meetings with, 207–8, 210, 299
 June 23, 1972 memo of, 208–10, 297–300, 407–8
 Watergate affidavit of, 297–300
Ward, M. D., 78
Washington Daily News, 143, 144
Washington Post, 74, 279, 296, 316, 393, 399, 400, 435–36, 437
 Bailley coverage in, 145, 150
 early Watergate break-in coverage in, 175, 185, 210–11, 283
 Watergate cover-up coverage in, 250
 wiretap story in, 280–82
 Woodward's failed tryout at, 84
 Woodward hired by, 85
 see also Woodward-Bernstein Moorer-Radford coverage; Woodward-Bernstein Watergate coverage
Washington Special Action Group (WSAG), 14, 16, 17
Washington Star, 143, 144, 145, 150, 153, 283

Watergate, the:
Oliver/Wells/Governors' telephone in, 129, 134, 137–38, 139
Ulasewicz's visit to, 106–7, 131
Watergate affair:
executive privilege invoked in, 242, 248, 249, 257, 261, 269, 312, 321–22, 328, 339, 341, 415
foreign reaction to, 410–11
March 30, 1972 meeting and, 123–26
Maureen Dean-Bailley-Rikan connection and, 130
media reaction to, 249, 253, 257, 271
Nixon's resignation as result of, 154
O'Brien investigation as seed of, 102
see also GEMSTONE plan; Saturday Night Massacre
Watergate break-in, first, 135–41
amateurism of, 135–36
approval of, 124–25
Dean as source of order for, 140–41, 239
Magruder's order for, 133
Oliver/Wells/Governors' telephone as target of, 134, 137–38, 139
photographs taken in, 136, 139
telephone tap in, 136–37, 139, 147
Watergate break-in, second, 154–60
address books seized in, 156, 159, 185, 284, 285
Dean as source of order for, 148, 177, 214, 239
events of, 154–60
Magruder's approval of, 147, 148, 188
Nixon's reaction to, 161–62, 175, 185, 187, 192–93, 199–204
participants in, 154
sloppiness of, 156
target of, 147–48, 157
Washington Post coverage of, 175, 185, 210–11
Wells's desk key found in, 149, 157, 158–59
Watergate burglars' trial, 218, 236, 237, 238, 239, 240
Watergate cover-up, 161–276
CIA in, 194, 195–98, 201, 202–4, 209–10, 214, 297, 299, 301–3, 407–8
Ehrlichman implicated by Dean in, 163, 176, 258, 261, 262, 273, 274, 276, 318
Haldeman implicated by Dean in, 163, 178, 250, 261, 262, 273, 274, 276, 318
"hang-out road" alternative to, 255–56, 270
Hunt's hush money in, 205–10, 212–14, 216
indictments for, 167, 180, 181, 184, 399–400
Liddy's document shredding in, 162, 176
Magruder's phone call to Dean and, 163, 168, 176
Magruder's role in, 163, 166–67, 169–70, 176, 183–84, 219–21, 273
Mitchell implicated by Dean in, 163, 190–91, 196–98, 214, 216, 240, 261–62, 270, 318, 321
Mitchell implicated by Magruder in, 163, 164–65, 176
Nixon implicated by Dean in, 163, 178, 272, 318

Watergate cover-up, (cont.)
Nixon's fear of complications as cause of, 191–92
Nixon's role in, 193, 195–204, 224–28, 241–76, 320–21
"smoking gun" tape and, 195, 198–201
"straying off the reservation" and, 221, 260
Watergate Special Prosecutor:
abolition of, 355
appointment of, 276, 338
constitutional status of, 339
in disposition of Nixon's White House tapes, 428–29
indictments by, 167, 180, 184
Nixon on, 222
see also Cox, Archibald; Jaworski, Leon
Watts, William, 86
Weathermen, 98
Weir, Raymond J., 16, 19, 20, 21, 22, 70
Welander, Robert O., 28, 50, 70, 76, 306, 390, 393
Buzhardt's and Stewart's questioning of, 62–64, 292, 293, 309, 374, 384, 397–98
character of, 36
files seized, 57
firing and sea command transfer of, 57, 58, 306
on Haig, 42, 43–44, 45
Haig and, 37, 58–60, 63
innocence claimed by, 40
investigation of Anderson leak and, 14–24
JCS-NSC dual role of, 34–35
in media's uncovering of Moorer-Radford affair, 374, 380, 381, 382, 384, 385, 386, 391
questioning of, by Ehrlichman and Young, 33–46, 61, 66, 292, 293, 374, 382, 384, 385, 391, 403, 408–9, 417, 432, 445–69
as Radford-Moorer information link, 13–14, 15, 23, 28, 31, 35–36, 38, 39, 40, 62, 393
retirement of, 402
Robinson replaced by, 13, 15, 29
Senate testimony of, 397–98, 401
on spying as JCS self-defense, 25–26
Woodward's questioning of, 306–7, 380, 382–83
Woodward's serving under, 76, 78, 80, 83
Wells, Bernard, 290–91
Wells, Ida M. "Maxie," 128, 134, 138
second Watergate break-in and desk key of, 148–49, 157, 158–59
West, Woody, 143, 144
Wheeler, Earle G., 11, 55
White House Communications Agency (WHCA), 80, 325
White House Domestic Council, 96, 100
White House Office of Security, 324–25
White House Years (Kissinger), 6
Whiting, Allen S., 279
Will (Liddy), 112, 116, 165, 176, 177, 434
Williams, Edward Bennett, 296
Wills, Frank, 155, 156, 157
Wilson, John, 312, 313, 314, 376
Winks, Robin, 75

Witness to Power (Ehrlichman), 57, 94, 237, 241
Wong, Albert, 325, 326
Woods, Joe, 94, 107
Woods, Rose Mary, 94, 323–24, 337
  eighteen-and-a-half-minute tape gap and, 364–67, 368, 370
  Nixon's White House tapes transcribed by, 341, 361, 363–64
Woodward, Alfred E., 71–72, 79
Woodward, Bob, 54, 69–85, 88–90
  Armstrong as Senate Watergate committee conduit for, 316–17, 332
  background of, 69, 71–72
  Bernstein's initial relationship with, 283
  in Book and Snake, 75
  character of, 80
  on Deep Throat's character, 284
  on Deep Throat's identity, 368–69
  early conservatism of, 72, 73, 74
  first wife of, *see* Woodward, Kathleen Middlekauff
  at *Montgomery County Sentinel*, 84, 85
  Navy briefing duties denied by, 70–71, 80–81, 83
  Navy career of, 69–71, 75–84
  Navy Commendation Medal awarded to, 78
  novel written by, 73
  in NROTC, 71, 73
  Pentagon assignment of, 69–71, 79–83, 85
  post-Watergate career of, 438–39
  self-image of, 72, 73–74, 76, 83
  in Vietnam War, 74, 77–78, 83
  wiretap story by Bernstein and, 280–82, 289–90
  at Yale, 69, 71, 73–75
  see also Deep Throat; Woodward-Bernstein Watergate coverage; Woodward-Haig connection
Woodward, Jane, 71
Woodward, Kathleen Middlekauff, 72–73, 74, 76–77, 79–80
Woodward-Bernstein, coverage of Moorer-Radford by, 306–7, 376, 379–83, 387–88, 394–95
Woodward-Bernstein Watergate coverage:
  Buzhardt's hearing of Nixon's White House tapes in, 362, 369–70
  CRP and Watergate burglars linked in, 286, 287
  Deep Throat first used in, 234, 280–81, 326
  deliberate erasure in Nixon's White House tapes in, 366–68
  Haig's protection of Nixon's White House tapes in, 405
  Hunt first named in, 185, 285

Woodward-Bernstein Watergate coverage, *(cont.)*
  Jaworski's appointment in, 358
  Nixon's resignation in, 414–16, 418, 419, 423
  Nixon's White House tapes in, 332–33
  Saturday Night Massacre in, 343, 348
  slush fund article in, 234
  on Walters's memo, 298, 300
Woodward-Haig connection, 68–89, 282–83
  briefing sessions and, 70–71, 83, 85, 285, 295, 369
  Deep Throat story as protection of, 283
  first meeting in, 88
  Haig as Woodward source in, 88–90
  Haig's denial of, 89
  Haig's staff meeting leak and, 437
  Nixon's ignorance of, 295
  Nixon's removal and, 283
  Post Op-Ed piece and, 435–36
  see also Deep Throat
Wright, Charles Alan, 339, 348–50, 351
Wright, USS, 75–76, 83

Yahya Khan, Agha Muhammad, 14
Yale University, 84
  CIA recruitment at, 74
  ROTC program at, 71, 73, 74
  secret societies of, 74–75
  Woodward at, 69, 71, 73–75
Yesbeck, Clota, 148, 149
Young, David R., 47, 50, 63, 115, 292, 305, 312, 373, 387
  on Anderson leak investigation team, 15, 16, 19, 20, 21, 22
  on Haig in Moorer-Radford affair, 58–60, 66
  Moorer-Radford report of, 49, 315, 374, 384, 385, 390, 402, 409, 417, 432
  Pentagon Papers investigation and, 113, 114
  as Plumber, 15
  Welander's confession to Ehrlichman and, 33–46, 61, 66, 292, 293, 374, 382, 386, 391, 401, 403, 408–9, 417, 432, 445–69

Ziegler, Ronald L., 106, 201, 250, 292, 294, 334–35, 355, 362, 386, 404, 416, 418, 419, 430, 432
  Haig and, 295, 437–38
  on "inoperative" previous statements, 274–75, 295
  in post-break-in events, 173, 174, 193
Zumwalt, Elmo R., Jr., 10, 17, 23, 25, 27, 28, 29, 36, 289, 307